# Microsoft® Excel 2010:
## Comprehensive

**SANDRA RITTMAN**
Long Beach City College

**LABYRINTH**
LEARNING™

El Sobrante, CA

*Microsoft Excel 2010: Comprehensive*
by Sandra Rittman

Copyright © 2011 by Labyrinth Learning

**LABYRINTH**
LEARNING™

Labyrinth Learning
P.O. Box 20818
El Sobrante, California 24820
800.522.9746
On the web at lablearning.com

President:
Brian Favro

Product Development Manager:
Jason Favro

Managing Editor:
Laura A. Lionello

Production Manager:
Rad Proctor

eLearning Production Manager:
Arl S. Nadel

Editorial/Production Team:
Pamela Beveridge, Belinda Breyer, Everett
Cowan, Alec Fehl, Sandy Jones,
PMG Media

Indexing: Joanne Sprott

Interior Design:
Mark Ong, Side-by-Side Studios

Cover Design:
Words At Work

ITEM:          1-59136-310-1
ISBN-13: 978-1-59136-310-1

Manufactured in the United States of America.

10 9 8 7 6 5 4 3 2

# Microsoft® Excel 2010:
## Comprehensive

# Contents in Brief

# Table of Contents

# Quick Reference Tables

# Keyboard Shortcuts

## DOCUMENT COMMANDS

| | |
|---|---|
| Help | `F1` |
| Name Manager dialog box | `Ctrl` + `F3` |
| Open | `Ctrl` + `O` |
| Print | `Ctrl` + `P` |
| Refresh all data sources | `Ctrl` + `Alt` + `F5` |
| Save | `Ctrl` + `S` |
| Select All | `Ctrl` + `A` |
| View macros | `Alt` + `F8` |

## EDITING COMMANDS

| | |
|---|---|
| Clear cell contents | `Delete` |
| Copy | `Ctrl` + `C` |
| Cut | `Ctrl` + `X` |
| Insert a line break | `Alt` + `Enter` |
| Insert comment | `Shift` + `F2` |
| Insert hyperlink | `Ctrl` + `K` |
| Paste | `Ctrl` + `V` |
| Place a chart on its own sheet | `F11` |
| Redo | `Ctrl` + `Y` |
| Select a column | `Ctrl` + `Spacebar` |
| Select a row | `Shift` + `Spacebar` |
| Select all | `Ctrl` + `A` |
| Undo | `Ctrl` + `Z` |

## FIND/REPLACE COMMANDS

| | |
|---|---|
| Find | `Ctrl` + `F` |
| Replace | `Ctrl` + `H` |

## FORMATTING COMMANDS

| | |
|---|---|
| Bold | `Ctrl` + `B` |
| Italic | `Ctrl` + `I` |
| Underline | `Ctrl` + `U` |

## FORMULA COMMANDS

| | |
|---|---|
| Autosum | `Alt` + `=` |
| Show formulas | `Ctrl` + `` ` `` |

# Preface

*Microsoft® Excel 2010: Comprehensive* is a complete survey of Microsoft Excel, with engaging content that prepares learners to succeed. Our brand new work-readiness exercises ensure students have the critical thinking skills necessary to succeed in today's world. The book includes:

- **Introductory Skills** – Introduction to Excel and the Ribbon interface; entering and editing entries; selecting cells and ranges; create and modify basic formula; format worksheets; import web data; and more
- **Intermediate Skills** – Sort worksheet rows; freeze headings; set print options; copy and move worksheets; copy formatting between worksheets; hide detail data; use Office templates; lock and unlock cells; and more
- **Advanced Skills** – Use PivotTables and PivotCharts; use the PMT and FV functions; group worksheets; use trendlines; create shared workbooks; track changes; use Windows Live SkyDrive; integrate Excel with other Office programs; and more

Content from this book is also available in two 24+-hr courses and in three 12+-hr courses.

| 24+ Hour Courses | 12+ Hour Courses |
| --- | --- |
| Microsoft Excel 2010: Introductory Skills | Microsoft Excel 2010: Level 1 |
| Microsoft Excel 2010: Advanced Skills | Microsoft Excel 2010: Level 2 |
| | Microsoft Excel 2010: Level 3 |

For almost two decades, Labyrinth Learning has been publishing easy-to-use textbooks that empower educators to teach complex subjects quickly and effectively, while enabling students to gain confidence, develop practical skills, and compete in a demanding job market. We add comprehensive support materials, assessment and learning management tools, and eLearning components to create true learning solutions for a wide variety of instructor-led, self-paced, and online courses.

Our textbooks follow the *Labyrinth Instruction Design,* our unique and proven approach that makes learning easy and effective for every learner. Our books begin with fundamental concepts and build through a systematic progression of exercises. Quick Reference Tables, precise callouts on screen captures, carefully selected illustrations, and minimal distraction combine to create a learning solution that is highly efficient and effective for both students and instructors.

This course is supported with *comprehensive instructor support* materials that include printable solution guides for side-by-side comparisons, test banks, customizable assessments, customizable PowerPoint presentations, detailed lesson plans, pre-formatted files for integration to leading learning management system, and more. Our unique WebSims allow students to perform realistic exercises for tasks that cannot be performed in the computer lab.

Our *eLab assessment and learning management tool* is available to supplement this course. eLab is an intuitive, affordable, web-based learning system that helps educators spend less time on course management and more time teaching. eLab integrates seamlessly with your Labyrinth textbook.

# Visual Conventions

This book uses many visual and typographic cues to guide students through the lessons. This page provides examples and describes the function of each cue.

**Type this text**

Anything you should type at the keyboard is printed in this typeface.

Tips, Notes, and Warnings are used throughout the text to draw attention to certain topics.

Command→
Command→
Command, etc.

This convention indicates how to give a command from the Ribbon. The commands are written: Ribbon Tab→Command Group→Command→ Subcommand.

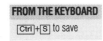

These margin notes indicate shortcut keys for executing a task described in the text.

# Exercise Progression

The exercises in this book build in complexity as students work through a lesson toward mastery of the skills taught.

- **Develop Your Skills** exercises are introduced immediately after concept discussions. They provide detailed, step-by-step tutorials.
- **Reinforce Your Skills** exercises provide additional hands-on practice with moderate assistance.
- **Apply Your Skills** exercises test students' skills by describing the correct results without providing specific instructions on how to achieve them.
- **Critical Thinking and Work-Readiness Skills** exercises are the most challenging. They provide generic instructions, allowing students to use their skills and creativity to achieve the results they envision.

# Acknowledgements

We are grateful to the instructors who have used Labyrinth titles and suggested improvements to us over the many years we have been writing and publishing books. This book has benefited greatly from the reviews and suggestions of the following instructors.

Darrell Abbey, *Cascadia Community College*

Tonya Bailey, *Laurel Technical Institute*

Jim Bandy, *Spencerian College*

Gene Carbonaro, *Long Beach City College*

Susan Carrier, *Mt San Jacinto College*

Richard Chambers, *Texas State Technical College*

Laura Collins-Galvan, *Fayetteville Technical Community College*

Susan Comtois, *Cambrian College of Applied Arts and Technology*

Rose Corgan, *Raymond Walters College – UC*

Brad Davis, *Santa Rosa Junior College*

William Eichenlaub, *S.E. Tech*

Dawn Followell, *Richland Community College*

Steven Fontaine, *Montachusette Regional Vocational Technical School*

Summer Garrett, *SJRCC*

Wahid Hamidy, *San Diego Miramar College*

Jeanne Horan, *South Seattle Community College*

Loretta Jarrell, *LTC-Baton Rouge Campus*

Pat Jarvis, *Truckee Meadows Community College*

Laurie Johnson, *Manhattan Area Technical College*

Teresa Jolly, *South Georgia Technical College*

Gwen Just, *Parkland College*

Jodi Kidd, *Ashland County-West Holmes Career Center*

Jeanne Lake, *Marshall Vo-Tech – Saline County Career Center*

Mark Larson, *Wisconsin Learning Center*

Sarah Lederstein, *Beth Yaakov*

Jayne Lowery, *Jackson State Community College*

Patricia McClain, *Pima Community College - NEC DT*

Marion Medcalf, *Centennial College*

Peter Meggison, *Massasoit Community College, Brockton, MA*

John Mims, *Central New Mexico Community College Workforce Training Center*

Amanda Odom, *Western Technology Center*

Paul Pendley, *Coastal Bend College*

Joseph Perret, *Pierce College*

Mary Peterson, *Tennessee Technology Center*

Kari Phillips, *Davis Applied Technology College*

Sharyn Putnik, *Tooele Applied Technology College*

Joann Santillo, *Mahoning County CTC*

Lisa Satterlee, *Northwest College*

Pamela Silvers, *A-B Tech*

Ericka Wiginton, *Southwest Technology Center*

Cally Youngberg, *Red Wing/Winona State College Southeast Technical*

# Exploring Excel 2010

## LEARNING OBJECTIVES

After studying this lesson, you will be able to:

- Explain ways Excel can help your productivity
- Navigate around the Excel window and issue commands
- Enter text and numbers into cells
- Distinguish between a text and a number entry in a cell
- Save, "save as," and close workbooks

In this lesson, you will develop fundamental Excel skills. This lesson will provide you with a solid understanding of Excel so you are prepared to master advanced features later. You will learn how to navigate around a worksheet, enter various types of data, and select cells.

# Building a Basic Spreadsheet

Welcome to Green Clean, a janitorial product supplier and cleaning service contractor to small businesses, shopping plazas, and office buildings. Green Clean uses environmentally friendly cleaning products and incorporates sustainability practices wherever possible, including efficient energy and water use, recycling and waste reduction, and reduced petroleum use in vehicles. In addition to providing green cleaning services, the company also sells its eco-friendly products directly to customers.

**green clean**

You will follow the steps with Green Clean employees as they use essential Excel features to complete tasks and projects.

Nicole Romero works as a payroll assistant at Green Clean. She needs to create a list of hours that cleaning service employees worked during the weekend (Friday through Sunday). Nicole's manager has asked her to compile the data from employee time sheets and report hours on a daily basis. Nicole decides that Excel is the right tool for this task and proceeds to organize the data in a worksheet, shown in the following illustration.

| | A | B | C | D | E |
|---|---|---|---|---|---|
| 1 | Service Employees Weekend Hours Worked | | | | |
| 2 | | | | | |
| 3 | Alton Mall | | Friday | Saturday | Sunday |
| 4 | | Barnes | 6 | 6 | 6 |
| 5 | | Chau | 8 | 8 | 8 |
| 6 | | Lee | 4 | 0 | 4 |
| 7 | | Olsen | 4 | 3 | 0 |
| 8 | | Total Hrs | | | |
| 9 | Century Bank | | | | |
| 10 | | Garcia | 3 | 5 | 0 |
| 11 | | Kimura | 3 | 4 | 0 |
| 12 | | Tan | 3 | 5 | 0 |
| 13 | | Total Hrs | | | |
| 14 | Newport Medical | | | | |
| 15 | | Kowalski | 8 | 6 | 8 |
| 16 | | Silva | 6 | 6 | 0 |
| 17 | | Wilson | 5 | 2 | 5 |
| 18 | | Total Hrs | | | |

Notice that Excel makes it easy for you to organize your data in columns and rows. The "Total Hrs" rows have been included in the example, although you will not learn how to create formulas to calculate totals in this lesson.

# 1.1 Presenting Excel 2010

**Video Lesson**   labyrinthelab.com/videos

Microsoft Office Excel is an electronic spreadsheet program that allows you to work with numbers and data much more efficiently than the pen-and-paper method. Excel is used in virtually all industries and many households for a variety of tasks such as:

- Creating and maintaining detailed budgets
- Keeping track of extensive customer lists
- Performing "what-if" scenarios and break-even analyses
- Determining the profitability of a business or sector
- Creating tables to organize information
- Tracking employee information
- Producing detailed charts to graphically display information
- Creating invoices or purchase orders
- Determining the future value of an investment, the present value of an annuity, or the payment for a loan
- Working with reports exported from small business accounting software programs such as Intuit's QuickBooks®

As you can see from this list, Excel is not just used to crunch numbers. It is a very powerful program that is used not only to work with numbers but also to maintain databases. If you have started a database in Excel, you can even import it into Microsoft Access (the program in the Microsoft Office Suite that is specialized for working with databases). Many people may use Excel to track their databases rather than Access because of its ease of use and because Access is not included in all of the Microsoft Office editions. If you are tracking multiple databases that you wish to include in reports and data queries, you will want to consider utilizing Access, though, as it really is designed to work with multiple tables of data.

Throughout the Excel lessons, the terms *spreadsheet* and *worksheet* will be used interchangeably.

## 1.2 Starting Excel

The method you use to start Excel depends in large part on whether you intend to create a new workbook or open an existing workbook. A workbook is a file containing one or more worksheets. To create a new workbook, use one of the following methods. (The item names in the menus may vary depending on your Windows version.) Once the Excel program has started, you can begin working in the new workbook that appears.

- Click the Start ⊞ button, choose the Microsoft Office folder from the All Programs menu, and choose Microsoft Office Excel 2010. (Depending on your installation of Microsoft Office, Microsoft Office Excel 2010 may appear on the All Programs menu.)
- Click the Microsoft Office Excel 2010 ⊠ button on the taskbar located to the right of the Start button. (This button may not appear on all computers.)

Use one of the following methods if you intend to open an existing Excel workbook. Once the Excel program has started, the desired workbook will open in an Excel window.

- Navigate to the desired document using Windows Explorer or Computer and double-click the workbook.
- Click the Start ⊞ button and point to Recent Items. You can choose the desired workbooks from the documents list, which displays the most-recently used documents.

### DEVELOP YOUR SKILLS 1.2.1
### Start Excel

*In this exercise, you will start the Excel program.*

1. **Start** your computer, if necessary, and the Windows Desktop will appear.

2. Click the **Start** ⊞ button and choose **Programs** (or All Programs).

3. Choose the **Microsoft Office** folder from the menu, and then choose **Microsoft Office Excel 2010**.
   *After a pause, the Excel program loads and the Excel window appears.*

4. **Maximize** ▫ the window, if necessary.

# 1.3 Exploring the Excel Program Window

**Video Lesson**    labyrinthelab.com/videos

When you launch Excel, you will see a blank workbook displayed. The window is filled with many objects and a space for you to create your spreadsheet. Using the figures that follow, you will have an opportunity to learn the names of some of the objects that you can see on your screen.

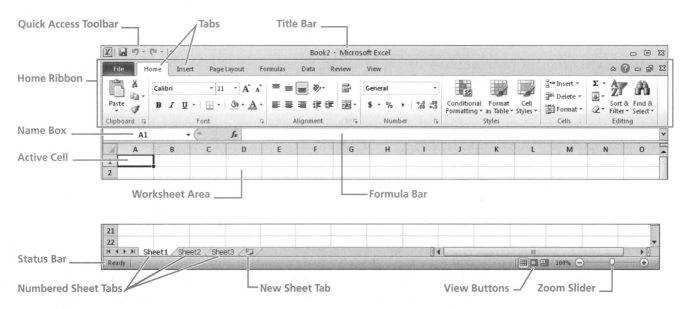

## Using Worksheets and Workbooks

Excel displays a blank workbook the moment you start the program. A workbook is composed of worksheets. A workbook is similar to a paper notebook with several sheets of paper. You enter text, numbers, formulas, charts, and other objects in worksheets. By default, Excel displays three worksheets in a new workbook, each accessible by a separate tab at the bottom of the screen. The maximum number of worksheets you can insert is limited only by the amount of memory available on your computer.

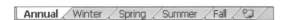

In this example, the sheet tabs are named so that you can organize data for each season as well as track annual information.

A worksheet has a grid structure with horizontal rows and vertical columns. A new worksheet has 16,384 columns and 1,048,576 rows. However, at any given time only a small number of the rows and columns are visible in the worksheet window. The intersection

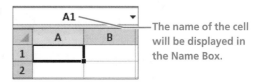

of each row and column is a cell. Each cell is identified by a reference. The reference is the column letter followed by the row number. For example, A1 is the reference of the cell in the top-left corner of the worksheet. So, this is called cell A1.

# Mousing Around in Excel

The shape of the mouse pointer will change as you move it around the Excel window. The shape of the pointer will let you know what will happen if you click over that spot.

| Mouse Pointer Shape | Function |
|---|---|
| ⊹ | Click to select a cell. |
| | Click and drag to select multiple cells. |
| ✛ | The fill handle pointer; dragging this pointer will copy the cell contents or the next values in a data series to adjacent cells. |
| ↖ | Allows you to perform a variety of tasks when clicked, such as issue a command from the Ribbon or select a new tab. |
| ⬌✛ | The move pointer; if you drag with this, it will move cell contents from one location to another. |
| ↕ ⟷ ⬃ | The resize pointers; dragging one of these pointers will allow you to change the height, width, or both dimensions of objects such as pictures, shapes, or charts. |
| ➡ ⬇ | Select a row or column. |
| I | Click with the I-beam pointer to enter text, such as in the Formula Bar. |

# Scrolling Along in a Worksheet

There are two scroll bars visible in the Excel window, both vertical and horizontal. They allow you to see other areas of the worksheet without changing which cell is active. There are three ways to use the scroll bars to view other areas of your spreadsheet.

Click between an arrow and the scroll box to move one "screen view" at a time.

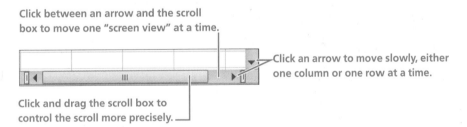

Click an arrow to move slowly, either one column or one row at a time.

Click and drag the scroll box to control the scroll more precisely.

# Navigating in a Worksheet

When you have a cell selected, it is surrounded by a thick line, which indicates that it is the active cell. You can change the active cell by clicking in another cell or by using the keyboard. This is important because data is entered into the active cell. The vertical and horizontal scroll bars let you navigate through a worksheet; however, scrolling does not change which cell is active. After scrolling, you will have to select which cell is to be active, either by clicking or using one of the keystrokes listed below.

You may type a cell reference in the Name Box and then tap [Enter] to navigate to that cell.

| Keystroke(s) | How the Highlight Moves |
|---|---|
| → ← ↑ ↓ | One cell right, left, up, or down |
| Home | Beginning of current row |
| Ctrl + Home | Home cell, usually cell A1 |
| Ctrl + End | Last cell in active part of worksheet |
| Page Down | Down one visible screen |
| Page Up | Up one visible screen |
| Alt + Page Down | One visible screen right |
| Alt + Page Up | One visible screen left |
| Ctrl + G | Displays Go To dialog box—enter cell reference and click OK |

### DEVELOP YOUR SKILLS 1.3.1
## Move the Selection and Explore the Excel Window

*In this exercise, you will practice selecting the active cell in a worksheet so that you can become comfortable enough with the program to begin to create a worksheet.*

### Navigate with the Mouse

1. Slide the **mouse pointer** over the screen and notice the thick **cross shape** ✛ when it is in the worksheet area.
   *If you click with this pointer shape, you will select a cell.*

2. Click the **cross-shaped pointer** on any cell and notice that the cell becomes active.

3. Move the selection five times by **clicking** in various cells.

### Navigate with the Keyboard

*Now that you have practiced using the mouse, it is time to learn how to use the keyboard to move about a worksheet. You should use the keys on your keyboard that are between the main part and the numeric keypad on the far right.*

4. Use the →, ←, ↑, and ↓ keys to position the highlight in **cell F10**.

5. **Tap** the Home key and see that the highlight moves to cell A10.
   *The Home key always makes the cell in column A of the current row active.*

6. **Press** Ctrl + Home to make A1 the active cell.

7. **Tap** the Page Down key two or three times.
   *Notice that Excel displays the next 25 or so rows (one "visible" screen's worth) each time you tap Page Down.*

8. **Press** and **hold down** the ↑ key until A1 is the active cell.

### Use the Scroll Bars

*The scroll bars allow you to see other areas of the Excel worksheet area without changing which cell is active.*

9. Click the **Scroll Right** ▶ button on the horizontal scroll bar until columns AA and AB are visible.
   *Excel labels the first 26 columns A–Z and the next 26 columns AA–AZ. A similar labeling scheme is used for the remaining columns out to the final column, XFD.*

10. Click the **Scroll Down** ▼ button on the vertical scroll bar until row 100 is visible.
    *Notice that the highlight has not moved. To move the highlight, you must click in a cell or use the keyboard.*

11. Take a few minutes to practice **scrolling** and **moving** the selection.

## Use the Go To Command

*As you learned in the preceding keystroke navigation table, you can use [Ctrl]+[G] to display the Go To box, where you can go to a specific cell by entering the desired cell reference in the Reference box and clicking OK. You can use [Ctrl]+[Home] to select cell A1.*

12. **Press** [Ctrl]+[G] to display the Go To dialog box.

13. Type **g250** in the Reference box and click **OK**.
    *Notice that cell references are not case sensitive.*

14. Use the **Go To** command to move to two or three different cells.

15. **Press** [Ctrl]+[Home] to return to cell A1.

## Navigate with the Name Box

16. Click the **Name Box** at the left of the Formula Bar.

17. Type **ab9** and **tap** [Enter].

18. **Press** [Ctrl]+[Home] to return to cell A1.

## Explore the Excel Window

*Now that you have learned how to select cells and move around in the window, it is time to explore the Excel window a bit further.*

19. Follow these steps to explore the Excel window:

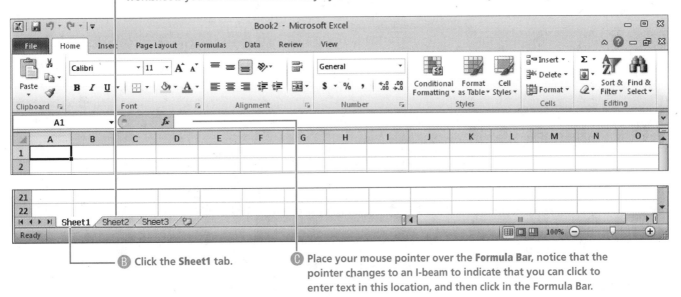

Ⓐ Click the **Sheet2** tab and notice that a different blank worksheet appears. The number of worksheets you can have is limited only by the amount of available memory in the computer.

Ⓑ Click the **Sheet1** tab.

Ⓒ Place your mouse pointer over the **Formula Bar**, notice that the pointer changes to an I-beam to indicate that you can click to enter text in this location, and then click in the Formula Bar.

20. Select any cell **other than** A1, the currently active cell, to exit the Formula Bar.

21. Select **cell A1**.
    *Leave the Excel window open.*

# 1.4 Working with Tabs and Ribbons

**Video Lesson**   labyrinthelab.com/videos

In Microsoft Office 2010, Excel does not have the traditional menu and toolbars with which computer users are familiar. You are able to access the commands that will allow you to effectively utilize Excel through the tabs, ribbons, and Office button located at the top of the window.

## The Quick Access Toolbar

The Quick Access Toolbar is located at the top-left corner of the window and contains commands that you use frequently. This toolbar can be customized using the Customize Quick Access Toolbar button. If you regularly use the Quick Print and Open commands, you may wish to add them to the Quick Access toolbar, as shown.

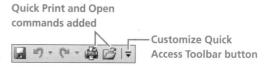

Quick Print and Open commands added

Customize Quick Access Toolbar button

## Displaying Tabs and Working with Ribbons

The tabs at the top of the Excel window organize the commands into eight categories. The commands appear on ribbons displayed across the screen. In order to view a different tab, you simply need to single-click it. The commands on the Ribbon can be chosen by a single-click as well.

Excel's Home Ribbon

The standard tabs along with the Ribbon are displayed in the preceding illustration. Additional contextual tabs will become visible as necessary. For instance, if you are working with a picture, a picture tab will appear.

The Ribbon with a contextual tab displayed. When a picture is selected, a special Picture Tools Format tab appears. All of the commands on this ribbon deal with the formatting of the picture.

Point to the Ribbon and slowly roll the mouse wheel to browse from one tab to another.

## The File Tab

The File tab on the Ribbon, when clicked, accesses a menu that allows you to issue file-management commands. File management simply means working with Excel on the level of the "file"—such as creating new files, opening existing files, saving the file you are working on, and printing the file.

The following illustration shows a special group of tabs on the menu, Info through Help. When one of these tabs is selected, the Backstage view displays a large window pane containing the various options. Some panes contain help for using the options.

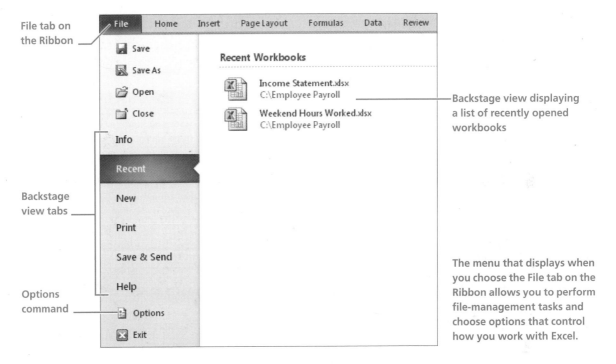

File tab on the Ribbon

Backstage view tabs

Options command

Backstage view displaying a list of recently opened workbooks

The menu that displays when you choose the File tab on the Ribbon allows you to perform file-management tasks and choose options that control how you work with Excel.

## Customizing the Ribbon

Microsoft Office users now may easily customize the Ribbon. The Customize Ribbon category in Excel Options allows you to rearrange the tab order, create a new tab, add a new group to an existing tab, add or remove commands, and export all customizations for use on other computers. The built-in tabs cannot be removed, but they may be hidden. An individual tab or all tabs and the Quick Access toolbar may be reset to their original default items.

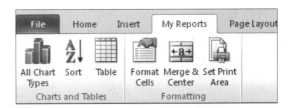

A custom tab added to the Ribbon with commands grouped according to the user's preference and workflow

## ScreenTips

A ScreenTip is a little window that appears to describe the function of the object at which you are pointing. ScreenTips appear when you rest your mouse pointer over an option on a ribbon, the Quick Access toolbar, or the Office button. Enhanced ScreenTips appear for some of the commands. An Enhanced ScreenTip is a larger window that is more descriptive than a ScreenTip and provides a link to an Excel help topic.

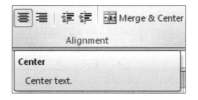

When you place your mouse pointer over an object on the Ribbon, a ScreenTip appears.

Sometimes you will see an Enhanced ScreenTip when you place your mouse pointer over an object. In this case, you receive an Enhanced ScreenTip explaining the function of the Margins command with a link to a help topic.

## Dialog Box Launchers

Many of the groups on the Ribbon have dialog box launchers 🔲. Clicking on the dialog box launcher will open a window that allows you to issue additional commands.

Clicking the dialog box launcher in the Font area of the Home ribbon will open the Format Cells dialog box with the Font tab displayed.

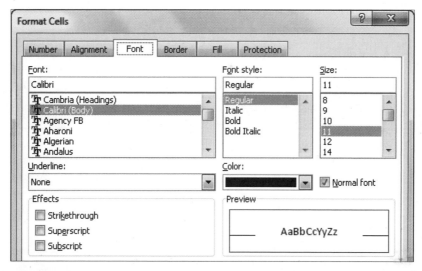

The Font tab of the Format Cells dialog box allows you to make changes to how the font appears in the selected cell(s).

## Hiding the Ribbon

There may be times when you do not want the Ribbon displayed at the top of the window. In order to hide it, simply click the Minimize the Ribbon button at the upper-right corner of the window, shown to the right. The button changes to become Expand the Ribbon. To display the Ribbon to issue a single command, click on the tab you wish to view. Once you have issued the command, the Ribbon will be hidden. To display the Ribbon permanently once again, click the Expand the Ribbon button.

| Task | Procedure |
|---|---|
| Customize the Quick Access toolbar with a standard command | ▪ Click the Customize Quick Access Toolbar button.<br>▪ Choose the desired command from the menu. |
| Customize the Quick Access toolbar with a Ribbon command | ▪ Right-click the Ribbon command you wish to add.<br>▪ Choose Add to Quick Access Toolbar. |
| Customize the Quick Access toolbar with a command not available on the Ribbon | ▪ Click the Customize Quick Access Toolbar ⊽ button on the Quick Access toolbar.<br>▪ Choose More Commands in the menu.<br>▪ Choose the category or tab from where you wish the command to come.<br>▪ Click the command you wish to add.<br>▪ Click Add. |
| Remove a button from the Quick Access toolbar | ▪ Right-click the button you wish to remove.<br>▪ Choose Remove from Quick Access Toolbar. |
| Customize the Ribbon | ▪ Choose File→Options 🖹.<br>▪ Choose the Customize Ribbon category to the left.<br>▪ Add or remove tabs, groups, and commands; rename tabs; change the tab order, or reset tabs to their original default items as desired. |
| Hide the Ribbon | ▪ Click the Minimize the Ribbon button at the upper-right corner of the window or double-click the tab of the currently displayed Ribbon. |
| Unhide the Ribbon | ▪ Click the Expand the Ribbon button at the upper-right corner of the window or double-click any of the tabs above the hidden Ribbon. |

## DEVELOP YOUR SKILLS 1.4.1

# Explore the Tabs, Ribbons, and the Quick Access Toolbar

*In this exercise, you will have the opportunity to explore the tabs and Ribbon at the top of the Excel window. In addition, you will add a button to the Quick Access toolbar that you believe is important to always have readily available.*

### Display the Page Layout Ribbon

*In the next few steps you will display the Page Layout tab of the Ribbon and open the Page Setup dialog box.*

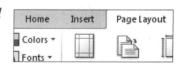

1. Click the **Page Layout tab** at the top of the window.
   *The Page Layout tab is displayed.*

2. Click the **dialog box launcher** at the bottom-right corner of the Page Setup group of the Ribbon.
   *The Page Setup dialog box appears.*

3. Click the **Cancel** button at the bottom of the dialog box to close it.

4. Move your **mouse pointer** over various commands on the Page Layout tab of the Ribbon to display their ScreenTips and explore what will occur if you choose to click them.

## Add a Button to the Quick Access Toolbar

*In this section, you will add a button to the Quick Access toolbar that will allow you to easily open another workbook.*

5. Follow these steps to add Open to the Quick Access toolbar:

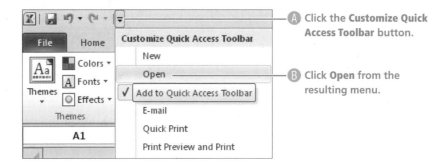

Ⓐ Click the **Customize Quick Access Toolbar** button.

Ⓑ Click **Open** from the resulting menu.

*Notice the ScreenTip that displays below the mouse pointer when you point at a menu option, explaining what will occur if you choose that option. The Open button will appear on the Quick Access toolbar.*

*The new button appears on the Quick Access toolbar.*

## Remove a Button from the Quick Access Toolbar

*In order to remove the Open button from the Quick Access toolbar, you will repeat the steps you took to add it.*

6. Click the **Customize Quick Access Toolbar** button.

7. Choose **Open** from the resulting menu.
   *Excel will essentially "remove the checkmark" from the Open option and remove the button from the toolbar. Leave the Excel window open, as you will continue to work with it in the next exercise.*

# 1.5 Entering Data in Excel

**Video Lesson**    labyrinthelab.com/videos

You can begin entering data the moment Excel is started. Data is entered into the active cell (the cell with the thick line around it). Text and numbers are used for different purposes in a worksheet. For instance, text entries cannot be used in calculations, whereas number entries can. Text is used for descriptive headings and entries that require alphabetic characters or a combination of alphabetic and numeric characters and spaces. Numbers can be entered directly or can be calculated using formulas. Excel recognizes the data you enter and decides whether the entry is text, a number, or a formula that performs a calculation.

## Data Types

Entries are defined as one of two main classifications: constant values or formulas. Constant values can be text, numeric, or a combination of both. The one thing that makes an entry constant is that the value does not change when other information changes. Conversely, formula entries display the results of calculations, and a result can change when a value in another cell changes.

$f_x$  1263

This entry is a constant value; it will not change as other cells are updated.

$f_x$  =SUM(C5:C8)

When a formula entry is used, it will refer to one or more cells and will change as the indicated cells are updated.

## Completing Cell Entries

Text and numbers are entered by positioning the highlight in the desired cell, typing the desired text or number, and completing the entry. You can use Enter, Tab, or any of the arrow keys (→, ←, ↑, ↓) to complete an entry. The position of the active cell following a cell entry depends on the method by which you complete the entry.

| Entry Completion Method | Where the Active Cell Will Appear |
|---|---|
| Enter | It will move down to the next cell. |
| Tab | It will move to the next cell to the right. |
| → ↑ ↓ ← | It will move to the next cell in the direction of the arrow key. |
| Esc | The entry will be deleted and the current cell will remain active. |

## The Enter and Cancel Buttons

The Enter ✔ and Cancel ✖ buttons appear on the Formula Bar whenever you enter or edit an entry. The Enter button completes the entry and keeps the highlight in the current cell. The Cancel button cancels the entry, as does the Esc key.

The Cancel and Enter buttons appear when an entry is being entered or edited.

| | A | B | C | D | E | F | G | H |
|---|---|---|---|---|---|---|---|---|
| 1 | Service Employees Weekend Hours Worked | | | | | | | |

A1    ▼    ✖ ✔ $f_x$  Service Employees Weekend Hours Worked

# Deleting and Replacing Entries

You can delete an entire entry after it has been completed by clicking in the cell and tapping ⎡Delete⎤. Likewise, you can replace an entry by clicking in the cell and typing a new entry. The new entry will replace the original entry.

# Long Text Entries

Text entries often do not fit in a cell. These entries are known as long entries. Excel uses the following rules when deciding how to display long entries:

- If the cell to the right of the long entry is empty, then the long entry displays over the adjacent cell.

- If the cell to the right of the long entry contains an entry, then Excel shortens, or truncates, the display of the long entry.

Keep in mind that Excel does not actually change the long entry; it simply truncates the display of the entry. You can always widen a column to accommodate a long entry.

| | A | B | C | D | E |
|---|---|---|---|---|---|
| 1 | Service Employees Weekend Hours Worked | | | | |
| 2 | | | | | |

The entry, Service Employees Weekend Hours Worked, is a long entry. The entire phrase is entered in cell A1, although it displays over cells A1-E1.

DEVELOP YOUR SKILLS 1.5.1
# Enter Text

*In this exercise, you will enter text into your worksheet.*

## Type a Long Entry

*First, you will have the opportunity to see how text can flow over empty cells to the right of its "home" cell.*

1. Make **cell A1** active by clicking the **mouse pointer** ✛ in it.

2. Type **Service Employees Weekend Hours Worked** and **tap** ⎡Enter⎤.
   *The text is entered in the cell and the highlight moves down to cell A2. Excel moves the highlight down when you tap* ⎡Enter⎤ *because most people enter data column by column. Notice that the entry displays over cells B1, C1, D1, and E1. The long entry would not display over these cells if they contained data.*

3. Click **cell A1** and note the appearance of the Formula Bar.

| A1 | ▾ | ● | $f_x$ | Service Employees Weekend Hours Worked |

*Notice that the Formula Bar displays the name of the active cell (A1) as well as its content. In this example, the cell's content is the title, Service Employees Weekend Hours Worked. The title is a long entry because it is wider than cell A1. Cells B1-E1 are empty so the long entry is displayed over them. Keep in mind, however, that the entire entry belongs to cell A1. This concept will be demonstrated in the next few steps.*

## Verify that the Entry Belongs to Cell A1

4. **Tap** the ⎡→⎤ key to make cell B1 active.

5. Look at the **Formula Bar** and notice that cell B1 is empty.
   *The long entry belongs to cell A1 even though it is displayed over cells A1–E1.*

## Type Additional Text Entries

6. Click in **cell C3**.

7. Type **Friday** and **tap** →️ once.
   *Notice that the entry is completed and the highlight moves to cell D3. You can always use the arrow keys to complete an entry and move the highlight in the desired direction.*

8. Type **Wednesday** in cell D3 and **tap** →️.

9. Type **Sunday** in cell E3 and **tap** ←️.
   *Notice that the display of* Wednesday *is shortened, or truncated.*
   *However, the Wednesday entry is still contained in its entirety in cell D3.*
   *A long entry is always truncated when the cell to the right contains text, a number, or a formula.*

   | Friday | Wednesd: | Sunday |
   |---|---|---|

10. Type **Saturday** in cell D3 and **tap** ⎯Enter⎯.
    *The new entry in cell D3 replaces the previous entry.*

11. **Enter** the remaining text entries shown in the following illustration.
    *If Excel proposes any entries for you as you type, simply continue typing. Leave the workbook open for the next exercise.*

|  | A | B | C | D | E |
|---|---|---|---|---|---|
| 1 | Service Employees Weekend Hours Worked | | | | |
| 2 | | | | | |
| 3 | Alton Mall | | Friday | Saturday | Sunday |
| 4 | | Barnes | | | |
| 5 | | Chau | | | |
| 6 | | Lee | | | |
| 7 | | Olsen | | | |
| 8 | | Total Hrs | | | |
| 9 | Century Bank | | | | |
| 10 | | Garcia | | | |
| 11 | | Kimura | | | |
| 12 | | Tan | | | |
| 13 | | Total Hrs | | | |
| 14 | Newport Medical | | | | |
| 15 | | Kowalski | | | |
| 16 | | Silva | | | |
| 17 | | Wilson | | | |
| 18 | | Total Hrs | | | |

# 1.6 Working with Numbers

**Video Lesson**　labyrinthelab.com/videos

Number entries can contain only the digits 0–9 and a few other characters. Excel initially right-aligns numbers in cells, although you can change this alignment. The following table lists characters that Excel accepts as part of a number entry.

| Valid Characters in Number Entries |
| --- |
| The digits 0–9 |
| The following characters: + – ( ) , / $ % . * |

Entering numbers using the numeric keypad is very quick. The keypad is designed like a calculator. It includes its own decimal point and an Enter key.

## Number Formats

It isn't necessary to type commas, dollar signs, and other number formats when entering numbers. It's easier to simply enter the numbers and use Excel's formatting commands to add the desired number format(s). You will not format numbers in this lesson.

## Decimals and Negative Numbers

You should always type a decimal point if the number you are entering requires one. Likewise, you should precede a negative number entry with a minus (–) sign or enclose it in parentheses ( ).

### DEVELOP YOUR SKILLS 1.6.1
### Enter Numbers

*In this exercise, you will practice entering numbers and canceling entries before completion.*

**Use the Enter Button**

1. Position the highlight in **cell C4**.

2. Type **6** but don't complete the entry.

3. Look at the Formula Bar and notice the **Cancel** ☒ and **Enter** ✔ buttons.
   *These buttons appear whenever you begin entering or editing data in a cell.*

4. Click the **Enter** ✔ button to complete the entry.
   *Notice that the highlight remains in cell C4. You can use the Enter button to complete entries, though it is more efficient to use the keyboard when building a worksheet. This is because the highlight automatically moves to the next cell. The Enter button is most useful when editing entries.*

## Use the Cancel Button and the [Esc] Key

5. Position the highlight in cell C5 and type **8**, but don't complete the entry.

6. Click the **Cancel** [X] button on the Formula Bar to cancel the entry.

7. Type **8** again, but this time **tap** [Esc] on the keyboard.
   *The [Esc] key has the same effect as the Cancel button.*

8. Type **8** once again, and this time **tap** [↓].
   *Notice that Excel right-aligns the number in the cell.*

9. **Enter** the remaining numbers shown in the illustration at right.

**TIP** — To use the numeric keypad to enter numbers, the [number lock] light must be on. If it's not, press the [Num Lock] key on the keypad.

|  | A | B | C | D | E |
|---|---|---|---|---|---|
| 1 | Service Employees Weekend Hours Worked | | | | |
| 2 | | | | | |
| 3 | Alton Mall | | Friday | Saturday | Sunday |
| 4 | | Barnes | 6 | 6 | 6 |
| 5 | | Chau | 8 | 8 | 8 |
| 6 | | Lee | 4 | 0 | 4 |
| 7 | | Olsen | 4 | 3 | 0 |
| 8 | | Total Hrs | | | |
| 9 | Century Bank | | | | |
| 10 | | Garcia | 3 | 5 | 0 |
| 11 | | Kimura | 3 | 4 | 0 |
| 12 | | Tan | 3 | 5 | 0 |
| 13 | | Total Hrs | | | |
| 14 | Newport Medical | | | | |
| 15 | | Kowalski | 8 | 6 | 8 |
| 16 | | Silva | 6 | 6 | 0 |
| 17 | | Wilson | 5 | 2 | 5 |
| 18 | | Total Hrs | | | |

10. Take a minute to verify that you have correctly entered all the numbers.
    *It is so important for you to be accurate when you are entering data into Excel. Learning how to use complex formulas and functions will not do you any good if your original data is inaccurate!*

# 1.7 Understanding Save Concepts

**Video Lesson** — labyrinthelab.com/videos

One important lesson to learn is to save your workbooks early and often! Power outages and careless accidents can result in lost data. The best protection is to save your workbooks every 10 or 15 minutes or after making significant changes. Workbooks are saved to file storage locations such as a USB drive, the Documents folder, a shared network drive, and websites on the Internet.

## Storing Your Exercise Files

Throughout this book, you will be referred to files in your "file storage location." You can store your exercise files on various media, such as on a USB flash drive, in the Documents folder, or to a network drive at a school or company. While some figures may display files on a USB flash drive, it is assumed that you will substitute your own location for that shown in the figures. See Storing Your Exercise Files for additional information on alternative storage media. Storing Your Exercise Files is available on the student web page for this book at labyrinthelab.com/excel10.

**NOTE** — In Windows XP, the folder is called My Documents. In Windows Vista and Windows 7, it is called Documents. Throughout this book we will use the word Documents when referring to this folder.

If you have not yet copied the student exercise files to your local file storage location, follow the instructions in Storing Your Exercise Files, located on the student web page for this book.

## The Save Command

The Save ![icon] button on the Quick Access toolbar or the File tab on the Ribbon initiates the Save command. If a document has been saved previously, Excel replaces the original version with the new, edited version. If a document has never been saved, Excel displays the Save As dialog box. The Save As dialog box lets you specify the name and storage location of the document. You can also use the Save As dialog box to make a copy of a document by saving it under a new name or to a different location. Your filenames can have up to 255 characters, including spaces. Your filenames, however, should be descriptive but brief enough to manage your files and share them on networks and the Internet effectively.

## Save As Options

In Excel, you are given multiple options as to how to save your workbook. How you save a workbook depends on how it will be used and who will be using it. If you are collaborating with someone who has a version earlier than Excel 2007 installed, you will need to save the file in the Excel 97-2003 Format. If you wish to publish your workbook and do not wish for others to make changes to it, you may save it as a PDF file for viewing in the Adobe Reader program. The default format is the Excel Workbook format, which is great to use if everyone who will be utilizing the file has Excel 2010 or 2007 installed.

The Save As command allows you to save a spreadsheet or entire workbook in various formats to use data in earlier versions of Excel or other applications.

| File | Home |
| --- | --- |
| 💾 Save | |
| 📁 Save As | |

Excel Workbook
Excel Macro-Enabled Workbook
Excel Binary Workbook
Excel 97-2003 Workbook
XML Data
Single File Web Page
Web Page
Excel Template
Excel Macro-Enabled Template
Excel 97-2003 Template
Text (Tab delimited)
Unicode Text
XML Spreadsheet 2003
Microsoft Excel 5.0/95 Workbook
CSV (Comma delimited)
Formatted Text (Space delimited)
Text (Macintosh)
Text (MS-DOS)
CSV (Macintosh)
CSV (MS-DOS)
DIF (Data Interchange Format)
SYLK (Symbolic Link)
Excel Add-In
Excel 97-2003 Add-In
PDF
XPS Document
OpenDocument Spreadsheet

## Locating Workbooks

The Save As dialog box lets you locate workbooks on your local drives and in network locations. The Documents folder in the hard drive of your local computer usually is the default location for saving a workbook. You must change the location if you do not want to save there. Once you save to or open a workbook from a different location, the default changes to that location. Always check the Save As dialog box for the current drive and folder before finishing the save.

## Issuing Commands from the Keyboard

There are many times when it is more convenient to issue a command from the keyboard than to chase it down with your mouse. These commands are termed keyboard shortcuts and can help you to be more efficient as you can enter these commands "on the fly" without removing your fingers from the keyboard. In this book, you will see keyboard shortcuts displayed in a special feature called From the Keyboard. Whenever you issue a keyboard command, you will first hold down the shortcut key ( Ctrl ,

**FROM THE KEYBOARD**
Ctrl + S to save

Alt, or Shift) and then tap the additional key to issue the command. This approach is similar to holding down the Shift key and then tapping a letter to make it capital. Throughout this book, you will be asked to use Ctrl + S to save your worksheet.

## *Key Tips*

While not every command has a keyboard shortcut assigned, you still can use the keyboard to choose any command on the Ribbon or Quick Access toolbar. When you tap the Alt key, numbered key tips display over buttons on the Quick Access toolbar and alphabetic key tips display over the Ribbon tabs. For example, the sequence for choosing the Save As command is Alt, F, A. You may wish to memorize your most frequently used commands.

Tapping Alt and then F (or using Alt + F) will display the File tab. ——

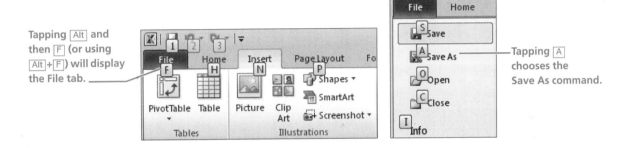

Tapping A chooses the Save As command.

## *AutoSave*

If your computer suddenly stops working, you may be able to recover some of your work. When switched on, the AutoSave feature saves your workbook to a default file storage location every ten minutes or at the interval you set. This is *not* the location where you save your workbooks. An autosave is performed only if you edited the workbook during the interval. If your computer freezes or loses power, the Document Recovery pane should display when you restart the computer and Excel. The pane contains one or more document versions you may recover. If you wish to keep a version other than the "Original" one you saved, you should then save it to your file storage location. Some of Excel's save options are shown in the following illustration.

Option that automatically creates a workbook recovery file at the specified interval

Option to allow you to recover the last autosave if you did not issue a save command

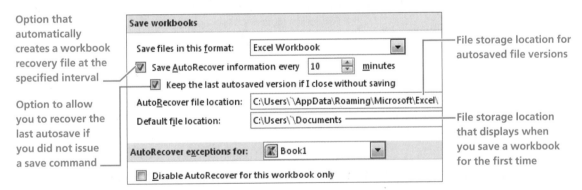

File storage location for autosaved file versions

File storage location that displays when you save a workbook for the first time

Use the Save command often for the best possible chance of recovering your most recent changes to a workbook. Changes made after the last autosave cannot be recovered.

## Managing Workbook File Versions

When the Keep the Last Autosaved Version If I Close Without Saving option is switched on, Excel maintains the last autosaved version for four days. The Info and Recent tabs in Backstage view allow you to recover autosaved versions or the unsaved version of a workbook after you close it.

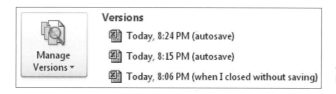

Autosaved workbook versions displayed in the Info tab of Backstage view

| QUICK REFERENCE | SAVING A WORKBOOK AND MANAGING WORKBOOK FILE VERSIONS |
|---|---|
| **Task** | **Procedure** |
| Save for the first time | ▪ Click Save 💾 on the Quick Access toolbar.<br>▪ Name the workbook and choose the location in which to save it.<br>▪ Click Save. |
| Save changes in the workbook | ▪ Click Save 💾 on the Quick Access toolbar. |
| Save in a new location or with a new name | ▪ Choose File→Save As 📇.<br>▪ Change the name of the workbook, the file storage location, or both.<br>▪ Click Save. |
| Save the workbook in the Excel 97-2003 Format | ▪ Choose File→Save As 📇.<br>▪ Enter the filename and navigate to the desired file storage location.<br>▪ Choose Excel 97-2003 from the Save as Type list.<br>▪ Click Save. |
| Use key tips to choose a command | ▪ Tap the Alt key to display key tips.<br>▪ Tap the letter or number key that corresponds to the desired tab on the Ribbon or Quick Access toolbar button.<br>▪ Tap the letter(s) in the key tip for the desired command on the Ribbon. |

| QUICK REFERENCE | SAVING A WORKBOOK AND MANAGING WORKBOOK FILE VERSIONS (continued) |
|---|---|
| **Task** | **Procedure** |
| Set autosave options | ■ Choose File→Options 🗎, and choose the Save category at the left in the Excel Options dialog box. |
| | ■ Place a checkmark next to Save AutoRecover Information Every, and type the desired number in the Minutes box. |
| | ■ Place a checkmark next to Keep the Last Autosaved Version If I Close Without Saving. |
| Recover an autosaved workbook version | ■ With the workbook file open, choose File→Info. |
| | ■ In the Info tab of Backstage view, click the version that displays the desired date and time. |
| Recover an unsaved workbook | ■ Perform one of the following: |
| | ◆ Choose File→Info. In the Info tab of Backstage view, click the Manage Versions menu ▼ button, and choose Recover Unsaved Workbooks. |
| | *or* |
| | ◆ Choose File→Recent. Choose Recover Unsaved Workbooks at the lower-right corner of the Recent tab of Backstage view. |
| | ■ In the Open dialog box, display the files in Details view. |
| | ■ Double-click the file displaying the desired filename, date, and time. |
| | ■ Click Save As in the message area above the worksheet, enter a filename, and choose your file storage location. |

DEVELOP YOUR SKILLS 1.7.1

# Save the Workbook

*In this exercise, you will save the workbook created in the previous exercises to your file storage location. You will also use key tips to select a command on the Ribbon and view Excel's options for saving workbooks.*

*Before You Begin: Navigate to the student web page for this book at labyrinthelab.com/excel10 and see the Downloading the Student Exercise Files section of Storing Your Exercise Files for instructions on how to retrieve the student exercise files for this book and to copy them to your file storage location.*

## Use the Mouse to Save

1. Click the **Save** 🖫 button on the Quick Access toolbar.
   *The Save As dialog box appears because this is the first time you are saving the workbook.*

2. Notice that the proposed name Book1 is highlighted in the File Name box.
   *The name may be Book2 or something similar. You may need to select the name to highlight it if you clicked elsewhere in the dialog box.*

3. **Type** the name **Weekend Hours Worked** and it will replace the proposed name.

   | File name: | Weekend Hours Worked |
   |---|---|
   | Save as type: | Excel Workbook |

4. Choose the Lesson 01 folder in your file storage location by **navigating** to the correct drive and folder.
   *See the online document, Storing Your Exercise Files, for specific instructions for your operating system.*

5. Click **Save** or **tap** Enter.
   *Notice that the filename appears in the Title Bar of the window to indicate that the workbook is saved.*

### Use Key Tips to Save As

6. **Tap** the ⌐Alt⌐ key.
   *Key tips display on the Quick Access toolbar and Ribbon.*

7. **Tap** the ⌐F⌐ key.
   *The File tab displays.*

8. **Tap** the ⌐A⌐ key.
   *The Save As dialog box displays.*

9. **Tap** ⌐Esc⌐ to cancel the dialog box without saving.

### Explore Save Options

10. Choose File→Options 🄱.

11. Choose the **Save** category at the left of the Excel Options dialog box.

12. Notice the settings under Save Workbooks
   *The two autorecovery options may be switched on, as indicated by checkmarks.*

13. On a classroom computer, click **Cancel** to close the dialog box without changing the default save options.
   *On a computer you own, you may place a checkmark next to Save AutoRecover Information Every and enter the desired number in the Minutes box. You may place a checkmark next to Keep the Last Autosaved Version If I Close Without Saving.*

   *Leave the workbook open for the next exercise.*

   | | Weekend Hours Worked - Microsoft Excel | |
   |---|---|---|

## 1.8 Closing and Starting New Workbooks

**Video Lesson**    labyrinthelab.com/videos

The Close 🗀 command is used to close an open workbook. When you close a workbook that has not been saved, Excel prompts you to save the changes. If you choose to save at the prompt and the workbook has previously been saved, Excel simply saves the changes and closes the workbook. If the workbook is new, Excel displays the Save As dialog box, allowing you to assign a name and file storage location to the workbook.

**FROM THE KEYBOARD**
⌐Ctrl⌐+⌐N⌐ to open a new, blank workbook

The New command on the File menu displays Backstage view, where you may start a new, blank workbook. You can create a new workbook at any time because multiple workbooks may be open simultaneously.

## Close the Workbook and Start a New Workbook

*In this exercise, you will close the workbook that you have been working on throughout this lesson. Then you will open a new, blank workbook.*

1. Choose **File→Close** 📁.

2. Click the **Save** or **Yes** button if Excel asks you if you want to save the changes.
   *Notice that no workbook appears in the Excel window. The Excel window always has this appearance when all workbooks have been closed.*

3. Choose **File→New**.

4. Follow these steps to create a new, blank workbook:

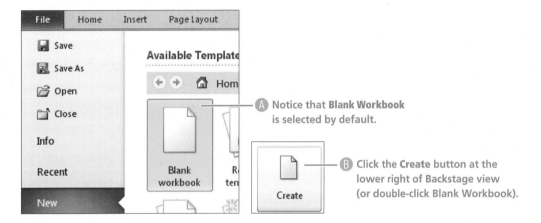

Ⓐ Notice that **Blank Workbook** is selected by default.

Ⓑ Click the **Create** button at the lower right of Backstage view (or double-click Blank Workbook).

*You will not enter any data into this workbook.*

# 1.9 Exiting from Excel

**Video Lesson** labyrinthelab.com/videos

You should exit Excel and other programs if you are certain you won't be using them for some time. This will free up memory for other programs. When you exit Excel, you will be prompted to save any workbooks that have unsaved edits. The Close command differs from the Exit command in that Close affects only the active workbook and leaves Excel open. Any other workbooks that are being used will remain open until you close them or exit Excel.

| QUICK REFERENCE | CLOSING WORKBOOKS AND EXITING EXCEL |
|---|---|
| **Task** | **Procedure** |
| Close the active workbook | ▪ Choose File→Close 📁. |
| | ▪ Respond if asked to save changes to the workbook. |
| Close all open workbooks and exit Excel | ▪ Choose File→Exit ☒. |
| | ▪ Respond if asked to save changes for any open workbooks. |

## Exit from Excel

*In this exercise, you will exit from the Excel program.*

1. Choose **File→Exit** ☒.

   *Excel will close without prompting you to save the workbook because you have not entered any data into it.*

# 1.10 Concepts Review

| Concepts Review | labyrinthelab.com/excel10 |

*To check your knowledge of the key concepts introduced in this lesson, complete the Concepts Review quiz by going to the URL listed above. If your classroom is using Labyrinth eLab, you may complete the Concepts Review quiz from within your eLab course.*

# Reinforce Your Skills

## Create a Workbook

*In this exercise, you will create a workbook. You will start Excel and then enter text and numbers that contain two decimal places.*

### Start Excel and Enter Text

1. Start Excel by selecting **All Programs→Microsoft Office→Microsoft Office Excel 2010** from the Start menu.
   *Notice that a blank workbook with three worksheets is displayed when you open Excel.*

2. Enter text in **rows 1 through 9** as shown in the following illustration.
   *Use the* Tab *and* Enter *keys as necessary to enter the data. Type the customer's name and address in cells B5, B6, and B7.*

|  | A | B | C | D | E |
|---|---|---|---|---|---|
| 1 | Order Tracking Sheet | | | | |
| 2 | | | | | |
| 3 | Order No. | 1552 | | | |
| 4 | | | | | |
| 5 | Sold to: | Empire Dry Cleaning | | | |
| 6 | | 1833 Franklin Highway | | | |
| 7 | | Huntington, WV 25716 | | | |
| 8 | | | | | |
| 9 | Item | In Stock? | Quantity | Price | Discount |

### Enter Decimal and Negative Numbers

3. In **cells A9 through E14**, enter the data shown in the illustration at right.
   *Type a decimal point (.) in the Price numbers and Discount numbers. Type a minus (–) sign before the Discount numbers.*

|  | A | B | C | D | E |
|---|---|---|---|---|---|
| 9 | Item | In Stock? | Quantity | Price | Discount |
| 10 | A423 | Y | 2 | 63.95 | -3.15 |
| 11 | A321 | Y | 4 | 28.95 | 0 |
| 12 | D928 | N | 16 | 5.85 | -0.59 |
| 13 | S251 | N | 8 | 3.09 | -0.31 |
| 14 | B444 | Y | 20 | 8.77 | -0.88 |

### Save the Workbook

4. Choose **Save** 📥 on the Quick Access toolbar.

5. **Type** the filename **rs-Order Tracking** and **navigate** to the Lesson 01 folder in your file storage location.

6. Click **Save** or **tap** Enter.
   *The workbook will be saved in the location that you specified. Leave the workbook open.*

# Explore the Excel Window and Save and Close Your Workbook

*In this exercise, you will take a look at the features of the Excel window before saving the changes and closing your new workbook.*

1. **Click** to display the Data tab of the Ribbon.
   *Look at the types of commands available. Many of them will be covered in later lessons of this book.*

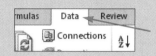

2. Select the **View** tab of the Ribbon.

3. Click the **Minimize the Ribbon** ⌃ button at the upper-right corner of the window to hide the Ribbon.

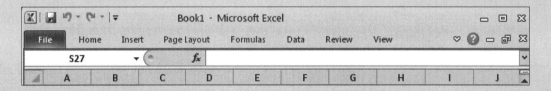

4. **Double-click** the Home tab to display the Ribbon once again.
   *Notice that the Home tab is displayed because you chose it to redisplay the Ribbon.*

5. Click **cell C5**, and then look at the **Formula Bar**.

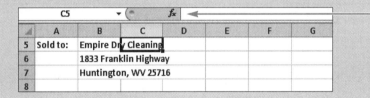

   *There is nothing displayed because the entire entry is contained in cell B5 and is simply spilling over cell C5 because it is empty.*

6. **Type** your name, and then click the **Enter** ✔ button.
   *Your name will now appear in cell C5, and the customer name in cell B5 will be truncated.*

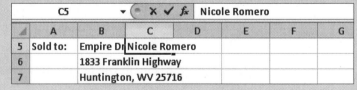

7. **Tap** ⎣Delete⎦.
   *Your name will be deleted, and the customer name from B5 will once again spill over the cells to the right.*

8. Select **cell A16** and **enter** your first and last names.

9. Use ⎣Ctrl⎦+⎣S⎦ to save the changes to the workbook.
   *The workbook saves to your same file storage location as before.*

10. Choose **File→Exit** to close Excel.

# Apply Your Skills

## Create a New Workbook

*In this exercise, you will create a new worksheet and then save and close the workbook.*

1. Start **Excel** by selecting **All Programs** from the Start menu.
   *A new, blank workbook appears.*

2. Create the **worksheet** shown in the following illustration and **type** your first and last names in **cell D1**.
   *Proofread all data. You will not create formulas to calculate totals in this exercise.*

| | A | B | C | D | E |
|---|---|---|---|---|---|
| 1 | Green Clean Q1 Expenses | | | Student Name | |
| 2 | | | | | |
| 3 | Item | | January | February | March |
| 4 | Building | Lease | 3000 | 3000 | 3000 |
| 5 | | Utilities | 1689 | 1572 | 1646 |
| 6 | | Phone | 250 | 242 | 329 |
| 7 | | Insurance | 8696 | 0 | 0 |
| 8 | | Total | | | |
| 9 | | | | | |
| 10 | Equipment | | 1211 | 506 | 4890 |
| 11 | | | | | |
| 12 | Salaries | Mgmt | 4500 | 4500 | 4500 |
| 13 | | Full time | 20658 | 19777 | 21422 |
| 14 | | Part time | 24656 | 25980 | 25316 |
| 15 | | Total | | | |
| 16 | | | | | |
| 17 | Supplies | Office | 1963 | 2432 | 1784 |
| 18 | | Vehicle | 872 | 944 | 903 |
| 19 | | Total | | | |
| 20 | | | | | |
| 21 | Other | Fuel | | | |
| 22 | | Marketing | 500 | 300 | 200 |
| 23 | | Uniforms | 63 | 101 | 83 |
| 24 | | Misc | 162 | 471 | 65 |
| 25 | | Total | | | |

3. **Save** the workbook with the name **as-Q1 Expenses** in **your** Lesson 01 folder and then **exit** Excel.

# Critical Thinking & Work-Readiness Skills

*In the course of working through the following Microsoft Office-based Critical Thinking exercises, you will also be utilizing various work-readiness skills, some of which are listed next to each exercise. Go to* labyrinthelab.com/workreadiness *to learn more about the work-readiness skills.*

## 1.1 Enter Missing Data into a Worksheet

Nicole's manager at Green Clean mentions the importance of the spreadsheet for daily reporting of timesheet hours for employees. Hearing this, Nicole realizes that doing a good job every day on this report will be appreciated. She decides from now on to double-check that she has transferred the numbers correctly before she shows it to her manager. Sure enough, she sees that Tan's Friday number should have been 4, and that Silva's Saturday number should have been 3. Open ct-Timesheet Hours (Lesson 01 folder), enter the corrections, and save the corrected workbook as **ct-Timesheet Hours Revised**.

## 1.2 Enter New Data into a Worksheet

Nicole begins to understand that mileage for employees driving to jobs is a big concern. Trying to anticipate her manager's needs, she decides that a handy reminder of the mileage to each customer might be useful. Using Google Maps and MapQuest, she figures out the mileage from Green Clean headquarters to each of the locations. The distances are as follows: Alton Mall, 10 miles; Century Bank, 12.5 miles; and Newport Medical, 24 miles. She wants to get her manager's feedback before going any further with her idea. Open ct-Timesheet Hours Revised, if necessary, and insert these values in column B next to each facility. Do not be concerned that the column A entries do not display completely. Save the edited worksheet as **ct-Mileage** in your Lesson 01 folder. Close the workbook but do not exit Excel.

## 1.3 Use the Numeric Keypad

Now that she has proven she can create accurate spreadsheets, Nicole is asked to put together additional spreadsheets. Nicole sees that streamlining the way she does data entry will help her handle her workload. She decides to practice using the numeric keypad. Create a new, blank workbook. Practice data entry, reading numbers from various exercises in this lesson and entering the data down a column of the blank worksheet using the numeric keypad. Practice until you feel comfortable. (There is no need to save your work.) Why should Nicole (and you) pay attention to speed as well as accuracy when creating spreadsheets? Type your answer in a Word document named **ct-Questions** saved to your Lesson 01 folder.

# Editing, Viewing, and Printing Worksheets

In this lesson, you will expand on basic skills in Excel. You will learn various methods of editing worksheets: replacing and deleting entries, using Undo and Redo, working with AutoCorrect, and more. You will also learn about printing Excel worksheets and working with different views. When you have finished this lesson, you will have developed the skills necessary to produce carefully edited and proofed worksheets.

## LEARNING OBJECTIVES

After studying this lesson, you will be able to:

- Use a variety of techniques to select, move, and copy cells and ranges
- Clear cell contents, including formatting
- Complete cell entries automatically
- Work with various Excel views and the zoom feature
- Print your worksheet and change workbook properties

# Creating a Basic List in Excel

Ken Hazell is the human resources manager of Green Clean, a janitorial product supplier and cleaning service contractor. He realizes that Excel can be used as a simple database to maintain lists of employees, product inventory, or other items. He and other managers use Excel's view options to work with data and preview how the worksheet will look when printed.

| Green Clean | | | | |
|---|---|---|---|---|
| Management and Support Roster | | | | |
| | | | | |
| Name | Phone | Position | Employment Date | On Call |
| Tommy Choi | 619-555-3224 | President | | |
| Mary Wright | 858-555-3098 | VP, Sales and Marketing | 5/22/2007 | Monday |
| Derek Navarro | 619-555-3309 | VP, Operations | 3/30/2009 | Tuesday |
| Isabella Riso-Neff | 858-555-0211 | Risk Management Director | 4/13/2009 | Wednesday |
| Kenneth Hazell | 619-555-3224 | Human Resources Director | 7/17/2006 | Thursday |
| D'Andre Adams | 760-555-3876 | Facilities Services Manager | 12/7/2005 | Friday |
| Talos Bouras | 858-555-1002 | Sales Manager | 5/10/2004 | Saturday |
| Michael Chowdery | 858-555-0021 | Purchasing Manager | 10/26/2009 | Sunday |
| Ahn Tran | 760-555-0728 | Office Manager | 6/26/2006 | |
| Jenna Mann | 951-555-0826 | Administrative Assistant | 3/15/2010 | |
| Nicole Romero | 858-555-4987 | Payroll Assistant | 5/25/2009 | |
| Amy Wyatt | 619-555-4016 | Customer Service Rep | 8/17/2009 | |

Ken will use this spreadsheet to organize the management and support employees' phone numbers, dates of employment, and the evening that each manager is on call in case of emergency.

| | A | B | C | D | E |
|---|---|---|---|---|---|
| | | | Click to add header | | |
| 1 | Green Clean | | | | |
| 2 | Management and Support Roster | | | | |
| 3 | | | | | |
| 4 | Name | Phone | Position | Employment Date | On Call |
| 5 | Tommy Choi | 619-555-3224 | President | | |
| 6 | Mary Wright | 858-555-3098 | VP, Sales and Marketing | 5/22/2007 | Monday |
| 7 | Derek Navarro | 619-555-3309 | VP, Operations | 3/30/2009 | Tuesday |
| 8 | Isabella Riso-Neff | 858-555-0211 | Risk Management Director | 4/13/2009 | Wednesday |
| 9 | Kenneth Hazell | 619-555-3224 | Human Resources Director | 7/17/2006 | Thursday |
| 10 | D'Andre Adams | 760-555-3876 | Facilities Services Manager | 12/7/2005 | Friday |
| 11 | Talos Bouras | 858-555-1002 | Sales Manager | 5/10/2004 | Saturday |
| 12 | Michael Chowdery | 858-555-0021 | Purchasing Manager | 10/26/2009 | Sunday |
| 13 | Ahn Tran | 760-555-0728 | Office Manager | 6/26/2006 | |

Ken previews the worksheet in Page Layout view prior to printing it.

# 2.1 Opening Workbooks

**Video Lesson**  labyrinthelab.com/videos

**FROM THE KEYBOARD**
Ctrl+O to open

The File→Open command displays the Open dialog box. The Open dialog box lets you navigate to any file storage location and open previously saved workbooks. Once a workbook is open, you can browse it, print it, and make editing changes. The organization and layout of the Open dialog box are similar to those of the Save As dialog box.

### DEVELOP YOUR SKILLS 2.1.1
## Open the Workbook

*In this exercise, you will open a workbook that lists various employees.*

1. Start **Excel**.

2. Click the **File** tab on the Ribbon and choose the **Open** command.
   *The Open dialog box is displayed.*

In future lessons, this command will be written, Choose File→Open.

3. **Navigate** to your file storage location (such as a USB flash drive).

4. **Double-click** the Lesson 02 folder to open it.

5. Select the Management Roster workbook and click **Open**.

You can also double-click a document in the Open dialog box to open it.

# 2.2 Editing Entries

**Video Lesson**  labyrinthelab.com/videos

You can edit the active cell by clicking in the Formula Bar and making the desired changes. You can also double-click a cell and edit the contents directly there. This technique is known as in-cell editing.

## Replacing Entries

Editing an entry is efficient if the entry is so long that retyping it would be time-consuming. Editing can also be helpful when working with complex formulas and other functions that are difficult to re-create. If the entry requires little typing, however, it is usually easier to simply retype it. If you retype an entry, the new entry will replace whatever is contained in the cell.

# Deleting Characters

Use the Delete and Backspace keys to edit entries in the Formula Bar and within a cell. The Delete key removes the character to the right of the insertion point, while the Backspace key removes the character to the left of the insertion point.

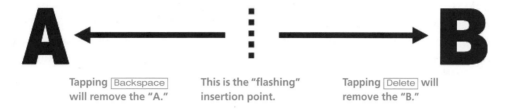

| Tapping Backspace will remove the "A." | This is the "flashing" insertion point. | Tapping Delete will remove the "B." |

---

## DEVELOP YOUR SKILLS 2.2.1
## Edit Entries

*In this exercise, you will use the Formula Bar to revise the contents of cell A2. You will also edit cells B3 and B15 directly in the cells.*

### Edit in the Formula Bar

1. Click **cell A2** to select it.

2. Follow these steps to edit cell A2 using the Formula Bar:

Ⓐ Click in the **Formula Bar** just to the right of the word *List*.

Ⓑ Tap Backspace four times to remove the word *List*, and then type **Roster**.

Ⓒ Click the Enter button.

### Replace an Entry

3. Click **cell D4**.

4. Type **Employment Date** and **tap** Enter.
   *The entry* Employment Date *replaces the entry* Starting Date. *Notice that the cell formatting (underlining the word) has been applied to the new entry as well. Also note that the new entry is cut off or truncated because the cell to the right contains an entry.*

### Use In-Cell Editing

5. **Double-click** cell A8 (the cell with the name Isabella Riso).

6. Use the mouse or the → key to position the flashing **insertion point** to the right of the last name, Riso.

7. Type **–Neff**, and then **tap** Enter to complete the change.
   *The entry should now read Isabella Riso-Neff.*

8. Click the **Save** 🖫 button to update the changes.
   *Clicking the Save button automatically saves changes to a workbook that has previously been saved.*

# 2.3 Selecting Cells and Ranges

**Video Lesson**  labyrinthelab.com/videos

When you want to change something in a worksheet—for instance, move, copy, delete, format, or print specific data—you must first select the cell(s). The most efficient way to select cells is with the mouse, though you can also use the keyboard method. You can select one or many cells. A group of contiguous (adjacent) cells is called a range. Entire columns or rows may be selected by clicking or dragging the column headings (such as A, B, C) or row headings (such as 1, 2, 3).

## Excel Ranges

Each cell has a reference. For example, A1 refers to the first cell in a worksheet. Likewise, a range reference specifies the cells included within a range. The range reference includes the first and last cells in the range separated by a colon (:). For example, the range A4:E4 includes all cells between A4 and E4 inclusive. The following illustration highlights several ranges and their corresponding range references.

| | A6 | ▼ | $f_x$ | Mary Wright | | |
|---|---|---|---|---|---|---|
| | **A** | **B** | **C** | | **D** | **E** |
| **1** | Green Clean | | | | | |
| **2** | Management and Support Roster | | | | | |
| **3** | | | | | | |
| **4** | Name | Phone | Position | | Employment Date | On Call |
| **5** | Tommy Choi | 619-555-3224 | President | | | |
| **6** | Mary Wright | 858-555-3098 | VP, Sales and Marketing | | 5/22/2007 | |
| **7** | Derek Navarro | 619-555-3309 | VP, Operations | | 3/30/2009 | |
| **8** | Isabella Riso-Neff | 858-555-0211 | Risk Management Director | | 4/13/2009 | |
| **9** | Kenneth Hazell | 619-555-3224 | Human Resources Director | | 7/17/2006 | |
| **10** | D'Andre Adams | 760-555-3876 | Facilities Services Manager | | 12/7/2005 | |
| **11** | Talos Bouras | 858-555-1002 | Sales Manager | | 5/10/2004 | |
| **12** | Michael Chowdery | 858-555-0021 | Purchasing Manager | | 10/26/2009 | |
| **13** | Ahn Tran | 760-555-0728 | Office Manager | | 6/26/2006 | |
| **14** | Jenna Mann | 951-555-0826 | Administrative Assistant | | 3/15/2010 | |

*Range A1:A2* — rows 1–2, column A

*Range A4:E4* — row 4

*Range A6:D10* — rows 6–10

The selected ranges in the worksheet are shaded, as displayed above. In addition, the first cell in the last range selected, A6, shows no shading and has an outline around it. This cell display indicates that it is the active cell, which is displayed in the Name Box and Formula Bar.

The following Quick Reference table describes selection techniques in Excel.

| QUICK REFERENCE | SELECTING CELLS AND RANGES |
|---|---|
| **Techniques** | **How to Do It** |
| Select a range | Drag the mouse pointer over the desired cells. |
| Select several ranges | Select a range, and then press Ctrl while selecting additional range(s). |
| Select an entire column | Click a column heading or press Ctrl+Spacebar. |

| Techniques | How to Do It |
|---|---|
| Select an entire row | Click a row heading or press Shift + Spacebar. |
| Select multiple columns or rows | Drag the mouse pointer over the desired column or row headings. |
| Select an entire worksheet | Click the Select All button ◢ at the top-left corner of the worksheet or press Ctrl + A. |
| Select a range with Shift | Position the highlight in the first cell you wish to select, press Shift, and click the last cell in the range. |
| Extend or decrease a selection with Shift | Press Shift while tapping an arrow key. |

### DEVELOP YOUR SKILLS 2.3.1
## Practice Making Selections

*In this exercise, you will practice selecting multiple ranges and entire rows and columns using the mouse. You will also use the Shift and Ctrl keys to practice selecting cell ranges.*

### Click and Drag to Select a Range

1. Position the **mouse pointer** ✛ over **cell A4**.

2. **Press** and **hold down** the left mouse button while dragging the mouse to the right until the **range A4:E4** is selected, and then **release** the mouse button.
   *Notice that for each range that is selected, the corresponding row and column headings are displayed in orange.*

3. **Click** once anywhere in the worksheet to deselect the cells.

### Select Multiple Ranges

4. Follow these steps to select two ranges:

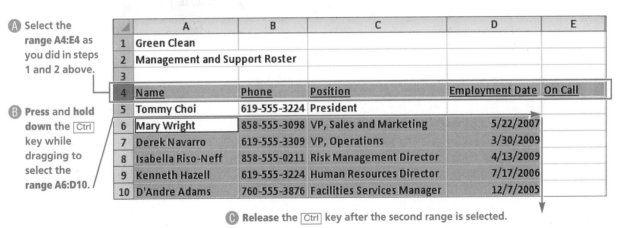

Ⓐ Select the range A4:E4 as you did in steps 1 and 2 above.

Ⓑ **Press** and **hold down** the Ctrl key while dragging to select the range A6:D10.

| ◢ | A | B | C | D | E |
|---|---|---|---|---|---|
| 1 | Green Clean | | | | |
| 2 | Management and Support Roster | | | | |
| 3 | | | | | |
| 4 | Name | Phone | Position | Employment Date | On Call |
| 5 | Tommy Choi | 619-555-3224 | President | | |
| 6 | Mary Wright | 858-555-3098 | VP, Sales and Marketing | 5/22/2007 | |
| 7 | Derek Navarro | 619-555-3309 | VP, Operations | 3/30/2009 | |
| 8 | Isabella Riso-Neff | 858-555-0211 | Risk Management Director | 4/13/2009 | |
| 9 | Kenneth Hazell | 619-555-3224 | Human Resources Director | 7/17/2006 | |
| 10 | D'Andre Adams | 760-555-3876 | Facilities Services Manager | 12/7/2005 | |

Ⓒ Release the Ctrl key after the second range is selected.

*Both the A4:E4 and A6:D10 ranges are selected now. The Ctrl key lets you select more than one range at the same time.*

5. **Press** and **hold down** the Ctrl key while you select another range, and then **release** the Ctrl key.

*You should now have three ranges selected.*

6. Make sure you have **released** the Ctrl key, and then **click** once anywhere on the worksheet to deselect the ranges.

*The highlighting of the previous selections disappears.*

## Select Entire Rows and Columns

7. Follow these steps to select various rows and columns:

Ⓐ Click the **column A** heading to select the entire column.

Ⓑ Position the mouse pointer on the **column C** heading and drag to the right until **columns C, D, and E** are selected.

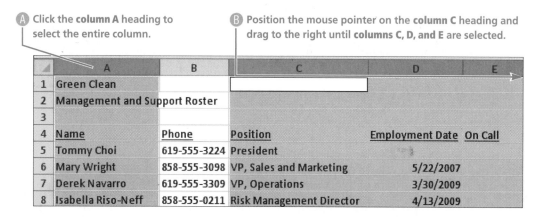

*Column A will be deselected because you were not holding down the Ctrl key.*

Ⓒ Click the **Select All** button to select the entire worksheet.

Ⓓ Click the **row 1** heading to select the entire row.

Ⓔ Drag the mouse pointer down over the headings from **row 6 to row 10** to select them.

*Only rows 6–10 will be selected because you did not hold down Ctrl.*

## Use Keyboard Techniques

8. Follow these steps to use keyboard techniques to select cells:

(A) Click cell A4.

| | A | B | C | D | E |
|---|---|---|---|---|---|
| 4 | Name | Phone | Position | Employment Date | On Call |
| 5 | Tommy Choi | 619-555-3224 | President | | |
| 6 | Mary Wright | 858-555-3098 | VP, Sales and Marketing | 5/22/2007 | |
| 7 | Derek Navarro | 619-555-3309 | VP, Operations | 3/30/2009 | |
| 8 | Isabella Riso-Neff | 858-555-0211 | Risk Management Director | 4/13/2009 | |
| 9 | Kenneth Hazell | 619-555-3224 | Human Resources Director | 7/17/2006 | |
| 10 | D'Andre Adams | 760-555-3876 | Facilities Services Manager | 12/7/2005 | |
| 11 | Talos Bouras | 858-555-1002 | Sales Manager | 5/10/2004 | |
| 12 | Michael Chowdery | 858-555-0021 | Purchasing Manager | 10/26/2009 | |
| 13 | Ahn Tran | 760-555-0728 | Office Manager | 6/26/2006 | |
| 14 | Jenna Mann | 951-555-0826 | Administrative Assistant | 3/15/2010 | |
| 15 | Nicole Romero | 858-555-4987 | Payroll Assistant | 5/25/2009 | |
| 16 | Amy Wyatt | 619-555-4016 | Customer Service Rep | 8/17/2009 | |

(B) **Press** and **hold down** the [Shift] key and click **cell E16** to select the range A4:E16.

(C) Click **cell A12.**

| | A | B | C | D |
|---|---|---|---|---|
| 12 | Michael Chowdery | 858-555-0021 | Purchasing Manager | 10/26/2009 |
| 13 | Ahn Tran | 760-555-0728 | Office Manager | 6/26/2006 |
| 14 | Jenna Mann | 951-555-0826 | Administrative Assistant | 3/15/2010 |
| 15 | Nicole Romero | 858-555-4987 | Payroll Assistant | 5/25/2009 |
| 16 | Amy Wyatt | 619-555-4016 | Customer Service Rep | 8/17/2009 |

(D) **Press** and **hold down** the [Shift] key, and then **tap** [→] three times and [↓] four times.

*The range A12:D16 is selected. Notice that the [Shift] key techniques give you precise control when selecting. You should use the [Shift] key techniques if you find selecting with the mouse difficult or if you have a large range to select that is not entirely visible on your screen.*

9. Take a few moments to practice selection techniques. See if you can select a specific portion of a worksheet.

# 2.4 Working with Cut, Copy, and Paste

**Video Lesson**   labyrinthelab.com/videos

**FROM THE KEYBOARD**
Ctrl+C to copy
Ctrl+X to cut
Ctrl+V to paste

The Cut, Copy, and Paste commands are available in all Office suite applications. With Cut, Copy, and Paste, you can move or copy cells within a worksheet, between worksheets, or between different Office applications. For example, you could use the Copy command to copy a range from one worksheet and the Paste command to paste the range into another worksheet. Cut, Copy, and Paste are most efficient for moving or copying cells a long distance within a worksheet or between worksheets. Cut, Copy, and Paste are easy to use if you remember the following guidelines:

- You must select cells before issuing a Cut or Copy command.
- You must position the highlight at the desired location before issuing the Paste command. The highlight's position is important because the range you paste will overwrite any cells in the paste area.

You need only to select the upper-left cell of the destination range before pasting a copied range. It is not necessary to select the entire destination range.

## Marquee and Paste Options Button

A marquee (animated dashed line) surrounds the selected cell(s) after you choose the Cut or Copy command. The marquee disappears upon the next action you take after pasting.

The Paste Options  button displays at the lower-right corner of the destination cell(s) after a paste action. Its drop-down list allows you to customize what will be pasted, such as only the cell contents or their formatting. The button disappears upon the next action you take. You will not work with paste options in this lesson.

Tap the Esc key to remove the marquee manually.

You can also right-click on a cell or range of cells in order to get a shortcut menu specific to the selection. The Cut, Copy, and Paste commands are available on this menu as well. There are many ways to issue commands; your job is to simply figure out which method works best for you!

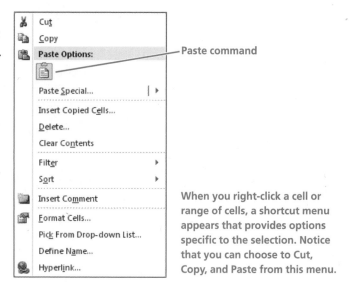

When you right-click a cell or range of cells, a shortcut menu appears that provides options specific to the selection. Notice that you can choose to Cut, Copy, and Paste from this menu.

# The Office Clipboard

The Office Clipboard lets you collect items from any Office worksheet or program and paste them into any other Office document. For example, you can collect a paragraph from a Word document, data from an Excel worksheet, and a graphic from a PowerPoint slide and then paste them all into a new Word document. The Office Clipboard can also be used within a single application like Excel to collect several items and then paste them as desired. The Office Clipboard can hold up to 24 items.

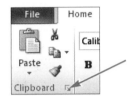

The Office Clipboard containing a copied graphic and two text blocks

## How It Works

You can place multiple items on the Office Clipboard using the standard Cut and Copy commands; however, the Office Clipboard task pane must first be displayed. It is displayed by clicking the launcher button in the Clipboard area of the Home tab. Once text or other objects are on the Clipboard, you may paste any item to one or more selected cells in a worksheet.

# Moving and Copying Cells via Drag and Drop

Drag and Drop produces the same results as Cut, Copy, and Paste. However, Drag and Drop is usually more efficient if you are moving or copying entries a short distance within the same worksheet. If the original location and

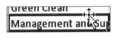

The mouse pointer changes to a four-pointed arrow as you point at the dark line surrounding the selected cell or range. Dragging the selection will move it to another location in the worksheet.

new destination are both visible in the current window, then it is usually easier to use Drag and Drop. With Drag and Drop, you select the cells you wish to move or copy, and then you point to the dark line around the selected range and drag the range to the desired destination. If you press the Ctrl key while dragging the selected area, the cells are copied to the destination. Drag and Drop does not place items on the Office Clipboard, however, so you will want to use either the Cut or the Copy command if you wish to work with the Office Clipboard.

# Editing Cells via Right-Dragging

Right-dragging is a variation of the drag and drop technique. Many beginners have trouble using drag and drop because they have difficulty controlling the mouse. This difficulty is compounded if they are trying to copy entries using drag and drop. This is because copying requires the Ctrl key to be held while the selected range is dragged. With the right-drag method, the right mouse button is used when dragging. When the right mouse button is released at the desti-

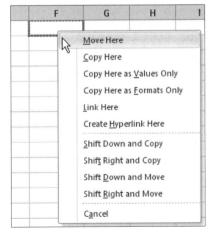

When you right-drag and drop, you will receive a pop-up menu at the destination so that you can choose whether to move or copy the data. You may cancel the action and then repeat the right-drag and drop if the indicated destination is not what you wanted.

nation, a pop-up menu appears. The pop-up menu gives you several options including Move, Copy, and Cancel. This approach provides more control because there is no need to use the Ctrl key when copying and you have the option of canceling the move or copy.

| Command | Explanation | Procedure |
|---|---|---|
| Cut | The Cut command removes entries from selected cells and places them on the Office Clipboard. | ■ Select what you wish to move.<br>■ Choose Home→Clipboard→Cut ✂ from the Ribbon, or press Ctrl+X. |
| Copy | The Copy command also places entries on the Office Clipboard, but it leaves a copy of the entries in the original cells. | ■ Select what you wish to copy.<br>■ Choose Home→Clipboard→Copy 📋 from the Ribbon or press Ctrl+C. |
| Paste | The Paste command pastes entries from the Office Clipboard to worksheet cells beginning at the highlight location. | ■ Click once where you wish the clipboard contents to be pasted.<br>■ Choose Home→Clipboard→ Paste from the Ribbon, or press Ctrl+V. |

# Move and Copy Selections

*In this exercise, you will have the opportunity to use the Cut, Copy, and Paste commands as well as drag and drop to move and copy selections.*

## Copy and Paste

1. Click **cell A1** to select it.

2. Display the **Home** tab, locate the **Clipboard** command group, and click the **Copy** 📋 button on the Ribbon.
   *A marquee will surround the selection that you have copied and placed on the clipboard.*

3. Click **cell C2**.

4. Choose **Home→Clipboard→Paste** from the Ribbon to **paste** the selection in cell C2.
   *The Paste command consists of two parts. Make certain to click the button in the upper part. If you accidentally click the drop-down arrow in the lower part of the command, you may still choose Paste from the list.*

|   | A | B | C | D |
|---|---|---|---|---|
| 1 | Green Clean | | | |
| 2 | Management and Support Roster | | Green Clean | |
| 3 | | | | 📋 (Ctrl) ▾ |

The contents of cell A1 will remain there as well as appear in cell C2 when you choose to copy the selection. Notice the marquee surrounding the cell that is being copied and the Paste Options button that appears to the lower right of the cell in which the selection was pasted.

## Cut and Paste

5. **Right-click** cell C2.
   *When you right-click a cell, a shortcut menu appears with options specific to the cell, as well as the Mini toolbar.*

6. Choose **Cut** from the shortcut menu.

7. **Right-click** cell E2 and choose **Paste** 📋 under Paste Options from the shortcut menu.

| C | D | E |
|---|---|---|
|   |   |   |
|   |   | Green Clean |

Cell C2 will now be empty because the contents were moved to cell E2.

## Drag and Drop

8. Follow these steps to move the contents of cell E2 via the drag-and-drop method:

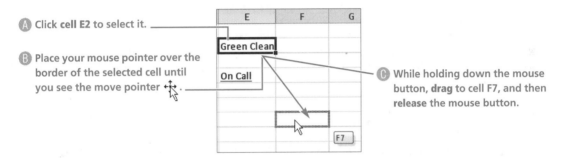

Ⓐ Click **cell E2** to select it.

Ⓑ Place your mouse pointer over the border of the selected cell until you see the move pointer ⊹.

Ⓒ While holding down the mouse button, **drag** to cell F7, and then **release** the mouse button.

*When you drag a cell with this method, Excel shows what cell the selection will be dropped into by displaying it on a ScreenTip as well as placing a highlight around the cell.*

## Right-Drag a Selection

9. Select **cell E4**, and then place your mouse pointer over the border of the selected cell until you see the move pointer as shown at right.

10. Start **dragging** with the **right** (not the left) mouse button. Keep the right mouse button held down until told to release it in the next step.

11. Drag down to **cell F5**, and then **release** the right mouse button.
    *A pop-up menu appears, listing your choices for the right-drag.*

12. Choose **Copy Here** from the pop-up menu.
    *The contents of cell E4 remain in the cell and are copied to the destination cell, F5. Do not save, but keep the workbook open. In the next exercise, you will undo some recent actions.*

# 2.5 Using Undo and Redo

**Video Lesson**    labyrinthelab.com/videos

Excel's Undo 🔄 button lets you reverse actions that have occurred in Excel. You can reverse simple actions such as accidentally deleting a cell's content or more complex actions such as deleting an entire row. Most actions can be undone, but those that cannot include printing and saving workbooks. The Undo command can become your best friend when you have to undo an action that you are not sure how you issued. Don't you wish life had an undo button at times?

The Redo 🔄 button reverses an Undo command. Use Redo when you undo an action but then decide to go through with that action after all. The Redo button will be visible on the Quick Access toolbar only after you have undone an action.

## Undoing Multiple Actions

**FROM THE KEYBOARD**

Ctrl+Z to undo
Ctrl+Y to redo

Clicking the arrow ▾ on the Undo button displays a list of actions that can be undone. You can undo multiple actions by dragging the mouse over the desired actions. However, you must undo actions in the order in which they appear on the drop-down list. For example, you cannot skip the first and second items to undo only the third item.

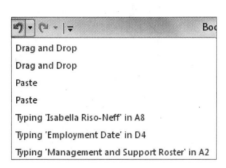

When you click the arrow on the Undo button, you will see a list of previous actions with the most recent at the top.

### *Limitations to "Undoing"*

In Excel, there are times when the Undo command will not work. If you click the File tab on the Ribbon and choose any command (such as saving a workbook), it cannot be undone. When an action cannot be undone, Excel will change the Undo ScreenTip to "Can't Undo."

| QUICK REFERENCE | UNDOING AND REDOING ACTIONS |
|---|---|
| **Task** | **Procedure** |
| Undo the last action | ■ Click the Undo 🔄 button on the Quick Access toolbar or tap Ctrl+Z. |
| Undo a series of actions | ■ Click the drop-down arrow 🔄 ▾ on the Undo button to display a list of previous actions.<br>■ Choose the last command that you wish to have undone. |
| Redo an undone action | ■ Click the Redo 🔄 button on the Quick Access toolbar. |

## Reverse Actions

*In this exercise, you will delete the contents of a column and then use Undo to reverse the deletion. When you do, the original data will display in the column again. You will also use Redo to reverse an Undo command.*

### Delete the Column Contents

1. Click the **column A** heading to select the entire column.

2. **Tap** [Delete].
   *All of the contents in column A have been deleted! There are many times that you will use Undo in order to reverse an action you did not wish to make.*

### Use Undo and Redo

3. Click **Undo** 🔄 to restore the entry.

4. Follow these steps to undo the last four commands from the previous section:

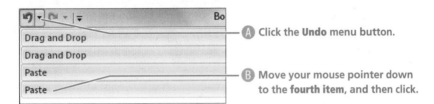

Ⓐ Click the **Undo** menu button.

Ⓑ Move your mouse pointer down to the **fourth item**, and then click.

*Excel undoes your last four commands.*

5. Click the **Redo** 🔄 button four times to restore the four actions that you "undid."

6. Use [Ctrl]+[S] to save the changes, but don't close the workbook.
   *You must hold down the [Ctrl] key first and then tap the [S] to issue the Save command.*

# 2.6 Clearing Cell Contents and Formats

**Video Lesson**   labyrinthelab.com/videos

**FROM THE KEYBOARD**

Delete to clear cell contents

In Excel, you can format cell content by changing the font style, size, and color. You can also add enhancements such as bold, italics, and underline. Cells with numeric data can be formatted as currency, dates, times, percents, and more. In this lesson, you will learn how to clear existing formatting.

Clicking the Clear ⟨button⟩ button displays a menu that lets you clear content, formats, and comments from cells. The submenu also contains a Clear All option that clears all of these items from the selected cell(s).

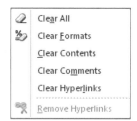

| | |
|---|---|
| ⟨icon⟩ | Clear All |
| ⟨icon⟩ | Clear Formats |
| | Clear Contents |
| | Clear Comments |
| | Clear Hyperlinks |
| ⟨icon⟩ | Remove Hyperlinks |

Clicking the Clear button in the Editing group of the Home ribbon will display a menu that shows all of the options for clearing cell contents.

## Excel's Options for Clearing Cells

| | |
|---|---|
| Clear Contents | Clearing the content has the same effect as tapping the Delete key. The cell contents are deleted, but any format applied to the cell remains and will be in effect when new data is entered in the cell. |
| Clear Formats | The clear Formats option removes all text and number formats, leaving unformatted entries in the cell(s). |
| Clear Comments | You can insert comments in cells to document your worksheet. The Clear Comments option also removes comments from the selected cells. |
| Clear Hyperlinks | Clearing a hyperlink leaves the entry in the cell but removes its link to a workbook object, a web address, or an external document. |
| Clear All | This command will clear everything listed above. |

One of the most useful functions of Excel's Clear command is removing numeric value formats. Once a cell is formatted as a particular numeric format, such as a date or currency, Excel remembers that formatting even if the cell contents are deleted.

| QUICK REFERENCE | CLEARING CELL CONTENTS AND FORMATTING |
|---|---|
| **Task** | **Procedure** |
| Clear the contents of a cell | ■ Select the cell or range that you wish to clear.<br>■ Choose Home→Editing→Clear ⟨button⟩ from the Ribbon.<br>■ Choose Clear Contents from the resulting menu. |
| Clear the formatting from a cell | ■ Select the cell or range that you wish to clear.<br>■ Choose Home→Editing→Clear ⟨button⟩ from the Ribbon.<br>■ Choose Clear Formats from the resulting menu. |
| Clear contents and formatting from a cell | ■ Select the cell or range that you wish to clear.<br>■ Choose Home→Editing→Clear ⟨button⟩ from the Ribbon.<br>■ Choose Clear All from the resulting menu. |

## Clear Cell Contents and Formatting

*In this exercise, you will use the Clear command to delete cell contents and cell formats.*

1. Click **cell F5**.

2. Choose **Home→Editing→Clear** [🖋️▾] from the Ribbon and choose **Clear Formats**.
   *The contents of the cell were underlined, a type of formatting. When you choose to clear only the formats, the contents will remain and only the formatting is removed. Notice that the contents are no longer underlined.*

3. Click the **Undo** [↩] button on the Quick Access toolbar.

4. Ensure that **cell F5** is selected, click the **Clear** [🖋️▾] button, and choose **Clear All**.

5. **Type** your name and **tap** [Enter].
   *Notice that the contents are no longer underlined in cell F5 because you cleared "all" (formatting and contents) from it.*

6. Use [Ctrl]+[Z] to undo the typing of your name.

7. Click **cell F7** and **tap** [Delete].
   *The entry* Green Clean *is deleted. The* [Delete] *key functions the same as if you had clicked the Clear button and chosen Clear Contents. Any formatting will remain in the cell.*

8. **Save** [💾] the workbook.

# 2.7 Using Auto Features

| Video Lesson | labyrinthelab.com/videos |

Excel offers "auto" features that help you to work more efficiently. AutoFill allows you to quickly fill a range of cells. AutoComplete makes it easy to enter long entries by typing an acronym or a series of characters, which are "converted" to the desired entry. AutoCorrect can also assist in correcting commonly misspelled words.

## Working with AutoFill

AutoFill allows you to quickly extend a series, copy data, or copy a formula into adjacent cells by selecting cells and dragging the fill handle. If the selected cell does not contain data that AutoFill recognizes as a series, the data will simply be copied into the adjacent cells. The fill handle is a small black square at the bottom-right corner of the selected cell or cell range. A black cross appears when you position the mouse pointer on the fill handle. You can drag the fill handle to fill adjacent cells to accomplish the following:

- **Copy an entry**—If the entry in the active cell is a number, a formula, or a text entry, the fill handle copies the entry to adjacent cells.

- **Expand a repeating series of numbers**—If you select two or more cells containing numbers, Excel assumes you want to expand a repeating series. For example, if you select two cells containing the numbers 5 and 10 and drag the fill handle, Excel will fill the adjacent cells with the numbers 15, 20, 25, etc.

- **AutoFill of date entries**—If the active cell contains any type of date entry, Excel will determine the increment of the date value and fill in the adjacent cells. For example, if the current cell contains the entry May and you drag the fill handle, AutoFill will insert the entries Jun, Jul, and Aug in the adjacent cells.

The following table and illustrations provide examples of series that AutoFill can extend.

| Selected Cells | Extended Series |
|---|---|
| Mon | Tue, Wed, Thu |
| Monday | Tuesday, Wednesday, Thursday |
| Jan | Feb, Mar, Apr |
| January | February, March, April |
| Jan, Apr | Jul, Oct, Jan |
| 1, 2 | 3, 4, 5, 6 |
| 100, 125 | 150, 175, 200 |
| 1/10/11 | 1/11/11, 1/12/11, 1/13/11 |
| 1/15/11, 2/15/11 | 3/15/11, 4/15/11, 5/15/11 |
| 1st Qtr | 2nd Qtr, 3rd Qtr, 4th Qtr |

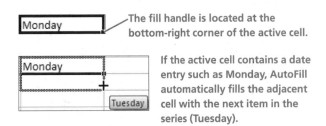

The fill handle is located at the bottom-right corner of the active cell.

If the active cell contains a date entry such as Monday, AutoFill automatically fills the adjacent cell with the next item in the series (Tuesday).

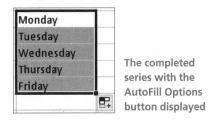

The completed series with the AutoFill Options button displayed

## AutoComplete vs. AutoFill

The AutoComplete feature is useful when you want the same entry repeated more than once in a column. AutoFill allows you to select a cell and fill in entries either by completing a series or copying the source cell, whereas AutoComplete works within a cell as you type. If the first few characters you type match another entry in the column, then AutoComplete will offer to complete the entry for you. You accept the offer by tapping Tab or Enter, or reject the offer by typing the remainder of the entry yourself.

| 16 | Amy Wyatt | 619-555-4016 | Customer Service Rep |
| 17 | Brian Simpson | 858-555-3718 | Customer Service Rep |

In this situation, a "c" was typed and the AutoComplete feature kicked into gear, suggesting that you may be interested in completing the entry as *Customer Service Rep* because you have already typed that entry earlier in the column. In order to accept *Customer Service Rep* as the entry, you would simply tap Tab to move to the next cell.

AutoComplete will complete the entry "case sensitive" to match capitalization from the existing column entry.

# Use the AutoComplete and AutoFill Features

*In this exercise, you will enter two new employees in the worksheet and use AutoComplete to aid in your entries. In addition, you will look at how to use AutoFill to complete a series of the days of the week.*

## Use AutoComplete

1. Click **cell A17** and type **Brian Simpson**, and then **tap** Tab to move to the next cell to the right.

2. Type **858-555-3718** and **tap** Tab.

3. Type **c** and notice that Excel suggests *Customer Service Rep* as the entry. **Tap** Tab to accept the suggestion and move to the next cell to the right.
   *Notice that the entry will be capitalized just as it is in the cell above.*

4. **Type** today's date, and then **tap** Enter.
   *Notice that when you tap* Enter, *the highlight moves to cell A18 where you can begin typing the next entry of the list.*

5. Type **Leisa Malimali** and **tap** Tab.

6. Type **619-555-4017** and **tap** Tab.

7. Type **S** in **cell C18**.
   *Excel will suggest* Sales Manager *from a previous row. In this case, Leisa is a sales assistant, so you will need to continue typing your entry. Make sure that you have typed a capital* S *as it will not pull from the previous entries.*

8. Continue typing **ales Assistant** and **tap** Tab.
   *Excel will replace the AutoComplete suggestion with the entry that you type,* Sales Assistant.

9. **Type** today's date and **tap** Enter.

## Use AutoFill to Expand a Series

*In this section of the exercise, you will fill in the column showing the manager responsible for being on emergency call each evening.*

10. Click **cell E6**.

11. Type **Monday**, and then click the **Enter** ✔ button.
    *Now that cell E6 contains Monday, Excel will recognize it as the beginning of the series, Tuesday, Wednesday, Thursday, and so forth. E6 will remain the active cell.*

12. Follow these steps to fill the adjacent cells:

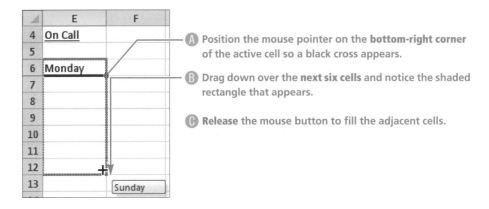

Ⓐ Position the mouse pointer on the **bottom-right corner** of the active cell so a black cross appears.

Ⓑ Drag down over the **next six cells** and notice the shaded rectangle that appears.

Ⓒ **Release** the mouse button to fill the adjacent cells.

*Excel recognizes days of the week (Monday), quarters (1st Qtr, Quarter 1, First Quarter), months (January), and other date values as the beginning of a series. You can expand any of these series with the fill handle.*

13. Click in the **Name Box** to the left of the Formula Bar, type **A1**, and **tap** Enter.

14. **Save** 🖫 the changes and leave the workbook **open**.

## Auto Fill Options

Video Lesson    labyrinthelab.com/videos

The Auto Fill Options 🖳 button appears below your filled selection after you fill cells in a worksheet. A menu of fill options appears when you click the button.

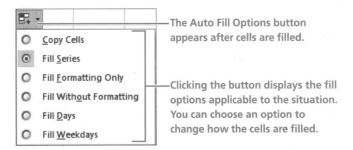

The Auto Fill Options button appears after cells are filled.

Clicking the button displays the fill options applicable to the situation. You can choose an option to change how the cells are filled.

If you choose Fill Without Formatting, you can fill cells without copying the formatting from the original cell. Fill Formatting Only copies the formatting but not the contents from the source cells.

## Use Auto Fill Options

*In this exercise, you will use Auto Fill Options to fill a data series without applying the source cell's formatting. You also will fill by applying only the formatting so that you may enter different data in cells.*

1. Click the **Sheet2** tab at the bottom of the window.

2. With **cell A1** selected, **drag** the fill handle to **cell D1**.

   *The data series expands to Year 1 – Q4, and the bold and shaded formatting from cell A1 is applied to the other series cells.*

   | | A | B | C | D |
   |---|---|---|---|---|
   | 1 | Year 1-Q1 | Year 1-Q2 | Year 1-Q3 | Year 1-Q4 |

3. Click the **Auto Fill Options** 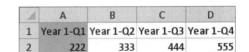 button at the lower-right corner of cell D1 and choose **Fill Without Formatting**.

   *The formatting is removed from B1:D1.*

4. **Deselect** the cells to view the actual formatting.

5. Select the **range A1:D1**.

6. **Drag** the fill handle in D1 down to **D7**.

7. Click the **Auto Fill Options** button and choose **Fill Formatting Only**.

   *The contents are removed from A2:D7, but the formatting is still applied.*

8. Enter numbers of your choice in **cells A2:D2**.

   *Notice that the formatting matches that of A1:D1.*

   | | A | B | C | D |
   |---|---|---|---|---|
   | 1 | Year 1-Q1 | Year 1-Q2 | Year 1-Q3 | Year 1-Q4 |
   | 2 | 222 | 333 | 444 | 555 |

9. Select the **Sheet1** tab of the workbook.

10. **Save** the changes and leave the workbook **open**.

# 2.8 Exploring the Many Views of Excel

**Video Lesson**   labyrinthelab.com/videos

Changing the view in Excel does not change how the worksheet will print. For instance, if you change the zoom to 300%, the worksheet will appear much larger on the screen but will still print normally. There are other views in Excel that will aid you in working with your file and assist you in making changes to the final printed worksheet. This lesson will cover Page Layout view and Zoom. Remember that your Ribbon may appear differently, depending on the size of your Excel window. There is an additional view option, , Page Break Preview, that allows you to set where pages will break when printed.

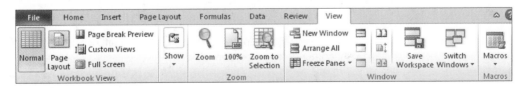

The View tab on the Ribbon provides options to view your workbook, show or hide screen items, control the zoom, and view multiple areas of the workbook at once.

## Working in Page Layout View

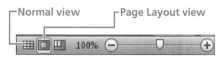

Page Layout view allows you to see how your spreadsheet will appear when you print it, page by page. You may edit your worksheet in this view. You also can add headers and footers with text, page numbering, and other items that print at the top and bottom of every page. You may use either the View ribbon or the view buttons in the lower-right corner of the worksheet window to switch between the Normal and Page Layout views.

The view buttons displayed in the lower-right corner of the worksheet window

## Zooming the View

The Zoom control lets you zoom in to get a close-up view of a worksheet and zoom out to see the full view. Zooming changes the size of the onscreen worksheet but has no effect on the printed worksheet. You can zoom from 10% to 400%.

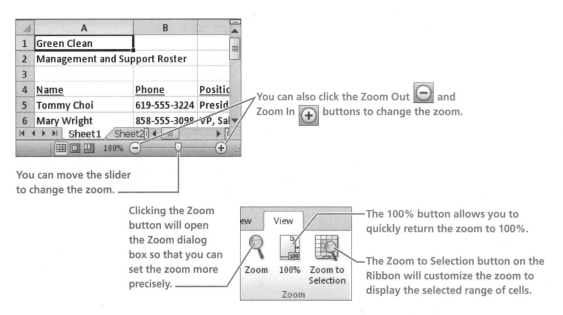

You can move the slider to change the zoom.

You can also click the Zoom Out and Zoom In buttons to change the zoom.

Clicking the Zoom button will open the Zoom dialog box so that you can set the zoom more precisely.

The 100% button allows you to quickly return the zoom to 100%.

The Zoom to Selection button on the Ribbon will customize the zoom to display the selected range of cells.

| QUICK REFERENCE | WORKING WITH EXCEL'S VIEWS |
|---|---|
| **Task** | **Procedure** |
| Change the zoom of a worksheet | ▪ Click and drag the zoom slider at the bottom-right corner of the worksheet window. |
| Zoom by increments | ▪ Click the Zoom In and Zoom Out buttons on the View toolbar. |
| Zoom in to a selection | ▪ Select the range you wish to zoom in on.<br>▪ Choose View→Zoom→Zoom to Selection from the Ribbon. |
| View a worksheet in Page Layout view | ▪ Choose View→Workbook Views→Page Layout from the Ribbon.<br>*or*<br>▪ Choose the Page Layout view button to the left of the zoom slider in the lower-right corner of the worksheet window. |

# Change Views and Use the Zoom Control

*In this exercise, you will practice using commands to change the zoom and switch between Page Layout and Normal views.*

## Change the Zoom

1. Follow these steps to adjust the zoom percentage:

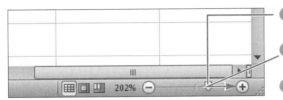

- **A** Place your mouse pointer over the **zoom slider** in the lower-right corner of the Excel window.
- **B** **Click** and **drag** the mouse pointer to the right until it is at approximately **200%**.
- **C** **Release** the mouse button.

2. Click the **Zoom Out** ⊖ button several times until the zoom displays **100%**.

3. Drag to select the **range A1:C18**.

4. Choose **View→Zoom→Zoom to Selection** 🔍 from the Ribbon.

5. Choose **View→Zoom→100%** 🔳 from the Ribbon.

## Switch Between Page Layout and Normal Views

6. Choose **View→Workbook Views→Page Layout View** 📄 from the Ribbon.
   *This view displays the worksheet as if printed on paper so that you may check that it fits on one page before printing.*

7. Choose **View→Workbook Views→Normal View** ▦ from the Ribbon.

8. Click the **Page Layout** 📃 button on the toolbar at the left of the zoom slider in the lower-right corner of the worksheet window.
   *The view buttons allow you to quickly toggle between views. The workbook may be printed from either Page Layout or Normal view.*

## Check That Data Fit on One Page

9. **Scroll down** to view the bottom of the page and then **scroll up** to the top of the page.

10. Scroll to the **right**.
    *The grayed areas will not print. They indicate which rows and columns would extend to additional printed pages if data were in them. Notice that all data in range A1:E18 do fit on one page.*

11. **Scroll back** to the left so that columns A–E are in view

## Edit in Page Layout View

12. **Delete** the contents of **cell A1**.
    *You may edit the worksheet in Page Layout view just as you would in Normal view.*

13. **Undo** ↩ the change.

14. **Save** 💾 the workbook.
    *The current workbook view is saved and would reappear the next time the workbook is opened. Leave the workbook open for the next exercise.*

## 2.9 Printing Worksheets

**Video Lesson**     labyrinthelab.com/videos

Excel gives you several ways to print your work. The method you choose depends on what you want to print. When you display the Print tab on the File menu, Backstage view displays a column of print options. The Print dialog box, familiar to users of previous Excel versions, has been eliminated. You may print specified pages, a selected range, or all data in the entire workbook. Additional choices include printing multiple copies and collating document pages in sets.

The Quick Print  button can be added to the Quick Access toolbar. When clicked, it will print one copy of the entire worksheet. For large workbooks in which you frequently want to print only a certain selection, you can print a selection or set a print area. Before printing, you can preview in Backstage view or Page Layout view to see what is going to be printed. Additional page setup options such as changing the print orientation, printing column headings on every page, setting the print area, and many others are accessible from Backstage view or the Page Layout ribbon.

The light gridlines displayed around cells in Normal and Page Layout views do not print.

### Print Preview

You have learned to use Page Layout view to preview the worksheet prior to printing. This view lets you see exactly how a worksheet will look when printed. Previewing can save time, paper, and wear and tear on your printer. It is especially useful when printing large worksheets and those with charts and intricate formatting. It is always wise to preview a large or complex worksheet before sending it to the printer.

In previous Excel versions, users also could display a separate Print Preview screen. Now, to save you time when you are ready to print, the Print tab of Backstage view displays a preview along with print options. The preview displays the overall look of the page that will be printed. You will usually need to zoom in to read any text. Scroll bars allow you to navigate to various areas of the zoomed-in page. The print preview is a very valuable tool for looking at how your worksheet will look when printed, but you are not able to edit your worksheet when you are in print preview mode (you will want to use Page Layout view for this purpose).

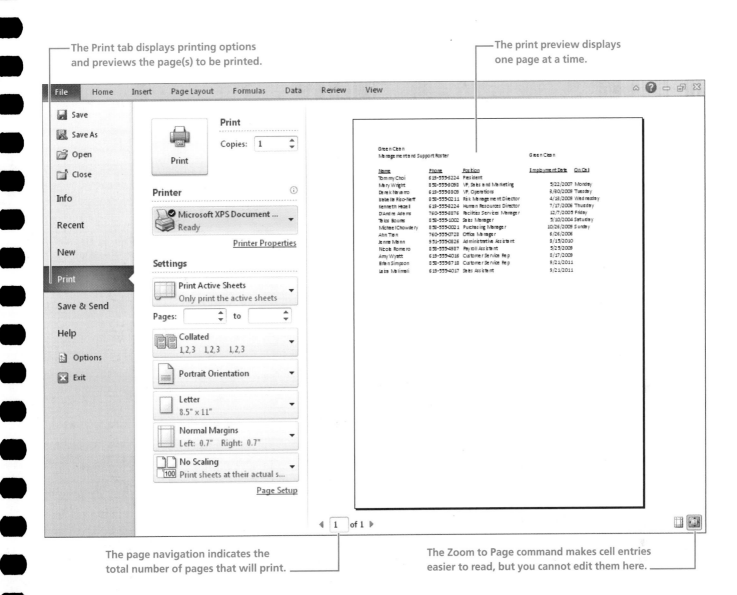

The Print tab displays printing options and previews the page(s) to be printed.

The print preview displays one page at a time.

The page navigation indicates the total number of pages that will print.

The Zoom to Page command makes cell entries easier to read, but you cannot edit them here.

## Print the Worksheet

You can customize your Quick Access toolbar to include the Quick Print button, which sends the entire worksheet to the current printer using whatever print options are currently in effect. You must use the Print command on the File menu if you want to change printers, adjust the number of copies to be printed, or set other printing options such as printing only selected cells. The following illustration explains the most important options available in the Print tab of Backstage view.

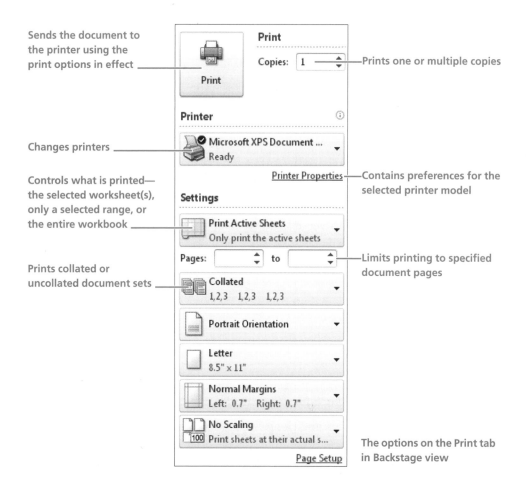

Sends the document to the printer using the print options in effect

Prints one or multiple copies

Changes printers

Contains preferences for the selected printer model

Controls what is printed—the selected worksheet(s), only a selected range, or the entire workbook

Prints collated or uncollated document sets

Limits printing to specified document pages

The options on the Print tab in Backstage view

## Printing Selections

FROM THE KEYBOARD
Ctrl + P to print

Many times you will want to print only a range of cells. You can do this by selecting the desired cells, choosing the Print command, choosing to print the selection, and clicking Print. You may also use this technique to print nonadjacent selections within a worksheet. Nonadjacent selections print on separate pages.

To print a selection, you must select the cell range before issuing the Print command.

| QUICK REFERENCE | PRINTING IN EXCEL |
| --- | --- |
| **Task** | **Procedure** |
| Preview how a worksheet will appear when printed | ▪ Choose File→Print or display Page Layout view. |
| Print a worksheet using default settings | ▪ Add the Quick Print 🖨 button on the Quick Access toolbar, if necessary.<br>▪ Click the Quick Print 🖨 button on the Quick Access toolbar. |

| Task | Procedure |
|---|---|
| Open the Print tab in Backstage view to make changes to printing options before printing | ▪ Choose File→Print. |
| Close the Print tab of Backstage view without printing | ▪ Tap the [Esc] key or choose any tab from the Ribbon. |
| Print a selection | ▪ Highlight the selection you wish to print.<br>▪ Choose File→Print.<br>▪ Under Settings, choose Print Selection from the Print What list.<br>▪ Click Print. |

## DEVELOP YOUR SKILLS 2.9.1

# Preview and Print a Worksheet

*In this exercise, you will preview the worksheet you have been working on in the Print tab of Backstage view and send it to the printer.*

### Preview How Your Worksheet Will Print

1. Choose **File→Print**.
   *The File tab of Backstage view displays, and a preview of page 1 displays at the right of the window. Notice that the page navigation option at the bottom-left corner of the preview indicates that you are viewing page 1 of 1 page total in the document.*

2. Click the **Zoom to Page** 🖼 button at the lower-right corner of the preview to zoom in on your worksheet.

3. Use the **scroll bars** to view the zoomed-in view.

4. Click the **Zoom to Page** 🖼 button again to zoom out.

### Print Your Worksheet

5. Look at the options available at the left of the File tab of Backstage view, and then click **Print** at the top-left corner of the options to print the worksheet.

6. **Tap** [Ctrl]+[S] to save the changes and leave the workbook open.

# 2.10 Editing Workbook Properties

Video Lesson   labyrinthelab.com/videos

Certain information about a workbook is saved along with the workbook contents. You can view these file properties while a workbook is open in Excel. The Windows operating system also displays document properties for a selected file.

## Standard Properties

The Info tab of Backstage view displays a group of standard properties associated with Microsoft Office files. The file size, creation date, date last modified, and author name properties are included automatically. The default author name is the User Name set in Microsoft Office, although you may change the author name if you wish. You may enter a title, subject, categories, and comments about the workbook. Any tags, or keywords, that you enter may help users search for the document in a folder, drive, or the entire computer. For example, a roster of management employees could be tagged as *management, employee,* and *contact.*

| Properties ▾ | |
| --- | --- |
| Size | 11.9KB |
| Title | Add a title |
| Tags | management, employ... |
| Categories | Employtees |
| **Related Dates** | |
| Last Modified | Today, 2:13 PM |
| Created | Yesterday, 4:10 PM |
| Last Printed | Today, 2:09 PM |
| **Related People** | |
| Author | Office 2010 |
| | Add an author |
| Last Modified By | Office 2010 |
| **Related Documents** | |
| 📁 Open File Location | |

You may add properties, such as tags to identify and organize workbooks, in the Info tab of Backstage view.

## Advanced Properties

In Backstage view, you can use the Show All Properties link to display an expanded properties list. These additional properties include Comments, project Status, and Manager. You can access two other views by displaying the Properties menu in Backstage view. The menu choices include a

**Show Document Panel**
Edit properties in the Document Panel above the workbook.

**Advanced Properties**
Show the Properties dialog box.

The Properties menu in the Info tab of Backstage view gives access to advanced and custom properties.

basic Document Properties panel that displays above the active worksheet and a Properties dialog box where you may create additional properties on its Custom tab. Custom properties do not display in Backstage view. If you know how to use a computer programming language such as Visual Basic for Applications (VBA), you can create code using custom properties to perform additional tasks in workbooks.

| Task | Procedure |
|---|---|
| Set the username | ■ Choose File→Options. |
| | ■ Enter the desired name in the User Name box in the General options window. |
| Edit standard properties | ■ Choose File→Info. |
| | ■ Add or change the desired properties at the right of Backstage view, or choose Properties menu ▼→Show Document Panel to work with properties while viewing the active worksheet. |
| Expand the Properties list | ■ Choose File→Info from the Ribbon. |
| | ■ Choose Properties menu ▼→Show All Properties. |
| Edit standard, advanced, and custom properties | ■ Choose File→Info. |
| | ■ Choose Properties menu ▼→Advanced Properties. |
| | ■ Click the appropriate tab in the Properties dialog box and edit the desired items. |

## DEVELOP YOUR SKILLS 2.10.1

# Edit Workbook Properties

*In this exercise, you will verify the Microsoft Office user name, display document properties in various ways, and enter several properties.*

## Verify the User Name

1. Choose **File→Options** 📄.
   *The General options category already should be selected in the categories at the left.*

2. Read the existing User Name at the bottom of the options window. (Your User Name will differ from the illustration.)
   *This is the user name set for all Microsoft Office documents. Do not change it unless your instructor directs you to do so.*

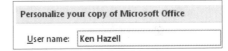

3. Click **Cancel** to exit Excel Options.

## Enter Standard Properties

4. Follow these steps to enter tags, a category, and an additional author for the workbook file:

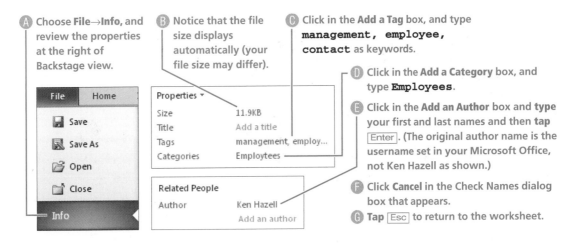

Ⓐ Choose **File→Info**, and review the properties at the right of Backstage view.

Ⓑ Notice that the file size displays automatically (your file size may differ).

Ⓒ Click in the **Add a Tag** box, and type **management, employee, contact** as keywords.

Ⓓ Click in the **Add a Category** box, and type **Employees**.

Ⓔ Click in the **Add an Author** box and **type** your first and last names and then **tap** ⎡Enter⎤. (The original author name is the username set in your Microsoft Office, not Ken Hazell as shown.)

Ⓕ Click **Cancel** in the Check Names dialog box that appears.

Ⓖ Tap ⎡Esc⎤ to return to the worksheet.

## Expand the Properties

5. Click the **File** tab, and then click **Info,** if necessary.
*The Info tab should be displayed in Backstage view.*

6. Choose **Show All Properties** at the bottom-right of Backstage view. (**Scroll down** to locate the command, if necessary.)

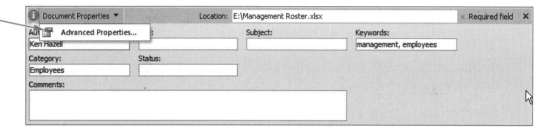

7. **Scroll** the expanded list of properties, which include Comments, Status, and Manager.

## Explore Advanced and Custom Properties

8. Choose **Properties** above the properties list and choose **Show Document Panel**.
*After a few moments, the panel displays above the active worksheet with the properties you entered. You can edit properties in the panel, if you prefer.*

9. Click **Document Properties** in the upper-left corner of the panel and choose **Advanced Properties**.

*The Management Roster Properties dialog box displays.*

10. **Click** each tab in the dialog box to view the workbook details available, ending with the Custom tab displayed.

*A custom property may be selected from the list or a name entered to create a new property. After the property's type and value are specified, the Add button is enabled. Remember that custom properties will not display in Backstage view.*

11. Click **Cancel** to exit the dialog box without saving any changes.

12. Close the **Document Properties** panel.

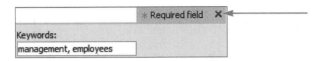

13. **Save** ⊞ the changes and **close** ⊠ the workbook.

## 2.11 Concepts Review

Concepts Review    labyrinthelab.com/excel10

*To check your knowledge of the key concepts introduced in this lesson, complete the Concepts Review quiz by going to the URL listed above. If your classroom is using Labyrinth eLab, you may complete the Concepts Review quiz from within your eLab course.*

# Reinforce Your Skills

REINFORCE YOUR SKILLS 2.1

## Edit a Worksheet

*In this exercise, you will edit a worksheet. This exercise demonstrates that sometimes it is easier to replace entries, whereas at other times it is easier to edit them.*

### Replace Several Entries

1. Start **Excel** and choose **File→Open** 📂 from the Ribbon.

2. **Navigate** to the Lesson 02 folder in your file storage location and **open** rs-Customers.

3. Select **cell B4**.

4. Type **Ralph** and **tap** [Enter].
   *Notice that it is easy to replace the entry because the name Ralph is easy to type.*

5. **Replace** the name *Calvin* in **cell B6** with the name **Stephen**.

### Edit Using the Formula Bar

6. Select **cell D4**.

7. Click in the **Formula Bar** just in front of the telephone prefix *333*.

8. **Tap** [Delete] three times to remove the prefix.

9. Type **222** and **complete** ✔ the entry.

10. **Change** the area code in cell D8 from *814* to **914**.
    *In these entries, it was easier to edit than to retype entire phone numbers.*

### Use In-Cell and "Your Choice" Editing

11. **Double-click** cell E4.

12. Use [→] or [←] to position the **insertion point** in front of the word *Lane*.

13. **Tap** [Delete] four times to remove the word *Lane*.

14. Type **Reservoir** and complete the entry.

15. Edit the next five addresses using either the Formula Bar or in-cell editing. The required changes appear bold in the following table.

| Cell | Make These Changes |
|------|--------------------|
| E5 | 2900 **Carleton** Drive, San Mateo, CA 94401 |
| E6 | **2300** Palm Drive, Miami, FL 33147 |
| E7 | 888 Wilson Street, **Concord**, CA 94565 |
| E8 | 320 Main Street, **Pittsburgh**, PA 17951 |
| E9 | **5120** 132$^{nd}$ Street, Los Angeles, CA **90045** |

16. **Save** the workbook.
    *Leave the workbook open as you will use it for Reinforce Your Skills 2.2*

# Use AutoComplete and AutoFill

*In this exercise, you will add data to the worksheet you created in the previous exercise by using AutoComplete and AutoFill. You also will use Auto Fill Options to restrict a fill action.*

*Before You Begin: You must have completed Reinforce Your Skills 2.1 and the rs-Customers workbook should be open.*

## Use AutoComplete

1. Select **cell B10**, and type **ja**.
   *Notice that AutoComplete does not suggest an entry when you only type a "j" as there are two "j" entries in the column.*

2. **Tap** [Tab] to accept the suggested entry of Jack.

3. Using the following figure, complete the customer's information, using **AutoComplete** in column F.

| ▲ | A | B | C | D | E | F |
|---|---|---|---|---|---|---|
| 9 | | Judy | Alioto | (213) 222-3344 | 132nd Street, Los Angeles, CA 95544 | West |
| 10 | | Jack | LaRue | (360) 444-0489 | 359 Peninsula Avenue, Port Angeles, WA 98363 | West |

## Use AutoFill to Extend a Series

4. Select **cell A4**.
   *Before using AutoFill, you must first select the cell that you will be using as the basis for the fill information.*

5. Place your mouse pointer over the **fill handle** at the bottom-right corner of the selected cell, **drag** down through cell A10, and then **release** the mouse button when the ScreenTip shows C-07.

| ▲ | A | B |
|---|---|---|
| 3 | Customer # | Firstna |
| 4 | C-01 | Burt |
| 5 | | Willie |
| 6 | | Calvin |
| 7 | | Susan |
| 8 | | Jack |
| 9 | | Judy |
| 10 | | Jack |
| 11 | | [C-07] |
| 12 | | |

| ▲ | A |
|---|---|
| 3 | Customer # |
| 4 | C-01 |
| 5 | C-02 |
| 6 | C-03 |
| 7 | C-04 |
| 8 | C-05 |
| 9 | C-06 |
| 10 | C-07 |

*Notice that Excel recognizes C-01 as the beginning of a series (C-02, C-03, C-04, …).*

### Enter Additional Customers

6. Enter the following three customers, in rows 11–13, into the list, using **AutoFill** and **AutoComplete** when possible.

| | A | B | C | D | E | F |
|---|---|---|---|---|---|---|
| 10 | C-07 | Jack | LaRue | (360) 444-0489 | 359 Peninsula Avenue, Port Angeles, WA 983 | West |
| 11 | C-08 | Edgar | Martinez | (206) 111-1111 | 11 Mariners Way Seattle, WA 98101 | West |
| 12 | C-09 | Trevor | Hoffman | (619) 555-1111 | 51 Camino de Padres, San Diego, CA 92101 | West |
| 13 | C-10 | Derek | Jeffries | (212) 222-5555 | 2 York Avenue, New York, NY 10002 | East |

### Use an Auto Fill Option

7. Select **cell A3**.
   *You will apply its bold and blue text formatting to the other column labels.*

8. **Drag** the fill handle in cell A3 to the right through cell F3, and then **release** the mouse button.

| 3 | Customer # | Firstname | Lastname | Phone | Address | Region |

*The cells are filled with Customer # because both the contents and formatting are copied by default.*

9. Click the **Auto Fill Options** button at the lower-right corner of cell F3 and choose **Fill Formatting Only** from the list.
   *The contents of range B3:F3 return to their former entries and only the formatting is applied.*

10. **Deselect** the cells by clicking on any other cell.

11. Use Ctrl + S to **save** your workbook. Leave the workbook open for the next exercise.

---

### REINFORCE YOUR SKILLS 2.3

## Move and Copy Cell Contents

*In this exercise, you will use the workbook from Reinforce Your Skills 2.2 and move and copy the contents of cells.*

*Before You Begin: You must have completed Reinforce Your Skills 2.1 and Reinforce Your Skills 2.2, and the rs-Customers workbook should be open.*

### Use Keyboard Shortcuts

1. Select **cell E1**.

2. Choose **Home→Clipboard→Cut** from the Ribbon.

3. Select **cell A1**, and choose **Home→Clipboard→Paste** from the Ribbon.

4. Select the range **A11:F11**, and **copy** the range using the keyboard command Ctrl + C.

5. Select **cell A14**, and paste the range using Ctrl + V.
   *This approach can come in handy if you have a new entry that is very similar to an existing one!*

6. Use Ctrl + Z to **undo** the Paste command.

### Copy Using the Context Menu

7. Select **cell D6**.

8. Taking care to avoid the fill handle, **point** at the dark line surrounding the cell, press the **right** mouse button, and **drag** down to cell D7.
*The pop-up, or context, menu appears when you release the mouse button.*

9. Choose **Copy Here** from the shortcut menu.
*The phone number from cell D6 is copied to cell D7.*

10. Edit the last four digits of the phone number in cell D7 to **3535**.

11. Use Ctrl + Home to return to cell A1.

12. **Close** ⊠ the workbook, choosing to **save** your workbook.

---

**REINFORCE YOUR SKILLS 2.4**

# Preview a Worksheet, Print, and Edit a Workbook Property

*In this exercise, you will use the workbook from Reinforce Your Skills 2.3 to preview and then print a selection from the workbook. You will view workbook properties and edit one of them.*

*Before You Begin: You must have completed Reinforce Your Skills 2.1, 2.2, and 2.3, and the rs-Customers workbook should be open.*

### Preview in Page Layout View

1. Click the **Page Layout** ▢ button on the toolbar at the left of the zoom slider in the lower-right corner of the worksheet window.

2. Look at the Status Bar at the bottom-left corner of the **Page Layout** window to verify that the worksheet fits on one page.
*The Status Bar should indicate Page: 1 of 1.*

3. Check the overall look of data on the page.
*Some text in the Address column is truncated (cut off). Normally you would correct any problem discovered during the preview, but you may leave the text as is in this lesson.*

### Cancel a Print

4. Choose **File→Print**.
*A preview displays at the right of the Print tab in Backstage view.*

5. Take a moment to look at the print options but **do not** change them.

6. **Tap** the Esc key to cancel the print and return to Page Layout view.

## Print a Selection

7. Click the **Normal view** ⊞ button on the toolbar at the left of the zoom slider in the lower-right corner of the worksheet window.
   *You will print just the last names and phone numbers in the next steps. You could have selected the range in Page Layout view also.*

8. Select the **range C3:D13**.

9. Use ⌈Ctrl⌉+⌈P⌉ to display the Print tab of Backstage view.

10. Follow these steps to print the selected range:

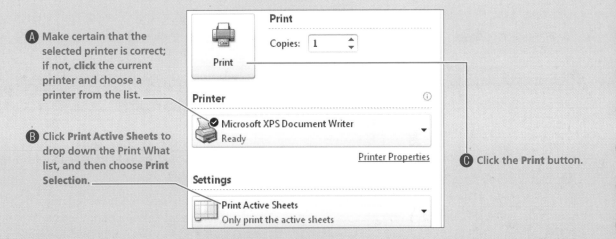

Ⓐ Make certain that the selected printer is correct; if not, **click** the current printer and choose a printer from the list.

Ⓑ Click **Print Active Sheets** to drop down the Print What list, and then choose **Print Selection**.

**Print**

Copies: 1

**Printer** ⓘ

✓ Microsoft XPS Document Writer
Ready

Printer Properties

Ⓒ Click the **Print** button.

**Settings**

Print Active Sheets
Only print the active sheets

*Only the selected range prints. Excel displays a page break (dashed line) to the right of column F in Normal view to indicate the edge of page 1.*

11. **Scroll down** to view the page break at the bottom of the page (after row 52, depending on your printer).
    *These page breaks disappear from Normal view when the workbook is closed, but Page Layout view always shows you the page break locations.*

12. Use ⌈Ctrl⌉+⌈Home⌉ to go to cell A1.

## Edit a Workbook Property

13. Choose **File→Info** to display Backstage view.

14. Enter the keywords **customers, contacts** in the Tags box under Properties at the right of Backstage view.

15. Click the **File** tab to exit Backstage view.

16. **Save** 🖫 the changes and **close** the workbook.

# Apply Your Skills

## Edit a Worksheet, Use Page Layout View, and Edit a Workbook Property

*In this exercise, you will edit a worksheet in both Normal and Page Layout views. You will also use AutoFill to extend a series.*

1. **Open** the workbook named as-Bonuses from the Lesson 02 folder in your file storage location.

2. Edit the title in **cell A1** to read **Site Safety Bonuses**.

3. **AutoFill** the months February through June in **cells C3:G3**.

4. **Edit** the label in **cell A3** to **Employee Name**.

5. **Change** the name Garcia, H. in **cell A5** to **Wilson, T**.

6. View the worksheet in **Page Layout view**.

7. While in Page Layout view, **edit** the label in **cell A8** to read **Grand Total** and **complete** the entry.

8. **AutoFill** just the contents without the formatting from the range **F4:F7** to **G4:G7**. *The values in range G4:G7 should appear black when you are done.*

9. Change the entry in **cell G4** to **300**.

10. Change the **Author** workbook property from the existing user name to your first and last names.

11. **Save** the changes and **close** the workbook.

# Select, Move, and Copy in a Worksheet

*In this exercise, you will practice selecting various ranges and cells in order to move and copy them.*

1. **Open** the workbook named as-Carpet Products from the Lesson 02 folder in your file storage location.

2. Select **A6:D19**; try using the Shift technique.

3. Place your **mouse pointer** over the edge of the selection until you see the move pointer, and then **click** and **drag up** until the top left of the selection is in row 3.
   *The selection will now be contained in the range A3:D16.*

4. Select **B3:D3** and issue the **Cut** command.

5. Click **cell B4** and issue the **Paste** command.

6. **Copy** the contents of **B4:D4** into **B12:D12**.

7. **Save** the workbook and leave it **open** for the next exercise.

| | A | B | C | D |
|---|---|---|---|---|
| 1 | Green Clean | | | |
| 2 | Carpet Products | | | |
| 3 | | | | |
| 4 | CARPET CLEANING SOLUTIONS | Type | Size | Price |
| 5 | EarthWise Carpet Cleaner | Concentrate | 64 ounces | $17.50 |
| 6 | EarthWise Carpet Cleaner | | 32 ounces | $9.85 |
| 7 | EarthWise Carpet Cleaner | Spray | 16 ounces | $4.50 |
| 8 | GBS All Purpose Carpet | Liquid | 120 ounces | $11.95 |
| 9 | GBS Dry Powder Cleaner | Powder | 16 ounces | $4.25 |
| 10 | Taz Carpet and Upholstery | Liquid | Gallon | $7.95 |
| 11 | | | | |
| 12 | CARPET STAIN REMOVERS | Type | Size | Price |
| 13 | EarthWise Carpet Stain Remover | Concentrate | 64 ounces | $9.95 |
| 14 | EarthWise Carpet Stain Remover | Concentrate | 32 ounces | $5.50 |
| 15 | EarthWise Carpet Stain Remover | Spray | 16 ounces | $4.65 |
| 16 | Carpet Bright Stain Eliminator | Spray | 32 ounces | $7.35 |

# Work with Undo, Clear, and AutoComplete

*In this exercise, you will work with the workbook from Apply Your Skills 2.2 to clear formatting, undo commands, and use AutoComplete.*

*Before You Begin: You must have completed Apply Your Skills 2.1 and 2.2, and the as-Carpet Products workbook should be open.*

1. Select **column D** by clicking the column header.

2. Choose **Home→Editing→Clear→Clear Formats** from the Ribbon.
   *Notice that the numbers remain in column D, but they are no longer formatted as currency.*

3. Click the **Undo** button on the Quick Access toolbar to bring back the cleared formatting.

4. Click **cell B6** and type **c**, observing the AutoComplete option that appears.

5. **Tap** Enter to accept the AutoComplete suggestion.

6. Select the **range A10:D10** and **tap** Delete to clear the contents of the cells.

7. Choose **File→Print**.

8. Check the print preview in the **Print** tab of Backstage view to make certain that the worksheet will print on one page.

9. **Print** the worksheet.

10. **Save** the changes to the workbook and **exit** from Excel.

| | A | B | C | D |
|---|---|---|---|---|
| 1 | Green Clean | | | |
| 2 | Carpet Products | | | |
| 3 | | | | |
| 4 | CARPET CLEANING SOLUTIONS | Type | Size | Price |
| 5 | EarthWise Carpet Cleaner | Concentrate | 64 ounces | $17.50 |
| 6 | EarthWise Carpet Cleaner | Concentrate | 32 ounces | $9.85 |
| 7 | EarthWise Carpet Cleaner | Spray | 16 ounces | $4.50 |
| 8 | GBS All Purpose Carpet | Liquid | 120 ounces | $11.95 |
| 9 | GBS Dry Powder Cleaner | Powder | 16 ounces | $4.25 |
| 10 | | | | |
| 11 | | | | |
| 12 | CARPET STAIN REMOVERS | Type | Size | Price |
| 13 | EarthWise Carpet Stain Remover | Concentrate | 64 ounces | $9.95 |
| 14 | EarthWise Carpet Stain Remover | Concentrate | 32 ounces | $5.50 |
| 15 | EarthWise Carpet Stain Remover | Spray | 16 ounces | $4.65 |
| 16 | Carpet Bright Stain Eliminator | Spray | 32 ounces | $7.35 |

# Critical Thinking & Work-Readiness Skills

*In the course of working through the following Microsoft Office-based Critical Thinking exercises, you will also be utilizing various work-readiness skills, some of which are listed next to each exercise. Go to labyrinthelab.com/ workreadiness to learn more about the work-readiness skills.*

## 2.1 Edit and Replace Entries

**WORK-READINESS SKILLS APPLIED**

- Making decisions
- Showing responsibility
- Knowing how to learn

Ken asks Jenna Mann to update the birthday list for Green Clean employees. Jenna finds the current birthday list in a Microsoft Excel file. She decides to contact each employee personally, as an excuse to introduce herself, as well as to verify the dates. Open ct-Birthdays (Lesson 02 folder) and make these edits: change Mary Wright's birthday to March 2; delete all information for Michael Tsang and Joe Smith; change Mary Jones to **Amy Wyatt** and her birthday of June 26; and add Alan Sedgwick and his birthday of September 25 at the end of the list. Save the file as **ct-Birthday Update**. If working in a group, discuss why a company might want to recognize birthdays. If working alone, type your answer in a Word document named **ct-Questions** saved to your Lesson 02 folder.

## 2.2 Edit and Print a Workbook

**WORK-READINESS SKILLS APPLIED**

- Acquiring and using information
- Exercising leadership
- Interpreting and communicating information

Ken decides to add a column to Jenna's birthday worksheet for monthly highlights (a job completed, a customer compliment, etc.) at the November employee meeting. Open ct-Birthday Update, if necessary. Add a column labeled **Highlight** and add the following:

**Mary Wright – Congratulations on deal with Hall Properties; Amy Wyatt – Congratulations on recent marriage; Jenna Mann – Thanks for updating birthday list; Talos Bouras – Happy birthday!; Michael Chowdery – Welcome, will report to Derek.**

Proofread your work and correct as necessary. Print preview the birthday list with the new column. Print the document. Save the file as **ct-Birthday Highlights** in your Lesson 02 folder.

## 2.3 Rearrange Data and use Auto Features

**WORK-READINESS SKILLS APPLIED**

- Organizing and maintaining information
- Seeing things in the mind's eye
- Showing responsibility

Ken wants an employee roster. Also, every employee has a quarterly "green" project to complete and Ken would like to track these. Open ct-Birthdays Highlights, if necessary. Select just the employee names and copy them to the Clipboard. Open ct-Employee Roster (Lesson 13 folder), and paste the names into column B. Select the names Kenneth Hazell through Alan Sedgwick, and move the names up one cell to eliminate the blank cell. Label column A as **Empoyee #**. Create a unique number for each employee in the Employee # column, starting with EN-001. Then, assign each employee randomly to one of the following: **Light Bulb Replacement**, **Product Improvement**, **Commute Reduction**. Save file as **ct-Employee Roster and Project** in your Lesson 02 folder and close all files.

# Working with Formulas and Functions

## LEARNING OBJECTIVES

After studying this lesson, you will be able to:

- Create formulas to calculate values, utilizing the proper syntax and order of operations
- Employ a variety of methods to use the IF logical function and statistical functions that determine the sum, average, count, maximum, and minimum of a range of numbers
- Use relative, absolute, and mixed cell references in formulas
- Modify and copy formulas
- Display the formulas contained within cells rather than the resulting values

The magic of the Excel spreadsheet lies in its ability to crunch numbers and make sense of data. The heart of this magic lies in the formulas and functions that are used for this number crunching. In this lesson, you will be introduced to creating and modifying basic formulas and functions in Excel. You will learn how to reference cells in formulas as well as how to use another automated feature of Excel, AutoSum. With an IF function, you may flag a cell with a text label, display a value, or perform a calculation when specific criteria are satisfied.

# Creating a Spreadsheet with Formulas

Green Clean earns revenue by selling janitorial products and contracts for cleaning services. Talos Bouras is a sales manager. He wants to set up a workbook with two worksheets, one to track commissions and the other to report how the projected profit would change based on costs and an increase or decrease in sales. He will create the necessary formulas for the workbook calculations.

**green clean**

| | A | B | C | D | E |
|---|---|---|---|---|---|
| 1 | | Sales Department | | | |
| 2 | | Projected Net Profit | | | |
| 3 | | Base | 2% | 5% | -5% |
| 4 | Product Sales | $ 53,200 | 54,264 | 55,860 | 50,540 |
| 5 | Contracts | 241,000 | 245,820 | 258,111 | 245,205 |
| 6 | Total Revenue | $ 294,200 | $ 300,084 | $ 313,971 | $ 295,745 |
| 7 | | | | | |
| 8 | Fixed Operating Cost | 101,400 | 101,400 | 101,400 | 101,400 |
| 9 | Marketing Expense | 15,000 | 15,000 | 15,000 | 15,000 |
| 10 | Commissions | 27,824 | 28,380 | 29,721 | 28,058 |
| 11 | Total Costs | $ 144,224 | $ 144,780 | $ 146,121 | $ 144,458 |
| 12 | | | | | |
| 13 | Gross Profit | $ 149,976 | $ 155,304 | $ 167,850 | $ 151,287 |
| 14 | Net Profit | $ 138,353 | $ 143,267 | $ 154,841 | $ 139,562 |
| 15 | Gross Profit vs. Revenue | 51.0% | 51.8% | 53.5% | 51.2% |
| 16 | | | | | |
| 17 | Contracts | 482 | | | |
| 18 | Average Contract | 500 | Marketing | 15,000 | |
| 19 | Product Commission Rate | 7% | Fixed Cost | 101,400 | |
| 20 | Contract Commission Rate | 10% | Tax Rate | 7.75% | |

The Profit Projection worksheet reports the effect of various sales projections and costs on net profit. When Talos changes the numbers in rows 17–20, the formulas recalculate the results in rows 4–15 automatically.

| | A | B | C | D | E | F | G |
|---|---|---|---|---|---|---|---|
| 1 | | Sales Department | | | | | |
| 2 | | First Quarter Commissions | | | | | |
| 3 | | | | | | | |
| 4 | Sales Team Member | January | February | March | Qtr 1 Total | Sales | Met Goal? |
| 5 | Talos Bouras | 250 | 486 | 415 | 1151 | 28775 | |
| 6 | Leisa Malimali | 74 | 88 | 101 | 263 | 6575 | |
| 7 | Brian Simpson | 389 | 303 | 422 | 1114 | 27850 | |
| 8 | Amy Wyatt | 346 | 381 | 502 | 1229 | 30725 | Yes |
| 9 | Monthly Total | 1059 | 1258 | 1440 | 3757 | | |
| 10 | | | | | | | |
| 11 | Average | 264.75 | 314.5 | 360 | 939.25 | | |
| 12 | Maximum | 389 | 486 | 502 | 1229 | | |
| 13 | Minimum | 74 | 88 | 101 | 263 | | |
| 14 | Count | 4 | 4 | 4 | 4 | | |
| 15 | Goal | | | | | 30000 | |

The Qtr 1 Commissions worksheet sums the monthly totals for all team members and each team member's quarterly sales. Formulas also calculate the monthly average, maximum, minimum, and item count. The IF function returns a message if the sales goal is met or leaves the cell blank if not met.

## 3.1 Working with Formulas and Functions

**Video Lesson**   labyrinthelab.com/videos

A formula is simply a math problem done in Excel. You can add, subtract, multiply, divide, and group numbers and cell contents in order to make your data work for you. A function is a prewritten formula that helps to simplify complex procedures, both for numbers and for text. For instance, a function can be used to sum a group of numbers, to determine the payment amount on a loan, and to convert a number to text.

### Using AutoSum to Create a SUM Formula

**FROM THE KEYBOARD**
Alt + = for Autosum

The power of Excel becomes apparent when you begin using formulas and functions. The most common type of calculation is summing a column or row of numbers. In fact, this type of calculation is so common that Excel provides the AutoSum feature specifically for this purpose.

The $\Sigma$ button on the Home tab, also known as Sum, automatically sums a column or row of numbers. When you click AutoSum, Excel starts the formula for you by entering =SUM() and proposes a range of adjacent cells within parentheses. Excel will first look upward for a range to sum, and if a range is not found there, it will next look left. You can accept the proposed range or drag in the worksheet to select a different range. You can see the formula, such as =SUM(B5:B8), in the Formula Bar as you edit cell contents. Then, the calculation result displays in the cell after you complete the entry. Empty cells in the sum range are ignored in the calculation.

If your Excel window is smaller, the button may be displayed like this: $\Sigma$ ▾.

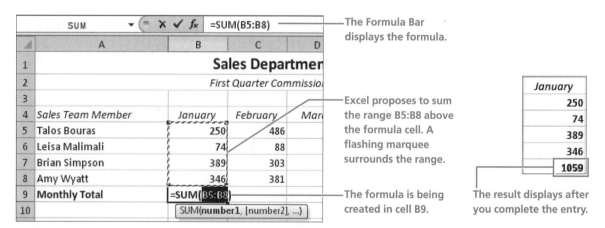

The Formula Bar displays the formula.

Excel proposes to sum the range B5:B8 above the formula cell. A flashing marquee surrounds the range.

The formula is being created in cell B9.

The result displays after you complete the entry.

## AVERAGE, COUNT, COUNTA, MAX, and MIN Functions

The AutoSum button does not stop at simply summing a group of numbers. The following statistical functions are also available on the AutoSum drop-down list: average, count numbers, maximum, and minimum.

An additional Count command equal to the COUNTA function in formulas is available on the Status Bar. The following table describes these functions. The COUNTA function counts all nonblank cells in the specified range. At times, you will want use COUNTA to count all entries, whether or not they contain numbers. You could use the Count Numbers command, equal to the COUNT function, when it is important to identify any non-number cells as possible errors.

| AutoSum and/or Status Bar Function | How Function Appears in Formula | Description |
|---|---|---|
| Sum | SUM | Adds the values in the cells indicated in the formula |
| Average | AVERAGE | Averages the values in the cells indicated in the formula by dividing the sum total by the number of values |
| Count Numbers or Numerical Count | COUNT | Counts the number of values in the cells indicated in the formula; cells containing text and blank cells are ignored |
| Count | COUNTA | Counts the number of nonblank cells in the cells indicated in the formula; cells containing text are included; empty cells are ignored |
| Max or Maximum | MAX | Returns the maximum (highest) value in the cells indicated in the formula |
| Min or Minimum | MIN | Returns the minimum (lowest) value in the cells indicated in the formula |

 Once you have entered a formula in a cell, you can use AutoFill to copy it to adjacent cells.

## Status Bar Functions and Customization

The Status Bar, which is displayed at the bottom of the Excel window, allows you to view information about a range of numbers without actually inserting a function formula in the worksheet. You can customize the Status Bar to display the following functions: Average, Count, Numerical Count, Minimum, Maximum, and Sum. To customize the Status Bar, right-click anywhere on it and click to add or remove features. Other than functions, you can also customize additional features of the Status Bar, such as Zoom, Signatures, Overtype Mode, and Macro Recording.

The range B5:B8 is selected in the worksheet.

| ◢ | A | B | C |
|---|---|---|---|
| 1 | | **Sales Depa** | |
| 2 | | *First Quarter Cor* | |
| 3 | | | |
| 4 | *Sales Team Member* | *January* | *February* |
| 5 | Talos Bouras | 250 | 486 |
| 6 | Leisa Malimali | 74 | 88 |
| 7 | Brian Simpson | 389 | 303 |
| 8 | Amy Wyatt | 346 | 381 |
| 9 | **Monthly Total** | **1059** | **1258** |

By default, Excel displays in the Status Bar the average, count of values, and sum of the selected range.

Right-clicking the Status Bar displays a menu from which you can add items to or delete them from the Status Bar.

**Customize Status Bar**

| | | |
|---|---|---|
| ✓ | Cell Mode | Ready |
| ✓ | Signatures | Off |
| ✓ | Information Management Policy | Off |
| ✓ | Permissions | Off |
| | Caps Lock | Off |
| | Num Lock | Off |
| ✓ | Scroll Lock | Off |
| ✓ | Fixed Decimal | Off |
| | Overtype Mode | |
| ✓ | End Mode | |
| | Macro Recording | Not Recording |
| ✓ | Selection Mode | |
| ✓ | Page Number | |
| ✓ | Average | 264.75 |
| ✓ | Count | 4 |
| | Numerical Count | |
| | Minimum | |
| | Maximum | |
| ✓ | Sum | 1059 |
| ✓ | Upload Status | |
| ✓ | View Shortcuts | |
| ✓ | Zoom | 100% |
| ✓ | Zoom Slider | |

---

| QUICK REFERENCE | USING AUTOSUM AND THE STATUS BAR FUNCTIONS |
|---|---|
| **Task** | **Procedure** |
| AutoSum a range of cells | ▪ Click in the cell where you want the sum to appear. |
| | ▪ Choose Home→Editing→AutoSum **Σ** from the Ribbon. |
| | ▪ If the proposed range is correct, tap [Enter] or click the AutoSum button to complete the function. |
| | ▪ If the proposed range is incorrect, click and drag to select the correct range before tapping [Enter]. |
| AutoSum across columns or down rows | ▪ Select the cell range in the row below or column to the right of the data where you want the sums to appear. |
| | ▪ Choose Home→Editing→AutoSum **Σ** from the Ribbon. |
| Use Status Bar functions | ▪ Right-click the Status Bar and add or remove the desired functions, if necessary. |
| | ▪ Drag to select the range of cells to which you wish to apply the function. |
| | ▪ Look at the Status Bar at the bottom of your Excel window to view the average, count of values, and sum of the selected range. |

# Use AutoSum and Status Bar Functions

*In this exercise, you will use AutoSum to calculate the monthly commission total for the sales team as well as the quarterly total for each sales team member. You will also explore the functions on the Status Bar.*

## Open an Excel File

1. Start **Excel**.

2. **Open** the Commissions workbook from the Lesson 03 folder in your file storage location.
*Take a look at the workbook. There are two tabs at the bottom of the window: Qtr 1 Commissions and Profit Projection. You will first work with the commissions worksheet to calculate monthly and quarterly commission totals. You also will find the average, maximum, minimum, and count of numbers for each month.*

## Use AutoSum

3. With the Qtr 1 Commissions worksheet displayed, select **cell B9**.

4. Choose **Home→Editing→Sum** $\Sigma$ from the Ribbon.
*Excel displays a marquee (marching ants) around the part of the spreadsheet where it thinks the formula should be applied. You can change this selection as necessary.*

5. Follow these steps to complete the Sum formula.

Ⓐ Notice the **formula**, which is a sum of numbers in the range B5:B8.

Ⓑ The **flashing marquee** surrounds the range B5:B8, which AutoSum determines to be the most likely range for the formula.

Ⓒ Click the **Enter** ✔ button on the Formula Bar to complete the entry. The total should be 1059.

## Override the Range AutoSum Proposes

6. Select **cell E7** and choose **Home→Editing→Sum** $\Sigma$ from the Ribbon.
   *Notice that, as there are no values above cell E7, Excel looked to the left to find a range to sum, B7:D7. Now, assume that you wanted only cells B7:C7 to be summed.*

7. Follow these steps to override the proposed range:

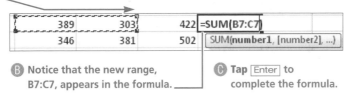

Ⓐ Position the mouse pointer on **cell B7**; **drag to the right to select the range B7:C7**.

| 389 | 303 | 422 | =SUM(B7:C7) | |
| 346 | 381 | 502 | SUM(**number1**, [number2], ...) | |

Ⓑ Notice that the new range, B7:C7, appears in the formula.

Ⓒ Tap [Enter] to complete the formula.

8. **Undo** ↺ the formula.

## Use AutoFill to Extend a Formula

*You can use AutoFill to extend a formula just as you would use it to extend a series of days in the week.*

9. Follow these steps to AutoFill the formula in cell B9 into the cells to its right:

Ⓐ Select **cell B9.**

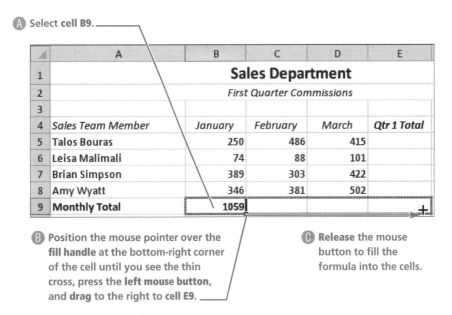

| ◢ | A | B | C | D | E |
|---|---|---|---|---|---|
| 1 | | **Sales Department** | | | |
| 2 | | *First Quarter Commissions* | | | |
| 3 | | | | | |
| 4 | *Sales Team Member* | *January* | *February* | *March* | *Qtr 1 Total* |
| 5 | **Talos Bouras** | 250 | 486 | 415 | |
| 6 | **Leisa Malimali** | 74 | 88 | 101 | |
| 7 | **Brian Simpson** | 389 | 303 | 422 | |
| 8 | **Amy Wyatt** | 346 | 381 | 502 | |
| 9 | **Monthly Total** | 1059 | | | + |

Ⓑ Position the mouse pointer over the **fill handle** at the bottom-right corner of the cell until you see the thin cross, press the **left mouse button**, and **drag** to the right to **cell E9.**

Ⓒ **Release** the mouse button to fill the formula into the cells.

*Cell E9 displays 0 because the cells above it are empty. You can create formulas that include empty cells and then enter data later.*

## Calculate the Quarterly Totals

10. Select the **range E5:E8**.

11. Choose **Home→Editing→Sum** $\boxed{\Sigma}$ from the Ribbon.
    *Excel created a formula in each cell of the selected range without requiring you to complete the formulas.*

| Qtr 1 Total |
|---:|
| 1151 |
| 263 |
| 1114 |
| 1229 |
| 3757 |

12. **Delete** the formulas in **range B9:E9** and **range E5:E8**.
    *The data are returned to their original state. Next you will create all formulas at once by selecting the data and the empty cells to the right and below the data.*

## Sum Columns and Rows Simultaneously

13. Select the **range B5:E9** and click **Sum** $\boxed{\Sigma}$.
    *The formula results appear in B9:D9 and E5:E9. This procedure is the most efficient to use when the data are arranged in this way.*

## Explore Statistical Functions with AutoSum

14. Select **cell B11**.

15. On the Home ribbon in the Editing group, click the **drop-down arrow** at the right of the **AutoSum** button.

    $\boxed{\Sigma \text{ AutoSum } \blacktriangledown}$

16. Choose **Average** from the drop-down menu.
    *Excel proposes the range B5:B10, which is incorrect.*

17. Select the correct **range B5:B8** and **tap** $\boxed{\text{Enter}}$ to complete the entry.
    *The result should equal 264.75.*

18. Select **cell B12**.

19. Choose **Home→Editing** $\boxed{\Sigma \text{ AutoSum } \blacktriangledown}$ **menu** ▼**→Max** from the Ribbon.
    *Max means Maximum.*

20. Select the correct **range B5:B8** and **tap** $\boxed{\text{Enter}}$ to display the highest value in the range you chose.

21. Select **cell B13** and choose **Home→Editing→AutoSum menu** ▼**→Min** from the Ribbon.
    *Min means Minimum, or the lowest value.*

22. Correct the range to **B5:B8** and then click **Enter** ✓ on the Formula Bar to complete the entry.

23. Select **cell B14** and choose **Home→Editing** $\boxed{\Sigma \text{ AutoSum } \blacktriangledown}$ **menu** ▼ from the Ribbon.

24. Choose **Count Numbers** from the menu, correct the range to **B5:B8**, and click **Enter** on the Formula Bar to complete the entry.

    *Notice that the function COUNT is used in the formula. This function counts all cells in the range that contain a number. You can use this function to check that all cells have a number.*

25. Select **cell B6** and **delete** the contents.

    *The formula recalculates the count as 3 and recalculates the average because one cell in the range is now blank.*

26. **Undo** 🔄 the deletion.

**Use Status Bar Functions**

27. Select the **range B5:B8**.

28. Look at the Status Bar in the lower-right corner of the window to see the **sum value** displayed.

29. **Save** 💾 the workbook and keep it **open** for the next exercise.

| | B | C |
|---|---|---|
| | January | February |
| | 250 | 486 |
| | 74 | 88 |
| | 389 | 303 |
| | 346 | 381 |
| | 1059 | 1258 |
| | | |
| | 264.75 | 314.5 |
| | 389 | 486 |
| | 74 | 88 |
| | =COUNT(B5:B8 | |

✓ ƒ× | =COUNT(B5:B8

COUNT(**value1**, [value2], …)

Average: 264.75        Count: 4        Sum: 1059

---

## 3.2 Creating Formulas

**Video Lesson**    labyrinthelab.com/videos

You have already learned how to compute totals with AutoSum. AutoSum provides a convenient method for summing a range of numbers. However, you will need to use many other types of formulas in Excel. In fact, many worksheets, such as financial models, require hundreds or even thousands of complex formulas.

### Beginning Character in Formulas

As you saw in the AutoSum discussion in the previous section, functions begin with an equals (=) sign. If you are typing a formula in a cell, it is recommended that you also begin it with an equals (=) sign, even though you can begin it with a plus (+) or a minus (–) sign. It is best to adopt one method in order to create consistency.

### Cell and Range References

Formulas derive their power from the use of cell and range references. For example, in the previous exercise, you used AutoSum to insert the formula =SUM(B5:B8) in cell B9. Because the range reference (B5:B8) was used in the formula, you were able to copy the formula across the row using the fill handle. There are two important benefits to using references in formulas.

■ When references are used, formulas can be copied to other cells.

■ Because a reference refers to a cell or a range of cells, the formula results are automatically recalculated when the data is changed in the referenced cell(s).

Do not type results of calculations directly into cells. Always use formulas.

# The Language of Excel Formulas

Formulas can include the standard arithmetic operators shown in the following table. You can also use spaces within formulas to improve their appearance and readability. Notice that each formula in the table begins with an equals (=) sign. Also, keep in mind that each formula is entered into the same cell that displays the resulting calculation.

| QUICK REFERENCE | USING ARITHMETIC OPERATORS IN FORMULAS | |
|---|---|---|
| **Operator** | **Example** | **Comments** |
| + (addition) | =B7+B11 | Adds the values in B7 and B11 |
| – (subtraction) | =B7–B11 | Subtracts the value in B11 from the value in B7 |
| * (multiplication) | =B7*B11 | Multiplies the values in B7 and B11 |
| / (division) | =B7/B11 | Divides the value in B7 by the value in B11 |
| ^ (exponentiation) | =B7^3 | Raises the value in B7 to the third power (B7*B7*B7) |
| % (percent) | =B7*10% | Multiplies the value in B7 by 10% (0.10) |
| ( ) (grouping) | =B7/(C4–C2) | Subtracts the value in C2 from the value in C4 and then divides B7 by the subtraction result |

When typing a cell reference in a formula, you can simply type the column letter in lowercase and Excel will capitalize it for you.

# "Please Excuse My Dear Aunt Sally"

Excel formulas follow the algebraic hierarchy. This means that the formula completes operations in a specific order. You can memorize this hierarchy with the mnemonic "Please Excuse My Dear Aunt Sally":

| Please | Parentheses (grouping symbols) |
|---|---|
| Excuse | Exponents |
| My | Multiplication |
| Dear | Division |
| Aunt | Addition |
| Sally | Subtraction |

To control the order of operations, you can use parentheses to cause Excel to add or subtract before multiplying or dividing. Take a look at the following examples to see how the order of operations works with and without parentheses and how the resulting value will be different.

| =53+ 7*5 = 53+35 = 88 | Multiplication then addition |
|---|---|
| =(53+7)*5 = (60)*5 = 300 | Parentheses then multiplication |

Excel includes two additional items in the order of operations between parentheses and exponents. At the beginning of a formula, a minus (–) sign is interpreted as a negative. You may need to use parentheses around an operation that includes a negative number to ensure a correct answer. A percent sign is also considered as an operator.

| =–4*2          = –8 | Negative number multiplied by positive number |
|---|---|
| =2+50%+3^2 = 2.5+9 = 11.5 | Percent then exponent |

## Use the Keyboard to Create Formulas

*In this exercise, you will use the keyboard to enter formulas into the spreadsheet.*

1. Click the **Profit Projection** sheet tab at the bottom of the Excel window.

   | ◄ ◄ ► ► | Qtr 1 Commissions | Profit Projection ◄

2. Select **cell B5** and view its formula in the Formula Bar.
   *This formula multiplies the number of contracts (B17) by the average contract revenue (B18).*

3. Select **cell B6** and use **AutoSum** to sum the sales in the **range B4:B5**.

4. Select **cell B11** and **sum** the costs in the **range B8:B10**.
   *The total costs result is not correct, but you will enter data in cells B9 and B10 in the next exercise.*

5. Select **cell B13**, the Gross Profit for the Base column.

6. Type **=B6–B11** in the cell, and then **tap** [Enter] to complete the formula.
   *In order to calculate the gross profit, you need to subtract the total costs (B11) from total revenue (B6).*

7. Select **cell B15**, Gross Profit vs. Revenue.

8. Type **=b13/b6** in the cell, and then **tap** [Enter] to complete the formula.
   *Formulas are not case sensitive. Notice that regardless of whether you type the cell references as upper- or lowercase, the formula will work properly. In this worksheet, the cell has been formatted to display a percentage for you.*

9. **Save** 🖫 the workbook and keep it **open** for the next exercise.

# 3.3 Using Cell References in Formulas

| Video Lesson | labyrinthelab.com/videos |

A cell reference identifies which cell or range of cells contains the values to use in a formula. Cell references are one of three types: relative, absolute, or mixed. All formulas use the relative cell reference unless you specifically instruct Excel to use another type. You used relative cell references in the formulas you created in the last exercise. As this lesson continues, you will learn about the other two types of cell references.

## Relative Cell References

A relative cell reference means the cell is *relative* to the cell that contains the formula. For example, when you create a formula in cell C3 to calculate A3 minus B3 ( =A3–B3), Excel finds that the first value is two cells to the left of the formula. The second value is one cell to the left of the formula.

When you copy a formula, the cell references update automatically and refer to new cells relative to the new formula cell. For example, if you copied the formula mentioned in the previous paragraph down to cell C4, the new formula would be A4 minus B4 ( =A4–B4). The first and second values are still relative to the same number of cells to the left of the formula cell.

| ⬐ | A | B | C | D | E |
|---|---|---|---|---|---|
| 11 | Total Costs | =SUM(B8:B10) | =SUM(C8:C10) | =SUM(D8:D10) | =SUM(E8:E10) |
| 12 | | | | | |
| 13 | Gross Profit | =B6-B11 | =C6-C11 | =D6-D11 | =E6-E11 |

Notice that when a formula utilizing relative cell references in column B is copied through to column E, the cells referenced in the copied formulas will refer to cells relative to where they are pasted.

## Point Mode

One potential danger that can occur when typing formulas is accidentally typing the incorrect cell reference. This is easy to do, especially if the worksheet is complex. Point mode can help you avoid this problem. With point mode, you can insert a cell reference in a formula by clicking the desired cell as you are typing the formula. Likewise, you can insert a range reference in a formula by dragging over the desired cells. You will use point mode in the next exercise.

## Absolute Cell References

You have been using relative references thus far in this course. Relative references are convenient because they update automatically when formulas are moved or copied. In some situations, you may not want references updated when a formula is moved or copied. You must use absolute or mixed references in these situations. Absolute references always refer to the same cell, regardless of which cell the formula is moved or copied to. You can refer to cells on other worksheets or in other workbooks as well.

### Creating Absolute References

You create absolute references by placing dollar signs in front of the column and row components of the reference, for example, $C$1. You can type the dollar signs as you enter a formula or add them later by editing the formula. The following illustration shows an example of how absolute references are used in formulas.

| ⬐ | A | B | C | D | E |
|---|---|---|---|---|---|
| 14 | Net Profit | =B13*(1-$D$20) | =C13*(1-$D$20) | =D13*(1-$D$20) | =E13*(1-$D$20) |

Cell B14 displays a formula that has both a relative cell reference (B13) and an absolute cell reference ($D$20).

When copied to cell C14, the relative cell reference will refer to the cell relative to where it is pasted (C13), but the absolute cell reference will remain the same.

## Mixed References

You can mix relative and absolute references within a reference. For example, the reference $C1 is a combination of an absolute reference to column C and a relative reference to row 1. Mixed references are useful when copying many types of formulas.

## Using the F4 Function Key

You make a reference absolute or mixed by typing dollar signs while entering the reference. You can also use the F4 function key to insert the dollar signs. You may do so right after typing the cell reference or by clicking for an insertion point in the cell reference in the Formula Bar. The first time you tap F4, dollar signs are placed in front of both the column and row components of the reference. If you tap F4 again, the dollar sign is removed from the column component, thus creating a mixed reference. If you tap F4 a third time, a dollar sign is placed in front of just the column component and removed from the row component. One more tap of F4 will return you to a relative cell reference. The following table indicates what happens to a cell reference when its formula is copied and pasted to the next column or row.

| Cell Reference | Type | Copy-and-Paste Action | Result When Pasted |
|---|---|---|---|
| B6 | Relative | One column to the right | C6 |
| B6 | Relative | One row down | B7 |
| $B$6 | Absolute | One column to the right | $B$6 |
| $B$6 | Absolute | One row down | $B$6 |
| $B6 | Mixed | One column to the right | $B6 |
| $B6 | Mixed | One row down | $B7 |
| B$6 | Mixed | One column to the right | C$6 |
| B$6 | Mixed | One row down | B$6 |

## What-If Analysis

Another great advantage to using cell references in formulas is that it allows you to perform what-if analyses. A what-if analysis is as simple as changing the value in a cell that is referenced in a formula and observing the overall change in the data. You can perform these simple analyses at any time by replacing the value(s) in referenced cells. The Undo command can come in very handy when performing a what-if analysis as it provides a quick way to return the worksheet to the original values. If you wish to perform an extensive what-if analysis and not worry about losing your original data, you may wish to save your workbook under a different name as a "practice" file.

## Create Formulas Using Cell References

*In this exercise, you will use absolute cell references to create formulas that can be copied to other cells.*

### Enter a Formula Using Point Mode

1. Select **cell B9** and type **=** to begin a formula.

2. Select **cell D18** and **tap** the F4 function key.

If you have a keyboard that uses the function keys for other purposes, you may have to tap the F Lock key to be able to utilize F4 for absolute or mixed references in Excel.

*Tapping F4 will make the D18 cell reference an absolute by adding the $ symbol to both the column and row references. Take a look at the Formula Bar and you will see $D$18. A formula can consist of just one cell reference. In this case, you want the marketing expense always to reflect the value in cell D18.*

3. **Tap** Enter to complete the formula.

## Calculate the Commissions Using Order of Operations

*You will enter a more complex formula to calculate the total commissions for product sales and contract sales. You want Excel to perform calculations in the following order. First, multiply product sales (B4) by their commission rate (B19). Second, multiply contract sales (B5) by their commission rate (B20). Last, add the two products together.*

4. Select **cell B10** and type **=** to begin a formula.

5. Select **cell B4** and type **\***.

6. Select **cell B19** and **tap** [F4].

7. Type **+** to continue the formula.

8. Select **cell B5** and type **\***.

9. Select **cell B20** and **tap** [F4].

10. Click the **Enter** ✅ button to complete the formula.
    *The result should equal 27,824. You have used point mode to create a formula containing both relative and absolute cell references. Notice how the formula appears in the Formula Bar: =B4 \* $B$19 + B5 \* $B$20. No matter where you copy and paste this formula, the formula always will reference the commission rates in cells B19 and B20.*

## Calculate the Net Profit Using Parentheses

*You will create the formula =B13 \* (1 - $D$20) to calculate the net profit. The gross profit in cell B13 will be multiplied by a factor that takes into account a tax on profits. The calculation in parentheses means "100% minus 7.75%," or 92.25%. The gross profit in cell B13 then will be multiplied by 92.25%.*

11. Select **cell B14** and type **=** to begin a formula.

12. Select **cell B13** and type **\*(1−** to continue the formula.

13. Select **cell D20** and **tap** [F4].

14. Type **)** and **tap** [Enter] to complete the formula.
    *The result should be $138,353.*

## Project a Sales Increase

*You will create the formula =$B$4 \* (1 + C$3) to project a 2 percent increase over the base product sales. The sales in cell B4 will be multiplied by (100% + 2%), or 102%. Notice that, when the formula is copied across the row later, the absolute reference will always refer to $B$4 as the base sales. The percentage of increase or decrease will change from C$3 to D$3 or E$3, the corresponding percentage over each column.*

15. Select **cell C4** and type **=** to begin a formula.

16. Select **cell B4** and **tap** [F4].

17. Type **\*(1+** to continue the formula.

18. Select **cell C3** and **tap** [F4] two times to create the C$3 mixed cell reference.

19. Type **)** and **tap** [Enter] to complete the formula.
    *The result should equal 54,264.*

20. Select **cell C5**.

21. Repeat the above procedure to project a **2 percent increase** for base contract sales.
    *The result should equal 245,820.*

22. **Save** 💾 the changes.

23. Compare your worksheet formulas and their results with the following illustrations.

| | A | B | C | D | E |
|---|---|---|---|---|---|
| 1 | | **Sales Department** | | | |
| 2 | | *Projected Net Profit* | | | |
| 3 | | *Base* | *2%* | *5%* | *-5%* |
| 4 | Product Sales | $  53,200 | $  54,264 | | |
| 5 | Contracts | $  241,000 | $  245,820 | | |
| 6 | **Total Revenue** | $  **294,200** | $  **300,084** | $  - | $  - |
| 7 | | | | | |
| 8 | Fixed Operating Cost | $  101,400 | | | |
| 9 | Marketing Expense | $  15,000 | | | |
| 10 | Commissions | $  27,824 | | | |
| 11 | Total Costs | $  **144,224** | | | |
| 12 | | | | | |
| 13 | Gross Profit | $  149,976 | | | |
| 14 | Net Profit | $  138,353 | | | |
| 15 | Gross Profit vs. Revenue | $  1 | | | |
| 16 | | | | | |
| 17 | Contracts | $  482 | | | |
| 18 | Average Contract | $  500 | Marketing | $  15,000 | |
| 19 | Product Commission Rate | 7% | Fixed Cost | $  101,400 | |
| 20 | Contract Commission Rate | 10% | Tax Rate | 7.75% | |

| | A | B | C | D | E |
|---|---|---|---|---|---|
| 1 | | **Sales Department** | | | |
| 2 | | *Projected Net Profit* | | | |
| 3 | | *Base* | *0.02* | *0.05* | *-0.05* |
| 4 | Product Sales | 53200 | =$B$4*(1+C$3) | | |
| 5 | Contracts | 241000 | =B5*(1+C$3) | | |
| 6 | Total Revenue | =SUM(B4:B5) | =SUM(C4:C5) | =SUM(D4:D5) | =SUM(E4:E5) |
| 7 | | | | | |
| 8 | Fixed Operating Cost | =D19 | | | |
| 9 | Marketing Expense | =$D$18 | | | |
| 10 | Commissions | =B4*$B$19+B5*$B$20 | | | |
| 11 | Total Costs | =SUM(B8:B10) | | | |
| 12 | | | | | |
| 13 | Gross Profit | =B6-B11 | | | |
| 14 | Net Profit | =B13*(1-$D$20) | | | |
| 15 | Gross Profit vs. Revenue | =B13/B6 | | | |

# 3.4 Modifying and Copying Formulas

**Video Lesson** labyrinthelab.com/videos

You can modify and copy formulas in much the same way that you edit and copy cells.

## Modifying Formulas

You can edit a formula either in the Formula Bar or by double-clicking the formula cell to complete an in-cell edit. If you select a cell and enter a new formula, it replaces the previous contents of the cell.

When you select a formula to edit it, you will see colored lines around all of the cells that are referenced by the formula. This feature can help you to visually determine whether the formula is correct.

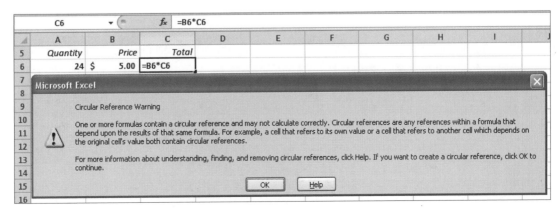

The formula in B14 is selected for editing (as indicated by the insertion point in the cell). Excel graphically displays the cells that are being referenced by the formula, B13 and D20.

## Circular References

You may inadvertently use a circular reference when creating or editing a formula. A circular reference occurs when the formula refers to its own cell or to another formula that refers to that cell. For example, a formula in cell C6 is =B6*C6. Excel cannot complete the calculation because cell C6 is the formula cell, not a reference to a value. When Excel displays a Circular Reference Warning message, you may either click OK to read the circular reference help topic or click Cancel to close the warning. Either option allows the circular reference to remain in the formula until you correct the formula.

You must correct the formula manually after you close Help or the Circular Reference Warning message.

# Copying Formulas

You can use either the Copy and Paste commands with formulas or AutoFill in order to copy them to new cells. You can copy formulas to one cell at a time or to a range of cells using either method.

If you use Auto Fill, the Auto Fill Options 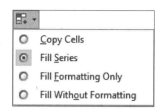 button will appear once you have released the mouse button. Clicking this button will allow you to customize your fill. The Fill Series option displays in the list if you AutoFill a value but does not display for a formula.

You can change what was copied in the cells through AutoFill by clicking the Auto Fill Options button and choosing a different option.

## Modify and Copy Formulas

*In this exercise, you will use techniques to modify and copy formulas in order to complete your profit projection.*

### Modify Formulas and Correct a Circular Reference

1. Select **cell B8**, and then follow these steps to edit the formula in the Formula Bar:

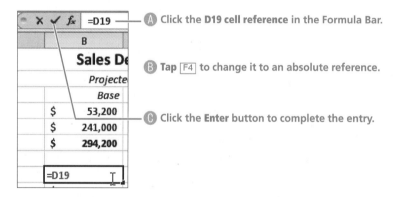

    Ⓐ Click the **D19 cell reference** in the Formula Bar.

    Ⓑ Tap F4 to change it to an absolute reference.

    Ⓒ Click the **Enter** button to complete the entry.

2. **Double-click** cell C6 to begin an in-cell edit.
   *Notice that the cell references are displayed in color in the formula and on the worksheet.*

3. Follow these steps to complete an in-cell edit:

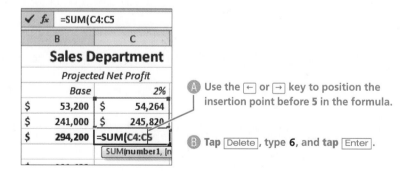

    Ⓐ Use the ← or → key to position the insertion point before **5** in the formula.

    Ⓑ Tap Delete, type **6**, and tap Enter.

*Excel displays a Circular Reference Warning message because you referred to C6, the formula cell itself.*

4. Choose **OK** in the Circular Reference Warning message.

5. **Undo** 🔄 the change.

## Use Copy and Paste Commands to Copy a Formula

6. Select **cell B14** and then use Ctrl+C to **copy** the formula.

7. Select **cell C14** and then use Ctrl+V to **paste** the formula in the new cell.
   *This method works great if you need to copy a formula to just one cell. You can use these commands to copy a formula to a range of cells as well.*

8. Select the **range D14:E14** and then use Ctrl+V.
   *The formula that you copied in step 6 is now pasted to the range of cells selected.*

9. **Tap** Esc to cancel the marquee around cell B14.

10. Select **cell D14** and look at the formula in the Formula Bar.

| D14 | ▼ | *fx* | =D13*(1-$D$20) | |
|---|---|---|---|---|
| | A | B | C | D |
| 13 | Gross Profit | $ 149,976 | | |
| 14 | Net Profit | $ 138,353 | $ - | $ ⊹ - |

*Notice that the relative cell reference now indicates cell D13, whereas the absolute cell reference is still looking to cell D20.*

## Use AutoFill to Copy Formulas

11. Follow these steps to copy the formula from cell C4 to the range D4:E4.

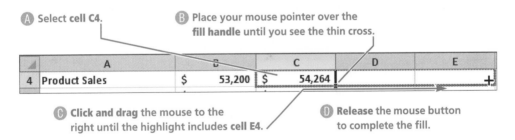

Ⓐ Select **cell C4**.

Ⓑ Place your mouse pointer over the **fill handle** until you see the thin cross.

| | A | B | C | D | E |
|---|---|---|---|---|---|
| 4 | Product Sales | $ 53,200 | $ 54,264 | | |

Ⓒ **Click and drag** the mouse to the right until the highlight includes **cell E4**.

Ⓓ **Release** the mouse button to complete the fill.

12. Use **AutoFill** to copy the formula from **cell C5** to the **range D5:E5**.
    *Next, you will use AutoFill to copy formulas from B8:B15 all the way through C8:E15.*

13. Select the **range B8:B15**.

14. Place your mouse pointer over the **fill handle** at the bottom right of the selected range.

15. When you see the thin cross ✚, **drag** to the **right** until the highlight includes the cells in **column E** and then release the mouse.

| | A | B | C | D | E | |
|---|---|---|---|---|---|---|
| 8 | Fixed Operating Cost | $ 101,400 | $ 101,400 | $ 101,400 | $ 101,400 | |
| 9 | Marketing Expense | $ 15,000 | $ 15,000 | $ 15,000 | $ 15,000 | |
| 10 | Commissions | $ 27,824 | $ 28,380 | $ 29,215 | $ 26,433 | |
| 11 | Total Costs | $ 144,224 | $ 144,780 | $ 145,615 | $ 142,833 | |
| 12 | | | | | | |
| 13 | Gross Profit | $ 149,976 | $ 155,304 | $ 163,295 | $ 136,657 | |
| 14 | Net Profit | $ 138,353 | $ 143,267 | $ 150,639 | $ 126,066 | |
| 15 | Gross Profit vs. Revenue | 51.0% | 51.8% | 52.9% | 48.9% | |
| 16 | | | | | | |

16. **Deselect** the filled range.

*Make it a habit to deselect highlighted cells after performing an action. This step will help avoid unintended changes to cell contents.*

17. **Save** 💾 the changes and leave the workbook **open**.

# 3.5 Displaying and Printing Formulas

**Video Lesson**  labyrinthelab.com/videos

FROM THE KEYBOARD

Ctrl + ` to show formulas

Excel normally displays the results of formulas in worksheet cells. However, you may need to display the actual formulas from time to time. Displaying formulas, especially in complex financial worksheets, can help you understand how a worksheet functions, enabling you to "debug" the worksheet and locate potential problems.

To display formulas, you will use the Show Formulas command on the Formulas tab of the Ribbon. You can edit a formula in this view, but you will need to show values again to see the result. To view the values once again, choose Show Formulas again.

While formulas are displayed, Excel automatically widens columns to show more of the cell contents. You can print the formula display as you would any other worksheet. You may wish to switch to landscape orientation, which prints the worksheet across the wide edge of the paper.

Depending on your monitor size, the buttons may appear as only icons, without the text descriptors, or as large buttons.

| B | C | D |
|---|---|---|
| **Sales Department** | | |
| *Projected Net Profit* | | |
| Base | 0.02 | 0.05 |
| 53200 | =$B$4*(1+C$3) | =$B$4*(1+D$3) |
| =B17*B18 | =$B$5*(1+C$3) | =$B$5*(1+D$3) |
| =SUM(B4:B5) | =SUM(C4:C5) | =SUM(D4:D5) |
| | | |
| =$D$19 | =$D$19 | =$D$19 |
| 15000 | 15000 | 15000 |
| =B4*$B$19+B5*$B$20 | =C4*$B$19+C5*$B$20 | =D4*$B$19+D5*$B$20 |
| =SUM(B8:B10) | =SUM(C8:C10) | =SUM(D8:D10) |
| | | |
| =B6-B11 | =C6-C11 | =D6-D11 |
| =B13*(1-$D$20) | =C13*(1-$D$20) | =D13*(1-$D$20) |
| =B13/B6 | =C13/C6 | =D13/D6 |

When you choose to show formulas, you will see the formulas in the cells rather than the values as before. If a cell does not contain a formula, the contents will be visible in this view.

## QUICK REFERENCE    VIEWING AND PRINTING FORMULAS

| Task | Procedure |
|---|---|
| Display or hide the formulas in a workbook | ■ Choose Formulas→Formula Auditing→Show Formulas from the Ribbon. |
| Change paper orientation to print across the wide edge | ■ Choose Page Layout→Page Setup→Orientation→Landscape from the Ribbon. |
| Print displayed formulas | ■ Choose File→Print. |
| | ■ Choose any desired options in the Print tab and click Print. |

## DEVELOP YOUR SKILLS 3.5.1

# Display Formulas in a Worksheet

*In this exercise, you will display the formulas in the profit projection worksheet to see how it is constructed and to be able to troubleshoot any potentially inaccurate formulas.*

1. Choose **Formulas→Formula Auditing→Show Formulas** from the Ribbon.
   *Take a look at the worksheet. You can use this feature to examine your formulas more closely.*

2. Choose **Formulas→Formula Auditing→Show Formulas** from the Ribbon.
   *The values will be displayed once again.*

# 3.6 Using Formula AutoComplete

**Video Lesson**    labyrinthelab.com/videos

Excel includes a feature that assists you in creating and editing formulas. Formula AutoComplete will jump into action once you have typed an equals (=) sign and the beginning letters of a function in a cell. It works by displaying a list of functions beginning with the typed letters below the active cell.

## Functions Defined

A function is a predefined formula that performs calculations or returns a desired result. Excel has more than 400 built-in functions. You construct functions using a set of basic rules known as syntax. Fortunately, most functions use the same or similar syntax. This syntax also applies to the MIN, MAX, AVERAGE, COUNT, and COUNTA functions.

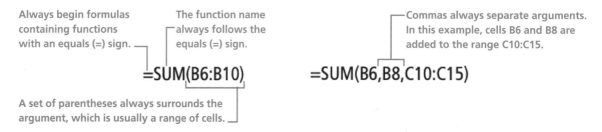

Always begin formulas containing functions with an equals (=) sign.

The function name always follows the equals (=) sign.

A set of parentheses always surrounds the argument, which is usually a range of cells.

Commas always separate arguments. In this example, cells B6 and B8 are added to the range C10:C15.

=SUM(B6:B10)        =SUM(B6,B8,C10:C15)

| QUICK REFERENCE | USING FORMULA AUTOCOMPLETE TO ENTER A FORMULA INTO A CELL |
|---|---|
| **Task** | **Procedure** |
| Use Formula AutoComplete | ■ Type an equals (=) sign and begin typing the desired formula. |
| | ■ Double-click the formula once you see it in the list. |
| | ■ Select the range to which you wish to apply the formula. |
| | ■ Type a closed parenthesis, ), to finish the formula. |
| | ■ Complete the entry. |

### DEVELOP YOUR SKILLS 3.6.1
## Use Formula AutoComplete

*In this exercise, you will have an opportunity to use the Formula AutoComplete feature to create a formula.*

1. Display the **Qtr 1 Commissions** worksheet by clicking the sheet tab.

   ⟨ ◀ ▶ ⟩ | **Qtr 1 Commissions** / Profit Projection /

2. Select **cell C11**.

3. Type **=ave** and observe the list that results.

| =AVE | | | | | | | | |
|---|---|---|---|---|---|---|---|---|
| ƒ AVEDEV | | | | | | | | |
| ƒ AVERAGE | Returns the average (arithmetic mean) of its arguments, which can be numbers or names, arrays, or references that contain numbers | | | | | | | |
| ƒ AVERAGEA | | | | | | | | |
| ƒ AVERAGEIF | | | | | | | | |
| ƒ AVERAGEIFS | | | | | | | | |

*When you use Formula AutoComplete, Excel will show you a list of functions that begin with the letters you type in. If you click on a function in the list, a ScreenTip will describe the function.*

4. **Double-click** AVERAGE in the list.
   *Excel will fill in the function name for you. It will be up to you to select the range next.*

5. Drag to select **cells C5:C8** as the range for the formula.

You do not include total rows or columns when completing most functions.

6. **Tap** ⎡Enter⎤ to complete the function.
   *Notice that Excel added the parenthesis at the end of the formula for you. The result should be 314.5.*

7. Select **cell C11** and use the fill handle to **copy** the function to the **range D11:E11**.

| ▲ | A | B | C | D | E |
|---|---|---|---|---|---|
| 11 | Average | 264.75 | 314.5 | 360 | 939.25 |
| 12 | Maximum | 389 | | | |

*You now have the average commission for each month and the entire quarter.*

8. **Save** 💾 the changes and leave the workbook **open**.

# 3.7 Using Insert Function

**Video Lesson**  labyrinthelab.com/videos

The Insert Function $f_x$ button displays the Insert Function dialog box. This dialog box provides access to all of Excel's built-in functions. It allows you to locate a function by typing a description or searching by category. When you locate the desired function and click OK, Excel displays the Function Arguments box. The Function Arguments box helps you enter arguments in functions. The Insert Function box and the Function Arguments box are shown in the following illustrations.

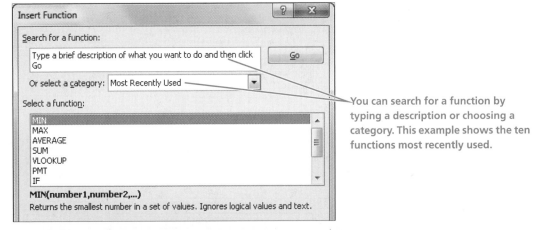

You can search for a function by typing a description or choosing a category. This example shows the ten functions most recently used.

The Function Arguments box appears when you choose a function and click OK.

You can type the argument (typically a range) in this box or select the desired range in the worksheet.

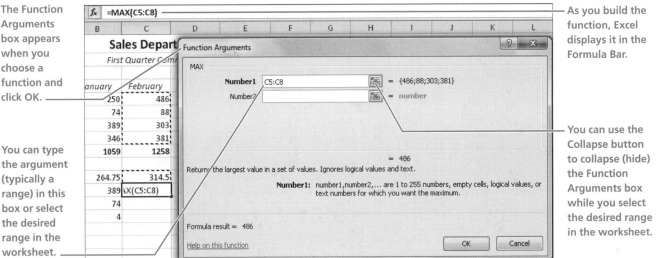

As you build the function, Excel displays it in the Formula Bar.

You can use the Collapse button to collapse (hide) the Function Arguments box while you select the desired range in the worksheet.

 The Function Arguments dialog box can be moved by dragging its title bar to view the desired range on the worksheet.

| Task | Procedure |
|---|---|
| Create a function using the Insert Function command | ■ Select the cell(s) in which you wish to enter a function.<br>■ Click the Insert Function [fx] button on the Formula Bar.<br>■ Choose the desired function and click OK.<br>■ Select the range to which you wish to apply the function.<br>■ Click OK. |

## DEVELOP YOUR SKILLS 3.7.1

# Use Insert Function

*In this exercise, you will complete the commissions worksheet by using the Insert Function command to create both the maximum and minimum functions.*

1. Select **cell C12**.

2. Follow these steps to create the Maximum function:

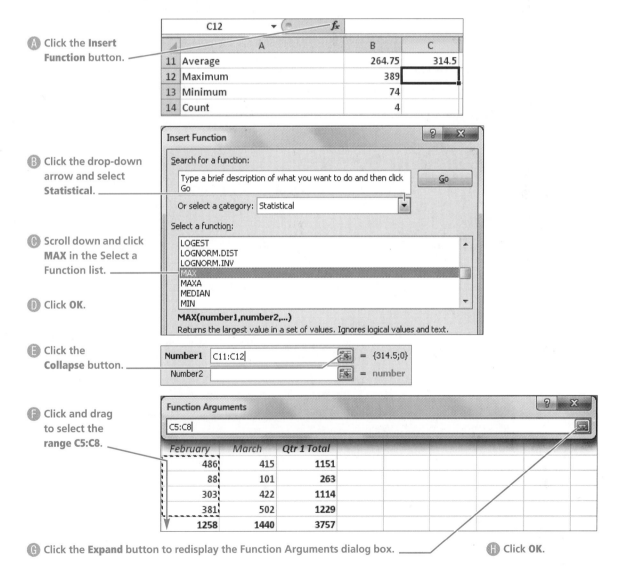

A. Click the **Insert Function** button.

B. Click the drop-down arrow and select **Statistical**.

C. Scroll down and click **MAX** in the Select a Function list.

D. Click **OK**.

E. Click the **Collapse** button.

F. Click and drag to select the range **C5:C8**.

G. Click the **Expand** button to redisplay the Function Arguments dialog box.

H. Click **OK**.

3. Using the procedure from **step 2**, create the **Minimum** function in **cell C13**.

4. Create the **Count** function in **cell C14**.

5. Select the **range C12:C14** and **copy** the formulas to the **range D12:E14**.

| ◢ | A | B | C | D | E |
|---|---|---|---|---|---|
| 11 | Average | 264.75 | 314.5 | 360 | 939.25 |
| 12 | Maximum | 389 | 486 | 502 | 1377 |
| 13 | Minimum | 74 | 88 | 101 | 263 |
| 14 | Count | 4 | 4 | 4 | 12 |

6. **Save** 💾 the changes and leave the workbook **open**.

# 3.8 Creating Formulas with the IF Function

**Video Lesson**   labyrinthelab.com/videos

Excel's IF function displays a value or message based on a logical test you design. Depending on the result of the logical test, the IF function displays whatever you choose for a true or false result. For example, you may check to see whether the purchase amount is greater than $200. If true, a discount is calculated; if false, the text *No discount* is displayed.

## IF Function Syntax

**NOTE**

If you type the IF formula directly in its cell, you must add quotation (") marks around text arguments. If you use the Insert Function command, Excel will add the quotation marks for you.

The generic parts of the IF function are shown in the following table.

| Function | Syntax |
|---|---|
| IF | IF(logical_test, value_if_true, value_if_false) |

The following table outlines the arguments of the IF function.

| Argument | Description |
|---|---|
| logical_test | The condition being checked using a comparison operator, such as =, >, <, >=, <=, or <> (not equal to) |
| value_if_true | The value, text in quotation (") marks, or calculation returned if the logical test result is found to be true |
| value_if_false | The value, text in quotation (") marks, or calculation returned if the logical test result is found to be false |

# How the IF Function Works

The formula =IF(C6>=200,C6*D6,0) is used as an example to explain the function result. Excel performs the logical test to determine whether the value in C6 is greater than or equal to 200. A value of 200 or more would evaluate as true. Any of the following would evaluate as false: the value 50, a blank cell, or text entered in cell C6. If the logical test proves true, the calculation C6*D6 is performed and the result displays in the formula cell. If the calculation proves false, the value 0 (zero) displays instead.

You may specify various actions to be performed for the value_if_true and value_if_false arguments. You may display a text message or leave the cell blank. You may create complex calculations and even use other functions in arguments within an IF function, called nesting. Two examples that display text are shown in the following table.

| Formula | Action If True | Action If False |
| --- | --- | --- |
| IF(F3>150000, "Over Budget", "Within Budget") | The text *Over Budget* displays | The text *Within Budget* displays |
| IF(D6<=30,"","Late") | The cell displays blank | The text *Late* displays |

If you type "" (quotation marks without a space between) as the value_if_true or value_if_false argument, Excel leaves the cell blank.

DEVELOP YOUR SKILLS 3.8.1
## Use the IF Function

*In this exercise, you will use the IF function to display a text message when a salesperson achieves at least $30,000 in quarterly sales.*

### Create an IF Formula to Display a Message

1. Click the **Qtr 1 Commissions** sheet tab at the bottom of the Excel window if the sheet is not already displayed.

2. **Enter** the column heading **Sales** in cell F4 and **Met Goal?** in cell G4.

3. Enter values in the **range F5:F8** as shown at right.

4. Enter **Goal** in **cell A15** and **30000** in **cell F15**.
   *You will create a formula that compares the value in the Sales cell with the goal of $30,000. If sales are equal or greater, the message Yes displays. Otherwise, the cell displays No.*

|  | F | G |
| --- | --- | --- |
| 4 | Sales | Met Goal? |
| 5 | 28775 | |
| 6 | 6575 | |
| 7 | 27850 | |
| 8 | 30725 | |

5. Select **cell G5** and click the **Insert Function** $f_x$ button in the Formula Bar.

6. Follow these steps to find the IF function:

Ⓐ **Choose Logical** from the Or Select a Category list.

Ⓑ **Double-click** the IF function.

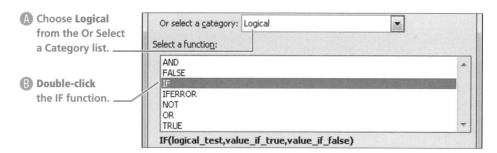

*The Function Arguments dialog box appears for the IF function.*

7. If necessary, move the Function Arguments dialog box out of the way by **dragging** its title bar until you can see column G.

8. Follow these steps to specify the IF function arguments:

Ⓐ Select **cell F5** in the worksheet, use Shift + > to type >, and then type = (greater than or equal to).

Ⓑ Select **cell F15** (the $30,000 goal amount) and **tap** F4 to convert the cell to an absolute cell reference. (The reference must be absolute because the copied formula always should refer to this cell.)

Ⓒ Click in the **Value_If_True box**, type **Yes**, and **tap** Tab. (Excel adds the quotation marks for you.)

Ⓓ Enter **No** in the Value_If_False box.

Ⓔ **Tap** Enter to choose **OK**.

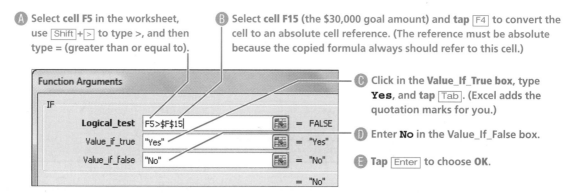

9. Review the completed formula in the Formula Bar.
   *The formula is =IF(F5>=$F$15,"Yes","No"). The message No appears in cell G5 because Talos Bouras' sales are not at least $30,000, the value in cell F15. The value_if_false argument applies.*

10. Use **AutoFill** to copy the formula in **cell G5** down to the **range G6:G8**.
   *The cell for Amy Wyatt displays Yes as specified by your value_if_true argument. The cells for all other salespeople display No.*

## Edit the IF Function

*Now you will edit the value_if_false argument to "" to display no message.*

11. Select **cell G5**.

12. In the Formula Bar, **click** between the quotation (") mark and the N, and **tap** Delete twice to delete *No*.

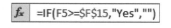

13. Click **Enter** ✓ in the Formula Bar to complete the formula.
   *Now cell G5 does not display any message because the value_if_false argument contains no text.*

14. Use **AutoFill** to copy the formula in **cell G5** down to the **range G6:G8**.

   *Notice that the cells that previously displayed No in column G now display no message, as shown in the illustration below. The salespeople who met goal are easier to identify.*

| | A | B | C | D | E | F | G |
|---|---|---|---|---|---|---|---|
| 4 | Sales Team Member | January | February | March | Qtr 1 Total | Sales | Met Goal? |
| 5 | Talos Bouras | 250 | 486 | 415 | 1151 | 28775 | |
| 6 | Leisa Malimali | 74 | 88 | 101 | 263 | 6575 | |
| 7 | Brian Simpson | 389 | 303 | 422 | 1114 | 27850 | |
| 8 | Amy Wyatt | 346 | 381 | 502 | 1229 | 30725 | Yes |
| 9 | Monthly Total | 1059 | 1258 | 1440 | 3757 | | |
| 10 | | | | | | | |
| 11 | Average | 264.75 | 314.5 | 360 | 939.25 | | |
| 12 | Maximum | 389 | 486 | 502 | 1377 | | |
| 13 | Minimum | 74 | 88 | 101 | 263 | | |
| 14 | Count | 4 | 4 | 4 | 12 | | |
| 15 | Goal | | | | | 30000 | |

15. **Save** 💾 the changes and **close** the workbook.

# 3.9 Concepts Review

Concepts Review    [labyrinthelab.com/excel10](labyrinthelab.com/excel10)

*To check your knowledge of the key concepts introduced in this lesson, complete the Concepts Review quiz by going to the URL listed above. If your classroom is using Labyrinth eLab, you may complete the Concepts Review quiz from within your eLab course.*

# Reinforce Your Skills

## Use the AutoSum Function

*In this exercise, you will use AutoSum to compute totals.*

1. **Open** the rs-Benefit Plan workbook from the Lesson 03 folder in your file storage location.

2. Select **cell C10**, and then choose **Home→Editing→Sum** $\Sigma$ from the Ribbon.
   *Notice that Excel proposes the formula =SUM(C8:C9). Excel proposes this incorrect formula because there are empty cells in the range you are to sum.*

3. **Drag** the mouse pointer over the **range C5:C9**.
   *The flashing marquee will surround the range C5:C9.*

4. **Complete** the entry.
   *The total should equal 650.*

| Amount | Con |
|--------|-----|
| 100 | |
| | |
| | |
| 350 | |
| 200 | |
| =SUM(C5:C9) | |

5. Use the techniques described in the preceding steps to compute the **totals** in **cells E10, G10**, and **I10**.

6. **Save** 💾 the changes to your workbook and **close** it.

## Create Simple Formulas

*In this exercise, you will create formulas using the keyboard as well as the point-and-click method.*

1. **Open** the rs-Orders and Returns workbook from the Lesson 03 folder in your file storage location.

2. Select **cell B18**.

3. Type **=**.

4. Select **cell B4** and and type **+**.

5. Select **cell B9** and type **+**.

6. Select **cell B14** and **tap** ⏎Enter.

7. Use **AutoFill** to copy the formula to **cells C18** and **D18**.

8. Using the techniques described in the preceding steps, create a formula in **cell B19** that **totals** the exchanges from all three sales categories.

9. Create another formula in **cell B20** that **totals** the returns from all three sales categories.

10. Use **AutoFill** to copy the formulas into the appropriate cells.

11. Take a few minutes to examine the formulas in the Formula Bar.

12. **Save** 💾 the changes and **close** the workbook.

# Use Formula AutoComplete, AutoFill, and Display Formulas

*In this exercise, you will calculate averages by using the Formula AutoComplete feature. You will also display formulas and preview them in Page Layout View. You will explore the Landscape and Portrait print settings.*

## Use AutoComplete

1. **Open** the rs-Service Contracts workbook from the Lesson 03 folder in your file storage location.

2. Select **cell A10** and **edit** the label to read **Green Clean Service Contracts - Prior Year**.

3. Select **cell B2** and use **AutoFill** to copy the series Qtr 2, Qtr 3, and Qtr 4 into the **range C2:E2**.

4. Select **cell B8**.

5. Begin **typing** the formula **=aver**, and then **tap** [Tab] to choose **AVERAGE** as the function.

6. Drag to select **B3:B6**, and then **tap** [Enter].
   *The result should equal 33.*

7. Use the **fill handle** to copy the formula across **row 8**.

8. Select **cell B17**.

9. Use **Formula AutoComplete** to average the **range B12:B15**.
   *The result should equal 23.5. Remember that, you can type the function name and arguments in lowercase and Excel will convert them to uppercase.*

10. Use the **fill handle** to copy the formula across **row 17**.

11. Select **cell B20**.

12. Use **point mode** to enter the formula =B7-B16, and **complete** the entry.
    *The result should equal 38.*

13. Use the **fill handle** to copy the formula across **row 20**.

## Display Formulas and Preview in Page Layout View

14. Use [Ctrl]+[`] to display the worksheet formulas.
    *The grave accent [`] key is above the [Tab] key.*

15. Choose **View→Workbook Views→Page Layout** 🖹 from the Ribbon.

16. Take a few minutes to look at the way the data and formulas display.
    *Notice that Excel widened the columns so that most of the cell contents display. In this view, the worksheet fits on two pages.*

17. Choose **Page Layout→Page Setup→Orientation→Landscape** from the Ribbon.
    *Landscape orientation prints across the wide edge of the paper, which is useful for printing the formula view. Now the formulas fit on one page.*

18. Choose **Page Layout→Page Setup→Orientation→Portrait** from the Ribbon.
    *Portrait orientation prints across the narrow edge of the paper, which is acceptable for printing this worksheet while formulas are hidden.*

19. Click the **Normal View** button in the view toolbar at the bottom-right corner of the window.

20. Use `Ctrl`+`` ` `` to **hide** the formulas.

21. **Save** 💾 the changes and **close** the workbook.

REINFORCE YOUR SKILLS 3.4

# Use Absolute References and Perform a What-If Analysis

*In this exercise, you will create a worksheet that calculates commissions as total sales multiplied by the commission rate. You will change the commission rate to see the impact this change has on the total sales. You will use an absolute reference when referencing the commission rate.*

1. Start a **new** workbook, and set up the worksheet shown to the right. **Type** all numbers as shown.

2. Select **cell C6**, and **enter** the formula **=B6*$C$3** in the cell.
   *The result should be 2200. Cell C3 needs an absolute reference because you will copy the formula down the column and because the new formulas must also reference C3.*

|   | A | B | C |
|---|---|---|---|
| 1 | January Commission Report | | |
| 2 | | | |
| 3 | Commission Rate | | 5% |
| 4 | | | |
| 5 | | Sales | Commission |
| 6 | Bouras | 44000 | |
| 7 | Malimali | 17000 | |
| 8 | Simpson | 41000 | |
| 9 | Wyatt | 36000 | |

3. Use the **fill handle** to copy the formula down the column to **cells C7 through C9**.

4. Select **cell C3**, and change the percentage to **3%**.
   *By this time, you should see the benefit of setting up values first (such as the commission rate) and referencing them in formulas. This step allows you to perform what-if analyses. In most cases, you will need absolute references when referencing variables in this manner. Absolute references are necessary whenever you copy a formula that references a variable in a fixed location.*

|   | A | B | C |
|---|---|---|---|
| 1 | January Commission Report | | |
| 2 | | | |
| 3 | Commission Rate | | 3% |
| 4 | | | |
| 5 | | Sales | Commission |
| 6 | Bouras | 44000 | 1320 |
| 7 | Malimali | 17000 | 510 |
| 8 | Simpson | 41000 | 1230 |
| 9 | Wyatt | 36000 | 1080 |

5. **Save** 💾 as `rs-January Commissions` in the Lesson 03 folder and continue with the next exercise.

# Use COUNT and COUNTA Functions

*In this exercise, you will create formulas using the COUNT and COUNTA functions.*

*Before You Begin: You must have completed Reinforce Your Skills 3.4 and the rs-January Commissions workbook should be open.*

1. Type **Count** in **cell A11**.

2. Type **CountA** in **cell A12**.

3. Select **cell B11** and begin **typing** the formula **=cou**.

4. Read the description of the COUNT function in the list that appears.
   *The COUNT function counts the cells containing numbers in the specified range.*

5. **Tap** Tab to select **COUNT** in the list.

6. Drag to select **B5:B9** and **tap** Enter.
   *The result should equal 4. The label in cell B5 is ignored.*

7. Select **cell B12** and repeat the above procedure, this time selecting the **COUNTA** function.
   *The result should equal 5, including the label in cell B5. The COUNTA function counts all nonblank cells in the specified range.*

8. Select **cell B7** and **delete** the contents.
   *The result is one less for both the COUNT and COUNTA formulas. Any blank cells are ignored.*

9. Leaving **cell B7** as blank, **save** 🖫 the changes, and **close** the workbook.

| ◢ | A | B | C |
|---|---|---|---|
| 1 | January Commission Report | | |
| 2 | | | |
| 3 | Commission Rate | | 3% |
| 4 | | | |
| 5 | | Sales | Commission |
| 6 | Bouras | 44000 | 1320 |
| 7 | Malimali | | 0 |
| 8 | Simpson | 41000 | 1230 |
| 9 | Wyatt | 36000 | 1080 |
| 10 | | | |
| 11 | Count | 3 | |
| 12 | CountA | 4 | |

# Use the IF Function

*In this exercise, you will use the IF function to display a message if a project is going over budget as compared to the budget objective.*

## Add Budget Data to the Worksheet

1. **Open** the rs-Website Budget workbook from the Lesson 03 folder.

2. Enter **Budget Objective** in **cell A7** and **20000** in **cell B7**.

## Create an IF Function

3. Select **cell C6** and click the **Insert Function** button in the Formula Bar.

4. Select the **IF** function from the Most Recently Used or Logical category and click **OK**.
   *The Function Arguments dialog box displays.*

5. For the Logical Test entry, select **cell B7** in the worksheet, and use ⎡Shift⎤+⎡>⎤ for the greater-than symbol.

6. Select **cell B6** and **tap** ⎡Tab⎤ to complete the entry.

7. Type **Within Budget** in the Value If True box and **tap** ⎡Tab⎤.

8. Type **Exceeds Budget** in the Value If False box and **tap** ⎡Enter⎤.
   *The result displays as* Within Budget.

9. **Change** the value in cell B7 from $20,000 to 15000.
   *Now the IF function result displays* Exceeds Budget.

10. **Save** 🖫 the changes and **close** the workbook.

# Apply Your Skills

## Create Simple Formulas

*In this exercise, you will develop a worksheet with simple formulas.*

1. **Open** the as-Credit Lines workbook from the Lesson 03 folder in your file storage location.

2. Follow these guidelines to create the following worksheet:
   - **Enter** all remaining text and number entries.
   - Use **formulas** in **columns D** and **F** to calculate subtotals and new balances. Calculate each **subtotal** as the previous balance plus new charges. Calculate each **new balance** as the subtotal minus the payment amount.
   - Use **AutoSum** to calculate totals for the **range B10:F10**.

| ▲ | A | B | C | D | E | F |
|---|---|---|---|---|---|---|
| 1 | Green Clean - Credit Lines | | | | | |
| 2 | | | | | | |
| 3 | Customer | Previous Balance | New Charges | Subtotal | Payment Amount | New Balance |
| 4 | Abel Printing Inc. | 104 | 50 | | 154 | |
| 5 | Charley's Restaurant | 230 | 85 | | 315 | |
| 6 | Hightower Electric | 58 | 116 | | 0 | |
| 7 | Mendez Foods | 423 | 320 | | 423 | |
| 8 | Ota Beverage Supply | 140 | 65 | | 0 | |
| 9 | Sara Yang, CPA | 97 | 43 | | 100 | |
| 10 | Total Credit | | | | | |

3. Issue the command to display the **formulas**.
   *Notice that the column widths are automatically increased to accommodate the width of the formulas. This will cause the worksheet to print on two pages.*

4. Display **Page Layout** view to preview how formulas will print; **print** the formulas.

5. **Hide** the formulas and then display **Normal view**.

6. **Save** 🖫 the changes and **close** the workbook.

# Use AutoSum, MIN, and MAX

*In this exercise, you will create a new worksheet that includes text and numbers. You will enter formulas and functions. Finally, you will save, print, and close the workbook.*

1. Follow these guidelines to create the worksheet shown:

   - **Enter** the text and numbers as shown in the following illustration.

   - Use the **generic formulas** shown below to calculate the interest charge in column E and the new balance in column F. Use **parentheses** in the Interest Charge formula to change the order of the calculation. You want Excel to subtract the payments from the beginning balance and then multiply the result by 1.5%. **Don't type** the words *Beginning Balance*, *Charges*, etc., in the formulas; use the appropriate cell references. Use **Auto-Fill** to extend the formulas from **row 4 through row 9**.

     Interest Charge = 1.5% * (Beginning Balance – Payments)

     New Balance = Beginning Balance + Charges – Payments + Interest Charge

   - Use **AutoSum** to calculate the totals in **row 10**.

   - Use the **MAX** and **MIN** functions to calculate the highest and lowest numbers in **rows 11** and **12**.

| | A | B | C | D | E | F | |
|---|---|---|---|---|---|---|---|
| 1 | Green Clean - Accounts Receivable | | | | | | |
| 2 | | | | | | | |
| 3 | Customer | Beg. Bal. | Charges | Payments | Interest | New Balance | |
| 4 | R202 | 2000 | 2300 | 1000 | | | |
| 5 | R314 | 2450 | 100 | 2450 | | | |
| 6 | R572 | 5400 | 2190 | 3000 | | | |
| 7 | W016 | 3450 | 500 | 1450 | | | |
| 8 | W215 | 100 | 3400 | 100 | | | |
| 9 | W264 | 1600 | 600 | 0 | | | |
| 10 | Totals | | | | | | |
| 11 | Highest | | | | | | |
| 12 | Lowest | | | | | | |

2. Display the formulas in **Page Layout** view.

3. Change to **Landscape** orientation; **print** the formulas.
   *The formulas will print on one page.*

4. **Hide** the formulas and then display **Normal view**.

5. **Save** 💾 with the name **as-Accounts Receivable** in the Lesson 03 folder and **close** the workbook.

# Use Absolute References

*In this exercise, you will create formulas using absolute references.*

1. **Open** the as-Jan Price Change workbook from the Lesson 03 folder.

2. Follow these guidelines to complete the following worksheet:

   ■ **Enter** the text entries as shown. Enter the numbers in **column B** and the percentage in **cell B3**.

   ■ Use the **generic formula** shown below to calculate the discounted price in **cell C6**. Use an **absolute reference** when referring to the discount rate in **cell B3**. Remember that you are calculating the discounted price, so your formula must subtract the discount rate in **cell B3** from 1.

   Discounted Price = Original Price * (1 – Discount Rate)

   ■ **Copy** the formula in **cell C6** down the column.

   *Cell C6 was formatted for you so it displays the price with two decimal places.*

3. Change the percentage in **cell B3** to **10%**, and watch the worksheet recalculate.

4. Change the percentage in **cell B3** back to **15%**, and watch the worksheet recalculate.

5. **Print** the worksheet.

6. **Display** the formulas; **print** the formulas.
   *The formulas will print on one page.*

7. **Hide** the formulas and then make certain Normal view is displayed.

8. **Save** 💾 the changes and **close** the workbook.

| ▲ | A | B | C |
|---|---|---|---|
| 1 | January Price Changes | | |
| 2 | | | |
| 3 | January Discount Rate | 15% | |
| 4 | | | |
| 5 | | Original Price | Discounted Price |
| 6 | Bamboo Ware Plates | 3.65 | |
| 7 | Biograde Garbage Bags, 25 | 1.89 | |
| 8 | Biograde Garbage Bags, 50 | 3.69 | |
| 9 | Biograde Garbage Bags, 100 | 6.89 | |
| 10 | Green Earth Scrub Pads | 2.25 | |
| 11 | Reusable Cloths, 2 dozen | 2.49 | |
| 12 | Reusable Cloths, 4 dozen | 4.69 | |

# Create a Financial Report

*In this exercise, you will create a worksheet by entering data, creating formulas, and using absolute references. You will also save, print a section of, and close the workbook.*

1. **Open** the as-Projected Net Profit workbook from the Lesson 03 folder.

2. Use these guidelines to create the financial report at right:

   | | A | B | C | D | E |
   |---|---|---|---|---|---|
   | 1 | Projected Net Profit | | | | |
   | 2 | | | | | |
   | 3 | | Q1 | Q2 | Q3 | Q4 |
   | 4 | Revenue | 345000 | 390000 | 480000 | 500000 |
   | 5 | | | | | |
   | 6 | Employee Costs | | | | |
   | 7 | Capital Expenditures | | | | |
   | 8 | Manufacturing | | | | |
   | 9 | Marketing & Sales | | | | |
   | 10 | Total Costs | | | | |
   | 11 | | | | | |
   | 12 | Gross Profit | | | | |
   | 13 | Net Profit | | | | |
   | 14 | | | | | |
   | 15 | Employee Costs | 18% | | | |
   | 16 | Capital Expenditures | 22% | | | |
   | 17 | Manufacturing | 17% | | | |
   | 18 | Marketing & Sales | 16% | | | |
   | 19 | Tax Rate | 40% | | | |

   - **Type** the headings, labels, and numbers as shown in the illustration to the right. Use **AutoFill** whenever possible to copy cells or complete a series (for example, with the Q1, Q2, Q3, and Q4 headings).

   - Use a **formula** to calculate the employee costs in **cell B6**. The formula should calculate the revenue in **cell B4** multiplied by the percentage in **cell B15**. Use a **mixed reference** to refer to the revenue in **cell B4** and an **absolute reference** to refer to the cost percentage in **cell B15**. Use **formulas** to calculate the other costs in the **range B7:B9**. Each formula should multiply the revenue in **row 4** by the related cost percentage in **rows 16–18**.

   - Use **AutoSum** to calculate the total cost in **cell B10**.

   - Calculate the **gross profit** in **cell B12** as **Revenue – Total Costs**.

   - Calculate the **net profit** in **cell B13** as **Gross Profit * (1 – Tax Rate)**. Once again, use an **absolute reference** when referring to the tax rate in **cell B19**.

   - Copy the cost and profit formulas from Q1 across the rows to Q2, Q3, and Q4. You must use the correct cell references in formulas to get the correct results for this exercise.

3. Perform a **what-if analysis** on your worksheet by changing the employee costs percentage in **row 15** to **25%**. Make certain that the report recalculates correctly when the value is changed.

4. Display the formulas in **Page Layout** view.

5. Change to **Landscape** orientation; **print** the formulas.
   *The formulas will print on one page.*

6. **Hide** the formulas and then display **Normal view**.

7. Select the **range A3:E13** and **print** just that area.

8. **Save** 🖫 the changes and **close** the workbook.

# Use the SUM, AVERAGE, and IF Functions

*In this exercise, you will create an IF function to indicate whether a department met the safety goal each month. You will create formulas to total the safety incidents in a six-month period and calculate the average number of incidents per month.*

1. **Open** the as-Safety Goal workbook from the Lesson 03 folder.

2. Enter **January** in **cell A6**; **AutoFill** down **column A** to display the months January through June.

3. Enter the data in the **range B5:B11** and **cells C5, A12**, and **A14**, referring to the illustration at the end of this exercise.

4. **Sum** the total safety incidents for January through June in **cell B12**.

5. Use the **IF** function to create a formula in **cell C6** that indicates whether the department met its goal of no safety incidents during the month. Display **Met Goal** if the incidents are equal to zero (0). Display **Not Met** if the incidents are more than 0.

6. **Copy** the formula down the column for the months **February through June**.

7. Use the **AVERAGE** function to create a formula in **cell B14** that finds the average number of safety incidents per month during January through June.

8. **Display** and **print** the worksheet formulas.

9. **Save** 💾 the changes and **close** the workbook.

| | A | B | C |
|---|---|---|---|
| 1 | Green Clean | | |
| 2 | Safety Scores | | |
| 3 | Operations Department | | |
| 4 | January-June | | |
| 5 | | Incidents | Goal Met? |
| 6 | January | 0 | Met Goal |
| 7 | February | 3 | Not Met |
| 8 | March | 1 | Not Met |
| 9 | April | 2 | Not Met |
| 10 | May | 0 | Met Goal |
| 11 | June | 0 | Met Goal |
| 12 | Total | 6 | |
| 13 | | | |
| 14 | Average Incidents | 1 | |

# Critical Thinking & Work-Readiness Skills

*In the course of working through the following Microsoft Office-based Critical Thinking exercises, you will also be utilizing various work-readiness skills, some of which are listed next to each exercise. Go to labyrinthelab.com/workreadiness to learn more about the work-readiness skills.*

## 3.1 Calculate Totals

**WORK-READINESS SKILLS APPLIED**

- Reasoning
- Evaluating information
- Using computers to process information

Sales manager Talos Bouras needs to analyze his customer base so he knows where his best chances for new sales contacts will be. Open ct-Customer Base (Lesson 03 folder). Calculate the number of projects and total billings for each company type listed in column A. Save your changes as **ct-Customer Base Totals** in the Lesson 03 folder. Which company type has the largest billings? Which customer type has the largest billing per company? If working in a group, discuss these questions. If working alone, type your answers in a Word document named **ct-Questions** saved to your Lesson 03 folder.

## 3.2 Create Formulas to Calculate Averages

**WORK-READINESS SKILLS APPLIED**

- Reasoning
- Using arithmetic/mathematics
- Thinking creatively

Talos Bouras also wants to know the average number of projects and average billings per company type. He is thinking of adding a new type of customer—health care—to his base, but first he wants to be sure that the new customer type will perform at least as well as his current average customer type. Open ct-Customer Base Totals, if necessary, and calculate these averages. Do not be concerned about formatting the formula results. Save the file in your Lesson 03 folder as **ct-Customer Base Averages**. If Talos wants the average of total billings per customer to rise over time, what categories of customers should he pursue and which should he deemphasize? Why would knowing his average number of projects and billings help him make decisions in the future? If working in a group, discuss these questions. If working alone, type your answers in a Word document named **ct-Questions2** saved to your Lesson 03 folder.

## 3.3 Use Absolute Cell References

**WORK-READINESS SKILLS APPLIED**

- Reasoning
- Thinking creatively
- Using arithmetic/mathematics

Green Clean is raising prices across the board by 4.5 percent in the new year. Open ct-Customer Base Averages, if necessary. Use an absolute reference to calculate the new amount of billings for each company if increased by 4.5 percent. (Hint: Calculate total billings plus 4.5 percent of total billings.) In another column, calculate each company type if the billings are increased to 7.5 percent. Save the file as **ct-Customer Base Projections**. What factors go into deciding to raise prices and commit to a 7.5 percent target increase in billings? If working in a group, discuss this question. If working alone, type your answer in a Word document named **ct-Questions3** saved to your Lesson 03 folder.

# Formatting the Contents of Cells

## LEARNING OBJECTIVES

After studying this lesson, you will be able to:

■ Format worksheets using a variety of methods and apply workbook themes

■ Control text to align and fit within cells

■ Format cells with borders, fill colors, and cell styles

■ Work with date functions and create custom number formats

■ Apply conditional formatting to flag positive and negative trends

In this lesson, you will learn how to use several of Excel's formatting features to enhance your worksheets. You will also learn powerful tools and techniques such as AutoFormat and the Format Painter. Moreover, you will learn to use Excel's Conditional Formatting tool, which may be used to format values that fall within an acceptable range, thus drawing attention to those values. By the end of this lesson, you will have developed the skills necessary to produce professional-looking worksheets.

**Student Resources**    labyrinthelab.com/excel10

# Formatting with Excel

Tommy Choi is the president of Green Clean, a janitorial product supplier and cleaning service contractor. The company's accountant drafted an income statement, which Tommy will use to compare revenues and expenses for each quarter of the year. He will use many of Excel's formatting features to make the spreadsheet easier to read and understand. Tommy especially wants the text to align better and the numbers to clearly indicate dollar and percent amounts. He will create a workbook theme so that uniform formatting may be applied to Green Clean's other worksheets.

| | A | B | C | D | E |
|---|---|---|---|---|---|
| 1 | Green Clean | | | | |
| 2 | Income Statement | | | | |
| 3 | 3rd Quarter [Current Year] | | | | |
| 4 | | July | August | September | Quarter Total |
| 5 | REVENUES | | | | |
| 6 | Sales | 254723 | 261378 | 188684 | 704785 |
| 7 | Finance Charge Revenue | 4702 | 3982 | 3370 | 12054 |
| 8 | Total Revenues | 259425 | 265360 | 192054 | 716839 |

| | A | B | C | D | E |
|---|---|---|---|---|---|
| 1 | | | Green Clean | | |
| 2 | | | Income Statement | | |
| 3 | | | 3rd Quarter [Current Year] | | |
| 4 | | July | August | September | Quarter Total |
| 5 | REVENUES | | | | |
| 6 | Sales | $ 254,723 | $ 261,378 | $ 188,684 | $ 704,785 |
| 7 | Finance Charge Revenue | 4,702 | 3,982 | 3,370 | 12,054 |
| 8 | Total Revenues | $ 259,425 | $ 265,360 | 192054 | $ 716,839 |

The top figure represents the Revenues portion of the Income Statement before you work your formatting magic. The bottom figure shows how the worksheet will appear at the end of the lesson.

# 4.1 Formatting Worksheets

**Video Lesson** labyrinthelab.com/videos

Formatting deals with changing how the data in your worksheet looks, not with changing the data itself. In Excel and other Microsoft Office programs, you can format text by changing the font, font size, and font color. You can also apply various font enhancements, including bold, italic, and underline. To format cells, select the desired cell(s) and apply formats using buttons on the Home tab of the Ribbon, by using the Format Cells dialog box, or by using the Mini toolbar that appears when you right-click a cell or select text.

## Formatting Entries with the Ribbon

The Font group on the Home tab of the Ribbon provides you with many popular formatting commands.

The Font group on the Home tab of the Ribbon makes finding formatting options easy.

## Using the Mini Toolbar

The Mini toolbar, a feature common to several applications in the Office Suite, will appear when text is selected. It will appear transparent until you move the mouse pointer over it. If you right-click a cell, the Mini toolbar will appear nontransparent, ready to use. The Mini toolbar will allow you to format the selected text without needing the Home tab of the Ribbon to be displayed. This feature can be extremely convenient when you are primarily working with another tab of the Ribbon.

If you select text, the Mini toolbar will appear transparent.

Once the mouse pointer is placed over the Mini toolbar or you right-click a cell, the Mini toolbar will appear "solid."

The Mini toolbar will appear when text is selected, such as when "REVENUES" is selected above.

## Live Preview

**FROM THE KEYBOARD**

Ctrl+B for bold
Ctrl+I for italicize
Ctrl+U for underline

In Office, you can preview how many formatting changes will look before actually issuing the command. Where this feature is available, you will see how the selected area will look when you place your mouse pointer over the formatting option.

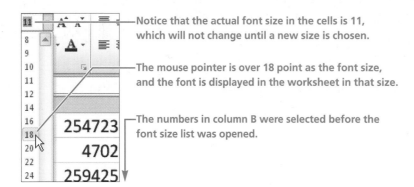

Notice that the actual font size in the cells is 11, which will not change until a new size is chosen.

The mouse pointer is over 18 point as the font size, and the font is displayed in the worksheet in that size.

The numbers in column B were selected before the font size list was opened.

# Format Cells with the Ribbon and Mini Toolbar

*In this exercise, you will begin to format the worksheet by using both the Ribbon and the Mini toolbar.*

## Open an Excel File

1. Start **Excel**.

2. **Open** the Income Statement workbook from the Lesson 04 folder in your file storage location.
   *You will see a worksheet displayed that contains all of the data and formulas but that is very much in need of some "beautification!" We will begin by changing the font size of the entire worksheet.*

## Use the Ribbon to Format

*In this section, you will first select the entire worksheet. This means that any formatting that is applied will affect every cell in the whole worksheet.*

3. Follow these steps to change the font size of the entire worksheet:

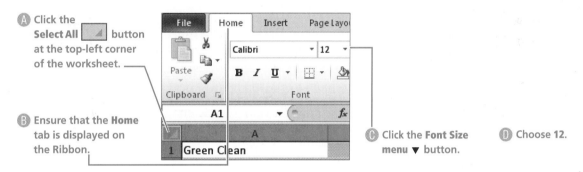

Ⓐ Click the **Select All** button at the top-left corner of the worksheet.

Ⓑ Ensure that the **Home** tab is displayed on the Ribbon.

Ⓒ Click the **Font Size menu ▼** button.

Ⓓ Choose **12**.

   *Notice that as you move the mouse pointer over the font size list, Excel will allow you to preview how the worksheet would appear if each font size were selected.*

## Use the Mini Toolbar to Format

4. Select **cell A5**.

5. **Double-click** the word *REVENUES* in **cell A5** two times.
   *The first time you double-click, the cell will be available for editing; the second time, REVENUES will be selected and a translucent Mini toolbar will appear above the selection.*

6. **Move** the mouse pointer over the **Mini toolbar**.
   *When you move your mouse pointer over the transparent Mini toolbar, it will become visible and you can choose an option.*

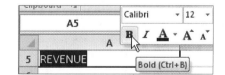

7. Click the **Bold** **B** button.

8. **Right-click** cell A10.
   *Right-clicking a cell will also display the Mini toolbar.*

9. Click the **Bold** **B** button on the Mini toolbar.

10. Use Ctrl + S to **save** the changes to the workbook and then continue with the next exercise.

# 4.2 Using Excel's Alignment and Indent Features

Video Lesson    labyrinthelab.com/videos

Excel allows you to alter how the text is aligned within cells. In addition to the standard left, center, and right horizontal alignments, you can indent the contents within a cell from either edge.

## Aligning Entries

The Align Text Left ▤, Center ▦, and Align Text Right ▤ buttons on the Home tab of the Ribbon let you align entries within cells. By default, text entries are left aligned and number entries are right aligned. To change alignment, select the cell(s) and click the desired alignment button.

## Indenting Cell Entries

The Increase Indent ▤ button and Decrease Indent ▤ button in the Alignment group on the Home tab of the Ribbon let you offset entries from the edges of cells. If a cell entry is left aligned, it will indent from the left edge, and if it is right aligned, it will indent from the right edge. Indenting is useful for conveying the hierarchy of entries. The following illustration shows indented cells.

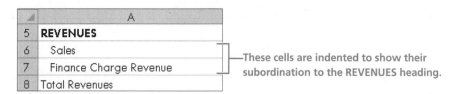

These cells are indented to show their subordination to the REVENUES heading.

| QUICK REFERENCE | WORKING WITH ALIGNMENTS AND INDENTS |
|---|---|
| **Task** | **Procedure** |
| Change the alignment in cells | ▪ Select the cells in which you wish to change the alignment.<br>▪ Click the appropriate button in the Alignment group on the Home tab of the Ribbon. |
| Indent a cell or range of cells | ▪ Select the cells that you wish to indent.<br>▪ Click the appropriate button in the Alignment group on the Home tab of the Ribbon. |

# Work with Alignment and Indent

*In this exercise, you will set the alignment in cells as well as indent entries.*

## Change the Alignment in Cells

1. Select the **range B4:E4**.

2. Choose **Home→Alignment→Align Text Right** ≣ from the Ribbon.

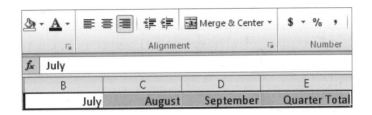

## Indent Cell Entries

3. Follow these steps to indent entries in a range of cells:

Ⓐ Select the range A6:A7.

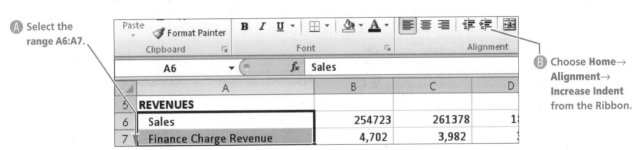

Ⓑ Choose **Home→ Alignment→ Increase Indent** from the Ribbon.

4. Select the **range A11:A22**, taking care not to include **cell A23** in the selection.

5. Choose **Home→Alignment→Increase Indent** ⧈ from the Ribbon.
   *Now the types of revenue and expenses have been "set off" from the left edge of the cell.*

6. **Save** 💾 the changes to the workbook.

# 4.3 Using Excel's Text Control Options

Video Lesson    labyrinthelab.com/videos

The Alignment group on the Home tab of the Ribbon provides options that allow you to merge cells and wrap lengthy text within a cell entry. You can insert a line break to place text on separate lines in a cell.

## Merging and Splitting Cells

Excel's merge cells options allow you to combine cells. Merged cells behave as one large cell, and you can merge cells both vertically and horizontally. The merged cell takes on the name of the top left cell in the merged range. For example, if you merge cells A1:E1, the resulting merged cell will be named A1.

### Merge & Center Command

The Merge & Center 🔲 button merges selected cells and changes the alignment of the merged cell to center. This technique is often used to center a heading across columns. The Merge & Center command can format cells on only one row at a time. You would need to repeat the command for each heading on separate rows. You split a merged and centered cell by clicking the Merge & Center button again.

|  | A | B | C | D | E |
|---|---|---|---|---|---|
| 1 | Green Clean | | | | |

Cells A1:E1 selected and ready to be merged

|  | A | B | C | D | E |
|---|---|---|---|---|---|
| 1 | Green Clean | | | | |

The merged and centered cell A1 that results

### Merging Cells

The Merge & Center menu contains additional merging options. The menu is accessed by clicking the ▼ arrow on the Merge & Center button.

The Merge Across command merges cells without centering the contents. You may select cells in multiple rows and merge across each row with one command, as shown in the following illustration.

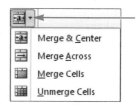

|  | A | B | C |
|---|---|---|---|
| 28 | | | |
| 29 | Note: Compare contract sales with 2nd Quarter | | |
| 30 | See attached details for supply expense | | |
| 31 | | | |

The range A29:C30 was selected and then the cells in each row were merged across the row. The gridline between cells A29 and A30 indicates that their contents are in separate rows.

The Merge Across command can be used to merge multiple headings across their rows in one step, after which they may be center aligned.

The Merge Cells command allows you to merge cells both across rows and down columns. In general, you should avoid merging any cells unless they are titles or headings at the top of the worksheet. Merged cells can restrict your ability to work with individual rows and columns. Also, some data will be lost if you merge multiple cells containing data.

### Splitting Cells

Merged cells may be split again by clicking the Merge & Center button on the Ribbon or by choosing Unmerge Cells from the Merge & Center menu.

# Wrapping Text

The Wrap Text option forces text to wrap within a cell as it would in a word-processing document. This is a good option to use when text is truncated (cut off) by the cell entry to the right and widening the column is not practical. The row height increases to accommodate the additional lines of wrapped text.

| 28 | | |
| --- | --- | --- |
| 29 | Note: Compare contract sales with 2nd Quarter | |
| 30 | | |

The height of row 29 has increased to display all of the text wrapped in one cell.

### Entering a Line Break

You can force text to display on the next line of a cell by inserting a line break. This feature is particularly useful for dividing a column heading to maintain a narrow column width, as shown in the illustration below.

FROM THE KEYBOARD

Alt + Enter to insert a line break

| | September | Quarter Total |
| --- | --- | --- |
| | $ 188,684 | $ 704,785 |

A line break may be erased by moving the insertion point to the end of the line and tapping Delete. You may need to insert a space between words after removing the line break.

# Shrinking Text to Fit Within a Cell

There may be times when changing the width of a column or wrapping text is not appropriate, yet you still want all of the text within the cell to be displayed. The Shrink to Fit option allows you to reduce the text size of the cell entry to whatever fits the existing cell width. Shrink to Fit is not available on the Ribbon but rather is in the Alignment tab of the Format Cells dialog box.

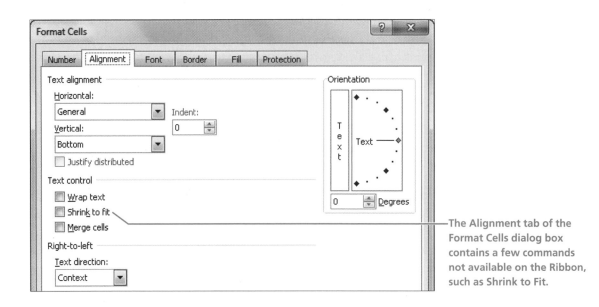

The Alignment tab of the Format Cells dialog box contains a few commands not available on the Ribbon, such as Shrink to Fit.

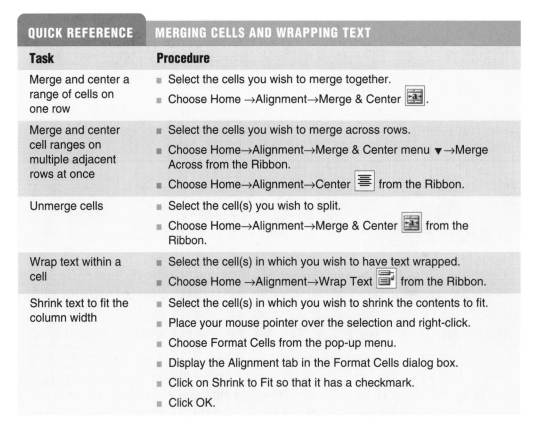

| QUICK REFERENCE | MERGING CELLS AND WRAPPING TEXT |
|---|---|
| **Task** | **Procedure** |
| Merge and center a range of cells on one row | ▪ Select the cells you wish to merge together. <br> ▪ Choose Home →Alignment→Merge & Center ⊞. |
| Merge and center cell ranges on multiple adjacent rows at once | ▪ Select the cells you wish to merge across rows. <br> ▪ Choose Home→Alignment→Merge & Center menu ▼→Merge Across from the Ribbon. <br> ▪ Choose Home→Alignment→Center ≡ from the Ribbon. |
| Unmerge cells | ▪ Select the cell(s) you wish to split. <br> ▪ Choose Home→Alignment→Merge & Center ⊞ from the Ribbon. |
| Wrap text within a cell | ▪ Select the cell(s) in which you wish to have text wrapped. <br> ▪ Choose Home →Alignment→Wrap Text ⊞ from the Ribbon. |
| Shrink text to fit the column width | ▪ Select the cell(s) in which you wish to shrink the contents to fit. <br> ▪ Place your mouse pointer over the selection and right-click. <br> ▪ Choose Format Cells from the pop-up menu. <br> ▪ Display the Alignment tab in the Format Cells dialog box. <br> ▪ Click on Shrink to Fit so that it has a checkmark. <br> ▪ Click OK. |

## Control Text in Cells

*In this exercise, you will have the opportunity to merge and center cells as well as wrap text within a cell.*

### Merge and Center a Range of Cells

1. Select the **range A1:E1**.

2. Choose **Home→Alignment→Merge & Center**  from the Ribbon.
   *The entry from cell A1 is now centered over columns A through E.*

3. Select **cell C1**.
   *Notice that A1 is displayed in the Name Box. While cell C1 is merged with A1, B1, D1, and E1, it essentially no longer exists!*

### Merge and Center on Multiple Adjacent Rows

4. Select the **range A2:E3**.

5. Choose **Home→Alignment→Merge & Center menu ▾→Merge Across** from the Ribbon.

6. Choose **Home→Alignment→Center** ☰ from the Ribbon.
   *You may find this method more efficient than selecting and merging cells one row at a time.*

### Wrap Text within a Cell

7. Select **cell A29**.

8. Choose **Home→Alignment→Wrap Text** from the Ribbon.

9. Follow these steps to manually enter a line break in a cell:

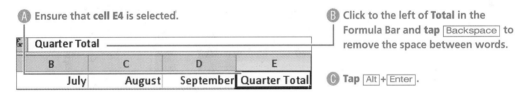

10. **Tap** Enter to complete the entry.
    *Excel applies wrapped text formatting to the cell and applies the line break where you tapped* Alt + Enter.

11. **Save** 💾 the changes to the workbook.

# 4.4 Formatting Numbers

**Video Lesson**　labyrinthelab.com/videos

Excel lets you format numbers in a variety of ways. Number formats change the way numbers are displayed, though they do not change the actual numbers. Once a number formatting has been applied to a cell, it remains with the cell—even if the contents are deleted. The following table describes the most common number formats.

| Number Format | Description |
|---|---|
| General | Numbers are formatted with the General format by default. This format does not apply any special formats to the numbers. |
| Comma Style | The Comma Style format inserts a comma after every third digit in the number. This format also inserts a decimal point and two decimal places, which can be removed if desired. |
| Currency | The Currency format is the same as the Comma Style format, except that it adds a dollar ($) sign in front of the number. |
| Accounting | The Accounting format is the same as Currency format, except that the dollar sign is placed at the left edge of the cell. |
| Percent Style | The Percent Style, also known as Percentage, inserts a percent (%) sign to the right of the number. The percentage is calculated by multiplying the number by 100. |

If you begin an entry with a dollar sign, the Currency format will automatically be applied.

The following table provides several examples of formatted numbers.

| Number Entered | Format | How the Number Is Displayed |
|---|---|---|
| 5347.82 | General | 5347.82 |
| 5347.82 | Comma with 0 decimal places | 5,348 |
| 5347.82 | Comma with 2 decimal places | 5,347.82 |
| 5347.82 | Currency with 0 decimal places | $5,347 |
| 5347.82 | Currency with 2 decimal places | $5,347.82 |
| .5347 | Percentage with 0 decimal places | 53% |
| .5347 | Percentage with 2 decimal places | 53.47% |

## Using the Number Command Group

The Number command group on the Home tab of the Ribbon allows you to format your numbers in a variety of ways, with the most common styles displayed as buttons. The top area of the group displays the number formatting of the selected cell(s). Clicking the menu button to the right of the current number formatting displays a menu of additional number format choices.

If you click the dialog box launcher button in the Number group, the Format Cells dialog box will appear with the Number tab displayed.

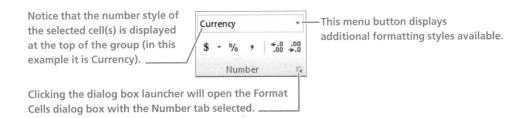

Notice that the number style of the selected cell(s) is displayed at the top of the group (in this example it is Currency).

This menu button displays additional formatting styles available.

Clicking the dialog box launcher will open the Format Cells dialog box with the Number tab selected.

## Using Accounting and Currency Styles

There are two number styles that apply currency symbols (such as dollar signs) to numbers. You will notice a difference in where the dollar sign is placed based on the style you select. If you choose the Accounting style, currency symbols will appear fixed at the left of the cells. The Currency style, on the other hand, will display the currency symbol in front of the number in the cell.

In the Accounting style, the dollar sign will be fixed at the left edge of the cell.

In the Currency style, the dollar sign will be placed in front of the number.

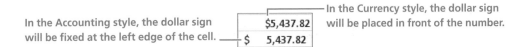

## Applying the Percent Style

The Percent Style, also named Percentage in Excel, adds a percent sign (%) after the number. Depending on when you format the cell, you will enter a whole number or a decimal number. To achieve the correct result in the cell entry, follow one of the two procedures explained below.

■ Select the cells that you wish to format as Percent Style and apply the formatting. If you format the cells first, you can type 25 and it will be formatted as 25%.

■ Type the value in the cell first, and then apply the Percent Style formatting. If you type in the value first, you will need to type it in as a decimal. For instance, you will need to type in .25 in order for it to format properly as 25%. If you type in 25 and then apply Percent Style formatting, it will appear as 2500%.

## How Numbers Display in Cells

You have seen that text entered in a cell spills over onto the empty cells to its right when the text cannot fit within its cell width. Numbers, on the other hand, do not spill over. Formula results that contain decimal numbers will display as many decimal places as can fit in the cell (see the illustration below).

| 27 | Net Income to Total Revenues | 0.271361665 | 0.311508894 | -0.038452727 | 0.203218575 |

Formula results will display as many decimal places as possible in the cell.

At times, a number combined with its formatting cannot fit within the cell width. For example, the number 254723 displays in a cell. After being formatted as Currency, the number should display as $254,423.00 but now cannot fit. Instead, you will see number signs (###) displayed across the cell width. There is no need to worry because the number is not lost; it just cannot display. The number display can be restored by increasing the column width. Other possible solutions include decreasing the decimal places and reducing the font size.

| ◢ | A | B | C | D | E |
|---|---|---|---|---|---|
| 6 | Sales | ########## | ########## | ########## | ########## |

The number signs (###) indicate numbers that cannot display within the cell width.

## Adjusting Decimal Places

Most preset number formats, such as Comma Style, display two decimal places by default. You can adjust the number of decimal places displayed in the cell by using the Increase Decimal and Decrease Decimal buttons on the Ribbon. For example, clicking the Decrease Decimal button twice changes the number display from two to no decimal places in the selected cell(s). The number display is rounded up when necessary. For example, 525.83 would display as 526 when formatted with no decimal places, and 82.33 would display as 82. The actual number in the cell, however, is not changed and remains accurate when used in calculations.

## Displaying Negative Numbers

Negative number displays can be either preceded by a minus sign or surrounded by parentheses. You can also display negative numbers in red. The Currency option and Number option in the Format Cells dialog box let you choose the format for negative numbers.

The negative number format you choose affects the alignment of numbers in the cells. If the format displays negative numbers in parentheses, a small space equal to the width of a closing parenthesis appears on the right edge of cells containing positive numbers. Excel does this so the decimal points are aligned in columns containing both positive and negative numbers.

| | | | | | |
|---|---|---|---|---|---|
| 16 | Insurance | 8696 | 0 | 9534 | 18230 |
| 17 | Rent | 8000 | 8000 | 9000 | 25000 |
| 18 | Supplies | 1263 | 2458 | -22 | 3699 |
| 19 | Telephone | 300 | 300 | 300 | 900 |
| 20 | Utilities | 1689 | 1782 | 1824 | 5295 |
| 21 | Vehicle Expenses | 17823 | 18622 | 26781 | 63226 |
| 22 | Wages | 125622 | 124300 | 124015 | 373937 |
| 23 | Total Expenses | 189027 | 182698 | 199439 | 571164 |
| 24 | | | | | |
| 25 | Net Income (Loss) | 70398 | 82662 | -7385 | 145675 |

When the numbers are formatted as General style, the negative numbers will be displayed with a minus sign in front of them.

| | | | | | |
|---|---|---|---|---|---|
| 16 | Insurance | 8,696.00 | 0.00 | 9,534.00 | 18,230.00 |
| 17 | Rent | 8,000.00 | 8,000.00 | 9,000.00 | 25,000.00 |
| 18 | Supplies | 1,263.00 | 2,458.00 | (22.00) | 3,699.00 |
| 19 | Telephone | 300.00 | 300.00 | 300.00 | 900.00 |
| 20 | Utilities | 1,689.00 | 1,782.00 | 1,824.00 | 5,295.00 |
| 21 | Vehicle Expenses | 17,823.00 | 18,622.00 | 26,781.00 | 63,226.00 |
| 22 | Wages | 125,622.00 | 124,300.00 | 124,015.00 | 373,937.00 |
| 23 | Total Expenses | 189,027.00 | 182,698.00 | 199,439.00 | 571,164.00 |
| 24 | | | | | |
| 25 | Net Income (Loss) | 70,398.00 | 82,662.00 | (7,385.00) | 145,675.00 |

When you choose the Comma Style format, you can accept the default negative number format with parentheses or change it to display a minus sign in the Format Cells dialog box. If you choose to format negative numbers with parentheses, the positive numbers will be set a bit further from the right edge of the cell in order for the decimal points to be aligned. Notice also that the cell containing the number 0 is displayed with a hyphen (-).

# Format Numbers

*In this exercise, you will apply various number formatting options to the worksheet.*

## Use the Accounting and Currency Styles

1. Follow these steps to apply the Accounting format to a range of cells:

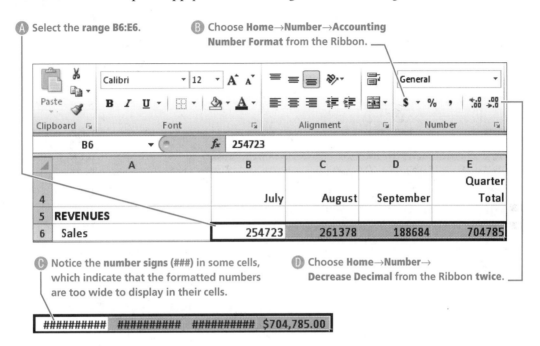

Ⓐ Select the **range B6:E6**.

Ⓑ Choose **Home→Number→Accounting Number Format** from the Ribbon.

Ⓒ Notice the **number signs (###)** in some cells, which indicate that the formatted numbers are too wide to display in their cells.

Ⓓ Choose **Home→Number→ Decrease Decimal** from the Ribbon **twice**.

*Notice that the Accounting format displays the dollar sign as fixed at the left edge of the cells. "Custom" is displayed as the number format on the Ribbon because you changed the number of decimal places of the Accounting format.*

2. Select the **range B7:E7**.

3. Choose **Home→Number→Comma Style** ⬚ from the Ribbon.

4. Choose **Home→ Number→Decrease Decimal** ⬚ from the Ribbon twice.

5. Select the **range B8:E8, hold down** ⬚Ctrl⬚, and select the **range B11:E11**.
   *Remember that by using* ⬚Ctrl⬚, *you can select multiple ranges to which you can apply formatting.*

6. Choose **Home→Accounting Number Format** ⬚$⬚ from the Ribbon.

7. Choose **Home→Decrease Decimal** ⬚ from the Ribbon twice.

8. **Repeat** the above steps to apply **Accounting Number Format** with **no decimals** to the ranges **A23:E23** and **A25:E25**.

## Use Comma Style

9. Select the **range B12:E22**.

10. Apply **Comma Style formatting** with **no decimals** to the selection.
    *Notice that the 0 entry in cell C16 now displays as a hyphen (–) with Comma Style formatting applied.*

### Use Percent Style

11. Select the **range B27:E27**.

12. Choose **Home→Number→Percent Style** 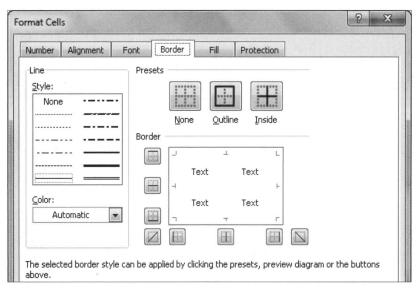 from the Ribbon.

13. Choose **Home→Number→Increase Decimal** from the Ribbon.
    *The percentages are formatted with one decimal place.*

14. **Save** the changes to the workbook.

## 4.5 Using the Format Cells Dialog Box

**Video Lesson**   labyrinthelab.com/videos

The Format Cells dialog box contains six tabs that allow you to format different aspects of your worksheet: Number, Alignment, Font, Border, Fill, and Protection. Some options in this dialog box are not available on the Ribbon. Therefore, using the dialog box may be more convenient when you are setting complex formatting.

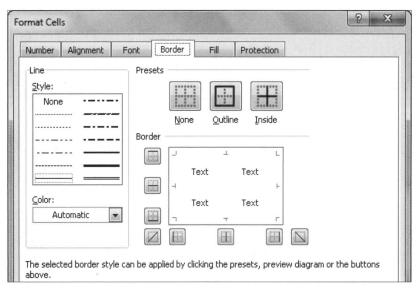

The Border tab of the Format Cells dialog box allows you to set the borders for the selected cells. In this example, the preview in the Border section shows that a line will appear around the entire selection as well as between each row that is selected.

# 4.6 Applying Borders and Fills to Cells

Borders are lines around the cell edges that print as well as display in the worksheet. Do not confuse these with the nonprinting gridlines that display in Normal view. Fills are background shading and pattern effects that fill entire cells. You can apply borders and fills using options on the Ribbon or in the Format Cells dialog box. Borders and fills should provide consistency, call attention to important details, and make the worksheet easier to understand. Keep in mind that "less is more" when applying colors and other formatting.

## Applying Borders

The Borders button on the Home tab of the Ribbon lets you add borders to cell edges. When you click the Borders menu ▼ button, a list of options appears. You can apply one of these border Quick Styles to all selected cells by choosing it from the list. You can also choose More Borders from the bottom of the list to display the Borders tab of the Format Cells dialog box.

The image displayed on the Borders button on the Ribbon will change based on the last border applied. This feature makes it easy to apply the same border formatting throughout the workbook.

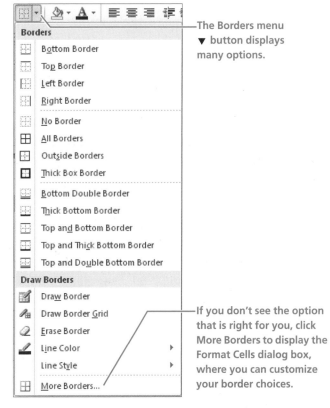

The Borders menu ▼ button displays many options.

If you don't see the option that is right for you, click More Borders to display the Format Cells dialog box, where you can customize your border choices.

## Applying Fill Colors and Patterns

The Fill Color button on the Home tab of the Ribbon lets you fill the background of selected cells with color. When you click the Fill Color menu button, a palette of colors appears. You can apply a color to all selected cells by choosing it from the palette. The fill color is independent of the font color used to format text and numbers. The Format Cells dialog box has a Fill tab that lets you apply fill colors and a variety of patterns and effects.

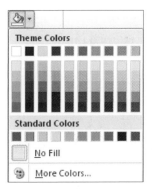

This palette of colors results when you click the Fill Color menu ▼ button. The color you choose will fill the cell but will not affect the color of the font.

Printing a test version of a worksheet allows you to see how your color choices will print, especially important for grayscale printers.

# Format with the Format Cells Dialog Box

*In this exercise, you will apply borders and fill coloring to the worksheet.*

## Apply Borders to a Selection

1. Select the **range A1:E27**.
   *When you choose A1, you will actually be choosing the entire merged cell that spans across column E.*

2. Choose **Home→Font→Borders menu ▾→More Borders** from the Ribbon.

3. Follow these steps to apply the border formatting:

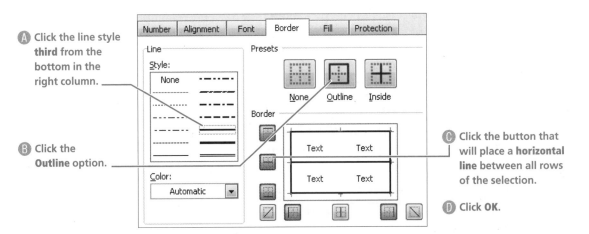

Ⓐ Click the line style **third** from the bottom in the right column.

Ⓑ Click the **Outline** option.

Ⓒ Click the button that will place a **horizontal line** between all rows of the selection.

Ⓓ Click **OK**.

*Notice that the Borders button now displays the icon* ⊞*, which represents the More Borders option on the Borders menu. It will always display the last option selected from the Borders menu.*

4. Use ⌈Ctrl⌉+⌈Z⌉ to undo the borders.

5. Select the **range B7:E7, hold down** the ⌈Ctrl⌉ key, and select the **range B22:E22**. Then **release** the ⌈Ctrl⌉ key.

6. Click the **Borders menu ▾** button.

7. Choose the **Bottom Border** option to place a border along the bottom of the selected cells.
   *A border will appear along the bottom of both of the selected ranges. The Borders button will now display the Bottom Border icon.*

8. Select the **range B25:E25**.

9. Click the **Borders menu ▾ button** and choose **Top and Double Bottom Border**.

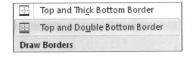

10. Select the **range A5:E5**, **hold down** the Ctrl key, and select **A10:E10**. Then **release** the Ctrl key.

11. Follow these steps to apply a fill color to the selected ranges:

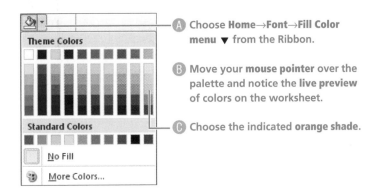

A) Choose **Home→Font→Fill Color menu ▼** from the Ribbon.

B) Move your **mouse pointer** over the palette and notice the **live preview** of colors on the worksheet.

C) Choose the indicated **orange shade**.

12. **Click away** from the selection to view the color in the selected ranges.
*Notice that the cells are now orange, but the text has remained black.*

13. **Save** 💾 the changes to the workbook.

## 4.7 Working with Format Painter and Quick Styles

**Video Lesson**  labyrinthelab.com/videos

Excel has two features, shared with several other Office Suite applications, that allow you to apply formatting quickly to cells. The Format Painter applies formatting from existing worksheet cells. You already have worked with Quick Styles when applying predefined borders. Now you will apply predefined formats as cell styles.

### The Format Painter Tool

There may be times when you want to copy the formatting from one cell to another without copying the contents. The Format Painter lets you copy text formats and number formats from one cell to another. This tool can be extremely helpful if you have a cell to which many formatting options have been applied and you do not wish to apply each option individually to another cell or range of cells.

# Applying Quick Styles to Cells

You can apply Excel's built-in cell styles, also called Quick Styles, or create your own styles for a uniform worksheet design. A cell style's formatting may include the font, number format, borders, and fill.

New cell styles that you create appear in the Custom section of the styles list. They are based on the workbook theme, so the colors change automatically to match any new theme that is applied. Among the built-in styles, only the Themed Cell Styles change colors. Any styles that you create or edit apply only to the currently open workbook. The Merge Styles command in the styles list allows you to import styles created in a different workbook into a currently open workbook.

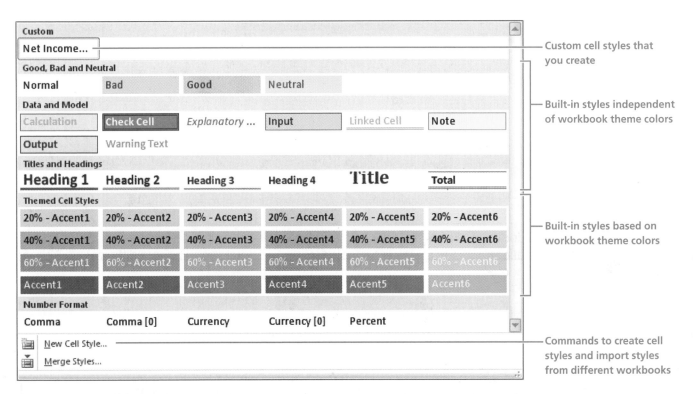

Custom cell styles that you create

Built-in styles independent of workbook theme colors

Built-in styles based on workbook theme colors

Commands to create cell styles and import styles from different workbooks

| QUICK REFERENCE | WORKING WITH FORMAT PAINTER AND CELL STYLES |
|---|---|
| **Task** | **Procedure** |
| Copy formats to one other cell or range | ■ Click the cell that has the format(s) you wish to copy.<br>■ Choose Home →Clipboard→Format Painter from the Ribbon.<br>■ Select the cell or range to which you wish to copy the format(s). |
| Copy formats to multiple locations | ■ Click the cell that has the format(s) you wish to copy.<br>■ Double-click the Home →Clipboard→Format Painter button.<br>■ Select the cells or ranges to which you wish to copy the format(s).<br>■ When you are finished, click the Format Painter button to turn it off. |
| Apply a cell style (Quick Style) to a cell or range of cells | ■ Select the cells to which you wish to apply the cell style.<br>■ Choose Home→Styles→Cell Styles from the Ribbon.<br>■ Select the desired style from the list. |

| Task | Procedure |
|---|---|
| Create a cell style | ■ Choose Home→Styles→Cell Styles →New Cell Style from the Ribbon. |
| | ■ Click the Format button in the Style dialog box and select the desired formatting options in the Format Cells dialog box. |
| | ■ Click OK. |
| | ■ Name the style in the Style dialog box and select the formatting categories to be included. |
| Modify a cell style | ■ Choose Home→Styles→Cell Styles  from the Ribbon. |
| | ■ Right-click the desired style from the list and choose Modify to edit the existing style or Duplicate to create a new style based on the existing style. |
| | ■ Click the Format button in the Style dialog box and select the desired formatting options in the Format Cells dialog box. |
| | ■ Click OK. |
| | ■ Name the style in the Style dialog box, if necessary, and select the formatting categories to be included. |
| Import cell styles from a different workbook | ■ Open the workbook from which you wish to import styles. |
| | ■ In the destination workbook, choose Home→Styles→Cell Styles→Merge Styles from the Ribbon. |
| | ■ Choose the source workbook name. |

When you double-click Format Painter, you can scroll through the worksheet to reach the desired location(s). You can even click a sheet tab to copy formatting to a different worksheet in the workbook.

## DEVELOP YOUR SKILLS 4.7.1

# Change Formatting with Format Painter and Cell Styles

*In this exercise, you will copy the formatting from one cell to a range of cells. You also will apply cell styles and create a custom style.*

## Copy Formatting with Format Painter

1. Select **cell A10**.
   *You must first select the cell from which you wish to copy the formatting.*

2. Choose **Home→Clipboard→Format Painter** button from the Ribbon.

3. Select the **range A25:E25**.
   *The formatting from A10 is applied to the entire range of A25:E25. Notice that the General number formatting is also applied.*

4. Choose **Home→Number→Accounting Number Format** $ from the Ribbon.

5. Choose **Home→Number→Decrease Decimal** from the Ribbon twice.

## Apply Cell Styles

6. Select **cell A29**.

7. Follow these steps to apply a built-in cell style:

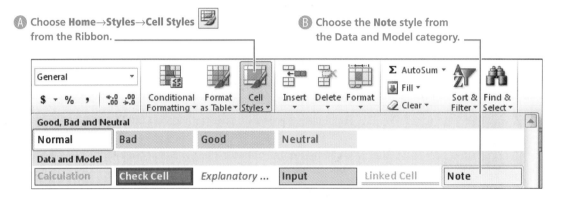

(A) Choose **Home→Styles→Cell Styles** from the Ribbon.

(B) Choose the **Note** style from the Data and Model category.

*The built-in cell styles include ratings, data and model formats, titles and headings, styles matching the workbook theme, and number formats. Your styles may differ.*

8. Select the **range A1:E3**.

9. Choose **Home→Styles→Cell Styles** from the Ribbon. Then, from the Themed Cell Styles category, select **40% - Accent5**.
   *The cell style is in the fifth color palette from the left.*

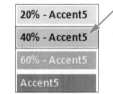

10. **Deselect** the range.

## Create a Custom Cell Style

11. Choose **Home→Styles→Cell Styles** from the Ribbon.

12. Choose **New Cell Style** at the bottom of the styles list.

13. Follow these steps to begin creating a cell style:

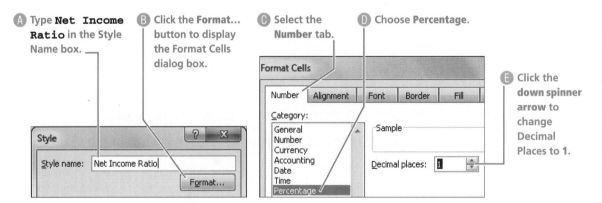

(A) Type **Net Income Ratio** in the Style Name box.

(B) Click the **Format...** button to display the Format Cells dialog box.

(C) Select the **Number** tab.

(D) Choose **Percentage**.

(E) Click the **down spinner arrow** to change Decimal Places to **1**.

14. With the Format Cells dialog box still displayed, select the **Fill** tab.

15. Choose the **fourth color** in the **last column** of the theme colors palette.

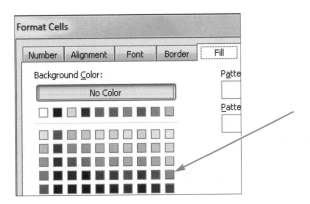

16. Follow these steps to set the text characteristics for the cell style:

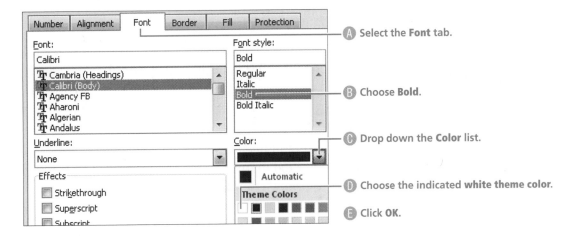

- (A) Select the **Font** tab.
- (B) Choose **Bold**.
- (C) Drop down the **Color** list.
- (D) Choose the indicated **white theme color**.
- (E) Click **OK**.

17. Notice that your changes are shown in the **Style** dialog box.

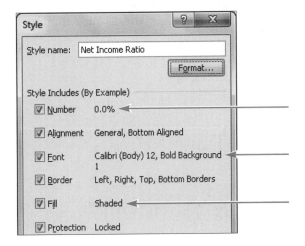

*All the categories with a checkmark will be applied to the style. You can remove the checkmark from any formatting you don't want to use.*

18. Click **OK** to close the Style dialog box.

19. Select the **range A27:E27**.

20. Choose **Home→Styles→Cell Styles** 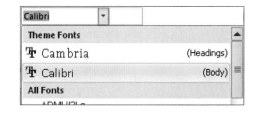 from the Ribbon. Then, from the Custom category, select your **Net Income Ratio** style.
    *With the time it took to set the formatting, you can easily understand why cell styles are useful. Using the Merge Styles command, you can also import them into other workbooks.*

21. **Deselect** the range.

22. **Save** the changes to the workbook.

# 4.8 Formatting with Themes

| Video Lesson | labyrinthelab.com/videos |
|---|---|

Themes allow you to apply formatting easily to your entire workbook. A variety of new theme designs are provided in Excel 2010. All themes have been developed by designers at Microsoft to help you maintain a unified design. You can, however, modify a theme by changing the font set, color palette, or graphic effect design. You can save the modifications as a custom theme that can be reused with other workbooks.

There is good advice that you should heed when using different font styles—do not use too many of them on one worksheet. You can "overformat" your worksheet! Themes allow you to choose a set of compatible fonts, one for headings and one for body text. These theme fonts for the currently selected theme are identified at the top of the Font list. Likewise, the ten theme colors display at the top of a list when you are applying colors. Individual worksheet cells to which you applied nontheme fonts do not change font when a new theme is applied to the workbook.

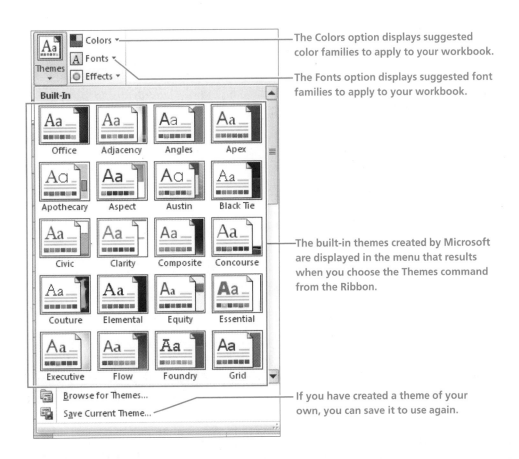

The Colors option displays suggested color families to apply to your workbook.

The Fonts option displays suggested font families to apply to your workbook.

The built-in themes created by Microsoft are displayed in the menu that results when you choose the Themes command from the Ribbon.

If you have created a theme of your own, you can save it to use again.

| QUICK REFERENCE | APPLYING, MODIFYING, AND SAVING A THEME |
| --- | --- |
| **Task** | **Procedure** |
| Apply a theme to a workbook | ■ Open the workbook to which you wish to apply the theme. <br> ■ Choose Page Layout →Themes→Themes [Aa] from the Ribbon. <br> ■ Choose a theme to apply. |
| Modify and save a theme | ■ Choose Page Layout→Themes→Themes [Aa] from the Ribbon. <br> ■ Choose a theme. <br> ■ Change the Colors, Fonts, and Effect options in the Themes group of the Page Layout ribbon as desired. <br> ■ Choose Page Layout→Themes→Themes→Save Current Theme from the Ribbon. <br> ■ Enter a theme name and click Save. |

# Use Themes in a Workbook

*In this exercise, you will apply a theme to the workbook. You also will modify a theme and explore how it would be saved.*

## Change the Theme

1. Click the **Page Layout view** button in the Status Bar at the lower-right corner of the window.
   *The view buttons are to the left of the zoom slider.*

2. Choose **Page Layout→Themes→Themes** from the Ribbon.
   *Office is the default theme applied to new workbooks.*

3. Point at various **themes** and observe the effect that Live Preview displays in the worksheet.
   *Notice that you can scroll down to display additional themes.*

4. Choose the **Executive** theme.
   *The colors and font in the workbook now correspond to those indicated in the theme.*

5. Look at the left in the **Status Bar** to see that this theme displays the worksheet on one page.

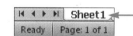

## Modify and Explore Saving a Theme

6. Choose **Page Layout→Themes→** **A** Fonts ▾ from the Ribbon.

7. Point at various **font families** and observe the effect that Live Preview displays in the worksheet.

8. Choose the **Thatch** theme fonts.

9. Choose **Page Layout→Themes→Themes→Save Current Theme** from the Ribbon.
   *The Save Current Theme dialog box displays. Notice the default folder for saving themes on your system. You could enter a filename to save the modified theme.*

10. Click **Cancel** and do *not* save the theme.

11. **Save** the changes to the workbook.

## 4.9 Inserting Date Functions and Formatting

**Video Lesson** labyrinthelab.com/videos

As you have learned, statistical functions like SUM and AVERAGE are very useful in summarizing data. Now you will insert a function that will always display today's date. Excel will determine the date to display according to your computer's clock feature.

## Working with Dates

Dates are used in workbooks in two ways. First, you can simply type and display dates in cells using various formats such as 11/20/14; November 20, 2014; or 20-Nov-14. Second, you can use dates in formulas. For example, you may want to compute the number of days an invoice is past due. You calculate this as the difference between the current date and the original invoice date.

## Date Serial Numbers

When you enter a date in a cell, Excel converts the date to a serial number between 1 and 2,958,525. These numbers correspond to the 10-millennium period from January 1, 1900, through December 31, 9999. The date January 1, 1900, is assigned the serial number 1; January 2, 1900, is assigned the serial number 2; and December 31, 9999, is assigned the serial number 2,958,525. When dates are converted to numbers, you can use the numbers/dates in calculations. Best of all, serial numbers are created for you automatically!

## Entering Dates

Excel performs the following steps when you enter a date in a cell:

- It recognizes the entry as a date if you enter it using a standard date format such as 11/20/14; November 20, 2014; or 20-Nov-14.
- It converts the date to a serial number between 1 and 2,958,525.
- It formats the serial number entry with the same date format you used when you entered the date.

This roundabout process occurs behind the scenes so you never see it happening. The benefit of converting dates to numbers and then formatting them with a date format is that the dates can be used in calculations.

# Inserting Date and Time Functions

In this lesson, you will see the value of using date and time functions in Excel.

## About Date Functions

The current date is often required in worksheets. You may also want to show the date the worksheet was created or printed. The following details apply in general to dates you insert with date functions:

- You can insert a date function rather than typing the date in a worksheet.
- Some date functions produce the current date and, depending on the specific function, can update automatically.
- You insert date functions with the Insert Function dialog box or by typing the function in the result cell.
- Date functions are not case sensitive so you can type the formula in lowercase.

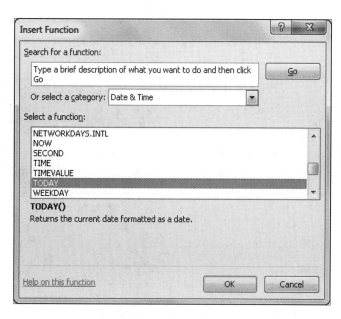

In the Date & Time function category, Excel provides a variety of functions. Notice that there is a description of the selected function displayed below the list.

The following table discusses three of the most common date and time functions.

| Function | Description |
|---|---|
| TODAY( ) | This function displays the current system date and calculates the serial number. The date updates automatically when the worksheet is recalculated or reopened. |
| NOW( ) | This function displays the current system date and time and calculates the serial number. The date and time update automatically when the worksheet is recalculated or reopened. |
| DATE(year,month,day) | This function returns a specific date displayed in the default date format and calculates the serial number. The date does not update when the worksheet is recalculated or reopened. |

## DEVELOP YOUR SKILLS 4.9.1

# Use the TODAY Function and Format a Date

*In this exercise, you will create formulas that will calculate the current date and you will learn how to format dates.*

## Create Labels

1. Enter the **text labels** in the **range B29:E29** using Alt + Enter, and **align right** as shown in the following illustration.

| ⬚ | A | B | C | D | E |
|---|---|---|---|---|---|
| 29 | Note: Compare contract sales with 2nd Quarter | Date Created | Date Reviewed | Elapsed Days | Date Printed |

## Type and Format a Date

2. Select **cell C30**.

3. Type **9/1/14** in the cell, and then click **Enter** ✓ on the Formula Bar.
   *Look at the Number group on the Home tab of the Ribbon. The number format style displayed is Date, which Excel formatted for you when you typed the number in the date format.*

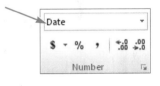

4. Display the **Home** tab of the Ribbon.

5. Click the **dialog box launcher** ▣ in the Number group of the Home tab.
   *The Format Cells dialog box will open with the Number tab displayed.*

6. Follow these steps to change the date format:

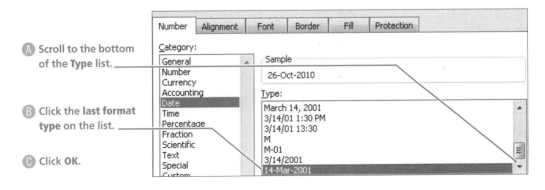

Ⓐ Scroll to the bottom of the **Type** list.

Ⓑ Click the **last format type** on the list.

Ⓒ Click **OK**.

7. Ensure that **cell C30** is still selected, and then **tap** Delete.
   *Look at the Number group on the Home tab of the Ribbon and notice that even when you remove the contents of the cell (the date you typed in), the number format for the cell will remain as Date.*

## Use the TODAY Function and Calculate Dates

8. Follow these steps to enter the TODAY function:

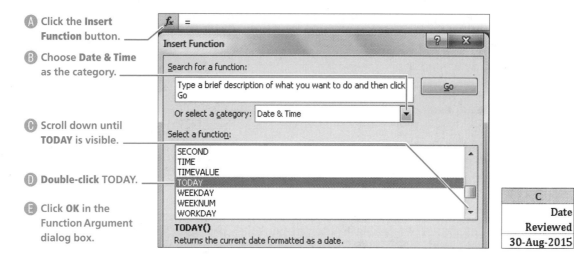

Ⓐ Click the **Insert Function** button.

Ⓑ Choose **Date & Time** as the category.

Ⓒ Scroll down until **TODAY** is visible.

Ⓓ **Double-click** TODAY.

Ⓔ Click **OK** in the Function Argument dialog box.

*The date will appear with the number formatting you set for the cell.*

9. Select **cell B30**, and **enter** the date that is four days prior to today.

10. Use **Format Painter** to apply the date format from **cell C30** to **cell B30**.

11. Select **cell D30**, and **enter** the formula **=C30–B30**.
    *The result should equal 4. You can create formulas that calculate dates in various ways.*

## Use the NOW Function

12. Select **cell E30**, type **=now(** and **tap** Enter to complete the formula.
    *Excel adds the ending parenthesis for the function formula for you. Number signs ( # # # ) display across the cell width. You will recall that this means the date is too long to fit.*

13. **Right-click** cell E30, and choose **Format Cells** in the context menu.

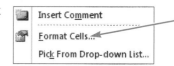

14. Select the **Alignment** tab in the Format Cells dialog box.

15. Place a **checkmark** next to Shrink to Fit and click **OK**.

*The NOW function displays the current date and time, which is updated the next time you open the worksheet. Your dates will be different from those shown.*

16. Save 💾 the changes to the workbook.

# 4.10 Creating Custom Formats

**Video Lesson**   labyrinthelab.com/videos

Excel's predefined number format options usually are sufficient, but occasionally you may need a modified format. For example, you may want a date to display the year as two digits instead of four. An identification or account number may need to be displayed with preceding zeros, such as 0004842. The Format Cells dialog box includes a Type box in which you can edit an existing number format or create a new one.

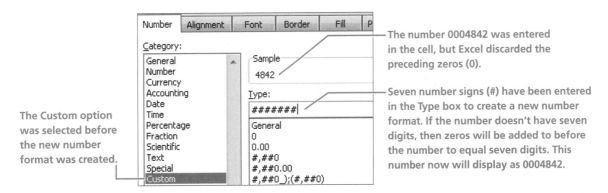

The Custom option was selected before the new number format was created.

The number 0004842 was entered in the cell, but Excel discarded the preceding zeros (0).

Seven number signs (#) have been entered in the Type box to create a new number format. If the number doesn't have seven digits, then zeros will be added to before the number to equal seven digits. This number now will display as 0004842.

| QUICK REFERENCE | CREATING CUSTOM NUMBER FORMATS |
|---|---|
| **Task** | **Procedure** |
| Modify an existing number format to create a custom format | ▪ Select the cell or range to which you wish to apply a custom number format. |
| | ▪ Click the dialog box launcher ⬚ on the Number group of the Home tab. |
| | ▪ Select the Custom category in the Format Cells dialog box. |
| | ▪ Choose an existing format from the list that is closest to the desired formatting. |
| | ▪ Edit the formatting in the Type box, and the Sample number displays the result. |
| | ▪ Click OK, and the new format will be added to the bottom of the Custom list. |

## DEVELOP YOUR SKILLS 4.10.1
## Modify a Date Format

*In this exercise, you will edit the date format currently applied to the NOW function formula.*

1. Select **cell E30**.

2. Click the **dialog box launcher** ⬚ on the Number group of the Home tab.
   *The Format Cells dialog box displays the Number tab.*

3. Verify that the **Custom** category is selected, and **m/d/yyyy h:mm** is the currently selected format.

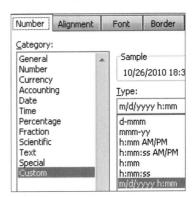

4. In the **Type** box, **edit** the format to be **m/d/yy h:mm AM/PM** and then click **OK**.

*The custom date format is applied to cell E30.*

5. **Save** 💾 the changes to the workbook.

# 4.11 Working with Conditional Formatting

**Video Lesson**     labyrinthelab.com/videos

The Conditional Formatting ▦ command applies formatting to cells that meet criteria that you set. Conditional formats are activated only when the criteria are met. For example, you may assign a yellow fill to a cell when its value is greater than 12. You may apply conditional formatting to cells containing values, text, dates, blanks, or errors. Conditional formats are often used as alerts. They draw attention to better-than-expected results or values that fall outside an acceptable range. Conditional formatting must be set in one worksheet at a time within a workbook.

New to Excel 2010 is the ability to create conditional formatting that refers to a cell in a different sheet of the workbook. For example, you can compare a trainee's test score with the average score for all trainees located in a summary worksheet. Conditional formatting cannot refer to cells in another workbook.

## Using Presets and Multiple Conditions

You can choose from conditional formatting presets on the Conditional Formatting menu for frequently used criteria, such as Greater Than, Equal To, Above Average, and Top 10 Items. You may set any number of conditional formats and create multiple rules to check for more than one condition in a cell. Do so with care to ensure that the formatting result is accurate and useful. Conditional formatting rules are applied in the priority order you set. The Stop If True option, when selected in any rule, prevents further formatting by the remaining rules after a criterion is evaluated as True.

## Creating a Conditional Formatting Rule

If no preset item on the Conditional Formatting menu has your desired criteria or formatting, you may create a new conditional formatting rule. For example, you may wish to base conditional formatting on the result of a formula. The following illustration defines the parts of the New Formatting Rule dialog box. The options vary in the lower half of the dialog box depending on the rule type you select.

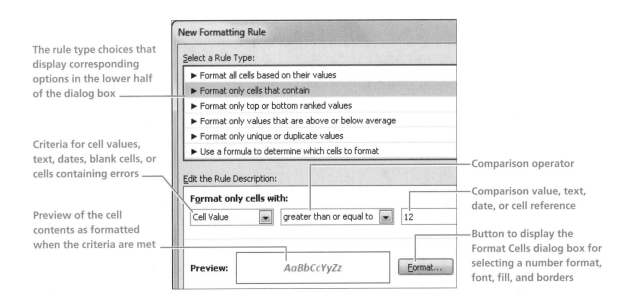

The rule type choices that display corresponding options in the lower half of the dialog box

Criteria for cell values, text, dates, blank cells, or cells containing errors

Comparison operator

Comparison value, text, date, or cell reference

Preview of the cell contents as formatted when the criteria are met

Button to display the Format Cells dialog box for selecting a number format, font, fill, and borders

## Formatting with Graphics

You can choose to conditionally format cells with data bars, a color scale, or an icon set. These graphics identify values that are average, above average, and below average in the selected cell range. You may select a menu preset or create a custom rule using any of these visual aids. After bars, colors, or icons are applied with conditional formatting, you may filter to display only items that are formatted with a specific color or icon. For example, you may filter a column in a list for cells

| | July | August | September |
|---|---|---|---|
| $ | 254,723 | $ 261,378 | $ 188,684 |
| | 4,702 | 3,982 | 3,370 |
| ✓ | $ 259,425 | ✓ $ 265,360 | ✗ $ 192,054 |

Conditional formatting with data bars, a color scale, or icons helps you to categorize data, identify trends, and highlight trouble areas.

containing a red icon to view only the cells with below-average results. You will not use filtering in this lesson.

Use consistent formatting and limit the use of data bars, color scales, and icon sets on one worksheet. Using multiple styles in adjacent rows or columns, as in the preceding figure, could confuse the reader.

## The Conditional Formatting Rules Manager

Conditional formatting rules can be created, edited, rearranged, and deleted within the Conditional Formatting Rules Manager dialog box. The following illustration displays the rules set within an entire worksheet.

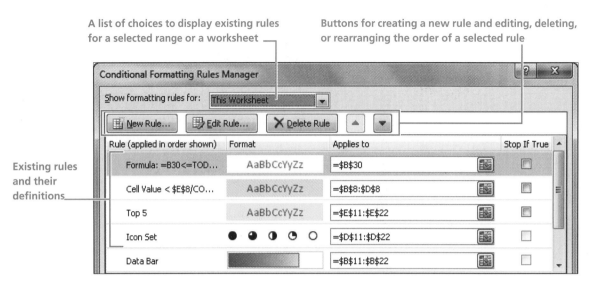

A list of choices to display existing rules for a selected range or a worksheet

Buttons for creating a new rule and editing, deleting, or rearranging the order of a selected rule

Existing rules and their definitions

The Conditional Formatting Rules Manager dialog box allows you to work with all rules applied to a selected range or a worksheet.

| QUICK REFERENCE | APPLYING CONDITIONAL FORMATTING |
|---|---|
| **Task** | **Procedure** |
| Apply preset conditional formatting | ■ Select the cells to receive formatting. |
| | ■ Choose Home→Styles→Conditional Formatting ⊞ from the Ribbon, display a preset menu, and choose a command. |
| | ■ Edit options in the preset rule dialog box, if desired. |
| Create a conditional formatting rule | ■ Select the cells to receive formatting. |
| | ■ Choose Home→Styles→Conditional Formatting→New Rule from the Ribbon. |
| | ■ Choose a rule type and formatting options in the New Formatting Rule dialog box. |
| Apply conditional formatting with data bars, a color scale, or an icon set | ■ Select the cells to receive formatting. |
| | ■ Choose Home→Styles→Conditional Formatting→Data Bars or Color Scales or Icon Sets from the Ribbon. |
| | ■ Choose a preset item on the command's submenu or More Rules to create a custom rule. |
| Clear conditional formatting from specific cells | ■ Select specific cells from which to remove formatting. |
| | ■ Choose Home→Styles→Conditional Formatting→Clear Rules→Clear Rules from Selected Cells from the Ribbon. |
| Clear all conditional formatting from a worksheet | ■ Display the desired worksheet. |
| | ■ Choose Home→Styles→Conditional Formatting→Clear Rules→Clear Rules from Entire Sheet from the Ribbon. |
| Manage conditional formatting rules | ■ Choose Home→Styles→Conditional Formatting→Manage Rules from the Ribbon to display the Conditional Formatting Rules Manager dialog box. |
| | ■ Choose Current Selection or a worksheet from the Show Formatting Rules For list. |
| | ■ Use buttons in the dialog box to create a new rule, or select an existing rule and edit, delete, or change its order. |

# Apply Conditional Formatting

*In this exercise, you will apply various types of conditional formatting to cell ranges. You also will create a conditional formatting rule and remove conditional formatting from a range.*

## Use a Preset to Apply Highlight Formatting

1. Select the **range B8:D8**, taking care **not** to select the total in cell E8.

2. Choose **Home→Styles→Conditional Formatting→Highlight Cells Rules→Less Than** from the Ribbon.
   *The Less Than dialog box appears with the suggested value $228,707. This is the average of the lowest and highest values in the range. You will change this to a formula that averages all three values in the range.*

3. Follow these steps to begin the formula:
   *You will build the formula =$E$8/COUNT($B$8:$D$8).*

   Ⓐ **Drag** the title bar of the **Less Than** dialog box so that row 8 of the worksheet is visible.

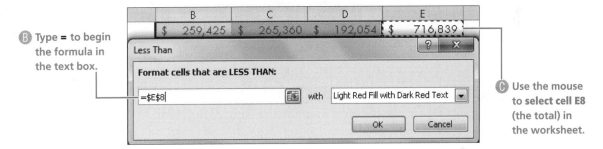

   Ⓑ Type **=** to begin the formula in the text box.

   Ⓒ Use the mouse to select **cell E8** (the total) in the worksheet.

4. Continue typing **/count (** in the formula.

5. Select the **range B8:D8** in the worksheet.

6. Type **)** to complete the formula.

7. Drop down the **With** list to review the other formatting choices, and leave **Light Red Fill with Dark Red Text** selected.

8. Click **OK**.

9. **Deselect** the range to see that cell D8 is formatted in red as below average.
   *The color red often is used to highlight "bad" results. Yellow is used to indicate "average," and green means "good."*

## Create a Conditional Formatting Rule

10. Select **cell B19**, and **tap** Delete to erase its contents.

11. Taking care not to select the totals in row 23, select the **range B11:D22**.
    *You selected the July, August, and September expenses.*

12. Choose **Home→Styles→Conditional Formatting→Highlight Cells Rules→More Rules** from the Ribbon.
    *The New Formatting Rule dialog box appears. Format Only Cells That Contain is the selected rule type.*

13. Follow these steps to create a custom conditional formatting rule:

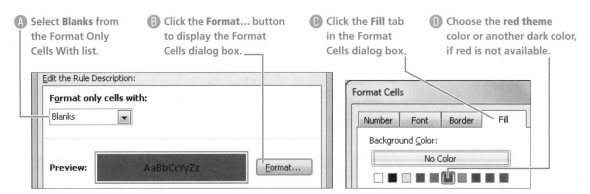

Ⓐ Select **Blanks** from the Format Only Cells With list.

Ⓑ Click the **Format...** button to display the Format Cells dialog box.

Ⓒ Click the **Fill** tab in the Format Cells dialog box.

Ⓓ Choose the **red theme** color or another dark color, if red is not available.

14. Click **OK** to exit the Format Cells dialog box.
    *Notice the red fill in the Preview box of the New Formatting Rule dialog box.*

15. Click **OK** to exit the New Formatting Rule dialog box.
    *The conditional formatting is applied to cell B19, the blank cell, to draw attention to a potential error.*

## Format with Data Bars and Icons

*You will select the expense values in one column at a time and apply conditional formatting. Selecting the entire range of July through September cells would compare each value with the Quarter Total, which is not the result you need.*

16. Select the **range B11:B22** and choose **Home→Styles→Conditional Formatting→Data Bars→Blue Data Bar** from the Ribbon.
    *The data bars display each part of the July total expenses like a bar chart inside the cells as shown at right. Wages is a very high percentage of total expenses.*

17. Select the **range C11:D22** and choose **Home→Styles→Conditional Formatting→Icon Sets→5 Quarters (black and white circles)** from the Ribbon.

| B |
|---:|
| $ 500 |
| 14,723 |
| 2,450 |
| 6,750 |
| 1,211 |
| 8,696 |
| 8,000 |
| 1,263 |
| |
| 1,689 |
| 17,823 |
| 125,622 |
| $ 188,727 |

18. Change the value in cell C20 to **50000**.

| | | | |
|---|---:|---|---:|
| ○ | 300 | ○ | 300 |
| ◐ | 50,000 | ○ | 1,824 |
| ○ | 18,622 | ◔ | 26,781 |
| ● | 124,300 | ● | 124,015 |
| $ | 230,916 | $ | 199,439 |

*The amount of fill within each circle helps you compare expenses in relation to the total and to each other.*

19. Click **Undo** 🔄 to restore the value in cell C20.

## Format with a Top Rule

20. Select the **range E11:E22** and choose **Home→Styles→Conditional Formatting→ Top/Bottom Rules→Top 10 Items**.

21. Change 10 to **5** in the Top 10 Items dialog box, choose **Yellow Fill with Dark Yellow Text** from the With list, and click **OK**.
*The highest five values are highlighted in the Quarter Total column. Mixing highlights, data*

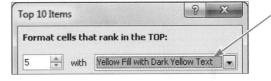

bars, *color scales, and icon sets on one worksheet could make the data look confusing. Normally, for consistency, you would limit the styles.*

## Format Using a Formula

*In the next few steps, you will enter a formula that compares the date created to another date. If the result of this logical test is true, the cell's text will change to red.*

22. Select **cell B30**, and choose **Home→Styles→Conditional Formatting→New Rule** from the Ribbon.
*The New Formatting Rule dialog box displays.*

23. Follow these steps to create a conditional formatting rule using a formula:

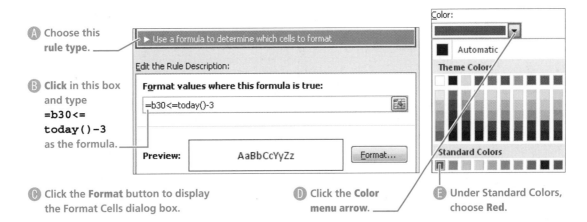

A **Choose this rule type.**

B **Click** in this box and type **=b30<= today()-3** as the formula.

C Click the **Format** button to display the Format Cells dialog box.

D Click the **Color** menu arrow.

E Under Standard Colors, choose **Red**.

24. Click **OK** in the Format Cells dialog box, and click **OK** in the Edit Formatting Rule dialog box.
*The formula tests whether the creation date in cell B30 is three or more days before today's date. The logical test result is true, so red was applied to the text in cell B30.*

25. Select the **range C11:C22** and choose **Home→Styles→Conditional Formatting→ Clear Rules→Clear Rules from Selected Cells** from the Ribbon.
    *The icons disappear from the range. Conditional formats may be removed from a selected range or from the entire worksheet.*

26. **Save** 🖫 the changes, and **close** the workbook.

# 4.12 Concepts Review

| Concepts Review | <u>labyrinthelab.com/excel10</u> |
|---|---|

*To check your knowledge of the key concepts introduced in this lesson, complete the Concepts Review quiz by going to the URL listed above. If your classroom is using Labyrinth eLab, you may complete the Concepts Review quiz from within your eLab course.*

# Reinforce Your Skills

## Format a Worksheet with the Ribbon and Mini Toolbar

*In this exercise, you will format a worksheet using commands available on the Home tab of the Ribbon and on the Mini toolbar.*

### Format Text

1. **Open** the rs-Eco Kids Club Budget Formatting workbook from the Lesson 04 folder in your file storage location.

2. Change the **font** for the entire worksheet to one of your choice.
   *Remember that cells to which a nontheme font is applied would not change font if you were to choose a different workbook theme.*

3. Select **A1**, **A7**, and **A15** using the ⌜Ctrl⌟ key.

4. Choose **Home→Font→Bold** B from the Ribbon.

5. **Right-click** cell B25 and choose **Bold** B from the Mini toolbar.

### Format Numbers

6. Select the **ranges B8:D8**, **B13:D13**, and **B16:D16** using the ⌜Ctrl⌟ key.

7. Choose **Home→Number→Accounting Number Format** $ from the Ribbon.
   *Leave the default two decimal places as is.*

8. Select the **range B24:D25**.

9. **Right-click** a selected cell, and choose **Accounting Number Format** $ from the Mini toolbar.

10. Select the **range B9:D12**.

11. Using the method of your choice, apply **Comma Style** with **two decimal places** to the selection.

12. Select the **range B17:D23**.

13. Use ⌜Ctrl⌟+⌜Y⌟ to repeat the most recent action.
    *Comma Style is applied to the selection. You can use ⌜Ctrl⌟+⌜Y⌟ or the Mini toolbar if selecting multiple ranges is not convenient.*

14. Select **cell D4**.

15. Taking care not to choose Accounting Number Format, choose **Home→Number→Number Format menu ▾** button and choose **Currency** from the list.
    *Notice that the dollar sign ($) displays next to the number. Compare this to the dollar sign placement in cell C8, to which you applied Accounting Number Format.*

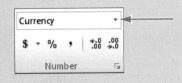

16. **Save** 🖫 the changes, and **close** the workbook.

# Align Data and Copy Formats

*In this exercise, you will change the alignment within cells and copy formatting from one cell to others.*

1. **Open** the rs-Eco Kids Club Budget Alignment workbook from the Lesson 04 folder in your file storage location.

2. Select **cell A4** and **right-align** the entry.

3. Select **cell B24**.

4. Choose **Home→Clipboard→Format Painter** 🖌 from the Ribbon.

5. Select the **range B25:D25**.
   *The formatting from cell B24 is applied to the range B25:D25.*

6. **Save** 💾 the changes and **close** the workbook.

# Work with Text Control Options

*In this exercise, you will merge and center entries, use the Shrink to Fit feature, and insert line breaks to control text.*

## Merge and Center Titles and Split Cells

1. **Open** the rs-Eco Kids Club Budget Text Control workbook.

2. Select the **range A1:D1**.

3. Choose **Home→Alignment→Merge & Center** ▦ from the Ribbon.

4. With the range still selected, choose **Home→Alignment→Merge & Center**.
   *Choosing the command again splits, or unmerges, the cells.*

5. Select the **range A1:D2**.

6. Choose **Home→Alignment→Merge & Center menu ▼→Merge Across** from the Ribbon.
   *The Merge Across command allows you to merge multiple rows at once.*

7. **Center-align** the selection.

## Use Shrink to Fit

8. Select the **range B6:D6**.

9. Choose **Home→Alignment→dialog box launcher** ⌧ from the Ribbon.

10. Place a checkmark in the **Shrink to Fit** box under Text Control, as shown at right, and then click **OK**.
    *The contents of the cells shrunk to fit into the cells with the current width, but the text is hard to read.*

11. **Undo** ↶ the text shrink to fit.

### Insert Line Breaks

12. **Double-click** cell B6 to begin in-cell editing.

13. Move the **insertion point** just to the left of the *A* in *Actual*, and **tap** ⌷Backspace⌷ to remove the space between words.

14. Use ⌷Alt⌷ + ⌷Enter⌷ to insert a line break.

15. Repeat the above steps to insert a line break in the text of **cells C6** and **D6**.

16. **Align** the text in the **range B6:D6** with the numbers in the columns.

17. **Save** 🖫 the changes, and **close** the workbook.

---

**REINFORCE YOUR SKILLS 4.4**

# Work with Dates, Cell Styles, and Themes

*In this exercise, you will enter a date function that will calculate the current date for you. You will apply cell styles to worksheet cells and change the fonts in the workbook theme.*

### Insert and Format Today's Date

1. **Open** the rs-Eco Kids Club Budget Date Function workbook.

2. Select **cell B4**.

3. Click the **Insert Function** 𝑓ₓ button.

4. Choose the **Date & Time** category if you do not see the TODAY function in the Most Recently Used category.

5. **Scroll down**, and then click to select the **TODAY** function.

6. Click **OK**.

7. Click **OK** again in the Function Arguments window.
   *The date will be returned in the default MM/DD/YYYY format.*

8. Choose **Home→Number→dialog box launcher** 🗗 from the Ribbon.

9. Display the **Number** tab in the Format Cells dialog box, **scroll down** if necessary, and then choose the format that will display the date as in the example **1-Jan-15.**
   *Excel uses March 14, 2001, as its "example date" in the Type list of the Format Cells dialog box. Rest assured that the date displayed will not be March 14, 2001, unless that is the date entered in the cell or the date resulting from a formula you may have created.*

### Apply Cell Styles

10. Make certain that **cell B4** is still selected, and then choose **Home→Styles→Cell Styles** from the Ribbon.

11. Choose an appropriate **Quick Style** from the list to draw attention to the date.

12. Select the **ranges A7:D7, A15:D15, and A25:D25** using the ⌷Ctrl⌷ key.

13. Choose **Home→Styles→Cell Styles from the Ribbon**, and then choose an appropriate **Themed Cell Style** from the list.

### Change the Theme Fonts

14. Choose **Page Layout→Themes→Fonts** 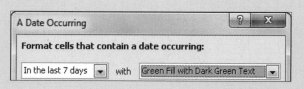 from the Ribbon.

15. Point at various **font themes** to preview the workbook, and then choose a **font** theme. *Remember that you can scroll to view all the font themes.*

16. Evaluate how the data appear, and change the **font theme**, if necessary, until you are satisfied.

17. Add any **formatting** that you think enhances the workbook design.

18. **Save** 🖫 the changes, and **close** the workbook.

---

**REINFORCE YOUR SKILLS 4.5**

# Apply Conditional Formatting and Manage Rules

*In this exercise, you will apply conditional formatting to cell ranges to analyze trends. You will use the Conditional Formatting Manager to edit, rearrange, and delete conditional formatting rules.*

### Create Formulas

1. **Open** the rs-Shipping Fee Analysis workbook.

2. Select **cell F4**, and **enter** the formula **=d4-e4**.
   *The result should be (37.00). The formula calculates the amount that the estimated shipping fee collected from the customer was over or under the actual fee paid.*

3. **Copy** the difference formula in **cell F4** down the column for all orders in **rows 5 through 18**.

4. Select the **range D19:F19**, and use **AutoSum** to total the values in each column. **Bold** all entries in **row 19**.

5. **Right-align** the **column headings** in **row 3**.

### Use a Date Preset

6. Select the **range B4:B18**.

7. Choose **Home→Styles→Conditional Formatting→Highlight Cells Rules→A Date Occurring** from the Ribbon.
   *The A Date Occurring dialog box appears with the Yesterday option displayed.*

8. Choose in **In the Last 7 Days** from the date list, and choose **Green Fill with Dark Green Text** from the With list.
   *The last four dates are highlighted in column B of the worksheet.*

### Apply and Customize an Icon Set

9. Select the **range F4:F18**.

10. Choose **Home→Styles→Conditional Formatting→Icon Sets→3 Symbols (Circled)** from the Ribbon.
    *Displaying three icons makes the list look cluttered. You want to draw attention to the largest negative amounts.*

11. With the **range F4:F18** still selected, follow these steps to remove two icons from the display:

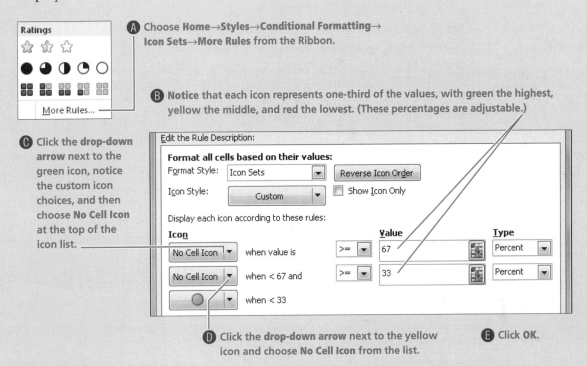

**A** Choose **Home→Styles→Conditional Formatting→ Icon Sets→More Rules** from the Ribbon.

**B** **Notice** that each icon represents one-third of the values, with green the highest, yellow the middle, and red the lowest. (These percentages are adjustable.)

**C** Click the **drop-down arrow** next to the green icon, notice the custom icon choices, and then choose **No Cell Icon** at the top of the icon list.

**D** Click the **drop-down arrow** next to the yellow icon and choose **No Cell Icon** from the list.

**E** Click **OK**.

*Now only red icons display to focus attention on three undesirable amounts in cells F4, F6, and F16.*

## Apply a Color Scale

12. Select the **range E4:E18**.

13. Choose **Home→Styles→ Conditional Formatting→Color Scales→Green-White Color Scale** from the Ribbon. *The Actual Shipping values are highlighted with shades of green. The darkest green highlights the highest value, the shades become lighter as the values decrease, and the lowest value displays a white background.*

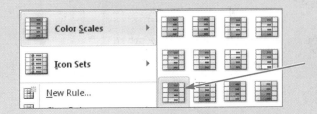

## Create a Text Rule

14. Select the **range C4:C18**.

15. Choose **Home→Styles→Conditional Formatting→Highlight Cells Rules→Text That Contains** from the Ribbon.

16. Type **11** in the Format Cells that Contain the Text box, choose **Yellow Fill with Dark Yellow Text** from the With list, and then click **OK**.

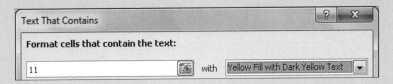

**17. Deselect** the range, and analyze the results.

*Notice that the highlighted cells indicate a pattern. The three worst values marked in the Difference column also are highlighted in dark green as the highest Actual Shipping charges. The yellow highlights in the Shipped Via column show that vendor 11 shipped these three orders. Conditional formatting makes important data and trends clear.*

| | C | D | E | F |
|---|---|---|---|---|
| 3 | Shipped Via | Estimated Shipping | Actual Shipping | Difference |
| 4 | 11 | 125.00 | 162.00 | (37.00) |
| 5 | 22 | 10.00 | 8.95 | 1.05 |
| 6 | 11 | 100.00 | 142.65 | (42.65) |
| 7 | 33 | 50.00 | 50.00 | - |
| 8 | 44 | 10.00 | 17.45 | (7.45) |
| 9 | 44 | 16.00 | 13.25 | 2.75 |
| 10 | 33 | 82.00 | 64.00 | 18.00 |
| 11 | 22 | 40.00 | 23.75 | 16.25 |
| 12 | 33 | 5.00 | 4.95 | 0.05 |
| 13 | 22 | 42.00 | 48.75 | (6.75) |
| 14 | 11 | 100.00 | 100.00 | - |
| 15 | 44 | 52.50 | 46.25 | 6.25 |
| 16 | 11 | 200.00 | 240.00 | (40.00) |

## Apply, Edit, and Rearrange Multiple Rules

**18.** Select the **range C4:C18**.

**19.** Choose **Home→Styles→Conditional Formatting→ Highlight Cells Rules→Duplicate Values** from the Ribbon, choose options to **format duplicate values with a green fill with dark green text**, and click **OK**.

*All vendor numbers in column C are duplicates. The second rule overwrites the yellow highlighting created by the first rule. You will arrange rules to prevent this.*

**20.** Choose **Home→Styles→Conditional Formatting→Manage Rules** from the Ribbon. *The Manage Rules command is at the bottom of the Conditional Formatting menu.*

**21.** Follow these steps in the Conditional Formatting Rules Manager dialog box to rearrange the two rules applied to range C4:C18:

Ⓐ **Drop down** the Show Formatting Rules For list and choose **This Worksheet** to display all conditional formatting rules.

Ⓑ Select the **Cell Value Contains '11'** rule (the second rule in the list), and then click the **Move Up** button.

**Conditional Formatting Rules Manager**

Show formatting rules for: This Worksheet

| New Rule... | Edit Rule... | Delete Rule | ▲ | ▼ |

| Rule (applied in order shown) | Format | Applies to | Stop If True |
|---|---|---|---|
| Cell Value = 11 | AaBbCcYyZz | =$C$4:$C$18 | ☑ |
| Duplicate Values | AaBbCcYyZz | =$C$4:$C$18 | ☐ |
| Graded Color Scale | | =$E$4:$E$18 | ☐ |
| Icon Set | ● | =$F$4:$F$18 | ☐ |
| Icon Set | ● ● ● | =$F$4:$F$18 | ☐ |

Ⓒ Click to add a checkmark in the **Stop If True** box for the **Cell Value Contains '11'** rule.

Ⓓ Click OK.

*Conditional Formatting rules are applied in the order listed. The Stop If True option in the first rule prevents the green formatting from being applied by the Duplicate Values rule.*

## Delete a Conditional Formatting Rule

22. Choose **Home→Styles→Conditional Formatting→Manage Rules** from the Ribbon.

23. **Drop down** the Show Formatting Rules For list and choose **This Worksheet**.

24. Select the Icon Set rule that displays **three icons**.

| Icon Set | ● ○ ○ | =$F$4:$F$18 | | □ |
|---|---|---|---|---|

*This rule is no longer needed because you customized the icons.*

25. Click the **Delete Rule** button at the top of the dialog box, and then click **OK**.
*Your worksheet should resemble the following illustration. Your dates in column B will differ.*

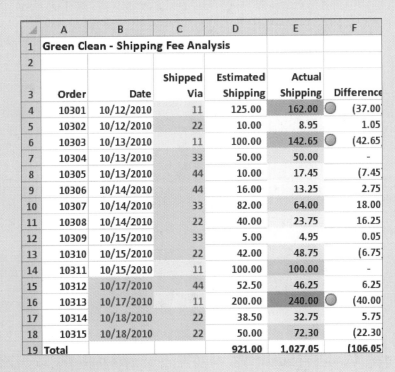

| | A | B | C | D | E | F |
|---|---|---|---|---|---|---|
| 1 | Green Clean - Shipping Fee Analysis | | | | | |
| 2 | | | | | | |
| 3 | Order | Date | Shipped Via | Estimated Shipping | Actual Shipping | Difference |
| 4 | 10301 | 10/12/2010 | 11 | 125.00 | 162.00 ○ | (37.00) |
| 5 | 10302 | 10/12/2010 | 22 | 10.00 | 8.95 | 1.05 |
| 6 | 10303 | 10/13/2010 | 11 | 100.00 | 142.65 ○ | (42.65) |
| 7 | 10304 | 10/13/2010 | 33 | 50.00 | 50.00 | - |
| 8 | 10305 | 10/13/2010 | 44 | 10.00 | 17.45 | (7.45) |
| 9 | 10306 | 10/14/2010 | 44 | 16.00 | 13.25 | 2.75 |
| 10 | 10307 | 10/14/2010 | 33 | 82.00 | 64.00 | 18.00 |
| 11 | 10308 | 10/14/2010 | 22 | 40.00 | 23.75 | 16.25 |
| 12 | 10309 | 10/15/2010 | 33 | 5.00 | 4.95 | 0.05 |
| 13 | 10310 | 10/15/2010 | 22 | 42.00 | 48.75 | (6.75) |
| 14 | 10311 | 10/15/2010 | 11 | 100.00 | 100.00 | - |
| 15 | 10312 | 10/17/2010 | 44 | 52.50 | 46.25 | 6.25 |
| 16 | 10313 | 10/17/2010 | 11 | 200.00 | 240.00 ○ | (40.00) |
| 17 | 10314 | 10/18/2010 | 22 | 38.50 | 32.75 | 5.75 |
| 18 | 10315 | 10/18/2010 | 22 | 50.00 | 72.30 | (22.30) |
| 19 | Total | | | 921.00 | 1,027.05 | (106.05) |

26. **Save** 🖫 the changes, and **close** the workbook.

# Apply Your Skills

## Format Text and Numbers

*In this exercise, you will format text and numbers.*

1. **Open** the as-Green Clean Inventory workbook from the Lesson 04 folder in your file storage location.

2. Format **cell D5** in **Currency Style** with **two decimals**.

3. Format the **range D6:D9** in **Number** style from the Number Format list in the Ribbon.

4. Format the **range E5:E10** in **Comma Style** with **zero decimals**.

5. Apply **bold** formatting to the entries in **rows 4** and **10**.

6. Format the title in **cell A1** with **bold**, and change the font size to **14**.

7. **Save** 💾 the changes to the workbook, and continue with the next exercise.

| | A | B | C | D | E |
|---|---|---|---|---|---|
| 1 | **Green Clean Inventory** | | | | |
| 2 | Carpet Products | | | | |
| 3 | | | | | |
| 4 | CARPET CLEANING SOLUTIONS | Type | Size | Price | Quantity |
| 5 | EarthWise Carpet Cleaner | Concentrate | 64 ounces | $17.50 | 224 |
| 6 | EarthWise Carpet Cleaner | Concentrate | 32 ounces | 9.85 | 468 |
| 7 | EarthWise Carpet Cleaner | Spray | 16 ounces | 4.50 | 201 |
| 8 | GBS All Purpose Carpet | Liquid | 120 ounces | 11.95 | 53 |
| 9 | GBS Dry Powder Cleaner | Powder | 16 ounces | 4.25 | 134 |
| 10 | **Total Inventory** | | | | 1,080 |
| 11 | | | | | |
| 12 | CARPET STAIN REMOVERS | Type | Size | Retail Price | Quantity |
| 13 | EarthWise Carpet Stain Remover | Concentrate | 64 ounces | 9.95 | 251 |
| 14 | EarthWise Carpet Stain Remover | Concentrate | 32 ounces | 5.5 | 131 |
| 15 | EarthWise Carpet Stain Remover | Spray | 16 ounces | 4.65 | 192 |
| 16 | Carpet Bright Stain Eliminator | Spray | 32 ounces | 7.35 | 62 |
| 17 | Total Inventory | | | | 636 |

# Align and Control Text, Add Borders, and Use Format Painter

*In this exercise, you will center the titles across worksheet columns, insert line breaks to wrap text, apply borders to a cell, and use Format Painter.*

*Before You Begin: You must have completed Apply Your Skills 4.1, and the as-Green Clean Inventory workbook should be open.*

1. **Merge** and **center** the titles in **cells A1** and **A2** across **columns A through E**.

2. Change **cell D4** to `Retail Price` and insert a **line break** so that each word is on a separate line in the entry.

3. **Right-align** the entries in **cells D4** and **E4**.

4. Place a **single border** along the top of the **cell E10** and a **double line border** along the bottom.

5. Use **Format Painter** to apply the formatting from the **range A4:E4** to the **range A12:E12**.

6. Use **Format Painter** to apply the following formatting:
   - From cell D5 to **cell D13**
   - From cell D6 to the **range D14:D16**
   - From cell E5 to the **range E13:E16**
   - From cell E10 to **cell E17**

7. **Save** 💾 the changes to the workbook, and continue with the next exercise.

| | A | B | C | D | E |
|---|---|---|---|---|---|
| 1 | **Green Clean Inventory** | | | | |
| 2 | Carpet Products | | | | |
| 3 | | | | | |
| 4 | **CARPET CLEANING SOLUTIONS** | **Type** | **Size** | **Retail Price** | **Quantity** |
| 5 | EarthWise Carpet Cleaner | Concentrate | 64 ounces | $17.50 | 224 |
| 6 | EarthWise Carpet Cleaner | Concentrate | 32 ounces | 9.85 | 468 |
| 7 | EarthWise Carpet Cleaner | Spray | 16 ounces | 4.50 | 201 |
| 8 | GBS All Purpose Carpet | Liquid | 120 ounces | 11.95 | 53 |
| 9 | GBS Dry Powder Cleaner | Powder | 16 ounces | 4.25 | 134 |
| 10 | Total Inventory | | | | 1,080 |
| 11 | | | | | |
| 12 | **CARPET STAIN REMOVERS** | **Type** | **Size** | **Retail Price** | **Quantity** |
| 13 | EarthWise Carpet Stain Remover | Concentrate | 64 ounces | $9.95 | 251 |
| 14 | EarthWise Carpet Stain Remover | Concentrate | 32 ounces | 5.50 | 131 |
| 15 | EarthWise Carpet Stain Remover | Spray | 16 ounces | 4.65 | 192 |
| 16 | Carpet Bright Stain Eliminator | Spray | 32 ounces | 7.35 | 62 |
| 17 | Total Inventory | | | | 636 |

# Change the Theme, Apply Color to Cells, and Create Conditional Formatting

*In this exercise, you will indent cell entries, center the title across worksheet columns, apply a border to cells, and use Format Painter. You will apply a conditional formatting rule to highlight low quantities of products in the inventory.*

*Before You Begin: You must have completed Apply Your Skills 4.2, and the as-Green Clean Inventory workbook should be open.*

1. Apply the **fill color** of your choice to the **merged range A1:A2**.

2. Change the **font color** in the **ranges A5:C9** and **A13:C16**.

3. Apply the **Sketchbook** theme to the workbook. (This theme is in the From Office.com group of the menu. If unavailable, choose an appropriate theme from the Built-In group.)

4. Use **Page Layout view** or the **Print** tab in Backstage view to ensure that the worksheet fits on one page.

5. Create a **conditional formatting rule** that highlights any values below 150 in the Quantity column, but do not include the total inventory cells.

6. **Save** 🖫 the changes, and **close** the workbook.

| | A | B | C | D | E |
|---|---|---|---|---|---|
| 1 | **Green Clean Inventory** | | | | |
| 2 | Carpet Products | | | | |
| 3 | | | | | |
| 4 | **CARPET CLEANING SOLUTION** | Type | Size | Retail Price | Quantity |
| 5 | EarthWise Carpet Cleaner | Concentrate | 64 ounces | $17.50 | 224 |
| 6 | EarthWise Carpet Cleaner | Concentrate | 32 ounces | 9.85 | 468 |
| 7 | EarthWise Carpet Cleaner | Spray | 16 ounces | 4.50 | 201 |
| 8 | GBS All Purpose Carpet | Liquid | 120 ounces | 11.95 | 53 |
| 9 | GBS Dry Powder Cleaner | Powder | 16 ounces | 4.25 | 134 |
| 10 | **Total Inventory** | | | | **1,080** |
| 11 | | | | | |
| 12 | **CARPET STAIN REMOVERS** | Type | Size | Retail Price | Quantity |
| 13 | EarthWise Carpet Stain Remover | Concentrate | 64 ounces | $9.95 | 251 |
| 14 | EarthWise Carpet Stain Remover | Concentrate | 32 ounces | 5.50 | 131 |
| 15 | EarthWise Carpet Stain Remover | Spray | 16 ounces | 4.65 | 192 |
| 16 | Carpet Bright Stain Eliminator | Spray | 32 ounces | 7.35 | 62 |
| 17 | **Total Inventory** | | | | **636** |

# Critical Thinking & Work-Readiness Skills

*In the course of working through the following Microsoft Office-based Critical Thinking exercises, you will also be utilizing various work-readiness skills, some of which are listed next to each exercise. Go to labyrinthelab.com/ workreadiness to learn more about the work-readiness skills.*

## 4.1 Format Text in an Excel Spreadsheet

Green Clean (and any organization in which you may be employed) has design preferences and standards. This exercise will help you build your formatting ability according to Green Clean's standards. Open ct-Customer Base (Lesson 04 folder). Practice the following skills:

- Right-align the column headings in columns B-F.
- Indent companies A-K in column A.
- Merge the range A1:F1, and type **First Quarter Sales** in the merged cell. Apply appropriate text formatting to this title.
- Text wrap your full name and today's date in cell A20.

Save your work as **ct-Customer Base1** in your Lesson 04 folder.

**WORK-READINESS SKILLS APPLIED**

- Seeing things in the mind's eye
- Organizing and maintaining information
- Reading

## 4.2 Display Numbers in an Excel Spreadsheet

Green Clean uses numbers in spreadsheets for a variety of purposes: currency style for their price lists, quantities for order forms, and accounting styles and negative numbers for budgeting. Open ct-Customer Base1, if necessary, and resave it as **ct-CustomerBase2**. You realize that to work with all of the company's spreadsheets, you need to practice formatting numbers, noting accounting, currency, percent, and negative numbers styles. Select the range D4:D18. From the Number group on the Home tab of the Ribbon, select different number styles. Note the various foreign currency styles on the Accounting Number Format menu. Remember these styles do not calculate exchange rates. Select the range F3:F18 and format the range to show tenths of a percent (0.1%). Select cell D18.

**WORK-READINESS SKILLS APPLIED**

- Reasoning
- Organizing and maintaining information
- Applying technology

## 4.3 Use Format Painter and Insert the Date

Green Clean plans to acquire several small cleaning companies. In anticipation of adding a lot of data to Customer Base spreadsheet you decide to hone your spreadsheet skills. Open ct-Customer Base2, if necessary, and save it as **ct-CustomerBase3**. Using the Format Painter, change the column C entries to look like those in column B. Think about how Format Painter can help you be consistent and efficient. Then, returning to the Excel spreadsheet, insert today's date in cell B20 and the time in cell C20. Practice inserting date and time functions. If working alone, format the date and time at least three different ways. If working in a group, discuss the usefulness of date and time stamping. Save the changes to your spreadsheet and close the file.

**WORK-READINESS SKILLS APPLIED**

- Seeing things in the mind's eye
- Organizing and maintaining information
- Showing responsibility

# Changing the Appearance of Worksheets

## LEARNING OBJECTIVES

After studying this lesson, you will be able to:

■ Insert, delete, move, copy, and rename worksheets in a workbook

■ Modify column width and row height

■ Insert, delete, hide, and unhide columns and rows

■ Set the vertical alignment and rotate text

■ Find and replace data and formatting, and use AutoCorrect effectively

In this lesson, you will learn techniques for changing the structure of worksheets as it relates to worksheet tab order, rows, columns, and additional cell alignment options. In addition, you will learn about time-saving features such as Find and Replace. After you complete this lesson, you will have learned many basics you need to work with Excel.

# Changing Workbook Tabs, Columns, and Rows

Safety is an important concern at Green Clean, the janitorial product supplier and cleaning service contractor. Isabella Riso-Neff is the risk management director. She prepares company policies and procedures for legal compliance, contracts, insurance, Worker's Compensation, and workplace safety. Isabella is coordinating with Ken Hazell, the human resources director, to formalize the safety training program at Green Clean.

Isabella will organize the structure of a workbook containing multiple worksheets. A worksheet will contain a list of learning objectives for the training topic. Test questions will be created for each objective to assess an employee's knowledge and performance regarding the objective. The worksheet will show the number of test questions in each category as well as the total and percentage. Isabella will work with entire rows and columns to organize the worksheet, find and replace text and formats, and vertically align and rotate headings.

| | A | B | C | D | E | F | G | H |
|---|---|---|---|---|---|---|---|---|
| 1 | | Green Clean | | | | | | |
| 2 | | Safety Training - Chemicals | | | | | | |
| 3 | | | Exam Categories | | | | | |
| 4 | | Performance Objectives | Knowledge | Comprehension | Performance | Analysis | Total | Percentage |
| 5 | | | (Number of Items) | | | | | |
| 6 | 1. | *Identify and mix hazardous materials safely.* | | | | | | |
| 7 | | a. Understand and follow steps on material safety data sheets (MSDS) correctly. | 2 | 1 | 2 | | 5 | 10% |
| 8 | | b. Identify hazardous materials | | 2 | 2 | 1 | 5 | 10% |

Column widths and row heights are adjusted to display the cell contents. The text for the exam categories is rotated 90 degrees to fit the columns on one page.

| | | | C | D | E | F | G | H |
|---|---|---|---|---|---|---|---|---|
| 24 | | a. Demonstrate first aid procedures for various given incidents. | | 2 | 2 | 2 | 0 | 0% |
| 25 | | b. Demonstrate the use of an emergency wash station. | | 2 | 2 | 2 | 2 | 4% |
| 26 | | Total | 7 | 20 | 29 | 11 | 52 | 100% |
| 27 | | Percentage | 13% | 38% | 56% | 21% | 100% | |
| 28 | | | | | | | | |

Chemicals / Lifting / Garbage / Floors / Notes

Worksheet tabs are copied, rearranged, and colored to clearly identify the workbook structure.

# 5.1 Managing Worksheets

**Video Lesson**    labyrinthelab.com/videos

As you begin to work with more complex workbooks, you will need to be comfortable with workbook management and navigating among multiple worksheets. You can organize a workbook by inserting, deleting, and rearranging worksheets. You also can rename worksheet tabs and apply colors to them.

## Inserting and Deleting Worksheets

**FROM THE KEYBOARD**
Shift + F11 to insert a worksheet

Although Excel displays three worksheets in a new workbook by default, you can insert as many new worksheets as your available computer memory allows. Excel makes it very easy to insert a new worksheet with the Insert Worksheet button located at the far right corner of the worksheet tabs. You may also insert multiple worksheets before any worksheet tab. To clean up the appearance of your workbook, you may wish to delete unused worksheets. You may also select multiple worksheets for deletion at one time. Realize, though, that deleting a worksheet cannot be undone!

## Rearranging, Copying, Renaming, and Coloring Worksheet Tabs

Sheet tabs can be placed in any order simply by dragging. You can duplicate a worksheet by holding Ctrl and dragging its tab to the desired location. This copying feature is useful in creating sheets for recurring time periods, such as quarters of the year, or categories, as you will do in this lesson. You can also rename a worksheet tab to give it a more descriptive name. If you want to organize your workbook a bit more, you can change the color of the tabs. The active worksheet tab name will be displayed in bold. Take a look at the following figure to learn more about worksheet tabs.

The navigation buttons to the left of the sheet tabs are extremely useful when you navigate through a large number of worksheets whose tabs cannot display all at once.

When clicked, the Insert Worksheet button automatically inserts a new sheet to the right of the existing sheet tabs.

The name of the active worksheet is displayed in bold.

These Sheet2 and Sheet3 tabs are unused and can be deleted to clean up the workbook.

You cannot undo the Delete worksheet command. If you issue the command by mistake, however, you can close the workbook without saving it and then reopen it to recover the lost worksheet.

# Hiding and Unhiding Worksheets

You can hide a worksheet from view. For example, you may temporarily want to work with only certain sheets or prefer not to call attention to data on a specific worksheet. Be aware, however, that anyone using your workbook could unhide the sheet. You can hide and unhide worksheets using commands on the Ribbon or from the context menu that displays after you right-click a sheet tab.

| QUICK REFERENCE | MANAGING WORKSHEETS |
|---|---|
| **Task** | **Procedure** |
| Activate a worksheet | ■ Click the desired worksheet tab. |
| Rename a worksheet | ■ Double-click the worksheet tab to be renamed. |
| | ■ Type a new name and tap [Enter]. |
| Change the worksheet tab color | ■ Right-click the desired sheet tab. |
| | ■ Choose Tab Color from the context menu and click the desired color. |
| Insert a worksheet to the right of existing sheet tabs | ■ Click the Insert Worksheet button to the right of the last tab displayed. |
| Insert a worksheet before the active sheet tab | ■ Choose Home→Cells→Insert→Insert menu ▼→Insert Sheet from the Ribbon. |
| Insert multiple worksheets before the active sheet tab | ■ Select the desired worksheet tab, hold down [Shift], and then click a sheet tab at the right to equal the number of worksheets that you wish to insert. |
| | ■ Choose Home→Cells→Insert menu ▼→Insert Sheet from the Ribbon. |
| Delete a worksheet | ■ Right-click the tab of the worksheet you wish to delete. |
| | ■ Choose Delete from the context menu. |
| Delete multiple worksheets | ■ Select the first worksheet tab to be deleted, hold down [Ctrl], and then click each additional sheet tab that you wish to delete. (Or, hold down [Shift] and select the last in a range of tabs.) |
| | ■ Choose Home→Cells→Delete menu ▼→Delete Sheet from the Ribbon. |
| | ■ Click Delete in the dialog box that appears. |
| Move a worksheet | ■ Drag the worksheet tab to the desired position in the worksheet order. |
| Copy a worksheet | ■ Select the sheet to be copied. |
| | ■ Hold down [Ctrl] while dragging the tab of the sheet you wish to copy. |
| | ■ Release the mouse button, and then release [Ctrl] when the new tab is in the desired position. |
| Hide a worksheet | ■ Select the worksheet tab. |
| | ■ Choose Home→Cells→Format→Hide & Unhide→Hide Sheet from the Ribbon, or right-click the sheet tab and choose Hide from the context menu. |
| Unhide a worksheet | ■ Choose Home→Cells→Format→Hide & Unhide→Unhide Sheet from the Ribbon (or right-click the sheet tab and choose Unhide from the context menu), and choose the sheet to be unhidden. |

# Modify Workbook Sheet Order and Sheet Tabs

*In this exercise, you will insert and move a new worksheet, delete a sheet, and copy a sheet. You will rename worksheet tabs and change their color. Finally, you will hide and unhide a worksheet.*

## Rename Sheet Tabs

1. **Open** the Safety Training workbook from the Lesson 05 folder in your file storage location.

2. Follow these steps to rename Sheet1:

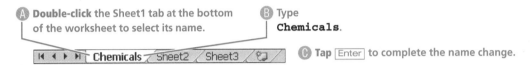

**A** **Double-click** the Sheet1 tab at the bottom of the worksheet to select its name.
**B** Type **Chemicals**.
**C** Tap [Enter] to complete the name change.

3. **Rename** Sheet2 to **Lifting**.

## Insert, Move, and Delete Sheets

4. Click the **Insert Worksheet** button to the right of the sheet tabs.
   *A new sheet appears to the right of the existing sheets.*

5. **Rename** the new sheet as **Notes**.

6. Drag the **Notes** sheet to the left of **Sheet3**.

*Notice that the mouse pointer displays an empty sheet icon as you drag to the desired position indicated by the small triangle ▼. Drag again if the Notes sheet does not display between Lifting and Sheet3 after you release the mouse button.*

7. **Right-click** Sheet3, and choose **Delete** from the context menu.
   *Excel does not ask you to confirm the deletion because the worksheet is empty.*

8. Click the **Lifting** sheet tab to select the sheet.

9. **Hold down** [Shift] and select the **Notes** tab.
   *Both tabs are selected. Next, you will insert two sheets, the number of sheets selected.*

10. Choose **Home→Cells→Insert menu ▼→Insert Sheet** from the Ribbon.

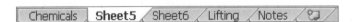

*Two new sheets were inserted before the Lifting sheet. Your sheet numbers may be different.*

11. With Sheet5 currently selected, **hold down** [Ctrl] and select the **Sheet6** tab.
    *The [Ctrl] key allows you select nonadjacent sheets for deletion, while the [Shift] key selects all sheets between the active sheet tab and the next tab you select.*

12. Choose **Home→Cells→Delete menu ▾→Delete Sheet** from the Ribbon.
    *The two sheets are deleted.*

13. **Save** 🖫 the changes to the workbook.

## Copy the Lifting Sheet

14. Click the **Lifting** sheet tab to select the sheet.

15. **Hold down** Ctrl, drag the **Lifting** tab to the right to position it between Lifting and Notes, and **release** Ctrl.

*Notice that the mouse pointer displays a sheet icon containing a plus sign ( + ) as you drag, indicating that you are copying the sheet. The duplicated sheet is named Lifting (2).*

16. **Rename** Lifting (2) to **Garbage**.

17. Repeat **steps 14–16** to copy the **Garbage** sheet and **rename** it to **Floors**.

18. In **cell A2** of the Floors sheet, edit *Lifting and Motion* to read **Floors**.

| | A | B |
|---|---|---|
| 1 | | Green Clean |
| 2 | | Safety Training - Floors |

19. Select the **Garbage** sheet.

20. In **cell A2**, edit *Lifting and Motion* to read **Garbage**.

## Change the Sheet Tab Color

21. **Right-click** the Chemicals sheet, point to Tab Color in the context menu, and choose the **orange theme color** from the palette, as shown.

22. Repeat the above step to apply a **blue theme shade** to the **Lifting sheet** tab.

23. Apply a **green theme shade** to the **Garbage** sheet tab.

24. Apply a **brown theme shade** to the **Floors** tab.
    *You will leave the Notes tab in its original gray shade.*

25. Select the **Chemicals** tab.
    *Notice that the text of the currently selected tab turns bold and its color reduces to a subtle orange band below the text.*

### Hide and Unhide a Worksheet

26. **Right-click** the Notes sheet tab and choose **Hide** from the context menu, as shown at right.
*The worksheet and its tab disappear.*

27. Choose **Home→Cells→Format** from the Ribbon.

28. Trace down to **Visibility**, point to **Hide & Unhide**, and choose **Unhide Sheet** from the submenu that appears.

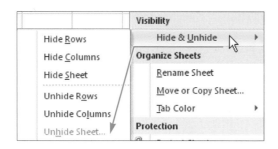

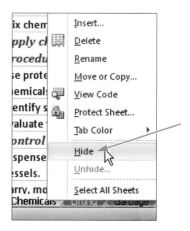

*The Unhide dialog box displays. The Notes sheet already is selected because it is the only one available to be unhidden.*

29. Click **OK**.

30. **Save** the changes to the workbook and continue with the next topic.

# 5.2 Modifying Columns and Rows

**Video Lesson** labyrinthelab.com/videos

As you have seen, many entries do not fit within the default column width. Worksheets can also appear overcrowded with the standard row heights, which may tempt you to insert blank rows to make the worksheet more readable. The problem with this "fix," though, is that it can cause problems down the road when you begin to use some of Excel's more powerful features. In this lesson, you will use more time-saving techniques to fix column width and row height issues, such as changing multiple columns and rows at the same time and using AutoFit to let Excel figure out the best width or height. Both of these commands simply require you to select multiple columns or rows before issuing the command.

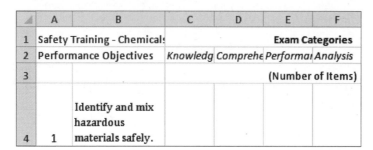

You can see that you have a lot of work to do here in resizing rows and columns!

# Column Widths and Row Heights

There are a variety of methods for changing widths of columns and heights of rows. They can be performed on either one or multiple columns or rows. One efficient way to adjust widths and heights is to simply drag the heading lines of the column(s) or row(s).

## Standard Column Widths and Row Heights

Each column in a new worksheet has a standard width of 8.43 characters, where the default text setting is Calibri 11 point. Each row has a standard height of 15 points, which is approximately one-fifth of an inch.

## AutoFit

You can adjust both column widths and row heights with the AutoFit command. AutoFit adjusts column widths to fit the widest entry in a column. Likewise, AutoFit adjusts row heights to accommodate the tallest entry in a row. The following Quick Reference table discusses AutoFit options and other commands for setting column widths and row heights.

| | A | | B |
|---|---|---|---|
| 1 | Safety Training - Chemicals | | |
| 2 | Performance Objectives | | |
| 3 | | | |

When you point to the border between columns or rows, a double-pointed arrow lets you know you can manually drag to change its size or double-click to issue the AutoFit command.

| QUICK REFERENCE | CHANGING COLUMN WIDTHS AND ROW HEIGHTS |
|---|---|
| **Technique** | **Procedure** |
| Set a precise column width | ▪ Select the column for which you wish to change the width.<br>▪ Choose Home→Cells→Format→Column Width from the Ribbon.<br>▪ Type the column width you desire. |
| Set column widths with AutoFit using the Ribbon | ▪ Select the column(s) for which you wish to change the width.<br>▪ Choose Home→Cells→Format→AutoFit Column Width from the Ribbon. |
| Set column widths with AutoFit by double-clicking | ▪ Select a single column or multiple columns for which you wish to change the width.<br>▪ Position the mouse pointer between any two selected headings or to the right of the selected single column heading. Double-click only when you see the double arrow mouse pointer to AutoFit all selected columns. |
| Set a precise row height | ▪ Select the row for which you wish to change the height.<br>▪ Choose Home→Cells→Format→Row Height from the Ribbon.<br>▪ Type the row height you desire. |
| Set row heights with AutoFit | ▪ Select the row for which you wish to change the height.<br>▪ Choose Home→Cells→Format→AutoFit Row Height from the Ribbon. You can also select multiple rows and double-click between any two selected headings to AutoFit all selected rows. |
| Manually adjust column widths and row heights | ▪ Select one or more columns or rows and drag the column or row heading line instead of double-clicking it. |

# Change Column Width and Row Height

*In this exercise, you will change the column width and row height to ensure that the cell entries fit properly.*

1. Display the **Chemicals** worksheet of the Safety Training workbook.

## Adjust Column Widths

2. Follow these steps to resize column A:

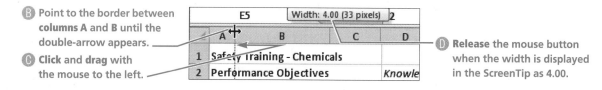

Ⓐ Place the **mouse pointer** to the right of column A until the double-arrow mouse pointer appears, and then **double-click**.

*Notice that the column is resized to fit the widest entry, which is in row 1. You will be merging and centering the title in row 1, so this column is too wide for your use.*

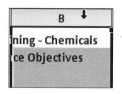

Ⓑ Point to the border between **columns A and B** until the double-arrow appears.

Ⓒ **Click** and **drag** with the mouse to the left.

Ⓓ **Release** the mouse button when the width is displayed in the ScreenTip as 4.00.

## Set a Precise Column Width

3. Click the **column B heading** to select the entire column.

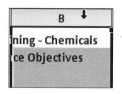

4. Follow these steps to precisely set the column width:

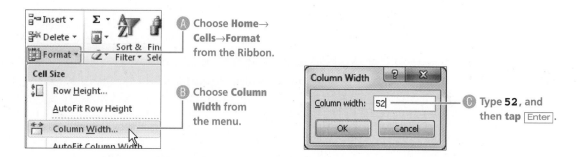

Ⓐ Choose **Home→ Cells→Format** from the Ribbon.

Ⓑ Choose **Column Width** from the menu.

Ⓒ Type **52**, and then **tap** Enter.

*The column has been sized much larger to accommodate the larger cell entries, which have "spread out" because the cells are formatted to wrap text.*

5. Click the **heading** for **row 4** and drag down through **row 24**.

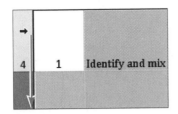

*Rows 4 through 24 should now be selected. Any command issued will apply to all selected rows.*

6. **Point** between two of the selected rows to display the double-arrow pointer and **double-click**.

   *All of the selected rows shrink to fit the tallest entry. You can choose Home→ Cells→Format→AutoFit Row Height from the Ribbon if you have difficulty keeping the mouse still while double-clicking.*

7. **Save** 💾 the changes to the workbook.

# 5.3 Inserting and Deleting Columns, Rows, and Cells

**Video Lesson** labyrinthelab.com/videos

You can insert and delete columns, rows, and cells as needed in your worksheets. You probably figure that you will have plenty of rows and columns because you start out with more than 1,000,000 and 16,000 of them, respectively. The ability to insert and delete will come in handy when you want to restructure your worksheet after it has been created.

## Inserting and Deleting Rows and Columns

Excel lets you insert and delete rows and columns. This feature gives you the flexibility to restructure your worksheets after they have been set up. The Quick Reference table in this section discusses the various procedures used to insert and delete rows and columns.

Formulas using SUM, AVERAGE, and other similar functions will update automatically to take into account inserted and deleted rows and columns with two exceptions. If you insert a row above the first row in the range and its formula, you will need to edit the formula to include that row. Likewise, you will need to edit the formula if you insert a column to the left of the first column in the formula range. The following illustration shows how the inserted row has no effect on the SUM formulas.

| | A | B | C | D | E |
|---|---|---|---|---|---|
| 1 | | Solvents | Cleaners | Polishes | Total |
| 2 | | 2 | 2 | 2 | |
| 3 | In Stock | 2 | 2 | 2 | 6 |
| 4 | Ordered | 2 | 2 | 2 | 6 |
| 5 | Damaged | 2 | 2 | 2 | 6 |
| 6 | Total | =SUM(B3:B5) | | 6 | 18 |

A new row 2 was inserted above the range included in the original SUM formula. Notice that the SUM formula does not include the new row because it is above the cell that began the original range. The totals are still 6 rather than 8. If a new row were inserted between rows 3 and 4, the function would be automatically updated to include the new row because it is within the range of the formula. The totals would then be 8.

**WARNING**

Excel does not alert you to an inserted row or column outside the original range used in a formula.

# Inserting and Deleting Cells

If you want to insert or delete only cells, not entire rows or columns, you need to issue a command to insert or delete cells. This command will allow you to add or remove a "chunk" or range of cells from your worksheet. However, this command may cause problems because it alters the structure of your entire worksheet. For this reason, use this feature cautiously.

## Shift Cells Option

When you add or remove a range of cells from your worksheet, you will need to tell Excel how to shift the surrounding cells to either make room for the addition or fill the space from the deletion.

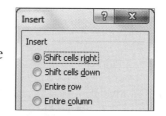

There are four Shift Cells options for you to choose from when you insert cells.

## The Appearance of the Cells Group Commands

The buttons in the Cells group of the Home tab of the Ribbon will appear differently depending on the size of your Excel window (which may be determined by the size of your monitor).

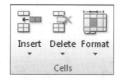 

The figure on the left displays how the Cells group buttons will be displayed in a larger window, whereas the figure on the right displays the buttons as displayed in a smaller window. In the exercise steps, you will see the illustrations depicting the larger Ribbon buttons.

| QUICK REFERENCE | INSERTING AND DELETING ROWS, COLUMNS, AND CELLS |
|---|---|
| **Task** | **Procedure** |
| Insert rows | ■ Select the number of rows you wish to insert (the same number of new rows will be inserted above the selected rows). |
| | ■ Choose Home→Cells→Insert from the Ribbon, or right-click the selection and choose Insert from the context menu. |
| Insert columns | ■ Select the number of columns you wish to insert (the same number of new columns will be inserted to the left of the selected columns). |
| | ■ Choose Home→Cells→Insert from the Ribbon, or right-click the selection and choose Insert from the context menu. |
| Delete rows | ■ Select the rows you wish to delete. |
| | ■ Right-click the selection and choose Delete. |

| QUICK REFERENCE | INSERTING AND DELETING ROWS, COLUMNS, AND CELLS (continued) |
|---|---|
| **Task** | **Procedure** |
| Delete columns | ■ Select the columns you wish to delete.<br>■ Right-click the selection and choose Delete. |
| Insert cells | ■ Select the cells in the worksheet where you want the inserted cells to appear.<br>■ Choose Home→Cells→Insert from the Ribbon, or right-click the selection and choose Insert from the context menu.<br>■ Choose the desired Shift Cells option. |
| Delete cells | ■ Select the cells you wish to delete.<br>■ Choose Home→Cells→Delete from the Ribbon, or right-click the selection and choose Delete from the context menu.<br>■ Choose the desired Shift Cells option. |

DEVELOP YOUR SKILLS 5.3.1

# Add and Remove Rows, Columns, and Cells

*In this exercise, you will insert and delete rows, as well as insert cells into the worksheet.*

## Delete Unnecessary Rows

1. Select **rows 15** and **24**, using the Ctrl key to select **nonadjacent** rows.
   *The rows in which there are no objectives listed are now selected.*
2. With both rows still selected, **right-click** row 24 and choose **Delete** from the context menu.
   *The data below a deleted row moves up one row.*

## Add Another Row to the Sheet

3. Select **row 6**.
   *When you choose to insert a row, the new row will be placed above the row you have selected.*
4. **Point** (don't click) over the **Home→Cells→Insert** button on the Ribbon as shown.

   *Notice that when you place the mouse pointer over the Insert button, there is a line that divides it into two halves. If you click above or to the left of the line (depending on how large the Ribbon appears on your computer), a new cell, row, or column will be inserted above or to the left of your selection. If you click below or to the right of the line, a menu appears from which you can select a command.*
5. Click the **Insert** button (not the menu ▾ button).
6. **Enter** the text in the following illustration into the appropriate cells.

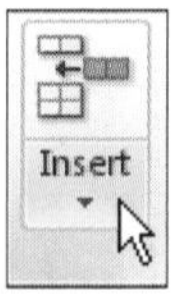

| | A | B | C | D | E | F |
|---|---|---|---|---|---|---|
| 6 | b. | Identify hazardous materials. | | 2 | 2 | 1 |

7. Follow these steps to copy the necessary formulas:

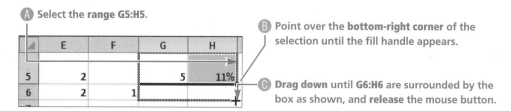

Ⓐ Select the **range G5:H5**.

Ⓑ Point over the **bottom-right corner** of the selection until the fill handle appears.

Ⓒ **Drag down** until **G6:H6** are surrounded by the box as shown, and **release** the mouse button.

*All of the formulas and functions have automatically been updated to include the correct cell addresses because cell references were used in creating the worksheet formulas. The percentages in column H recalculated to include the new values, and cell H5 now displays 10%.*

### Insert a Row Outside a Formula Range

8. Select **cell C24** and view its formula in the Formula Bar, and then select **cell C25** and view its formula.
   *The C24 formula is =SUM(C4:C23), and the C25 formula is =C24/$G$24. The related worksheet formulas have automatically been updated as a result of the previous steps. The formulas include the correct cell addresses because the deleted and inserted rows were within the original ranges of the formulas.*

9. Insert a **new row** at **row 4**.

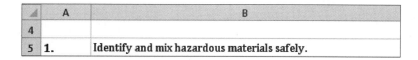

10. Select **cell C25** and view its formula in the Formula Bar.
    *The formula adjusted to =SUM(C5:C24) because the data moved down one row. However, the formula did not update to include cell C4 from the newly created row. That row is above the first cell of the original range in the formula. You would need to edit formulas if you wanted to include row 4.*

11. **Undo** the inserted row 4.

### Insert Cells into the Worksheet

*You have discovered that you want to merge and center the contents of cell A1 over the entire worksheet. You will need to "bump" everything in columns C through H down one row.*

12. Select the **range C1:H1**.

13. Follow these steps to insert the cells and shift your existing data down:

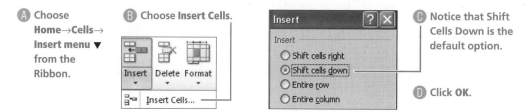

Ⓐ Choose **Home→Cells→ Insert menu ▼** from the Ribbon.

Ⓑ Choose **Insert Cells**.

Ⓒ Notice that Shift Cells Down is the default option.

Ⓓ Click **OK**.

14. Select the **range A3:B3**.

15. Choose **Home→Cells→Insert** 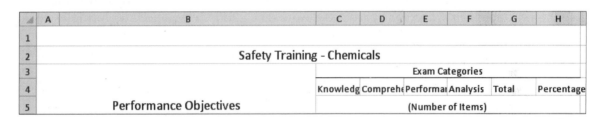 from the Ribbon.
*Everything in columns A and B, below cells A3 and B3, is shifted down one cell.*

16. Select **row 1** and choose **Home→Cells→Insert** from the Ribbon again.
*Because you selected an entire row first, a new row is inserted.*

## Time to Format!

*Now that you have changed the structure of the worksheet a bit, you will do some formatting to make it more presentable.*

17. Follow these steps to merge and center a range:
    - Select the **range A1:H1**.
    - Choose **Home→Alignment→Merge & Center** from the Ribbon.
    - While the merged range is still selected, change the font size to **16**.

    *There is nothing in this cell at this time, but you will add a text title later.*

18. **Merge & Center** the **range A2:H2** and change the font size to **14**.

19. **Merge & Center** the **range A3:B5** and change the font size to **14**.
    *Notice that the Merge & Center command works to merge both columns and rows at once.*

20. **Merge & Center** the **range C3:H3** and place a **border** along the bottom of the cells.

21. **Merge & Center** the **range C5:H5**.

22. **Right-align** the **range B26:B27**.
    *Once you are done formatting, your worksheet should resemble the following figure.*

| A | B | C | D | E | F | G | H |
|---|---|---|---|---|---|---|---|
| 1 | | | | | | | |
| 2 | | Safety Training - Chemicals | | | | | |
| 3 | | | | Exam Categories | | | |
| 4 | | Knowledg | Compreh | Performa | Analysis | Total | Percentage |
| 5 | Performance Objectives | | | (Number of Items) | | | |

23. Use Ctrl + S to **save** the changes to the workbook.

# 5.4 Formatting and Hiding Columns and Rows

**Video Lesson** labyrinthelab.com/videos

You can format, hide, and unhide columns and rows by first selecting the desired columns or rows. You can make your selection in several ways: clicking a single column or row heading, dragging to select adjacent headings, or holding the Ctrl key while you click each nonadjacent heading.

## Formatting All Cells in a Column or Row Simultaneously

Once you have selected the desired row or column, you apply any formatting just as you would to a single cell or range. The formatting is applied to every cell across the row or down the column to the end of the worksheet. The advantage to formatting entire rows or columns is that the formatting already is applied consistently to every cell when you enter data. Some settings, such as column width or row height, automatically apply to every cell in the column or row.

## Hiding Columns and Rows

There may be times when you wish to hide certain rows or columns from view. The hidden rows and columns will not be visible, nor will they print. However, the hidden rows and columns will still be part of the worksheet, and their values and formulas could still be referenced by other formulas in the visible rows and columns. Hiding rows and columns can be useful when you want to focus attention on other parts of the worksheet.

| A | B | C | D | E | G | H |
|---|---|---|---|---|---|---|
| 2 | Safety Training - Chemicals | | | | | |

Notice that column F and row 1 are not visible once the Hide command is issued.

## Unhiding Columns and Rows

After rows or columns have been hidden, you must issue an Unhide command to make them visible once again. Before the command to unhide rows is issued, you must select at least one row above and one row below the hidden ones. Likewise, you must select at least one column to the left and one to the right of the hidden ones before issuing the Unhide command. If you have hidden column A or row 1, you will need to drag to select from row 2 up to the column headings or from column B left through the row headings.

| Task | Procedure |
|---|---|
| Hide columns or rows | ■ Select the column(s) or row(s) you wish to hide.<br>■ Choose Home→Cells→Format→Hide & Unhide→Hide Columns or Hide Rows from the Ribbon, or right-click the column heading and choose Hide from the context menu. |
| Unhide columns or rows | ■ Select the columns to the left and right or the rows above and below the column(s) or row(s) you wish to unhide.<br>■ Choose Home→Cells→Format→Hide & Unhide→Unhide Columns or Unhide Rows from the Ribbon, or right-click the column heading and choose Unhide from the context menu. |

### DEVELOP YOUR SKILLS 5.4.1

## Hide, Unhide, and Format Columns and Rows

*In this exercise, you will hide and unhide rows and columns. You also will format all cells in a column simultaneously.*

### Hide Multiple Columns and a Row

*You will hide the number of questions in individual categories so that only the total and percentage columns display. You will also hide row 1 because you have yet to enter anything in it.*

1. Follow these steps to hide columns C through F:

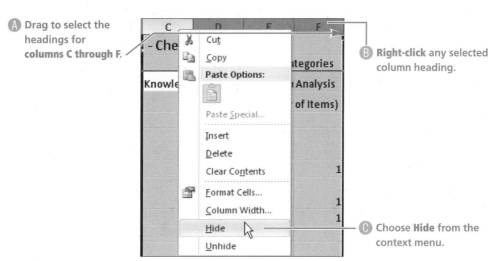

A Drag to select the headings for **columns C through F.**

B **Right-click** any selected column heading.

C Choose **Hide** from the context menu.

*Columns C through F are no longer visible. They are still a part of the worksheet and can be revealed again with a simple Unhide command.*

2. **Right-click** the row 1 heading, and then choose **Hide** from the context menu.

## Unhide the Hidden Columns and Row

3. Follow these steps to unhide columns C through F:

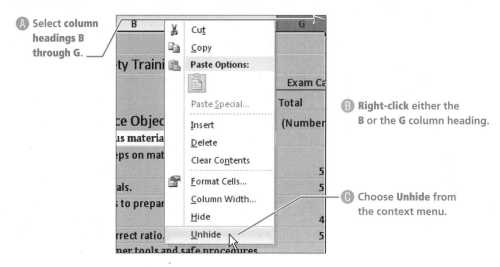

**A** Select **column headings B through G**.

**B** **Right-click** either the **B** or the **G** column heading.

**C** Choose **Unhide** from the context menu.

*Remember that to unhide a column you must first select the columns to the left and right of the hidden column (or the rows above and below a hidden row).*

4. Follow these steps to unhide row 1:

**A** Select from **row heading 2** up to the **Select All** button.

**B** **Right-click** over row heading 2.

**C** Choose **Unhide** from the context menu.

*Row 1 is visible once again.*

## Apply Percent Style to All Cells in a Column

5. Click the **column heading** for **column H**.
   *Notice that the Number Format box in the Number group of the Home tab indicates that the column currently is in General number format, except for cells that have been formatted manually in rows 7–27.*

6. Choose **Home→Number→Percent Style** % from the Ribbon.
   *The Number Format box in the Number group of the Home tab now displays Percentage. All numbers in the column are formatted as percentages, but text entries are unaffected.*

7. Enter **50** in cell H29 to verify that the percentage format is applied.

8. **Undo** the entry.

9. **Save** the changes to the workbook.

## 5.5 Changing Vertical Alignment and Rotating Text

Video Lesson    labyrinthelab.com/videos

You have already learned many techniques for arranging data. Now you will be expanding on that knowledge and learning how to change the vertical alignment and rotate the contents of cells.

### Setting Vertical Alignment

Vertical alignment positions the cell contents between the top and bottom of the cell. Vertical alignment options include top, bottom, center, and justify. The default alignment is bottom. The Justify option is useful with multiple-line entries. For example, the Justify option evenly distributes unused space between lines in a multiple-line entry so text fills the cell from the top edge to the bottom edge. Vertical alignment is set by choosing the Top Align, Middle Align, and Bottom Align buttons in the Alignment group on the Home tab of the Ribbon. You can also choose those options and Justify via the Alignment dialog box launcher button in the Ribbon.

### Rotating Text

The Orientation option on the Ribbon has several rotation options that you can apply to text in a cell. When column headings are extra wide, making the worksheet spread out too far horizontally, you might consider rotating the text to save room. The decision to rotate text to improve a worksheet's appearance must be balanced with how easily the text may be read. Text can be rotated more precisely from 0 to 90 degrees using the Orientation option on the Alignment tab in the Format Cells dialog box. Excel increases the row height to accommodate the rotated text.

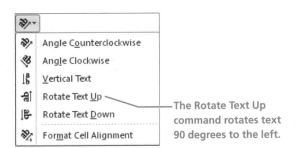

The Rotate Text Up command rotates text 90 degrees to the left.

Orienting the column headings allows the column widths to be narrower.

| Task | Procedure |
|------|-----------|
| Set cell content to align vertically with the top, middle, or bottom of a cell | ■ Select the cell(s) in which you wish to change the vertical alignment.<br>■ Choose Home→Alignment→Top Align, Middle Align, or Bottom Align from the Ribbon. |
| Set cell content to justify vertically within a cell | ■ Select the cell(s) in which you wish to change the vertical alignment.<br>■ Choose Home→Alignment dialog box launcher 🔲 from the Ribbon.<br>■ Click the Vertical drop-down arrow under Text Alignment and choose Justify from the list. |
| Rotate text within a cell using a preset option | ■ Select the cell(s) in which you wish to rotate text.<br>■ Choose Home→Alignment→Orientation 📐▾ from the Ribbon and select the desired preset from the list. |
| Rotate text within a cell using a precise number of degrees | ■ Select the cell(s) in which you wish to rotate text.<br>■ Choose Home→Alignment dialog box launcher 🔲 from the Ribbon.<br>■ Choose the desired text rotation in the Orientation section of the Alignment tab in the Format Cells dialog box. |

**DEVELOP YOUR SKILLS 5.5.1**

# Rotate Text and Change Its Vertical Alignment

*In this exercise, you will rotate the categories at the top of the worksheet as well as change the vertical alignment in cells.*

## Rotate Text

1. Select the **range C4:H4**.

2. Choose **Home→Alignment→Orientation** 📐▾→**Rotate Text Up** from the Ribbon.

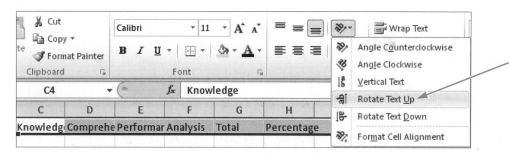

*The headings are rotated in their cells. Normally, the row height would increase automatically to AutoFit the headings. The merged text in row 3 prevented that from happening in this case.*

3. Point at the bottom of the **row 4 header** until the double-arrow pointer displays and then **double-click**. *The row height increases so that all rotated text is visible. If you have difficulty positioning the mouse pointer precisely, you may select row 4 and then choose Home→Cells→Format→AutoFit Row Height from the Ribbon.*

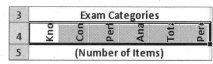

4. Follow these steps to AutoFit columns C through H:

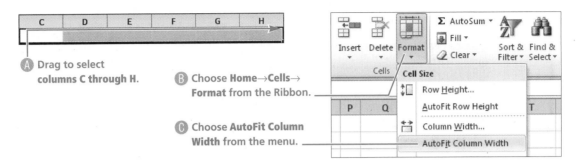

Ⓐ Drag to select
columns C through H.

Ⓑ Choose **Home→Cells→**
**Format** from the Ribbon.

Ⓒ Choose **AutoFit Column**
**Width** from the menu.

## Change Vertical Alignment

5. Select **cell A3**.
   *Remember, this is a vertically and horizontally merged cell so it is quite large.*

6. Choose **Home→Alignment→Middle Align** ≡ from the top row of the Ribbon.

7. Select the **range A6:H25**.

8. Choose **Home→Alignment→Top Align** ≡ from the Ribbon.
   *The text in the performance objective rows now aligns at the top of cells, which makes it easier to read across the rows. You have decided that the alphabet letters in column A should be aligned at the right of their cells.*

9. Select the **range A7:A10**.

10. Choose **Home→Alignment→Align Text Right** ≡ from the Ribbon.

11. Use **Format Painter** to copy the formatting from **cell A10** to the other alphabet letters in **ranges A12:A14, A16:A17, A19:A22,** and **A24:A25**.
    *Rows 3 through 7 of your worksheet should resemble the following illustration.*

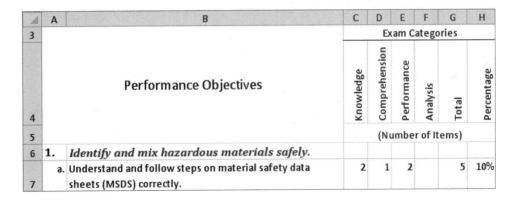

12. **Save** 🔲 the changes to the workbook.

## 5.6 Using Excel's Find and Replace Commands

**Video Lesson** labyrinthelab.com/videos

Excel's Find command performs searches on a worksheet or an entire workbook. It can search for a particular word, number, cell reference, formula, or format. Find is often the quickest way to locate an item in a workbook. The Replace feature helps you to find an item and replace it with a specified item.

Excel searches for text without regard to case. For example, a search for *green* will find all occurrences of *green* and *Green*. Unlike Microsoft Word in the Office Suite, Excel replaces text only with the exact case you type. Replacing *Green* with *blue* does not capitalize the "b" to match case in the original word. This is one reason you will want to use the Replace All command with care.

### Replacing Cell Formats

**FROM THE KEYBOARD**

Ctrl+F to find
Ctrl+H to replace

Excel lets you find and replace not just text but also cell formats. For example, you may want to search all worksheets and workbooks for cells formatted with Currency style with no decimals and replace that format with Currency style with two decimals. Finding and replacing cell formats can be a big time-saver, especially with large worksheets and multiple-sheet workbooks.

**TIP** Find and replace options remain set after the Find and Replace dialog box is closed unless you have cleared the options. If Excel does not find the text you want, check that you have removed any undesired formatting options.

You can limit the Find and Replace command to specific areas of a workbook.

You can find and replace items with specific cell formats.

Always use the Replace All button with care.

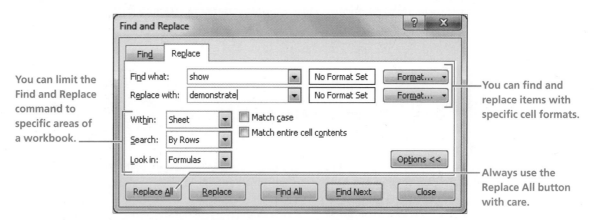

| Task | Procedure |
|------|-----------|
| Find text or formatting | ■ Choose Home→Editing→Find & Select →Find from the Ribbon.<br>■ Type in the text you wish to find, or choose the appropriate formatting.<br>■ Choose either to find the next instance of the text or formatting by clicking Find Next or to find all instances by clicking Find All.<br>■ Click Close when you are through with the Find feature |
| Find and replace text or formatting | ■ Choose Home→Editing→Find & Select →Replace from the Ribbon.<br>■ Type in or choose the formatting that you wish to find and have replaced.<br>■ Type in the text or choose the formatting that will replace the indicated text or formatting.<br>■ Click Close when you are through with the Replace feature. |
| Clear all find and replace options | ■ Delete the Find What and Replace With entries in the Find and Replace dialog box.<br>■ Click the drop-down arrow on the top Format button, and choose Clear Find Format.<br>■ Click the drop-down arrow on the bottom Format button, and choose Clear Replace Format. |

## DEVELOP YOUR SKILLS 5.6.1

# Find and Replace Entries

*In this exercise, you will find and replace text as well as formatting.*

## Find and Replace Text

1. Choose **Home→Editing→Find & Select** →**Replace** from the Ribbon.
   *The Find and Replace dialog box opens.*

2. Follow these steps to prepare to replace all instances of *Show* with *Demonstrate*.

Ⓐ Type **Show** in the Find What field.

Ⓑ Tap Tab, and then type **Demonstrate** in the Replace With field.

Ⓒ Click **Find Next** to see the next place that *Show* appears in your worksheet.

Ⓓ Click **Replace** to replace just this one instance of *Show*.

Ⓔ Click **Replace All** to replace every remaining instance of *Show* in the worksheet.

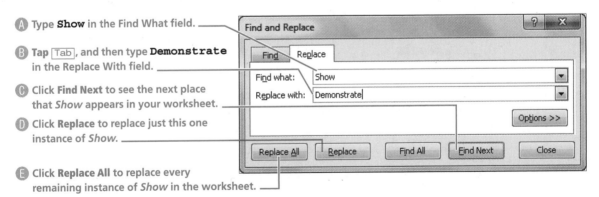

3. Click **OK** to acknowledge the total number of replacements.

*After replacing all, Excel will let you know the total number of replacements. Leave the Find and Replace dialog box open for the next step.*

## Find and Replace Formatting

4. Click the **Options** button in the Find and Replace dialog box.
   *Excel expands the dialog box to display additional Find and Replace settings.*

5. Follow these steps to set the formatting to be found:

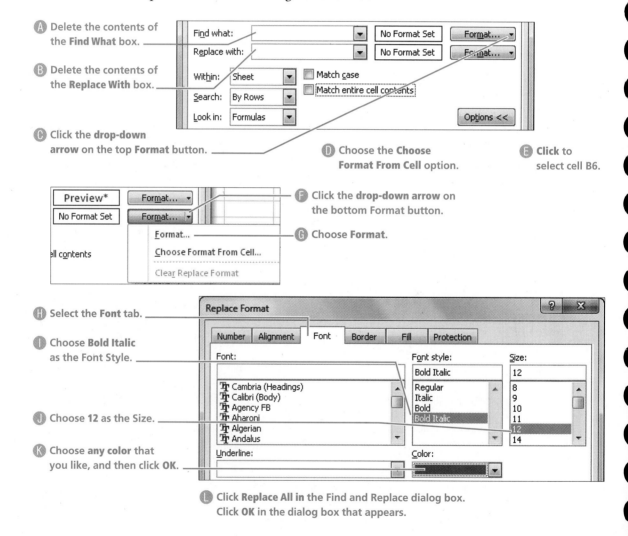

Ⓐ Delete the contents of the **Find What** box.

Ⓑ Delete the contents of the **Replace With** box.

Ⓒ Click the **drop-down arrow** on the top Format button.

Ⓓ Choose the **Choose Format From Cell** option.

Ⓔ **Click** to select cell B6.

Ⓕ Click the **drop-down arrow** on the bottom Format button.

Ⓖ Choose **Format**.

Ⓗ Select the **Font** tab.

Ⓘ Choose **Bold Italic** as the Font Style.

Ⓙ Choose **12** as the Size.

Ⓚ Choose **any color** that you like, and then click **OK**.

Ⓛ Click **Replace All** in the Find and Replace dialog box. Click **OK** in the dialog box that appears.

*All instances of formatting that are the same as that in cell B6 are replaced with the new formatting that you have chosen.*

## Clear Find and Replace Criteria

*The find and replace criteria remain set even after the dialog box is closed. You must clear the criteria from the dialog box before performing another find or replace operation. (Exiting Excel also clears the dialog box.)*

6. Click the **drop-down arrow** on the top Format button and choose **Clear Find Format**.

7. Click the **drop-down arrow** on the bottom Format button and choose **Clear Replace Format**.

8. Click **Close** to exit the Find and Replace dialog box.

9. **Save** 💾 the changes to the workbook.

## 5.7 Using AutoCorrect

Video Lesson  labyrinthelab.com/videos

Excel's AutoCorrect feature can improve the speed and accuracy of entering text. AutoCorrect is most useful for replacing abbreviations with a full phrase of up to 255 characters. For example, you could set up AutoCorrect to substitute *United States Government* whenever you type *usg*. AutoCorrect also automatically corrects common misspellings and typographical errors. For example, the word *the* is often misspelled as *teh*, and the word *and* is often misspelled as *adn*. These and other common spelling mistakes are fixed automatically. Auto-Correct also automatically capitalizes the first letter of a day if you type it in lowercase. For example, if you type *sunday* and complete the entry, AutoCorrect will enter *Sunday* in the cell. Finally, AutoCorrect fixes words that have two initial capital letters by switching the second letter to lowercase.

The AutoCorrect dialog box allows you to customize how the AutoCorrect feature will work for you.

 AutoCorrect entries are shared by all programs in the Microsoft Office Suite, so if you've already added some in Word, they are available for you to use in Excel as well.

# Expanding AutoCorrect Entries

AutoCorrect goes into action when you type a word in a text entry and tap Spacebar or when you complete a text entry. The word or entry is compared with all entries in the AutoCorrect table. The AutoCorrect table contains a list of words and their replacement phrases. If the word you type matches an entry in the AutoCorrect table, a phrase from the table is substituted for the word. This is known as expanding the AutoCorrect entry.

# Undoing AutoCorrect Entries

There may be times that AutoCorrect replaces an entry against your wishes. AutoCorrect is treated as a single "character," meaning that it is viewed by the Undo feature the same as if you typed an "a" or tapped Delete. Therefore, you can use Undo to reverse an AutoCorrect entry.

# Creating and Editing AutoCorrect Entries

The AutoCorrect dialog box allows you to add entries to the AutoCorrect table, delete entries from the table, and set other AutoCorrect options. To add an entry, type the desired abbreviation in the Replace box and the desired expansion for the abbreviation in the With box.

 If you create the abbreviation using uppercase letters, it will not work if you type it in lower-case letters later. Type all abbreviations in lowercase so you don't have to remember to type them in upper- or lowercase in the worksheet.

| QUICK REFERENCE | USING AUTOCORRECT |
|---|---|
| **Task** | **Procedure** |
| Modify AutoCorrect options | ■ Choose File→Options 🔲. |
| | ■ Click the Proofing option from the left-side menu. |
| | ■ Click AutoCorrect Options. |
| | ■ Make any desired changes to the AutoCorrect feature. |
| | ■ Click OK. |
| | ■ Click OK to close the Excel Options window. |

## DEVELOP YOUR SKILLS 5.7.1
# Use AutoCorrect

*In this exercise, you will train AutoCorrect to replace an abbreviation with a phrase and learn how to override AutoCorrect.*

**Observe How AutoCorrect Works**

1. Select **cell A1**.

2. Type **teh cat adn dog ran fast**, and then **tap** Enter.
   *Notice that both of the spelling errors have been corrected by AutoCorrect.*

## Override an AutoCorrect Command

3. Click **cell A1**, type **adn** and **tap** Spacebar.
*AutoCorrect has corrected the misspelling.*

4. Use Ctrl + Z to **undo** the last command.
*Undo will reverse the last command, in this case AutoCorrect.*

5. **Tap** Esc to cancel the entry.

## Create an AutoCorrect Entry

6. Choose **File→Options** 📄.

7. Follow these steps to display the AutoCorrect dialog box:

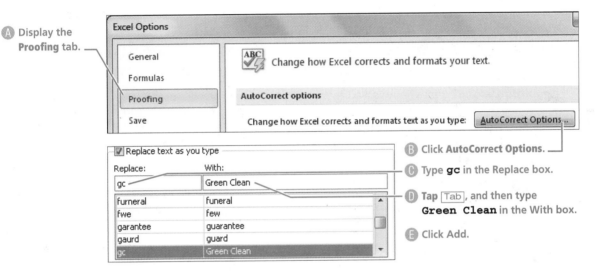

Ⓐ Display the **Proofing** tab.

Ⓑ Click **AutoCorrect Options.**

Ⓒ Type **gc** in the Replace box.

Ⓓ **Tap** Tab, and then type **Green Clean** in the With box.

Ⓔ Click Add.

*Your entry will be added to the list.*

8. Click **OK** in the AutoCorrect dialog box.

9. Click **OK** in the Excel Options dialog box.

## Use an AutoCorrect Entry

10. Ensure that **cell A1** is still selected, type **gc** and **tap** Enter.
*The AutoCorrect entry that you created is entered into the cell.*

## Delete an AutoCorrect Entry

*It is important for you to delete the AutoCorrect entry you just created. Otherwise it will still be there when the next student uses the computer.*

11. Choose **File→Options**, and display the **Proofing** tab.

12. Click **AutoCorrect Options**.

13. Follow these steps to delete the AutoCorrect entry you have created:

A Type **gc** in the Replace box.

B Click **Delete**, and then tap Enter.

C Click **OK**.

14. **Save** 💾 the changes and **close** the workbook.

# 5.8 Concepts Review

**Concepts Review**  labyrinthelab.com/excel10

*To check your knowledge of the key concepts introduced in this lesson, complete the Concepts Review quiz by going to the URL listed above. If your classroom is using Labyrinth eLab, you may complete the Concepts Review quiz from within your eLab course.*

# Reinforce Your Skills

## Manage Worksheets

*In this exercise, you will start with a new, blank workbook. You will organize the workbook by renaming, inserting, deleting, rearranging, and copying its worksheets.*

### Rename Sheet Tabs

1. Use Ctrl + N to start a **new**, blank workbook if one is not already displayed.

2. **Double-click** the Sheet1 tab, type **April**, and **tap** Enter.

3. **Rename** the Sheet3 tab to **March**.

### Delete a Sheet

4. **Right-click** the Sheet2 tab and select **Delete** from the context menu.

### Insert and Move Sheets

5. Choose **Home→Cells→Insert menu ▾→Insert Sheet** from the Ribbon.
   *The new sheet is added before the currently active sheet.*

6. **Rename** the new sheet to **February**.

7. Click the **Insert Sheet** button at the right of the sheet tabs.
   *The new sheet is added as the last sheet.*

8. **Rename** the new sheet to **January**.

9. **Drag and drop** the sheet tabs to arrange them in month sequence from January through April.

### Copy a Sheet

10. **Hold down** the Ctrl key and **drag** the April sheet tab to the right.
    *A new April (2) sheet tab should display when you release the mouse and Ctrl.*

11. **Rename** the April (2) sheet tab to **May**.

12. **Copy** the May sheet to create a **June** sheet.

13. **Save** 🖫 as **rs-Tabs** in the Lesson 05 folder and **close** the workbook.

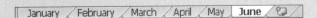

# Insert and Delete Rows

*In this exercise, you will modify a sales invoice worksheet by removing and inserting line items.*

1. **Open** the rs-Sales Invoice workbook from the Lesson 05 folder in your file storage location.

## Create Formulas

2. Select **cell D7**, and **enter** a formula that calculates the Extension as the Quantity multiplied by the Unit Price.
   *The result should be 122.5.*

3. **Copy** the Extension formula down through **rows 8–11**.

4. Use **AutoSum** to compute the subtotal for the extension in **column D**.

5. Calculate the **Sales Tax** as the Subtotal multiplied by 7.75%.

6. Calculate the **Total** as the Subtotal plus the Sales Tax.

7. Select all of the numbers in **columns C–D** and change the number format to **Comma Style** with **two decimals**.

8. Apply **Accounting Number Format** to **cell D14** so the total contains a dollar sign ($).

## Delete a Row and Insert New Rows

*The customer has decided to cancel one product from the order and add two other products.*

9. Select **row 9** by clicking the row heading.

10. Choose **Home→Cells→Delete** 🗐 (taking care not to click the menu ▾ button) from the Ribbon.
    *Notice that if you select the entire row, you can simply click the Delete command without having to choose the menu button and the Delete Sheet Rows command. The Subtotal, Sales Tax, and Total automatically recalculated to omit the deleted row.*

11. **Drag** to select the **row headings** for **rows 10** and **11**.

12. Choose **Home→Cells→Insert** 🗐 from the Ribbon.
    *Notice that the first blank record was inserted at row 10 and the prior contents of row 10 shifted down two rows.*

13. Add the following two items:

| ▲ | A | B | C |
|---|---|---|---|
| 10 | GBS All Purpose Carpet | 3 | 11.95 |
| 11 | Handy Trash Liners | 24 | 2.85 |

14. Use the **fill handle** to copy the formula in **cell D9** to **cells D10** and **D11**.

15. Select **cell D13** and notice that the **SUM** function has been updated automatically to include the values in cells D10 and D11 that were added when you inserted the rows.
    *Excel adjusted the formula reference because the rows inserted were within the range referenced in the formula.*

## Enter the Current Date

16. Use the **TODAY** function to insert the current date in **A3**.

17. Format the date with the **date format** of your choice.

18. Insert a **blank row** between the date and the customer name.
    *Your workbook should resemble the following illustration.*

| ◢ | A | B | C | D |
|---|---|---|---|---|
| 1 | **Green Clean** | | | |
| 2 | *Sales Invoice* | | | |
| 3 | October 22, 2010 | | | |
| 4 | | | | |
| 5 | *Customer:* | **Heartwell Laboratories** | | |
| 6 | | | | |
| 7 | **Item** | **Quantity** | **Unit Price** | **Extension** |
| 8 | EarthWise Carpet Clea | 7 | 17.50 | 122.50 |
| 9 | EarthWise Carpet Clea | 16 | 9.85 | 157.60 |
| 10 | EarthWise Carpet Stair | 10 | 5.50 | 55.00 |
| 11 | GBS All Purpose Carpe | 3 | 11.95 | 35.85 |
| 12 | Handy Trash Liners | 24 | 2.85 | 68.40 |
| 13 | Carpet Bright Stain Elir | 6 | 7.35 | 44.10 |
| 14 | **Subtotal** | | | 483.45 |
| 15 | Sales Tax | | | 37.47 |
| 16 | **Total** | | | **$ 520.92** |
| 17 | | | | |
| 18 | *Thank you for your business!* | | | |

19. **Save** 💾 the changes to the workbook and continue to the next exercise.

### REINFORCE YOUR SKILLS 5.3

# Adjust Column and Row Properties

*In this exercise, you will insert and format a column, adjust column widths, and hide a row.*

*Before You Begin: You must have completed Reinforce Your Skills 5.2. The rs-Sales Invoice workbook should be open.*

### Insert and Format a Column

1. Select **column A** by clicking the column heading.

2. Choose **Home→Cells→Insert** ⊞ from the Ribbon.
   *To accommodate the new column A, the previous column headings increased by one letter. The titles that were in the range A1:A3 now are in the range B1:B3.*

3. While **column A** is still selected, **center-align** all the cells in the column.
   *All entries that you type in the next step will be center aligned.*

4. **Enter** the following data in **column A**, as shown at right.

| ◢ | A |
|---|---|
| 7 | **Item No.** |
| 8 | 14335 |
| 9 | 14043 |
| 10 | 29322 |
| 11 | 29566 |
| 12 | 35800 |
| 13 | 38720 |

### Change Column Widths

5. **Point** at the border to the right of the **column B heading** until the pointer displays a two-headed arrow and **double-click**.
   *You just AutoFit the column width, and all text in column B should be visible.*

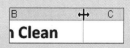

6. **Center-align** the titles and date in the **range B1:B3**.

7. Select **columns C through E**.

8. Point at the border between the **column D** and E **headings** and **double-click**.
   *The columns are sized to fit the widest entry. The customer name in Column C is a long entry that made the column too wide, so you will adjust the column width manually.*

9. **Point** at the border to the right of the **column C heading** and drag until the ScreenTip indicates that the width is approximately 10.00.

### Hide a Row

10. Select **row 5**.

11. Choose **Home→Cells→Format** ▦ **→Hide & Unhide→Hide Rows** from the Ribbon.
    *The company name in row 5 is now hidden from view.*

12. **Save** 🖫 the changes and **close** the workbook.

---

### REINFORCE YOUR SKILLS 5.4

# Use Find and Replace

*In this exercise, you will experiment with finding and replacing contents and formats.*

### Find and Replace Contents

1. **Open** the rs-Quarterly Sales workbook from the Lesson 05 folder.
   *You wish to change Region to Area in headings but not in region numbers, such as Region 1.*

2. Choose **Home→Editing→Find & Select** 🔍 **→Replace** from the Ribbon.

3. Enter `region` in the Find What box and `Area` in the Replace With box.
   *You do not have to use a capital "R" in the Find What box. If you want the replacement text to be capitalized, though, you must type it that way in the Replace With box.*

4. Click **Find Next**.
   *Using the Replace All command would not give the correct result because you want to leave the Region 1, Region 2, and Region 3 entries as is. If the dialog box covers the worksheet data, you may drag the title bar at the top of the dialog box to move it out of the way.*

5. Replace only the entries in **cells B4** and **E4**; leave the dialog box **open**.

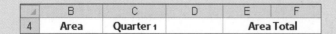

| | B | C | D | E | F |
|---|---|---|---|---|---|
| 4 | Area | Quarter 1 | | Area Total | |

*If you replaced an entry that you did not want to change, you can click Undo in the Quick Access toolbar without closing the Find and Replace dialog box.*

6. Enter `region 1` in the Find What box and `East` in the Replace With box.

7. Click the **Find All** button, and then **click** each of the occurrences at the bottom of the dialog box to review the contents of each cell.

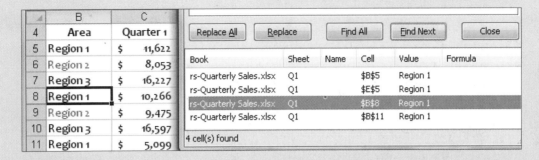

*The Find All command reports that four occurrences were found. You may enlarge the dialog box by dragging its bottom border down. After reviewing the possible replacements, you decide that using Replace All is acceptable.*

8. Click **Replace All**. Then, click **OK** to acknowledge the number of replacements made.

9. Make the following additional replacements:
   - Replace *Region 2* with **Central**.
   - Replace *Region 3* with **West**.

10. **Close** the **Find and Replace** dialog box, and review the replacements.

## Find and Replace Formats

11. Use Ctrl + H to display the **Find and Replace** dialog box.

12. **Delete** the entries in the **Find What** and **Replace With** boxes.

13. Click the **Options** button to expand the dialog box, if necessary.

14. Click the **drop-down arrow** on the Format button in the Find What row, and then click the **Choose Format From Cell** command on the menu.

15. Select **cell B6**.

16. Click the **Format** button for the Replace With box (not the drop-down button) to display the **Replace Format** dialog box.

17. Display the **Font** tab, choose to make the Font style **Regular** and the color **black**, if not already selected, and then click **OK**.

18. Choose to **Replace All**.

19. Click **OK** to acknowledge the number of replacements made.

## Clear All Find and Replace Settings

20. Use the **Format** menus to clear all find and replace settings.
    *The two preview boxes should display No Format Set when you are finished.*

21. **Close** the Find and Replace dialog box.

22. **Save** the changes to the workbook and continue to the next exercise.

# Use AutoCorrect

*In this exercise, you will edit a worksheet by creating, using, and deleting AutoCorrect entries.*

*Before You Begin: You must have completed Reinforce Your Skills 5.4. The rs-Quarterly Sales workbook should be open.*

## Create AutoCorrect Entries

1. Choose **File→Options** ▣.

2. Click the **Proofing** option along the left-side menu, and then click **AutoCorrect Options**.

3. In the Replace box, type **aw** and **tap** Tab.
   *Remember to type the abbreviation in lowercase.*

4. In the With box, type **Amy Wyatt**.

5. Click the **Add** button.
   *Do not click the OK button right now as you are going to create a few more AutoCorrect entries.*

6. **Create** the following entries. Click **OK** when you are finished.

   | | |
   |---|---|
   | lm | Leisa Malimali |
   | bs | Brian Simpson |

7. Click **OK** to close the Excel Options window.

## Use AutoCorrect Entries

8. Select **cell A5**.

9. Type **aw** and **tap** Spacebar.
   *The sales rep's name appears in the cell.*

10. Select **cell A8**.

11. Type **bs** and **tap** Tab.

12. Using **AutoCorrect**, enter Leisa Malimali's name in **cell A11**.

13. Using the method of your choice, either AutoCorrect or the fill handle, **enter** the same sales rep's name in the two blank cells below each name.

14. AutoFit **column A** so the names are visible.

| | Sales Rep | Area |
|---|---|---|
| 4 | **Sales Rep** | **Area** |
| 5 | Amy Wyatt | East |
| 6 | Amy Wyatt | Central |
| 7 | Amy Wyatt | West |
| 8 | Brian Simpson | East |
| 9 | Brian Simpson | Central |
| 10 | Brian Simpson | West |
| 11 | Leisa Malimali | East |
| 12 | Leisa Malimali | Central |
| 13 | Leisa Malimali | West |

## Delete AutoCorrect Entries

*Remember that the AutoCorrect entries that you create can be used in all Office applications. You may find that you do not want a name to appear each time you type its shortcut. You will now delete the AutoCorrect entries that were created.*

15. Choose **File→Options**.

16. Click the **Proofing** option along the left-side menu, and then click **AutoCorrect Options**.

17. In the **Replace** box, type **aw**.
    *The AutoCorrect entry appears in the With box next to its abbreviation in the Replace box.*

18. Click the **Delete** button under the AutoCorrect entry list.

19. **Delete** the AutoCorrect entries for *lm* and *bs*.
    *In order to have the correct "With" entry appear, you will need to remove the previous name from the With box before typing the next shortcut entry in the Replace box.*

20. When you have finished deleting all three entries, click **OK**.

21. Click **OK** to close the Excel Options window.

22. **Save** 🖫 the changes and **close** the workbook.

# Apply Your Skills

## Restructure an Accounts Receivable Report

*In this exercise, you will insert and move columns and rows, create a formula, and apply a theme to the report.*

1. **Open** the as-Accounts Receivable workbook from the Lesson 05 folder in your file storage location.

2. Use the **DATE** function to insert the the date **October 14, 2014** in **cell E4**.

3. **Delete** the empty cells in **row 8**.

4. Insert **two columns** between columns A and B. Enter the **customer numbers** and **invoice numbers** shown in the illustration at the end of the exercise. Also, enter the headings in the **range B6:C6**, and **wrap** the text within the cells. Align the data as shown in the illustration.

5. Format the entries in column D in **Currency Style** with **no decimals**.

6. Enter a formula in **cell F7** that calculates the number of days since the invoice was issued (date in row 4 minus the invoice date). Make certain to use **absolute** and **relative** cell references correctly in the formula. Use **AutoFill** to extend the formula.

7. Use formulas in **column F** to calculate the number of days the invoices are past due. Assume the terms are **net 30 days**. Your formulas should subtract 30 from the number of days since the invoice was issued.

8. Apply a **border** to the left of each column in **columns B through G**.

9. Apply the **theme** of your choice to change the formatting of the workbook.

10. **AutoFit** all data columns.

11. Increase the row height of **rows 7 through 12** to add some extra space among the entries.

12. **Rename** the sheet tab as **Aging Report** and **delete** the unused sheet tabs.
    *Your completed worksheet should look similar to the following illustration. However, the formatting may be different based on the theme you chose.*

| ▲ | A | B | C | D | E | F | G |
|---|---|---|---|---|---|---|---|
| 1 | | | Green Clean | | | | |
| 2 | | | Accounts Receivable Aging Report | | | | |
| 3 | | | | | | | |
| 4 | | | | | | Report Date: | 10/8/2014 |
| 5 | | | | | | | |
| 6 | Customer Name | Customer Number | Invoice Number | Invoice Amount | Invoice Date | Days After Invoice Date | Days Past Due |
| 7 | Castro Screenprinting | R202 | 189 | $234 | 8/1/2014 | 68 | 38 |
| 8 | Lucas Mfg., Inc. | R314 | 155 | $980 | 9/1/2014 | 37 | 7 |
| 9 | MAA Medical Labs | R572 | 130 | $469 | 8/15/2014 | 54 | 24 |
| 10 | Medina Electrical Supply | W016 | 246 | $345 | 7/20/2014 | 80 | 50 |
| 11 | Molly's Dance Studio | W215 | 228 | $765 | 8/21/2014 | 48 | 18 |
| 12 | Sosa Marine, Inc. | W264 | 210 | $123 | 7/9/2014 | 91 | 61 |
| 13 | | | | | | | |

|◄ ◄ ► ►| Aging Report

13. **Print** the worksheet when you have finished.

14. **Save** 💾 the changes and **close** the workbook.

## APPLY YOUR SKILLS 5.2

# Vertically Align and Rotate Text

*In this exercise, you will create a worksheet, create formulas, and change the vertical alignment and text rotation.*

1. **Open** a new Excel file and **enter** all text, numbers, and dates as shown in the illustration at the end of this exercise. Follow these guidelines to create the large paragraph shown near the top of the worksheet:

   - Merge and center the **range A2:H2**.
   - Set the height of **row 2** to 75.00 points.
   - Turn on the **Wrap Text** option.
   - Change the **vertical alignment** to center and the **horizontal alignment** to left.
   - **Type** the text in the large merged cell.

2. Rotate the text in **F5:H5** up 90 degrees. Use Alt+Enter to force line breaks in the **range F4:H4**.

3. Follow these guidelines to format the worksheet:
   - Merge and center each of the following ranges: **A4:A5**, **F4:F5**, **G4:G5**, and **H4:H5**.
   - Merge and center the ranges **A1:H1**, **B4:C4**, and **D4:E4**.
   - Apply the borders as shown in the illustration, including a border around the **range A12:H13**.

4. Use formulas in **column F** to calculate the number of days between the two assessments.

5. Use formulas in **column G** to calculate the point increase between the two assessment scores.

6. Use formulas to calculate the percentage increase in **column H**. The percentage increase is calculated as the point increase in column G divided by the first assessment score in **column C**.

7. Use the **AVERAGE** function to calculate the averages in **cells F12** and **H13**.

8. Format the percentage increases in **column H** as **Percent Style** with **no decimals**. Apply additional formatting to numbers, dates, and text as desired. Adjust row heights and column widths similar to those shown below.

9. **Print** the worksheet when you have finished.

10. **Save** 💾 with the name **as-Performance Assessments** in the Lesson 05 folder and **close** the workbook.

| | A | B | C | D | E | F | G | H |
|---|---|---|---|---|---|---|---|---|
| 1 | **Safety Performance Assessments** | | | | | | | |
| 2 | This worksheet computes the percentage increase in assessment scores for employees who have been receiving basic safety training The average number of days required to achieve the results is also shown. | | | | | | | |
| 3 | | | | | | | | |
| 4 | | Assessment 1 | | Assessment 2 | | Number of Days Between Tests | Point Increase | Percentage Increase |
| 5 | **Employee** | Date | Score | Date | Score | | | |
| 6 | Barnes, S. | 3-Feb | 78 | 30-Mar | 87 | 55 | 9 | 12% |
| 7 | Garcia, B. | 5-Feb | 77 | 28-Mar | 82 | 51 | 5 | 6% |
| 8 | Lee, K. | 5-Feb | 65 | 5-Apr | 80 | 59 | 15 | 23% |
| 9 | Olsen, M. | 10-Mar | 64 | 1-Apr | 72 | 22 | 8 | 13% |
| 10 | Tan, Q. | 12-Mar | 68 | 2-Apr | 78 | 21 | 10 | 15% |
| 11 | Wilson, T. | 1-Feb | 72 | 10-Mar | 88 | 37 | 16 | 22% |
| 12 | **Average Days** | | | | | 41 | | |
| 13 | **Average Increase** | | | | | | | 15% |

# Use Find and Replace

*In this exercise, you will find and replace both text and formatting in a worksheet.*

1. **Open** the as-Excel Training Objectives workbook from the Lesson 05 folder in your file storage location.

2. Using **Find and Replace**, change the formatting in **cell B6** and every other cell with the same formatting so that they are no longer italicized and are blue (you choose the exact shade of blue) rather than a dark shade of red.

3. Find every instance of the word *learner* and replace it with `employee`.

4. Adjust the **row heights** as necessary.

5. **Print** the worksheet when you are finished.

6. **Save** 🖫 the changes and **close** the workbook.

# Critical Thinking & Work-Readiness Skills

*In the course of working through the following Microsoft Office-based Critical Thinking exercises, you will also be utilizing various work-readiness skills, some of which are listed next to each exercise. Go to* labyrinthelab.com/ workreadiness *to learn more about the work-readiness skills.*

## 5.1 Add a Column to a Worksheet

**WORK-READINESS SKILLS APPLIED**

- Organizing and maintaining information
- Improving or designing systems
- Thinking creatively

Open ct-Safety Training (Lesson 05 folder). Insert a column immediately to the right of the Performance column (under Exam Categories). Label the column **Team Participation** to reflect the new cooperative behaviors Green Clean wants to encourage. Indicate that there will be one item for each of the performance objectives. Adjust column widths for size and appearance. Print preview to ensure that the columns fit across one page width. Save the file as **ct-Safety Training Team** and close it. Why might Green Clean add a Team Participation category to their safety training program? If working in a group, discuss this question. If working alone, type your answer in a Word document named **ct-Questions** saved to your Lesson 05 folder.

## 5.2 Proofread a Worksheet and Add a Row

**WORK-READINESS SKILLS APPLIED**

- Applying technology to a task
- Solving problems
- Writing

While accurate data and consistent formatting help readers understand a worksheet, well written text also contributes to that goal. Open ct-Safety Training Team, if necessary. Find all instances of the characters *mix* and change them to *blend*, making certain to match the case of the original word. Add *paln* to the AutoCorrect list to be replaced by *plan*. Then, insert a new row for objective 6. Type **Create team paln** to see how Excel responds, then remove *plan* from AutoCorrect. Next, explore the use of the Spelling checker located on the Review tab of the Ribbon, and make any corrections needed. Save with the name **ct-Safety Training Plan** in your Lesson 05 folder. If working in a group, discuss why Green Clean might want to have a plan that specifies the roles for each team member. Discuss how other Microsoft Office tools can help you create and monitor a team plan. If working alone, type your answers in a Word document named **ct-Questions2** saved to your Lesson 05 folder.

## 5.3 Adjust Column and Row Formatting

**WORK-READINESS SKILLS APPLIED**

- Organizing and maintaining information
- Applying technology to a task
- Solving problems

Open ct-Safety Training Plan, if necessary. Format all column B cells identically. Delete the row containing objective 3c. Autofit the height of all rows containing data, and then review all row heights for consistency. Delete the Sheet2 and Sheet3 worksheet tabs. Save your file as **ct-Safety Training Final** in your Lesson 05 folder, and then close it.

# Charting and Transmitting Worksheet Data

## LESSON OUTLINE

## LEARNING OBJECTIVES

After studying this lesson, you will be able to:

- Create a variety of different types of charts
- Move and size embedded charts
- Modify, format, and print charts
- Send a worksheet or workbook via email
- Import web data into a worksheet

In this lesson, you will use Excel's charting features to create various types of charts. Charting is an important skill to have when using worksheets because comparisons, trends, and other relationships are often conveyed more effectively with charts. You will use Excel to create column charts, line charts, and pie charts. In addition, you will learn how to edit and format legends, data labels, and other chart objects to communicate data clearly. A worksheet or workbook, including its charts, can be sent via email to others who need the information or who are collaborating on a group project. Excel also allows you to copy data from a web page into a worksheet.

# Charting Sales Performance

Mary Wright is the vice president, sales and marketing, of Green Clean. Her company earns revenue by selling janitorial products and contracts for cleaning services. Mary has asked sales manager Talos Bouras to prepare several charts depicting revenue for the most recent fiscal year. Mary wants charts that compare sales in the various quarters, the growth trend throughout the year, and the contributions of each sales team member to the company sales. Talos will work together with administrative assistant Jenna Mann in using Excel's features to produce accurate and easy-to-understand charts that meet Mary's high standards.

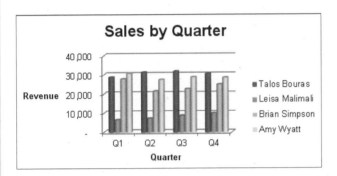

A column chart that compares the sales that sales team members achieved in each quarter of the year

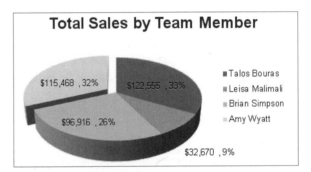

A pie chart that displays the portion of total yearly sales that each sales team member contributed

A line chart that indicates the sales trend upward or downward from quarter to quarter

# 6.1 Creating Charts in Excel

**Video Lesson**    labyrinthelab.com/videos

Numerical data is often easier to interpret when presented in a chart. You can embed a chart in a worksheet so that it appears alongside the worksheet data, or you can place the chart on a separate worksheet. Putting the chart on a separate worksheet prevents the chart from cluttering the data worksheet. Regardless of their placement, charts are always linked to the data from which they are created. Thus, charts are automatically updated when worksheet data changes. Charts are made up of individual objects including the chart title, legend, plot area, value axis, category axis, and data series. You can apply options and enhancements to each object.

## Integrated Chart Engine

A chart engine is integrated within the suite of Office programs. You can create a chart in Microsoft Word or PowerPoint as well as in Excel. Once you have mastered the topics in this lesson, you will be able to understand how to create charts in those other Microsoft Office applications as well! When a chart is created in Word or PowerPoint, it is actually saved and stored as an Excel chart. You can create charts in Access, but the chart engine is different.

## Creating New Charts

When you create a chart, you have the option of either embedding it into the current worksheet where the data is or placing it on a separate sheet of its own. You may want to embed the chart if it can fit on one printed page with the worksheet data. A large or complex chart may display better on its own sheet. An embedded chart can be moved to its own sheet, and a chart on a separate sheet can be moved to embed on a worksheet.

### Embedding a Chart in the Worksheet

Embedded charts can be created by choosing the chart type from the Insert tab of the Ribbon. If you want to see the entire list of chart types displayed before you make your choice, you can open the Insert Chart dialog box. To avoid covering the worksheet data, you can move and resize an embedded chart.

### Creating a Chart on a Separate Sheet

**FROM THE KEYBOARD**

F11 to create a chart on its own sheet

To place a full-size chart on its own sheet, simply select the source range of cells in the worksheet and then tap the F11 key. A new sheet with a generic name, such as Chart1, will be created before the active worksheet in the workbook tab order. When you use the F11 key, the chart on the new sheet will be based on the default chart type, but you can change the type after creating the chart. You can choose the chart type while creating an embedded chart, if you prefer, and then use the Move Chart command in the Ribbon to relocate the chart from the worksheet to its own sheet.

## Choosing the Proper Data Source

It is important to select the proper data on which to base your chart. In addition to selecting the basic data for the chart, you will also want to determine whether or not to select any "total" rows to include in the chart. You will not usually include both individual category data and totals because the individual data will appear distorted, as shown on the next page in the illustration to the right. You should also make certain that you select the proper row and column headings for your column and bar charts. If you notice that any of these important pieces are missing, you will need to reselect your source data.

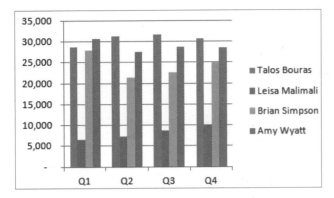

The data in this column chart correctly compare the sales among the four sales team members during each of four quarters.

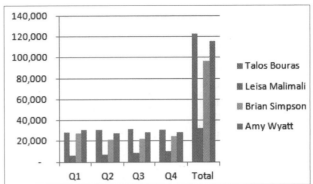

Including the total sales in the chart shrinks the columns for the individual sales team members. Comparing their data is more difficult, and their sales may seem bad as compared with the totals.

# Chart Types

Excel provides 11 major chart types. Each chart type also has several subtypes from which you can choose. Excel has a chart type for most data-display needs.

## Built-In Chart Types

Each chart type represents data in a different manner. You can present the same data in completely different ways by changing the chart type. For this reason, you should always use the chart type that most effectively represents your data. The three most common chart types are column, pie, and line. You will be creating all three types in this lesson.

## User-Defined Charts

Excel lets you create and save customized charts to meet your particular needs. For example, you can create a customized chart that contains the name of your company and its color(s) in the background and use it as the template for all new charts of that type.

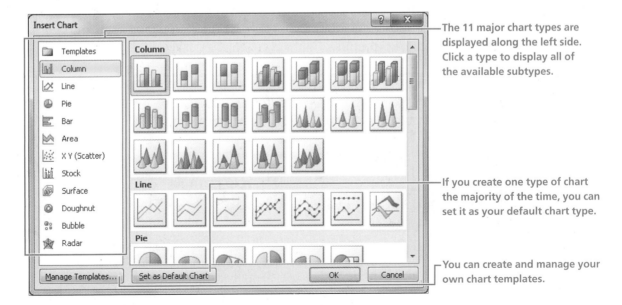

The 11 major chart types are displayed along the left side. Click a type to display all of the available subtypes.

If you create one type of chart the majority of the time, you can set it as your default chart type.

You can create and manage your own chart templates.

# Column Charts and Bar Charts

Column charts compare values (numbers) using vertical bars. Bar charts compare values using horizontal bars. Each column or bar represents a value from the worksheet. Column charts and bar charts are most useful for comparing sets of values (called data series). Column and bar charts can be created in 2-D or 3-D formats.

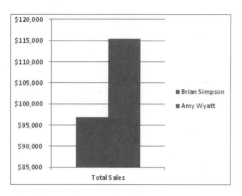
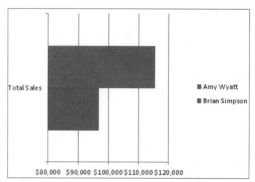

The column chart on the left and the bar chart on the right both display the same data to compare total sales for two people, but the chart types are different. The number of dollar values on the bar chart axis has been modified to accommodate the bar length.

# Category Axis and Value Axis

The horizontal line that forms the base of a column chart is the category axis. The category axis typically measures units of time such as days, months, and quarters, although it can also measure products, people, tests, and other categories. The vertical line on the left side of a column chart is the value axis. The value axis typically measures values such as dollars. Most chart types (including column and bar charts) have a category and a value axis.

# Legend

The box containing a text description for each data series is the legend. The text labels usually are taken from the first column or first row of the selected worksheet data.

The following illustrations show the worksheet data and one of the two column charts you will create in the next exercise. The illustrations show the objects included on most column charts and the corresponding data used to create the chart. Take a few minutes to study the following illustrations carefully.

| | A | B | C | D | E | F |
|---|---|---|---|---|---|---|
| 2 | Quarterly and Total Sales - Fiscal Year | | | | | |
| 3 | | | | | | |
| 4 | | Q1 | Q2 | Q3 | Q4 | Total Sales |
| 5 | Talos Bouras | 28,775 | 31,342 | 31,763 | 30,675 | $ 122,555 |
| 6 | Leisa Malimali | 6,575 | 7,304 | 8,768 | 10,023 | $ 32,670 |
| 7 | Brian Simpson | 27,850 | 21,471 | 22,634 | 24,961 | $ 96,916 |
| 8 | Amy Wyatt | 30,725 | 27,444 | 28,802 | 28,497 | $ 115,468 |
| 10 | Quarter Total | $ 93,925 | $ 87,561 | $ 91,967 | $ 94,156 | $ 367,609 |

The following chart was created using the selected data shown here. Notice that the Total row and column were not included in the selection. The column chart compares the sales numbers for the individual quarters, but it does not include the total sales from row 10 nor column F.

This is the vertical value axis. Excel created the numbering scale (0–35,000) after it determined the range of values included in the chart.

This is the horizontal category axis. The category axis labels (Q1, Q2, Q3, and Q4) were taken from row 4, the first row of the selected worksheet range.

Notice the chart columns. The columns represent values from the various data series. The first data series is the Talos Bouras numbers in row 5. The first column in each group of four columns represents his sales for that quarter.

The legend identifies each data series in the chart columns. The four names in the legend were taken from column A, the first column of the selected worksheet range.

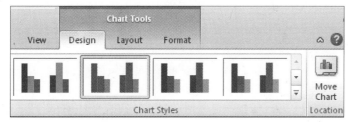

Notice that the chart includes a chart title (Sales by Quarter), a value axis title (Revenue), and a category axis title (Quarter).

## Chart and Axis Titles

Excel allows you to create titles for your charts as well as the value and category axes. If you choose a range of information that includes what appears to Excel to be a title, Excel will include it in the new chart. You can always edit this title if it is not correct.

## The Chart Tools

When a chart is selected, various Chart Tools will be displayed as additional tabs on the Ribbon. These tabs allow you to make changes to the design, layout, and formatting of the chart.

When a chart is selected, the Chart Tools will be displayed, adding the Design, Layout, and Format tabs to the Ribbon.

These additional Ribbon tabs are called contextual tabs.

| Task | Procedure |
|---|---|
| Create a chart | ■ Enter the data you wish to chart into Excel.<br>■ Select the data range for the chart.<br>■ Display the Insert tab of the Ribbon.<br>■ Choose the type of chart from the Charts group. |
| Move an existing chart to its own sheet | ■ Right-click a blank area of the chart and choose Move Chart from the context menu.<br>■ Choose New Sheet in the Move Chart dialog box and rename the sheet, if desired. |
| Move a chart from its own sheet to a worksheet as an embedded object | ■ Right-click a blank area of the chart and choose Move Chart from the context menu.<br>■ Choose Object In and select the desired worksheet in the Move Chart dialog box. |
| Add a title to a chart | ■ Select the chart to which you wish to add a title.<br>■ Choose Layout→Labels→Chart Title from the Ribbon to display the title options.<br>■ Choose how you wish the title to appear.<br>■ Select the default title "Chart Title," and type in the title you wish for your chart. |
| Add axis titles to a chart | ■ Select the chart to which you wish to add an axis title.<br>■ Choose Layout→Labels→Axis Titles from the Ribbon to display the axis options.<br>■ Choose whether you wish to apply a horizontal or vertical axis title.<br>■ Choose how you wish the title to appear.<br>■ Select the default title "Axis Title," and type the title you wish for your axis.<br>■ Repeat these steps for the other axis. |

## DEVELOP YOUR SKILLS 6.1.1

# Create Charts

*In this exercise, you will create two column charts. The 2-D column chart will display on a separate sheet and the clustered cylinder chart will be embedded in the worksheet.*

### Create a 2-D Column Chart on a New Sheet

1. **Open** the Sales Performance Charts workbook from the Lesson 06 folder in your file storage location.

2. Select the **range A4:E8** in the Sales by Quarter worksheet.

3. **Tap** the F11 key.
   *Tapping F11 creates a new sheet before the Sales by Quarter sheet in the workbook tab order. The new chart fills the area on the sheet and the chart is based on the default chart type of Clustered Column. Notice that the Chart Tools display on the Ribbon; they can be used to modify the chart.*

4. **Double-click** the new chart tab, type **Sales by Rep**, and **tap** Enter to rename the sheet.

Sales by Rep / Sales by Quarter

## Create an Embedded Column Chart

5. Display the **Sales by Quarter** worksheet and make certain the **range A4:E8** is still selected.

6. Follow these steps to create a clustered cylinder column chart:

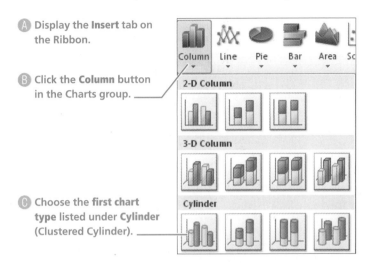

Ⓐ Display the **Insert** tab on the Ribbon.

Ⓑ Click the **Column** button in the Charts group.

Ⓒ Choose the **first chart type** listed under **Cylinder** (Clustered Cylinder).

*The chart will appear embedded in the Sales by Quarter worksheet with the default properties for the clustered column chart type displayed. The data in the chart is based on the range of cells you preselected.*

7. Look at the Ribbon to see that the **Chart Tools** are now displayed and the **Design** tab is active.
*Notice that the chart is covering part of the data. In the next exercise, you will learn how to move charts within a sheet.*

## Edit the Chart and Axis Titles

8. Choose **Chart Tools→Layout→Labels→Chart Title** ▦ **→Above Chart** from the Ribbon.

9. Follow these steps to title the chart:

Ⓐ **Select** the default title, *Chart Title.*

Ⓑ **Type** the new title as shown here.

Ⓒ **Click** in a blank area of the chart to accept the new title.

10. Choose **Layout→Labels→Axis Titles** ▦ **→Primary Horizontal Axis Title→Title Below Axis** from the Ribbon.

11. **Drag** to select the default title, *Axis Title.*

12. **Type** in the new horizontal axis title, **Quarter**, and then **click away** to accept the new title.

13. Choose **Layout→Labels→Axis Titles** 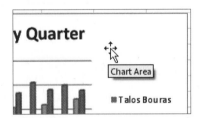 **→Primary Vertical Axis Title→Horizontal Title** from the Ribbon.

14. Notice that the default title placeholder, *Axis Title*, is selected.

15. **Type** the new vertical axis title, **Revenue**, and then **click** outside the title box to accept the new title.

16. **Save** the changes and leave the workbook **open** for the next exercise.

# 6.2 Moving and Sizing Embedded Charts

**Video Lesson**  labyrinthelab.com/videos

When a chart is selected, it is surrounded by a light border with sizing handles displayed. A selected chart can be both moved and resized.

## Moving Embedded Charts

Charts that are embedded in a worksheet can easily be moved to a new location. A chart can be moved by a simple drag, but you need to ensure that you click the chart area and not a separate element. Regardless of whether a chart is embedded within a worksheet or moved to a separate tab, the chart data will automatically update when values are changed in the source data.

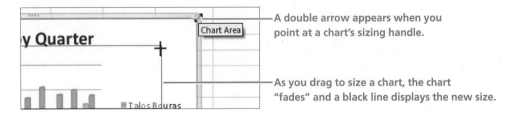

A four-pointed arrow indicates that you can drag to move this selected chart.

## Sizing Embedded Charts

To size a chart, it must first be selected. You simply need to drag a sizing handle when the double-arrow mouse pointer is displayed. In order to change a chart size proportionately, hold Shift while dragging a corner handle.

A double arrow appears when you point at a chart's sizing handle.

As you drag to size a chart, the chart "fades" and a black line displays the new size.

# Deleting Charts

Deleting an embedded chart is a very simple process—just select the chart area and tap [Delete]. You can always use the Undo command if you delete an embedded chart by mistake. You delete a chart that is on its own tab by deleting the worksheet. This action cannot be undone, so Excel warns you with a prompt to confirm the deletion.

| QUICK REFERENCE | MOVING AND SIZING EMBEDDED CHARTS AND DELETING CHARTS |
|---|---|
| **Task** | **Procedure** |
| Move an embedded chart | Drag the selected chart to a new location with the move pointer while it is positioned over the chart area. |
| Change the chart size | Drag any sizing handle (hold down [Shift] while dragging a corner handle to resize proportionally). |
| Delete a chart | Embedded Chart: Select the chart, and then tap the [Delete] key. |
| | Worksheet Chart: Delete the worksheet. |

## DEVELOP YOUR SKILLS 6.2.1
## Size and Move an Embedded Chart

*In this exercise, you will move and resize the embedded column chart that you created in the previous exercise. You will also copy a sheet containing an embedded chart and delete the chart.*

### Size a Chart

1. **Click once** on the chart area of the embedded chart in the Sales by Quarter sheet to select the chart.
   *Sizing handles appear around the border of the chart.*

2. Follow these steps to resize the chart to be smaller:

Ⓐ Place the mouse pointer over the **upper-right sizing handle** until you see the double-pointed arrow (not a four-pointed arrow).

Ⓑ **Press and hold** [Shift] while you drag the sizing handle down and to the left.

Ⓒ **Release** the mouse button about one-half inch from the corner in order to decrease the size by one-half inch; **release** the [Shift] key.

*Notice that Excel resized the width and height proportionately because you held down the [Shift] key as you resized the chart.*

## Move a Chart

3. Follow these steps to move the chart and center it below the worksheet data:

Ⓐ Place the mouse pointer over a blank area of the chart so that a **four-pointed arrow** appears.

Ⓑ Drag the chart **down and to the left** until it is just below row 11 and centered within **columns A through F.**

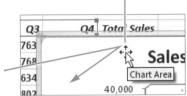

Ⓒ **Release** the mouse button when you are satisfied with the chart position.

*You will see a rectangle "ghost" as you drag, showing you where the chart will land if you release the mouse button at that location.*

## Copy a Sheet

4. **Hold down** the ⌈Ctrl⌉ key; **drag** the Sales by Quarter sheet tab to the right and then **release** the mouse and ⌈Ctrl⌉ key.

*The duplicate sheet is named Sales by Quarter (2).*

5. **Rename** the Sales by Quarter (2) sheet to **Team Totals**.

## Delete an Embedded Chart

6. **Click once** to select the column chart in the Team Totals sheet and **tap** ⌈Delete⌉. *Excel deletes the embedded chart.*

7. Use ⌈Ctrl⌉+⌈Z⌉ to undo the **Delete** command. *The embedded chart reappears on the worksheet. You can restore an embedded chart right after it is deleted.*

8. Use ⌈Ctrl⌉+⌈Y⌉ to redo the **Delete** command. *The chart is once again deleted. (You will create a pie chart here in a later exercise.)*

9. Use ⌈Ctrl⌉+⌈S⌉ to **save** your workbook, and leave it **open** for the next exercise.

# 6.3 Exploring Other Chart Types

**Video Lesson** labyrinthelab.com/videos

In the previous section, you learned about column and bar charts. Now you will explore line and pie charts and how they can make your data work for you.

## Line Charts

Line charts are most useful for comparing trends over a period of time. For example, line charts are often used to show stock market activity where the upward or downward trend is important. Like column charts, line charts have category and value axes. Line charts also use the same or similar objects as column charts. The following illustration shows a line chart that depicts the trend in quarter sales throughout the year. Data labels indicate the value for each time period along the line plotted on the chart. Take a moment to study the following figures.

| | A | B | C | D | E | F |
|---|---|---|---|---|---|---|
| 1 | **Sales Department** | | | | | |
| 2 | *Quarterly and Total Sales - Fiscal Year* | | | | | |
| 3 | | | | | | |
| 4 | | *Q1* | *Q2* | *Q3* | *Q4* | *Total Sales* |
| 5 | Talos Bouras | 28,775 | 31,342 | 31,763 | 30,675 | $ 122,555 |
| 6 | Leisa Malimali | 6,575 | 7,304 | 8,768 | 10,023 | $ 32,670 |
| 7 | Brian Simpson | 27,850 | 21,471 | 22,634 | 24,961 | $ 96,916 |
| 8 | Amy Wyatt | 30,725 | 27,444 | 28,802 | 28,497 | $ 115,468 |
| 10 | **Quarter Total** | $ 93,925 | $ 87,561 | $ 91,967 | $ 94,156 | $ 367,609 |

The following chart was created using the selected data shown here. Notice that the data is in two separate ranges. You use the Ctrl key to select these nonadjacent ranges so that you can chart just the totals and the Q1–Q4 labels.

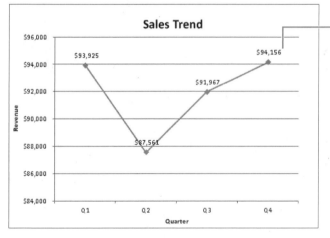

This is a data label. Data labels show the precise value of the various data points. You can use data labels with any chart type.

The line chart clearly depicts the downward and upward trend in sales volume.

# Create a Line Chart

*In this exercise, you will create a line chart that displays the total sales.*

*Before You Begin: The Sales by Quarter worksheet should be displayed.*

## Create a Line Chart

1. Follow these steps to select the data for the line chart on the Sales by Quarter worksheet:

Ⓐ Select the **range A4:E4** (do not select cell F4).

Ⓑ **Press and hold down** Ctrl while selecting the range A10:E10 (do not select cell F10). Both ranges should be selected.

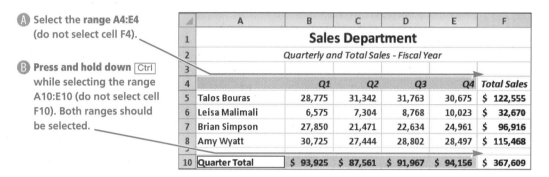

| | A | B | C | D | E | F |
|---|---|---|---|---|---|---|
| 1 | | **Sales Department** | | | | |
| 2 | | *Quarterly and Total Sales - Fiscal Year* | | | | |
| 3 | | | | | | |
| 4 | | **Q1** | **Q2** | **Q3** | **Q4** | **Total Sales** |
| 5 | Talos Bouras | 28,775 | 31,342 | 31,763 | 30,675 | $ 122,555 |
| 6 | Leisa Malimali | 6,575 | 7,304 | 8,768 | 10,023 | $ 32,670 |
| 7 | Brian Simpson | 27,850 | 21,471 | 22,634 | 24,961 | $ 96,916 |
| 8 | Amy Wyatt | 30,725 | 27,444 | 28,802 | 28,497 | $ 115,468 |
| 10 | Quarter Total | $ 93,925 | $ 87,561 | $ 91,967 | $ 94,156 | $ 367,609 |

2. Choose **Insert→Charts→Line** 〰️ **→Line with Markers** from the Ribbon, as shown.

   *Excel creates an embedded line chart in the current worksheet. Notice the light border and sizing handles, indicating the chart is selected. The Chart Tools contextual tabs are also visible on the Ribbon.*

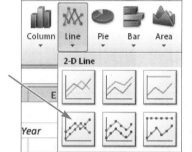

## Move the Chart

*Now you will move the chart to its own worksheet.*

3. Follow these steps to move the chart:

   - Make certain the chart is **selected** (displays handles), which also makes the Chart Tools contextual tabs visible.

   - Choose **Design→Location→Move Chart** 📊 from the Ribbon.

   *The Move Chart dialog box appears. In this dialog box, you can choose where to place the chart as well as provide a name for a new sheet if you wish to create one.*

4. Follow these steps to move the chart to its own sheet:

Ⓐ Drag to select the existing **New Sheet** entry and type **Sales Trend** as the name for the new sheet.

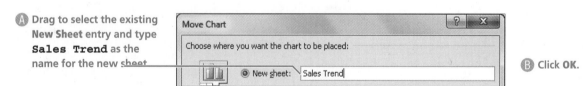

Ⓑ Click **OK**.

*The chart now appears on its own worksheet.*

## Edit the Chart

5. Click the **Title** text box once to select it, and then **triple-click** on Quarter Total to select the entire entry.

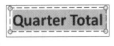

6. Type **Sales Trend**, and then **click** another area of the chart.

7. Choose **Layout→Labels→Axis Titles** 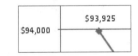 **→Primary Horizontal Axis Title→Title Below Axis** from the Ribbon.
*Excel provides a text box below the horizontal axis with a default name of* Axis Title *displayed.*

8. **Drag** to select the default horizontal axis title.

9. **Type** the new horizontal axis title, **Quarter**, and then **click away** to accept the new title.

10. Choose **Layout→Labels→Axis Titles** 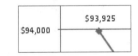 **→Primary Vertical Axis Title→Rotated Title** from the Ribbon.

11. **Triple-click** to select the default vertical axis title.

12. Type **Revenue** as the new vertical axis title, and then **click away** to accept the new title.

13. Choose **Layout→Labels→Data Labels** 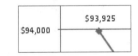 **→Above** from the Ribbon.
*Excel displays the values above the data points on the chart.*

14. Use ⌃Ctrl + S to **save** your worksheet, and leave it **open** for the next exercise.

# Pie Charts

**Video Lesson**   labyrinthelab.com/videos

Pie charts are useful for comparing parts of a whole. For example, pie charts are often used in budgets to show how funds are allocated. You typically select only two sets of data when creating pie charts: the values to be represented by the pie slices and the labels to identify the slices. The following illustration shows a worksheet and an accompanying 3-D pie chart with data labels applied. Notice that the worksheet has a Total Sales column.

|   | A | B | C | D | E | F |
|---|---|---|---|---|---|---|
| 4 |   | Q1 | Q2 | Q3 | Q4 | Total Sales |
| 5 | Talos Bouras | 28,775 | 31,342 | 31,763 | 30,675 | $ 122,555 |
| 6 | Leisa Malimali | 6,575 | 7,304 | 8,768 | 10,023 | $ 32,670 |
| 7 | Brian Simpson | 27,850 | 21,471 | 22,634 | 24,961 | $ 96,916 |
| 8 | Amy Wyatt | 30,725 | 27,444 | 28,802 | 28,497 | $ 115,468 |
| 10 | Quarter Total | $ 93,925 | $ 87,561 | $ 91,967 | $ 94,156 | $ 367,609 |

The names in column A will become labels in the legend. The numbers in column F will determine the sizes of the slices.

Excel calculates the percentages based on the numbers you select.

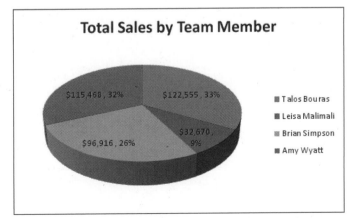

## Exploding Pie Slices

There are times when you may want to draw attention to a particular slice of the pie chart. You can make one slice explode from the chart simply by dragging it away from the other slices.

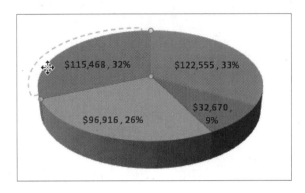

Notice that as you drag a slice out to give it an exploded effect, Excel will show with a dashed line where it will land.

## Rotating and Elevating Pie Charts

You have the option to change the rotation and perspective (also known as elevation) of pie charts in order to display data in a different position or change the angle at which it is viewed. The 3-D Rotation button on the Layout tab of the Ribbon will open a dialog box that allows changes to the rotation and perspective to take place.

### DEVELOP YOUR SKILLS 6.3.2
## Create a Pie Chart

*In this exercise, you will create a pie chart with the same data used for the line chart and leave it embedded in the Team Totals worksheet.*

*Before You Begin: The Team Totals worksheet should be displayed.*

#### Insert the Pie Chart

1. Follow these steps to select the range for the chart on the Team Totals worksheet:

Ⓐ Drag to select **A4:A8**.

Ⓑ While **holding** Ctrl, drag to select **F4:F8**.

| | A | B | C | D | E | F |
|---|---|---|---|---|---|---|
| 4 | | Q1 | Q2 | Q3 | Q4 | Total Sales |
| 5 | Talos Bouras | 28,775 | 31,342 | 31,763 | 30,675 | $ 122,555 |
| 6 | Leisa Malimali | 6,575 | 7,304 | 8,768 | 10,023 | $ 32,670 |
| 7 | Brian Simpson | 27,850 | 21,471 | 22,634 | 24,961 | $ 96,916 |
| 8 | Amy Wyatt | 30,725 | 27,444 | 28,802 | 28,497 | $ 115,468 |
| 10 | Quarter Total | $ 93,925 | $ 87,561 | $ 91,967 | $ 94,156 | $ 367,609 |

2. Choose **Insert→Charts→Pie** 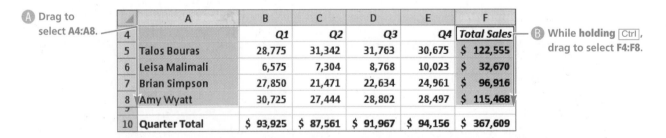 **→3-D Pie→Pie in 3-D** from the Ribbon.

3. Place the **mouse pointer** over the chart area so that the **four-pointed arrow appears**, and then **drag** it **down** and to the **left** until it is below row 11 and centered between columns A through F.
   *Notice that the cell F4 entry, Total Sales, is used as the chart title.*

4. **Edit** the chart title to read **Total Sales by Team Member**, clicking outside of the Title box to accept the new title.

5. Choose **Layout→Labels→Data Labels** 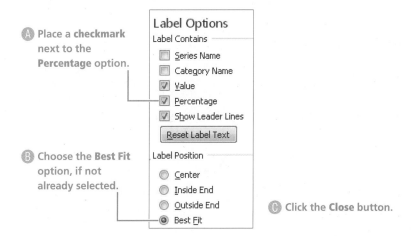**→More Data Label Options** from the Ribbon.
   *The Format Data Labels dialog box appears.*

6. Follow these steps to format the data labels:

Ⓐ Place a **checkmark** next to the **Percentage** option.

Ⓑ Choose the **Best Fit** option, if not already selected.

Ⓒ Click the **Close** button.

*Excel displays both the value and the percentage in each pie slice wherever they "best fit."*

## Explode a Pie Slice

7. **Click** the slice representing Amy Wyatt's sales, and then **pause** and **click** it again.
   *The first click will select all slices, and the second click will select just the slice for Amy Wyatt.*

8. Place the **mouse pointer** over the Amy Wyatt slice until you see a **move pointer**, and then **drag** away from the pie chart slightly and **release**.
   *Notice that as you drag the pie slice away from the main chart, a dashed line appears where the slice will land if you release the mouse button.*

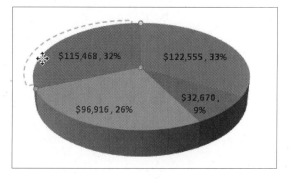

9. Use ⌜Ctrl⌝+⌜S⌝ to **save** your worksheet, and leave it **open** for the next exercise.

# 6.4 Modifying Existing Charts

**Video Lesson**   labyrinthelab.com/videos

You can modify any chart object after the chart has been created. You can change the size, font, color, and placement of titles; format the numbers on the value axis; change the background color of the chart area; and more. You can also add or remove objects such as legends and data labels. You can even move an embedded chart to a separate worksheet and vice versa. These changes are made with the Chart Tools, which are grouped onto three contextual Ribbon tabs that appear when a chart is selected: Design, Layout, and Format. The following table describes the various Chart Tools available to modify your charts.

| QUICK REFERENCE | USING CHART TOOLS ON THE RIBBON |
| --- | --- |
| **Contextual Tab** | **Command Groups on the Tab** |
| Design | ■ *Type* allows you to change the type of chart, set the default chart type, and save a chart as a template. |
| | ■ *Data* allows you to switch the data displayed on rows and columns and to reselect the data for the chart. |
| | ■ *Chart Layouts* allows you to change the overall layout of the chart. |
| | ■ *Chart Styles* allows you to choose a preset style for your chart. |
| | ■ *Location* allows you to switch a chart from being embedded to being placed on a sheet and vice versa. |
| | ■ *Mode* allows you to switch the display mode for charts. |
| Layout | ■ *Current Selection* allows you to select a specific chart element and apply formatting to it. |
| | ■ *Insert* allows you to insert objects into your chart. |
| | ■ *Labels* allows you to make changes to various labels on your chart, such as the title and data labels. |
| | ■ *Axes* allows you to choose whether to display axes and gridlines, as well as to set the properties for them. |
| | ■ *Background* allows you to change the background formatting, such as fill color, for the chart. |
| | ■ *Analysis* allows you to analyze the data displayed within the chart. |
| | ■ *Properties* allows you to change the name of the chart. |
| Format | ■ *Current Selection* allows you to select a specific chart element and apply formatting to it. |
| | ■ *Shape Styles* allows you to visually make changes to the selected chart element. |
| | ■ *WordArt Styles* allows you to apply WordArt to text labels in your chart. |
| | ■ *Arrange* allows you to change how your chart is arranged in relation to other objects in your worksheet. |
| | ■ *Size* allows you to change the size of your chart by typing in exact values. |

## Changing the Chart Type

There are so many chart types available that you may wish to explore other options before making a final decision. It is easy to change the type of an existing chart by using the Change Chart Type dialog box.

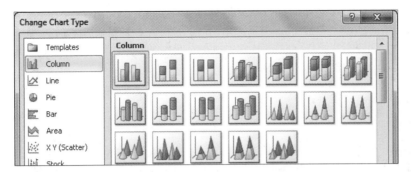

In the Change Chart Type dialog box, you can choose from many preset chart types if you wish to change the type of an existing chart.

## Reselecting Data

You may decide after creating a chart that some source data is missing or data that should be excluded. The Select Data command displays the Select Data Source dialog box, where you may change the data range for the entire chart. The recommended reselection method is to collapse the dialog box and drag in the worksheet. The following illustration shows that the Chart Data Range reference =Sales!$A$4:$E$8 includes the worksheet name followed by an exclamation (!) point. You also can add, edit, or remove a single data series or edit the category axis labels. The Switch Row/Column option swaps the data in the vertical and horizontal axes of the chart. You could use this option when values display along the horizontal axis and you would rather have them on the vertical axis.

The worksheet name followed by an exclamation (!) point in the data range

The Collapse button

The command to switch data between vertical and horizontal chart axes

A data series selected and ready to be edited or removed

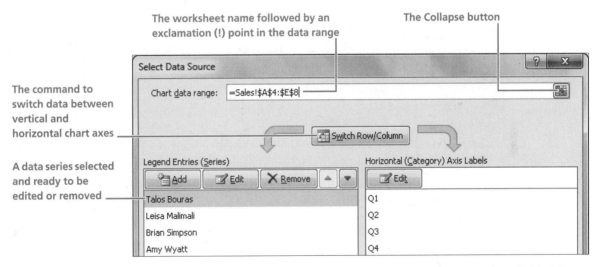

The Select Data Source dialog box allows you to change the range of cells for individual data series or the entire chart.

Using the arrow keys while attempting to edit a data range in a text box results in unwanted characters. For best results, reselect a data range by dragging in the worksheet.

## Modifying Chart Elements

Charts are made up of various elements. For example, the legends, titles, and columns are all types of elements. You must select an element before you can perform an action on it. You can select an element by clicking it with the mouse. Once selected, you can delete, move, size, and format the element. You delete a selected element by tapping the ⌈Delete⌉ key, move a selected element by dragging it with the mouse when you see the move pointer, and change the size by dragging a sizing handle.

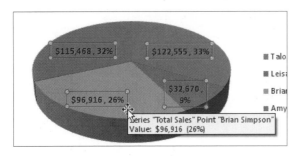

In this illustration, the data labels are the selected element, and the ScreenTip indicates that the mouse is pointing at the data label for Brian Simpson.

# Formatting Chart Elements

You can modify any chart element after the chart has been created by using the visual Chart Tools on the Ribbon. As an alternative, you can double-click the chart element to display a Format dialog box with many options for that element. For example, options in the Format Data Series dialog box allow you to adjust the column bar width; change the space between bars; and apply a fill, border, or other visual effects.

## *Previewing Formatting Before Applying*

You can preview how a formatting change would appear in a worksheet cell before actually issuing the command to apply it. The same is true with the Chart Tools Format ribbon in Excel. If you place the mouse pointer over a button on one of the options in the Shape Styles or WordArt Styles group, a preview displays how the change will look in your chart.

| QUICK REFERENCE | MODIFYING EXISTING CHARTS |
|---|---|
| **Task** | **Procedure** |
| Change the chart type | ■ Select the chart you wish to change to a different type. |
| | ■ Choose Design→Change Chart Type from the Ribbon. |
| | ■ Browse the types available and double-click the desired type. |
| Reselect a data range for the entire chart | ■ Select the chart. |
| | ■ Choose Design→Data→Select Data from the Ribbon. |
| | ■ Click the Collapse ⬚ button at the right of Chart Data Range in the Select Data Source dialog box. |
| | ■ Drag in the worksheet to select the new data range. |
| | ■ Click the Expand ⬚ button at the right of Chart Data Range in the Select Data Source dialog box. |

| Task | Procedure |
|------|-----------|
| Reselect the range for a data series | ▪ Select the chart. |
| | ▪ Choose Design→Data→Select Data from the Ribbon. |
| | ▪ Select the desired item under Legend Entries (Series) in the Select Data Source dialog box and click Edit. |
| | ▪ Drag to select the entire Series Name or Series Values entry in the Edit Series dialog box. |
| | ▪ Drag in the worksheet to select the new range and click OK. |
| Delete a chart element | ▪ Select the desired chart element and tap ⌷ Delete ⌷. |
| Format an element on an existing chart | ▪ Select the chart element that you wish to format. |
| | ▪ Display the Design, Layout, or Format tab of the Ribbon. |
| | ▪ Choose the appropriate formatting command from the Ribbon. |

## DEVELOP YOUR SKILLS 6.4.1
# Modify a Chart

*In this exercise, you will change a chart type and then apply various formatting features to it.*

*Before You Begin: The Sales by Rep worksheet should be displayed.*

### Change a Chart Type

1. Click anywhere within the column chart on the **Sales by Rep** sheet to select the chart and display the **Chart Tools** Ribbon tabs.

2. Choose **Design→Type→Change Chart Type** 📊 from the Ribbon.
   *The Change Chart Type dialog box appears.*

3. Follow these steps to change the chart type:

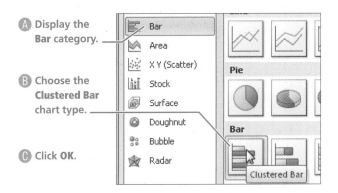

Ⓐ Display the **Bar** category.

Ⓑ Choose the **Clustered Bar** chart type.

Ⓒ Click **OK**.

## Reselect Data

4. Choose **Design→Data→Select Data** 🗔 from the Ribbon.

   *The Select Data Source dialog box appears with the Chart Data Range as ='Sales by Quarter'
   !$A$4:$E$8. You want to compare sales performance without including sales manager Talos Bouras.
   You will reselect the range to include the labels in row 4 and the data for the other three sales team
   members.*

5. Follow these steps to reselect the chart data range:

Ⓐ Click the **Collapse** button or drag the title bar of the dialog box, as necessary, to view the worksheet data.

Ⓑ Drag to select the **range A4:E4.**

Ⓒ **Hold down** [Ctrl] and select the **range A6:E8.**

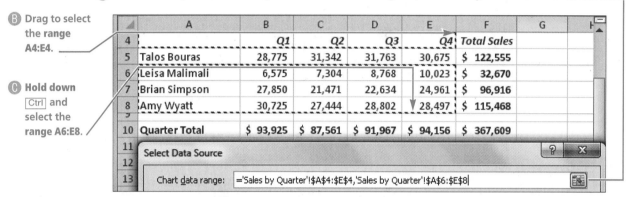

Ⓓ Click the **Expand** 🖾 button at the right of the range in the Select Data Source dialog box if you collapsed the box.

*The Legend Entries (Series) should list Leisa Malimali, Brian Simpson, and Amy Wyatt.*

6. Click **OK**.

7. Select one of the column bars for Leisa Malimali and **tap** [Delete].

   *Now two data series display in the chart. Any chart element can be deleted in this way.*

## Format a Chart Using the Ribbon

8. **Click** anywhere within the top bar in the chart, which represents the Amy Wyatt data series.

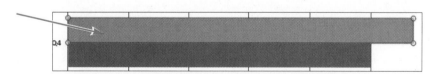

*Make certain that you single-click because that selects Amy Wyatt's data series for all four quarters and
leaves the current tab displayed. If you double-click, the Design tab with the current style displays on
the Ribbon. In this case, it won't matter as you are already viewing the Design tab, but it could cause
you to take extra steps if you were already working on the Format tab.*

9. Follow these steps to apply formatting to the Amy Wyatt data series:

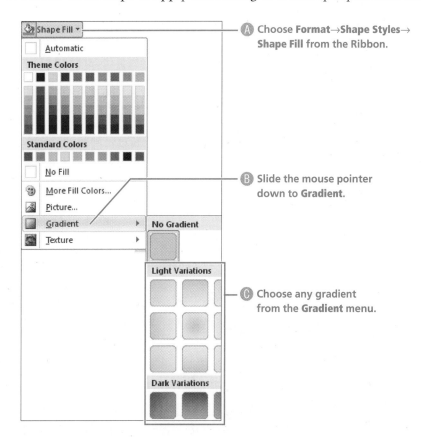

Ⓐ Choose **Format→Shape Styles→ Shape Fill** from the Ribbon.

Ⓑ Slide the mouse pointer down to **Gradient**.

Ⓒ Choose any gradient from the **Gradient** menu.

10. **Click** anywhere within the chart area to select it.
*Remember that any formatting you choose will apply only to the chart element you have selected.*

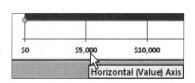

11. Choose **Format→Shape Styles→Shape Outline** 🖊️ **→Weight** from the Ribbon.

12. Point at various line weights to preview how they would look in the chart; then choose **3 pt** from the list.

13. Choose **Format→Shape Styles→Shape Outline** 🖊️ from the Ribbon, and then apply the color of your choice.
*A line now appears around the entire chart area. In the next few steps, you will be changing the number format of the value axis.*

## Format Axis Numbers

14. **Double-click** on any of the values in the horizontal axis at the bottom of the chart.
*The Format Axis dialog box displays. If the Format Plot Area or other dialog box displays, close it and again double-click a value on the horizontal axis.*

15. Follow these steps to format the axis numbers as Currency:

Ⓐ Choose **Number** at the left of the dialog box.

Ⓑ Choose the **Currency** category.

Ⓒ Click **Close**.

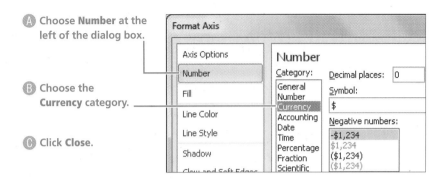

*The numbers on the axis now display with dollar ($) signs.*

### Add a Chart Title

16. Choose **Layout→Labels→Chart Title**  **→Above Chart** from the Ribbon.

17. Change the default chart title to **Sales by Rep**.

18. **Save** 🖫 the changes, and leave the workbook **open**.

| Sales by Rep |

# 6.5 Applying Layouts and Styles to Charts

**Video Lesson**   labyrinthelab.com/videos

Chart layouts, also known as quick layouts, are designs that contain various chart elements. Choosing a chart layout saves time versus adding and formatting chart elements one at a time. Chart Quick Styles are based on the theme applied to your workbook. There are many preset styles that you can apply to charts. The layouts and styles displayed on the Design tab of the Ribbon are based on the type of chart that you currently have selected. In the figures displayed below, you can see that the layouts and styles available for column charts are different from those available for pie charts.

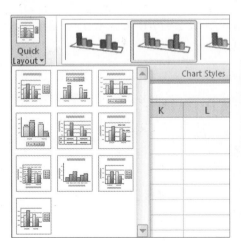

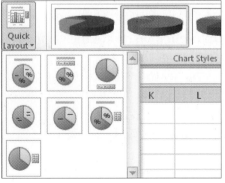

The chart layouts and styles available through Excel's Design tab of the Ribbon will change based on the type of chart you have selected.

## Formatting Attributes Controlled by the Selected Style

When you choose a style for your chart, the colors and effects (such as fill effects) will change to match the style selected. Data in worksheet cells is not affected by any styles that you apply to charts. Excel does not allow you to create your own styles, but you can save the formatting from a selected chart as a template to use as the basis for future charts.

## Viewing All Available Layouts and Styles for a Chart Type

The Ribbon will display just a few of the layouts and styles available for the selected chart type. To view the entire gallery, click the More button to expand the Chart Layouts or Chart Styles group of the Ribbon.

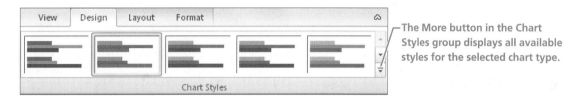

The More button in the Chart Styles group displays all available styles for the selected chart type.

| QUICK REFERENCE | APPLYING A LAYOUT AND STYLE TO A CHART |
|---|---|
| **Task** | **Procedure** |
| Apply a layout or style to a chart | ■ Select the chart to which you wish to apply a layout or style. |
| | ■ Choose the Design tab from the Ribbon. |
| | ■ Click the More ▽ button in the Chart Layouts or Chart Styles group to display the full array of available choices. |
| | ■ Click to choose the layout or style you wish to apply. |

## DEVELOP YOUR SKILLS 6.5.1
## Apply a Layout and a Style to a Chart

*In this exercise, you will apply a quick layout and Quick Style to the bar chart you created in the last exercise.*

*Before You Begin: The Sales by Rep sheet should be displayed.*

### Apply a Workbook Theme

1. Choose **Page Layout**→**Themes**→**Themes** [Aa]→**Origin** from the Ribbon.

2. **Click** each of the workbook tabs and view the result.
   *A uniform color scheme, font set, and graphic effects are applied to all worksheet data and charts. The chart style that you apply later in this exercise will match the workbook theme.*

### Change the Chart Layout

3. Select the **Sales by Rep** sheet.

4. **Click** in the chart area of the **Sales by Rep** chart to select the chart.

5. Choose **Design→Chart Layouts→More** ⏷ from the Ribbon.
   *Excel displays all of the chart layout choices for this type of chart.*

6. **Click once** to apply the layout of your choice and view the result in the chart.

7. Choose **Design→Chart Layouts→More** ⏷ from the Ribbon.

8. Choose **Layout 2** in the list.
   *A Screen Tip displays the layout name as you point at each layout. You will need to reenter any title that is not within the data range specified for the chart.*

9. If the default chart title displays at the top of the chart, change it to **Sales by Rep**.

## Change the Chart Style

10. Choose **Design→Chart Styles→More** ⏷ from the Ribbon.
    *Excel displays all of the available chart styles for this type of chart. The gallery styles match the color scheme and graphic effects from the currently applied workbook theme.*

11. **Click once** to apply a chart style you find attractive.
    *If there were data on this worksheet, the data would not be affected by the new chart style.*

12. Repeat **steps 10 and 11** if you wish to apply a different chart style.

13. **Save** 💾 the changes and leave the workbook **open**.

# 6.6 Previewing and Printing Charts

**Video Lesson**   labyrinthelab.com/videos

The Print command is used to preview and print charts. If a chart is embedded, you can print the entire worksheet or select and print just the chart. If a chart is on a separate worksheet, you must first display the sheet before issuing the Print command. In the preview on the Print tab in Backstage view, the chart will display in black and white or in color, depending on the type of printer selected.

Color fills and borders may not provide good contrast in charts printed on grayscale printers. Consider using shades of gray or black-and-white pattern fills.

| QUICK REFERENCE | PRINTING CHARTS |
|---|---|
| **Task** | **Procedure** |
| Preview how a chart will look when printed | ▪ Select the chart by either clicking it if it is embedded or displaying the sheet on which it is placed.<br>▪ Choose File→Print and look at the preview in Backstage view. |
| Print a chart | ▪ After using the above steps to preview the chart, select printing options in the Print tab of Backstage view.<br>▪ Click Print. |

## Preview and Print a Chart

*In this exercise, you will preview the pie chart you created in the last exercise and print the column chart.*

*Before You Begin: The Team Totals worksheet should be displayed.*

1. **Click once** to select the pie chart on the **Team Totals** worksheet.

2. Choose **File→Print**.
   *The pie chart appears in the preview of the Print tab in Backstage view.*

3. **Tap** ⌐Esc¬ to exit Backstage view without printing.

4. **Click** in a cell away from the pie chart to **deselect** the chart.

5. Choose **File→Print**.
   *Notice that when the chart is not selected, Excel will print the worksheet along with the embedded chart.*

6. **Tap** ⌐Esc¬ to exit Backstage view without printing.

7. Display the **Sales Trend** worksheet.

8. Choose **File→Print**, select an appropriate printer, click **Print**, and retrieve the printout.
   *Excel will print one copy of your chart to the default printer.*

9. Keep the workbook **open**.

# 6.7 Emailing a Workbook

**Video Lesson** labyrinthelab.com/videos

When you want to send an Excel workbook to someone by email, you have two choices. You may send the entire workbook as an attachment, or you may send a single worksheet as the body of the email message. Each method has its uses. Sending a worksheet as an email message may cause some formatting to be lost. However, if you just need to transmit a single worksheet, sending it as the body of an email message may be more convenient for the recipient to quickly view and print.

If you need to send a multisheet workbook, you must use the attachment method.

## Attaching a Workbook

You may send email from within Excel if you previously set up a Microsoft Outlook or Windows Live Mail email account. After you give the Send as Attachment command, an email message window appears with the workbook file already attached. You simply enter the recipient's email address and type your message. You may edit the subject line and attach more files, if desired. You may attach Excel workbooks from within most other email programs if you do not have an Outlook or Windows Mail account.

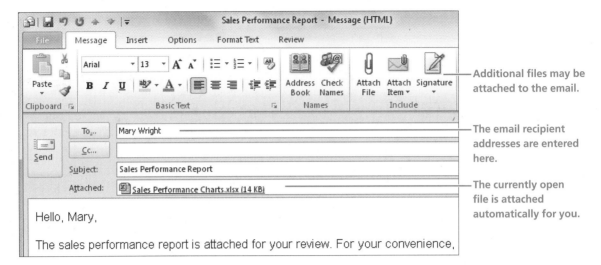

Additional files may be attached to the email.

The email recipient addresses are entered here.

The currently open file is attached automatically for you.

A Microsoft Outlook email message window

## Inserting a Worksheet in an Email Message

The Send to Mail Recipient  command has an option to place the currently displayed worksheet in the email message area. You fill in the email address, a subject for the message, and a short introduction to the worksheet before sending the message. The Introduction box will not be available in an email program other than Outlook.

The Send to Mail Recipient command does not appear on the Ribbon. You must add it to the Quick Access toolbar.

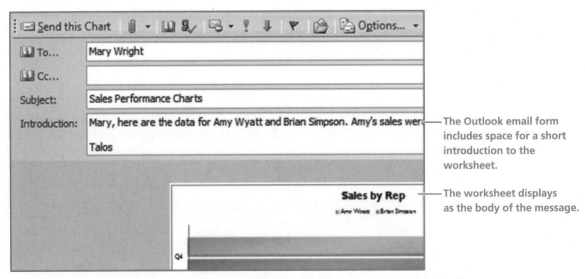

The Outlook email form includes space for a short introduction to the worksheet.

The worksheet displays as the body of the message.

Sending one worksheet as the message body in Outlook

| Task | Procedure |
|---|---|
| Add the Send to Mail Recipient command to the Quick Access toolbar | ■ Choose File→Options→Quick Access toolbar.<br>■ Choose Commands Not in the Ribbon from the Choose Commands From list.<br>■ Scroll down the list, select Send to Mail Recipient, and click the Add button. |
| Send an entire workbook as an attachment to an Outlook email message | ■ Open the workbook file you wish to send by email.<br>■ Choose File→Save & Send→Send Using E-mail→Send as Attachment (or click the Send to Mail Recipient button on the Quick Access toolbar, choose Send the Entire Workbook as an Attachment, and click OK).<br>■ Address the message and revise the default subject (the document name) for the message, if desired.<br>■ Click the Send button on the message window.<br>■ Close the message window. |
| Send a single worksheet as an Outlook email message | ■ Display the worksheet you wish to send by email.<br>■ Click the Send to Mail Recipient button on the Quick Access toolbar, choose Send the Current Sheet as the Message Body, and click OK.<br>■ Enter the email recipient(s), subject, and a brief introduction.<br>■ Click the Send This Sheet button on the email form toolbar.<br>■ Click the Send to Mail Recipient button on the Quick Access toolbar to hide the email window. |

## DEVELOP YOUR SKILLS 6.7.1
# Send a Workbook via Email

*In this exercise, you will set up a workbook to be emailed as an attachment. Because an email account may not be available on your computer, you will not actually send the message.*

*Before You Begin: The Sales Performance Charts workbook should be open. Outlook or another email program compatible with Microsoft Office should be installed.*

1. Choose **File→Save & Send**, make certain **Send Using E-mail** is the selected category, and click **Send as Attachment** at the right of Backstage view.
   *After a few moments, a new message is created in an Outlook message window (or another program set as the default email program for your computer). Notice that the Excel workbook is already attached. Its filename is visible in the Attached box.*

2. Address the message to **Mary Wright** (for a fictitious person in your email contacts list).

3. Change the message **subject** to **Sales Performance Report**.

4. Click in the **body** of the message and type the following text:

**Hello Mary,**
**The sales performance report is attached for your review.**
**For your convenience, charts have been created for data comparison.**
**Regards, Talos**

*A Send button may not be available in the email form. Because many computer classrooms are not equipped with email accounts, at this point you will close the message rather than send it.*

5. **Close** the email program window.

6. Leave the workbook **open** for the next exercise.

## 6.8 Importing Data into Excel via a Web Query

**Video Lesson**   labyrinthelab.com/videos

Many web pages are created using a table structure. Some data may change frequently, such as stock quotes on an external web page or weekly sales numbers on an organization's intranet. The From Web command is used to create a web query that retrieves this type of data into a worksheet. You can set the data to refresh once when the workbook is opened or as frequently as every minute while the workbook is open. You may add a previously saved web query to any worksheet. Excel includes connections to a few "refreshable" queries, which may be accessed with the Existing Connections command on the Ribbon.

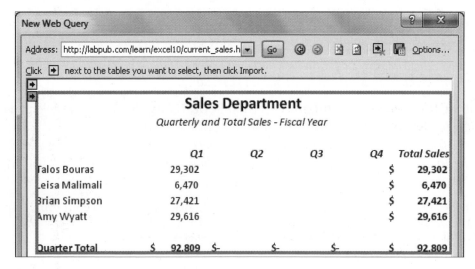

Selecting the table data from a web page to include in a web query

| QUICK REFERENCE | IMPORTING DATA VIA A WEB QUERY |
|---|---|
| **Task** | **Procedure** |
| Create a web query and import data to a worksheet | ■ Display the worksheet into which you wish to import the web data. |
| | ■ Ensure that your Internet connection is active. |
| | ■ Choose Data→Get External Data→From Web  from the Ribbon. |
| | ■ Enter the web page address and click one or more yellow arrows to select table areas on the web page. |
| | ■ Click Options, choose the desired formatting or other options in the Web Query Options dialog box, and click OK. |
| | ■ Click the Save Query button on the toolbar in the New Web Query dialog box, navigate to the desired location, and enter the filename. |
| | ■ Click Import in the New Web Query dialog box. |
| | ■ Choose a starting cell in the existing worksheet or choose New Worksheet as the destination. |
| | ■ Click the Properties button and select the desired refresh or other options in the External Data Range Properties dialog box. |
| | ■ Click OK in the Import Data dialog box. |
| Use a previously saved web query | ■ Choose Data→Get External Data→Existing Connections from the Ribbon. |
| | ■ Choose an existing connection from the list or click Browse for More and navigate to the desired web query file. |
| | ■ Choose the desired location for the data in the Import Data dialog box. |

DEVELOP YOUR SKILLS 6.8.1

# Import Data from a Web Page

*In this exercise, you will create a web query that places the current Quarter 1 sales from a web page into a worksheet.*

*Before You Begin: Your Internet connection should be active and the Sales Performance Charts workbook should be open.*

## Create a Web Query

1. Click the **Insert Worksheet** button to the right of the sheet tabs and **rename** the new sheet to **Current Sales**.

2. Choose **Data→Get External Data→From Web** from the Ribbon.
   *In the New Web Query dialog box, Internet Explorer connects with the web.*

3. Enter **labyrinthelab.com/excel10** into the address bar and **tap** [Enter].
   *Internet Explorer displays the homepage for your textbook.*

4. From the left navigation bar, choose **Lessons 1–6** and then **Lesson 6**; then, click the **Current Sales** link on the web page.
   *This page displays an Excel workbook that was saved as a web page.*

5. Follow these steps to select the data on the web page:

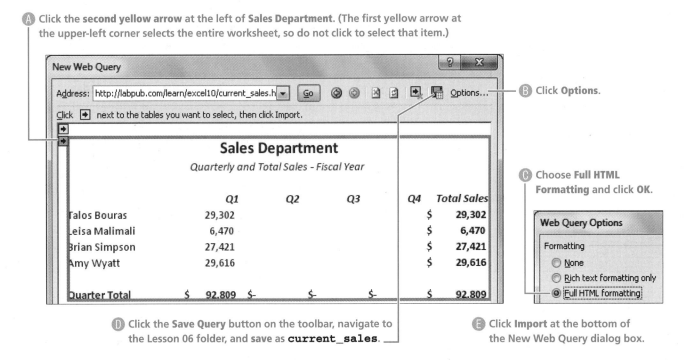

Ⓐ Click the **second yellow arrow** at the left of **Sales Department**. (The first yellow arrow at the upper-left corner selects the entire worksheet, so do not click to select that item.)

Ⓑ Click **Options**.

Ⓒ Choose **Full HTML Formatting** and click **OK**.

Ⓓ Click the **Save Query** button on the toolbar, navigate to the Lesson 06 folder, and **save** as **current_sales**.

Ⓔ Click **Import** at the bottom of the New Web Query dialog box.

## Import the Data

6. If a warning appears, read the warning in the Microsoft Office Excel Security Notice dialog box and click **OK** to confirm that you trust the website source.

7. In the Import Data dialog box, verify that **=$A$1 (cell A1)** in the existing worksheet is selected, and click **Properties**.

8. Review the Refresh Control and other properties available in the External Data Range Properties dialog box; click **Cancel** without making any changes.
   *You could set the data to refresh automatically with a frequency of your choice.*

9. Click **OK** in the Import Data dialog box.
   *The imported data displays on the worksheet. Notice that the data retained its formatting because you selected the Full HTML Formatting option. The Refresh All command on the Ribbon allows you to update the worksheet data manually if the source web page is revised. You could use the saved web query again in another worksheet.*

10. **Save** 💾 the changes and **close** the workbook.

# 6.9 Concepts Review

**Concepts Review**   labyrinthelab.com/excel10

*To check your knowledge of the key concepts introduced in this lesson, complete the Concepts Review quiz by going to the URL listed above. If your classroom is using Labyrinth eLab, you may complete the Concepts Review quiz from within your eLab course.*

# Reinforce Your Skills

## Create a Column Chart

*In this exercise, you will create a column chart to compare total new customers by time period. You will move and format the chart. Then you will switch the row and column data to compare the data by customer source category.*

### Create a Stacked Column Chart

1. **Open** the rs-Service Contracts Comparison workbook from the Lesson 06 folder.

2. Select the **range A3:E7**, taking care not to include the totals in row 8.

3. Choose **Insert→Charts→Column→2-D Column→Stacked Column** from the Ribbon.
   *The chart shows a column for each quarter with the four customer source categories stacked in a column. The stacked column chart is not as cluttered as a clustered column chart, which requires 16 columns to present the same data but allows more precise comparison of single categories.*

### Move and Format the Chart

4. **Point** at the chart area and drag the chart down and to the left until the upper-left corner is at **cell A11**.

5. Choose **Design→Chart Layouts→Layout 3** from the Ribbon.
   *ScreenTips help you to locate Layout 3 in the list. The legend is moved below the horizontal axis and a title text box is added above the chart.*

### Link the Chart Title to a Cell

6. **Click** in the chart title text box.
   *The entry =″Chart Title″ appears in the Formula Bar.*

7. Type **=** to begin a formula.

8. Click **cell A3** in the worksheet and **tap** Enter.
   *You just linked the chart title to the contents of cell A3 in Sheet1. The entry =Sheet1!$A$3 appears in the Formula Bar. Notice that Customer Source now appears in the chart title text box. The chart title would be updated if you edited the text in cell A3.*

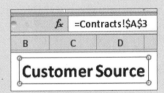

## Switch Row/Column Data

*Notice that the chart's horizontal axis displays the quarters of the year and the legend contains the customer source categories. Each column represents the total new customers in one quarter for comparison among time periods.*

9. Choose **Design→Data→Switch Row/Column** from the Ribbon.

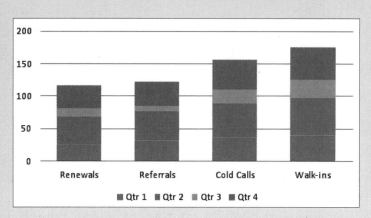

*The data reverse so the horizontal category axis displays the customer source categories. Each column represents the total new customers in a customer source category for comparison among categories.*

10. **Save** 🖫 the changes and **close** the workbook.

### REINFORCE YOUR SKILLS 6.2
## Adjust a Chart

*In this exercise, you will correct the data source range and convert a column chart to a line chart. The chart is formatted with a grayscale chart style suitable for printing on a grayscale printer.*

### Correct a Data Range

1. **Open** the rs-Chart Conversion workbook from the Lesson 06 folder.
   *An embedded column chart has been created on the Service Contracts sheet.*

2. Inspect the chart to locate an error in the way data are labeled.

*The categories on the horizontal axis are labeled 1 through 4 rather than Qtr 1 through Qtr 4. Excel used a default number series, which indicates a common error.*

3. **Select** the chart and notice that the chart data range does not include the category labels in row 3.

| | A | B | C | D | E |
|---|---|---|---|---|---|
| 3 | **Customer Source** | **Qtr 1** | **Qtr 2** | **Qtr 3** | **Qtr 4** |
| 4 | Renewals | 47 | 37 | 33 | 44 |
| 5 | Referrals | 22 | 28 | 30 | 32 |
| 6 | Cold Calls | 26 | 17 | 25 | 22 |
| 7 | Walk-ins | 18 | 20 | 15 | 17 |

4. Choose **Design→Data→Select Data** from the Ribbon; drag the **Select Data Source** dialog box to view the worksheet data, if necessary.
*You learned earlier in this lesson to reselect the chart data range. In the next step, you will use an alternative method to reselect just the horizontal axis labels.*

5. Click the **Edit** button in the Horizontal (Category) Axis Labels area of the dialog box.

6. Select the **range B3:E3** in the worksheet, click **OK** to exit the Axis Labels dialog box, and click **OK** again.
*The category axis labels are shown correctly on the chart.*

## Convert the Chart to a Line Chart

*Suppose you are interested in seeing only the trends in customer source rather than the numbers in individual quarters. You can easily convert the column chart to a line chart.*

7. Choose **Design→Type→Change Chart Type** 📊 from the Ribbon.

8. Choose **Line with Markers** in the Line category and click **OK**.

9. Choose **Layout→Labels→Data Labels** 📊→ **None** from the Ribbon.

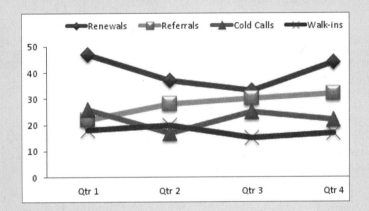

*The line chart shows downward and upward trends.*

10. **Deselect** the chart and **save** 💾 the changes.

11. Display the **print preview** in Backstage view, **print**, and **close** the workbook.
*Both the worksheet and the chart should print on a single page.*

# Create Pie Charts

*In this exercise, you will create two pie charts to illustrate employee salaries. The charts will show how salary cost is divided among departments and how one department's salaries are allocated. You will embed the first chart and place the second chart on a separate sheet.*

## Create the Company Chart

1. **Open** the rs-Payroll Expenses workbook from the Lesson 06 folder.

2. Use the Ctrl key to select the **ranges B3:E3** and **B9:E9**.

3. Choose **Insert→Charts→Pie→2-D Pie→Pie** from the Ribbon.
   *If you included the totals in column F by mistake, either delete and reinsert the chart or use the Select Data command in the Design ribbon to reselect the data source range.*

4. Move the chart to **row 11** below the worksheet data.

## Format the Company Chart

5. Choose **Layout→Labels→Data Labels** 📊→**More Data Labels Options** from the Ribbon.
   *The Format Data Labels dialog box displays the Label Options.*

6. Place a checkmark next to **Category Name and Percentage**, remove the checkmark from **Value**, and click **Close**.
   *Notice that the data label does not fit inside the smallest pie slice. This is OK, but an option can make the labels look uniform.*

7. Choose **Layout→Labels→Data Labels** 📊→**Inside End** from the Ribbon.
   *This data labels option causes all data labels to fit inside their pie slices.*

8. Click in the legend and **tap** Delete.
   *The legend is unnecessary because the department names are in the data labels.*

9. Choose **Layout→Labels→Chart Title** 📊→**Above Chart** from the Ribbon.

10. Select the default **chart title** text and use the Enter key while typing **Payroll Expenses by Department** to create a two-line title, as shown.

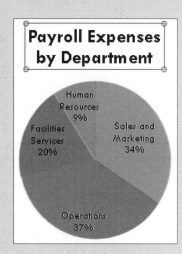

## Create a Pie Chart for the Sales and Marketing Department

11. Select the **range A3:B8**.
    *Using the* Ctrl *key is unnecessary because columns A and B are adjacent.*

12. Choose **Insert→Charts→Pie→2-D Pie→Pie** from the Ribbon.
    *Notice that the text in cell B3 is used as the chart title because B3 is the first cell in the data series.*

13. Choose **Design→Chart Layouts→Layout 1** from the Ribbon.
    *Layout 1 removes the legend and adds data labels with categories and percentages.*

## Move the Department Chart to Its Own Sheet

14. Choose **Design→Location→Move Chart** 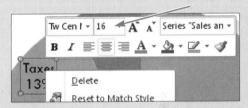 from the Ribbon.
    *The Move Chart dialog box is displayed. You can move a chart to a new sheet or as an embedded object to an existing sheet.*

15. Select the **text entry** (such as Chart1) next to New Sheet, type **Sales and Marketing**, and **tap** Enter to choose **OK**.
    *The new sheet containing the chart appears before Sheet1 in the workbook tab order.*

16. Choose **Design→Chart Styles→More** ⏷ from the Ribbon and choose an attractive Quick Style.
    *You may want to choose a grayscale Quick Style if you plan to print on a grayscale printer. The styles in the last row contain a black background, which you should avoid printing to conserve printer toner or ink.*

17. **Right-click** a data label to select all data labels and choose a **larger font size** from the Mini toolbar.
    *Some data labels may appear outside their pie slices, depending on the font you chose.*

18. **Save** 💾 the changes and **close** the workbook.

# Create a Doughnut Chart

*In this exercise, you will create a doughnut chart. Like pie charts, doughnut charts are useful for comparing parts of a whole. However, doughnut charts can contain more than one data series. Each ring in a doughnut chart represents a data series. The chart you create will compare the quarter 4 sales with total sales.*

## Create the Chart

1. **Open** the rs-Sales Comparison workbook from the Lesson 06 folder.

2. Take a few moments to determine the ranges that need to be selected in order to create a chart that **compares Qtr 4 sales** with the **total product sales**.

3. Use the Ctrl key to select the **ranges A3:A7 and E3:F7**.

4. Choose **Insert→Charts→Other Charts**  **→Doughnut→ Doughnut** from the Ribbon.
   *The Total data series appears in the outer ring of the chart. The Qtr 4 data series is in the inner ring. You will add formatting in the next few steps to identify the data clearly.*

## Format Data Labels and the Title

5. Choose **Design→Chart Layouts→Layout 6** from the Ribbon.
   *The layout adds a default chart title and data labels with percentages.*

6. **Click once** on the data label for total **Cold Calls (21%)**, and then click again to select just that label.

7. **Choose Layout→Labels→Data Labels** 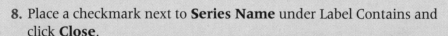 **→More Data Label Options** from the Ribbon.
   *The Format Data Label dialog box appears with the Label Options displayed.*

8. Place a checkmark next to **Series Name** under Label Contains and click **Close**.

9. Select only the **Cold Calls** label for Qtr 4 (24%) and **repeat** the previous step to add the series name to the label.
   *If labels were displayed for all data series names, the labels would overlap. Formatting at least one label on each ring, however, is important for identifying the time period that each ring represents.*

10. Change the default **chart title** to `Sales Source` (the contents of cell A3 on the worksheet).

## Move and Size the Chart

11. **Drag** the chart below the worksheet data and make certain all the data are visible.

12. Follow these steps to resize the chart width:

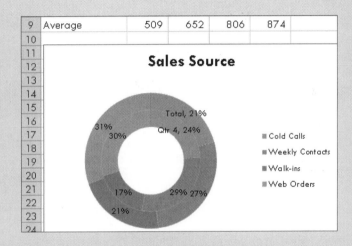

**A** Point at the **middle resizing handle** on the right edge of the chart frame until the mouse changes to a **double-pointed arrow**.

**B** **Drag to the left** until the right edge of the chart aligns with the right edge of **column** F.

13. **Save** 🖫 the changes, and **close** the workbook.

# Email a Worksheet

*In this exercise, you will place a worksheet into the body of an email message.*

*Before You Begin: The Send to Mail Recipient command should be available on the Quick Access toolbar or you must have rights to add the command.*

1. **Open** the rs-E-mail Chart workbook from the Lesson 06 folder and display the Sales by Rep chart sheet. (If a message appears about data connections above the worksheet, click Enable Content.)

2. Verify that the **Send to Mail Recipient** command is installed on the Quick Access toolbar. If it is not, follow these steps to install the command:

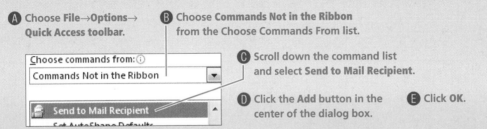

Ⓐ Choose **File→Options→ Quick Access toolbar.**

Ⓑ Choose **Commands Not in the Ribbon** from the Choose Commands From list.

Ⓒ Scroll down the command list and select **Send to Mail Recipient.**

Ⓓ Click the **Add** button in the center of the dialog box.

Ⓔ Click **OK.**

3. Click the **Send to Mail Recipient** button on the Quick Access toolbar.
   *A prompt appears, telling you about the two options for sending the entire workbook or a single worksheet.*

4. Choose the **Send the Current Sheet as the Message Body** option and click **OK**. (If a message appears about connections, click Enable Content.)
   *An Outlook (or other default email program) message window appears, in which you can address the message. The active worksheet appears in the message body.*

**5.** Follow these steps to set up the email message:

Ⓐ Type **Mary Wright** in the **To** box and assume that this name is set up with an email address in your contacts list.

Ⓑ Change the **subject line** as shown here.

Ⓒ If using Outlook, enter the **introductory message** as shown here.

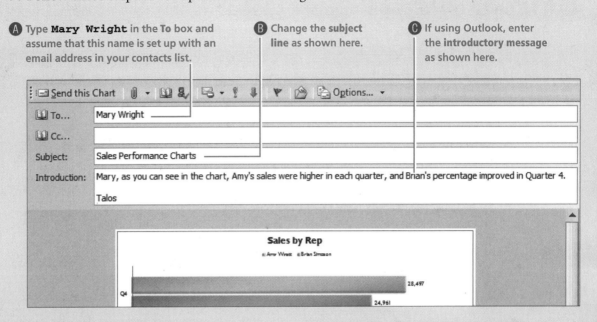

*The Send This Chart button may not be available at the upper-left corner of the email form. Because many computer classrooms are not equipped with email accounts, at this point, you will close the message rather than send it.*

**6.** Click the **Send to Mail Recipient** 🖼 button on the Quick Access toolbar.
*The button toggles between the email message window and the Excel workbook window when a worksheet is in the message body.*

**7. Close** the workbook. Do **not** save when asked if you wish to save.
*An email message cannot be saved in a workbook.*

# Apply Your Skills

## Create a Line Chart

*In this exercise, you will create a line chart on a separate sheet, rename the sheet tabs, and print a chart.*

| | A | B |
|---|---|---|
| 1 | Green Clean Web Orders | |
| 2 | Product Sales | |
| 3 | | |
| 4 | Date | Web Orders |
| 5 | Mar-15 | 92 |
| 6 | Apr-15 | 146 |
| 7 | May-15 | 122 |
| 8 | Jun-15 | 154 |
| 9 | Jul-15 | 128 |
| 10 | Aug-15 | 140 |
| 11 | Sep-15 | 231 |
| 12 | Oct-15 | 245 |
| 13 | Nov-15 | 258 |
| 14 | Dec-15 | 244 |
| 15 | Jan-16 | 231 |
| 16 | Feb-16 | 176 |
| 17 | **Total** | **2,167** |

1. Start a **new** workbook and create the worksheet shown at right:
   - **Enter** dates for the actual previous 12 months rather than the dates shown.
   - Use **AutoFill** to expand the date series.
   - **Resize** the column widths as necessary.

2. **Format** the dates so that they are displayed as *Mar-15* without the year (your year may be different).

3. Use the worksheet data to create the following chart:
   - Set up the **axis labels** and **title** as shown (your years may be different).
   - Do **not** include a legend.

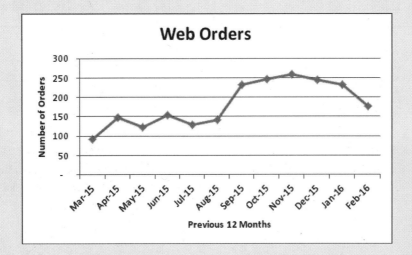

4. Place the **chart** on a separate sheet, naming it **Web Orders Trend**. *The dates will not appear slanted after the chart is moved.*

5. **Rename** the Sheet1 tab to **Supporting Data**.

6. **Print** the chart.

7. **Save** 💾 with the name **as-Web Orders** in the Lesson 06 folder and **close** the workbook.

# Create a Worksheet and Pie Chart

*In this exercise, you will create a worksheet and a pie chart based on the data in the worksheet. You will also apply a style to the worksheet; insert formulas in the worksheet; and move, resize, and explode a piece of the pie chart.*

1. Use these guidelines to create the worksheet and chart shown in the following illustration:

   ■ **Type** all numbers and text entries as shown, but use formulas to calculate the New Balance in **column E** and the Totals, Highest, and Lowest values in **rows 9–11**. The formula for New Balance is New Balance = Beginning Balance + Purchases – Payments. Calculate the Totals in **row 9** with AutoSum, and use the MAX and MIN functions for the Highest and Lowest calculations in **rows 10 and 11**.

   ■ Use the font size of your choice for the title **cell A1**, merge and center the title across the worksheet, and then format the workbook with the theme of your choice. Apply a cell style to the cells in **row 3** and add a border around the data in **rows 9–11**.

   ■ Create the embedded 3-D pie chart shown in the illustration. The pie chart slices represent the new balance percentages of each customer. The pie chart does not represent any of the data in **rows 9–11**.

   ■ Adjust the position and size of the embedded chart as shown in the illustration.

   ■ **Explode** the largest slice.

   ■ Format all pie slice data labels as italic by using a command on the Mini toolbar or the Home tab of the Ribbon.

2. **Print** the worksheet and embedded chart on a **single page**.

3. **Save** with the name **as-Accounts Receivable Report** in the Lesson 06 folder and **close** the workbook.

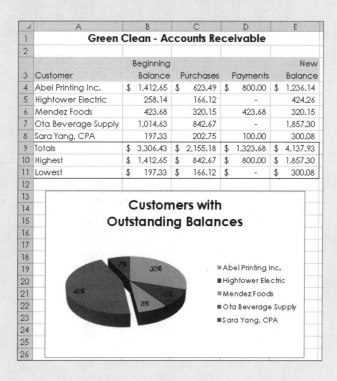

# Create a Column Chart and Edit Worksheets

*In this exercise, you will create a column chart embedded in the worksheet and then move, resize, and print the chart.*

1. **Create** the worksheet and embedded column chart shown in the following illustration. Use the font size of your choice for the title in **cell A1** and enter the actual year instead of the words *Current Year*. Notice that the column chart is 2-D. The differences in **row 6** are simply the Revenues numbers minus the Expenses numbers. Choose an appropriate chart layout so the negative numbers dip below the category axis in the chart as shown. Move the legend to the top of the chart as shown.

| | A | B | C | D | E | F | G | H |
|---|---|---|---|---|---|---|---|---|
| 1 | Net Income - Current Year | | | | | | | |
| 2 | | | | | | | | |
| 3 | | January | February | March | April | May | June | Total |
| 4 | Revenues | $259,425 | $265,360 | $192,054 | $259,425 | $265,360 | $161,054 | $1,402,678 |
| 5 | Expenses | 188,727 | 182,698 | 207,045 | 188,727 | 182,698 | 214,775 | 1,164,670 |
| 6 | Net Income (Loss) | $ 70,698 | $ 82,662 | $ (14,991) | $ 70,698 | $ 82,662 | $ (53,721) | $ 238,008 |
| 7 | | | | | | | | |

2. Change the **chart colors** to shades of gray, suitable for printing on a grayscale printer.

3. Move the chart to a **separate sheet**, and **rename** the sheet tab to **Net Income Chart**.

4. **Rename** the worksheet tab to **Net Income Analysis**.

5. **Delete** the unused sheet tabs, Sheet2 and Sheet3.

6. Add the **color** of your choice to the **Net Income Analysis** sheet tab.

7. **Preview** the worksheet to ensure that it fits on one page and then **print** the worksheet and chart.

8. **Save** with the name **as-Net Income Analysis** in the Lesson 06 folder and **close** the workbook.

# Send a Workbook via Email

*In this exercise, you will email a workbook to yourself.*

You should not perform this exercise if your computer cannot send and receive email.

*Before You Begin: You must have completed Apply Your Skills 6.3. Your Internet connection should be active. You must have an email account in Microsoft Outlook or other default email program that works within Microsoft Office on your computer.*

1. **Open** the as-Net Income Analysis workbook from the Lesson 06 folder.

2. Attach the entire **workbook** to an email message to yourself at your own email address.

3. Change the **subject line** to `Sending a Workbook via Email`.

4. In the **message area**, enter a greeting, a line describing the file, and a closing with your name.

5. **Send** the message.

6. Display your Inbox in **Outlook** (or other email program you used) and click the **Send/Receive** button every 30 seconds until the message you sent arrives.

7. **Print** the message after it appears in your Inbox. (It is not necessary to print the attachment.)

8. **Close** the Outlook (or other email) program window.

9. **Close** the workbook. Do **not** save when asked if you wish to save.

# Critical Thinking & Work-Readiness Skills

In the course of working through the following Microsoft Office-based Critical Thinking exercises, you will also be utilizing various work-readiness skills, some of which are listed next to each exercise. Go to labyrinthelab.com/workreadiness to learn more about the work-readiness skills.

## 6.1 Analyze Data Using an Embedded Column Chart

**WORK-READINESS SKILLS APPLIED**

- Seeing things in the mind's eye
- Reading
- Interpreting and communicating information

As part of an effort to reduce costs and environmental impact, Talos Bouras is tasked with reporting the delivery reps' driving activities. Open ct-Rep Driving Data (Lesson 06 folder). Create an embedded column chart that displays the miles driven by each driver. Title the chart appropriately. Label each driver at the base of the appropriate chart column. Use data labels to display the number of miles driven at the top of the appropriate column. Remove the legend. Create a similar chart to graph the total expenses for each driver. Save the file as **ct-Rep Driving Charts**. If working in a group, present your results. Answer questions such as: Who drove the most? Who drives the most efficiently? If working alone, type your answers in a Word document named **ct-Questions** saved to your Lesson 06 folder. Close the workbook.

## 6.2 Display Test Results Using a Pie Chart

**WORK-READINESS SKILLS APPLIED**

- Seeing things in the mind's eye
- Reading
- Interpreting and communicating information

Open ct-Test Results (Lesson 06 folder). On a separate worksheet, create a 3-D pie chart showing the percentage of contribution for each cleaner category to the overall total produced. Apply an appropriate style to the chart. Include appropriate data labels and give the chart a title. Change the 3-D rotation of the chart so the largest slice is in front. Determine whether or not to display the legend. Explode the largest slice. Change the sheet name to **Test Pie Chart** and save the file as **ct-Test Pie Chart** in your Lesson 06 folder. If working in a group, present your results. Discuss what cleaning product creates the most waste. Can you think of any alternative cleaning products that might be used? If working alone, type your answers in a Word document named **ct-Questions2** saved to your Lesson 06 folder.

## 6.3 Chart Sales Trends

**WORK-READINESS SKILLS APPLIED**

- Seeing things in the mind's eye
- Interpreting and communicating information
- Using computers to process information

Green Clean's sales results are in! Your job is to chart the sales data so that your manager can discuss the implications in a team meeting. Open the the Microsoft Word document named ct-Sales Results (Lesson 06 folder). Enter the information shown into a new Excel workbook. Type the actual current year, and calculate the totals. Review the data to determine the significant trends in sales performance. Create an embedded pie chart with appropriate labeling for one of these trends. Show other results in a columnar chart on a separate sheet. Keep in mind the data relationships that each chart type can best display. Save the file as **ct-Sales Charts** in your Lesson 06 folder. Why might you (or your manager) want to see the information displayed both ways? Type your answer in a Word document named **ct-Questions3** saved to your Lesson 06 folder.

# Working with Large Worksheets

## LEARNING OBJECTIVES

After studying this lesson, you will be able to:

■ Sort worksheet rows in alphabetic and numeric order

■ View nonadjacent areas of large worksheets and view multiple worksheets simultaneously

■ Set printing options to center and fit the worksheet on one page

■ Set options to print a worksheet on multiple pages

In this lesson, you will learn several techniques for working with large worksheets. You will sort the worksheet rows in alphabetic or numeric order. You will freeze headings, split the worksheet window to compare data from separate areas of the worksheet, and view two worksheets side by side. You will set print options, including margins, scaling, headers, and footers. For worksheets that cannot print on one page, you will set headings to print on each page and adjust page breaks.

# Managing Large Worksheets

My Virtual Campus
Corporation sells its
web application, a social
networking intranet, to
colleges and universities.
Students, alumni, faculty,

and staff can use this website to communicate with others, advertise campus events, collaborate on
projects, post job opportunities, and so forth. Roxana Ortega is a sales analyst who provides support
to college and university accounts to ensure customer satisfaction and build new product sales. She
has created an Excel workbook containing website usage data for Seaview College.

Roxana will sort the records by category. She will set worksheet views to compare data in her large
worksheet more easily. To prepare for printing the worksheet, Roxana will set several options for
reading the data across multiple pages. These options include a header and titles in rows and columns
that print on every page to label the data.

Names sorted
alphabetically
within the
Alumni
category

| ⬒ | A | B | C | D | E | F |
|---|---|---|---|---|---|---|
| 1 | Seaview College Usage Report | | | | | |
| 2 | | | | Year 1 | | |
| 3 | | | | | | |
| 4 | Last Name | First Name | Category | Jan | Feb | Mar |
| 5 | Do | Alan | Alumni | 0.0 | 0.0 | 0.0 |
| 6 | Johnson | Chriss | Alumni | 0.0 | 0.0 | 3.5 |
| 7 | Nguyen | Jimmy | Alumni | 0.0 | 2.0 | 0.0 |
| 8 | Amal | Asan | Faculty | 1.5 | 0.0 | 0.0 |
| 9 | Kim | Tae Joon | Faculty | 0.0 | 0.0 | 0.0 |
| 10 | Kissinger | Dorothy | Faculty | 14.0 | 17.5 | 36.0 |

The usage report sorted by category with names alphabetized
within each category

Header ——— Years 1-2, Seaview College Usage Report

Title rows

Seaview College Usage Report

| Last Name | First Name | Category | Aug | Sep | Oct | Nov | Dec | Totals |
|---|---|---|---|---|---|---|---|---|
| Do | Alan | Alumni | 0.0 | 0.0 | 2.5 | 0.0 | 3.0 | 79.0 |
| Johnson | Chriss | Alumni | 2.0 | 4.5 | 11.5 | 13.0 | 7.0 | 84.5 |
| Nguyen | Jimmy | Alumni | 0.0 | 0.0 | 0.0 | 2.0 | 3.0 | 24.5 |

Title columns

Page 2 of the printed report with a header and repeating titles that identify the data on every page

# 7.1 Sorting Worksheet Data

**Video Lesson**    labyrinthelab.com/videos

When your worksheet must be organized in alphabetic or numeric order, Excel can easily sort the list. Rather than adding new records by inserting blank rows one by one within the list, you may enter the records at the end of the list and then sort the entire list. Excel can order the list based on the data in any single column that you select. For example, you may sort by name, date, item number, or dollar amount. By using the Sort command on the Ribbon, you may sort by multiple columns. In the following example, records with the same last name are then sorted by first name.

An unsorted list

| Last Name | First Name |
|-----------|-----------|
| Do | Alan |
| Johnson | Chriss |
| Nguyen | Jimmy |
| Amal | Asan |
| Kim | Tae Joon |
| Kissinger | Dorothy |
| Lang | Thomas |
| Malinski | Ashton |

| Last Name | First Name | Category |
|-----------|-----------|----------|
| Abbott | Ami | Student |
| Amal | Asan | Faculty |
| Basinger | Stephon | Student |
| Do | Alan | Alumni |
| Do | Ty | Staff |
| Garcia Moreno | Juan | Staff |
| Harris | Patti | Staff |
| Johnson | Chriss | Alumni |

The list after sorting on two columns with names in alphabetic order

A sort is performed on all adjacent rows. If your worksheet contains totals below the data rows, insert a blank row between the two sections to avoid including the total row in the sort. You may, however, select only certain rows to sort when necessary.

If a sorting problem arises and Undo is unavailable, just close the workbook without saving it. Reopen the workbook to restore its original appearance.

## Sorting by a Single Column

The Sort A to Z $\boxed{\overset{A}{\underset{Z}{\downarrow}}}$ and Sort Z to A $\boxed{\overset{Z}{\underset{A}{\downarrow}}}$ buttons let you sort quickly by one column. Sort A to Z will sort records in ascending order from lowest to highest, and Sort Z to A sorts in descending order from highest to lowest. Excel sorts all rows in the contiguous list unless it determines that the list has a header row. A header row is the row at the top of a list that contains column headings.

If you often perform sorts, remember that you may add the Sort A to Z and Sort Z to A buttons to the Quick Access toolbar.

## Sorting Selected Rows

If the list contains rows you do not want included in the sort, you must select the rows you *do* want sorted before selecting one of the sort buttons. Excel will use column A as the sort key by default.

To keep the data together for each record, always select *one cell* in a column or *entire rows* before sorting. Do not attempt to sort by highlighting several cells in one column, such as the last names. The names would be in sequence, but the other cells belonging to each record would not move—a data disaster.

| QUICK REFERENCE | SORTING WORKSHEET DATA |
|---|---|
| **Task** | **Procedure** |
| Sort by a single column | ■ Select one cell in the desired column on or under the header row.<br>■ Choose Data→Sort & Filter and choose one of the following from the Ribbon:<br>  ◆ Sort A to Z $\boxed{\substack{A \\ Z}\downarrow}$<br>  ◆ Sort Z to A $\boxed{\substack{Z \\ A}\downarrow}$ |
| Sort selected rows by a single column | ■ Select a cell in the sort key column.<br>■ Select the rows to be sorted.<br>■ Choose Data→Sort & Filter and choose one of the following from the Ribbon:<br>  ◆ Sort A to Z $\boxed{\substack{A \\ Z}\downarrow}$<br>  ◆ Sort Z to A $\boxed{\substack{Z \\ A}\downarrow}$ |
| Sort by multiple columns | ■ Choose Data→Sort & Filter→Sort $\boxed{\substack{A Z \\ Z A}}$ from the Ribbon.<br>■ Choose the first column to be sorted from the Sort By list and change the Sort On and Order settings, if necessary.<br>■ Click the Add Level button to add a second sort category and change its settings, if necessary.<br>■ If desired, add more sort levels.<br>■ If the list to be sorted has a header row, place a checkmark next to My Data Has Headers.<br>■ Click OK. |

## DEVELOP YOUR SKILLS 7.1.1
# Sort by One Column

*In this exercise, you will use the sort buttons to sort a list in a workbook.*

### Sort Entire Lists

1. **Open** the Seaview College Usage Report workbook from the Lesson 07 folder in your file storage location.

2. If necessary, **maximize** 🔲 the window and click the **Years 1-2** sheet tab to display the worksheet.

3. Take a few moments to browse through this worksheet.
   *Notice that this worksheet is very large and contains monthly hours of website usage for a two-year period. You will use this worksheet throughout this lesson.*

4. Scroll to the top of the worksheet and select **cell A5**.
   *Notice that the rows are not in alphabetical order. In the next few steps, you will sort rows 5–42. The rows will be sorted by last name in column A because you selected a cell in this column. Keep in mind, however, that all the data in each row will stay together. Before you begin, notice that row 5 (Thomas Lang) has the Faculty category in cell C5 and the value 4.5 in cell D5.*

5. Choose **Data→Sort & Filter→Sort A to Z** [A↓Z] from the Ribbon. (Take care not to confuse this button with the Sort button on the Ribbon. Cancel the Sort dialog box if you opened it by mistake.)
*The Ami Abbott row is now on top because it is the first row in alphabetic order. Also notice that the entire rows have been rearranged. For example, the Thomas Lang row is now in the middle of the list and his data, Faculty and 4.5, are still part of that row. Notice that the header row 4 was not included in the sort. Finally, notice that the total row 44 was not included because a blank row separates the totals from the data rows.*

6. Choose **Data→Sort & Filter→Sort Z to A** [Z↓A] from the Ribbon to reverse the sort order.

7. **Scroll** to the right until the totals on the right side of the spreadsheet are visible, as shown at right.

8. Select **cell AB5**.

9. Choose **Data→Sort & Filter→Sort A to Z** [A↓Z] from the Ribbon to sort the rows based on the total hours in column AB.
*The Sort A to Z and Sort Z to A buttons always sort rows based on the column that contains the pointer.*

| Z | AA | AB | AC |
|---|---|---|---|
| | | | |
| | | | |
| Nov | Dec | Totals | |
| 0.0 | 3.0 | 79.0 | |
| 13.0 | 7.0 | 84.5 | |
| 2.0 | 3.0 | 24.5 | |
| 15.0 | 8.5 | 99.0 | |

10. Choose **Data→Sort & Filter→Sort Z to A** [Z↓A] from the Ribbon to sort in descending order based on total hours.

11. Scroll to the left until **column A** is visible.

12. Select **cell A5**, and then choose the **Sort A to Z** [A↓Z] button.

13. **Save** [💾] the changes.

## Inadvertently Include Totals in a Sort

*A blank row separates the list from the totals rows. Let's see what happens without a blank row.*

14. **Scroll down**, as shown in the following illustration, until the **totals** are visible.

| 40 | Sufi | Seri | Student | 7.0 | 2.0 | 16.0 | 4.5 | 13.0 | 8.0 | |
|---|---|---|---|---|---|---|---|---|---|---|
| 41 | Tejani | Sabrina | Student | 10.0 | 8.5 | 16.0 | 8.0 | 10.0 | 0.0 | |
| 42 | Zorn | Paul | Student | 13.0 | 8.0 | 4.0 | 2.0 | 14.0 | 3.5 | |
| 43 | | | | | | | | | | |
| 44 | **Month Totals** | | | 303.5 | 366.5 | 396.0 | 292.0 | 327.5 | 199.0 | |
| 45 | | | | | | | | | | |

15. Point to the row selector for **row 43, right-click**, and choose **Delete** from the pop-up (or context) menu.
*The blank row is deleted, and the rows containing totals now are a part of the list.*

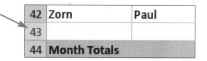

| 42 | Zorn | Paul |
|---|---|---|
| 43 | | |
| 44 | **Month Totals** | |

16. Select **cell A39**, and then choose **Data→Sort & Filter→Sort A to Z** [A↓Z] from the Ribbon.
*Notice that Excel included the totals rows in the sort with one total row now in row 34.*

17. **Undo** [↶] the sort.
*Next you will select rows 5–42 and sort. Because the first and last rows do not display on the same screen, dragging to select rows would be difficult.*

## Sort Selected Rows

*When no blank row separates the list from the totals, select only the rows to be sorted.*

18. Select **cell A5** to set column A as the sort key.

19. Follow these steps to select rows 5–42:

Ⓐ Click the row selector for **row 5.**

Ⓑ **Scroll down** until the bottom of the list is visible.

Ⓒ **Hold down** Shift and select the row selector for **row 42.**

| 4 | Last Name | First Name | Category | Jan |
|---|---|---|---|---|
| 5 | Abbott | Ami | Student | 18.5 |
| 6 | Amal | Asan | Faculty | 1.5 |
| 41 | Tejani | Tabriz | Faculty | 0.0 |
| 42 | Zorn | Paul | Student | 13.0 |
| 43 | **Month Totals** | | | 303.5 |

Ⓓ **Release the** Shift key.

*Rows 5–42 should appear highlighted. Make certain that entire rows are selected. If you select only certain cells in the rows, such as the names in the range A5:A42 , Excel will sort only those cells. The data would not match the names and would be useless.*

20. Choose **Data→Sort & Filter→Sort A to Z** ↓ from the Ribbon.
    *Only the selected student data rows are sorted. You did not include the totals in your selection.*

21. **Right-click** the row selector for **row 43**, and choose **Insert** from the context menu to insert a blank row that separates the data from the totals row.
    *Inserting the blank row will ensure that totals are not included in future sorts. The student data should appear sorted alphabetically by last name. If you had a problem with sorting, close the workbook without saving and reopen it.*

22. **Save** the workbook and leave it **open**.

# Sorting by Multiple Columns

| **Video Lesson** | labyrinthelab.com/videos |
|---|---|

The Sort dialog box is used to specify multiple sort keys for multiple-column sorts. For example, a worksheet displays last names in column A and first names in column B. Using the Sort dialog box, you may instruct Excel to sort the rows by last name and then by first name. This way, all rows with the same last name, such as Do, will be grouped together. Then those rows would be sorted by first name within each group (Do, Alan, followed by Do, Melissa, and then Do, Ty). You may sort by more than two columns when necessary. You display the Sort dialog box with the Data→Sort & Filter→Sort command.

### DEVELOP YOUR SKILLS 7.1.2
## Sort by Multiple Columns

*In this exercise, you will use the Sort dialog box to perform a two-column sort and a three-column sort.*

1. **Select** any cell in the data list.

2. Choose **Data→Sort & Filter→Sort** from the Ribbon.
   *The Sort dialog box appears.*

3. Follow these steps to sort the list by last name and then by first name:

Ⓐ If necessary, choose **Last Name** from the Sort By list.

Ⓑ Make certain **Values** is the **Sort On** setting.

Ⓒ Make certain **A to Z** is the Order setting.

Ⓓ Click the **Add Level** button to add a second sort category.

Ⓔ Choose **First Name** for the second sort, and make certain that **Values** and **A to Z** are set for this sort.

Ⓕ Make certain the **My Data Has Headers** option box is checked. (This option indicates that the list has a header row.)

Ⓖ Click **OK** to perform the two-column sort.

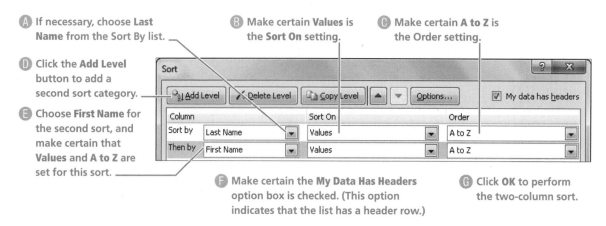

*Notice that the records with last name Do are sorted alphabetically by first name. Check that other records with the same last name are then sorted by first name.*

*Next you will add Category for a three-column sort.*

4. Choose **Data→Sort & Filter→Sort** ![icon] from the Ribbon.
   *The specifications for the two-level sort still display in the Sort dialog box.*

5. Follow these steps to add a sort category and move it up in the sort order:

Ⓐ Click the **Add Level** button.

Ⓑ Choose **Category** for the sort, and make certain that **Values** and **A to Z** are set for this sort.

Ⓒ Click the **Move Up** button to move Category to the top level. (If Category is not at the top, click the button again.)

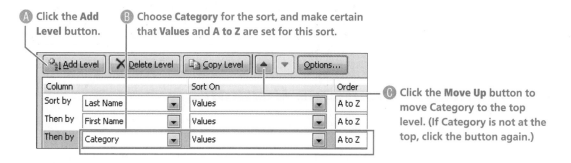

6. Click **OK**.
   *The records are first sorted by category and then by last name within each category. Any duplicate last names are sorted by first name.*

7. **Save** ![icon] the changes, and leave the workbook **open**.

# 7.2 Using Flexible Worksheet Views

**Video Lesson** labyrinthelab.com/videos

Excel allows you to view two areas of a large worksheet that normally could not display together. When done, you may restore the worksheet to its original view. The Freeze Panes and Split commands affect only how the worksheet displays. The worksheet prints as usual. When a workbook is opened, each worksheet displays the view that was in effect when the workbook was last saved. The New Window and Arrange All commands display two or more areas of a large worksheet in separate windows that may be scrolled simultaneously. Two or more worksheets in the same workbook or different workbooks can also be viewed at once. The multiple-window layout may be saved as a workspace for reuse later.

## Freezing Rows or Columns

When you scroll to the right on a wide worksheet, the headings in column A are no longer visible as you bring the next columns into view. As you scroll down, the row containing the column headings disappears. Without the headings, you cannot identify the person or category to which the data belong. Freezing the headings helps you keep your place as you scroll to the right or down the worksheet. When you give the Freeze Panes command, Excel freezes all rows above the selected cell and all columns to the left of the selected cell. You may freeze rows, columns, or both. The following illustration shows a cell selected before freezing headings in both rows and columns.

Use the Freeze Panes command to lock the headings in all worksheets that have more rows or columns than can fit on one screen.

| | A | B | C | D | E | F | G |
|---|---|---|---|---|---|---|---|
| 1 | Seaview College Usage Report | | | | | | |
| 2 | | | | Year 1 | | | |
| 3 | | | | | | | |
| 4 | Last Name | First Name | Category | Jan | Feb | Mar | Apr |
| 5 | Do | Alan | Alumni | 0.0 | 0.0 | 0.0 | 0.0 |
| 6 | Johnson | Chriss | Alumni | 0.0 | 0.0 | 3.5 | 0.0 |
| 7 | Nguyen | Jimmy | Alumni | 0.0 | 2.0 | 0.0 | 0.0 |

Selecting a cell before giving the Freeze Panes command tells Excel where you want the panes frozen.

Before freezing

| | A | B | C | K | L | M | N |
|---|---|---|---|---|---|---|---|
| 1 | Seaview College Usage Report | | | | | | |
| 2 | | | | | | | |
| 3 | | | | | | | |
| 4 | Last Name | First Name | Category | Aug | Sep | Oct | Nov |
| 18 | Harris | Patti | Staff | 4.5 | 6.5 | 3.0 | 0.5 |
| 19 | Johnson | Riley | Staff | 25.5 | 10.0 | 8.5 | 16.0 |
| 20 | Ly | Cindy | Staff | 0.0 | 0.0 | 0.0 | 0.0 |

After freezing: As you scroll, rows above and columns to the left of the selected cell are frozen.

# Freeze Rows and Columns

*In this exercise, you will freeze both rows and columns, rows only, and columns only.*

## Freeze Rows and Columns

1. Scroll to the **right** until the totals column on the right side of the spreadsheet is visible.
   *Columns A and B, which contain the users' names, dropped off the window. Without those headings, you cannot identify the person belonging to the data.*

   | | Y | Z | AA | AB |
   |---|---|---|---|---|
   | 1 | | | | |
   | 2 | | | | |
   | 3 | | | | |
   | 4 | Oct | Nov | Dec | Totals |
   | 5 | 2.5 | 0.0 | 3.0 | 79.0 |
   | 6 | 11.5 | 13.0 | 7.0 | 84.5 |
   | 7 | 0.0 | 2.0 | 3.0 | 24.5 |

2. Tap [Ctrl]+[Home] to move the highlight to **cell A1**.
   *This keystroke combination is useful when you work with large worksheets.*

3. Select **cell D5**.
   *This cell is below the headings in rows 1–4 and to the right of the headings in columns A–C.*

4. Choose **View→Window→Freeze Panes** ▦ menu ▾, and then choose **Freeze Panes** from the Ribbon.
   *The area above and to the left of cell D5 is frozen, indicated by a horizontal and a vertical separation line.*

5. Scroll to the **right** until the totals on the right side of the spreadsheet are in view.
   *The frozen columns A–C remain visible to identify the people belonging to the totals.*

6. Tap [Ctrl]+[Home] on the keyboard to jump back to the home cell, and notice that the highlight moves to cell D5 instead of A1.
   *Cell D5 is now the home cell because you froze the window panes at that location.*

7. Select **cell B5**.
   *Notice that you could edit this cell if desired. Frozen columns and rows still are available for editing.*

8. **Scroll down** until the monthly totals are visible as shown below.

   | | A | B | C | D | E | F | G |
   |---|---|---|---|---|---|---|---|
   | 1 | Seaview College Usage Report | | | | | | |
   | 2 | | | | Year 1 | | | |
   | 3 | | | | | | | |
   | 4 | Last Name | First Name | Category | Jan | Feb | Mar | Apr |
   | 41 | Tejani | Sabrina | Student | 10.0 | 8.5 | 16.0 | 8.0 |
   | 42 | Zorn | Paul | Student | 13.0 | 8.0 | 4.0 | 2.0 |
   | 43 | | | | | | | |
   | 44 | Month Totals | | | 303.5 | 366.5 | 396.0 | 292.0 |

   *The frozen rows 1–4 remain visible to identify the year and months belonging to the totals.*

   *Let's say you ask, "What are the total usage hours for years 1 and 2?" The frozen panes will make it easier to locate this information.*

9. Scroll to the **right** until the totals on the right side of the spreadsheet are visible.

| | A | B | C | Y | Z | AA | AB |
|---|---|---|---|---|---|---|---|
| 1 | Seaview College Usage Report | | | | | | |
| 2 | | | | | | | |
| 3 | | | | | | | |
| 4 | Last Name | First Name | Category | Oct | Nov | Dec | Totals |
| 41 | Tejani | Sabrina | Student | 3.0 | 0.0 | 0.0 | 126.0 |
| 42 | Zorn | Paul | Student | 8.0 | 0.0 | 0.0 | 75.0 |
| 43 | | | | | | | |
| 44 | Month Totals | | | 483.5 | 591.5 | 440.0 | 7964.5 |

*The usage total is 7964.5 hours. Freezing the headings helped you identify the totals cells.*

10. Choose **File→Print**, and view the print preview at the right of Backstage view.
*The frozen panes do not affect printing. The entire worksheet would print. You will learn to repeat row and column headings on each printed page of large worksheets later in this lesson.*

11. **Tap** [Esc] to exit the view without printing.

12. Choose **View→Window→Freeze Panes** 🖽 **menu ▾**, and then choose **Unfreeze Panes** from the Ribbon.
*Excel unfreezes the heading rows and columns and restores the worksheet to its original view.*

## Freeze Rows Only

*Now you will select a cell that has no columns to the left of it. This tells Excel to freeze only rows.*

13. Select **cell A5**, and then choose **View→Window→Freeze Panes** 🖽 **menu ▾**→Freeze Panes from the Ribbon.
*Rows 1–4 are frozen, but no columns are frozen.*

14. Scroll **down** and **right** to verify that only rows are frozen.
*When all columns of a worksheet fit in the window, you may freeze rows only.*

15. **Unfreeze** the panes.

## Freeze Columns Only

16. Select **cell D1**, and then choose **View→Window→Freeze Panes** 🖽 **menu ▾**→Freeze Panes from the Ribbon.
*Columns A–C are frozen, but no rows are frozen.*

17. Scroll **down** and **right** to verify that only columns are frozen.
*When all rows of a worksheet fit in the window, you may freeze columns only.*

18. **Unfreeze** the panes.

19. **Tap** [Ctrl]+[Home] to return the pointer to **cell A1**; leave the workbook **open**.
*You do not need to save because you made no changes in this exercise.*

# Splitting the Worksheet Window

Video Lesson    labyrinthelab.com/videos

At times, you will want to split the window to scroll within two areas of a worksheet. For example, a manager may want to compare data in rows 3–15 with rows 203–215. Use the Split command for this purpose. As with the Freeze Panes command, you should select the appropriate cell before choosing Split. To divide the window into two panes, select the first cell in a row or column. You may display four panes by selecting any other cell, but displaying two panes usually is sufficient. Using the same Split command, which now displays a highlight, removes the split. This type of command is called a *toggle*. Click it once to switch the command on and again to switch it off.

## *Splitting Compared to Freezing*

Freezing is useful to keep headings always visible. However, you may not easily view two nonadjacent groups of data. Splitting the window allows you to view two or four nonadjacent groups. Each pane has its own set of scroll bars. You may drag the split bar to adjust the number of rows or columns displayed in each pane. The following illustrations contrast a split window with a frozen window.

**A split window**

| | A | B |
|---|---|---|
| 9 | Kim | Tae Joon |
| 10 | Kissinger | Dorothy |
| 15 | Tejani | Tabriz |
| 16 | Do | Ty |
| 17 | Garcia Moreno | Juan |

Split bar

Each pane may be scrolled to view nonadjacent areas of the worksheet.

**A frozen window**

| | A | B | C | K | L |
|---|---|---|---|---|---|
| 1 | Seaview College Usage Report | | | | |
| 2 | | | | | |
| 3 | | | | | |
| 4 | Last Name | First Name | Category | Aug | Sep |
| 18 | Harris | Patti | Staff | 4.5 | 6.5 |
| 19 | Johnson | Riley | Staff | 25.5 | 10.0 |

Headings remain visible, but the ability to view nonadjacent areas is limited.

Use only Split or Freeze, not both together. One does not operate correctly when the other is in effect.

| QUICK REFERENCE | CONTROLLING WORKSHEET VIEWS |
|---|---|
| **Task** | **Procedure** |
| Freeze columns and rows | ▪ Select the cell below and to the right of the area to be frozen.<br>▪ Choose View→Window→Freeze Panes menu ▼→Freeze Panes from the Ribbon. |
| Freeze columns | ▪ Select the first cell in the column to the right of the column(s) to be frozen.<br>▪ Choose View→Window→Freeze Panes menu ▼→Freeze Panes from the Ribbon. |
| Freeze rows | ▪ Select the first cell in the row below the row(s) to be frozen.<br>▪ Choose View→Window→Freeze Panes menu ▼→Freeze Panes from the Ribbon. |
| Unfreeze all | ▪ Choose View→Window→Freeze Panes menu ▼→Unfreeze Panes from the Ribbon. |

| Task | Procedure |
|---|---|
| Split a window between columns or rows | ■ Select the first cell in the column or row in which the split is to occur. <br> ■ Choose View→Window→Split ⊞ from the Ribbon. |
| Adjust a split | ■ Drag the split bar that divides the window panes. |
| Remove a split | ■ Choose View→Window→Split ⊞ from the Ribbon. |
| Enlarge or shrink the worksheet view | ■ Drag the Zoom slider at the bottom-right corner of the worksheet window. |

## DEVELOP YOUR SKILLS 7.2.2
# Split the Worksheet Window

*In this exercise, you will split a worksheet window into two panes to scroll and compare data in two areas. You also will split the window into four panes so that column headings display to identify the total row data.*

*Before You Begin: The Seaview College Usage Report workbook should be open and the Years 1–2 sheet active. The list should appear sorted by category and then last name within the category. Records with the same last name are then sorted by first name. No rows or columns should be frozen.*

## Split between Columns

1. Follow these steps to split the window between columns:

Ⓐ Select **cell H1**.

Ⓑ Choose **View→Window→Split** ⊞ from the Ribbon.

|  | A | B | C | D | E | F | G | H | I | J |
|---|---|---|---|---|---|---|---|---|---|---|
| 1 | Seaview College Usage Report | | | | | | | | | |
| 2 | | | | Year 1 | | | | | | |
| 3 | | | | | | | | | | |
| 4 | Last Name | First Name | Category | Jan | Feb | Mar | Apr | May | Jun | Jul |
| 5 | Do | Alan | Alumni | 0.0 | 0.0 | 0.0 | 0.0 | 0.0 | 0.0 | 0.0 |
| 6 | Johnson | Chriss | Alumni | 0.0 | 0.0 | 3.5 | 0.0 | 0.0 | 0.0 | 2.0 |

*The window displays two panes with a gray split bar between them.*

2. In the pane on the right, drag the **scroll box** in the horizontal scroll bar to the right until **column K** is the first column visible, as shown in the following illustration.

| G | K | L | M | N |
|---|---|---|---|---|
| | | | | |
| | | | | |
| | | | | |
| Apr | Aug | Sep | Oct | Nov |
| 0.0 | 0.0 | 6.0 | 14.5 | 18.0 |
| 0.0 | 3.0 | 0.0 | 2.0 | 0.0 |
| 0.0 | 2.5 | 0.0 | 3.0 | 0.0 |

The pane displays the year 2 data.

*Compare the Alumni usage pattern for January through April with August through November of year 1. All alumni increased their hours, especially Alan Do.*

3. In the left pane, scroll **right** until **column K** is the first column visible.

   *Notice that the headings in columns A–C are no longer visible. They cannot be frozen while the window is split. You are comparing usage patterns for the entire list, so viewing the names is not necessary.*

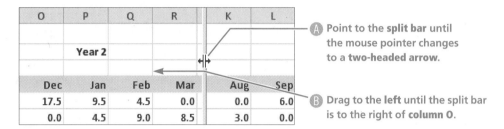

4. Follow these steps to move the split bar:

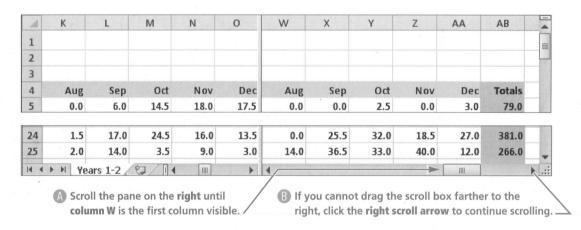

Ⓐ Point to the **split bar** until the mouse pointer changes to a **two-headed arrow**.

Ⓑ Drag to the **left** until the split bar is to the right of **column O**.

5. Follow these steps to display Aug-Dec for year 2 in the pane at the right:

| | K | L | M | N | O | W | X | Y | Z | AA | AB | |
|---|---|---|---|---|---|---|---|---|---|---|---|---|
| 1 | | | | | | | | | | | | |
| 2 | | | | | | | | | | | | |
| 3 | | | | | | | | | | | | |
| 4 | Aug | Sep | Oct | Nov | Dec | Aug | Sep | Oct | Nov | Dec | **Totals** | |
| 5 | 0.0 | 6.0 | 14.5 | 18.0 | 17.5 | 0.0 | 0.0 | 2.5 | 0.0 | 3.0 | 79.0 | |
| 24 | 1.5 | 17.0 | 24.5 | 16.0 | 13.5 | 0.0 | 25.5 | 32.0 | 18.5 | 27.0 | 381.0 | |
| 25 | 2.0 | 14.0 | 3.5 | 9.0 | 3.0 | 14.0 | 36.5 | 33.0 | 40.0 | 12.0 | 266.0 | |

| ◄ ◄ ► ►| | Years 1-2 |

Ⓐ Scroll the pane on the **right** until **column W** is the first column visible.

Ⓑ If you cannot drag the scroll box farther to the right, click the **right scroll arrow** to continue scrolling.

*The left pane should display Aug–Dec of year 1, and the right pane should display Aug–Dec of year 2 and the totals column.*

6. Scroll **down** until the month totals in **row 44** are in view.

| 42 | 3.0 | 0.0 | 0.0 | 0.0 | 0.0 | 0.0 | 3.5 | 8.0 | 0.0 | 0.0 | 75.0 | |
|---|---|---|---|---|---|---|---|---|---|---|---|---|
| 43 | | | | | | | | | | | | |
| 44 | 215.5 | 282.0 | 379.5 | 378.0 | 310.5 | 2?2.5 | 428.5 | 483.5 | 591.5 | 4?0.0 | 7964.5 | |

| ◄ ◄ ► ►| | Years 1-2 |

*Compare the month totals in the range K44:O44 with the same months in the range W44:AA44 to see that usage increased for each month in year 2. This comparison is more difficult because you cannot see the month names in row 4.*

7. Choose **View→Window→Split** 🔲 from the Ribbon to remove the split and restore the worksheet to its original view.

   *Unlike Freeze Panes, the Split command toggles on and off when you click the same button.*

## Split between Rows and Columns

8. Scroll **up**, select **cell P5**, and choose **View→Window→ Split** from the Ribbon.

   *This time, the window split into four panes because the pointer was not in the first cell of a row or column. The row 4 labels are in the upper panes because you selected a cell in row 5.*

| N | O | P | Q |
|---|---|---|---|
| | | Year 2 | |
| Nov | Dec | Jan | Feb |
| 18.0 | 17.5 | 9.5 | 4.5 |
| 0.0 | 0.0 | 4.5 | 9.0 |

9. Scroll the **lower-right** pane until **column W** is the first column visible, and then scroll **down** to view the month totals in **row 44**.

| | K | L | M | N | O | W | X | Y | Z | AA | AB |
|---|---|---|---|---|---|---|---|---|---|---|---|
| 2 | | | | | | | | | | | |
| 3 | | | | | | | | | | | |
| 4 | Aug | Sep | Oct | Nov | Dec | Aug | Sep | Oct | Nov | Dec | Totals |
| 44 | 215.5 | 282.0 | 379.5 | 378.0 | 310.5 | 272.5 | 428.5 | 483.5 | 591.5 | 440.0 | 7964.5 |
| 45 | | | | | | | | | | | |
| 46 | | | | | | | | | | | |

⎸◂ ▸ ⎹ Summary | Years 1 ◂ | | ▸ | ◂ | | ▸

*With the month names visible, comparing each month's hours between year 1 and year 2 is easier.*

10. Choose **View→Window→Split** ⊟ from the Ribbon to remove the split.

11. Tap ⎡Ctrl⎤+⎡Home⎤ to return the pointer to **cell A1**.

12. **Save** 💾 the change you made in the previous step, and leave the workbook **open**.

# Viewing Worksheets in Multiple Windows

**Video Lesson**   labyrinthelab.com/videos

As an alternative to splitting the worksheet window, you may display two areas of a large worksheet at once in separate windows within Excel. You can even display two or more worksheets in this way. The worksheets may be from the same workbook or different workbooks. This method allows you to compare, copy, or move data between worksheet areas more easily. Each window is numbered, and only one window can be active at one time. The New Window command on the Ribbon is used to add worksheet windows, and the Arrange All command displays them side by side, stacked top to bottom, or cascaded in layers with their title bars visible for selection.

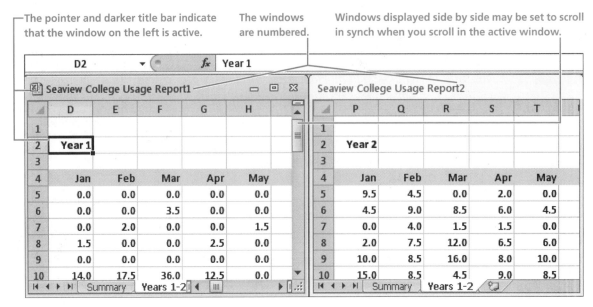

The pointer and darker title bar indicate that the window on the left is active.

The windows are numbered.

Windows displayed side by side may be set to scroll in synch when you scroll in the active window.

Two areas of the same workbook displayed as tiles in order to compare data between two years

The commands of the Window group in the View Ribbon

## Synchronous Scrolling

Once windows are arranged, they may be scrolled independently with the scroll bars in each window. You may want to use synchronous scrolling so that the view in all windows moves simultaneously in the same direction as you scroll in the active window. This feature keeps the rows or columns aligned in the windows to help you compare data. To use synchronous scrolling, the windows must be set to be viewed side by side.

## Saving the Layout as a Workspace

The Save Workspace command saves your multiple-window layout as a file separate from the workbook containing the data. The workbook still must be saved if you change any data and then close it. When you reopen the workspace file from your file storage location, any worksheets contained in the saved workspace will open in their respective windows ready for you to resume work.

| Task | Procedure |
|---|---|
| View two areas of the same worksheet | ■ Choose View→Window→New Window 🖼 from the Ribbon.<br>■ Choose View→Window→Switch Windows menu ▾ from the Ribbon, and select the desired active window from the list.<br>■ Choose View→Window→View Side by Side 🖽 from the Ribbon. The active window will appear on top or at the left. |
| View two worksheets from the same workbook | ■ Display the first worksheet.<br>■ Choose View→Window→New Window 🖼 from the Ribbon.<br>■ Click the tab of the second worksheet in the new window.<br>■ Arrange the windows as desired. |
| View two worksheets from different workbooks | ■ Display the first worksheet.<br>■ Chose File→Open, and navigate to the desired workbook.<br>■ Arrange the windows as desired. |
| Scroll windows synchronously | ■ Use one of the previous procedures to set up two or more windows.<br>■ Choose View→Window→View Side by Side 🖽 from the Ribbon.<br>■ If Synchronous Scrolling does not turn on automatically, choose View→Window→Synchronous Scrolling from the Ribbon. |
| Arrange windows | ■ Choose View→Window→Arrange All 🖺, and select a display option from the list. |
| Save a multiple-window layout | ■ Choose View→Window→Save Workspace 🖼 from the Ribbon, type a filename, and navigate to the desired file storage location. |

# Arrange Multiple Worksheet Windows

*In this exercise, you will view nonadjacent areas of a worksheet in separate windows and scroll them synchronously. You will arrange two worksheets from a workbook to view them simultaneously and then save the view as a workspace.*

## View Areas of the Same Worksheet

1. Display the **Years 1–2** worksheet in the Seaview College Usage Report workbook, if necessary.

2. Choose **View→Window→New Window** 🖼 from the Ribbon.
   *The Excel title bar displays Seaview College Usage Report:2 to indicate the window you just created.*

3. Choose **View→Window→Switch Windows** 🖼 **menu** ▾ from the Ribbon, and select **Seaview College Usage Report:1** from the list.
   *The Seaview College Usage Report:1 window now is the active window.*

4. Choose **View→Window→View Side by Side** 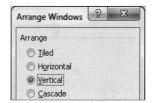 from the Ribbon.

*The Seaview College Usage Report:1 window appears on top of the other window because it was active when you chose the side-by-side view. (Depending on your computer monitor size and screen resolution, the windows may be displayed left to right.)*

5. Choose **View→Window→Arrange All**  from the Ribbon, choose **Vertical**, and click **OK**.

*The windows are arranged left to right rather than top to bottom.*

## Use Independent and Synchronous Scrolling

*Synchronous scrolling is turned on when you arrange windows side by side. Both windows display the year 1 data; so first you will scroll one window independently to display the year 2 data.*

6. Choose **View→Window→Synchronous Scrolling** in the Ribbon to toggle off synchronous scrolling.

*The Synchronous Scrolling toggle button now should not appear highlighted.*

7. Select **cell D5** in the Seaview College Usage Report:1 window, and choose **View→ Window→Freeze Panes→Freeze Panes** from the Ribbon.

8. Click in the **Seaview College Usage Report:2** window, select **cell D5**, and **freeze** the panes.

9. Scroll the Seaview College Usage Report:2 window to the **right** until **column P** appears, as shown in the illustration below.

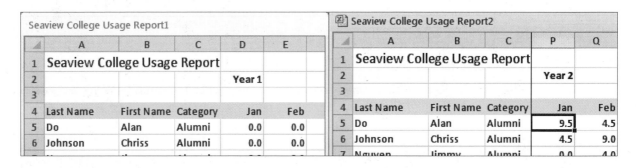

*The Jan, Feb, and other month columns display for year 1 and year 2. You scrolled a window independently from the other.*

10. Choose **View→Window→Synchronous Scrolling** in the Ribbon to toggle on synchronous scrolling.

11. Click in the **Seaview College Usage Report:1** window, scroll to the **right**, and watch the Seaview College Usage Report:2 window scroll as well.

*The columns for the same months remain in view in both windows for easy comparison of the data between the two years.*

12. Scroll **down** in one of the windows, and notice that synchronized scrolling displays the same rows in each window.

13. Click in the **Seaview College Usage Report:2** window, and **close** it.

### View Worksheets in the Same Workbook

14. Choose **View→Window→New Window** ⊞ from the Ribbon.

15. Click the **Summary** sheet tab in the Seaview College Usage Report:2 window.

16. Choose **View→Window→Arrange All**, choose **Tiled**, and click **OK**.
    *The Summary sheet and Years 1–2 sheet display side by side. Synchronous Scrolling is off, so you could scroll the Years 1–2 window and refer to the summary totals in the other window.*

### Save the Layout as a Workspace

17. Choose **View→Window→Save Workspace** ⊞ from the Ribbon, and save as **Seaview College Workspace** in the Lesson 07 folder in your file storage location.
    *The current window layout will be displayed the next time you open the workspace file.*

18. **Close** ⊠ the Summary sheet window, and maximize the Years 1–2 sheet window.

    | Seaview College Usage Report      ⬓ ⧉ ⊠ |
    | --- |

19. **Unfreeze** the panes.

20. Leave the workbook **open**.
    *You do not need to save because you did not make any changes to the workbook.*

## Creating Custom Worksheet Views

You can save certain display settings and print settings as custom views to redisplay at a later time. The display settings may include the currently selected cell or range, column widths, row heights, hidden rows and columns, filters, and window size. Print settings may include margins, headers and footers, print area, and sheet settings in the Page Setup dialog box. You can create multiple custom views in a worksheet. A view, however, can be applied only to the worksheet for which you created the custom view.

To manage custom views, include the worksheet name when creating a custom view name.

| QUICK REFERENCE | CREATING AND DISPLAYING CUSTOM WORKSHEET VIEWS |
| --- | --- |
| **Task** | **Procedure** |
| Create a custom view | ▪ Change the worksheet display and print settings as desired.<br>▪ Choose View→Workbook Views→Custom Views from the Ribbon.<br>▪ In the Custom Views dialog box, click Add.<br>▪ Enter a view name, and select the desired options. |
| Display a custom view | ▪ Choose View→Workbook Views→Custom Views from the Ribbon.<br>▪ Double-click the desired view in the Custom Views dialog box. |

# 7.3 Printing Multipage Worksheets

**Video Lesson**  labyrinthelab.com/videos

Excel provides a number of options for improving the format of large printed worksheets. For example, you may adjust settings such as:

- Decreasing the page margins or page scale to include more rows and columns
- Centering the worksheet on the page
- Printing pages horizontally (landscape) or vertically (portrait)
- Printing only a selected range of worksheet cells
- Adding a header and footer to label pages

## Setting Print Format in Page Layout View

Previously in this lesson, you edited a worksheet in Normal view and used the print preview in Backstage view to see how the worksheet would look as printed. The print preview allows you to view one page at a time. As an alternative, display Page Layout view, which can preview multiple printed pages. As you choose a printing option from the Ribbon, you can view the result immediately. You also may edit the worksheet in Page Layout view. You may change the view by using the View Ribbon or the view buttons in the Status Bar at the lower-right corner of the window.

The view buttons displayed in the lower-right corner of the worksheet window

DEVELOP YOUR SKILLS 7.3.1
## Display Page Layout View

*In this exercise, you will preview the worksheet in Page Layout view.*

1. **Tap** [Ctrl] + [Home] to move the pointer to cell A1, if necessary.

2. Choose **View→Workbook Views→Page Layout** 📄 from the Ribbon.
   *The worksheet displays as it would print on paper. The Status Bar at the lower left of the window displays Page: 1 of 3 to show that the cell pointer is in page 1 of three pages total.*

3. Drag the **scroll box** in the **horizontal scroll bar** to the right to view pages 2 and 3.

4. Drag the **scroll box** in the **vertical scroll bar** down to view the bottom of the pages.

5. Drag the **slider** in the **Zoom** control in the lower-right corner of the window to about **25%**.
   *The worksheet shrinks dramatically. Dimmed pages will not print, as those columns and rows are empty in the worksheet. The zoom level affects only how you are viewing the worksheet, not its printed appearance.*

6. Drag the Zoom slider to about **40%**.

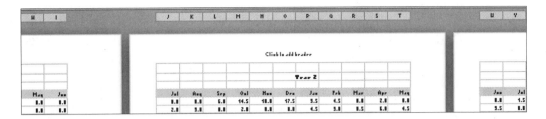

*The three pages should almost fill the view. If necessary, use a different zoom percentage to adjust for your computer monitor.*

7. Choose **View→Worksheet Views→Normal** from the Ribbon to return to Normal view.

8. Click the **Page Layout view** button in the Status Bar at the lower-right corner of the window.
*The view returns to the zoom percentage that you set previously. Notice how the columns fall on the pages. Page breaks split up the yearly data, and pages 2 and 3 are without headings to identify the person belonging to each row. You will resolve these problems in the next exercises.*

9. **Save** the changes, and leave the workbook **open**.

## Page Layout Ribbon

Video Lesson    labyrinthelab.com/videos

The print options are accessed on the Page Layout Ribbon in the Page Setup, Scale to Fit, and Sheet Options command groups. You may change the page orientation, adjust margins, and scale the worksheet size. As an alternative, the Page Setup dialog box available in prior Excel versions is launched by clicking the launcher button in the lower-right corner of the command group. You will use the Page Setup dialog box occasionally for commands not located on the Ribbon.

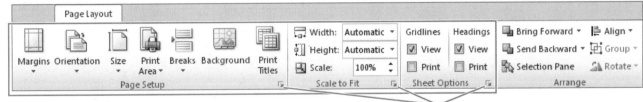

The Page Layout Ribbon with printing options in the Page Setup, Scale to Fit, and Sheet Options command groups.

Excel users who prefer changing settings in the Page Setup dialog box may click here.

# Sizing Options

The Page Setup and Scale to Fit command groups on the Page Layout Ribbon contain several options to help fit large worksheets on printed pages. Four useful sizing options are shown in the following illustration.

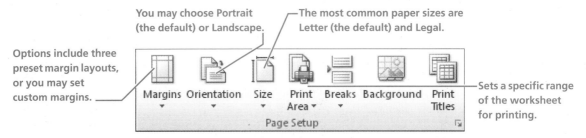

You may choose Portrait (the default) or Landscape.

The most common paper sizes are Letter (the default) and Legal.

Options include three preset margin layouts, or you may set custom margins.

Sets a specific range of the worksheet for printing.

Margins    Orientation    Size    Print Area    Breaks    Background    Print Titles

Page Setup

 You can use the orientation, margin presets, paper size, and scaling presets available in the Print tab of Backstage view to correct the worksheet size just before printing.

## *Margins*

The margins determine the space between the edge of the paper and the worksheet. You may choose from three preset margin layouts—Normal, Wide, and Narrow—as well as a Custom Margins option. Choose Narrow to fit more columns and rows on the printed page. Choose Custom Margins to launch the Page Setup dialog box with the Margins tab displayed. On this tab you may set specific worksheet margins and center the worksheet horizontally and vertically on the paper. Header and footer margins are covered later in this lesson. The illustration below describes the dialog box options.

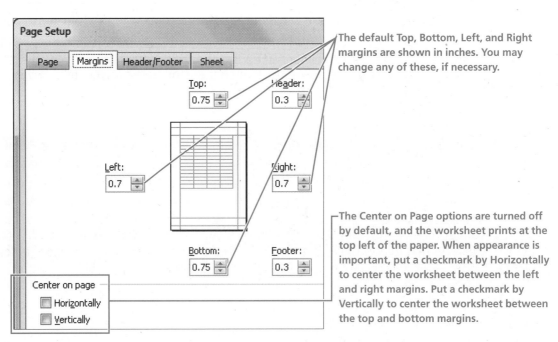

The default Top, Bottom, Left, and Right margins are shown in inches. You may change any of these, if necessary.

The Center on Page options are turned off by default, and the worksheet prints at the top left of the paper. When appearance is important, put a checkmark by Horizontally to center the worksheet between the left and right margins. Put a checkmark by Vertically to center the worksheet between the top and bottom margins.

## Orientation

 The orientation indicates the direction of printing. Portrait is the default and prints across the narrow edge of the paper. Landscape orientation prints across the wide edge of the paper and is useful with wide worksheets like the Years 1–2 worksheet in the Seaview College Usage Report workbook. The orientation of each worksheet may be set individually in a workbook.

Portrait orientation

Landscape orientation

## Size

The Size option refers to the paper size. The default is Letter 8.5" × 11" paper. You can fit more columns on the page using Legal 8.5" × 14" paper, but keep in mind that the larger size paper may be more difficult to store.

## Print Area

To reduce the number of printed pages or to leave out nonessential cells, you may set any range of cells in the worksheet as the print area. The Set Print Area command makes the range permanent until you set a different range or choose Clear Print Area to restore the entire worksheet for printing. Use Set Print Area if you plan to print a specific range most of the time.

## Scale to Fit

The Scale to Fit command group on the Page Layout Ribbon provides automated scaling options to shrink the worksheet for printing.

- **Width**—You may reduce the size of a worksheet containing many columns to fit its width on one, two, or more pages, as appropriate. When a few worksheet columns spill onto the next printed page, set the Width to one page less.
- **Height**—You may set the Height for one page less when a few rows spill onto another page. Reduce the size of a worksheet containing many rows to fit its height on one, two, or more pages, as appropriate.
- **Scale**—To shrink the width and height in the same proportion, set the Scale to less than 100%. Note that, for legibility, you may scale a small worksheet to greater than 100%. To use Scale, the Width and Height must be set to Automatic. Keep in mind that a scaled worksheet may fit on fewer pages, but the text may be too small to read.

 To reset the Height and Width to normal size, choose Automatic from each drop-down list. Make certain to change Scale to 100%, as the percentage does not reset automatically. The Undo command cannot reverse any Scale to Fit settings.

| Task | Procedure |
|------|-----------|
| Display Page Layout view | ▪ Choose View→Workbook Views→Page Layout  from the Ribbon or click the Page Layout view button in the lower-right corner of the window. |
| Change to preset margins | ▪ Choose Page Layout→Page Setup→Margins ▦ menu ▼ and choose Normal, Narrow, or Wide from the Ribbon. |
| Change specific margins | ▪ Choose Page Layout→Page Setup→Margins ▦ menu ▼ and choose Custom Margins from the Ribbon. |
| | ▪ Change the Top, Bottom, Left, or Right margin in the Page Setup dialog box. |
| Center the worksheet on printed page(s) | ▪ Click the dialog box launcher ▣ button in the bottom-right corner of the Page Setup command group of the Page Layout Ribbon. |
| | ▪ Choose the Margins tab in the Page Layout dialog box. |
| | ▪ Under Center on Page, place a checkmark next to Horizontally to center between the left and right margins. |
| | ▪ Under Center on Page, place a checkmark next to Vertically to center between the top and bottom margins. |
| Change the orientation | ▪ Choose Page Layout→Page Setup→Orientation ▤ menu ▼ and choose Portrait or Landscape from the Ribbon. |
| Change paper size | ▪ Choose Page Layout→Page Setup→Size ▯ menu ▼ and choose a paper size from the Ribbon. |
| Scale the worksheet to fit on fewer pages | ▪ Choose Page Layout→Scale to Fit, select 100% in the Scale box, type the desired percentage, and tap Enter. |
| Scale the worksheet width or height | ▪ Choose Page Layout→Scale to Fit→Width menu ▼ or Height menu ▼ and set the desired number of pages. |
| Set a print range | ▪ Select the desired cells. |
| | ▪ Choose Page Layout→Page Setup→Print Area ▣ menu ▼→Set Print Area from the Ribbon. |
| Remove the print range | ▪ Choose Page Layout→Page Setup→Print Area ▣ menu ▼→Clear Print Area from the Ribbon. The entire worksheet area containing data is restored as the print area. |

# Use Sizing Options

*In this exercise, you will change the orientation and margins. You also will scale a worksheet to print on fewer pages. You will use commands on the Ribbon as well as in the Page Setup dialog box.*

### Switch to Landscape Orientation

1. Verify that the Seaview College Usage Report workbook is open from the previous exercise.

   The **Years 1–2** worksheet should be displayed in **Page Layout view** at about **40%** zoom. *Notice that the pages appear in portrait orientation with the narrow edge of the paper on top.*

If the worksheet does not display the page edges, the current view might be set to Normal. Switch to Page Layout view. You may choose printing options in Normal view, but you cannot see the results.

2. Choose **Page Layout→Page Setup→Orientation** 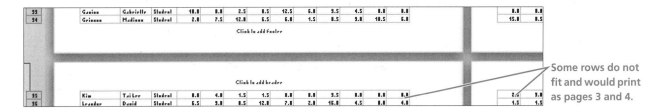 **menu ▾→Landscape** from the Ribbon.

*By printing along the wide edge of the page, you have reduced the worksheet width to two pages. A few rows, however, still spill down onto additional pages.*

Some rows do not fit and would print as pages 3 and 4.

3. **Save** 🖫 the change to the workbook.

## Change Margins

4. Choose **Page Layout→Page Setup→Margins** 🗔 **menu ▾→Narrow** from the Ribbon.

5. Experiment with the choices in the **Margins** 🗔 **menu ▾** by choosing **Wide**, then **Normal**, and then returning to **Narrow**.

*Decreasing the margins allows more columns and rows to fit on a page, but the rows still do not fit onto one page in height.*

6. **Save** 🖫 the changes to the workbook.

## Use the Scale to Fit Options

7. Examine the **Years 1–2** worksheet.

*Recall that this worksheet still does not fit on one page in height. Notice that the worksheet is significantly wider than it is tall.*

8. Choose **100%** in the Scale box in the Scale to Fit command group of the Page Layout Ribbon, type **54**, and **tap** ⌅Enter⌅.

*Both the width and height were scaled to almost half size to fit on one page. As you can see, it wasn't such a good idea to compress a two-page worksheet onto one page. The printed worksheet would be unreadable. The Scale option works best when only a few columns or rows spill over to an extra page.*

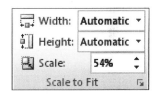

9. Choose **54%** in the Scale box in the Scale to Fit command group of the Page Layout Ribbon, type **100**, and **tap** ⌅Enter⌅.

*You must reset the Scale to Fit options manually because Undo cannot reverse them. Next, you will instruct Excel to shrink the rows to fit on one page in height without affecting the width.*

10. Choose **Page Layout→Scale to Fit→Height menu ▾→1** page from the Ribbon.

*Your worksheet now fits on 1 page high and 1.5 pages wide. The width changed in proportion to the height that you chose. The Status Bar should display Page: 1 of 2. If you change the Width or Height, the Scale option becomes unavailable, and the opposite also is true.*

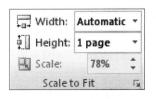

11. **Save** 🖫 the changes to the workbook.

## Set the Print Area

*Assume that you want to print only part of the worksheet.*

12. Click the **Normal** view button in the lower-right corner of the window.

13. Select **cells A1:H13**.

14. Choose **Page Layout→Page Setup→Print Area** 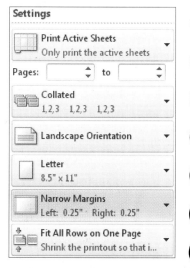 menu ▼→**Set Print Area** from the Ribbon.
    *The print area appears surrounded by a fence border.*

## Preview the Printout

15. Choose **File→Print**.
    *Excel would print only the cells that you set as the print area.*

16. Look at the **Settings** area in the lower-left corner of Backstage view.
    *Notice that settings you chose, such as Landscape Orientation and Narrow Margins, are shown. You could change a setting from its drop-down list in Backstage view and observe the effect in the print preview. This feature is useful when you discover a sizing error just before printing.*

17. Click the **Page Layout** tab on the Ribbon to close Backstage view.

18. Choose **Page Layout→Page Setup→Print Area** 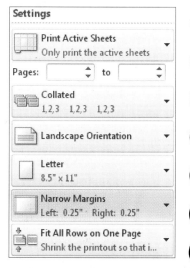 menu ▼→**Clear Print Area** from the Ribbon.
    *The fence border disappears because the print area is reset to include all cells containing data in the entire worksheet.*

19. Select any cell to deselect the highlighted cells.

## Center the Summary Worksheet

*You will center the Summary worksheet on the printed page in the next steps.*

20. Display the **Summary** sheet of the workbook in Page Layout view.

21. Choose **Page Layout→Page Setup→Margins** menu ▼→**Custom Margins** from the Ribbon.

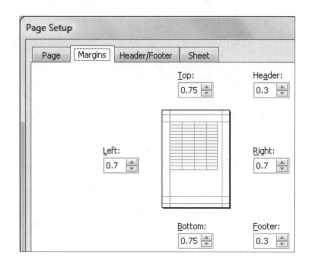

*The Page Setup dialog box opens with the Margins tab displayed. The default margin settings in inches for Top, Bottom, Left, and Right may be different in your dialog box, depending on the printer that you use. The margins may be adjusted individually.*

22. In the Center on Page area at the lower-left corner, place a checkmark next to **Horizontally** and **Vertically**; then click **Print Preview** at the lower-right corner of the dialog box.
    *The print preview in Backstage view shows that the worksheet is centered between the left and right margins and between the top and bottom margins on the page. You could choose to center only horizontally, which aligns the worksheet at the top margin.*

23. Click the **Page Layout** tab on the Ribbon to exit Backstage view.
    *Notice that Page Layout view does not display horizontal and vertical centering. Only the print preview in Backstage view does.*

24. Display the **Years 1–2** worksheet.

25. **Save** 🖫 the changes to the workbook.

26. **Print** 🖨 the Years 1–2 worksheet.
    *Examine your printed worksheet for the settings you performed. Now you have learned a sequence of techniques you may use to size a large worksheet for printing.*

## Headers and Footers

Video Lesson    labyrinthelab.com/videos

Headers print at the top of every page, and footers print at the bottom of every page. They identify the worksheet name, page number, and so on. Excel provides a variety of predesigned headers and footers from which you may choose. You may even create customized headers and footers to suit your particular needs and create a different header and footer on odd and even pages for double-sided printing. The following illustration contains a header.

| Years 1-2, Seaview College Usage Report | | Page 1 of 3 | | | | Author: Roxana Ortega | |
|---|---|---|---|---|---|---|---|
| **Seaview College Usage Report** | | | | | | | |
| | | Year 1 | | | | | |
| | | | | | | | |
| Last Name | First Name | Category | Jan | Feb | Mar | Apr | May | Jun |
| Do | Alan | Alumni | 0.0 | 0.0 | 0.0 | 0.0 | 0.0 | 0.0 |
| Johnson | Chriss | Alumni | 0.0 | 0.0 | 3.5 | 0.0 | 0.0 | 0.0 |

The three sections of this header print on every page and include
the worksheet tab name, workbook name, page number, and text.

 Use Page Layout view or the print preview in Backstage view to see headers and footers. They do not display in Normal view.

## Creating and Formatting Headers and Footers

Headers and footers are created most conveniently in Page Layout view. Excel divides headers and footers into left, center, and right sections of the page. You need not fill in all three sections. To activate a section, just click in it to display the Design Ribbon filled with header and footer options. Once you activate a section, there are three ways to add content to it:

- Choose a predesigned item from the Header or Footer drop-down lists in the Header & Footer command group.

- Insert an element from the Ribbon.

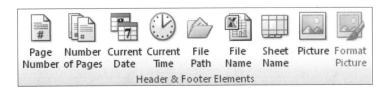

The Header & Footer Elements command group in the
Header & Footer Tools Design tab on the Ribbon

Options include the workbook filename, worksheet tab name, current date, time, and page number. When you choose an option from the Header & Footer Elements command group, Excel displays a code to represent the item. For example, the code *&[Date]* rather than the actual date displays because the current date will change. When you click outside the header section, Excel converts *&[Date]* to the actual date.

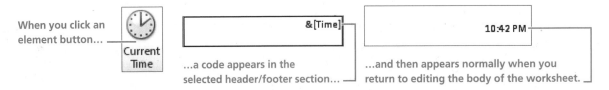

When you click an element button... **Current Time** ...a code appears in the selected header/footer section... &[Time] ...and then appears normally when you return to editing the body of the worksheet. 10:42 PM

- Type your own custom text.

Excel allows you to use a combination of these methods to create header/footer content. You may also format headers and footers. For example, you may change the font, size, and color.

| QUICK REFERENCE | CREATING HEADERS AND FOOTERS |
|---|---|
| **Task** | **Procedure** |
| Display Page Layout view | ■ Choose View→Workbook Views→Page Layout ⊡ from the Ribbon or click the Page Layout view button from the Status Bar at the lower-right corner of the window. |
| Select a predesigned page header or footer | ■ Display Page Layout view ⊡ from the Status Bar.<br>■ Select Click to Add Header above the worksheet or Click to Add Footer below the worksheet.<br>■ Choose Design→Header & Footer→Header menu ▼ or Footer menu ▼, and then choose a predesigned item in the Ribbon. |
| Create a custom page header or footer | ■ Display Page Layout view ⊡ from the Status Bar.<br>■ Select the left, center, or right header section above the worksheet or footer section below the worksheet.<br>■ Type text and set options from the Header & Footer Elements command group on the Ribbon. |

| Task | Procedure |
|---|---|
| Set header and footer margins | ■ Click the dialog box launcher ⬜ button in the bottom-right corner of the Page Setup command group of the Page Layout Ribbon. |
| | ■ Choose the Margins tab in the Page Setup dialog box. |
| | ■ Change the Header or Footer margin. |
| Create a different header and/or footer to print on page 1 | ■ Choose Page Layout→Page Setup→dialog box launcher from the Ribbon. |
| | ■ Click the Header/Footer tab in the Page Setup dialog box. |
| | ■ Place a checkmark next to Different First Page, and click OK. |
| | ■ Display the worksheet in Page Layout view, and create the desired headers and/or footers on page 1 and page 2. Any of these may be left blank, if desired. |
| Create different headers and/or footers to print on odd and even pages | ■ Choose Page Layout→Page Setup→dialog box launcher from the Ribbon. |
| | ■ Click the Header/Footer tab in the Page Setup dialog box. |
| | ■ Place a checkmark next to Different Odd and Even Pages, and click OK. |
| | ■ Display the worksheet in Page Layout view, create the desired header and/or footer on an odd page, and then create the desired header and/or footer on an even page. |
| Remove a header or footer | ■ Select any section of the header or footer, choose Design→Header & Footer→Header menu ▼ or Footer menu ▼, and choose (None) from the Ribbon. |

## DEVELOP YOUR SKILLS 7.3.3
# Set the Header and Footer

*In this exercise, you will select predefined headers and footers, remove a footer, create custom headers and footers, and change the margins for these items.*

## Use Predefined Headers and Footers

1. Verify that the **Years 1–2** worksheet of the Seaview College Usage Report workbook is open from the previous exercise.

2. Choose **Page Layout view** from the Status Bar at the lower-right corner of the window.

3. Change the zoom level to about **75%**.

4. **Scroll up**, if necessary, to view the top of the page and choose **Click to Add Header**.

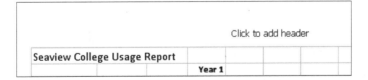

*The center header section is activated, and the Design Ribbon displays. (If it does not, click the Design tab on the Ribbon.)*

5. Choose **Design→Header & Footer→Header** 📄 **menu ▼** on the Ribbon, browse the available predefined header choices, and then choose **Page 1 of ?** from the list.
   *The predefined header consists of one center section and displays as* Page 1 of 2. *The page number is updated on every page. For example, the header displays* Page 2 of 2 *on the second page.*

6. Follow these steps to select a predefined footer:

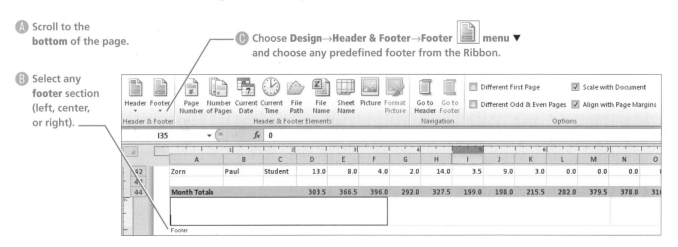

Ⓐ Scroll to the **bottom** of the page.

Ⓒ Choose **Design→Header & Footer→Footer** menu ▼ and choose any predefined footer from the Ribbon.

Ⓑ Select any **footer** section (left, center, or right).

*You may select any of the three sections before choosing a predefined header or footer.*

## Remove a Footer

7. Select any section of the footer.

8. Choose **Design→Header & Footer→Footer** menu ▼, and select **(None)** at the beginning of the menu in the Ribbon.
*The previous footer was removed because you chose (None). The footer area displays Click to Add Footer.*

## Create a Custom Header and Footer

9. **Scroll up** in the worksheet to display the header.
*Next, you will insert items in the header by clicking buttons on the Header & Footer Elements command group.*

10. Select the **left** header section (display the Design Ribbon, if necessary), click the **Sheet Name** button, **type** a comma, **tap** [Spacebar], and then click the **File Name** button.
*The footer section displays &[Tab], &[File]. When you click outside the section, the display changes to Years 1–2, Seaview College Usage Report. You may add text, punctuation, and spaces between elements. You may tap [Enter] and add text lines to the header section, but unexpected results may occur. Always check the header and footer in the print preview of Backstage view before printing.*

11. Select the **right** header section, **type** your name, and click **outside** the header.

12. Add the **current time** and **current date** to any section of the footer. Separate the two elements with punctuation or spaces so you can read each element easily.

## Change the Header and Footer Margins

13. Display the **Page Layout** Ribbon and click the **dialog box launcher** ⊡ button in the bottom-right corner of the Page Setup command group.
*If the commands on the Ribbon appear dimmed, make certain that the pointer is in a cell outside the header and footer.*

14. Follow these steps to change the header and footer margins:

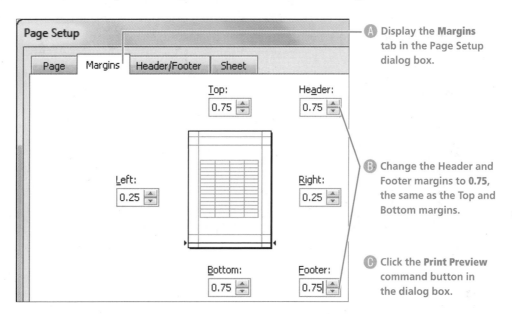

Ⓐ Display the **Margins** tab in the Page Setup dialog box.

Ⓑ Change the Header and Footer margins to **0.75**, the same as the Top and Bottom margins.

Ⓒ Click the **Print Preview** command button in the dialog box.

15. Examine the **header and footer** positions.
*Your header should look like the following illustration.*

~~Seaview College Usage Paper~~

*Now the header and footer are positioned farther from the top of the page but overlap the worksheet. You should always make the header and footer margins smaller than the top and bottom margins so that the header and footer print in the margin area.*

16. Click the **Page Setup** link at the bottom-left corner of Backstage view.
*This is another way to display the Page Setup dialog box.*

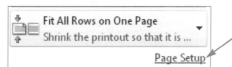

17. Change the **Header and Footer** margins to an appropriate position of your choice and check the position in the print preview.
*While typing the position, such as .3, in a text box, make certain to include the decimal point.*

18. Return to **Page Layout view** without printing.

19. **Save** 🖫 the changes and leave the workbook **open**.

# Adding a Watermark Image

Video Lesson    labyrinthelab.com/videos

A watermark is a lightly shaded notation such as *Confidential* or *Draft,* or a logo that appears behind document data. Excel does not include a watermark command as Microsoft Word does. You can, however, add a photo or transparent image you created in a graphics program to a header or footer to achieve a watermark effect on each page of the worksheet. The image must be larger than the header or footer area in which you place it. After the Picture command on the Header & Footer Tools Design toolbar is used to insert the image, the header or footer section displays &*[Picture]*. The image is not displayed in the worksheet until you deselect the header or footer. You can size and scale the image after inserting it in the worksheet. You also can change the brightness and contrast of some images with an acceptable result.

| 1.5 | 1.5 | 0.0 | 0.0 | 3.5 | 0.0 | 0.0 | 0.0 | 2.0 | 3.0 |
|---|---|---|---|---|---|---|---|---|---|
| 35.0 | 19.5 | 22.0 | 0.0 | 0.0 | 0.0 | 0.0 | 0.0 | 0.0 | 0.0 |
| 0.0 | 0.0 | 14.0 | 17.5 | 17.5 | 12.5 | 0.0 | 24.0 | 35.0 | 19.5 |
| 5.5 | 7.0 | 9.5 | 4.5 | 13.0 | 4.5 | 6.5 | 3.0 | 0.5 | 12.0 |
| 18.5 | 27.0 | 18.5 | 6.0 | 5.5 | 25.5 | 10.0 | 8.5 | 16.0 | 8.0 |
| 35.0 | 19.5 | 22.0 | 0.0 | 0.0 | 0.0 | 0.0 | 0.0 | 0.0 | 0.0 |

A logo watermark is displayed behind worksheet data on each printed page.

# Applying a Worksheet Background

The worksheet background normally appears white with the cell gridlines displayed. But, you can use a photo or other image to fill the background and then turn off the gridlines. For example, you can apply a background photo to promote your organization or products when you publish a workbook as a web page. The background image is repeated across and down the sheet, which requires that the original image be scaled appropriately and contrast well with the worksheet text colors. The image cannot be adjusted in Excel. You might want to temporarily display the word *Draft,* as shown in the illustration below and to the right. The background image, however, is not included on a printed worksheet.

**Seaview College Usage Report**

|  | Year 1 | Year 2 | Total |
|---|---|---|---|
| Alumni | 75.5 | 112.5 | 188.0 |
| Faculty | 569.0 | 907.5 | 1476.5 |

A photo background should contrast well with worksheet text.

**Seaview College Usage Report**

|  | Year 1 | Year 2 | Total |
|---|---|---|---|
| Alumni | 75.5 | 112.5 | 188.0 |
| Faculty | 569.0 | 907.5 | 1476.5 |

A background image can be used temporarily and then removed.

| QUICK REFERENCE | ADDING A WATERMARK AND BACKGROUND TO SHEETS |
|---|---|
| **Task** | **Procedure** |
| Add a watermark image to a worksheet | ■ Select the left, center, or right section of the header or footer.<br>■ Choose Design→Header & Footer Elements→Picture 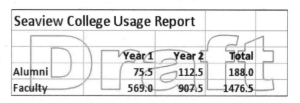, navigate to the desired image, and click Insert.<br>■ Choose Design→Header & Footer Elements→Format Picture and adjust the size, cropping, and image control as desired. |

| Task | Procedure |
|------|-----------|
| Remove a watermark image | ■ Click in the appropriate header or footer section, which selects &[Picture], and tap Delete. |
| Apply a repeating background to a worksheet | ■ Choose Page Layout→Page Setup→Background from the Ribbon, navigate to the desired image file, and click Insert. |
| Remove a background | ■ Choose Page Layout→Page Setup→Delete Background from the Ribbon. |

## DEVELOP YOUR SKILLS 7.3.4

# Apply a Watermark and Background to Sheets

*In this exercise, you will add a watermark effect to all pages of the Years 1–2 worksheet. You also will use a "Draft" image in the background of the Summary sheet to serve as a temporary reminder that the sheet is not final.*

### Add a Watermark Image

1. Display the **Years 1–2** sheet of the Seaview College Usage Report workbook in Page Layout view, if necessary.

2. Select the **center** section of the header.
   *The codes for the page numbering that you set in an earlier exercise are selected. You will replace the page numbering in the next step.*

3. Choose **Design→Header & Footer Elements→Picture** , navigate to the Lesson 07 folder in your file storage location, select **Company Watermark**, and click **Insert**.
   *The header section displays the code &[Picture], but the image is not displayed while the header is selected.*

4. Click any cell in the worksheet to deselect the header.
   *The image containing "My Virtual Campus" displays at about row 14 and is horizontally centered on the sheet because you selected the center header section. The image was created in Windows Paint and has a grayscale shade applied to contrast with the worksheet text. The image appears on every page of the worksheet.*

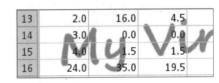

5. **Scroll right** to view the same watermark on page 2.
   *The watermark is layered under the cell contents, so the fill applied to cells in column AB partially covers the image.*

6. **Tap** Ctrl+P to display the Print tab of Backstage view, and notice in the print preview that the watermark would print.
   *A watermark displays only in Page Layout view and the print preview in Backstage view.*

7. **Tap** Esc to exit Backstage view without printing, and then **tap** Ctrl+Home to return to cell A1.

8. **Save** the changes.

### Apply a Background

*You will add the word "Draft" throughout the Summary sheet as a reminder that the sheet is not final. An image file has been created for this purpose.*

9. Display the **Summary** sheet of the Seaview College Usage Report in Normal view.

10. Choose **Page Layout→Page Setup→Background** 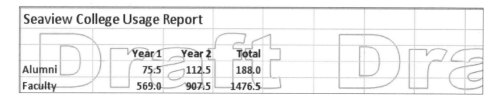 from the Ribbon, navigate to the Lesson 07 folder in your file storage location, select **Draft Image**, and click **Insert**.

*The word "Draft" repeats across and down the entire worksheet. Excel tiles as many copies of the image as will fit based on the image size.*

11. **Tap** [Ctrl] + [P] to display the Print tab of Backstage view, and notice in the print preview that the background would *not* print.

12. **Exit** from Backstage view without printing.

13. **Save** 💾 the changes, and leave the workbook **open**.

## Setting Title Rows and Columns

**Video Lesson**   labyrinthelab.com/videos

You may specify one or more rows as title rows and one or more columns as title columns. Title rows and columns are printed on every page of a worksheet. For example, recall that the Years 1–2 worksheet prints on multiple pages. Rows 1–4 contain worksheet titles and the column headings, and columns A–C contain the people and categories that describe the content of the various rows. Without that information, the data on the second page may be difficult to understand. This problem can be resolved by specifying rows 1–4 as title rows and columns A–C as title columns so that they appear on all pages. The title rows or columns are set in the Page Setup dialog box.

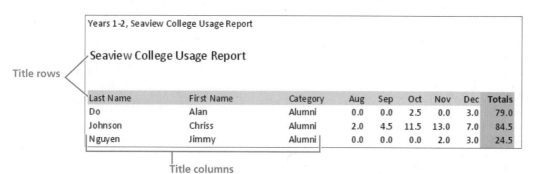

Page 2 of a printed worksheet with title rows and title columns repeating on every page

The Title Rows and Title Columns options are not available if you display the Page Setup dialog box from within the Print tab of Backstage view. To use these options, you must launch the Page Setup dialog box from the Page Layout Ribbon.

# Sheet Options

The Sheet command group of the Page Layout Ribbon contains options that affect the worksheet view and all printed pages of the worksheet. You may choose some options separately for viewing the worksheet and for printing.

## *Gridlines*

By default, light gray gridlines surround every cell in the worksheet view. Normally you should leave that option on, but you may view the worksheet without gridlines. By default, gridlines do not print. In large worksheets, you may find it useful to print with gridlines to help the eyes track data across rows and down columns.

| Gavins | Gabrielle | Student | 10.0 | 0.0 |
|--------|-----------|---------|------|-----|
| Grisson | Madison | Student | 2.0 | 7.5 |
| Kim | Tai Lee | Student | 0.0 | 4.0 |

The printed worksheet without gridlines (the default setting)

| Gavins | Gabrielle | Student | 10.0 |
|--------|-----------|---------|------|
| Grisson | Madison | Student | 2.0 |
| Kim | Tai Lee | Student | 0.0 |

The printed worksheet with gridlines

## *Headings*

By default, column headings (letters A, B, and so on) and row headings (numbers 1, 2, and so on) display in the worksheet view. You rarely would need to turn the display off. By default, these headings do not print. Including the headings may be useful for worksheet design, training, and group discussions.

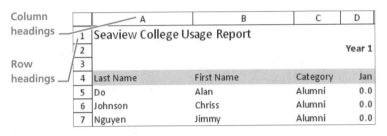

Column headings

Row headings

|   | A | B | C | D |
|---|---|---|---|---|
| 1 | Seaview College Usage Report | | | |
| 2 | | | | Year 1 |
| 3 | | | | |
| 4 | Last Name | First Name | Category | Jan |
| 5 | Do | Alan | Alumni | 0.0 |
| 6 | Johnson | Chriss | Alumni | 0.0 |
| 7 | Nguyen | Jimmy | Alumni | 0.0 |

The printed worksheet with column and row headings

| QUICK REFERENCE | SETTING TITLES, GRIDLINES, AND HEADINGS |
|-----------------|------------------------------------------|
| **Task** | **Procedure** |
| Print title rows on every page | ▪ Choose Page Layout→Page Setup→Print Titles from the Ribbon.<br>▪ Click in the Rows to Repeat at Top box.<br>▪ Drag to select the desired rows in the worksheet.<br>▪ Click Print Preview or OK. |
| Print title columns on every page | ▪ Choose Page Layout→Page Setup→Print Titles from the Ribbon.<br>▪ Click in the Columns to Repeat at Left box.<br>▪ Drag to select the desired columns in the worksheet.<br>▪ Click Print Preview or OK. |
| Print gridlines | ▪ Choose Page Layout→Sheet Options→Gridlines→Print from the Ribbon. |
| Print Excel column and row headings | ▪ Choose Page Layout→Sheet Options→Headings→Print from the Ribbon. |

## Set Sheet Options

*In this exercise, you will set options to print repeating title rows and title columns, gridlines, and row and column headings on a multipage worksheet.*

### Set Title Rows and Columns

1. Display the **Years 1–2** worksheet in Page Layout view at a zoom percentage that is comfortable for you.

2. Tap Ctrl + Home to jump to **cell A1**.

3. Choose **Page Layout→Page Setup→Print Titles** from the Ribbon.
   *The Page Setup dialog box displays with the Sheet tab active.*

4. Follow these steps to set title rows and title columns:

Ⓐ If necessary, drag the Page Setup dialog box by its title bar to make **columns A–C** and **rows 1–4** visible.

Ⓑ Click in the **Rows to Repeat at Top** box, which is currently empty.

Ⓒ Drag to select **rows 1–4**. A flashing marquee appears around the rows. The Rows to Repeat at Top box should display $1:$4.

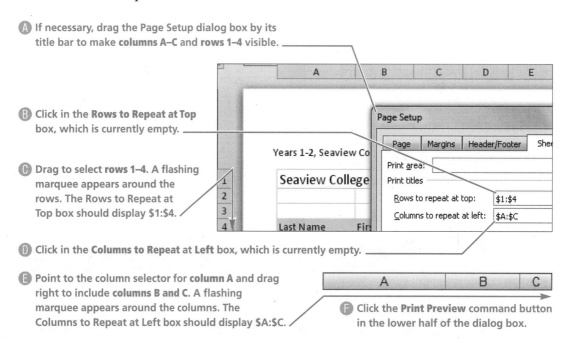

Ⓓ Click in the **Columns to Repeat** at **Left** box, which is currently empty.

Ⓔ Point to the column selector for **column A** and drag right to include **columns B and C**. A flashing marquee appears around the columns. The Columns to Repeat at Left box should display $A:$C.

Ⓕ Click the **Print Preview** command button in the lower half of the dialog box.

5. Click the **Next Page** button below the print preview in Backstage view, and then click the **Zoom to Page** button in the lower-right corner to zoom in.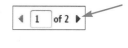
   *Examine the results for page 2 in the print preview. The title rows and columns repeat on every page of the printed worksheet. Now it is easier to identify the people, categories, and months that belong to each row of data on page 2.*

6. Click **Page Setup** at the bottom-left corner of Backstage view, select the **Sheet** tab in the Page Setup dialog box, and notice that the Print Titles section is unavailable.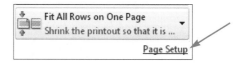
   *The Page Setup dialog box must be displayed through the Page Layout Ribbon if you want to set print titles.*

7. Click **Cancel** to exit the Page Setup dialog box.

8. **Exit** Backstage view without printing.

## Turn Gridlines and Headings On and Off

9. Click the **Normal** view button in the lower-right corner of the window.

10. Choose **Page Layout→Sheet Options→Gridlines→View** from the Ribbon to turn off the option.
    *The lines around the cells disappear. Occasionally you might want to turn off gridlines to help proofread or identify borders you applied manually around cells.*

11. Follow these steps to turn gridlines back on and to display gridlines and headings when you print:

Ⓐ Choose **Page Layout→Sheet Options→Gridlines→ View** from the Ribbon to turn on the option again. (The view options affect only how the worksheet displays and do not affect printing.)

Ⓑ Place a checkmark in the **Gridlines Print** option box.

Ⓒ Place a checkmark in the **Headings Print** option box.

*You do not see the effect of these last two settings in either Normal or Page Layout views.*

12. Choose **File→Print** and click the **Zoom to Page** button in the lower-right corner of Backstage view to zoom in, if necessary.
    *Gridlines appear as dotted lines but will print as solid lines. The column headings (A, B, and so on) and row headings (1, 2, and so on) also display above and to the left of the worksheet. You must display the print preview in Backstage view to see these effects.*

13. **Exit** Backstage view without printing.

14. **Save** the changes and leave the workbook **open**.

# Working with Page Breaks

**Video Lesson**  labyrinthelab.com/videos

You may use Page Break Preview to see where Excel's automatic page breaks occur in a worksheet and which part of the worksheet will be printed. This view also allows you to insert additional page breaks manually when they are needed. In Page Break Preview, the print area of the worksheet appears in white and nonprinting areas appear in gray.

The Page Break Preview button

## Adjusting Automatic Page Breaks

Excel formats most printed worksheets by inserting automatic page breaks when pages are full. An automatic page break appears as a dashed line.

| U | V | W | X | Y | Z | AA | AB | AC |
|---|---|---|---|---|---|---|---|---|
| 0.0 | 8.5 | 16.5 | 0.0 | 4.0 | 6.0 | 14.5 | 79.0 | |
| 0.0 | 0.0 | 14.5 | 6.0 | 14.5 | 18.0 | 17.5 | 177.5 | |
| 0.0 | 1.5 | 18.0 | 14.0 | 22.5 | 33.5 | 13.0 | 306.0 | |

Excel inserts an automatic page break, which appears as a dashed line.

At times, you may want to force a page break in a different place. For example, in the Years 1–2 worksheet, Excel splits a year by printing some of the year 2 month columns on the first page and the remaining month columns on the second page. All columns for a given year should be printed on the same page. You may adjust the location of a page break by clicking and dragging it in Page Break Preview. The page break then displays as a solid line, indicating that it is a manual page break.

| P | Q | R | S | T | U | V | W | X | Y | Z | AA | AB | AC |
|---|---|---|---|---|---|---|---|---|---|---|---|---|---|
| Year 2 | | | | | | | | | | | | | |
| Jan | Feb | Mar | Apr | May | Jun | Jul | Aug | Sep | Oct | Nov | Dec | Totals | |
| 9.5 | 4.5 | 0.0 | 2.0 | 0.0 | 0.0 | 1.5 | 0.0 | 0.0 | 2.5 | 0.0 | 3.0 | 79.0 | |
| 4.5 | 9.0 | 8.5 | 6.0 | 4.5 | 3.5 | 0.0 | 2.0 | 4.5 | 11.5 | 13.0 | 7.0 | 84.5 | |
| 0.0 | 4.0 | 1.5 | 1.5 | 0.0 | 0.0 | 3.5 | 0.0 | 0.0 | 0.0 | 2.0 | 3.0 | 24.5 | |

The two-headed arrow indicates that the page break is being dragged to the left.
A page break that you move or add appears as a solid line.

An automatic page break indicates that the page is filled, so you must move a vertical page break to the left to shift columns to the next page. Move a horizontal page break up to shift rows to the next page. You cannot increase columns or rows on a full page without adjusting other print options.

## Inserting and Removing Page Breaks

Even if the worksheet fits on one page, at times you may need to add a page break. For example, you might want the data for each six-month period to print on separate pages. You must select a cell in an appropriate column or row before issuing the Insert Page Break command. The page break appears as a solid line in the column to the left of the selected cell or the row above the selected cell. You may remove any page break that you set manually. If necessary, Excel will insert automatic page breaks after you remove manual page breaks.

| | A | B | C | D | E | F | G | H | I | J | K | L | M | N | O | P | Q |
|---|---|---|---|---|---|---|---|---|---|---|---|---|---|---|---|---|---|
| 1 | Seaview College Usage Report | | | | | | | | | | | | | | | | |
| 2 | | | | Year 1 | | | | | | | | | | | | Year 2 | |
| 3 | | | | | | | | | | | | | | | | | |
| 4 | Last Nai | First Na | Category | Jan | Feb | Mar | Apr | May | Jun | Jul | Aug | Sep | Oct | Nov | Dec | Jan | Fel |
| 5 | Do | Alan | Alumni | 0.0 | 0.0 | 0.0 | 0.0 | 0.0 | 0.0 | 0.0 | 0.0 | 6.0 | 14.5 | 18.0 | 17.5 | 9.5 | 4.! |
| 6 | Johnson | Chriss | Alumni | 0.0 | 0.0 | 3.5 | 0.0 | 0.0 | 0.0 | 2.0 | 3.0 | 0.0 | 2.0 | 0.0 | 0.0 | 4.5 | 9. |
| 7 | Nguyen | Jimmy | Alumni | 0.0 | 2.0 | 0.0 | 0.0 | 1.5 | 0.0 | 0.0 | 2.5 | 0.0 | 3.0 | 0.0 | 0.0 | 0.0 | 4. |

The worksheet with page breaks added manually, shown as solid lines

| Task | Procedure |
|---|---|
| Adjust an automatic page break | ■ Choose the Page Break Preview button from the Status Bar at the bottom-right corner of the window. <br> ■ Drag a vertical dashed automatic page break line to the left or a horizontal page break line up. <br> ■ Observe the page break change to a solid line to indicate a manual page break. |
| Add a manual page break | ■ Choose the Page Break Preview button from the Status Bar at the bottom-right corner of the window. <br> ■ Select a cell below or to the right of the desired page break location. <br> ■ Choose Page Layout→Page Setup→Breaks menu ▼→Insert Page Break from the Ribbon, or right-click the cell and choose Insert Page Break from the context menu. |
| Remove a manual page break | ■ Choose the Page Break Preview button from the Status Bar at the bottom-right corner. <br> ■ Select the cell to the right of the desired vertical page break line or below a horizontal page break line. <br> ■ Choose Page Layout→Page Setup→Breaks menu ▼→Remove Page Break from the Ribbon, or right-click the cell and choose Remove Page Break from the context menu. |

**DEVELOP YOUR SKILLS 7.3.6**

# Work with Page Breaks

*In this exercise, you will move, add, and remove a page break in Page Break Preview.*

## Display Page Break Preview

1. **Tap** Ctrl + Home to display **cell A1**, if necessary.

2. Choose the **Page Break Preview** button from the Status Bar at the bottom-right corner of the window.

3. If the Welcome to Page Break Preview dialog box appears, click **OK** to close the dialog box. *The words* Page 1 *and* Page 2 *on the worksheet indicate the area to be printed on each page. You should see a dark blue, dashed automatic page break line between columns V and W. The columns for the months of year 2 are split between two pages. You will adjust the page break to force the January column of year 2 to the next page.*

## Adjust a Page Break

4. Click anywhere on the **blue automatic page break line** and drag to the **left** until it is to the left of **column P.**

| P | Q | R | S | T | U | V | W | X | Y | Z | AA | AB | AC |
|---|---|---|---|---|---|---|---|---|---|---|---|---|---|
| **Year 2** | | | | | | | | | | | | | |
| Jan | Feb | Mar | Apr | May | Jun | Jul | Aug | Sep | Oct | Nov | Dec | Totals | |
| 9.5 | 4.5 | 0.0 | 2.0 | 0.0 | 0.0 | 1.5 | 0.0 | 0.0 | 2.5 | 0.0 | 3.0 | 79.0 | |
| 4.5 | 9.0 | 8.5 | 6.0 | 4.5 | 3.5 | 0.0 | 2.0 | 4.5 | 11.5 | 13.0 | 7.0 | 84.5 | |
| 0.0 | 4.0 | 1.5 | 1.5 | 0.0 | 0.0 | 3.5 | 0.0 | 0.0 | 0.0 | 2.0 | 3.0 | 24.5 | |

*The data for January through July will now print on page 2 along with the data for the rest of that year. The worksheet still fits on two pages.*

5. Select a cell anywhere on **page 1.**

6. Choose **File→Print**.

7. Click the **Zoom to Page** button at the lower-right corner of the print preview in Backstage view to zoom in, if necessary, and scroll page 1 to the right.
*Page 1 ends with column O, which contains the December data for year 1.*

8. Click the **Next Page** button below the print preview in Backstage view.
*Page 2 contains the names and categories in columns A–C and then displays column P containing the January data for year 2.*

9. **Exit** Backstage view without printing.

## Insert and Remove a Page Break

10. In **Page Break Preview**, select any cell in **column J**, which contains July data.

11. Choose **Page Layout→Page Setup→Breaks** menu ▾→ **Insert Page Break** from the Ribbon.
*A solid blue, manual page break line now appears to the left of column J.*

| H | I | J | K |
|---|---|---|---|
| | | | |
| | | | |
| May | Jun | Jul | Aug |
| 0.0 | 0.0 | 0.0 | 0.0 |
| 0.0 | 0.0 | 2.0 | 3.0 |

12. Point to any cell in **column V, right-click,** and choose **Insert Page Break** on the context menu.
*Do not move the pointer off column V as you right-click.*

*You may add or remove page breaks by choosing a command either on the Ribbon or in the context menu.*

13. Use either method you have just learned to add a page break to the left of **column AB.**
*The worksheet would now print on five pages. Next you will remove all but one page break.*

14. Select any cell in **column J.**

15. Choose **Page Layout→Page Setup→Breaks** menu ▾→**Remove Page Break** from the Ribbon.

16. Point to any cell in **column V, right-click,** and choose **Remove Page Break** in the context menu.

17. Use either method you have just learned to remove the page break to the left of **column AB**.

    *The worksheet should now contain only one page break to the left of column P.*

18. **Save** 🖫 your changes and **print** 🖶 the worksheet.

19. **Close** ⊠ the workbook.

## 7.4 Concepts Review

**Concepts Review**  labyrinthelab.com/excel10

*To check your knowledge of the key concepts introduced in this lesson, complete the Concepts Review quiz by going to the URL listed above. If your classroom is using Labyrinth eLab, you may complete the Concepts Review quiz from within your eLab course.*

# Reinforce Your Skills

## Insert Formulas and Sort Rows

*In this exercise, you will open a workbook that contains an accounts receivable aging report. You will create formulas to calculate the number of days the accounts are past due. You will also sort the rows.*

### Create the Formulas

1. **Open** the rs-Aging Report workbook from the Lesson 07 folder in your file storage location.

2. If necessary, **maximize** ☐ the window.

3. Type **7/1/14** in **cell B2**.
   *The date displays in Date format with the year as four digits. The year matches the invoice dates in column D.*

4. Select **cell F5** and enter the formula **=$B$2-D5**.
   *This formula calculates the number of days between July 1 and the invoice date. Cell B2 must be an absolute cell reference in the formula.*

5. Select **cell G5** and enter the formula **=F5-30**.
   *An invoice is considered past due if not paid within 30 days.*

6. Select the **range F5:G5**, and use the fill handle to copy the formulas down their columns for all customers.

| 157 | 127 |
|---|---|

### Sort the Rows

*Notice that the rows currently are unsorted.*

7. Select **cell A5** and choose **Data→Sort & Filter→Sort A to Z** ᴀ↓ from the Ribbon.
   *The rows are sorted by the account numbers in column A.*

8. Select **cell E5,** and choose **Date→Sort & Filter→Sort Z to A** ᴢ↓ from the Ribbon.
   *The rows are in descending order by the invoice amount. The largest amount should appear at the top of the list.*

9. Select **cell G5**, and choose **Data→Sort & Filter→Sort Z to A** ᴢ↓ from the Ribbon.
   *The rows now are sorted by the number of days past due from highest to lowest.*

10. **Save** 🖫 the changes and **close** ⊠ the workbook.

# Use Multiple Sort Keys

*In this exercise, you will use the Sort dialog box to sort worksheet rows using two sort keys. Then you will sort using three sort keys.*

1. **Open** the rs-Balance Due Report workbook from the Lesson 07 folder.
   *Notice that the list is currently sorted by the Account Number column.*

2. Select any data cell below the **row 3** headings.

## Sort on Two Sort Keys

3. Choose **Data→Sort & Filter→Sort** 🔳 from the Ribbon.
   *Excel will identify the list and select the correct rows. The header row will not be selected.*

4. Change the first Sort By level to **Outstanding Balance**, and set sorting on values in **Z to A** order.

5. Add a second level, set the Then By key to **Account Number** and sorting on values in **smallest to largest** order, and click **OK**.

| Lastname | Firstname | Account Number | Outstanding Balance |
|----------|-----------|----------------|---------------------|
| Ochoa | Carlos | 00012364 | Y |
| Smith | Sandra | 00012987 | Y |
| Carlton | Debra | 00013418 | Y |

*Take a moment to study the results. Notice that rows with an Outstanding Balance of "Y" move to the top of the list because you sorted in descending order. Records in the "Y" and "N" groups are then sorted by account number.*

## Sort on Three Sort Keys

6. Choose **Data→Sort & Filter→Sort** 🔳 from the Ribbon.
   *Now you will change the sort order within the Outstanding Balance groups to last name. Any same last names will then be sorted by first name.*

7. Change Then By to **Lastname** in the second level, with sorting on values in **A to Z** order.

8. Add a third level, set the Then By key to **Firstname**, with sorting on values in **A to Z** order, and then click **OK**.

| Lastname | Firstname | Account Number | Outstanding Balance |
|----------|-----------|----------------|---------------------|
| Adams | Latonya | 00014321 | Y |
| Carlton | Debra | 00013418 | Y |
| Carlton | Nico | 00028937 | Y |
| Dip | Visith | 00030279 | Y |

*Records in the "Y" and "N" groups are sorted by last name within each group. The same last names are grouped together and then sorted by first name (Carlton, Debra comes before Carlton, Nico).*

9. **Save** 🔳 the changes and **close** 🔳 the workbook.

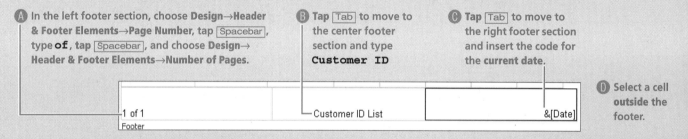

# Create a Custom Footer

*In this exercise, you will remove a footer and create a custom footer. You will also preview and print the worksheet.*

1. **Open** the rs-Customer ID List from the Lesson 07 folder.

2. Display **Page Layout view** by clicking its button in the lower-right corner of the window.

3. Select any section of the **footer**.
   *Next you will remove the existing footer.*

4. Choose **Design→Header & Footer→Footer** 📄 **menu ▼** and choose **(None)** from the top of the list.

5. Follow these steps to create a custom footer and format the footer:

Ⓐ In the left footer section, choose **Design→Header & Footer Elements→Page Number**, tap Spacebar, type **of**, tap Spacebar, and choose **Design→ Header & Footer Elements→Number of Pages**.

Ⓑ **Tap** Tab to move to the center footer section and type **Customer ID**

Ⓒ **Tap** Tab to move to the right footer section and insert the code for the **current date**.

Ⓓ Select a cell outside the footer.

-1 of 1
Footer

Customer ID List

&[Date]

*The custom footer displays below the worksheet in Page Layout view.*

6. Choose **File→Print**.
   *The footer is displayed in the print preview.*

7. **Print** 🖨 the worksheet.

8. **Save** 💾 the changes and **close** ✕ the workbook.

# Arrange Worksheet Windows

*In this exercise, you will open two workbooks and arrange the windows horizontally in order to compare expense data between sheets. You will also copy and paste data from one workbook to the other.*

## Open the Workbooks

1. **Open** the rs-Expenses Area 3 workbook from the Lesson 07 folder in your file storage location.

2. **Open** the rs-Expenses Area 5 workbook.

## Arrange Windows

3. Choose **View→Window→Switch Windows→2 rs-Expenses Area 3** from the Ribbon.
   *The Area 3 worksheet is in the active window.*

4. Choose **View→Window→Arrange All** from the Ribbon, select **Horizontal** in the Arrange Windows dialog box, and click **OK**.

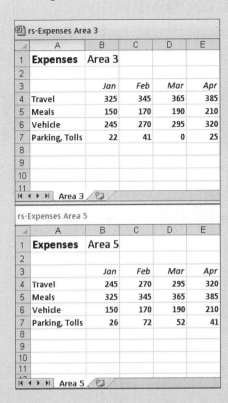

*The Area 3 worksheet window appears above the Area 5 worksheet window.*

5. Choose **View→Window→View Side by Side** 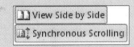 from the Ribbon; verify that the **Synchronous Scrolling** option is turned on in the Ribbon.

## Copy and Paste Data between Windows

6. In the **Area 3** worksheet in the top window, select and copy the column headings in the **range B3:N3**.

7. In the **Area 5** worksheet in the bottom window, select **cell B3** and paste.

8. Scroll in either window until **column N** is in view.
   *Both windows scroll in synch to display the Total column because the Synchronous Scrolling option is on.*

9. In the **Area 3** worksheet in the top window, select the **range N4:N7** and choose **Home→Editing→Sum** from the Ribbon.
   *The formula in each row sums the expense for January–December.*

10. Copy the **range N4:N7** and paste to **cell N4** in the **Area 5** worksheet.
    *You can copy and paste formulas as well as data to another sheet.*

11. **Save** the changes in each workbook and **close** them.

# Print a Large Worksheet on One Page

*In this exercise, you will set a worksheet to print on a single page. You will accomplish this by using landscape orientation and the Scale to Fit option. You also will add a header and experiment with paper size options.*

1. **Open** the rs-Volume Comparison workbook from the Lesson 07 folder.

2. Display **Page Layout view** by clicking its button in the lower-right corner of the window.
   *Notice that the worksheet currently is in portrait orientation with the narrow edge of the page on top.*

3. Drag the **Zoom** slider in the lower-right corner of the window to a percentage that allows you to see all the pages.
   *The worksheet is three pages wide and one page high. In the remainder of this exercise, you will adjust settings in the Page Layout Ribbon to fit this worksheet on a single page.*

   *During the remainder of this exercise, change the zoom level as needed.*

4. Choose **Page Layout→Page Setup→Orientation** menu ▼→**Landscape** from the Ribbon.
   *The worksheet now is two pages wide and one page high.*

## Change the Paper Size

5. Choose **Page Layout→Page Setup→Size** menu ▼→**Legal 8.5" x 14"** from the Ribbon.
   *More columns fit on page 1. Printing on wider paper and making a few other adjustments may fit a worksheet on fewer pages. Assume, however, that you want to use only letter-size paper because you find it inconvenient to switch paper in your printer and store wide printouts in notebooks and file folders.*

6. Change the paper size back to **Letter 8.5" x 11"**.

## Launch the Page Setup Dialog Box

7. Click the **dialog box launcher** button in the bottom-right corner of the Page Setup command group of the Page Layout Ribbon.
   *The Page Setup dialog box appears with the Page tab displayed. If a different tab is active, click the Page tab. Notice that the Orientation and Paper Size options are available in the dialog box as well as on the Ribbon. Also notice that the dialog box contains command buttons to jump to the Print tab of Backstage view and Print Preview.*

8. Click **Cancel** to exit the dialog box without making any changes.

## Scale the Worksheet and Add a Header

9. Choose **Page Layout→Scale to Fit→Width menu** ▼→**1 Page** from the Ribbon.
   *Now the worksheet fits on one page. The worksheet originally was one page high, so it is not necessary to change the Height option.*

10. Select any section of the **header**.

11. Choose the predefined header **Page 1 of ?**.

12. **Save** the changes and **close** the workbook.

# Apply Your Skills

## Sort on Multiple Sort Keys

*In this exercise, you will sort the rows in a worksheet using three sort keys.*

1. **Open** the as-Orders workbook from the Lesson 07 folder in your file storage location.

2. If necessary, **maximize** 🔲 the window.

3. Format the numbers in **column D** as **Comma style** with **no decimal places**.

4. **AutoFit** all column widths.
   *Notice that the rows are currently sorted by Sales in column D.*

5. Use the **Sort** dialog box to sort the rows using three sort keys: **key 1**, Area in smallest to largest order; **key 2**, Customer in A to Z order; and **key 3**, Sales in largest to smallest order. *The rows for each customer will be sorted within groups by modules according to their sales prices.*

   *Your completed worksheet should match the following example.*

| | A | B | C | D |
|---|---|---|---|---|
| 1 | Orders | | | |
| 2 | | | | |
| 3 | Area | Customer | Module | Sales |
| 4 | 1 | Draper University | Core 3 | 55,095 |
| 5 | 1 | Draper University | Billing | 16,650 |
| 6 | 1 | Draper University | Employment | 13,350 |
| 7 | 1 | Draper University | Support 3 | 4,950 |
| 8 | 1 | Western State College | Core 1 | 37,750 |
| 9 | 1 | Western State College | Billing | 15,595 |
| 10 | 1 | Western State College | Support 1 | 3,095 |
| 11 | 3 | Jennerstown Academy | Core 1 | 36,995 |
| 12 | 3 | Jennerstown Academy | Billing | 15,595 |
| 13 | 3 | Jennerstown Academy | Support 1 | 3,095 |
| 14 | 5 | North Chauwakeegan State | Core 2 | 52,795 |
| 15 | 5 | North Chauwakeegan State | Support 1 | 3,095 |
| 16 | 7 | University of Norwood | Core 3 | 56,095 |
| 17 | 7 | University of Norwood | Billing | 15,595 |
| 18 | 7 | University of Norwood | Support 2 | 3,295 |
| 19 | 7 | University of Norwood | Upgrade Protection | 895 |
| 20 | 8 | Olson College | Core 2 | 54,150 |
| 21 | 8 | Olson College | Billing | 15,595 |
| 22 | 8 | Olson College | Support 2 | 3,295 |
| 23 | 10 | Underwood College | Core 2 | 53,995 |
| 24 | 10 | Underwood College | Support 2 | 3,295 |
| 25 | 10 | Underwood College | Upgrade Protection | 895 |

6. **Save** 💾 the changes, **print** 🖨️ the worksheet, and **close** ⊠ the workbook.

# Print a Large Worksheet on One Page

*In this exercise, you will use the Page Layout Ribbon to format the worksheet so that it prints on one page. You also will include a header and footer.*

1. **Open** the as-Maria Fernandez Expenses workbook from the Lesson 07 folder.

2. Display the **Page Layout** Ribbon and change the orientation.

3. Change the **margins** or use the **Scale to Fit** options so that the worksheet will print on **one page**.

4. Add the **header and footer** shown in the following illustration. Use the **current date**.

5. **Type** your name in the footer.

6. Use **Print Preview** to review the worksheet before printing.
   *Your printed worksheet should fit on one page, as in the following example, showing the top and bottom of the page.*

as-Maria Fernandez Expenses

| Expenses | Maria Fernandez | | | Area 3 | | | | | | | | | |
|---|---|---|---|---|---|---|---|---|---|---|---|---|---|
| | January | February | March | April | May | June | July | August | September | October | November | December |
| Travel | 325 | 345 | 365 | 385 | 405 | 425 | 205 | 240 | 275 | 310 | 345 | 380 |
| Meals | 150 | 170 | 190 | 210 | 230 | 250 | 176 | 70 | 125 | 180 | 235 | 290 |
| Vehicle | 245 | 270 | 295 | 320 | 345 | 370 | 205 | 220 | 235 | 250 | 265 | 280 |
| Parking, Tolls | 22 | 41 | 0 | 25 | 39 | 7 | 26 | 72 | 52 | 41 | 38 | 47 |

| 11/13/2014 | 1 of 1 | Student Name |
|---|---|---|

7. **Save** 🖫 the changes, **print** 🖶 the worksheet, and **close** ⊠ the workbook.

# Print a Large Worksheet on Two Pages

*In this exercise, you will use the Page Layout Ribbon to format the worksheet so that it prints a title column and gridlines. You also will adjust the page break to balance the amount of data printed on each page.*

1. **Open** the as-David Sutton Expenses workbook from the Lesson 07 folder.

2. Display the **Page Layout** Ribbon and turn on **gridlines** for printing.

3. Set **column A** as a title column on every page.
   *Do not change the orientation from portrait.*

4. Adjust the page break so that **page 2** contains the July–December expenses.

5. **Save** 🖫 the changes, **print** 🖨 the worksheet, and **close** ⊠ the workbook.
   *Your two-page printout should match the following example.*

| | January | February | March | April | May | June |
|---|---|---|---|---|---|---|
| Travel | 245 | 270 | 295 | 320 | 345 | 370 |
| Meals | 325 | 345 | 365 | 385 | 405 | 425 |
| Vehicle | 150 | 170 | 190 | 210 | 230 | 250 |
| Parking, Tolls | 26 | 72 | 52 | 41 | 38 | 47 |

| | July | August | September | October | November | December |
|---|---|---|---|---|---|---|
| Travel | 205 | 220 | 235 | 250 | 265 | 280 |
| Meals | 205 | 240 | 275 | 310 | 345 | 380 |
| Vehicle | 15 | 70 | 125 | 180 | 235 | 290 |
| Parking, Tolls | 22 | 41 | 0 | 25 | 39 | 7 |

# Critical Thinking & Work-Readiness Skills

*In the course of working through the following Microsoft Office-based Critical Thinking exercises, you will also be utilizing various work-readiness skills, some of which are listed next to each exercise. Go to* labyrinthelab.com/workreadiness *to learn more about the work-readiness skills.*

## 7.1 View a Large Worksheet

**WORK-READINESS SKILLS APPLIED**

- Organizing and maintaining information
- Showing responsibility
- Solving problems

Roxana Ortega keeps My Virtual Campus Corporation records in Excel. Roxana soon realizes there are too many records to view on the screen at the same time. Open ct-Draper University Usage Report (Lesson 07 folder). Create a freeze pane for the last name, first name, and category. Use the scroll bar to view the Totals column in row 42, and then quickly move to the home cell. Scroll to view the totals in column AB. Save your workbook as **ct-Draper University Usage Report [Your Last Name]** in your Lesson 07 folder, and keep it open for the next exercise.

## 7.2 Sort a Large Worksheet

**WORK-READINESS SKILLS APPLIED**

- Organizing and maintaining information
- Using computers to process information
- Reasoning

Roxana wants to sort the records and analyze data at the end of the year to see who has the largest usage. Open **ct-Draper University Usage Report** (Lesson 07 folder), if necessary. Find the last data row and create a new blank row to separate the data from the total row. Custom sort the users by category alphabetically then by largest to smallest for the Totals column. Save your work, and keep the file open. If working in a group, discuss what questions the Sort feature can help answer about this worksheet. If working alone, type your response in a Word document named **ct-Questions** saved to your Lesson 07 folder.

## 7.3 Print a Large Worksheet

**WORK-READINESS SKILLS APPLIED**

- Organizing and maintaining information
- Showing responsibility
- Seeing things in the mind's eye

The data does not fit properly on one page. Roxana realizes the entire list can be printed on one or two pages if she uses page layout and print options, such as page orientation, margins, or page breaks. Help Roxana by opening ct-Draper University Usage Report [Your Last Name] (Lesson 07 folder), if necessary. Determine an appropriate layout that will print the worksheet on one or two pages; then set page layout and print options as necessary. Preview the layout to make certain all records will print correctly. Save and close your file when finished.

# Managing Multiple-Sheet Workbooks

## LEARNING OBJECTIVES

After studying this lesson, you will be able to:

- Change the default number of sheets for new workbooks
- Create formulas that summarize data from multiple worksheets
- Copy worksheets and their formats
- Create cell names for navigation and formulas
- Construct hyperlinks to worksheet cells and external documents
- Print multiple worksheets of a workbook

As you continue to work with Excel, you may find your workbooks growing in size and complexity. In this lesson, you will manage workbooks by copying and moving worksheets, as well as copying formatting from one worksheet to another. Workbooks may be organized with a summary worksheet and two or more detail worksheets, each containing data for one month, quarter, region, or other category. By using linked formulas on the summary worksheet, you will summarize information from the detail worksheets. You will use the power of defined names to identify cells, navigate worksheets more efficiently, and produce formulas that are easier to understand. You will create hyperlinks to navigate to areas within the workbook and to other documents. After selecting multiple worksheets, you will choose print options and print the selected worksheets using a single command.

# Tracking Project Expenses

My Virtual Campus Corporation, a social networking technology company, has developed a project budget. The project team will create and  market an optional My Career module for the company's web application. Anthony Ngo, the finance director, has allocated the total amount to various budget categories. Anthony needs a workbook that tracks the year-to-date expenditures and consolidates the information on a summary worksheet. The summary worksheet will give Anthony an instant overview of the amounts spent compared to the budget allocations. The workbook will be dynamic. Formulas in the summary worksheet will be linked to cells in the detail sheets, where all the necessary detail information will be stored. The following illustrations show the summary worksheet and three of the detail sheets that Anthony will create.

| | A | B |
|---|---|---|
| 1 | **Advertising Tracking Sheet** | |
| 2 | | |
| 3 | | Amount Spent |
| 4 | September | - |
| 5 | October | 2,000 |
| 6 | November | 6,075 |
| 7 | December | 1,200 |
| 8 | January | |
| 9 | February | |
| 10 | March | |
| 11 | April | |
| 12 | May | |
| 13 | June | |
| 14 | July | |
| 15 | August | |
| 16 | **Total** | **$9,275** |

| | A | B |
|---|---|---|
| 1 | **Equipment Tracking Sheet** | |
| 2 | | |
| 3 | | Amount Spent |
| 4 | September | 8,547 |
| 5 | October | 3,640 |
| 6 | November | 5,072 |
| 7 | December | 1,211 |
| 8 | January | |
| 9 | February | |
| 10 | March | |
| 11 | April | |
| 12 | May | |
| 13 | June | |
| 14 | July | |
| 15 | August | |
| 16 | **Total** | **$18,470** |

| | A | B | C |
|---|---|---|---|
| 1 | **Mileage Tracking Sheet** | | |
| 2 | | | |
| 3 | | Mileage | Amount Spent |
| 4 | September | 720 | 317 |
| 5 | October | 885 | 389 |
| 6 | November | 280 | 123 |
| 7 | December | 420 | 185 |
| 8 | January | | - |
| 9 | February | | - |
| 10 | March | | - |
| 11 | April | | - |
| 12 | May | | - |
| 13 | June | | - |
| 14 | July | | - |
| 15 | August | | - |
| 16 | **Total** | 2,305 | **$1,014** |

| | A | B | C |
|---|---|---|---|
| 1 | **My Virtual Campus** | | |
| 2 | **My Career  -  Budget and Expenses** | | |
| 3 | | | |
| 4 | **General and Capital Expenses** | **Budget Allocation** | **Year-to-Date Spent** |
| 5 | Advertising | 40,000 | 9,275 |
| 6 | Equipment | 25,000 | 18,470 |
| 7 | Mileage | 8,000 | 1,014 |

The summary worksheet tracks the totals from the detail sheets.

# 8.1 Using Multiple Worksheets

**Video Lesson**   labyrinthelab.com/videos

You may add worksheets in a workbook, limited only to the amount of available memory on your computer. Worksheets may also be deleted as necessary. Much like pages in a word processor document, multiple worksheets are a convenient way to organize your data logically into more manageable sections. Any worksheet can contain formulas that perform calculations on data contained in other worksheets. For example, you may set up a summary worksheet that totals data from multiple detail worksheets.

## Modifying the Default Number of Sheets

Each new workbook contains three worksheets. You may change the default number of sheets for new workbooks using the Excel Options dialog box. Changing the default number can save time if your workbooks typically contain only one worksheet or more than three sheets.

### DEVELOP YOUR SKILLS 8.1.1
## Change the Default for Sheets in Workbooks

*In this exercise, you will change the number of sheets in new workbooks, test the change, and restore the default to three.*

1. Start **Excel**.

2. Choose **File→Options** 🗈 to display the General options in the Excel Options dialog box.

3. Follow these steps to change the default number of sheets in a workbook:

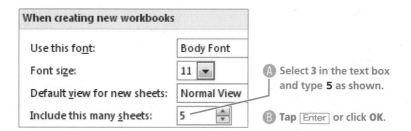

4. **Tap** [Ctrl]+[N] to start a new workbook.
   *Notice the five sheet tabs at the bottom of the worksheet window.*

5. Display the **Excel Options** dialog box again.

6. Change the default number of sheets back to **3** and click **OK**.

7. **Tap** [Ctrl]+[N] to verify that the number of sheets is three.

8. Taking care not to close the Excel program window, **close** 🗙 the open workbooks. Choose **not** to save if you are prompted to save either workbook.

# Selecting Multiple Sheets

Video Lesson    labyrinthelab.com/videos

Cell entries and formatting may be created in the same cell or range of multiple sheets simultaneously. This action is recommended when the sheets have an identical structure. After one sheet is displayed, holding the [Ctrl] key and clicking another sheet tab will add it to the selection. You can perform other simultaneous actions to the selected sheets, such as inserting a row.

| Summary | Advertising | Mileage | Sheet3 |

**Three of the four sheet tabs have a light background to indicate that they are selected.**

| QUICK REFERENCE | USING MULTIPLE SHEETS |
|---|---|
| **Task** | **Procedure** |
| Change the default number of sheets for new workbooks | ▪ Choose File →Options 📄 , and select the General category. <br> ▪ In the When Creating New Workbooks section, change Include This Many Sheets to the desired number of sheets. |
| Select multiple worksheets | ▪ Display the first sheet to be included in the selection. <br> ▪ Hold down [Ctrl] and click each additional sheet tab desired, or hold down [Shift] and click a sheet tab to include contiguous sheets. |
| Remove sheets from the selection | Follow one of these steps: <br> ▪ Hold down [Ctrl] and click a sheet tab to deselect it. <br> ▪ Click a sheet tab that is not in the selection to cancel a multiple selection. <br> ▪ Hold down [Shift] and click the first selected sheet tab to cancel a contiguous selection. |

## DEVELOP YOUR SKILLS 8.1.2
## Select Multiple Sheets

*In this exercise, you will select three worksheets and then format and enter data in the same cell of them all.*

1. **Open** the Project Budget workbook from the Lesson 08 folder in your file storage location.

2. **Maximize** 🔲 the window.

3. With the **Summary** sheet active, **hold down** [Ctrl] and click the **Mileage** sheet tab.
   *Both sheet tabs have a light background to indicate that they are selected. The Advertising sheet tab, which is not in the selection, has a dark background.*

4. **Hold down** [Ctrl] and click the **Mileage** sheet tab to remove it from the selection.
   *In the next steps, you will enter the word* Total *in cell A16 of the Summary, Advertising, and Mileage sheets.*

5. Follow these steps to select adjacent sheets:

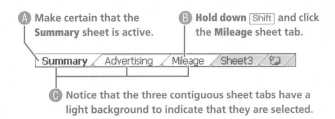

Ⓐ Make certain that the **Summary** sheet is active.

Ⓑ **Hold down** [Shift] and click the **Mileage** sheet tab.

| Summary | Advertising | Mileage | Sheet3 |

Ⓒ Notice that the three contiguous sheet tabs have a light background to indicate that they are selected.

6. Select **cell A16**, choose **Home→Font→Bold** B from the Ribbon, type **Total**, and tap ⌸Enter⌸.

7. **Hold down** ⌸Shift⌸ and click the **Summary** sheet tab to cancel the multiple sheet selection.

8. Display the **Mileage** sheet, and notice that the cell entry appears in **cell A16**.

9. **Save** 🖫 the changes, and leave the workbook **open**.

# 8.2 Linking Cells and Formulas

**Video Lesson** labyrinthelab.com/videos

Excel lets you link cells from different worksheets in the same workbook or in other workbooks. Linking lets you place values from a source worksheet into a destination worksheet. This powerful capability is the glue that binds worksheets together.

## Why Link Cells?

Linking is often used to create totals in summary worksheets from values in detail worksheets. This capability lets you keep detailed information in the detail sheets and see the totals in the summary worksheet. Linking generally reflects the needs of many organizations. For example, top-level managers usually are interested in seeing the big picture, while detailed information is needed at the departmental level. Because the original data are entered only once, linking ensures that all references to the data are accurate. If the contents of the original cells are changed, the appropriate cell in the summary worksheet updates automatically.

## Linking Formulas

You link cells by creating a linking formula in the summary worksheet. Linking formulas specify cells from the detail worksheets. You must use specific syntax—or language—when creating a linking formula.

### Creating Linking Formulas

As with normal formulas, before you create a linking formula, you must select the cell in the summary worksheet where you want the result to appear. Also as with all other formulas, a linking formula begins with the equals (=) sign. You may type a linking formula, but using the mouse to select cells is more accurate and highly recommended.

### Linking Cells from Other Worksheets in Formulas

The formulas shown will link the contents of one cell from a detail worksheet to a cell in the summary worksheet. The sheet name and cell reference are separated by an exclamation point (!). If the sheet name contains spaces or other nonalphabetic characters, the sheet name must be surrounded by single quotes ('), as in the second example.

You may create calculation formulas on a summary worksheet using data from one or more detail worksheets. The following example sums the sales from four quarterly sheets to result in the yearly total. Notice that you may use commas to separate the four cell references.

=SUM(Quarter1!D18, Quarter2!D18, Quarter3!D18, Quarter4!D18)

### Linking Cells from Other Workbooks in Formulas

If the source cell is in a different workbook, you must include the full workbook name in square brackets. Because the example workbook name contains a space, single quotes (') are included before the workbook name and after the worksheet name. Selecting the cell with the mouse will add all of this syntax for you.

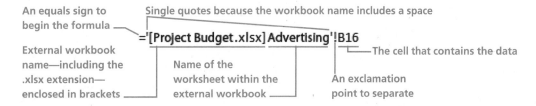

DEVELOP YOUR SKILLS 8.2.1
## Create a Linking Formula

*In this exercise, you will create a formula to link a cell in the Advertising worksheet to the Summary worksheet.*

**Browse the Workbook**

1. Display the **Summary** sheet of the Project Budget workbook.

2. Select **cell D2** and notice that the cell contains the TODAY function.
   *This cell will always display the current date.*

3. Review the expense categories in **column A** and the budget allocations in **column B**.
   *The budget allocations add up to $300,000, as shown in cell B16.*

4. Review **column C** and notice that the Year-to-Date Spent cells currently are blank.
   *The cells in column C will be linked to the year-to-date expenditure totals in the detail sheets, such as Advertising and others you will add.*

5. Review **column D**.
   *The Available Balance in column D will be the difference between the Budget Allocation in column B and the Year-to-Date Spent total in column C. Column D will show the remaining budgeted amount for each expense category.*

## Create a Total Formula in a Detail Worksheet

6. Display the **Advertising** worksheet.
   *The amount spent on advertising is entered for each month to date. You will link the total in cell B16 to cell C5 in the Summary worksheet.*

7. Select **cell B16**, use **Home→Editing→AutoSum** $\Sigma$, and **tap** Enter to calculate the column total.
   *The total should equal 8,075. Notice that AutoSum summed the entire range B4:B15. This is desirable because AutoSum will keep a running total as you enter data throughout the year.*

   *The text in cells A1 and B3 is smaller than that of other cells; you will apply formatting in a later exercise.*

## Create Linking Formulas Using Point Mode

*You may use point mode to create linking formulas as you do with other formulas.*

8. Display the **Summary** worksheet.

9. Select **cell C5** and type an equals (**=**) sign.
   *Excel displays the equals sign in the Formula Bar.*

10. Display the **Advertising** worksheet.
    *Excel displays the Advertising worksheet. The sheet name Advertising appears in the Formula Bar followed by an exclamation point.*

11. Select **cell B16**.
    *The linking formula =Advertising!B16 displays in the Formula Bar.*

12. Complete the formula by clicking the **Enter** ✓ button on the Formula Bar or **tapping** Enter.
    *Excel displays the Summary worksheet with the completed link in cell C5. The number 8,075 appears in cell C5. Notice that the formula instructs Excel to link to cell B16 in the Advertising worksheet. The exclamation point separates the two arguments (parts of the formula).*

13. Display the **Advertising** worksheet.

14. Select **cell B7** and type **1200**.
    *The total in cell B16 displays 9,275.*

15. Display the **Summary** worksheet.
    *Cell C5 now displays 9,275. The link is dynamic, always reflecting the current value in the source cell.*

16. **Save** 💾 the changes.

## Calculate the Available Balance

17. In the **Summary** worksheet, select **cell D5** and use point mode to subtract **cell C5** from **cell B5**.
    *If your result does not equal 30,725, make certain that the cell references in the formula are in the correct order for subtraction. You will complete the remaining formulas for columns C and D in a later exercise.*

18. **Save** 💾 the changes and leave the workbook **open**.

# 8.3 Copying Worksheets

**Video Lesson**   labyrinthelab.com/videos

The Project Budget workbook will eventually contain more expenditure worksheets with the same structure as the Advertising worksheet. Rather than inserting new blank sheets, you may use the Move or Copy Sheet command to copy an existing worksheet and then edit the duplicate.

## The Move or Copy Dialog Box

A *copied* worksheet created with the Move or Copy Sheet command is an exact duplicate of the original worksheet. The data, structure, print settings, and page setup settings are identical to the original worksheet. To move or copy a worksheet to another workbook, both workbooks must be open. Placing a checkmark in the Create a Copy box creates a *copy*. Leaving the box blank *moves* the selected worksheet. A worksheet moved to another workbook no longer exists in the original workbook.

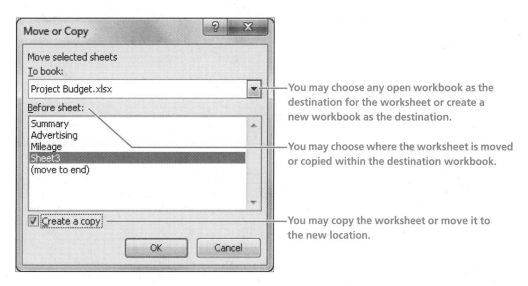

You may choose any open workbook as the destination for the worksheet or create a new workbook as the destination.

You may choose where the worksheet is moved or copied within the destination workbook.

You may copy the worksheet or move it to the new location.

| QUICK REFERENCE | COPYING AND MOVING WORKSHEETS |
|---|---|
| **Task** | **Procedure** |
| Copy or move a worksheet using a command | ■ Select the desired sheet tab to be copied or moved.<br>■ Choose Home→Cells→Format ▦ →Move or Copy Sheet from the Ribbon.<br>*or*<br>■ Right-click the sheet tab and choose Move or Copy from the pop-up (or context) menu.<br>■ Choose the destination workbook or (New Book) for a new blank workbook from the To Book list.<br>■ Select the worksheet position from the Before Sheet list.<br>■ To copy, place a checkmark in the Create a Copy box. To move, leave the box empty. |
| Copy or move a worksheet in the same workbook by dragging | ■ To move, drag the sheet tab to the desired location within the tabs.<br>■ To copy, hold down Ctrl and drag the sheet tab. |

# Create a Copy of a Worksheet

*In this exercise, you will make two copies of the Advertising worksheet to create new sheets named Equipment and Training Materials.*

Scroll through the sheet tabs using the ◄ and ► buttons if any tab is not visible during the exercise.

### Create the Equipment Worksheet

1. Display the **Advertising** worksheet in the Project Budget workbook.
   *The active worksheet always is the worksheet that is copied.*

2. Choose **Home→Cells→Format** [icon]**→Move or Copy Sheet** from the Ribbon.

3. Follow these steps to create a copy of the Postage worksheet.

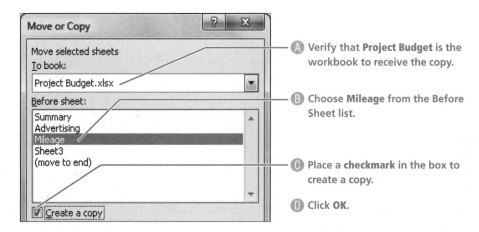

*Excel positions the duplicate worksheet before the Mileage sheet and names it Advertising (2).*

4. **Double-click** the Advertising (2) sheet tab, **type** the new name **Equipment**, and **tap** ⟨Enter⟩ to rename the sheet.

### Edit the Title and Number Entries in the Equipment Worksheet

5. **Double-click cell A1** to position the insertion point in the cell.

6. **Double-click** again on the word *Advertising* to select it.

7. **Type** the word **Equipment** and **complete** the entry.
   *The title now should read Equipment Tracking Sheet.*

8. Change the numbers in the **range B4:B7**, as shown in the illustration to the right.
   *Notice that cell B16 contains a sum formula. Copying a worksheet includes all cell contents and formatting from the original worksheet.*

9. **Save** [icon] the changes.

| | A | B |
|---|---|---|
| 1 | Equipment Tracking Sheet | |
| 2 | | |
| 3 | | Amount Spent |
| 4 | September | 8,547 |
| 5 | October | 3,640 |
| 6 | November | 5,072 |
| 7 | December | 1,211 |

## Create the Training Materials Worksheet

*Now you will use the context menu to select the Move or Copy Sheet command.*

10. Display the **Advertising** worksheet.

11. **Right-click** the **Advertising** sheet tab and choose **Move or Copy** from the context menu.

12. In the Move or Copy dialog box, choose **Sheet3** from the Before Sheet list, place a checkmark in the **Create a Copy** box, and *click* **OK**.

13. Change the name of the new sheet to **Training Materials**.
    *The sheet tabs should look like those shown. If necessary, drag a sheet tab to the correct position in the worksheet order.*

| Summary | Advertising | Equipment | Mileage | **Training Materials** | Sheet3 |

14. Edit the title in **cell A1** of the Training Materials worksheet and change the numbers in the **range B4:B7**, as shown in the illustration to the right.

| | A | B | C |
|---|---|---|---|
| 1 | Training Materials Tracking Sheet | | |
| 2 | | | |
| 3 | | Amount Spent | |
| 4 | September | 145 | |
| 5 | October | 1,620 | |
| 6 | November | (1,705) | |
| 7 | December | 730 | |

## Delete the Sheet3 Worksheet

*Recall that the default number of worksheets for a new workbook is three. You will now delete Sheet3, as it is not needed.*

15. Display the **Sheet3** worksheet.

16. **Right-click** the **Sheet3** tab and choose **Delete** from the context menu. Choose **Delete** in the Microsoft Excel dialog box to confirm.

| Summary | Advertising | Equipment | Mileage | **Training Materials** |

## Copy the Salaries Worksheet from a Different Workbook

*When you move or copy a worksheet to a different workbook, both files must be open.*

17. **Open** the Salaries workbook from the Lesson 8 folder.

18. **Right-click** the **Salaries** sheet tab and choose **Move or Copy** from the context menu.

19. Follow these steps to copy the Salaries worksheet:

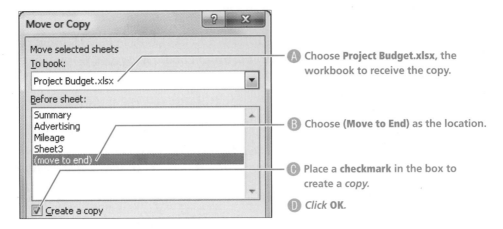

A. Choose **Project Budget.xlsx**, the workbook to receive the copy.

B. Choose **(Move to End)** as the location.

C. Place a **checkmark** in the box to create a *copy*.

D. *Click* **OK**.

*Excel positions the Salaries worksheet after the Training Materials worksheet in the Project Budget workbook. In the next exercise, you will correct the width of column G.*

20. **Close** ☒ the Salaries workbook without saving.

21. **Save** 💾 the changes to the Project Budget workbook and leave it **open**.

## Copying Formats between Worksheets

**Video Lesson**   labyrinthelab.com/videos

Excel provides three ways to copy just the cell formatting from one worksheet to another without copying the text or numbers in the cells:

- The Format Painter
- The Paste Options menu
- The Paste Special command

You may want to copy the format of titles, headings, and numbers from one worksheet to other sheets to give them a unified appearance. You also may want to copy formatting into new worksheets in which the data will be entered later.

### Format Painter

**FROM THE KEYBOARD**

Ctrl + A to select all

Use the Format Painter 🖌 tool on the Home Ribbon to copy formatting to cells in the target worksheet. You may select any of the following before using the Format Painter button: one or more cells, columns, or rows, or the entire worksheet. The column width or row height is not applied unless you select an entire column or row before using Format Painter.

Use the Select All ◢ button above the top-left corner of the worksheet to select the entire worksheet.

## Use Format Painter to Copy Formats

*In this exercise, you will use the Format Painter to copy formatting from the Summary worksheet to the Advertising worksheet. You also will apply formatting from the Advertising worksheet to the two worksheets you created in the previous exercise.*

### Copy Formatting from the Summary Worksheet to the Advertising Worksheet

1. Display the **Summary** worksheet in the Project Budget workbook and select **cell A2**.
   *You will copy the text format from this subheading to the heading in the Advertising worksheet.*

2. Choose **Home→Clipboard→Format Painter** 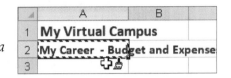 from the Ribbon.
   *Cell A2 displays a marquee, and the mouse pointer changes to a block cross with a paintbrush.*

3. Display the **Advertising** worksheet.

4. Select **cell A1**, and the format is copied to that cell.
   *The font in cell A1 now has the same dark blue color and size as the subheading in the Summary worksheet. Notice that you may switch to any worksheet after the Format Painter has been activated.*

5. Display the **Summary** worksheet and select **cell D4**.

6. Choose **Format Painter** from the Ribbon.

7. Display the **Advertising** worksheet and select **cell B3** to copy the format to that cell.

8. Display the **Summary** worksheet and select **cells A16** and **B16** (the cells in the Total row).

9. Choose F**ormat Painter** from the Ribbon.

10. Display the **Advertising** worksheet and select **cell A16** (the first cell in the Total row).
    *Bold and the Currency Style number format are copied to cells A16:B16.*

### Copy All Formats to Other Worksheets

*The Advertising, Equipment, and Training Materials sheets have an identical structure and format. You will use the Format Painter to copy all formatting— for text, numbers, column widths, and row heights— from the Advertising worksheet to the other sheets.*

11. Display the **Advertising** worksheet, if not already displayed.

12. Click the **Select All** button.
    *The entire Advertising worksheet is selected.*

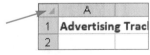

13. **Double-click** Format Painter on the Ribbon.
    *Double-clicking the Format Painter button lets you apply the format as many times as needed.*

14. Display the **Equipment** worksheet, and then click the **Select All** button.
    *Excel applies the Format Painter command to the entire selection. Notice that the Format Painter is still active.*

15. Display the **Training Materials** worksheet, and click the **Select All** ◢ button.
    *The entire worksheet has the same formatting as the Advertising worksheet. Notice that this technique creates consistent formatting among worksheets (provided they have an identical structure).*

16. Click **Format Painter** 🖌 on the Ribbon to deactivate it.

17. Click anywhere in the **worksheet** to deselect the cells.

### Deselect Cells

18. Take a few moments to review the various sheets and deselect highlighted cells.
    *Entire ranges may still appear selected from a previous use of Format Painter. Clearing the selections prevents cell contents from being changed or deleted accidentally.*

19. **Save** 🖫 the changes.

### Edit the Mileage Worksheet

20. Display the **Mileage** worksheet.
    *The numbers in column B are the number of miles driven in a given month. You will calculate the actual mileage expense in column C. The mileage expense is calculated as the number of miles multiplied by a cost of 44 cents per mile.*

21. Select **cell C4** and enter the formula **=B4\*.44**.
    *The result should equal 316.8 or 317. You will standardize the cell formatting in a moment.*

22. Use **Format Painter** 🖌 to copy the number and font formatting from **cell B4** to **cell C4**.

23. Use the **fill handle** to copy the formula and cell formatting down the column to **row 15**.
    *Some of the cells will display zeros or dashes (depending on the default settings on your computer) because some values have not yet been entered into column B.*

24. **Deselect** the highlighted cells.

25. **Save** 🖫 the changes and leave the workbook **open**.

## Paste Options

Video Lesson    labyrinthelab.com/videos

You may use the Copy command and options on the Paste menu in the Ribbon to control the type of formatting and content that are applied to the target cells, as described in the following examples:

- You apply just the column width from a selected cell to another column.
- You paste values without their formatting in order to apply different formatting manually.
- You copy cells arranged across a row and paste them down a column, or vice versa. This is known as *transposing* data.
- You paste formula results as values into a different workbook because the cells that the formulas refer to are not available there.

The options on the Paste menu will vary depending on the attributes of the copied selection. Clicking the Paste drop-down menu button in the Ribbon displays the menu. The Paste Options button appears at the lower-right corner of the destination cell(s) to customize after a copy-and-paste action is performed. When the button is clicked, the same options display as on the Paste menu in the Ribbon. The button disappears upon the next action you take.

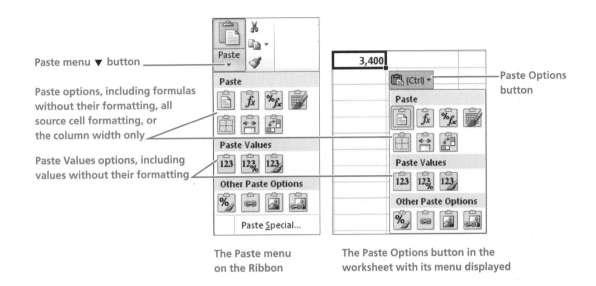

Paste menu ▼ button

Paste options, including formulas without their formatting, all source cell formatting, or the column width only

Paste Values options, including values without their formatting

Paste Options button

The Paste menu on the Ribbon

The Paste Options button in the worksheet with its menu displayed

You can hover the mouse over any button on the Paste menu to display its name in a pop-up box. Pointing to an option in the Paste menu displays a preview of the result in the worksheet. Any paste option may be used to perform a paste as well as change the result immediately after the paste operation. The buttons and their actions are listed in the following table.

| Button | Name | Paste Action in the Destination Cell |
|---|---|---|
| | Paste | Pastes the source cell's contents and applies all its formatting |
| | Formulas | Pastes the source cell's contents and applies the destination cell's formatting |
| | Formulas & Number Formatting | Pastes the source cell's contents, applies the source cell's number format, and applies all other destination cell formatting |
| | Keep Source Formatting | Pastes the source cell's contents and applies all its formatting |
| | No Borders | Pastes the source cell's contents and applies all its formatting except borders |
| | Keep Source Column Widths | Pastes the source cell's contents and applies the source cell's column width to the destination column |
| | Transpose | Pastes the source range's contents and formatting but reverses the row and column data |
| | Values | Pastes the value resulting from a formula (but not the formula) and applies the destination cell's formatting |
| | Values & Number Formatting | Pastes the value resulting from a formula (but not the formula), applies the source cell's number format, and applies all other destination cell formatting |
| | Values & Source Formatting | Pastes the value resulting from a formula (but not the formula) and applies the source cell's formatting |
| | Formatting | Applies the source cell's formatting but does not paste its contents |
| | Paste Link | Creates a linking formula to the source cell and applies the source cell's formatting |
| | Picture | Pastes a picture of the selected range as an object on top of the spreadsheet (or into other document, such as a Word document) |
| | Linked Picture | Pastes a picture of the selected range and creates a link to update the picture if any source cell is changed |

## Paste Special

The Paste Special command contains a dialog box with many of the same options that are on the Paste menu. The Operation options allow you to add a copied value to (or subtract it from) the existing value in the destination cell, multiply the values, or divide the destination values by their corresponding copied values. Other options include pasting only the comments, data validation rules, and conditional formatting applied to the copied cell(s).

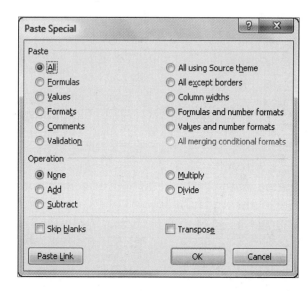

The Paste Special dialog box contains a wider range of options to limit the formatting to be transferred to the target cells.

| QUICK REFERENCE | USING FORMAT PAINTER, PASTE OPTIONS, AND PASTE SPECIAL |
|---|---|
| **Task** | **Procedure** |
| Copy formats to one other cell or range | ■ Click the cell that has the format(s) you wish to copy.<br>■ Choose Home→Clipboard→Format Painter ⟆ from the Ribbon.<br>■ Select the cell or range to which you wish to copy the format(s). |
| Copy formats to multiple locations | ■ Click the cell that has the format(s) you wish to copy.<br>■ Double-click the Home→Clipboard→Format Painter ⟆ button.<br>■ Select the cell or range to which you wish to copy the format(s).<br>■ When you are finished, click the Format Painter ⟆ button to turn it off. |
| Apply an option while pasting using the Ribbon | ■ Select a cell or range of cells, and choose Home→Clipboard→Copy from the Ribbon.<br>■ Choose Home→Clipboard→Paste menu ▼ from the Ribbon, and then choose the desired option from the list. |
| Apply an option after pasting | ■ Copy and paste the desired cell or range of cells.<br>■ Click the Paste Options button at the lower-right corner of the destination cell(s) and choose an option from the list. |
| Apply an option using Paste Special | ■ Select and copy a cell or range of cells.<br>■ Select the destination cell or range of cells.<br>■ Choose Clipboard→Paste menu ▼→Paste Special from the Ribbon.<br>■ Choose the desired option in the Paste Special dialog box. |

# Use Paste Options and Paste Special

*In this exercise, you will explore options to paste values. You will copy data from a column and paste it across a row, and you will add the values of copied cells to values in the corresponding destination cells. You will also copy only the column width formatting from one column to another column.*

## Explore Paste Options

1. Display the **Summary** worksheet.

2. Select the **range B4:B16**, and choose **Home→Clipboard→Copy**  from the Ribbon.
   *An animated marquee appears around the copied range B4:B16.*

3. Select **cell H4**, and then click the **Paste** drop-down menu button in the Clipboard group of the Ribbon.
   *The Paste menu appears.*

4. Follow these steps to view the result of various paste options:

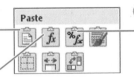

**A** Point at (but do not click) the **Paste** option, and notice that a normal paste is previewed in the range H4:H16.

**B** Point at **Formulas**, and notice that cell contents would be pasted without their bold or number formatting.

**C** Click the **Formulas & Number Formatting** button, and notice that bold formatting was not applied to the destination range.

5. **Undo** the paste.

## Copy Values without Formatting

6. Copy the **range B4:B16** if a marquee does not still display around the range.

7. Select **cell H4**, and choose **Home→Clipboard→Paste menu ▼** from the Ribbon.

8. Point at (but do not click) each **Paste Values** option to view its preview in the range H4:H16.

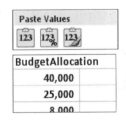

9. Choose **Values** [123] from the menu.
   *The cell contents are pasted without their formatting so that you may apply different formatting. Also, the cell H16 formula result, 300000, is pasted as a value. This capability would be useful if you planned to delete the cell containing the formula.*

## Transpose Data

*In the next steps, you will copy employee names down a column and paste them across a row in a different sheet.*

10. Select the **range A11:A15**, and choose **Home→Clipboard→Copy**  from the Ribbon.

11. Display the **Salaries** worksheet, select **cell B3**, and choose **Home→Clipboard→Paste** from the Ribbon.
    *The entries are pasted down column B. The values in the range B4:B7 have been overwritten. You realize that you wanted the employee names to be transposed across row 3 as column headings.*

12. Click the **Paste Options** button at the lower-right corner of the pasted range.

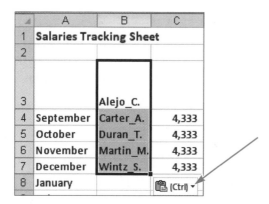

13. Choose **Transpose** in the paste options menu.

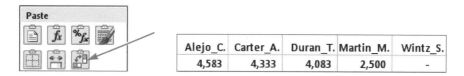

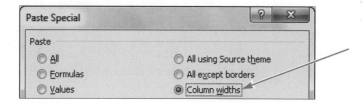

*The employee names are transposed across row 3, and the original values in the range B4:B7 are displayed. To limit formatting, the Paste Options button is used after a paste.*

14. **Right-align** the **range B3:F3** to align with the numbers below these employee names.

## Copy Only a Column Width

*Notice that the width of column G needs to be increased to display its contents correctly. You will copy the width from a similar column on another worksheet.*

15. Display the **Advertising** worksheet.

16. Select **cell B3** and choose **Copy** from the Ribbon.

17. Display the **Salaries** worksheet.

18. Select **cell G16** and choose **Home→Clipboard→Paste** [icon] menu ▼→**Paste Special** from the Ribbon.

19. Choose **Column Widths** and click **OK** in the Paste Special dialog box.

*Only the column width is applied from the source cell to all cells in column G. You could have chosen this option from the Paste menu.*

20. **Autofit** the height of **row 3**, if necessary.

### Add Copied Values to Destination Cells

*Next, you will use Paste Special to add the values from the range B5:B8 to corresponding cells in the range H5:H8.*

21. Display the **Summary** worksheet.

22. Select the **range B5:B8**, and use the keyboard shortcut $\boxed{\text{Ctrl}}$+$\boxed{\text{C}}$ to copy the range.

23. Select **cell H5**, and choose **Home→Clipboard→Paste menu ▼→Paste Special** from the Ribbon.

24. In the Paste Special dialog box, choose **Add** and then click **OK**.

*The value in cell B5 was added to the value in cell H5. The result in cell H5 should be 80,000. Each of the other values in the range B6:B8 was added to its corresponding cell in column H.*

25. **Save** 💾 the changes and leave the workbook **open**.

# 8.4 Naming Cells and Ranges

| Video Lesson | labyrinthelab.com/videos |
|---|---|

You may use a descriptive name instead of cell references in formulas and for worksheet navigation. Range names are easier to type, recognize, and remember. Excel refers to these as *defined names*. You may create a name for one cell or a range of cells.

## Naming Rules

Excel has a few rules for naming cells. Defined names:

- Must begin with a letter.
- Cannot resemble a cell reference, as in A3 or BC14.
- Cannot consist of the single letters C or R, which Excel interprets as column or row.
- Cannot contain spaces, hyphens, or symbols.
- May contain an underscore, period, or capital letter to connect words. Examples are Total_Sales, Total.Sales, and TotalSales.

## Creating Defined Names

Defined names are available throughout a workbook by default. You may define a name in one worksheet and use the name to navigate to its cell reference(s) from within any other worksheet. You may create names using any of the following methods.

### Name Box

You may create a name quickly by selecting the range and typing a name in the Name Box of the Formula Bar above the upper-left corner of the worksheet. You must tap Enter after typing the name. If you simply click outside the Name Box, the name will not be created.

The Name Box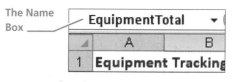

The Name Box may be widened to view an entire name by dragging the curved border between the Name Box and the Formula Box.

### New Name Dialog Box

The Define Name command displays the New Name dialog box, in which you may name a range and set its scope—or availability—to all worksheets in the workbook or just one worksheet. Usually you should leave Scope set to Workbook.

### Creating Cell Names from Row or Column Titles

You may use existing row or column titles to name individual cells. These cells usually are adjacent to the title cells. You select both the titles and the cells to which you wish to assign the names and then use the Create from Selection command to create the names.

The New Name dialog box

# Using Defined Names

Defined names are mainly used to navigate workbooks and create linking formulas or calculation formulas.

### Using Names to Navigate

Create defined names to move quickly to areas of the worksheet that you view or update frequently, such as a total, the first data cell at the top of a column, or a range of cells. To navigate to a named cell or range, you select its name from the Name list on the Formula Bar.

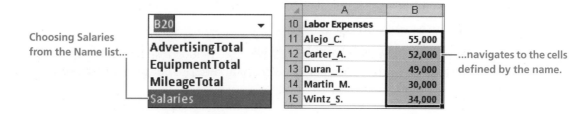

Choosing Salaries from the Name list... ...navigates to the cells defined by the name.

### Using Names in Formulas

Formulas containing defined names help others to understand what the formulas are calculating. For example, the formula =AdvertisingTotal+MileageTotal is easier to understand than =AC10+AD10. Workbook users might prefer the linking formula =AdvertisingTotal, which uses a defined name, rather than =Advertising!B16. You may substitute a defined name for cell references in any formula. You may type the defined name or select it from the Use in Formula list on the Ribbon.

If the error message #NAME? displays in a cell instead of the formula result, compare the spelling of the name in the formula with its spelling in the Name list and make certain the name was not deleted.

### DEVELOP YOUR SKILLS 8.4.1
## Create and Use Cell Names

*Navigating large workbooks becomes easier with defined names. In this exercise, you will create names for single cells and a cell range and then navigate to important areas of the workbook. You also will use defined names to create linking formulas.*

Scroll through the sheet tabs using the ⏮ and ⏭ buttons in the lower-left corner of the Excel window if any tab is not visible during the exercise.

### Create Names in the Name Box

1. Display the **Equipment** worksheet in the Project Budget workbook and select **cell B16**.

2. Follow these steps to name the cell:

Ⓐ Click in the **Name Box** at the left of the Formula Bar, which selects the B16 cell reference.

B16 ▾ ◉ *fx*

Ⓑ Type **EquipmentTotal** (do not include a space) and **tap** Enter.

*Remember that range names may include capital letters, underscores, or periods, but no spaces.*

*You must tap* Enter *after typing the name. If you simply click outside the Name Box, the name will not be created.*

3. Select any cell **other than** B16.

4. Select **cell B16** again.
   *The Name Box displays EquipmentTotal. The Name Box displays the defined name or reference for the active cell.*

5. Display the **Training Materials** worksheet and select **cell B16**.

6. Click in the **Name Box**.

7. Type **Training_Materials_Total** (do not include a space) and **tap** Enter.
   *The underscore character is inserted by holding down* Shift *and tapping the hyphen* - *key.*

8. To view the entire name, drag the **curved border** between the Name Box and the Formula Box to the right.

Training_Materi... ▾↔ *fx* =SU

### Create a Name in the New Name Dialog Box

9. Display the **Mileage** worksheet and select **cell C16**.

10. Choose **Formulas→Defined Names→Define Name** from the Ribbon.

11. In the New Name dialog box, **type** the name **MileageTotal**.
*Notice that the Scope option is set to Workbook, allowing the defined name to be selected from within any worksheet in this workbook.*

12. Click **OK**.

13. **Save** the changes.

### Use Names to Navigate

14. Choose **EquipmentTotal** from the Name list in the Formula Bar.
*The cell pointer moves to cell B16 in the Equipment worksheet.*

15. Navigate to **MileageTotal**.
*Navigation is quick, and you do not need to memorize cell addresses.*

### Use Names to Create Linking Formulas

*You will complete linking formulas on the Summary worksheet by using defined names.*

16. Display the **Summary** worksheet.

17. Select **cell C6**, choose **Formulas→Defined Names→Use in Formula** from the Ribbon, choose the defined name EquipmentTotal, and complete the formula.

18. Use the appropriate defined names to create linking formulas in **cells C7** and **C8**.

19. Use the **fill handle** to copy the formula in **D5** down to **D8**.
*Your totals should equal those shown.*

|   | A | B | C | D |
|---|---|---|---|---|
| 4 | **General and Capital Expenses** | **Budget Allocation** | **Year-to-Date Spent** | **Available Balance** |
| 5 | Advertising | 40,000 | 9,275 | 30,725 |
| 6 | Equipment | 25,000 | 18,470 | 6,530 |
| 7 | Mileage | 8,000 | 1,014 | 6,986 |
| 8 | Training Materials | 7,000 | 790 | 6,210 |

20. **Save** the changes and leave the workbook **open**.

## Modifying and Deleting Defined Names

**Video Lesson**   labyrinthelab.com/videos

**FROM THE KEYBOARD**
Ctrl + F3 to open the Name Manager dialog box

Use the Name Manager dialog box to view all defined names and edit their properties. The dialog box lists each defined name, the value(s) in the cell range, the cell reference(s), scope, and any comment you entered. You may add and delete names in Name Manager. Formula cells, however, display the error message *#NAME?#* after names have been deleted. You will need to edit the cell references in formulas that used any deleted name. You may select an existing name and edit the name or the cell(s) to which it refers by using the Collapse button.

If you copy a worksheet, Excel duplicates its defined names but assigns only a Worksheet scope. Neither the Name list on the Formula Box nor the Use in Formula list displays these names. You should re-create unique defined names that have a Workbook scope and delete the previous names having a Worksheet scope in the Name Manager.

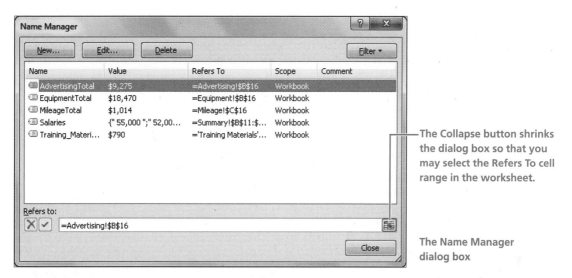

The Collapse button shrinks the dialog box so that you may select the Refers To cell range in the worksheet.

The Name Manager dialog box

To change the Refers To entry, use the Collapse button and point mode to select cells in the worksheet. Do not use arrow keys to edit the entry, as Excel would insert cell references rather than move the cursor.

| QUICK REFERENCE | USING NAMED CELLS AND RANGES |
| --- | --- |
| **Task** | **Procedure** |
| Name cells | ■ Select the range of cells, type a name in the Name Box on the Formula Bar, and tap Enter. |
| Create names from existing row or column titles | ■ Select the labels and the cells to which they will refer.<br>■ Choose Formulas→Defined Names→Create from Selection from the Ribbon.<br>■ Place a checkmark to indicate the location of the labels. |
| Change a defined name | ■ Choose Formulas→Defined Names→Name Manager from the Ribbon.<br>■ In the Name Manager dialog box, choose an existing name and click Edit.<br>■ Edit the name. |
| Change the range to which a name refers | ■ Choose Formulas→Defined Names→Name Manager from the Ribbon.<br>■ In the Name Manager dialog box, choose an existing name.<br>■ Click the Collapse button next to Refers To, select the new range in the worksheet, and click the Expand button.<br>■ Close the Name Manager dialog box, and click Yes to confirm the change. |
| Delete a defined name | ■ Choose Formulas→Defined Names→Name Manager from the Ribbon.<br>■ Choose an existing name, click Delete, and click OK to confirm the change. |

| Task | Procedure |
|------|-----------|
| Navigate to a defined range | ■ Choose the name from the Name list in the Formula Bar. |
| Use a defined name in a linking formula | ■ Select the cell to contain the summary formula.<br>■ Choose Formulas→Defined Names→Use in Formula 🔲 from the Ribbon, choose the defined name, and tap ⌷Enter⌷ to complete the formula. |
| Use one or more defined names in a calculation formula | ■ Select the cell to contain the formula.<br>■ Type the function beginning, such as =SUM(.<br>■ Choose Formulas→Defined Names→Use in Formula 🔲 from the Ribbon, choose the defined name, continue typing the formula and choosing defined names as needed, and tap ⌷Enter⌷ to complete the formula. |

## DEVELOP YOUR SKILLS 8.4.2

# Modify Defined Names and Create Names from Titles

*In this exercise, you will create a defined name, modify its Refers To range, and then delete the name. You will define names using text titles in a column. Finally, you will use defined names to create linking formulas.*

### Create a Defined Name and Modify Its Range

1. Display the **Salaries** worksheet, and select the **range C4:F15**.

2. Click in the **Name Box** at the left of the Formula Bar, type **Salary_Data**, and **tap** ⌷Enter⌷.
   *You realize that the salary numbers in column B are not included in the named range.*

3. **Deselect** the highlighted range.

4. Choose **Formulas→Defined Names→Name Manager** 🔲 from the Ribbon.

5. If necessary, drag the **Name Manager** dialog box by its title bar so the salary numbers are visible.

6. Follow these steps to change the Refers To range for Salary_Data:

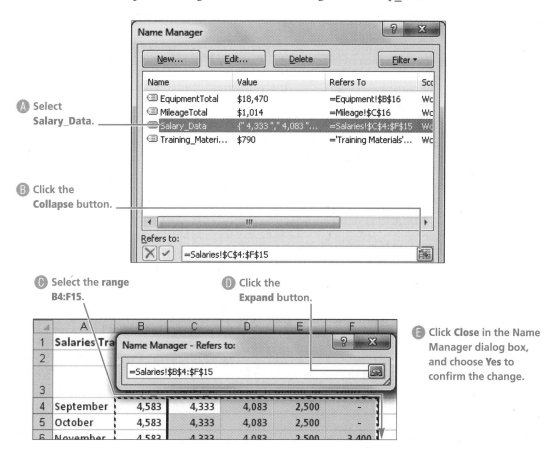

Ⓐ Select
Salary_Data.

Ⓑ Click the
Collapse button.

Ⓒ Select the **range**
**B4:F15**.

Ⓓ Click the
**Expand** button.

Ⓔ Click **Close** in the Name
Manager dialog box,
and choose **Yes** to
confirm the change.

7. Drop down the **Name** list at the left of the Formula Bar and choose **Salary_Data**.
   *The range B4:F15 is highlighted to indicate the Refers To area that you just set.*

8. **Deselect** the highlighted range.

## Delete a Defined Name

9. Choose **Formulas→Defined Names→Name Manager** 🖻 from the Ribbon.

10. Select **Salary_Data** in the Name Manager dialog box and click the **Delete** button above
    the defined names list.

11. Click **OK** to confirm the deletion; **close** the Name Manager dialog box.
    *Although no formulas were based on Salary_Data, take care in deleting defined names. Any formula
    cells that do use the deleted name would display the error message #NAME?#. Correcting the cell refer-
    ences in the formulas removes the error message.*

## Create Names from Titles in a Column

*Using a single command, you will assign names to each of the budgeted salary amounts in column B of the Summary worksheet.*

12. Display the **Summary** worksheet.

13. Select the **range A11:B15**, as shown to the right.
*Notice that each employee name in column A contains an underscore (_) because you will use these names as the basis for defined names. Remember that defined names may not include spaces.*

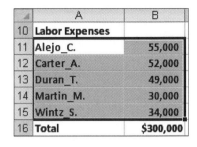

| | A | B |
|---|---|---|
| 10 | Labor Expenses | |
| 11 | Alejo_C. | 55,000 |
| 12 | Carter_A. | 52,000 |
| 13 | Duran_T. | 49,000 |
| 14 | Martin_M. | 30,000 |
| 15 | Wintz_S. | 34,000 |
| 16 | Total | $300,000 |

14. Choose **Formulas→Defined Names→Create from Selection** from the Ribbon.

15. In the Create Names from Selection dialog box, make certain a checkmark is in the **Left Column** box and click **OK**.
*Your choice specifies which cells should be used for the names. In this step, the cells in the left column (column A) are used to name the cells in column B.*

16. Select **cell B11** and notice that Alejo_C. appears in the Name box.
*The defined name Alejo_C. was assigned to this cell.*

17. Select **cell B12** and notice that this cell has been assigned the name Carter_A.

18. Click the **Name Box drop-down arrow** button and read the list of names.
*Notice that the defined names for each employee's salary now appear in the list. Defined names are sorted in alphabetic order.*

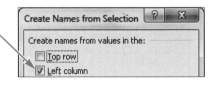

19. **Tap** [Esc] to collapse the Name list without making a selection.

## Insert Linking Formulas in the Salaries Worksheet

*You will use the names you just created to construct linking formulas in the Salaries worksheet. The linking formulas will reflect the budgeted amounts from column B of the Summary worksheet.*

20. Display the **Salaries** worksheet.

21. Select **cell B18**.
*Next you will use a command that quickly creates a linking formula.*

22. Choose **Formulas→Defined Names→Use in Formula** from the Ribbon, choose the defined name **Alejo_C.**, and **complete** the formula.
*The number 55000 appears. This is the budgeted salary amount for employee Alejo_C. from the Summary worksheet. A green triangle icon may display in the upper-left corner of the cell to indicate the formula cell is unprotected. You may ignore this icon.*

*Notice the linking formula in the Formula Bar. Excel added the equals (=) sign to the formula for you.*

23. Select **cell C18**, choose **Formulas→Defined Names→Use in Formula** from the Ribbon, choose the defined name **Carter_A.**, and click the **Enter** button in the Formula Bar to complete the formula.

24. Create linking formulas in **cells D18, E18, and F18** to match the names in **cells D3, E3, and F3**.

25. Use the **Format Painter** ✏ to copy the number formatting from **cell B7** to the **range B18:F18**.
*You may ignore any green triangle icons that may display in the upper-left corner of the cells.*

26. **Save** 💾 the changes and leave the workbook **open**.

## 8.5 Creating Hyperlinks

**Video Lesson**    labyrinthelab.com/videos

A hyperlink is a piece of text or a graphic that takes the user to another location when clicked. Web pages use hyperlinks to navigate from one web page to another. You may create hyperlinks in Excel worksheets that work just like the ones on web pages. Hyperlinks help others to navigate to important items of data or to documents outside the workbook. You create links with the Hyperlink command on the Ribbon.

**FROM THE KEYBOARD**
Ctrl + K to insert a hyperlink

| 6,986 | Mileage Details |
|-------|-----------------|

When a user clicks the Mileage Details hyperlink, the pointer jumps to a cell in a different worksheet.

## Types of Hyperlinks

You may create several types of links on a worksheet, including items inside or outside the workbook.

### Internal Hyperlinks

- **To cells in a workbook**—A hyperlink may point to a cell address or defined name in the workbook. You add hyperlink text or a graphic to a cell. The user may click the hyperlink on the worksheet rather than use the Name Box to navigate.

### Hyperlinks to External Sources

- **To another file**—A hyperlink can open a Word document containing information related to a workbook. Another hyperlink can open a different Excel workbook and point to a cell.

- **To a web page**—A hyperlink can point to a page on the web or on a corporate intranet. You may launch Internet Explorer and navigate to the desired web page from within the Insert Hyperlink dialog box. Excel then places the web page URL into the dialog box to save you the complexity of typing the URL or pasting it from the address bar.

- **To an email address**—A hyperlink can open an Office Outlook window to send an email message.

## Insert Hyperlink Dialog Box

You choose the link type in the Insert Hyperlink dialog box. The dialog box options change for each type of link except for two options that are always available: Text to Display is the text description that the user clicks to activate the hyperlink, and the optional ScreenTip displays an instruction or other text when the user points to the hyperlink. The following illustration shows the dialog box entries for jumping to a worksheet cell.

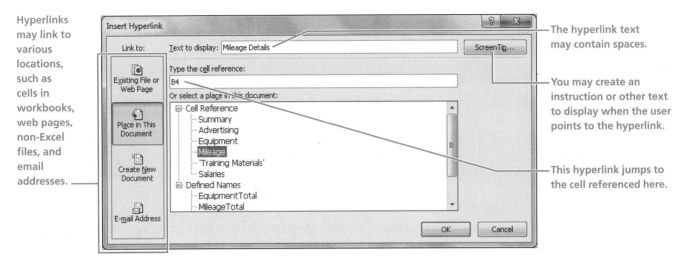

Hyperlinks may link to various locations, such as cells in workbooks, web pages, non-Excel files, and email addresses.

The hyperlink text may contain spaces.

You may create an instruction or other text to display when the user points to the hyperlink.

This hyperlink jumps to the cell referenced here.

Creating a hyperlink to jump to a cell in a different worksheet of the same workbook

## Editing and Removing Hyperlinks

You can change the default formatting for all hyperlink text in the workbook. You may edit a hyperlink to change the type of destination and specific location to which it points. For example, you may edit a hyperlink that points to a web page so that it points to a Word document (or some other type of file) instead. You must update the storage reference for a hyperlink if its linked file is moved to a different drive or folder. Although you may use the Remove Hyperlink command, you probably will find it more efficient to use Delete to erase the hyperlink contents from a cell.

| QUICK REFERENCE | CREATING, EDITING, AND REMOVING HYPERLINKS |
|---|---|
| **Task** | **Procedure** |
| Insert a hyperlink to a cell reference in the same workbook | ■ Select the cell or graphic to contain the hyperlink. <br> ■ Choose Insert→Links→Hyperlink from the Ribbon or use Ctrl+K from the keyboard. <br> ■ Choose the Place in This Document option. <br> ■ Type a brief description in the Text to Display box. <br> ■ Type the desired target cell in the Type the Cell Reference box. <br> ■ Choose the desired worksheet from the Cell Reference list. |
| Insert a hyperlink to a named cell or range in the same workbook | ■ Select the cell or graphic to contain the hyperlink. <br> ■ Choose Insert→Links→Hyperlink from the Ribbon or use Ctrl+K from the keyboard. <br> ■ Choose the Place in This Document option. <br> ■ Type a brief description in the Text to Display box. <br> ■ Choose the desired name from the Defined Names list. |

| Task | Procedure |
|------|-----------|
| Insert a hyperlink to a cell reference in a different workbook | ▪ Select the cell or graphic to contain the hyperlink. <br> ▪ Choose Insert→Links→Hyperlink from the Ribbon or use `Ctrl`+`K` from the keyboard. <br> ▪ Choose the Existing File or Web Page option. <br> ▪ Type a brief description in the Text to Display box. <br> ▪ Navigate to the desired file storage location and choose the desired file. <br> ▪ Click Bookmark to display the Select Place in Document dialog box. <br> ▪ Type the desired target cell in the Type in the Cell Reference box. <br> ▪ Choose the desired worksheet from the Cell Reference list and click OK. |
| Insert a hyperlink to a non-Excel file | ▪ Select the cell or graphic to contain the hyperlink. <br> ▪ Choose Insert→Links→Hyperlink from the Ribbon or use `Ctrl`+`K` from the keyboard. <br> ▪ Choose the Existing File or Web Page option. <br> ▪ Type a brief description in the Text to Display box. <br> ▪ Navigate to the desired file storage location and choose the desired file. |
| Insert a hyperlink to a web page | ▪ Select the cell or graphic to contain the hyperlink. <br> ▪ Choose Insert→Links→Hyperlink from the Ribbon or use `Ctrl`+`K` from the keyboard. <br> ▪ Choose the Existing File or Web Page option. <br> ▪ Type a brief description in the Text to Display box. <br> ▪ Click the Browse the Web button. <br> ▪ Navigate to the desired web page for the link. <br> ▪ Activate the Excel window, and the URL appears automatically in the Address text box of the Insert Hyperlink dialog box. |
| Edit an existing hyperlink | ▪ Right-click the hyperlink you wish to edit and choose Edit Hyperlink from the context menu. <br> ▪ Make the desired changes in the Edit Hyperlink dialog box and click OK. |
| Change default formatting for hyperlink text in a workbook | ▪ Select any cell in the workbook. <br> ▪ Choose Home→Styles→Cell Styles from the Ribbon. Under Data and Model, right click Hyperlink (or Followed Hyperlink) and choose Modify. <br> ▪ In Style box, click Format and change the font and fill, as desired. |
| Delete a hyperlink | ▪ Select the cell or graphic containing the hyperlink. <br> ▪ Right-click, and then choose Remove Hyperlink from the context menu. |

## Create Hyperlinks

*In this exercise, you will create one link to a cell on a worksheet and another link to a Word document. You will also edit one of the hyperlinks by adding a ScreenTip.*

### Create a Hyperlink to a Worksheet Cell

1. Display the **Summary** worksheet in the Project Budget workbook.

2. Select **cell E7** and choose **Insert→Links→Hyperlink** from the Ribbon.
*You will create a link that points to the first detail cell in the Mileage worksheet.*

3. Follow these steps to create the hyperlink:

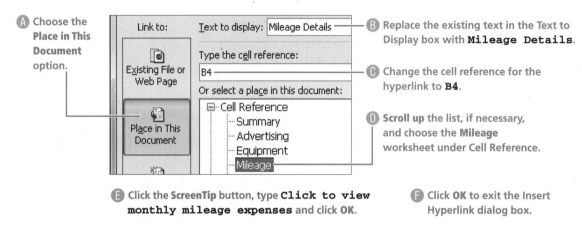

Ⓐ Choose the **Place in This Document** option.

Ⓑ Replace the existing text in the Text to Display box with **Mileage Details**.

Ⓒ Change the cell reference for the hyperlink to **B4**.

Ⓓ **Scroll up** the list, if necessary, and choose the **Mileage** worksheet under Cell Reference.

Ⓔ Click the **ScreenTip** button, type **Click to view monthly mileage expenses** and click **OK**.

Ⓕ Click **OK** to exit the Insert Hyperlink dialog box.

*A color change and underline indicate that cell E7 contains a hyperlink.*

### Create a Hyperlink to a File

4. Display the **Salaries** worksheet.

5. Select **cell G18** and choose **Insert→Links→Hyperlink** from the Ribbon.

6. Follow these steps to create a hyperlink to an external document:

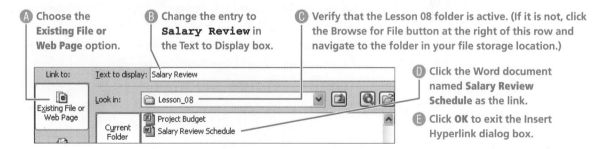

Ⓐ Choose the **Existing File or Web Page** option.

Ⓑ Change the entry to **Salary Review** in the Text to Display box.

Ⓒ Verify that the Lesson 08 folder is active. (If it is not, click the Browse for File button at the right of this row and navigate to the folder in your file storage location.)

Ⓓ Click the Word document named **Salary Review Schedule** as the link.

Ⓔ Click **OK** to exit the Insert Hyperlink dialog box.

*The text to display appears underlined to indicate its hyperlink status.*

### Edit a Hyperlink

7. Point the mouse on **cell G18** (but do **not** click) to display its ScreenTip.
*If you do not enter your own ScreenTip text, Excel displays the path to the hyperlink item, such as file:///F:\ Lesson 8\ Salary Review Schedule.docx.*

8. **Right-click** on the hyperlink display text in **cell G18** and choose **Edit Hyperlink** from the context menu.

9. In the Edit Hyperlink dialog box, click the **ScreenTip** button, type **Click to view schedule** and click **OK**.

10. Click **OK** to exit the Edit Hyperlink dialog box.

11. Point the mouse on **cell G18** (but do not click) to display your ScreenTip.

### Navigate with the Hyperlinks

12. Display the **Summary** worksheet and click the hyperlink in **cell E7**.
    *Excel jumps to cell B4 on the Mileage worksheet.*

13. Display the **Salaries** worksheet and click the hyperlink in **cell G18**.
    *Word launches and displays the linked document. Hyperlinks also may be created to other Excel workbooks or any other type of document file.*

14. **Close** [⊠] the Word window.

### Change the Appearance of Hyperlinks

*Notice that the hyperlink now displays purple text to indicate the hyperlink was followed.*

15. Choose **Home→Styles→Cell Styles** from the Ribbon.

16. Under Data and Model in the menu that appears, right-click **Followed Hyperlink** and choose **Modify.**

17. Click **Format** in the Style dialog box then choose the **Font** tab in the **Format Cells** dialog box.

18. Follow these steps to change the color in the Format Cells dialog box:

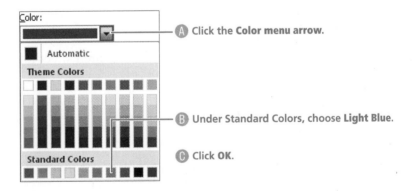

19. Click **OK** in the Style dialog box.
    *All followed hyperlinks in the workbook appear light blue.*

### Remove and Restore a Hyperlink

20. Display the **Summary** sheet.
    *Cell E7 contains a followed hyperlink.*

21. Right-click **cell E7**, and choose **Remove Hyperlink** from the context menu.
*The text "Mileage Details" changes to black, and the underline is removed to indicate that the text no longer links to another cell.*

22. **Tap** [Delete] to erase the text from cell E7.

23. Click **Undo** *twice* in the Quick Access toolbar to restore the hyperlink.

24. **Save** 🖫 the changes and leave the workbook **open**.

# 8.6 Printing Multiple-Sheet Workbooks

**Video Lesson**    labyrinthelab.com/videos

Excel prints the active worksheet when you choose the Quick Print 🖨 command. If you are working with a multiple-sheet workbook, you may use various techniques to set options and print multiple sheets at one time.

## Applying Page Setup Options to Multiple Sheets

You may adjust the margins, page orientation, headers and footers, and a variety of other settings that affect the printed worksheet. You may apply these settings to multiple worksheets by first using [Ctrl] to select nonadjacent sheet tabs or [Shift] to select adjacent sheet tabs.

## Printing All Sheets in a Workbook

You may print all sheets in a workbook by using [Shift] to select the sheet tabs and choosing the Quick Print command. As an alternative, you may print all sheets without selecting their tabs by choosing the Print Entire Workbook option in the Print Print tab of Backstage view.

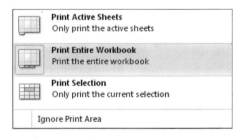

## Printing Selected Sheets

You may print only certain sheets by using [Ctrl] to select the desired sheet tabs and choosing Print or Quick Print.

### DEVELOP YOUR SKILLS 8.6.1
## Preview and Print Selected Sheets

*In this exercise, you will select multiple sheets, change their orientation, and preview them all at once.*

### Select Multiple Adjacent Sheets

1. Display the **Summary** worksheet in the Project Budget workbook.

2. With the **Summary** worksheet active, **hold down** [Shift] and click the **Mileage** sheet tab.

| Summary | Advertising | Equipment | Mileage | Training Materials | Salaries | ✎ |

*Four sheets appear selected. Using* [Shift] *selected the continuous range of sheets from the active sheet tab through the sheet tab that you clicked.*

3. Choose **Page Layout→Page Setup→Orientation→Landscape**.
   *The Training Materials and Salaries sheets remain in portrait orientation because you did not include them in the selected sheets.*

4. Choose **File→Print**.
   *Notice that the Print Active Sheets setting is selected. The bottom of the preview area displays "1 of 4," which indicates that four sheets are active and would print if you were to click Print. Do not print.*

5. Use the **Next Page** ▶ command to browse through the worksheets.
   *Notice that the orientation of the four sheets is landscape.*

6. Click the **Home** tab to exit Backstage view.

### Deselect Sheet Tabs

7. Click on any **unselected** sheet tab or **right-click** any sheet tab and choose **Ungroup Sheets** from the context menu.
   *Now only one sheet tab appears selected.*

### Select Multiple Nonadjacent Sheets

8. Display the **Advertising** worksheet.

9. **Hold down** [Ctrl], click the **Mileage** sheet tab, click the **Salaries** sheet tab, and then **release** [Ctrl].
   *Three sheets are selected. Using* [Ctrl] *allows you to select certain sheets in any order.*

10. **Ungroup** the sheets.
    *Now only one worksheet is active.*

### Select All Sheets in the Workbook for Printing

11. Choose **File→Print**.

12. In the Settings area of the Print tab, click **Print Active Sheets** and select **Print Entire Workbook** from the list.
    *You may use this option to print the entire workbook without first selecting the sheets. Do not print.*

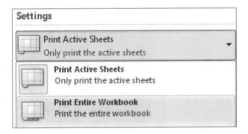

13. Click the **Home** tab to exit Backstage view without printing.

14. **Save** 🖫 and **close** ⊠ the workbook.

## 8.7 Concepts Review

Concepts Review    <u>labyrinthelab.com/excel10</u>

*To check your knowledge of the key concepts introduced in this lesson, complete the Concepts Review quiz by going to the URL listed above. If your classroom is using Labyrinth eLab, you may complete the Concepts Review quiz from within your eLab course.*

# Reinforce Your Skills

## Copy and Format Worksheets

*In this exercise, you will copy a worksheet twice to create three identical worksheets. You will then use the Format Painter to ensure consistent formatting among the sheets. Finally, you will name ranges and use the names in a formula.*

1. **Open** the rs-Sales Format workbook from the Lesson 8 folder in your file storage location.

2. **Maximize** ▣ the window.

3. Select **cell B10** and choose **Home→AutoSum** ▣ **menu ▾→Average** from the Ribbon. *Excel will propose the formula =Average(B4:B9). This range is incorrect because it includes the total sales in cell B8.*

4. Select the **range B4:B7** and click the **Enter** ☑ button on the Formula Bar to complete the formula.
   *The formula result is 72,750.*

5. Copy the formula to the **range C10:E10** for the other quarters.

6. **Deselect** the highlighted cells.

### Copy a Worksheet

*You will make two copies of the Eastern worksheet to be named Central and Western.*

7. **Right-click** the **Eastern** sheet tab and select **Move or Copy** from the context menu.

8. Make selections in the Move or Copy Sheet dialog box to place a copy after the **Eastern** worksheet and then click **OK**.

9. **Copy** the Eastern worksheet again and place the copy after the existing sheets.

10. **Rename** the new sheets as **Central** and **Western**.

11. Change the headings in **row 1** of the Central and Western sheets to **Central Region Sales** and **Western Region Sales**.

12. Change a few of the numbers in the Central and Western sheets so the sheets contain different data.

### Format a Worksheet

13. Display the **Eastern** worksheet, and then select **cell A1**.

14. Increase the font size to 14 and apply a **font color** ▣ to the text.

15. Select the **range B3:E3** and increase the size to **12**. Click the **Font Color** ▣ button (not its menu arrow) to apply the same color that you used in the previous step. **Right-align** the cell contents.

16. Format the **Average Sales** row in any way that you wish.

## Copy the Worksheet Formatting

17. Click the **Select All** ◢ button to select the entire worksheet.

18. **Double-click** the **Format Painter** 🖌 button on the Ribbon.

19. Display the **Central** worksheet.

20. Click the **Select All** ◢ button to copy the formats to that worksheet.
*The Format Painter should still be active, so you may apply formatting again.*

21. Display the **Western** worksheet and copy the formats to that worksheet.
*You were able to copy the formats in this manner because the sheets have an identical structure.*

22. Click the **Format Painter** 🖌 button on the Ribbon to deactivate it.

23. **Display** each worksheet and **deselect** the highlighted cells.

## Create Defined Names and Construct Formulas

24. Display the **Eastern** worksheet.

25. Select the **range B10:E10** and **tap** ⌨Delete to erase the average formulas.

26. Select the Q1 data in the **range B4:B7**.

27. Click in the **Name Box**, type **Quarter1**, and **tap** ⌨Enter.
*Remember that range names cannot contain spaces.*

28. Assign the name **Quarter2** to the **range C4:C7**.

29. Assign the name **Quarter3** to the **range D4:D7**.

30. Assign the name **Quarter4** to the **range E4:E7**.

31. Select **cell B10**, type the formula **=average(quarter1)**, and **tap** ⌨Enter to complete the formula.
*After you type =av Excel may propose the AVERAGE function, and you may double-click Average.
After you type a few letters of the defined name, Excel may propose Quarter1, and you may double-click Quarter1. The correct average, 72,750, should be displayed when you finish.*

32. Select **cell C10** and type **=average(** and then choose **Formulas→Defined Names→Use in Formula**, choose **Quarter2**, and **tap** ⌨Enter.

33. Enter an average formula in **cell D10** using the name **Quarter3**.

34. Enter an average formula in **cell E10** using the name **Quarter4**.

35. **Save** 💾 the changes and **close** ⊠ the workbook.

# Use Defined Names in Formulas

*Several of your co-workers have collaborated on the Sales Summary workbook. In this exercise, you will create the remaining linking formulas to link the regional sheets with the National summary worksheet. You will create calculation formulas using defined names and correct the cell references for an important defined name. You also will delete an unnecessary defined name.*

## Create Linking Formulas

1. **Open** the rs-Sales Summary workbook from the Lesson 8 folder.
   *Take a few moments to browse the National summary worksheet and the three regional detail sheets, Eastern, Central, and Western. The detail sheets include sales figures for each of the four quarters in the year.*

2. Choose **Formulas→Defined Names→Name Manager** 📇 from the Ribbon to view all defined names and their properties.

3. **Double-click** the **Refers To** column border to autofit the contents.

| Name | Value | Refers To | Scope |
|------|-------|-----------|-------|
| 📇 Central_Q1 | $241,000 | ='Central Region'!$B$8 | Workbook |
| 📇 Central_Q2 | $191,500 | ='Central Region'!$C$8 | Workbook |
| 📇 Central_Q3 | $145,000 | ='Central Region'!$D$8 | Workbook |

   *Notice the defined names for Quarters 1–4. The National worksheet contains linking formulas to each of the defined cells for Quarters 1, 2, and 3. You will create linking formulas for Quarter 4.*

4. Click the **Close** button to exit the Name Manager dialog box.

5. Display the **National** worksheet and select **cell E4**.
   *This cell will contain a linked formula to the total for Q4 on the Eastern Region worksheet.*

6. Choose **Formulas→Defined Names→Use in Formula** 📠 from the Ribbon, choose **Eastern_Q4**, and click the **Enter** button on the Formula Bar or **tap** ⎡Enter⎤ to complete the formula.

7. Create linking formulas in **cell E5** for the Central region and **cell E6** for the Western region, as shown at right.

| | Q4 |
|---|---|
| | 258,000 |
| | 211,000 |
| | 235,500 |
| $ | 704,500 |

## Create Calculation Formulas

*To help workbook users understand summing formulas more easily, you will use defined names rather than cell references to create totals formulas.*

8. Select **cell F4** in the National worksheet.

9. Choose **Formulas→Defined Names→Use in Formula** 📠→**Eastern_Q1** from the Ribbon.
   *The command automatically starts the formula with an equals (=) sign.*

10. Tap the plus (+) sign on the keypad.

11. Use Eastern_Q2 in the formula and **tap** the plus (+) sign on the keypad.

12. Use Eastern_Q3 in the formula and **tap** the plus (+) sign on the keypad.

13. Use **Eastern_Q4** in the formula.

14. Click the **Enter** button on the Formula Bar or **tap** Enter to complete the formula.

> =Eastern_Q1+ Eastern_Q2+Eastern_Q3+Eastern_Q4

*The total is $979,500.*

15. Use the procedure from the previous steps to create a total formula in **cell F5** for the Central region and **cell F6** for the Western region.

## Correct the Cell References for a Defined Name

16. Select **cell F7** in the **National** worksheet.
*Notice the formula in the Formula Bar. =SUM(Yearly_Total) includes a defined name, but the result displays as a dash (—) or 0. Something clearly is not correct.*

17. Choose **Formulas→Defined Names→Name Manager** 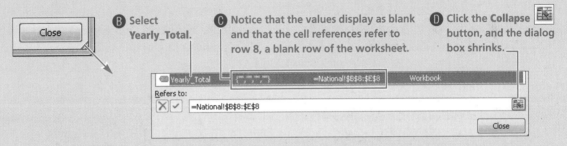 from the Ribbon and follow these steps to correct the error:

**A** If necessary, drag the corner of the dialog box down and right until **Yearly_Total** is visible.

**B** Select **Yearly_Total**.

**C** Notice that the values display as blank and that the cell references refer to row 8, a blank row of the worksheet.

**D** Click the **Collapse** button, and the dialog box shrinks.

18. Select the **range B7:E7** in the National worksheet.

19. Click the **Expand** button in the Name Manager: Refers To dialog box to return to Name Manager.

20. Click **Close** to exit Name Manager, and click **Yes** to confirm the change.
*The defined name now points to the correct cells, and the total displays as $2,659,000.*

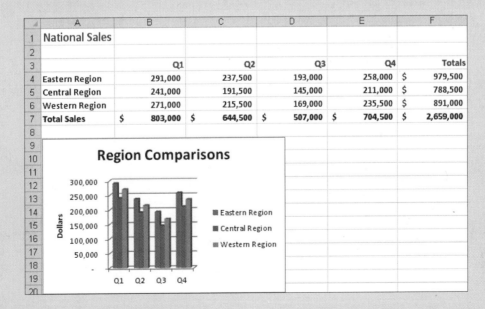

## Delete a Defined Name

*You will delete the defined name Region_Total because it is not needed.*

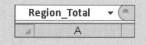

21. Choose **Region_Total** from the Name list in the Formula Bar.
*The pointer moves to cell F8 on the Western Region sheet. This cell is empty. Assume that you have verified that no workbook formula refers to Region_Total.*

22. Choose **Formulas→Defined Names→Name Manager**  from the Ribbon.

23. Select **Region_Total** from the list.

24. Click the **Delete** button at the top of the dialog box, and click **OK** to confirm the deletion.

25. **Close** the Name Manager dialog box.

26. **Save** the changes to the workbook and continue with the next exercise.

---

### REINFORCE YOUR SKILLS 8.3

## Create Hyperlinks

*You will continue working on the rs-Sales Summary workbook. In this exercise, you will create text hyperlinks for workbook navigation. You also will edit a hyperlink to correct the cell to which it points.*

*Before You Begin: You must have completed Reinforce Your Skills 8.2, and the rs-Sales Summary workbook should be open.*

### Create a Text Hyperlink

1. Select **cell D1** in the National worksheet.

2. Tap **Ctrl**+**K** to open the Insert Hyperlink dialog box.

3. Follow these steps to create a text hyperlink to the Eastern Region worksheet:

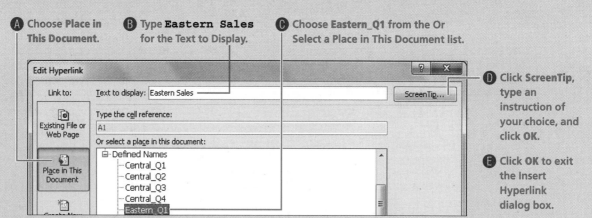

4. Test the hyperlink by clicking the display text in **cell D1**.
*The pointer moves to the Q1 total on the Eastern Region worksheet.*

## Create a Hyperlink from Existing Text

*You may use an existing cell entry as the hyperlink's text to display.*

5. Display the **National** worksheet and select **cell A5**.

6. Choose **Insert→Links→Hyperlink**  from the Ribbon.
   *Notice that "Central Region" appears in the Text to Display box. The text entry in the selected cell is used automatically.*

7. Change the Type the Cell Reference Entry to **A5** and click **OK**.
   *You must enter the cell reference. The address of the selected cell is not automatically displayed.*

## Edit a Hyperlink

*Now you realize that the recently created hyperlink refers to the wrong cell.*

8. **Right-click** the hyperlink in **cell A5**, notice the three hyperlink commands at the bottom of the context menu, and choose **Edit Hyperlink**.

9. Follow these steps to change the hyperlink reference:

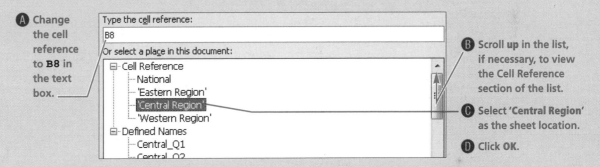

Ⓐ Change the cell reference to **B8** in the text box.

Ⓑ Scroll **up** in the list, if necessary, to view the Cell Reference section of the list.

Ⓒ Select **'Central Region'** as the sheet location.

Ⓓ Click **OK**.

10. Test the hyperlink by clicking its display text in **cell A5** of the **National** sheet.
    *The pointer moves to cell B8 on the Central Region sheet.*

11. Display the **National** worksheet.

12. **Save**  the changes to the workbook and continue with the next exercise.

# Format Multiple Worksheets for Printing

*In this exercise, you will create a header on all four sheets of a workbook.*

*Before You Begin: You may complete this exercise even if you did not complete Reinforce Your Skills 8.2 and Reinforce Your Skills 8.3. Open the rs-Sales Summary workbook from the Lesson 08 folder in your file storage location, if necessary.*

1. **Right-click** any **sheet tab** and choose **Select All Sheets** from the context menu.
   *The four sheet tabs are selected.*

2. Click the **Page Layout** button on the Status Bar at the lower-right corner of the window and drag the **Zoom** lever to the left until both the left and right edges of the page are visible.

   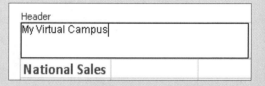

3. Use the **vertical scroll bar** to scroll to the top of the page.

## Add a Header to All Sheets

*Although it will appear that you are creating a header in the National worksheet, all selected sheets will contain the header.*

4. Click the **left** header section and type **My Virtual Campus**.
   *The contents of the header sections may not be displayed as you move among sections. They will be displayed after the header is deselected.*

   | Header | |
   | --- | --- |
   | My Virtual Campus | |
   | | |
   | **National Sales** | |

5. Click the **center** header section and choose **Design→Header & Footer Elements→Sheet Name**.

   | &[Tab] | | |
   | --- | --- | --- |
   | Eastern Sales | | |

   *The &[Tab] code places the worksheet name in the header.*

6. Click the **right** header section and choose **Design→Header & Footer Elements→ Current Date**.
   *The &[Date] code places the current date in the header.*

7. Select a **worksheet** cell, and the current date displays in the header.

8. Display the **Eastern Region** worksheet, and then display the **Central Region** worksheet and the **Western Region** worksheet.
   *The header displays in each worksheet and the appropriate sheet name appears in each header.*

## Print Headings on the Detail Sheets

9. Display the **Eastern Region** worksheet.
   *The four sheets are deselected. Eastern Region now is the selected sheet.*

10. **Hold down** ⌈Shift⌉ and click the **Western Region** worksheet.
    *The three detail sheets are selected.*

11. Choose **Page Layout→Sheet Options→Headings** and place a checkmark in the **Print** box.
    *You applied formatting only to the three selected sheets.*

12. Select all **four** sheet tabs and choose **File→Print**.

13. Use the **Next Page** command to browse through the pages in the Print tab of Backstage view.
    *The National worksheet does not display column and row headings because you did not include that worksheet in the selection.*

14. Click the **Home** tab of the Ribbon to exit Backstage view without printing.

15. **Save** 💾 the changes and **close** the workbook.

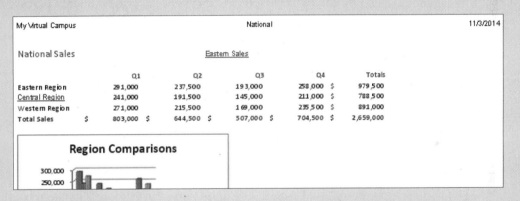

# Apply Your Skills

APPLY YOUR SKILLS 8.1

## Copy a Worksheet and Use Paste Options

*In this exercise, you will copy a worksheet from one workbook to another. You will use paste options to apply limited formatting to a worksheet. You will copy data and then transpose the data from columns to rows.*

### Copy a Worksheet to a Different Workbook

1. **Open** the as-Help Desk Tickets workbook from the Lesson 08 folder in your file storage location.

2. **Open** the as-Status Reports workbook from the Lesson 08 folder.

3. Copy the **Tickets Year 2** worksheet from the as-Status Reports workbook to the as-Help Desk Tickets workbook. Position the Tickets Year 2 sheet **after** the Tickets Year 1 sheet.

4. **Close** ☒ the as-Status Reports workbook.

### Paste Formatting

5. Copy the **range B3:E3** in the Tickets Year 1 sheet and paste the formatting (but not the cell contents) to the **same range** in the Tickets Year 2 sheet.

6. Copy only the **column widths** from columns A–E in the Tickets Year 1 worksheet to the **same columns** in the Tickets Year 2 worksheet.

### Transpose Data

7. In the **Tickets Year 2** worksheet, copy the **range A3:E6**, and paste to **cell G3**.

8. Use a paste option to transpose the **range G3:J7**. The data should reverse so that the months are displayed in the **range H3:J3** and the hours labels displayed in the range G4:G7, as shown in the illustration.

9. **Save** 🖫 the changes and **close** the workbook.

| ⊿ | A | B | C | D | E | F | G | H | I | J |
|---|---|---|---|---|---|---|---|---|---|---|
| 1 | Help Desk Trouble Ticket Report | | | | | | | | | |
| 2 | | | | | | | | | | |
| 3 | | 8 hours | 24 hours | 48 hours | Pending | | | January | February | March |
| 4 | January | 122 | 87 | 27 | 5 | | 8 hours | 122 | 253 | 365 |
| 5 | February | 253 | 118 | 35 | 3 | | 24 hours | 87 | 118 | 167 |
| 6 | March | 365 | 167 | 32 | 14 | | 48 hours | 27 | 35 | 32 |
| 7 | April | 385 | 124 | 51 | 6 | | Pending | 5 | 3 | 14 |
| 8 | May | 217 | 142 | 23 | 13 | | | | | |
| 9 | June | 116 | 58 | 30 | 2 | | | | | |
| 10 | July | 102 | 37 | 14 | 2 | | | | | |
| 11 | August | 76 | 26 | 10 | 0 | | | | | |
| 12 | September | 105 | 43 | 31 | 4 | | | | | |
| 13 | October | 247 | 102 | 25 | 9 | | | | | |
| 14 | November | 303 | 121 | 16 | 18 | | | | | |
| 15 | December | 185 | 96 | 22 | 9 | | | | | |
| 16 | | 2,476 | 1,121 | 316 | 85 | | | | | |

# Create a Linked Workbook

*In this exercise, you will create a new workbook that contains three worksheets. You will also create cell names and then use those names in linking formulas.*

1. Create a **new workbook** with the **three worksheets** shown in the illustrations at the end of this exercise. Name the summary worksheet **Totals** and name the detail sheets **Eastern** and **Central**.

2. **Enter** the numbers and text shown into the three sheets.

3. **Format** the titles, headings, and numbers as shown. Use the **Accounting** number format with **no decimal places** for the totals in all Totals rows. Set **font colors** of your choice. Ensure consistent formatting across the worksheets by using **Format Painter** and **Paste menu** options.

4. Use **AutoSum** to calculate the totals in all three sheets. The **SUM** formulas in the **Totals** row of the summary worksheet should sum the cells in **rows 4 and 5**, even though the cells are currently empty.

5. Create **defined names** for each total in **row 7** of the detail sheets. Name the totals in the Eastern worksheet **Eastern_January**, **Eastern_February**, and **Eastern_March**. Use similar names for the totals in the **Central** worksheet.

6. Use **linking formulas** to create links in **rows 4 and 5** of the summary worksheet to the totals in the detail sheets.

7. **Save** 💾 with the name **as-Regional Sales Q1** in the Lesson 8 folder; **close** the workbook.

|   | A | B | C | D |
|---|---|---|---|---|
| 1 | Quarter 1 Sales | | | |
| 2 | | | | |
| 3 | Region | January | February | March |
| 4 | Eastern | 71,745 | 57,495 | 69,035 |
| 5 | Central | 59,390 | 71,485 | 58,340 |
| 6 | Totals | $ 131,135 | $ 128,980 | $ 127,375 |

|   | A | B | C | D |
|---|---|---|---|---|
| 1 | Eastern Sales | | | |
| 2 | | | | |
| 3 | Account | January | February | March |
| 4 | Draper University | 71,745 | 16,650 | 13,350 |
| 5 | Western State College | - | 40,845 | 15,595 |
| 6 | Jennerstown Academy | - | - | 40,090 |
| 7 | Totals | $ 71,745 | $ 57,495 | $ 69,035 |

|   | A | B | C | D |
|---|---|---|---|---|
| 1 | Central Sales | | | |
| 2 | | | | |
| 3 | Account | January | February | March |
| 4 | North Chauwakeegan State | - | 55,890 | - |
| 5 | University of Norwood | 59,390 | 15,595 | 895 |
| 6 | Olson College | - | - | 57,445 |
| 7 | Totals | $ 59,390 | $ 71,485 | $ 58,340 |

# Create Hyperlinks and Print Multiple Sheets

*In this exercise, you will create hyperlinks for navigation. You will apply a print option to multiple sheets and print selected sheets. A header already has been created in all worksheets.*

*Before You Begin: Your Internet connection should be active.*

## Create Hyperlinks

1. **Open** the as-Peak Usage workbook from the Lesson 08 folder in your file storage location.

2. In the **range F4:F6** of the **Summary** sheet, create three text hyperlinks that navigate to **cell D4** in each detail sheet.

3. In **cell F1**, create a text hyperlink that navigates to the website www.lablearning.com.

4. Test the hyperlinks in the **range F4:F6**.

5. Test the hyperlink in **cell F1** and then **close** the displayed browser window.
   *An error message is displayed in the browser window if your computer is not connected to the Internet.*

## Set a Print Option and Print Selected Sheets

6. Select the **Week 1**, **Week 2**, and **Week 3** sheet tabs and choose to print gridlines from the Page Layout ribbon.

7. Select only the **Summary** and **Week 3** worksheets and display the print preview. The Summary sheet header should display "1 of 2 pages" and the Week 3 sheet header should display "2 of 2 pages."

8. **Print** 🖨 the two selected sheets.

9. **Save** 💾 the changes and **close** the workbook.

# Critical Thinking & Work-Readiness Skills

*In the course of working through the following Microsoft Office-based Critical Thinking exercises, you will also be utilizing various work-readiness skills, some of which are listed next to each exercise. Go to* labyrinthelab.com/ workreadiness *to learn more about the work-readiness skills.*

## 8.1 Use Worksheets for Supporting Documentation

Western State College is working on a project with My Virtual Campus and needs to set up the annual budget. Open ct-WSC (Lesson 08 folder). Rename Sheet1 to **Expenses** and Sheet2 to **Salaries**. Use Format Painter to copy the formatting from the Salaries worksheet to the Expenses sheet. Create a Summary worksheet containing identical formatting and formulas. Save your work as **ct-WSC [Your Last Name]**. Keep your file open. If working in a group, discuss how a consistent visual style can help in business communication. If working alone, type your answer in a Word document named **ct-Questions** saved to your Lesson 08 folder.

**WORK-READINESS SKILLS APPLIED**

- Organizing and maintaining information
- Interpreting and communicating information
- Participating as a member of a team

## 8.2 Link the Summary Sheet

WSC wants the summary sheet to show the combined budget for its project with My Virtual Campus. Included in the summary sheet will be the annual budget and up-to-date expenses for Advertising, Equipment, and Materials found in the Expenses sheet. Open ct-WSC [Your Last Name], if necessary. Link the summary budget and to-date expenses to the appropriate cells in the Expenses spreadsheet, preserving the cell formatting in the Summary sheet. WSC needs C. Alego and M. Martin from My Virtual Campus to work on this project. On the Summary sheet, create a hyperlink to the salary data for each of these employees. Save your work. If working in a group, brainstorm other possible business uses of linking in this project or more generally. If working alone, type your response in a Word document named **ct-Questions2** saved to your Lesson 08 folder.

**WORK-READINESS SKILLS APPLIED**

- Organizing and maintaining information
- Interpreting and communicating information
- Participating as a member of a team

## 8.3 Print a Summary with Supporting Worksheets

WSC wants to give the appropriate managers at My Virtual Campus a printout of the summary worksheet and supporting documentation. Use your same file and set up appropriate page layout options in order to print each worksheet on one page. Before printing, use print preview to view your work. Select and print all worksheets. Save your work, close the file, and exit Excel.

**WORK-READINESS SKILLS APPLIED**

- Solving problems
- Using computers to process information
- Applying technology to a task

# Creating Tables and Outlines

## LEARNING OBJECTIVES

After studying this lesson, you will be able to:

- Create and format tables from worksheet data
- Display totals and use other functions to perform calculations
- Sort data using various specifications
- Display specific data records by filtering
- Outline and group to summarize data

**E**xcel is often used to store lists of information. Excel tables provide a good structure for organizing such data and provide several tools to help you enter, view, and analyze information based on specific characteristics of the data. In this lesson, you will enter data into a table, format with a table style, and quickly create calculation formulas. Some formulas will include structured references that point to specific areas within the table. You will sort and filter the table contents to view data in various ways. You will also hide detail data using the outline and grouping commands to view just the summary data.

# Organizing Related Sales Data

Bruce Carter understands that his clients need to track and analyze their data easily. His company, My Virtual Campus Corporation, markets and maintains a social networking intranet to colleges and universities. As the sales manager, Bruce

analyzes the performance of his sales staff. He plans to organize related sales data using an Excel table. He will sort table data to view the "big picture" and filter employee data on specific criteria to display only relevant data. He also wants to count, sum sales totals, and calculate an average for the entire group. He feels confident that Excel tools will help him identify positive and negative trends in less time so he can lead his staff more effectively.

| | A | B | C | D | E | F | G | H | I | J |
|---|---|---|---|---|---|---|---|---|---|---|
| 1 | My Virtual Campus | | | | | | | | | |
| 2 | Sales Performance Table | | | | | | | | | |
| 3 | | | | | | | | | | |
| 4 | Last Name | First Name | Years | Review Date | Position | Region | State | ModSales | AppSales | Total Sales |
| 5 | Zain | Elizabeth | 7 | 1-Feb | Sales Account Mgr | Western | CA | 340,000 | 700,000 | 1,040,000 |
| 6 | Alvizo | Alex | 7 | 1-Mar | Senior Account Mgr | Western | CA | 602,000 | 622,000 | 1,224,000 |
| 7 | Clayton | Taneisha | 2 | 1-Mar | Sales Rep | Central | IL | 230,000 | 120,000 | 350,000 |
| 8 | Cray | Karen | 1 | 15-Apr | Sales Rep | Western | WA | 123,000 | 130,000 | 253,000 |
| 9 | Hill | Patricia | 1 | 1-Jun | Sales Rep | Central | IL | 120,000 | 170,000 | 290,000 |
| 10 | McGee | Olivia | 8 | 1-Jun | Senior Account Mgr | Eastern | MA | 317,000 | 513,000 | 830,000 |
| 11 | Fernandez | Maria | 1 | 15-Jun | Sales Account Mgr | Eastern | MA | 228,000 | 216,000 | 444,000 |
| 12 | Hasan | Taz | 3 | 15-Jul | Sales Account Mgr | Western | CA | 446,000 | 120,000 | 566,000 |
| 13 | Huy | Lin | 5 | 1-Aug | Senior Account Mgr | Central | IL | 234,000 | 560,000 | 794,000 |
| 14 | Sutton | David | 6 | 1-Sep | Sales Account Mgr | Central | CO | 162,000 | 151,000 | 313,000 |
| 15 | Williams | LaShaun | 3 | 1-Sep | Sales Account Mgr | Central | CO | 210,000 | 340,000 | 550,000 |
| 16 | Martinez | Carlos | 4 | 15-Sep | Senior Account Mgr | Eastern | FL | 450,000 | 450,000 | 900,000 |
| 17 | Mathis | Gerhardt | 3 | 15-Sep | Sales Rep | Western | CA | 156,000 | 160,000 | 316,000 |
| 18 | Knapp | mai | 2 | 15-Nov | Sales Rep | Eastern | FL | 140,000 | 130,000 | 270,000 |
| 19 | Total | | 4 | | 14 | | | 3,758,000 | 4,382,000 | 8,140,000 |
| 20 | | | Avg Years | | Total Sales Staff | | | Total Mod | Total App | |

The rows in this table are sorted by last name. The table also may be filtered by any column to display only certain data.

# 9.1 Understanding the Benefit of Tables

**Video Lesson** labyrinthelab.com/videos

You may still work with worksheet lists in the usual way, but at times you will want to convert a list into a table on the worksheet. Features specific to tables include the following:

- **Automatic expansion**—As you type more data rows at the bottom of the table or columns to the right, the table expands to include them. Cell formatting and formulas are copied automatically to the new rows.
- **Calculated columns**—Entering a formula in one cell automatically copies the formula to all cells in the table column. You need not autofill or copy.
- **Table styles**—Selecting any of the formatting presets in the table style library applies consistent formatting to the entire table. You must manually format cells in a worksheet list.
- **Filtering**—Filtering (displaying only those rows that meet certain criteria) is available immediately after you create a table, but you must turn on filtering in columns of a worksheet list. An improvement to Excel 2010 is that the filtering commands always are visible as you scroll down a table. They do not remain visible in a scrolled list unless you set the worksheet view to freeze panes.
- **Functions**—You may display a total row and create summary formulas instantly by choosing from a list of frequently used functions such as SUM and AVERAGE. All Excel functions may be used in tables.

# 9.2 Working with Tables

An Excel table manages related data. For example, a table can hold the sales performance data for each sales employee. The table data may be sorted, filtered, and calculated in various ways. Data are organized consistently throughout the table in rows and columns similar to the way data are structured in a table within a Microsoft Access database.

## Table Rows

In Excel, each row in a table (called a record in a database) holds a collection of facts about a certain person, event, or other item. For example, the sales performance table will have one row for each sales employee.

## Table Columns

Each column in a table (called a field in a database) contains one piece of information, such as last name or total sales achieved by the employee. For example, the sales performance table could have columns for each sales employee's last name, first name, position, and sales performance.

Each column contains one piece of data about the employee.

Each table row contains data about one person, event, or transaction—one row per employee in this example.

| | A | B | C | D |
|---|---|---|---|---|
| 4 | Last Name ▼ | First Name ▼ | Years ▼ | Review Date ▼ |
| 5 | **Alvizo** | Alex | 7 | 1-Mar |
| 6 | **Clayton** | Taneisha | 2 | 1-Mar |
| 7 | **Cray** | Karen | 1 | 15-Apr |

# 9.3 Creating a Table

**Video Lesson**   labyrinthelab.com/videos

You start a table by entering data in worksheet cells as you normally do. Do not use blank rows or columns to separate areas within the list because Excel does not include areas after blanks in a table. You may apply number formats and other formatting as desired. A worksheet may include more than one table and worksheet data outside of tables.

| | A | B | C |
|---|---|---|---|
| 4 | Company | Order Number | Amount |
| 5 | Blue Chip | 3056 | 56.97 |
| 6 | Razor Motors | 3057 | 30.16 |
| 7 | US Fuel | 3058 | 168.43 |
| 8 | Panda Foods | 3059 | 498.72 |

Worksheet cells ready to be converted to a table

## Converting a Range to a Table

You may convert a worksheet list to a table by selecting any cell in the list and choosing the Format As Table command from the Ribbon. Excel includes all adjacent cells in the table until a blank row and column are encountered. You may change the suggested table range if it is not correct. The table appears in place of the original cells. During the conversion process, you choose a table style, also known as a Quick Style. Many styles will format the table rows with alternating color bands. The Table Tools Design tab appears on the Ribbon after you create the table so you may apply additional formatting.

**FROM THE KEYBOARD**
Ctrl+T to create a table

You may change the table range if Excel guesses incorrectly.

The first row, containing column headings, will be used as the header row.

Create Table

Where is the data for your table?

=$A$4:$C$8

☑ My table has headers

| | A | B | C |
|---|---|---|---|
| 4 | Company ▼ | Order Number ▼ | Amount ▼ |
| 5 | Blue Chip | 3056 | 56.97 |
| 6 | Razor Motors | 3057 | 30.16 |
| 7 | US Fuel | 3058 | 168.43 |
| 8 | Panda Foods | 3059 | 498.72 |

Setting the range to be converted to a table       The table that results

Use Insert→Tables→Table ▦ from the Ribbon if you prefer to create a table and apply the default table style automatically.

# Creating a New Blank Table

As an alternative, you may start with blank cells in a table. After you select a range and choose the Format As Table command, the new table displays. Replace the generic column headings by typing your column labels and then enter the table data.

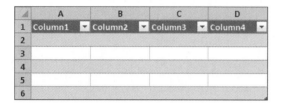

# Renaming a Table

Excel names tables as Table1, Table2, and so on. Although you may use the generic names, renaming with a more descriptive title is a good practice because table names often are used in formulas. As with defined names for a cell or a range, table names may not include spaces but may include multiple capital letters and underscores, as in OrderTable and Order_Table.

Table Name:
Order_Table

| QUICK REFERENCE | CREATING AND RENAMING TABLES |
|---|---|
| **Task** | **Procedure** |
| Create a table from an existing range | ■ Select the desired range in the worksheet. |
| | ■ Choose Home→Styles→Format As Table ⊞ from the Ribbon or use Ctrl+T from the keyboard. |
| | ■ Choose a table style from the list. |
| | ■ Change the suggested table range in the dialog box, if necessary. |
| | ■ Edit column headings in the first table row as necessary and type data if not already entered. |
| Rename a table | ■ Choose Design→Properties, click in the Table Name box to select the existing generic table name, type the new name (spaces are not allowed), and tap Enter. |

## DEVELOP YOUR SKILLS 9.3.1
## Create a Table

*In this exercise, you will create a table for My Virtual Campus Corporation's sales force. You will work with this table throughout the lesson.*

1. Start **Excel** and **open** the Sales Performance workbook from the Lesson 09 folder in your file storage location.

2. **Maximize** ⬜ the window.

### Format an Existing Range as a Table

3. Select **cell A4** in the Sales Performance Table worksheet.
   *Notice that the data in the range A4:I17 contain no blank rows or columns. You will convert this list from regular cells to a table.*

4. Choose **Home→Styles→Format As Table**  from the Ribbon.
   *The table style palette appears.*

5. Choose **Table Style Light 9** under the Light category. (The styles are in numerical order, and a pop-up ScreenTip should appear when you point to a style.)
   *The table will be formatted in blue with thin lines separating the rows.*

6. Make certain that the **Format As Table** dialog box options match the ones shown in the illustration, and click **OK**.
   *Although you selected only one cell in the range A4:I17, Excel suggests the entire range.*

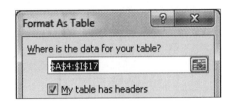

### Rename the Table

*The Table Tools Design tab appears on the Ribbon when a table cell is selected.*

7. Choose **Table Tools Design→Properties** and click in the **Table Name** box to select the existing generic table name. Taking care to type an underscore using ⎣Shift⎦+⎣-⎦ between the two words, type **Sales_Performance** and tap ⎣Enter⎦.
   *You should rename a table to provide a clear description of any table names used in formulas. Table names may include underscores and multiple capital letters, as in SalesPerformance, but may not include spaces.*

8. **Deselect** the highlighted table cells.

9. **Save** 💾 the changes, and leave the workbook **open**.

# Header Row

Video Lesson    labyrinthelab.com/videos

Always enter column headings as the first row of a table. Excel uses this as the header row. Excel uses the following rules for column headings.

- **One Item per Column**—Each column must contain one piece of information to enable full sorting and filtering. For example, create seven separate columns for last name, first name, middle initial, street address, city, state, and postal code.

- **Unique Headings**—Each heading should be different. For example, you cannot type Name as the same heading for two columns. Last Name and First Name are acceptable because the labels contain at least one different character.

- **Special Characters**—You may use spaces and multiple capital letters in column headings. Special characters such as underscore (_), comma (,), period (.), and dollar sign ($) also are allowed. Avoid using the "at" symbol (@), the pound sign (#), brackets ([ and ]), and single quotes ('), as those have special meanings in formulas.

With any table cell selected, the header row labels operate like frozen titles. They display in place of the column headings (A, B, C, and so on) as you scroll down the table.

The header row is frozen as you scroll so that column names remain visible.

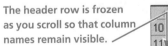

# Total Row

After you create a table, you may display the total row below the last table row. You may turn off its display, if desired. If the last table column contains numbers, a total is calculated automatically. If the last column contains text or dates, the nonblank entries in the column are counted (the total would display 3 in the following table).

| Company | Order Number | Amount |
|---|---|---|
| Blue Chip | 3056 | 56.97 |
| Razor Motors | 3057 | 30.16 |
| US Fuel | 3058 | 161.43 |
| Total | | 248.56 |

The total row displays below the last table row with an automatic sum in the last column.

## *Creating Summary Formulas*

A summary formula is a calculation displayed in the total row and based on the contents of its table column. You may create summary formulas very easily. Just choose from the total cell's list of commonly used functions such as SUM, AVERAGE, MIN, MAX, and COUNT. Excel performs the calculation on the entries in the table column, and you need not type anything or select any cells. By choosing More Functions in the list, you may access any other Excel function to create a custom formula or you may type the formula.

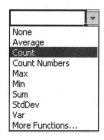

None
Average
Count
Count Numbers
Max
Min
Sum
StdDev
Var
More Functions...

The result of choosing AVERAGE

The result of choosing COUNT

The result of choosing SUM

| Years | Review Date | Position | Region | State | ModSales |
|---|---|---|---|---|---|
| 3 | 15-Sep | Sales Rep | Western | CA | 156,000 |
| 2 | 15-Nov | Sales Rep | Eastern | FL | 140,000 |
| 4 | | 14 | | | 3,758,000 |
| Avg Years | | Total Sales Staff | | | Total Mod |

An optional label typed below the table to explain the total

# Formatting a Table

The Table Tools Design Ribbon activates while any table cell is selected. You may change the table style, create a custom style and set it as the default, or clear the table style from the selected table. You also may turn on or remove the display of the header row and total row. Banded rows and columns contain a light fill and dark fill that alternate for each row or column for ease in reading across a record or down a category. You may set the first or last column to display differently than the others for emphasis. Apply other desired formatting such as bold, alignment, and number formats to selected cells as usual. Table formatting should be used sparingly to follow principles of effective design.

The First Column and Last Column options accent those columns to draw attention. Formatting options should be chosen sparingly to avoid confusing the reader.

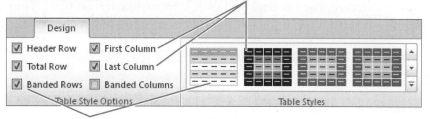

The table styles in the palette change to match the Table Style Options set on the Design tab of the Ribbon.

Banded rows alternate with a light and dark fill.

| QUICK REFERENCE | CHOOSING TOTAL ROW FORMULAS AND TABLE STYLE |
|---|---|
| **Task** | **Procedure** |
| Display/hide the header row or total row | ■ Select any cell in the table. |
| | ■ Choose Design→Table Style Options→Header Row or Total Row from the Ribbon. |
| Create a formula in the total row | ■ Select the desired cell in the total row. |
| | ■ Type a formula or choose the formula name or More Functions from the cell's formula list. |
| Change or remove a table style | ■ Select any cell in the table. |
| | ■ Choose Design→Table Styles→More ⬇ menu and choose a different table style or None from the Ribbon. |
| Emphasize data in a table | ■ Choose Design→Table Style Options and turn on/off First Column, Last Column, Banded Rows, and Banded Columns as desired. |

## DEVELOP YOUR SKILLS 9.3.2
# Create Totals and Format a Table

*In this exercise, you will view the header row and total row. You will create totals for some of the table columns. You also will change the table style.*

1. **Select** any cell in the table on the Sales Performance Table worksheet.

### Edit the Header Row

2. Review the column headings in **row 4**. (Choose **Design→Table Style Options→Header Row** from the Ribbon if the header row is not displayed.)

*Excel formatted the first row of column headings as the header row. Column headings may contain spaces. Each heading displays an AutoFilter button. You will learn how to filter using these buttons in a later topic of this lesson.*

3. **Double-click** the Date column heading and change *Date* to **Review Date**.

### Scroll with the Header Row Frozen

4. With any table cell selected, **scroll down** until the table column headings replace the worksheet column headings—A, B, C, and so on. Make certain that a table cell is selected if this does not occur.

| | Last Name ▼ | First Name ▼ | Years ▼ | Review Date ▼ | Posit |
|---|---|---|---|---|---|
| 7 | Clayton | Taneisha | 1.5 | 40238 | Sales |
| 8 | Cray | Karen | 1 | 40283 | Sales |
| 9 | Hill | Patricia | 0.5 | 40330 | Sales |

*The column headings freeze automatically as you scroll so they are always visible.*

5. **Scroll up** until row 1 is visible.

6. **Save** 🖫 the changes.

## Create Formulas in the Total Row

7. Choose **Design→Table Style Options→Total Row** from the Ribbon if the total row is not displayed in row 18.

8. Notice the total row in **row 18**.

| 18 | Total | | | | | | | | 4,252,000 |
|---|---|---|---|---|---|---|---|---|---|

*Excel added a total in the last column automatically because the column contains numbers. A total may be deleted just like the contents of any other cell if you do not want it to display.*

9. Select **cell C18** and follow these steps to create a formula:

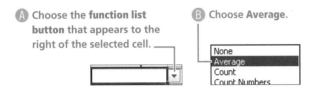

A Choose the **function list button** that appears to the right of the selected cell.

B Choose **Average**.

None
Average
Count
Count Numbers

*The average years employed displays as 4. Notice that you were not required to type an equals (=) sign or select cells to create the formula.*

10. Select **cell E18** and choose **Count** from the function list.
*The employees total 13. The COUNT function counts the number of nonblank entries in the table column.*

11. **Center-align** the contents of **cell E18**.

12. Select **cell H18** and choose **Sum** from the function list.

13. **Type** the following labels in **row 19**:

| 18 | Total | | 4 | | 13 | | | 3,618,000 | 4,252,000 |
|---|---|---|---|---|---|---|---|---|---|
| 19 | | | Avg Years | | Total Sales Staff | | | Total Mod | Total App |

*These labels describe the calculations in row 18. The labels are optional and are not actually part of the table because they are below the total row.*

14. **Center-align** the labels in **row 19**.

15. **Save** 💾 the changes.

## Change the Table Style

16. **Select** any table cell and choose **Design→Table Styles→More ▾ →Table Style Medium 16** from the Ribbon.
*Excel formats the table in blue with gray shaded bands on alternating rows. Notice that the Banded Rows option is selected in the Table Style Options group on the Ribbon.*

17. Choose **Design→Table Style Options** and place checkmarks next to **First Column** and **Last Column** in the Ribbon.
*The first and last columns now are highlighted with a blue fill color to draw attention.*

18. Choose **Design→Table Styles→More**  →**Table Style Medium 7** from the Ribbon.

19. Choose **Design→Table Style Options→Banded Rows** in the Ribbon to turn off alternating banded rows. Verify that the settings match those shown.

☑ Header Row   ☑ First Column
☑ Total Row    ☑ Last Column
☐ Banded Rows  ☐ Banded Columns

*The table is formatted in orange without shaded bands on alternating rows. The text in the first and last columns changed to bold. The table styles are designed to contrast text clearly against its background.*

20. **Save** 💾 the changes, and leave the workbook **open**.

## Adding and Deleting Rows and Columns

Video Lesson   labyrinthelab.com/videos

Tables are designed to help you add and delete records easily.

### Table Rows

You may insert a row anywhere in the table by selecting a cell below the desired location and choosing the Insert command from the Ribbon or the pop-up (or context) menu. Often it is easier to add records to the end of the table and then sort the list. After selecting the right-most cell in the last data row, you tap ⎾Tab⏌ to wrap to a new blank table row and continue using ⎾Tab⏌ after typing each cell entry. You use the Delete command from the Ribbon or context menu to remove rows after selecting a cell in the desired row(s).

| 450,000 |
| 160,000 |
| 4,252,000 |
| Total App |

More records may be entered by selecting the last data cell and tapping ⎾Tab⏌.

### Table Columns

You may insert a column anywhere in the table by first selecting a cell to the right of the desired location. To insert a column between other columns, you must display the Insert menu from the Ribbon or context menu and choose a command. You may simply type in the blank column to the right of the last column to add it to the table. The command for deleting a column varies based on the selected cell(s). The Delete command on the Ribbon may be used when entire columns are selected. You may select just one cell in each column to be deleted, but you must display the Delete menu from the Ribbon or context menu and choose a command.

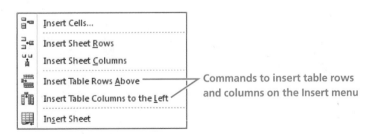

Insert Cells...
Insert Sheet Rows
Insert Sheet Columns
Insert Table Rows Above
Insert Table Columns to the Left
Insert Sheet

Commands to insert table rows and columns on the Insert menu

### *Automatic Extension*

The table extends to include new rows and column(s), calculations are updated, and consistent formatting is applied automatically.

The table will not extend to add the items shown in the illustration if you just select a cell and type.

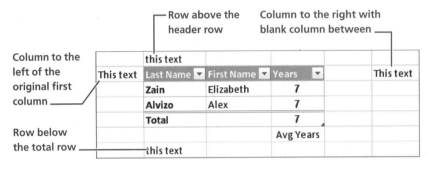

## Selecting Table Rows and Columns

At times you may need to select all cells in a table row or column. For example, cells must be selected before changing their text color. Selecting cells by dragging may be difficult in tables with many rows or columns. Selecting a table row or column is different from selecting a row or column in the worksheet, as follows:

- Selecting the row number selects the entire row through the end of the worksheet.
- Selecting with the arrow pointer *in* the first cell of a table row selects just the cells in the table row.
- Selecting the column letter selects the entire column through the end of the worksheet.
- Selecting with the arrow pointer in a table column heading selects just the cells in the table column.

Examine the pointer position in the following illustrations.

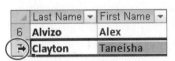
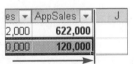

Placing the pointer on the 7 and clicking selects all row 7 cells through the end of the worksheet.

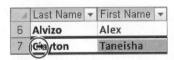

Placing the pointer inside the first cell in the row and clicking selects only cells in the table.

# Add and Delete Table Rows and Columns

*In this exercise, you will add a record to the table and explore commands to insert and delete rows and columns. You will select a row and a column in the table without including cells outside the table.*

## Add a Record to the Table

1. Select **cell I17** in the Sales Performance Table worksheet.
   *This is the last data cell in the table.*

2. **Tap** Tab, and the pointer wraps to a newly inserted row.

3. **Enter** the following record, **tapping** Tab after each cell except the last. **Tap** Enter to complete the last entry, 130000.
   *As you begin typing an entry, AutoComplete may fill in the remainder. Tap Tab to accept the entry and move to the next cell.*

Click Undo ↩ if you accidentally tap Tab after the last cell in the row.

| 18 | Knapp | Mai | 2 | 15-Nov | Sales Rep | Eastern | FL | 140,000 | **130,000** |

*Notice that the table expanded to include the new row, and formulas in the total row automatically recalculated to include the new numbers.*

4. **Save** 💾 the changes.

## Insert Rows and a Column Using the Ribbon

5. Select **cell E14**.

6. Choose **Home→Cells→Insert** 📑 from the Ribbon.

| 13 | Huy | Lin | 5 | 1-Aug | Senior Account Mgr | Centra |
| 14 | | | | | | |
| 15 | Sutton | David | 6 | 1-Sep | Sales Account Mgr | Centra |

*Excel inserts a blank table row above the selected cell. You may choose Insert without choosing its menu arrow ▼ when inserting one row.*

7. Select **cell K9** and type **Revised**. Type **Tuesday** in **cell K10**. (Do not enter this text in row 14.)

8. Select the **range E9:E10** and choose **Home→Cells→Insert menu ▼→Insert Table Rows Above** from the Ribbon. (Make certain to choose the menu arrow ▼ rather than Insert.)

| Sales Rep | | Western | WA | 123,000 | 130,000 | | |
| | | | | | | Revised |
| | | | | | | Tuesday |
| Sales Rep | | Central | IL | 120,000 | 170,000 | |

*Two rows are inserted above row 9. Notice that the text in cells K9 and K10 did not move. Rows and columns inserted in a table do not affect the cells outside the table.*

9. Select **cell D7** and choose **Home→Cells→Insert menu ▾→Insert Table Columns to the Left** from the Ribbon.

10. Select **cell D4** and replace the generic Column1 heading with **Phone**.

| Years | Phone | Review Date |
|---|---|---|
| 7 | | 1-Feb |
| 7 | | 1-Mar |

## Delete Rows and a Column Using the Context Menu

11. Point to any cell in table **row 16**, **right-click**, and choose **Delete→Table Rows** from the context menu.
*Table row 16 (a blank row) is deleted. You may insert or delete rows or columns using the context menu.*

12. Select the **range D9:D10**, **right-click**, and choose **Delete→Table Rows** from the context menu.
*Table rows 9 and 10 (blank rows) are deleted. The text in cells L9 and L10 is not affected by the deletion because those cells are outside the table.*

13. With the **range D9:D10** still selected, **right-click** and choose **Delete→Table Columns** from the context menu to delete column D.
*Now the table contains no blank rows or columns.*

14. **Select** any other table cell to deselect the highlighted cells.

15. **Save** 💾 the changes.

## Select a Table Row and Apply Cell Formatting

16. Point inside **cell A9** near its left border as shown at right until the pointer displays as an arrow and then **click**. (Do **not** click the 9 to the left of cell A9, which would select the entire row.)
*Excel selects the range A9:I9 within the table. Notice that cell K9 outside the table (containing Revised) is not selected.*

| 9 | ↦▥ | Patricia |
|---|---|---|

17. With the **range A9:I9** still selected, choose **Home→Styles→Cell Styles** ▦ **→Data and Model→Warning Text** from the Ribbon.
*Formatting may be applied to selected cells in a table.*

## Select Columns

18. In **cell D4**, point near the top of the Review Date column heading until the pointer displays an arrow, and **drag to select** both the Review Date and the Position table columns.
*Notice that the cells below the table are not included in the selection.*

| Review Date | Position |
|---|---|

19. **Select** any table cell to deselect the columns.

20. **Save** 💾 the changes.

# Calculated Columns

Video Lesson | labyrinthelab.com/videos

Any blank table column may become a calculated column. You create a formula in one cell, and Excel copies the formula to all of the other cells in the column automatically. If you do not want a calculated column, type text or a number in at least one cell before creating any unique formulas in the column.

## Converting a Table to a Range

You may convert a table to a normal range in the worksheet. Be aware that some table formatting may be lost if you convert the list back into a table at a later time.

## Printing a Table

The Print Selected Table option in the Print tab of Backstage view may be used to print a table without including the other cells on the worksheet. The option is available only when you select a cell in the table before displaying the Print tab.

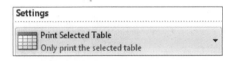

## Deleting a Table

You may delete a table by selecting all table cells, including the total row if visible, and tapping Delete or choosing the Delete Table Rows command.

The Undo ↺ command on the Quick Access toolbar can restore a deleted table.

| QUICK REFERENCE | EDITING, PRINTING, AND DELETING TABLES |
|---|---|
| **Task** | **Procedure** |
| Add records to a table | ▪ Select the last cell in the last data row and tap Tab. |
| | ▪ Type a cell entry, tap Tab, and continue this process until all records are added. |
| Insert one or more rows in a table | ▪ Select one cell or multiple cells below the desired location. |
| | ▪ Choose Home→Cells→Insert from the Ribbon to insert one row. |
| | *or* |
| | ▪ Choose Home→Cells→Insert menu ▼→Insert Table Rows Above from the Ribbon to insert multiple rows. |
| Delete one or more rows from a table | ▪ Select one cell in each row to be deleted. |
| | ▪ Choose Home→Cells→Delete from the Ribbon to delete one row. |
| | *or* |
| | ▪ Choose Home→Cells→Delete menu ▼→Delete Table Rows from the Ribbon to delete multiple rows. |

| Task | Procedure |
|------|-----------|
| Insert one or more columns in a table | ■ Type data or a formula in the column to the right of the last column.<br>*or*<br>■ Select one cell or multiple cells to the right of the desired location.<br>■ Choose Home→Cells→Insert menu ▼→Insert Table Columns to the Left from the Ribbon. |
| Delete one or more columns from a table | ■ Select one cell in each column to be deleted.<br>■ Choose Home→Cells→Delete menu ▼→Delete Table Columns from the Ribbon. |
| Select a table row | ■ Place the mouse inside the first cell of the row to display the arrow pointer and click. |
| Select a table column | ■ Place the mouse at the top of the table column heading to display the arrow pointer and click. |
| Create a calculated column | ■ Create a formula in any cell of a blank table column, and the formula copies to all other column cells automatically. |
| Convert a table to a normal range | ■ Select any cell in the table.<br>■ Choose Design→Tools→Convert to Range from the Ribbon. |
| Print a table only | ■ Select any cell in the table.<br>■ Choose File→Print, click the first option under Settings, and choose Print Selected Table from the list. |
| Delete a table | ■ Select all table cells, including the header row and table row.<br>■ Tap [Delete]. |

# Create a Calculated Column

*In this exercise, you will create a Total Sales column as a calculated column to sum the module software sales and education application sales for each employee.*

1. Select **cell J10**.

   *Column J is the blank column immediately to the right of the last table column. The table will expand to include this column after you enter something in it.*

2. Type **=** to begin the formula, and select **cell H10**.    | *f*x  =[@ModSales] |

   *Notice the cell reference in the Formula Bar. Excel uses a different type of reference for table cells. You will learn more about structured references in the next lesson topic.*

3. **Tap** [+] on the keypad, select **cell I10**, and select **Enter** ✔ to complete the formula.

   | Column ▼ |
   |---|
   | 1040000 |
   | 1224000 |
   | 350,000 |

   *The formula sums the module software sales and education application sales.*

   *Notice that the formula copied automatically for all other employees. This calculated column is now the last column in the table, so bolding transferred from column I to column J. A generic column heading displays.*

### Format the Calculated Column

4. Select **cell J19** and choose **Sum** from the cell's function list to display the column total.

5. Select the **range J5:J19** and format as **Comma Style** with **no decimal places**.

6. Select **cell J4** and replace the generic column heading with **Total Sales**.

7. Point at the border at the right of the **column J** heading until the two-pointed arrow appears, and then **double-click** the border to display the column heading completely.

8. **Save** 💾 the changes.

### Print Preview the Table

9. **Select** any cell in the table and choose **File→Print** to display the Print tab of Backstage view.

10. In the Settings area of Backstage view, click **Print Active Sheets** and choose **Print Selected Table** from the list. (Make certain a table cell is selected if the Print Selected Table option is not listed.)
    *Only one page containing just the table would print. The text in the ranges A1:A2, K9:K10, and C20:I20 would not print because those ranges are not within the table.*

11. Select the **Home** tab on the Ribbon to exit Backstage view without printing.

12. Delete the contents of **cells K9** and **K10**.

13. Select **cell D1** to place the pointer on page 1 of the worksheet.

14. **Save** 💾 the changes.

# 9.4 Understanding Structured References

Video Lesson    labyrinthelab.com/videos

Formulas in normal worksheet lists use cell references such as E7, but Excel uses structured references to refer to cells used in table formulas. Structured references allow formulas to adjust results automatically as rows and columns are added to or deleted from the table. They also adjust as you rename tables, edit column headings, and move or copy formulas. The generic syntax (language) of structured references allows you to create one formula in a calculated column so that the formula need not be copied to specific cells in the column as you must do in a normal worksheet range.

## Formulas with Structured References

To understand how structured references differ from cell references, compare the two formulas shown. They both contain references to total ModSales and AppSales for one employee. The first formula would be used in a normal worksheet range, and the second is used in the Total Sales calculated column of a table.

| ModSales | AppSales | Total Sales |
|---|---|---|
| 340,000 | 700,000 | 1,040,000 |

=H5+I5

A worksheet formula containing
relative cell references

| ModSales ▼ | AppSales ▼ | Total Sales ▼ |
|---|---|---|
| 340,000 | 700,000 | **1,040,000** |

=[@ModSales]+[@AppSales]

A table formula containing
structured references

The syntax, or language, used in table formulas has been simplified in Excel 2010. Previously, the table name and a row reference were included. The reference to cell H5 is converted to a structured reference containing brackets ([ ]) and the "at" symbol (@) in the table formula as explained in the following illustration.

Brackets surround the entire reference.

[@ModSales]

An "at" symbol (@)
precedes the name.

This is the heading in the column being referenced. (Additional
brackets would surround a name containing a space or underscore).

| QUICK REFERENCE | CREATING STRUCTURED REFERENCES IN TABLE FORMULAS |
|---|---|
| **Task** | **Procedure** |
| Create a structured reference | Use point mode to select a cell or a cell range while you create the table formulas. Excel creates the necessary structured references for you. |

DEVELOP YOUR SKILLS 9.4.1

# View Structured References

*In this exercise, you will review formulas in the Total Sales column that you created as a calculated column in the previous exercise. You also will view formulas in the table's total row.*

1. Select **cell J5**.

2. Review the addition formula containing two structured references for the values in the **ModSales** and **AppSales** columns.

   =[@ModSales]+[@AppSales]

3. Select **cell J6**.
   *The same formula displays for every cell in the calculated column. Any records added to the table would automatically include the formula.*

4. Select **cell H19** in the total row, and look at the formula in the Formula Bar.

   =SUBTOTAL(109,[ModSales])

   *This formula uses Excel's SUBTOTAL function, which consists of two arguments. The number 109 indicates the SUM function, and [ModSales] is a structured reference to the cells in the ModSales column.*

5. Select **cell C19** in the total row, and look at the formula in the Formula Bar.
   *The number 101 in the SUBTOTAL formula indicates the AVERAGE function, and [Years] refers to the cells in the Years column.*

   *Now you have learned to recognize some structured references that Excel created for you in formulas.*

# 9.5 Using Enhanced Sorting and Filtering in Lists and Tables

**Video Lesson**    labyrinthelab.com/videos

Excel's AutoFilter feature operates in the same manner for both lists and tables. A table automatically displays an AutoFilter button in each column heading to indicate that filtering is available. You may also display these buttons in a normal worksheet list. These column heading AutoFilter buttons provide additional sorting and filtering options not available on the Ribbon. The AutoFilter feature provides the capability to sort by color and to filter with a wide variety of color, text, number, and date options. These options help you analyze the data to spot trends and potential problems. Many Excel users filter large data sets, such as a product catalog. New to Excel 2010 is the capability to filter among up to 10,000 items in a column. The addition of a search box allows you to locate and add items quickly to the filter rather than scroll through the list to select them.

The Data→Sort & Filter→Filter [icon] command on the Ribbon turns on/off the display of the column heading list buttons for the selected table or list.

## Sorts

You can use the A to Z [icon] or Z to A [icon] commands to sort on one column in a worksheet list or table. Although these commands are available on the Data ribbon, you can easily access them via the column heading AutoFilter buttons. A column heading's AutoFilter button changes to indicate that the table or list is sorted based on that column. An up arrow indicates the sort is from lowest to highest, and a down arrow indicates highest to lowest. You may sort by a font color or fill color you applied manually, as well as by colors or icons created through conditional formatting. The Sort command on the Ribbon can sort on multiple columns. For example, you can sort by last name, then by first name, and then by middle name within duplicate names.

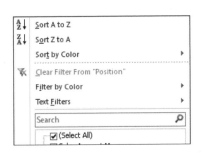

The sort and filter options for a text column

The arrow pointing up on the AutoFilter button indicates that the table is sorted by last name from lowest to highest.

A sorted table

## Sort a Table

*In this exercise, you will sort the table rows in alphabetic, numeric, and color order.*

*Before You Begin: If the column heading AutoFilter buttons do not display, select any table cell and choose Data→Sort & Filter→Filter.*

1. Follow these steps to sort by last name in the table on the Sales Performance Table worksheet.

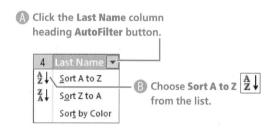

(A) Click the **Last Name** column heading **AutoFilter** button.

(B) Choose **Sort A to Z** from the list.

(C) Notice the sort indicator now shown on the button.

*The table rows are sorted in alphabetical order by last name. You could have used the identical sort command on the Data ribbon.*

2. Click the **Position** column heading **AutoFilter** button as shown at right, and then choose **Sort by Color→red color** box from the list.

*The table rows are sorted by color with the single row of red text displayed first.*

3. Choose the **Total Sales** column heading **AutoFilter** button→**Sort Largest to Smallest** from the list.

*The table rows are sorted by total sales from highest to lowest.*

4. **Save** the changes.

# Filters

**Video Lesson** labyrinthelab.com/videos

Filtering allows you to display only those rows that meet certain specifications that you choose. For example, you may display just the records for which the sales total is greater than $500,000 or display only records for employees with three years' experience. The records not meeting your specifications are hidden temporarily until you clear the filter. You may filter by text color, cell fill color, or cell contents including text, numbers, or dates. You can filter for a color or icon applied by conditional formatting. The column heading AutoFilter button displays a filter icon to alert you that the table is filtered and does not currently display all rows. The current filter setting appears in a screen tip when you hover the mouse over the button. You may filter on multiple columns using the AutoFilter buttons.

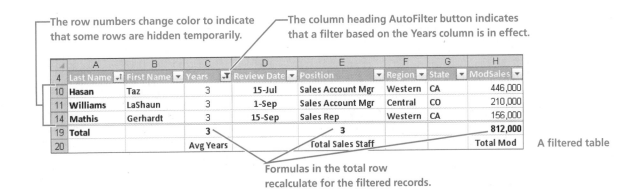

The row numbers change color to indicate that some rows are hidden temporarily.

The column heading AutoFilter button indicates that a filter based on the Years column is in effect.

| | A | B | C | D | E | F | G | H |
|---|---|---|---|---|---|---|---|---|
| 4 | Last Name | First Name | Years | Review Date | Position | Region | State | ModSales |
| 10 | Hasan | Taz | 3 | 15-Jul | Sales Account Mgr | Western | CA | 446,000 |
| 11 | Williams | LaShaun | 3 | 1-Sep | Sales Account Mgr | Central | CO | 210,000 |
| 14 | Mathis | Gerhardt | 3 | 15-Sep | Sales Rep | Western | CA | 156,000 |
| 19 | Total | | 3 | | 3 | | | 812,000 |
| 20 | | | Avg Years | | Total Sales Staff | | | Total Mod |

A filtered table

Formulas in the total row recalculate for the filtered records.

## Filtering with Multiple Criteria and Searches

An AutoFilter list contains all unique items in the column. After removing the checkmark from Select All, you may choose one or more items to include in the filter. In Excel 2010, a search can be performed on a column to locate the items to add to or delete from the filter criteria.

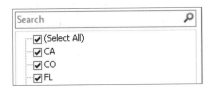

An AutoFilter list contains all items in the column before a search is performed.

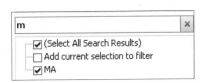

Typing "m" in the Search box locates MA, which then can be added to or deselected from the filter criteria.

# Custom Filters

The Custom Filter command, accessed via the column heading AutoFilter list, displays a dialog box that may be used to filter by two criteria in the same column. For example, you may filter for records with a review date between April 15 and June 15, using the And option as shown. The Or option displays every record that meets

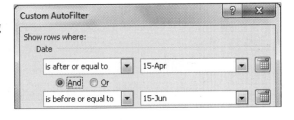

either one of the two criteria—the record need not meet both criteria. The dialog box also displays after you choose any text filter option or some of the number and date filter options. You may choose one or both specifications in the dialog box as needed. For example, specifying a beginning date of April 15 and leaving the ending date blank would locate all review dates from April 15 through the most recent date.

| Task | Procedure |
|---|---|
| Sort a table or list using an AutoFilter button | ▪ Select a cell in the table or list range and choose Data→Sort & Filter→Filter 🔽 to display column heading AutoFilter buttons, if necessary. |
| | ▪ Choose the column heading AutoFilter 🔽 button and one of the following from the list: |
| |    ◆ Sort A to Z or Smallest to Largest or Newest to Oldest 🔼 |
| |    ◆ Sort Z to A or Largest to Smallest or Oldest to Newest 🔽 |
| |    ◆ Sort by Color and the desired color or icon |
| |    ◆ Sort by Color→Custom Sort to sort on multiple columns without regard to color |
| Filter by selection in a table or list | ▪ Right-click the desired item in the column you want to filter. |
| | ▪ Choose Filter→Filter by Selected Cell's Value (or other characteristic) from the context menu. |
| Filter by a column's cell contents in a table or list | ▪ Choose the column heading AutoFilter 🔽 button. |
| | ▪ Choose Text Filters, Number Filters, or Date Filters and then choose the desired criterion from the list. |
| Filter by multiple criteria in the same column | ▪ Choose the column heading AutoFilter 🔽 button and do one of the following in the list: |
| |    ◆ Uncheck the column entries to be excluded from the filter; or uncheck the Select All box, and then check the column entries to be included. |
| |    ◆ Choose Text Filters, Number Filters, or Date Filters from the list, and choose an option. If the Custom AutoFilter dialog box is displayed, choose options for up to two criteria. |
| Filter using a search | ▪ Choose the column heading AutoFilter 🔽 button. |
| | ▪ Begin typing an entry in the Search box until the desired item appears. |
| | ▪ Uncheck any unwanted items, and click OK to apply the filter. |
| | ▪ If desired, search for another item, place a checkmark next to Add Current Selection to Filter (also uncheck Select All Search Results if you want to *exclude* the current search results), and click OK. |
| Clear filter criteria from one column | ▪ Choose the column heading filter 🔽 button→Clear Filter From "[column name]" from the list. |
| Clear filter criteria from all columns | ▪ Choose Data→Sort & Filter→Clear 🔽 from the Ribbon. |

# Filter a Table

*In this exercise, you will perform single-column and multicolumn filters using text, numbers, and dates.*

## Filter by Selection

1. **Right-click** any Eastern cell in the Region column and choose **Filter→Filter by Selected Cell's Value** from the context menu.
   *Four records containing Eastern in the Region column display, and the calculations in the total row change to reflect those records.*

2. **Select** any table cell and choose **Data→Sort & Filter→Clear** 🔻 from the Ribbon.
   *The table redisplays all 14 records.*

## Filter by Multiple Criteria in One Column

3. Follow these steps to filter for two job titles:

Ⓐ Choose the **Position** column heading **AutoFilter** button.

Ⓑ Choose **Sales Rep** from the list to uncheck that job title from the job positions to be displayed.

Ⓒ Click **OK**.

Ⓓ View the filtered list of nine records.

Ⓔ Hover the mouse pointer over the **Position** column heading **AutoFilter** button to display the filter criteria.

*The Position column heading AutoFilter button displays a filter icon to indicate that records have been filtered. Only the records for Sales Account Mgr and Senior Account Mgr are displayed, and the calculations changed in the total row. The sort order is still largest to smallest total sales.*

## Filter by Criteria in Two Columns

*You will filter the previous results further to view only the records for Massachusetts.*

4. Follow these steps to filter the previous results further:

Ⓐ Choose the **State** column heading **AutoFilter** button.

Ⓑ Uncheck (**Select All**) to deselect all states and then choose **MA** from the list.

Ⓒ Click **OK**.

Ⓓ **View** the filtered list of two records.

| Position | Region | State | ModSales |
|---|---|---|---|
| Senior Account Mgr | Eastern | MA | 317,000 |
| Sales Account Mgr | Eastern | MA | 228,000 |
| 2 | | | **545,000** |

Ⓔ Notice that both column headings display a **filter button** to indicate records have been filtered on two columns.

### Clear the Filters

5. Choose the **Position** column heading **AutoFilter**  button→**Clear Filter From "Position"** from the list.

6. Clear the filter from the State column.
   *The list is restored to all 14 records.*

### Filter by Text Criteria

7. Sort the table by **Last Name** in **A to Z order**.
   *Note that if two or more records had contained identical last names, you would use Data →Sort & Filter→ Sort on the Ribbon to perform a two-level sort on Last Name and First Name.*

8. **Save**  the change.
   *Next you will filter for records in which the last name begins with the letter M.*

9. Choose the **Last Name** column heading **AutoFilter** button→**Text Filters**→**Begins With** from the list.

10. In the **AutoFilter** dialog box, type **m** in the text box to the right of Begins With, and click **OK**.
    *Criteria are not case-sensitive—you may type M or m. Three last names begin with M.*

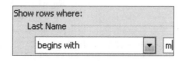

| 4 | Last Name | First Name |
|---|---|---|
| 13 | Martinez | Carlos |
| 14 | Mathis | Gerhardt |
| 15 | McGee | Olivia |

11. Choose the **Last Name** column heading **AutoFilter** button→ **Text Filters** from the list.
    *Notice that checkmarks display next to Text Filters and Begins With to indicate the current filter criteria. Read the other criteria options in the menu.*

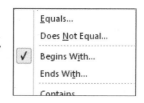

12. Choose the **Clear Filter From "Last Name"** command from the list.

### Filter by Number Criteria

*You want to reward California employees who made educational application sales of $450,000 or higher.*

13. Choose **AppSales** column heading **Auto-Filter button**→**Number Filters**→ **Greater Than Or Equal To**. In the Custom Auto-Filter dialog box, choose **450,000** from the list and click **OK**.
    *The filter displays five employees. You may choose from a list or type the criteria in the Custom Auto-Filter dialog box.*

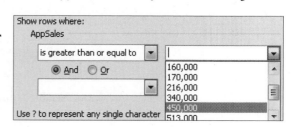

14. Also filter the **State** column for **California (CA)**.
    *Two employees in CA have application sales of $450,000 or greater.*

15. **Save**  the changes.

## Copy and Paste Filter Results

*Copying and pasting filtered rows allows you to save the results in the workbook for reference. The pasted cells are simply a worksheet list, although they could be converted to a table. These cells retain formatting from the table, but formulas are lost and those cells display the formula result as numbers or text.*

16. In **cell A22**, type **California Employees with >$450,000 Application Sales** and format this label in **italics**.

    *The greater than symbol (>) is created by holding down* Shift *and tapping* ⟨.⟩ *(period).*

17. Select the **range A4:J20**. Copy and paste to **cell A23** as shown.

| | A | B | C | D | E | F | G | H | I | J |
|---|---|---|---|---|---|---|---|---|---|---|
| 4 | Last Name | First Name | Years | Review Date | Position | Region | State | ModSales | AppSales | Total Sales |
| 5 | Alvizo | Alex | 7 | 1-Mar | Senior Account Mgr | Western | CA | 602,000 | 622,000 | 1,224,000 |
| 18 | Zain | Elizabeth | 7 | 1-Feb | Sales Account Mgr | Western | CA | 340,000 | 700,000 | 1,040,000 |
| 19 | Total | | 7 | | 2 | | | 942,000 | 1,322,000 | 2,264,000 |
| 20 | | | Avg Years | | Total Sales Staff | | | Total Mod | Total App | |
| 21 | | | | | | | | | | |
| 22 | *California Employees with >$450,000 Application Sales* | | | | | | | | | |
| 23 | Last Name | First Name | Years | Review Date | Position | Region | State | ModSales | AppSales | Total Sales |
| 24 | Alvizo | Alex | 7 | 1-Mar | Senior Account Mgr | Western | CA | 602,000 | 622,000 | 1,224,000 |
| 25 | Zain | Elizabeth | 7 | 1-Feb | Sales Account Mgr | Western | CA | 340,000 | 700,000 | 1,040,000 |
| 26 | Total | | 7 | | 2 | | | 942,000 | 1,322,000 | 2,264,000 |
| 27 | | | Avg Years | | Total Sales Staff | | | Total Mod | Total App | |

18. Select any table cell in **rows 4–9** and choose **Data→ Sort & Filter→Clear** 🔽 from the Ribbon.

    *The Ribbon command clears all filters from multiple columns at one time.*

## Filter by Searching

19. Choose the **Last Name** column heading **AutoFilter** 🔽 button.

20. Click in the **Search** box, type **sutton** and **tap** Enter.

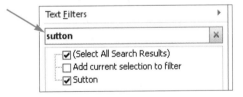

*The filter displays David Sutton's record. Searching for a name may be easier than scrolling to locate the name in a lengthy list.*

21. Choose the **Last Name** column heading **AutoFilter** 🔽 button.

22. Follow these steps to search for and add another name to the filter:

(A) Type **zain** in the Search box.

(B) Place a checkmark next to **Add Current Selection to Filter.**

(C) Click **OK.**

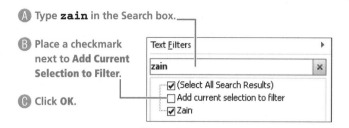

| Text Filters ▸ |
| --- |
| zain ✕ |
| ☑ (Select All Search Results) |
| ☐ Add current selection to filter |
| ☑ Zain |

*The filter displays Elizabeth Zain's record in addition to David Sutton's.*

23. **Clear** the filter.

## Explore Number and Date Criteria Options

24. Choose the **AppSales** column heading **AutoFilter** ▾ button→**Number Filters** and take a few moments to explore the other number criteria options.

25. Choose the **Review Date column heading AutoFilter** ▾ button→**Date Filters** and take a few moments to explore the date criteria options and choose at least one option.

26. Select any table cell and choose **Data→Sort & Filter→Clear** 🝖 from the Ribbon when you are done.
*The table should display 14 records sorted by last name.*

27. **Save** 🖫 the changes.

# 9.6 Using the Outline Feature

**Video Lesson**  labyrinthelab.com/videos

Excel's Outline feature helps you to control the display of detail data in worksheets. You may see the big picture while still being able to view the details when necessary. Outlining works best in normal worksheet ranges. The structure of tables limits the outlining options that you may use. If you repeatedly filter for a range of items, you may want to outline data to create groups rather than convert data to a table containing column heading AutoFilter buttons.

## How Outlines Work

When you create an outline for a worksheet list, Excel organizes the data into detail groups. This structure is displayed visually along the top border for columns and along the left border for rows. You may click the level number buttons to display various levels of detail, with 1 being the least detail and each higher number displaying more detail. The outline area also contains expand (+) and collapse (−) buttons you may click to display and hide individual groups of data. The following example shows an outlined worksheet.

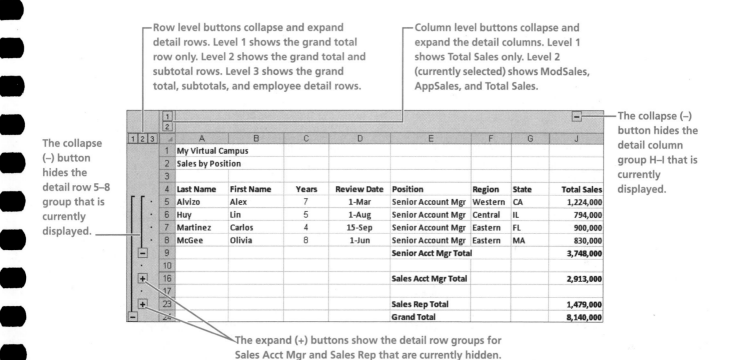

Row level buttons collapse and expand detail rows. Level 1 shows the grand total row only. Level 2 shows the grand total and subtotal rows. Level 3 shows the grand total, subtotals, and employee detail rows.

Column level buttons collapse and expand the detail columns. Level 1 shows Total Sales only. Level 2 (currently selected) shows ModSales, AppSales, and Total Sales.

The collapse (–) button hides the detail column group H–I that is currently displayed.

The collapse (–) button hides the detail row 5–8 group that is currently displayed.

The expand (+) buttons show the detail row groups for Sales Acct Mgr and Sales Rep that are currently hidden.

## Auto Outline

Excel can apply an outline to most worksheet lists automatically. The key to smooth automatic outlining is to arrange the detail and summary data consistently according to the following rules:

- **Detail Columns**—Detail data in columns must appear all to the right or left of the summary formulas.

- **Detail Rows**—If you want the outline to group detail rows, sort the list by category and insert a subtotal formula after each change within the category.

The more hierarchical your layout is, the more effective the resulting outline will be. Excel will try to outline all data related to summary formulas in the worksheet. If you are not satisfied with the results of the Auto Outline command, you may group rows and columns manually.

### DEVELOP YOUR SKILLS 9.6.1
## Outline a Worksheet Automatically

*In this exercise, you will use the Auto Outline command to outline a worksheet that contains summary formulas. Then you will collapse and expand the outline.*

1. Display the **Sales by Position** worksheet of the Sales Performance workbook.
   *This worksheet contains a normal list, not a table. The four senior account manager rows appear first in the list, followed by five sales account managers and then five sales reps. For outlining to be helpful, the data for each position should be together.*

## Create an Outline Automatically

*Excel can group the detail rows in an outline because a total row follows the detail rows for each position.*

2. Choose **Data→Outline→Group** 🔲 **menu ▾→Auto Outline** from the Ribbon. (The Group menu button may display as ➡.)
   *Excel automatically groups the rows and columns of the table, indicated by brackets to the left of and above the worksheet. On the left, notice that the rows are divided into three bracketed groups at Level 2 and one larger group at Level 1. Above the sheet, there is just one group bracketed for the columns. Excel reviewed the formulas on the worksheet to create these groupings.*

3. Use ⌨Ctrl⌨+⌨Home⌨ to move to **cell A1**.

4. Scroll down until **row 4** displays just below the Excel column heading letters.

5. Follow these steps to collapse and expand the display of all detail data:

   Ⓐ Click the **Level 1** button for columns. Notice that the ModSales and AppSales columns collapse, leaving only the Total Sales summary column visible. _____

   Ⓑ Click the **Level 1** button for the rows. This leaves only the grand total row visible. _____

   Ⓒ Click the **Level 2** button for the rows. This shows the grand total and subtotal rows. _____

   Ⓓ Click the **Level 3** button for the rows. This expands the view to show all detail rows. _____

6. Display **Level 2** for the rows.
   *Notice the expand ( + ) and collapse (−) buttons in the outline area. An outline level with a collapse button currently displays its detail data. An outline with an expand button has details that are not displayed.*

7. Follow these steps to expand individual groups of row detail data:

   Ⓐ Click the **expand (+)** button for the Senior Acct Mgr Total row to show its detail rows. _____

   Ⓑ Click the **expand (+)** button for the Sales Rep Total row to show its detail rows. _____

8. Click the **Level 3** button for the row groups.
   *This command reveals all detail row groups in the outline. You may use the expand and collapse buttons to display and hide individual groups. The Level 1, 2, and 3 buttons expand or collapse all groups in the level at once.*

9. **Save** 💾 the changes.

# Creating Groups Manually

Video Lesson    labyrinthelab.com/videos

When the detail rows do not include summary formulas or Excel simply does not outline the worksheet as you expected, you may group rows and columns manually. Row groups must be separated by a blank row, or Excel will combine all into one group. You select the rows or columns to be grouped and choose the Group command from the Ribbon. The selection is grouped in the outline or added to an existing adjacent group. You use a similar procedure to ungroup rows and columns manually. If desired, you may even ungroup rows and columns originally grouped by Excel's Auto Outline command.

| QUICK REFERENCE | GROUPING AND UNGROUPING IN LISTS AND TABLES |
|---|---|
| **Task** | **Procedure** |
| Automatically outline rows and columns | ■ Move columns of detail data all to the right or left of the summary formulas. <br> ■ Sort the list by category and insert a subtotal formula after each change of category if you want the outline to group detail rows. <br> ■ Choose Data→Outline→Group menu ▼→Auto Outline from the Ribbon. |
| Manually group rows or columns | ■ Insert a blank row between each section of rows to be grouped, if necessary. <br> ■ Select the detail row(s) or column(s) to be grouped. <br> ■ Choose Data→Outline→Group from the Ribbon and choose Rows or Columns. |
| Manually ungroup rows or columns | ■ Select the detail row(s) or column(s) to be ungrouped. <br> ■ Choose Data→Outline→Ungroup from the Ribbon and choose Rows or Columns. |
| Remove an entire outline | ■ Select any single worksheet cell. <br> ■ Choose Data→Outline→Ungroup menu ▼→Clear Outline from the Ribbon. |

## DEVELOP YOUR SKILLS 9.6.2
## Outline a Worksheet Manually

*In this exercise, you will create groups manually in a table that has no summary formulas for the rows.*

### Sort a List by Years

1. Display the **Sales by Years** worksheet of the Sales Performance workbook.

2. Select any cell in the Years column, choose **Data→Sort & Filter→Sort Largest to Smallest** ↯. <br> *The list is sorted by Years from 8 to 1.*

| 4 | Last Name | First Name | Years |
|---|---|---|---|
| 5 | McGee | Olivia | 8 |
| 6 | Alvizo | Alex | 7 |
| 7 | Zain | Elizabeth | 7 |
| 8 | Sutton | David | 6 |
| 9 | Huy | Lin | 5 |

## Create an Outline Automatically

3. Choose **Data→Outline→Group** 🔲 **menu ▾→Auto Outline** from the Ribbon.
   *Auto Outline grouped only columns H–I because Excel found total formulas in column J. The rows were not grouped because Excel found no summary formulas for them.*

4. Follow these steps to insert a blank row at row 10:

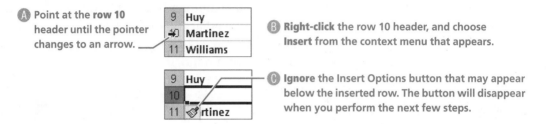

Ⓐ Point at the **row 10** header until the pointer changes to an arrow.

Ⓑ **Right-click** the row 10 header, and choose **Insert** from the context menu that appears.

Ⓒ **Ignore** the Insert Options button that may appear below the inserted row. The button will disappear when you perform the next few steps.

## Create Groups

*You will create one group for 1–4 years of experience and another group for 5–8 years. The blank row separates the two groups. Excel cannot create groups unless you insert blank rows between them.*

5. Select the **range C5:C9**.

6. Choose **Data→Outline→Group** 🔲, choose **Rows** from the Group dialog box, and click **OK**.

7. Select the **range C11:C19** and **group** the rows.

8. Experiment by clicking each **outline level** button, **expand** button, and **collapse** button to view the effects.
   *Outlining and grouping are alternatives to filtering.*

## Ungroup Rows

9. Select the **range E5:E9**, choose **Data→Outline→Ungroup** 🔲 from the Ribbon, and click **OK** in the Ungroup dialog box. (The Ungroup button may display as 🔲.)
   *When you select a cell range, the Ungroup command affects only outline levels that lie within the selected cells. Any cells outside the selection remain grouped.*

## Clear the Entire Outline

10. Select **cell E5** and choose **Data→Outline→Ungroup** 🔲 **menu ▾→Clear Outline** from the Ribbon.
    *When you select only one cell, all outline groups in the worksheet are cleared, including groups you created manually. You cannot undo after clearing the outline.*

11. Repeat **steps 5–7** to regroup the rows, and then **deselect** cells.

12. **Save** 💾 the changes.

# 9.7 Displaying Subtotals

**Video Lesson**    labyrinthelab.com/videos

The Subtotal ⊞ command creates subtotals and a grand total for numeric columns in a list. (The command is not available in tables.) You may specify the columns in which to display a subtotal. Excel automatically outlines rows of a list containing subtotals. The illustration shows the Sales by Region worksheet with subtotals displayed.

Excel automatically outlines the list after you create subtotals so that you may collapse or expand the details for each subtotaled group.

| | Region | State | ModSales | AppSales | Total Sales |
|---|---|---|---|---|---|
| 4 | **Region** | **State** | **ModSales** | **AppSales** | **Total Sales** |
| 5 | Central | CO | 162,000 | 151,000 | 313,000 |
| 6 | Central | CO | 210,000 | 340,000 | 550,000 |
| 7 | Central | IL | 120,000 | 170,000 | 290,000 |
| 8 | Central | IL | 230,000 | 120,000 | 350,000 |
| 9 | Central | IL | 234,000 | 560,000 | 794,000 |
| 10 | **Central Total** | | | | 2,297,000 |
| 11 | Eastern | FL | 140,000 | 130,000 | 270,000 |
| 12 | Eastern | FL | 450,000 | 450,000 | 900,000 |
| 13 | Eastern | MA | 228,000 | 216,000 | 444,000 |
| 14 | Eastern | MA | 317,000 | 513,000 | 830,000 |
| 15 | **Eastern Total** | | | | 2,444,000 |
| 16 | Western | CA | 156,000 | 160,000 | 316,000 |
| 17 | Western | CA | 340,000 | 700,000 | 1,040,000 |
| 18 | Western | CA | 446,000 | 120,000 | 566,000 |
| 19 | Western | CA | 602,000 | 622,000 | 1,224,000 |
| 20 | Western | WA | 123,000 | 130,000 | 253,000 |
| 21 | **Western Total** | | | | 3,399,000 |
| 22 | **Grand Total** | | | | 8,140,000 |

Subtotals were created in the Total Sales column for each region.

The grand total sums all detail cells in the column.

## Sorting the List

The first step in the subtotaling process is to sort the list on the column for which subtotals will be based. For example, sort on the State column if you want subtotals to appear each time the state changes. When you issue the Subtotal command, Excel groups all rows with the same state and calculates a subtotal for each group.

## The Subtotal Dialog Box

The Subtotal command on the Ribbon displays the Subtotal dialog box. The options in the dialog box determine the column for which subtotals are calculated and the function used in the calculations. The following illustration describes the options in the Subtotal dialog box.

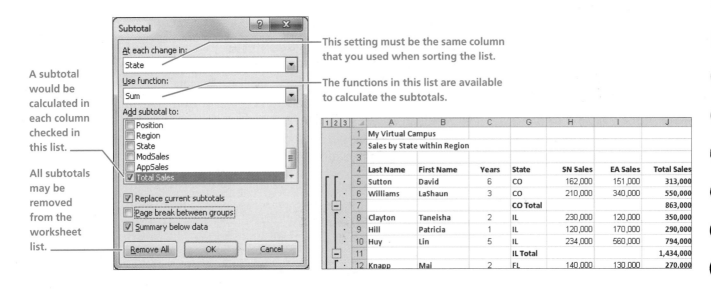

A subtotal would be calculated in each column checked in this list.

All subtotals may be removed from the worksheet list.

This setting must be the same column that you used when sorting the list.

The functions in this list are available to calculate the subtotals.

| QUICK REFERENCE | DISPLAYING AND REMOVING SUBTOTALS FROM WORKSHEET LISTS |
|---|---|
| **Task** | **Procedure** |
| Display subtotals | ■ Sort the list by the column on which you want subtotals to be based. |
| | ■ Choose Data→Outline→Subtotal from the Ribbon. |
| | ■ Set At Each Change In to the same column the sort is based on. |
| | ■ Choose the desired function from the Use Function drop-down list. |
| | ■ Choose the numeric columns you want subtotaled in the Add Subtotal To list. |
| Remove subtotals | ■ Choose Data→Outline→Subtotal from the Ribbon. |
| | ■ Click Remove All. |

## DEVELOP YOUR SKILLS 9.7.1

# Display Subtotals

*In this exercise, you will sort a worksheet list and display subtotals for each state. You also will use the Outline Bar to control the amount of detail displayed in the worksheet.*

### Sort a List by Region and State

1. Display the **Sales by State** worksheet of the Sales Performance workbook.

2. **Select** any cell in the list, choose **Data→Sort & Filter→Sort** [icon], set options to sort first by region and then by state as shown below, and click **OK**.

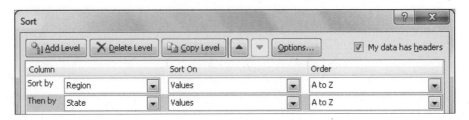

*The five Central rows are listed in state order, followed by four Eastern and then five Western rows. For subtotals to calculate correctly, the data for each state must be together. You could have sorted just by state without putting the states in region order.*

### Display Subtotals

3. Choose **Data→Outline→Subtotal** 🗏 from the Ribbon.
   *If an error message displays, make certain a cell is selected in the list.*

4. Follow these steps to set the subtotal options:

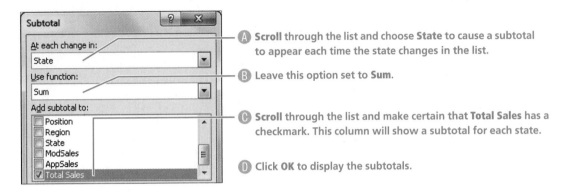

(A) **Scroll** through the list and choose **State** to cause a subtotal to appear each time the state changes in the list.

(B) Leave this option set to **Sum**.

(C) **Scroll** through the list and make certain that **Total Sales** has a checkmark. This column will show a subtotal for each state.

(D) Click **OK** to display the subtotals.

5. In **column J**, bold the six **subtotal** amounts and the **grand total** amount to make them stand out.
   *Take a few moments to review the subtotals and grand total before continuing.*

### Use the Outline Bar

6. Follow these steps to experiment with the Outline Bar for rows on the left side of the worksheet:

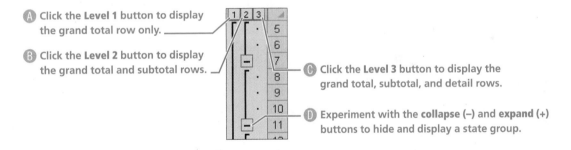

(A) Click the **Level 1** button to display the grand total row only.

(B) Click the **Level 2** button to display the grand total and subtotal rows.

(C) Click the **Level 3** button to display the grand total, subtotal, and detail rows.

(D) Experiment with the **collapse (–)** and **expand (+)** buttons to hide and display a state group.

*If you wanted to remove the subtotals from the list, you would use the Remove All button in the Subtotal dialog box. You will not remove subtotals in this exercise.*

7. **Save** 🖫 the changes changes, and **close** the workbook.

# 9.8 Concepts Review

Concepts Review    labyrinthelab.com/excel10

*To check your knowledge of the key concepts introduced in this lesson, complete the Concepts Review quiz by going to the URL listed above. If your classroom is using Labyrinth eLab, you may complete the Concepts Review quiz from within your eLab course.*

# Reinforce Your Skills

## Convert to a Table and Create Formulas

*In this exercise, you will convert a worksheet that tracks supporter information for a political campaign to a table. You will build total formulas, create a calculated column, and enter additional records.*

1. **Open** the rs-Reynolds Supporters workbook from the Lesson 09 folder in your file storage location. **Maximize** the window.

### Convert a Range to a Table

2. Select **cell A4**, choose **Home→Styles→Format As Table** from the Ribbon, choose a **table style**, and click **OK** to confirm the table range.
   *Your table style may be different from the one shown in the illustrations that follow.*

3. Choose **Design→Properties→Table Name** and change the existing name to **Contributions**.

4. Choose **Design→Table Style Options→Last Column** from the Ribbon.
   *The values in column G should appear bold.*

5. Select the column headings in **row 4** and **left-align** the text.
   *Left-aligning ensures that column headings are visible with their list buttons displayed.*

6. **Autofit** the table column widths so that all text is visible in the table.

### Create Formulas in the Total Row

7. Choose **Design→Table Style Options→Total Row** from the Ribbon to display the total row in row 20.

8. Select **cell E20** and choose **Count** from the total cell's list.

9. Select **cell F20** and choose **Average** from the total cell's list.

10. Format the **range F20:G20** in **Accounting** number format with **no decimal places**. (Do **not** select cell E20 because the calculation counts records rather than sums dollar amounts.)

| None |
| Average |
| Count |
| Count Numbers |
| Max |
| Min |
| Sum |
| StdDev |
| Var |
| More Functions... |
| 15 ▼ |

| 750 | 450 | 1,000 |
|-----|-----|-------|
| 15 | 404 | 9,075 |

### Create a Calculated Column

*You will build a formula that finds the difference between contributions for the current election and those for the last election.*

11. Select **cell H4**, type **Difference** as the column heading, and **autofit** the column width.

12. In **cell H5**, type an equals (**=**) sign.

13. Select **cell E5** and type a plus (**+**) sign.

14. Select **cell F5** and type a minus (**−**) sign.

15. Select **cell G5** and complete the formula.

16. With **cell H5** selected, **tap** F2 to display the formula in edit mode.
    *Notice the three structured references in the formula. Excel copied this formula to all cells in the column except the total row.*

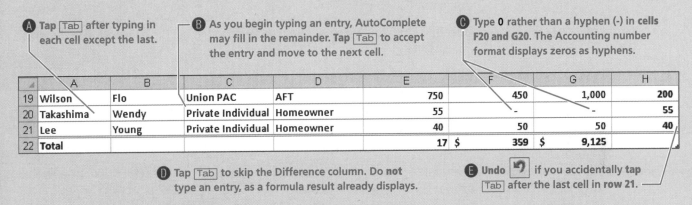

Difference ▾
=[@[Contribution 1]]+
[@[Contribution 2]]-
[@[Last Election
Contribution]]|

17. **Tap** Esc to exit edit mode without making any changes.

### Add Two Records

18. Select **cell H19** and **tap** Tab to create a new blank row.

19. Follow these steps to enter two records in rows 20–21:

**A** Tap Tab after typing in each cell except the last.

**B** As you begin typing an entry, AutoComplete may fill in the remainder. **Tap** Tab to accept the entry and move to the next cell.

**C** Type **0** rather than a hyphen (-) in cells **F20** and **G20**. The Accounting number format displays zeros as hyphens.

| | A | B | C | D | E | F | G | H |
|----|----------|-------|-------------------|-----------|------|-----|-------|-----|
| 19 | Wilson | Flo | Union PAC | AFT | 750 | 450 | 1,000 | 200 |
| 20 | Takashima | Wendy | Private Individual | Homeowner | 55 | - | - | 55 |
| 21 | Lee | Young | Private Individual | Homeowner | 40 | 50 | 50 | 40 |
| 22 | Total | | | | 17 $ | 359 $ | 9,125 | |

**D** Tap Tab to skip the Difference column. Do **not** type an entry, as a formula result already displays.

**E** Undo ↺ if you accidentally tap Tab after the last cell in **row 21**.

20. **Save** 💾 the changes and leave the workbook **open** for the next exercise.

### REINFORCE YOUR SKILLS 9.2

## Sort and Filter a Table

*In this exercise, you will sort table records and filter by number. You also will filter by icons created by a conditional formatting rule.*

*Before You Begin: You must have completed Reinforce Your Skills 9.1 and the rs-Reynolds Supporters workbook should be open. Your table style may look different from the one shown in the illustrations that follow.*

### Sort the Table

1. Choose the **Difference** column heading **AutoFilter** ▾ button→**Sort Largest to Smallest** ⤵ from the list.
   *The table rows are sorted from largest to smallest in value.*

### Filter by Number

2. Choose **Contribution 1** column heading **AutoFilter** ▾ button→**Number Filters**→**Above Average** from the list.
   *The filter displays seven records higher than the average contribution amount.*

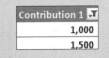

Contribution 1 ▾
1,000
1,500

3. Choose the **Contribution 1** column heading **AutoFilter** ⤓ button→**Number Filters**→**Top 10** from the list, and click **OK** in the Top 10 AutoFilter dialog box.
   *The filter displays the 10 highest difference amounts sorted from largest to smallest.*

4. Choose the **Contribution 1** column heading **AutoFilter** ⤓ button→**Clear Filter From "Contribution 1."**
   *The table view is restored to all 17 records.*

### Apply Conditional Formatting and Filter by Color

5. Select the **range E5:E21**.

6. Choose **Home→Styles→Conditional Formatting** 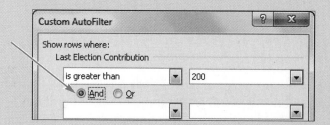**→Icon Sets** from the Ribbon, and choose **3 Stars** under the Ratings category.
*The conditional formatting rule applies a star icon to each cell, and the yellow solid star represents the highest values in the column.*

| Contribution 1 |
| --- |
| ☆ 1,000 |
| ⭐ 1,500 |
| ☆ 800 |
| ☆ 450 |

7. Choose the **Contribution 1** column heading **AutoFilter** ▾ **button→ Filter by Color**, and choose the solid yellow star from the Filter by Cell Icon list.
*Two records containing the solid yellow star display. You can filter by any icon created by conditional formatting to locate trends in the data.*

8. Sort the **Difference** column from **largest to smallest** if its column heading filter button does not display the sort icon.

9. **Save** 🖫 the changes and **close** the workbook.

---

### REINFORCE YOUR SKILLS 9.3

## Filter a List

*In this exercise, you will continue examining the Reynolds Supporters data as a list rather than a table. You will filter records by more than one criterion in a column.*

### Sort the List

1. **Open** the rs-Contribution List workbook from the Lesson 09 folder in your file storage location.

2. Select **cell A4**, and choose **Data→Sort & Filter→Filter** 🔻 from the Ribbon.
*Columns A–H in the list display the same column heading AutoFilter buttons as for a table.*

3. Choose the **Last Election Contribution** column heading **AutoFilter** ▾ button and choose Sort Largest to Smallest from the list.
*The rows are sorted from largest to smallest.*

### Filter by Two Criteria

4. Choose the **Last Election Contribution** column heading **AutoFilter** button**→Number Filters→Greater Than** from the Ribbon.

5. In the Custom Filter dialog box, enter **200** in the box to the right of Is Greater Than.
*Notice that the And option is selected, which allows you to select an additional criterion.*

Custom AutoFilter

Show rows where:
Last Election Contribution

| is greater than | ▾ | 200 | ▾ |
| ● And ○ Or | | | |
| | ▾ | | ▾ |

6. Click the **arrow** below the And option, and choose **Is Less Than** from the menu.

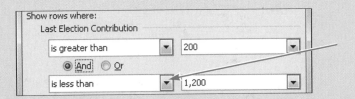

7. Enter **1200** in the box to the right of Is Less Than and click **OK**.
   *The filter displays five contribution records that meet the criteria you chose.*

| | A | B | C | D | E | F | G | H |
|---|---|---|---|---|---|---|---|---|
| 1 | Bobbi Fessler Reynolds for City Council | | | | | | | |
| 2 | Supporters Table | | | | | | | |
| 3 | | | | | | | | |
| 4 | Last Name | First Name | Contact Type | Organization | Contribution 1 | Contribution 2 | Last Election Contribution | Difference |
| 9 | Cho | Benjamin | Union PAC | IAFF | 750 | 250 | 1,000 | - |
| 12 | Campo | Maria | Union PAC | NEA | 800 | 1,000 | 1,000 | 800 |
| 15 | Wilson | Flo | Union PAC | AFT | 750 | 450 | 1,000 | 200 |
| 17 | Rogers | Thomasina | Business Owner | Steve's Auto Care | 350 | 250 | 500 | 100 |
| 19 | Pretinger | Deneice | Business Owner | Cablespace | 250 | 200 | 250 | 200 |

8. **Save** the changes, and leave the workbook **open** for the next exercise.

REINFORCE YOUR SKILLS 9.4

# Create Subtotals and Use Outlining Tools

*In this exercise, you will duplicate a worksheet and remove a filter. Then you will create subtotals for the contribution amounts by each type of contact.*

*Before You Begin: You must have completed Reinforce Your Skills 9.3, and the rs-Contribution List workbook should be open.*

## Copy the List Worksheet

1. Rename **Sheet1** of the rs-Contribution List workbook as **List**.

2. **Right-click** the List sheet tab and choose **Move or Copy** from the context menu.

3. Set the dialog box options as shown to create a copy, and click **OK**.

4. Rename the copied sheet as **Subtotals**.

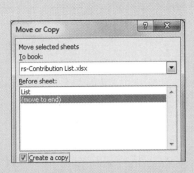

## Remove the Filter and Sort by Contact Type

5. Clear the filter from the **Last Election Contribution** column of the table.
   *All 17 records should be displayed, and they still are sorted by last election contribution in largest to smallest order.*

6. Sort by **Contact Type** in **A to Z** order.

## Create Subtotals

7. Choose **Data→Outline→Subtotal** 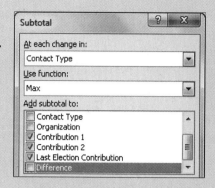 from the Ribbon, and set options as shown.

   *You will find the maximum contribution for each contact type in three columns of the worksheet list.*

8. Click the **collapse (–)** button for Private Individual Max and Union PAC Max in the outline area.

*Only the Business Owner detail rows display.*

9. Click the **Level 3** button in the upper-left corner of the worksheet to expand all detail rows.

10. Use an outline button to **collapse** the list to display just the **subtotals** and **grand maximum**.

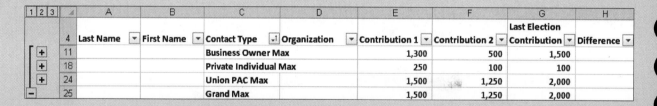

| | | | Last Name | First Name | Contact Type | Organization | Contribution 1 | Contribution 2 | Last Election Contribution | Difference |
|---|---|---|---|---|---|---|---|---|---|---|
| + | 11 | | | | Business Owner Max | | 1,300 | 500 | 1,500 | |
| + | 18 | | | | Private Individual Max | | 250 | 100 | 100 | |
| + | 24 | | | | Union PAC Max | | 1,500 | 1,250 | 2,000 | |
| − | 25 | | | | Grand Max | | 1,500 | 1,250 | 2,000 | |

*Notice that no formula results display in the Difference column. You did not choose to calculate that column while setting up the outline options.*

11. **Save** 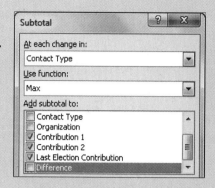 the changes and **close** the workbook.

# Apply Your Skills

## Convert to a Table and Create Formulas

*In this exercise, you will convert a worksheet range to a table. You will change a formula in the total row, create a calculated column, and add a record. You will also sort the table.*

1. **Open** the as-Westside Employee Compensation workbook from the Lesson 09 folder in your file storage location. **Maximize** the window.

2. **Convert** the worksheet range to a **banded row table** style of your choice.

3. **Rename** the table as `Retirement Plan` following Excel's rules for naming tables.

4. **Edit** column heading names as necessary and adjust **column widths**.

5. **Format** the numbers in **columns D and E** with **Comma Style**. You determine the number of decimal places.

6. Change the **formula** in the **total row** to one that averages the retirement plan contributions. Change the **label** in cell A18 to `Average`.

7. Create a **calculated column** that computes Retirement Plan Contributions divided by Compensation. Format the results with **Percent Style**. Use `% of Compensation` as the column heading.

8. Add the record for **Uyen** shown in the illustration.

9. Sort by **% of Compensation** from **largest to smallest**.

| | A | B | C | D | E | F |
|---|---|---|---|---|---|---|
| 1 | Westside Electric Supplies | | | | | |
| 2 | *Employee Compensation Table* | | | | | |
| 3 | | | | | | |
| 4 | Last Name | First Name | Category | Compensation | Retirement Plan Contributions | % of Compensation |
| 5 | Wilson | Larry | Salaried | 89,000 | 21,890 | 25% |
| 6 | Monroe | James | Hourly | 34,000 | 4,250 | 13% |
| 7 | Erickson | Bryan | Hourly | 38,000 | 4,500 | 12% |
| 8 | Barton | Lisa | Salaried | 51,000 | 6,000 | 12% |
| 9 | Zurlow | Jacob | Hourly | 30,000 | 3,450 | 12% |
| 10 | Jackson | Samuel | Salaried | 45,000 | 4,700 | 10% |
| 11 | Uyen | Ty | Salaried | 56,000 | 4,700 | 8% |
| 12 | Thomas | Lyn | Salaried | 34,000 | 2,700 | 8% |
| 13 | Ellison | Linda | Salaried | 32,000 | 2,500 | 8% |
| 14 | Parades | Lisa | Hourly | 31,000 | 2,300 | 7% |
| 15 | Chin | Raymond | Salaried | 56,000 | 3,450 | 6% |
| 16 | Watson | Guillermo | Hourly | 27,000 | 1,600 | 6% |
| 17 | Plavan | Jaime | Salaried | 45,000 | 1,900 | 4% |
| 18 | Hughes | Jason | Hourly | 23,000 | - | 0% |
| 19 | Average | | | | 4,567 | |

The completed Employee Compensation table

10. **Save** 💾 the changes and **close** the workbook.

# Sort and Filter a Table

*In this exercise, you will sort table records and filter by text and number.*

1. **Open** the as-Monrovia Media Sales workbook from the Lesson 09 folder. **Maximize** the window.

2. Sort by **Sales** from **most to least** as shown in the illustration.

3. **Filter** by **New York** in the Market column.

4. **Copy and paste** the filter results to **cell A21**.

5. In **cell A20**, **type** an appropriate title to describe the filter results.

6. **Clear** the filter.
   *Now you will complete another filter.*

7. **Filter** for units sold between **44 and 55 units**.

8. **Copy and paste** the filter results below the New York market filter results.

9. **Type** an appropriate title to describe the filter results.

10. **Clear** the filter.

11. Make certain that the table and two sets of pasted results will **print on one page**.

| | A | B | C | D | E | F | G |
|---|---|---|---|---|---|---|---|
| 1 | Monrovia Media | | | | | | |
| 2 | *Media Sales Table* | | | | | | |
| 3 | | | | | | | |
| 4 | Last Name | First Name | Units Sold | Week | Promotion | Market | Sales |
| 5 | Mathis | Gerhardt | 93 | 1-Aug | Senior Sales Rep | Cincinnati | 76,200 |
| 6 | Huy | Lin | 81 | 15-Sep | Sales Rep | Dallas | 65,200 |
| 7 | Zain | Elizabeth | 64 | 1-Feb | Senior Sales Rep | New York | 57,800 |
| 8 | Clayton | Taneisha | 79 | 1-Mar | Sales Rep | New York | 55,100 |
| 9 | Knapp | Mai | 62 | 15-Nov | Telemarketer | Dallas | 42,100 |
| 10 | McGee | Olivia | 62 | 1-Jun | Sales Rep | Phoenix | 31,700 |
| 11 | Smith | Jacqui | 55 | 15-Apr | Telemarketer | Phoenix | 31,200 |
| 12 | Alvizo | Alex | 47 | 1-Mar | Senior Sales Rep | Phoenix | 28,700 |
| 13 | Hasan | Taz | 47 | 15-Jul | Telemarketer | Las Vegas | 25,100 |
| 14 | Martinez | Carlos | 45 | 15-Sep | Senior Sales Rep | Las Vegas | 23,700 |
| 15 | Williams | LaShaun | 43 | 1-Sep | Las Vegas | Las Vegas | 20,200 |
| 16 | Richards | Paul | 43 | 15-Jun | Telemarketer | Las Vegas | 12,800 |
| 17 | Cray | Karen | 39 | 1-Sep | Telemarketer | New York | 11,590 |
| 18 | Hill | Patricia | 27 | 1-Jun | Sales Rep | Cincinnati | 9,000 |
| 19 | | | | | | | |
| 20 | *New York Market* | | | | | | |
| 21 | Last Name | First Name | Units Sold | Week | Promotion | Market | Sales |
| 22 | Zain | Elizabeth | 64 | 1-Feb | Senior Sales Rep | New York | 57,800 |

The completed Media Sales table

12. **Save** 💾 the changes and **close** the workbook.

# Outline a Worksheet and Use Subtotals

*In this exercise, you will sort records in a list that tracks monthly animal care expenses by cost, age, and health of the animals. You will outline the worksheet and display subtotals that calculate averages.*

1. **Open** the as-March Expenses workbook from the Lesson 09 folder.

2. Perform a **multicolumn sort** by Age and Health.
   *Now you will display subtotals as shown in the illustration below.*

3. Base **subtotals** on the animals' health.

4. Make subtotals **average** each of the cost columns.

5. **Bold** the subtotal and grand total amounts.
   *Now you will outline the worksheet.*

6. **Group** Shelter Cost and Veterinary Cost, but **do not** group the Total Costs column.

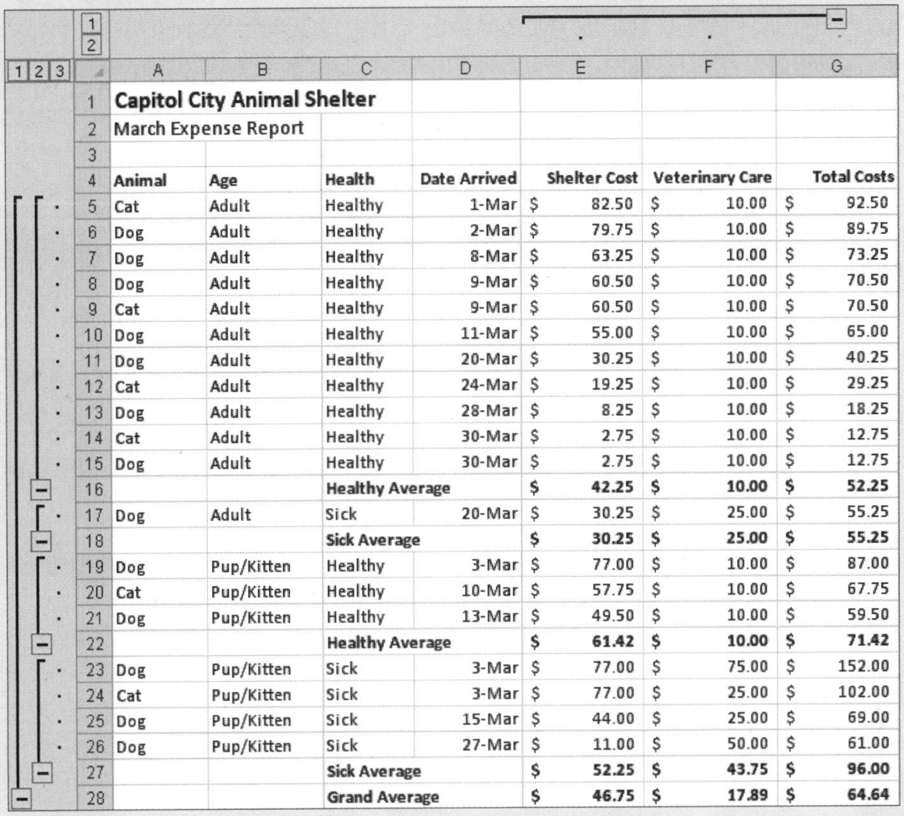

The outline after grouping

7. Use **outline buttons** to hide details for the two Pup/Kitten groups (not shown in the illustration).

8. Use **outline buttons** to hide the Shelter Cost and Veterinary Cost columns (not shown in the illustration).

9. **Save** 💾 the changes and **close** the workbook.

# Critical Thinking & Work-Readiness Skills

*In the course of working through the following Microsoft Office-based Critical Thinking exercises, you will also be utilizing various work-readiness skills, some of which are listed next to each exercise. Go to* labyrinthelab.com/workreadiness *to learn more about the work-readiness skills.*

## 9.1 Format Data

**WORK-READINESS SKILLS APPLIED**

- Seeing things in the mind's eye
- Using computers to process information
- Organizing and maintaining information\

Bruce Carter wants to analyze the data for My Virtual Campus Corporation's clients. He needs first to convert his data into a professional table and keep track of the number of schools he supports. Open ct-Customers (Lesson 09 folder). Convert the data to a table with the headings **Area**, **Customer**, **Module**, and **Sales**. Design the table in an appropriate professional style. Finally, create a total row and use it to calculate the number of customers. Save your work as **ct-Customers [Your Last Name]**. Keep the file open. If working in a group, discuss the differences between the Count and the Sum functions. If working alone, type your response in a Word document named **ct-Questions** saved to your Lesson 09 folder.

## 9.2 Add a Record and Sort

**WORK-READINESS SKILLS APPLIED**

- Solving problems
- Using computers to process information
- Organizing and maintaining information

Bruce realizes he needs to include Western State College to his list of customers. He then wants to analyze which customers are using the different modules. After adding the new data below to the end of the list in ct-Customers [Your Last Name], sort the Module column alphabetically. Revise the worksheet subtitle in cell A2 to **by Module**. Save your work and keep the file open.

| Area | Customer | Module | Sales |
|------|----------|--------|-------|
| 1 | Western State College | Support 1 | 3,095 |

## 9.3 Copy Data to a New Worksheet

**WORK-READINESS SKILLS APPLIED**

- Managing the self
- Using computers to process information
- Organizing and maintaining information

Bruce realizes he can copy the original data into a new worksheet and work with it without losing the original data. He will name both worksheets. Continue with ct-Customers [Your Last Name]. Make certain that the table has a total row. Rename the first worksheet to **Original**. Create a second worksheet by copying the first worksheet. Name the second worksheet **Test**. In the Test worksheet, perform a two-column sort by Customer and then by Sales. You choose the sort order. Revise the worksheet subtitle in cell A2 appropriately. Save and close the file.

# Adding Graphics to Worksheets

## LESSON OUTLINE

## LEARNING BJECTIVES

After studying this lesson, you will be able to:

- Use keywords to locate images in picture collections
- Insert and modify pictures and clip art on worksheets
- Draw, modify, and add text to shapes
- Customize SmartArt to convey ideas, processes, and data relationships

Enhancing your workbooks with graphics may help you illustrate the worksheet theme and call attention to important details. In this lesson, you will locate picture sources and then insert photos and clip art on worksheets. You will draw shapes using Excel's large gallery of drawing tools and move, size, rotate, and crop images. You will correct photos and apply special effects to images. With SmartArt, you will create text charts that visually demonstrate a process or relationship.

# Enhancing Data with Graphics

Recently promoted to a business analyst position, Kevin Hottel is eager to take on his next project. His company, My Virtual Campus Corporation, sells its social networking intranet to colleges and universities. The finance director is

concerned that the current year's sales are not as strong as the previous year's. Kevin has been asked to present several sales performance worksheets at a management strategy meeting. The data and charts already have been entered into the workbook. Kevin thinks that adding some graphics will highlight and connect the key points of his presentation. He will add graphics to several worksheets while applying some principles of good design. He will work with the graphics shown in the following illustration, including a picture file and a shape containing text.

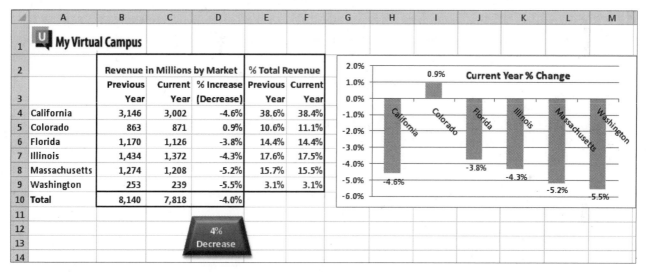

Along with the chart, this worksheet displays a picture and a shape with text.

# 10.1 Using Illustrations with Excel

**Video Lesson** labyrinthelab.com/videos

You can dress up your worksheets using the professionally designed clip art provided with Microsoft Office. You may also insert your own pictures, such as a company logo or a scanned picture.

## Design Principles

Graphics are fun to create, but that should not be the reason that you add them to a workbook. Before you add art, review the generally accepted design rules that follow.

- Each graphic should have a purpose, such as to call attention to an important number, summarize data, or contribute to the worksheet theme.
- Graphics should enhance and not distract or clutter the worksheet.
- The image colors, size, alignment, and other formatting should contribute toward a balanced appearance and consistent style with other worksheet objects.
- Copyright law prohibits the use of many images for commercial use without permission. However, there are also websites featuring copyright-free art. The clip art that comes with Excel is also free to use as long as you don't try to resell the clip art itself.

## The Illustrations Group on the Ribbon

To place a graphic on the worksheet, start with one of the tools in the Illustrations group on the Insert ribbon.

# 10.2 Inserting Pictures and Clip Art

The Picture  command adds an image saved as a file. Sources may include a digital camera, scanner, and purchased images. The Clip Art command adds a drawing or photo from a gallery of images available in Microsoft Office. You may adjust several image characteristics, including the sharpness, colors, and brightness. You may apply picture styles, such as a picture frame or blurred edges. Microsoft Office 2010 offers several new features for working with pictures. You can remove the background from a picture, apply a preset artistic effect, and capture a screen shot of another window to insert as a picture in a worksheet. Immediately after it is inserted, the picture or clip art image displays with sizing handles and a rotation lever, as shown in the illustration at right.

An inserted clip art image or picture displays sizing handles and a rotation lever.

# Inserting a Picture from a File

After you choose the Picture command from the Ribbon, Excel displays the Insert Picture dialog box, similar to the Open dialog box for workbooks. Navigate to the folder containing the desired picture and select its file. A variety of image file formats, including JPEG and TIFF, are compatible with Excel.

| QUICK REFERENCE | INSERTING IMAGES |
|---|---|
| **Task** | **Procedure** |
| Insert a picture | ■ Select a cell in the worksheet.<br>■ Choose Insert→Illustrations→Picture from the Ribbon.<br>■ In the Insert Picture dialog box, navigate to the drive and folder that contains the picture file.<br>■ Select the picture file and choose Insert. |
| Insert clip art | ■ Select a cell in the worksheet.<br>■ Choose Insert→Illustrations→Clip Art from the Ribbon to display the Clip Art task pane.<br>■ Type a keyword in the Search For box.<br>■ Choose the Results Should Be menu ▼, and place a checkmark next to the desired media types. Click on the task pane to collapse the menu.<br>■ Click Go.<br>■ Scroll through the clips that appear, and click or drag to move a clip to the worksheet. |
| Insert a screenshot of a non-Excel window into a worksheet | ■ Click in the desired window to be captured.<br>■ Switch to Excel, and do one of the following:<br>  ◆ Choose Insert→Illustrations→Screenshot from the Ribbon, and choose the desired window from the thumbnails list.<br>  *or*<br>  ◆ Choose Insert→Illustrations→Screenshot →Screen Clipping from the Ribbon, and drag to select the desired area of the window that appears. |

## DEVELOP YOUR SKILLS 10.2.1
## Insert a Picture

*In this exercise, you will add a picture to a worksheet.*

1. **Open** the Revenue Comparison workbook from the Lesson 10 folder in your file storage location.

2. **Maximize** ▣ the window.

3. **Display** each of the three worksheets to become familiar with their contents.
   *You will add a picture to the By Market worksheet.*

4. Display the **By Market** worksheet.

5. Select **cell B12**, and choose **Insert→Illustrations→Picture** from the Ribbon.

6. **Navigate** to the Lesson 10 folder in your file storage location.

7. Notice that none of the Excel workbook file names are displayed because the Files of Type option is set to **All Pictures**.

*Depending on your Windows version, the options may vary slightly from the illustration.*

8. Select the **MyVirtualCampus** file, and click **Insert**.
*The upper-left corner of the picture appears on cell B12, which you selected, but the picture is not attached to the cell. You will format this picture in a later exercise.*

| | A | B | C | D | E | F | G | H |
|---|---|---|---|---|---|---|---|---|
| 10 | Total | 8,140 | 7,818 | -4.0% | | | -6.0% | |
| 11 | | | | | | | | |
| 12 | | | | | | | | |
| 13 | | | | | | | | |
| 14 | | | | | | | | |
| 15 | | | | | | | | |
| 16 | | | | | | | | |

9. **Save** 💾 the changes to your workbook.

# Inserting a Screenshot

**Video Lesson**    labyrinthelab.com/videos

You can insert a screenshot of any other non-Excel window or a specific area of that window into a worksheet. For example, you can capture a certain area of a web page or Microsoft Word document. You may format the screenshot as you would any other picture.

**DEVELOP YOUR SKILLS 10.2.2**

## Insert a Screenshot

*In this exercise, you will open a Word document. Then you will take a screenshot of a specific area of the document to insert as a picture on a worksheet.*

### Open a Word Document

1. Choose **Start** ⊕ →**All Programs**→**Microsoft Office**→**Microsoft Word 2010**.
*The names on the Start menu may vary on your computer.*

2. In Word, open the **Expense Data** file from the Lesson 10 folder in your file storage location.
*This document contains a note about numbers to be used in the Revenue Comparison workbook.*

### Insert a Screenshot into a Worksheet

3. Click the **Excel** application button on the Windows taskbar at the bottom of the screen to switch to the Excel window.

4. Display the **Analysis** worksheet of the Revenue Comparison workbook.

5. Select **cell B15**.

6. Choose **Insert→Illustrations→Screenshot** 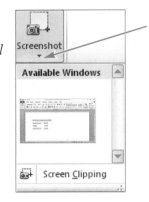 **menu ▾** from the Ribbon.
*Notice that the Available Windows section of the menu displays a thumbnail of the Word window. You could insert the entire window by selecting the thumbnail. Instead, you will select only the text area for the screenshot.*

7. Choose **Screen Clipping** from the menu.
*The Word window appears dimmed, and the mouse pointer appears as a plus (+) sign.*

8. Follow these steps to capture a screenshot area of the Word window:

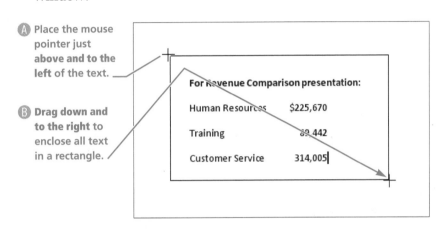

Ⓐ Place the mouse pointer just **above and to the left** of the text.

Ⓑ **Drag down and to the right** to enclose all text in a rectangle.

For Revenue Comparison presentation:

Human Resources    $225,670

Training    89,442

Customer Service    314,005

Ⓒ **Release** the mouse button to capture the screenshot.

*The Excel window appears, and your selection appears as a picture at cell B15. The insertion point (text cursor) may display in your screenshot; this is okay. If you are not satisfied with the image, tap* Delete *to erase it, and repeat steps 5–8.*

|  | A | B | C |
|---|---|---|---|
| 13 | **Marketing** | | |
| 14 | | | |
| 15 | | **For Revenue Comparison presentation:** | |
| 16 | | | |
| 17 | | Human Resources    $225,670 | |
| 18 | | Training    89,442 | |
| 19 | | | |
| 20 | | Customer Service    314,005 | |
| 21 | | | |

9. Switch to the **Word** window in the Windows taskbar, and **exit** Word.

10. **Save**  the changes to your workbook.

# Inserting Clip Art

**Video Lesson**  labyrinthelab.com/videos

The Clip Art ⊞ command on the Insert ribbon displays the Clip Art task pane. This pane lets you search for clip art using keywords. Every clip art image provided with Microsoft Office has a number of keywords associated with it that describe the image. For example, an image of a person using a laptop computer may be located using keywords such as *people, laptop,* and *computer.*

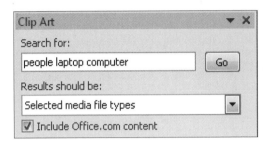

The Clip Art task pane lets you search Excel's large clip art collections.

## Clip Art Collections

The clip art that comes with Excel is from essentially two different sources. You may restrict the search to only the clip art collections installed with Microsoft Office on your computer, which are quite limited. Excel also can search a much larger collection on the Microsoft website. This web-based collection is only available when you are connected to the Internet and the Include Office.com Content option has a checkmark.

## Clip Art Types

Clip art comes in four different media types. However, only two of these types actually work with Excel. You may limit a clip art search to specific media types.

- **Illustrations**—These are drawings in a variety of designs and colors.
- **Photographs**—These are images from a camera.
- **Videos**—These are simple animations. They do not work in Excel, and an inserted video displays as a single still picture instead. (These videos do work in other Office applications, such as PowerPoint.)
- **Audio**—These are brief sound clips. Sound clips do not play directly in Excel but can be played in Windows Media Player or in some other Office applications.

### DEVELOP YOUR SKILLS 10.2.3
## Insert Clip Art

*In this exercise, you will search for clip art images and add one to a worksheet.*

1. Display the **Analysis** worksheet in the Revenue Comparison workbook, if necessary.

2. Select **cell C5**, and choose **Insert→Illustrations→Clip Art** ⊞ from the Ribbon.
   *The Clip Art task pane appears on the right of the Excel window. The selections from a previous search may display.*

3. Follow these steps to conduct a search:

Ⓐ **Type** the keywords `people laptop computer` in the Search For box.

Ⓑ Display the **Results Should Be** menu.

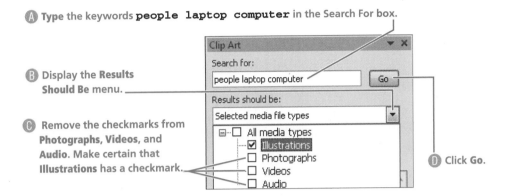

Ⓒ Remove the checkmarks from **Photographs**, **Videos**, and **Audio**. Make certain that **Illustrations** has a checkmark.

Ⓓ Click **Go.**

*After a pause, results of the search appear in the body of the Clip Art task pane.*

If you are not connected to the Internet, very few images will show in your search results. Choose any image if the one below is not available.

4. **Scroll** through the clips that appear and **click** the one shown at right. *The image displays at cell C5.*

5. **Close** the Clip Art task pane when you are finished.

6. **Save** 💾 the changes to your workbook.

## Moving, Sizing, and Rotating Images

**Video Lesson**   labyrinthelab.com/videos

When you select a picture or clip art image, sizing handles and a rotation handle appear. You can size, move, and rotate a selected object as described in the following illustrations.

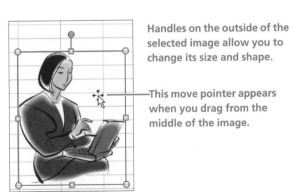

Handles on the outside of the selected image allow you to change its size and shape.

This move pointer appears when you drag from the middle of the image.

The Rotation handle allows you to rotate the image.

To delete a graphic, select it and tap Delete .

# Move, Rotate, and Size Images

*In this exercise, you will modify the appearance of the picture and clip art image you inserted in previous exercises.*

### Adjust Clip Art

1. Follow these steps to move, rotate, and size the laptop computer clip art image in the Analysis worksheet of the Revenue Comparison workbook:
   *Your image may be different from the one shown.*

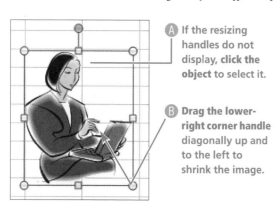

Ⓐ If the resizing handles do not display, **click the object** to select it.

Ⓑ **Drag the lower-right corner handle** diagonally up and to the left to shrink the image.

Ⓒ To rotate, **drag the circle** in the rotation handle to the **left**. (If your image is different, you may need to rotate to the right.)

Ⓓ **Point** anywhere in the image except on a resizing handle and drag to move so that the top of the image is near the top of **cell F3**. Then **tap** the arrow keys several times to nudge the image in small increments.

### Delete and Restore an Image

2. **Select** the laptop computer image and **tap** ⌷Delete⌷.
   *The image is removed.*

3. **Undo** 🔄 the delete.

### Adjust and Duplicate an Image

4. Display the **By Market** worksheet.

5. Follow these steps to size, move, and duplicate the image:

Ⓐ **Select** the picture to display its handles.

Ⓑ **Drag the upper-right corner handle** diagonally down and to the left to shrink the image.

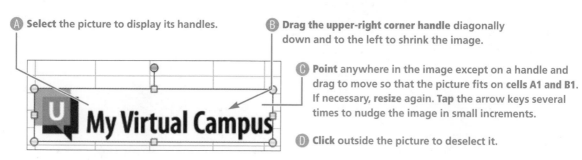

Ⓒ **Point** anywhere in the image except on a handle and drag to move so that the picture fits on **cells A1 and B1**. If necessary, **resize** again. **Tap** the arrow keys several times to nudge the image in small increments.

Ⓓ **Click** outside the picture to deselect it.

*The image should look similar to the following example.*

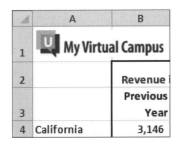

6. **Select** the picture, use `Ctrl`+`C` to copy, and then **deselect** the picture.

7. Display the **By Region** worksheet, select **cell A1**, and use `Ctrl`+`V` to paste.

8. Move the picture, if necessary, so that it fits attractively on **cells A1 and B1**.

9. **Deselect** the picture.

10. **Save** 💾 the changes to your workbook.

# Scaling and Cropping Images

**Video Lesson**   labyrinthelab.com/videos

When you select an image, various Picture Tools become available on the Ribbon. To adjust most characteristics, you will use the Format ribbon.

## *Scaling*

Scaling a picture reduces its overall size to a percentage of its original size. The effect is equal to having dragged a corner handle on the object. You can scale more precisely, however, by typing a number of inches in the Ribbon or using the spinner arrows to increase or decrease the scale in increments.

A picture at its original size

The picture scaled to 50 percent of its original size

Changing the height or width also changes the other dimension in the same proportion.

This button launches the Size and Properties dialog box.

The cropping and scaling options in the Format Ribbon

## Cropping

 If you want to use part of a picture or clip art image, you may use the Crop command. The object remains the same size, and you drag the handles inward to cut off one or more edges of the image.

The mouse pointer displays as the cropping tool.

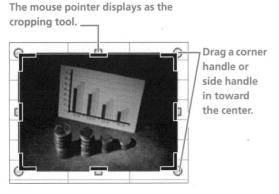

Drag a corner handle or side handle in toward the center.

The picture ready to be cropped

The picture after cropping each of its four sides

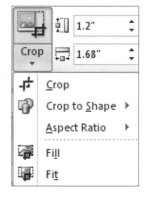

The Crop menu options

## The Format Picture Dialog Box

You may launch the Format Picture dialog box from the Format ribbon to set a number of options precisely when you need the same measurements for multiple objects or prefer not to use the mouse. In the Size category of the dialog box, you may set the height, width, rotation, and scale percentage. The object's original size also is listed. A separate Crop category contains settings for the crop dimensions.

The Size category of the Format Picture dialog box

## Resetting an Image

 If you want to start over, you may reset the image to its original characteristics by choosing a command from the Reset Picture menu on the Format ribbon or the Reset command in the Size category of the Format Picture dialog box. Use Undo to reverse only the previous change.

The Reset Picture & Size command removes all changes to the image. If you are satisfied with the size and cropping, you may want to copy and paste a duplicate image before experimenting with additional effects.

DEVELOP YOUR SKILLS 10.2.5
## Scale and Crop an Image

*In this exercise, you will scale a clip art image to smaller than its original size and crop the image.*

### Scale Using the Ribbon

1. Display the **Analysis** worksheet in the Revenue Comparison workbook.

2. Select **cell B3**, and choose **Insert→Illustrations→Clip Art** from the Ribbon.

3. In the Clip Art task pane, type **profit arrows** as the keyword. Place a checkmark next to **Include Office.com Content**. Set the Results Should Be option so that only **Illustrations** has a checkmark, and click **Go**.

4. **Scroll** through the results, and **click** the image shown to the right. If this image is not available, select an appropriate image for the worksheet. You may need to change the keyword to *profit* or *business* to choose a different image if no Internet connection is available.
   *The clip art image is displayed at cell B3.*

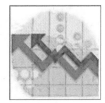

5. **Close** ☒ the Clip Art task pane.

6. If the profit arrows image does not display sizing handles, **select** the image.

7. Choose the **Format** ribbon if it is not already displayed.

8. Follow these steps to scale the image using the Ribbon:

Ⓐ In the Size group on the Format ribbon, click the ▼ spinner for **Shape Width** several times.

2.81"

2.98"

Size

Ⓑ In the Size group on the Format Ribbon, click the ▼ spinner for **Shape Height** several times. Notice that either command scales both the width and the height together. Your width and height may be different than shown.

## Scale Using the Format Picture Dialog Box

9. In the Size group on the Format ribbon, click the **dialog box launcher** button.

10. Follow these steps to scale the profit arrows image using the Size category of the Format Picture dialog box:

Ⓐ In the Scale section (not the Size and Rotate section), **drag** to select the current height and type **80**. Although the Width displays at its original percentage, notice that the Lock Aspect Ratio is turned on. The width will adjust in proportion to the height.

Ⓑ Tap ⌈Enter⌉ or choose Close to exit the dialog box.

*The image displays at 80 percent of its original size.*

11. **Right-click** the profit arrows image and choose **Size and Properties** from the pop-up (or context) menu.

12. In the Size and Properties dialog box, edit the scale width to **50** and **tap** ⌈Enter⌉. If you are using a different image than the one shown, use an appropriate percentage. *The image is half its original size. The height scales in proportion to the width that you set.*

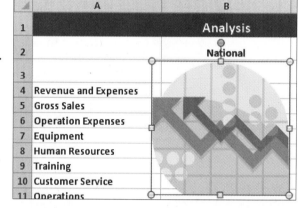

## Crop Using the Cropping Tool on the Ribbon

13. If the profit arrows image does not display sizing handles, **select** the image.

14. Choose **Format→Size→Crop** from the Ribbon.

15. Follow these steps to crop the image:

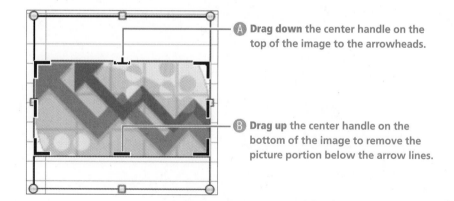

Ⓐ **Drag down** the center handle on the top of the image to the arrowheads.

Ⓑ **Drag up** the center handle on the bottom of the image to remove the picture portion below the arrow lines.

*Your cropped image may look similar to the following illustration.*

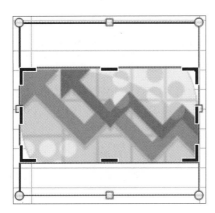

16. **Experiment** with the cropping handles until you are satisfied with the image. If needed, scale the image larger or smaller so that it balances well with other objects on the worksheet.

17. Click away from the image to deselect the cropping tool.

**Reset the Image to the Original Properties**

18. Select the **profit arrows** image, and choose **Format→Adjust→Reset Picture menu ▾→Reset Picture and Size** from the Ribbon.
    *All changes are removed, and the original image is restored.*

19. **Undo** 🔄 the reset.

20. Move the profit arrows image to **cell F11**.

21. **Click** outside the image to deselect it.

22. **Save** 💾 the changes to your workbook.

# Correcting Images and Applying Special Effects

**Video Lesson**   labyrinthelab.com/videos

The Picture Tools Format ribbon contains some options new to Excel 2010 so you may correct and enhance images. Now you can sharpen and soften photos and apply artistic effects to them. More options are available to adjust the brightness, contrast, and color of images. The background removal tool allows you to remove unwanted objects from a photo.

A color photo re-colored as grayscale

The same photo with increased contrast and the Plastic Wrap artistic effect

A photo with some background areas removed

## Picture Styles and Picture Effects

Continued from the previous Excel version, the Picture Styles group includes many options to frame an image or apply a reflection. With the Picture Effects, you may give the image a 3-D appearance by choosing a preset, which includes multiple effects. You also may choose a single effect, such as a shadow or a bevel. You may preview how any option will affect the selected image by passing the mouse pointer over the choices on the Ribbon.

A frame around a clip art image applied by a picture style

The Adjust group and Picture Styles group on the Format ribbon display when a clip art or picture image is selected.

The dialog box launcher in the Picture Styles group of the Format ribbon displays the Format Picture dialog box, where you may set some options more precisely than you can with the options available on the Ribbon. For example, you may set a contrast of 12%. You may also open the Format Picture dialog box by choosing a command on the menus in the Adjust group of the Ribbon.

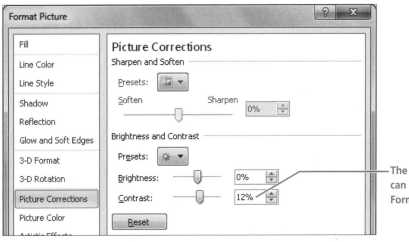

The contrast and other options can be adjusted precisely in the Format Picture dialog box

| QUICK REFERENCE | EDITING IMAGES |
| --- | --- |
| **Task** | **Procedure** |
| Scale an image | ■ Select the image and do one of the following:<br>   ◆ Choose Format→Size→Shape Height or Shape Width from the Ribbon and edit the size or use the spinner arrows.<br>   *or*<br>   ◆ Launch 🖾 the Format Picture dialog box from the Format ribbon, choose Height or Width under Scaling, and change the percentage. |
| Rotate an image | ■ Select the image and drag its rotation handle. |
| Crop an image | ■ Select the image and choose Format→Size→Crop 🖾 from the Ribbon and drag a cropping handle on the image. |
| Adjust image brightness and contrast | ■ Select the image, choose Format→Adjust→Corrections 🔆 menu ▼ from the Ribbon, and select a brightness and contrast preset option. |
| Adjust the image color | ■ Select the image, choose Format→Adjust→Color 🖾 menu ▼ from the Ribbon, and select a color saturation, color tone, or recolor preset option. |
| Set an option for an image precisely | ■ Select the image.<br>■ Choose FormatPicture Styles dialog box launcher 🖾 from the Ribbon.<br>■ Select the desired category in the Format Picture dialog box, and enter the value for the desired option. |
| Sharpen or soften a photo | ■ Select the photo, choose Format→Adjust→Corrections 🔆 menu ▼, and select a sharpen or soften preset option from the Ribbon. |
| Remove or restore background areas on a photo | ■ Select the photo.<br>■ Choose Format→Adjust→Remove Background 🖾 from the Ribbon.<br>■ Drag handles on the masking rectangle to select the area to be adjusted. Areas to be removed are masked in a single color.<br>■ To remove an object or area, choose Background Removal→Refine→Mark Areas to Remove from the Ribbon, and then click the pencil tool on an object or drag across an object until it displays the mask color.<br>■ To restore a removed object, choose Background Removal→Refine→Mark Areas to Keep from the Ribbon, and then click points on the object or drag across the object until its original color is restored.<br>■ When you are finished, choose Background Removal→Close→Keep Changes from the Ribbon (or choose Discard All Changes to cancel the background removal). |

| Task | Procedure |
|------|-----------|
| Apply an artistic effect to a photo | ▪ Select the photo, choose Format→Adjust→Artistic Effects menu ▼, and select a preset effect from the Ribbon. |
| Apply a picture style to an image | ▪ Select the image, choose Format→Picture Styles→More ⬚ menu from the Ribbon, and choose a style. |
| Apply a picture effect to an image | ▪ Choose Format→Picture Styles→Picture Effects 🖻 menu ▼ from the Ribbon, and choose a preset or other effect. |
| Reset an image to its original properties | ▪ Choose Format→Adjust→Reset Picture 🖼 from the Ribbon while the image is selected. |

## DEVELOP YOUR SKILLS 10.2.6
# Adjust Images and Apply Special Effects

*In this exercise, you will change the brightness and contrast of the profit arrows image and then recolor it with a theme color. You will apply a picture style and picture effects to images.*

1. Display the **Analysis** worksheet in the Revenue Comparison workbook.

2. Select the **profit arrows** picture.

### Adjust the Brightness and Contrast

3. Choose **Format→Adjust→Corrections** 🔆 **menu ▼** from the Ribbon, and **point** at the preset option in the center of the list.

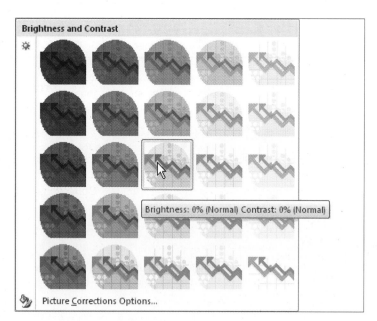

*The frame around this preset option indicates that it is the current setting. The ScreenTip shows that the brightness and contrast are normal at 0%. Notice that you could choose Picture Correction Options at the bottom of the menu to open the Format Picture dialog box. You could set a specific brightness or contrast percentage there.*

4. Point at a few other preset options to preview the effect on the image, and then choose **Brightness: +20% Contrast**: **–40%** in the top row.

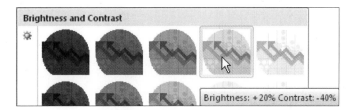

## Recolor an Image

5. Choose **Format→Adjust→Color** 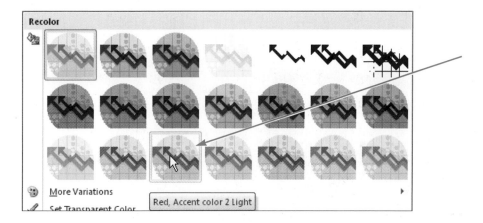 **menu ▼** from the Ribbon, **point** at various preset choices to preview the effect on the profit arrows image, and then choose **Red, Accent Color 2 Light** on the third row.

*The adjusted image is more muted than the original and contains shades of red.*

6. Feel free to **copy and paste** the profit image, drag the duplicate to **row 26**, and experiment with the other options in the Corrections and Color menus.

## Insert a Photo Image

7. Select **cell B3**, and choose **Insert→Illustrations→Clip Art** from the Ribbon.

8. Follow these steps to search for photo clips in the Clip Art task pane:

Ⓐ Type **business meeting women organizers** in the Search For box.

Ⓑ Drop down the **Results Should Be** list, and choose only **Photographs**.

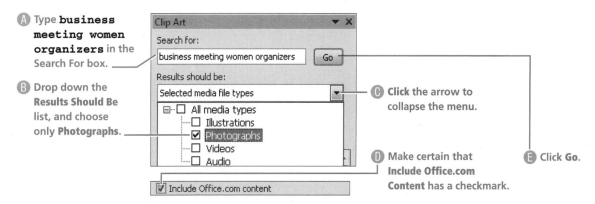

Ⓒ Click the arrow to collapse the menu.

Ⓓ Make certain that **Include Office.com Content** has a checkmark.

Ⓔ Click **Go**.

9. **Choose** the image of two women shown in the illustration. If this image is not available, choose an appropriate image for the worksheet.
*The image displays at cell B3 of the worksheet.*

10. **Close** ☒ the Clip Art task pane.

## Remove Background Areas from a Photo

*In the next steps, you will remove areas of the photo to focus attention on the two women.*

11. Choose **Format→Adjust→Remove Background** 🖼 from the Ribbon.
*The Background Removal tab appears at the right of the File tab. A masking rectangle appears on the image. Areas outside the rectangle are masked in a single color. Masked areas will be removed from the image.*

12. **Drag** the center handle of each side of the masking rectangle to surround the two women tightly, as shown in the illustration. (Do not be concerned if part of the clothing or hair is masked. A perfect image is not required in this exercise.)

*The suit jacket may be masked on the woman at the right. If a different object is masked, substitute that object in steps 13–15.*

13. Choose **Background Removal→Refine→Mark Areas to Keep** 🟢 from the Ribbon.

14. Place the **pencil tool pointer** near the top of the suit jacket (or another masked object if the suit jacket is not masked).

15. **Drag down** to the jacket sleeve to unmask part of the jacket. Continue **pointing and dragging** to unmask all areas of the suit jacket and any other area that you do not wish to mask.

    *You can choose Undo if your selection is incorrect. You could also use the Mark Areas to Remove command to mask additional areas of the image.*

16. When you are finished, choose **Background Removal→Close→Keep Changes** from the Ribbon.

17. With the photo image of two women still selected, choose **Format→ Size→Shape Height** from the Ribbon, type **1.5**, and **tap** Enter.

    *The image shrinks, and the width remains in proportion to the height. Ignore any changes to the masked areas that may occur from resizing the image. A perfect image is not required in this exercise.*

## Apply an Artistic Effect to a Photo

18. Select the photo on **cell I3**, and choose **Format→Adjust→Artistic Effects menu ▾→Plastic Wrap** from the Ribbon.

    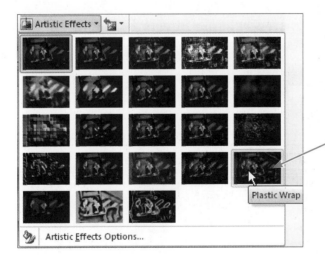

*The artistic effect options give a hand-drawn appearance to photos.*

### Add a Picture Style to an Image

19. **Select** the profit arrows image on **cell F11**.

20. Choose **Format→Picture Styles→Drop Shadow Rectangle** (the fourth choice from the left) from the Ribbon.
*The image displays a drop shadow effect, as shown in the following illustration.*

Picture Styles

21. Choose **Format→Picture Styles→ More** ⊽ **menu ▾** from the Ribbon, point to some of the menu items to preview their effects, and then **tap** [Esc] to cancel without making a selection.

### Apply a Picture Effect to an Image

22. **Select** the laptop computer image on **cell F3**.

23. **Drag** the scroll box in the horizontal scroll bar to the right so that the image will be visible as you display a menu.

24. Choose **Format→Picture Styles→Picture Effects** ▢ **menu ▾** from the Ribbon, and then follow these steps to choose a preset:

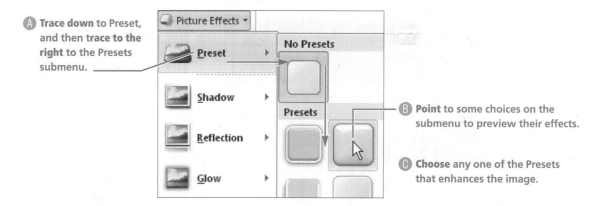

Ⓐ **Trace down** to Preset, and then **trace to the right** to the Presets submenu.

Ⓑ **Point** to some choices on the submenu to preview their effects.

Ⓒ **Choose** any one of the Presets that enhances the image.

*The preset picture effect that you chose may be different from the one shown here. While you may apply individual effects on the Picture Effects menu, such as a reflection or glow, the presets are quick and easy to use.*

A preset charcoal drawing picture effect

### Apply Effects to a Photo

25. Move the photo of two women from **cell B3** to overlap the profit arrows image on **cell F11**.

26. Apply one or two **effects** from the Format ribbon to the photo (artistic effect, color adjustment, picture style, or picture effect).
    *Your images and effects may differ from the illustration. You have created a variety of images on the worksheet. To maintain a consistent design throughout a workbook, remember to choose illustrations or photos that match in appearance.*

27. **Save** 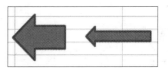 the changes to your workbook.

# 10.3  Getting into Shapes

**Video Lesson**    labyrinthelab.com/videos

With the Microsoft Office shape tools, you may draw lines, ovals, rectangles, arrows, and many other shapes. Lines and callouts containing text are particularly useful to emphasize areas of interest on worksheets and charts. The Shapes command is used to add these objects, and you may type text into any shape except lines, brackets, and braces. The following illustration highlights some categories on the Shapes menu.

The Text Box tool creates text that is not anchored within a cell.

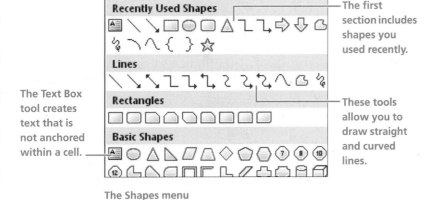

The Shapes menu

The first section includes shapes you used recently.

These tools allow you to draw straight and curved lines.

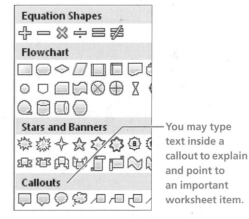

You may type text inside a callout to explain and point to an important worksheet item.

## Inserting Shapes

To draw a shape, choose the desired tool on the Shapes menu and then either click or drag in the worksheet. Clicking creates a shape of a predefined size, and dragging allows you to customize the width and height. You may use resizing handles on the shape or the Size commands on the Format ribbon to change the size after drawing. You may type text within the shape after drawing or selecting it. After you create or select a shape, the Drawing Tools appear on the Ribbon. The Format ribbon contains options to change the size, fill, and outline; add an effect; and insert more shapes.

Arrows drawn using the dragging method

## Constraining Objects

You may hold down the Shift key to draw shapes that remain in equal proportion of width to height. A rectangle is constrained to a square, and an oval is constrained to a circle. You also may constrain lines to 90- or 45-degree angles.

## Text Boxes

The Text Box A command creates a very useful object. Text boxes are slightly different from rectangle shapes, which display centered text. As you type in a text box, text is left aligned by default, and the text box lengthens automatically to display all the text. You may position a text box anywhere on a worksheet, even over worksheet entries, pictures, and other graphics.

A text box may be layered over a cell, picture, clip art, or shape.

## Applying Shape Styles and Effects

While a shape is selected, you may apply options from the Shape Styles group on the Format ribbon. You may apply one of the Quick Styles that are predesigned with a workbook theme color, outline, fill, and bevel effect. As an alternative, you may create a custom outline or fill. The Shape Effects menu contains options to angle, bevel, shadow, or reflect the image for a 3-D appearance. As in the Format Picture dialog box described for image settings earlier in this lesson, the options in the Format Shape dialog box are expanded in Excel 2010 so you may precisely customize a variety of shape settings.

| QUICK REFERENCE | INSERTING AND EDITING SHAPES |
|---|---|
| **Task** | **Procedure** |
| Insert a shape | ▪ Choose Insert→Illustrations→Shapes menu ▼, and choose a shape tool from the Ribbon. |
| | ▪ Click on the worksheet to create the shape or drag to control the shape's size. |
| | ▪ Hold down Shift while dragging to constrain the shape to a perfect square, circle, or 90- or 45-degree line. |
| Insert a text box | ▪ Choose Insert→Text→Text Box A from the Ribbon. |
| | ▪ Click in the worksheet and type the text. |
| Apply an outline or fill to a shape | ▪ Select the image, choose Format→Shape Styles, and choose a predesigned style from the Ribbon or choose Shape Fill or Shape Outline for custom settings. |
| Apply a shape effect | ▪ Choose Format→Shape Styles→Shape Effects menu ▼ from the Ribbon and choose a preset option or other effect while the shape is selected. |
| Set an option for a shape precisely | ▪ Select the shape. |
| | ▪ Choose Format→Shape Styles dialog box launcher from the Ribbon. |
| | ▪ Select the desired category in the Format Shape dialog box, and enter the value for the desired option. |

## Insert and Edit Shapes

*In this exercise, you will draw various shapes, including a callout and a text box. You will change the appearance of shapes, and you will apply a glow effect to one of the shapes.*

### Draw and Format an Oval

1. Display the **By Region** worksheet in the Revenue Comparison workbook.

2. Choose **Insert→Illustrations→Shapes menu ▾→Basic Shapes→Oval**  from the Ribbon.

3. Follow these steps to draw an oval on cell D5:

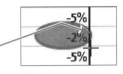

Ⓐ **Position** the mouse pointer slightly above and to the left of the number –2% and then **drag down and right**.

Ⓑ **Release** the mouse button to end the oval.

*The oval hides the number because the oval contains a fill.*

4. With the oval selected, choose **Format→Shape Styles→Shape Fill** 🖌 **menu ▾→No Fill** from the Ribbon.
*The number now appears through the oval.*

5. With the oval selected, choose **Format→Shape Styles→Shape Outline** 🖊 **menu ▾** from the Ribbon, pause the mouse over various orange shades, and **choose** one that will call attention to the circled number.

6. Move and resize the oval to center it over the number.

### Draw and Format a Callout Shape

7. Choose **Insert→Illustrations→Shapes→Callouts→Line Callout 1** 🔲 from the Ribbon.
*As an alternative, with the oval graphic still selected, you may choose Format→Insert Shapes→More* ⊟ *menu ▾ from the Ribbon and select the tool.*

8. Follow these steps to draw a callout on cell G9 in the By Region worksheet:

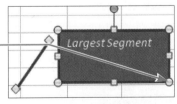

Ⓐ **Position** the mouse pointer in the center of cell **G9** and then **drag down and right**.

Ⓑ **Release** the mouse button to end the callout.

Ⓒ While the shape is still selected, **right-click** on the shape and choose **Italic** from the context menu. Type **Largest segment** but do **not** tap [Enter].

9. **Drag a handle** to resize the box so that the text fits on one line. If necessary, **drag the callout box** to move it slightly.

10. Choose **Format→Shape Styles→More** ⊟ **menu ▾**, trace down, and select **Moderate Effect – Red, Accent 2** (row 5, column 3).
*Your callout should contain italicized text, a graduated red fill, and a thin shadow. Using the preset effects saves time. Next you will move the callout line so that it points to the largest pie wedge in the chart.*

**11.** Follow these steps to rotate and lengthen the callout line:

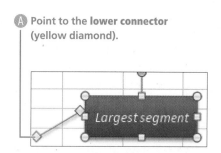

Ⓐ Point to the **lower connector** (yellow diamond).

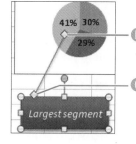

Ⓑ **Drag** the connector up and to the right until the line points to the 41% pie slice.

Ⓒ **Drag** the other connector to a position along the top of the callout box.

## Draw a Text Box

**12.** Display the **Analysis** worksheet in the workbook.

**13.** Choose **Insert→Illustrations→Shapes→Basic Shapes→Text Box** A from the Ribbon.
*The tool also is available by choosing Insert→Text→Text Box from the Ribbon.*

**14.** Follow these steps to draw a text box on the laptop computer image:

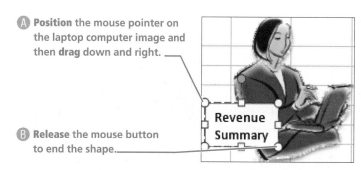

Ⓐ **Position** the mouse pointer on the laptop computer image and then **drag** down and right.

Ⓑ **Release** the mouse button to end the shape.

Ⓒ With the shape still selected, type **Revenue Summary** but do **not** tap Enter.

Ⓓ If necessary, **move and resize** the shape for an attractive appearance.

*To move a text box, point to its border rather than inside the shape.*

## Draw a Trapezoid

**15.** Display the **By Market** worksheet in the workbook.

**16.** Choose **Insert→Illustrations→Shapes→Basic Shapes→Trapezoid** △ from the Ribbon.

**17.** Follow these steps to draw a trapezoid on cell D12:

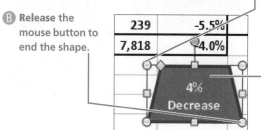

Ⓐ **Position** the mouse pointer slightly above and to the left of **cell D12** and then **drag** down and right.

Ⓑ **Release** the mouse button to end the shape.

Ⓒ **Right-click** the shape and choose Bold from the Mini toolbar. Choose Font Color menu ▼→Theme Colors→White, Background 1 (in the first row) from the Mini toolbar. Type **4%**, tap Enter, and type **Decrease**.

Ⓓ If necessary, **move and resize** the shape so that it is centered on **column D**.

**18.** With the trapezoid shape selected, choose **Format→Shape Styles→More** ▼ menu ▼, and select an appropriate red style from the Ribbon.

## Apply a Shape Effect

19. With the trapezoid selected, choose **Format→Shape Styles→Shape Effects** 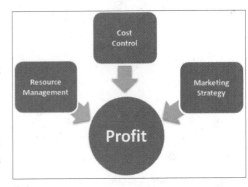 **menu ▾→ Bevel** from the Ribbon, **trace right and down**, preview each of the bevel choices, and choose one.

    *Because the shape has a bevel effect, the Soft Edges effects now are unavailable. The shape will not preview a change when you point to those effects on the menu.*

20. **Copy and paste** the trapezoid, move the duplicate to **row 26**, and choose **Format→ Shape Effects menu ▾→ No Bevel** from the Ribbon. **Preview** various effects from the Shape Effects menu, and choose one.

21. **Save** 💾 the changes to your workbook.

---

# 10.4 Illustrating with SmartArt

**Video Lesson** labyrinthelab.com/videos

Microsoft Office supplies an illustration category named SmartArt. Although you can use line, column, and pie charts to summarize worksheet data, you will use SmartArt to present ideas. For example, you might show several worksheets and charts to your executive team to outline areas of decreasing sales, but more important is the team's decision-making process to solve the problem. With SmartArt, you can illustrate a procedure, process, or decision tree. SmartArt includes charts to show relationships between ideas, illustrate an information cycle, and sequence various project workflow steps. Office 2010 includes more SmartArt design choices and a new Picture category.

SmartArt conveys ideas using brief text phrases.

## Using SmartArt

The Choose a SmartArt Graphic dialog box displays charts within categories. When you select a chart, its description displays to the right so that you may decide if it meets your presentation needs.

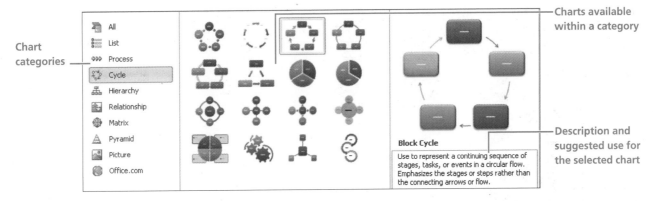

Charts available within a category

Chart categories

Description and suggested use for the selected chart

# Adding Text to SmartArt

After a SmartArt chart is inserted on the worksheet, you may select one of its graphics and begin typing text into it. Depending on the chart type, you may prefer to display the Text pane and enter all text as an outline. You are not restricted to the number of levels that display in the initial chart. You may add or delete levels and type as many items within a level as needed.

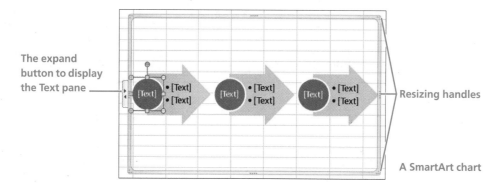

The expand button to display the Text pane

Resizing handles

A SmartArt chart

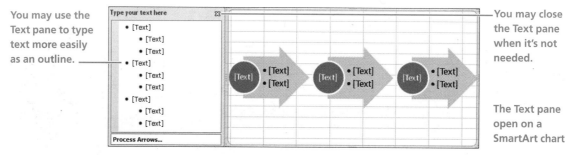

You may use the Text pane to type text more easily as an outline.

You may close the Text pane when it's not needed.

The Text pane open on a SmartArt chart

Keep text brief in SmartArt. Use short, descriptive phrases rather than complete sentences.

# Formatting SmartArt

The SmartArt Tools display when a SmartArt graphic is selected. You may change the chart's layout, colors, and number of shapes on the Design ribbon. There you also will find SmartArt Styles. These Quick Style designs combine shape fills, shadows, and 3-D effects that you can apply with the click of a button. You may use the Format ribbon to apply a shape style, outline, fill, or effect to one or multiple shapes in the SmartArt chart. As with other options, you may preview by pausing the mouse pointer over the choices on the Ribbon.

To delete an object in a SmartArt chart, select the object and tap ⌷Delete⌷. To delete an entire chart, select its frame and tap ⌷Delete⌷.

| Task | Procedure |
|------|-----------|
| Insert a SmartArt chart | ■ Choose Insert→Illustrations→SmartArt from the Ribbon.<br>■ In the Choose a SmartArt Graphic dialog box, choose a chart category, choose a specific chart type, and click OK. |
| Type text in a SmartArt chart | ■ Select a graphic in the chart and type text.<br>■ To type text for all chart graphics at one time, click the expand button on the left of the chart frame to display the Text pane, select all text, tap Delete, and then type the new text.<br>■ Use Tab to demote text to the next lower level and Shift+Tab to promote text to the next higher level. |
| Change the SmartArt chart style | ■ Click inside the SmartArt chart or on its frame.<br>■ Choose Design→SmartArt Styles→More menu ▼, and select a style from the Ribbon. |
| Apply an effect to a shape in SmartArt | ■ Select the desired shape(s) in the chart.<br>■ Choose an option from the Shape Styles, Shape Fill, Shape Outline, or Shape Effect menus on the Format ribbon. |

## DEVELOP YOUR SKILLS 10.4.1

# Insert SmartArt

*In this exercise, you will create a SmartArt graphic to convey a relationship. You will move, resize, and change colors on the graphic. You also will apply a style.*

1. Display the **Analysis** worksheet in the Revenue Comparison workbook.
   *You will convert the labels National and Sector to SmartArt to show a dynamic relationship.*

2. **Select** any cell and **tap** Home to display **column A**.

3. Select **cells B2:C2** and **tap** Delete to remove the labels.

### Insert an Arrow Ribbon and Add Text

4. Choose **Insert→Illustrations→SmartArt** from the Ribbon.
   *The Choose a SmartArt Graphic dialog box displays.*

5. Follow these steps to insert an arrow ribbon chart from the Choose a SmartArt Graphic dialog box:

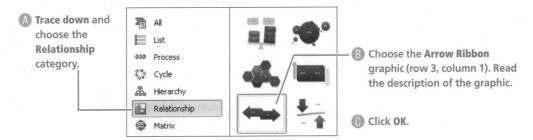

Ⓐ **Trace down** and choose the **Relationship** category.

Ⓑ Choose the **Arrow Ribbon** graphic (row 3, column 1). Read the description of the graphic.

Ⓒ Click **OK**.

*The arrow ribbon appears on the worksheet surrounded by a nonprinting frame. The SmartArt Tools appear on the Ribbon.*

## Format, Resize, and Move the Arrow Ribbon

*Make certain that the arrow ribbon graphic is still selected.*

6. Choose **Design→SmartArt Styles→Change Colors** 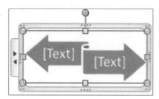 **menu ▾** from the Ribbon. Scroll down to **Accent 6**, preview several shades by pausing the mouse over them, and then **select** a shade appropriate for the worksheet.

*The graphic changes to the shade you chose.*

7. Select the **text box** on the left if not already selected, type **National**, and do **not** tap ⌷Enter⌷. Select the **text box** on the right, type **Sector**, and do **not** tap ⌷Enter⌷.

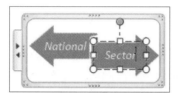

8. Follow these steps to change the text to italic:

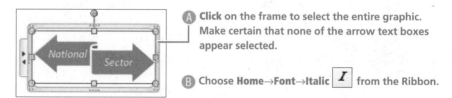

Ⓐ **Click** on the frame to select the entire graphic. Make certain that none of the arrow text boxes appear selected.

Ⓑ Choose **Home→Font→Italic** *I* from the Ribbon.

9. Follow these steps to shrink the graphic and move it into position:
*An arrow graphic is selected in the illustration to demonstrate the difference between the frame resizing handles and an object's resizing handles.*

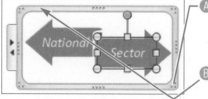

Ⓐ Point to the **lower-right corner resizing handle** on the frame and **drag up and left** to make the entire graphic smaller. Make certain that you do not select the resizing handle of an object inside the frame.

Ⓑ **Drag** the frame until the SmartArt is centered under the word *Analysis*.

*Your graphic may look slightly different from the following illustration.*

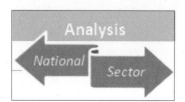

## Apply a SmartArt Style

10. If the SmartArt graphic does not display its frame, **click** anywhere in the graphic to select it.

11. Choose **Design→SmartArt Styles→More** ⊽ **menu ▾** from the Ribbon. Preview by pausing the mouse on each choice under Best Match for Document, and then select one. *Your choice may be different from the following one.*

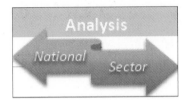

*You decide that the original effect looked better.*

12. **Undo** ↶ the style change.

13. **Save** 💾 the changes and **close** the workbook.

## 10.5 Concepts Review

Concepts Review    labyrinthelab.com/excel10

*To check your knowledge of the key concepts introduced in this lesson, complete the Concepts Review quiz by going to the URL listed above. If your classroom is using Labyrinth eLab, you may complete the Concepts Review quiz from within your eLab course.*

# Reinforce Your Skills

## Insert Clip Art and Shapes

*In this exercise, you will search Clip Art for appropriate graphics to illustrate your worksheet. You will create a text box and a shape. Then you will format the graphics to unify them with the workbook theme.*

### Insert Clip Art

1. **Open** the rs-Capital Expenses workbook from the Lesson 10 folder in your file storage location.

2. **Maximize** ☐ the window.

3. Select **cell A1**.
   *The clip art you insert in the next steps will be positioned on cell A1.*

4. Choose **Insert→Illustrations→ClipArt** ⊞ from the Ribbon to display the Clip Art task pane.

5. Follow these steps to conduct a search for a wedding clip art image in only two media type categories:

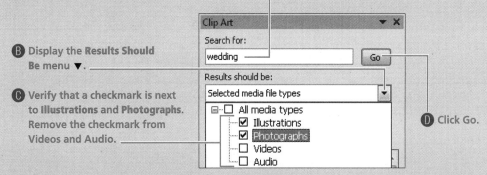

Ⓐ Type the keyword **wedding** in the Search For box.

Ⓑ Display the **Results Should Be menu ▼**.

Ⓒ Verify that a checkmark is next to **Illustrations** and **Photographs**. Remove the checkmark from Videos and Audio.

Ⓓ Click Go.

6. **Insert** an appropriate wedding clip art by selecting it from the results list.

7. **Close** the Clip Art task pane.

8. **Resize** the image to fit in column A by dragging the lower-right corner sizing handle.
   *The image's proportion of height to width is maintained when you use a corner handle.*

### Rotate Clip Art

9. Choose **Picture Tools Format→Arrange→Rotate** ⊿→**Flip Horizontal**.
   *The wedding clip art image reverses from left to right.*

## Draw a Text Box

10. Follow these steps to create a text box:

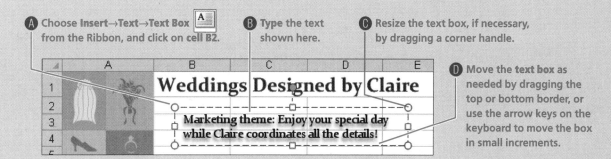

**A** Choose **Insert→Text→Text Box** from the Ribbon, and click on **cell B2**.

**B** Type the text shown here.

**C** Resize the text box, if necessary, by dragging a corner handle.

**D** Move the **text box** as needed by dragging the top or bottom border, or use the arrow keys on the keyboard to move the box in small increments.

## Draw an Arrow Shape

11. Choose **Insert→Illustrations→Shapes** menu ▾, and under Block Arrows, choose **Right Arrow**, as shown to the right.

12. Place the mouse pointer in **cell E15**, hold down Shift, and **drag to the right** until the arrow tip reaches the right edge of **column G**. **Release** the mouse and then **release** Shift. *The arrow's height should be in proportion to its width because you constrained the shape with* Shift.

13. While the arrow shape is still selected, choose **10 point** size from the Ribbon and type **Negative balance**.

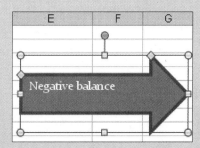

14. **Point** in the arrow shape and drag it to **cell A16**. **Resize** and **position** the arrow as shown.

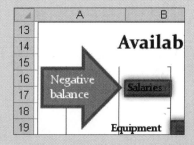

## Add a Shape Style to the Arrow

15. Choose **Drawing Tools Format→Shape Styles→More** ▾ from the Ribbon.

16. **Point** at the various green styles in the list to preview how the arrow would look, and then **select** a style that complements the other graphics.

## Color the Clip Art Image

17. Select the **wedding** clip art on cell A1.

18. Choose **Format→Adjust→Color** 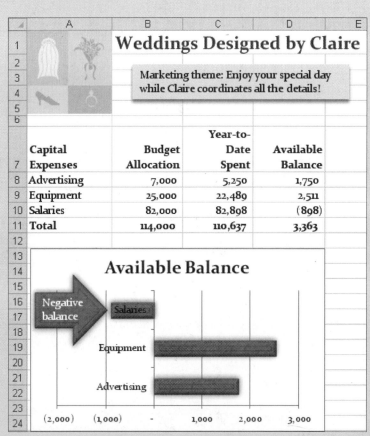 from the Ribbon, and choose a color that harmonizes with the other worksheet objects.

## Apply a Fill and Shape Effect to the Text Box

19. Select the text box on **row 3**, choose **Format→Shape Styles→Shape Fill** from the Ribbon, and choose a light shade of an appropriate theme color.
*A light fill shade provides good contrast so the text is easy to read.*

20. Choose **Format→Shape Styles→Shape Effects** from the Ribbon, choose **Shadow** in the menu, and choose an **Outer** shadow preset.
*Your worksheet should resemble the following illustration when you are finished. Your shape formatting may vary.*

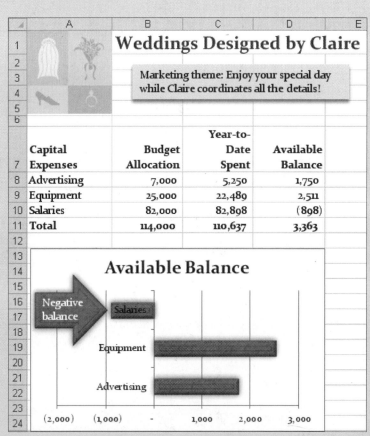

21. **Save** the changes and **close** the workbook.

# Insert and Format SmartArt

*In this exercise, you will insert a SmartArt diagram and type text into an outline that automatically pours the text into the graphics. Then you will change the diagram layout and style.*

1. **Open** the rs-Premium Soccer workbook from the Lesson 10 folder.

2. **Maximize** 🔲 the window.

## Insert a List Graphic and Add Text

*You will group the labels from column A into a more dynamic list.*

3. Choose **Insert→Illustrations→SmartArt**  from the Ribbon. In the Choose a SmartArt Graphic dialog box, choose the **List** category on the left, choose **Bending Picture Accent List** as shown, and then click **OK**.
*This chart contains circle placeholders for pictures, but you will not add pictures.*

4. Click the **expand** button as shown to display the Text pane, if not already displayed.

*You could type text directly in the graphics, but you probably will find it easier to enter all the text in the outline pane found next to the Text pane.*

5. Follow these steps to type the text:

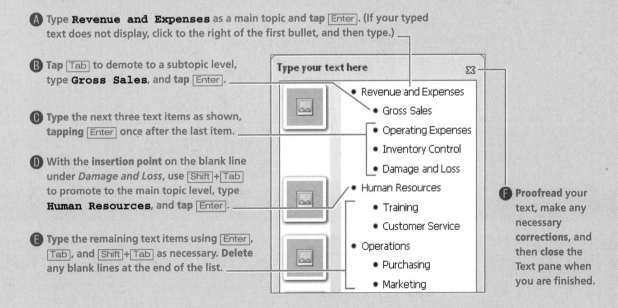

Ⓐ Type **Revenue and Expenses** as a main topic and tap Enter. (If your typed text does not display, click to the right of the first bullet, and then type.)

Ⓑ Tap Tab to demote to a subtopic level, type **Gross Sales**, and tap Enter.

Ⓒ Type the next three text items as shown, tapping Enter once after the last item.

Ⓓ With the **insertion point** on the blank line under *Damage and Loss*, use Shift + Tab to promote to the main topic level, type **Human Resources**, and tap Enter.

Ⓔ Type the remaining text items using Enter, Tab, and Shift + Tab as necessary. **Delete** any blank lines at the end of the list.

Ⓕ **Proofread** your text, make any necessary **corrections**, and then **close** the Text pane when you are finished.

*The SmartArt graphic should look like the following illustration.*

## Add More Text

6. To add a fourth main topic, click the **Expand** button to display the Text pane once again.

7. **Click** to the right of the last entry, *Marketing*, and **tap** Enter.

8. Use Shift + Tab to promote to a main topic and type **Publications**.

9. Create the two subtopics **Print** and **Web Page** and then **close** the Text pane.
   *The fourth text box displays below the others. In the next few steps, you will improve the design by changing the SmartArt layout and style.*

## Format the SmartArt Graphic

10. Choose **Design→Layouts→More** ⊽ **→Hierarchy List** layout from the Ribbon.
    *You may change layouts easily, but keep in mind that some layouts will not display all items from the previous layout. You may also use the Ribbon to change colors, styles, and the number of shapes in the graphic.*

11. Choose **Design→SmartArt Styles→More** ⊽ from the Ribbon. Under Best Match for Document, choose **Intense Effect**.
    *The SmartArt graphic should look like the following illustration.*

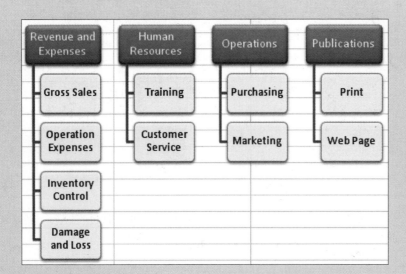

12. **Delete** the text labels in the **worksheet range A3:A13**.

13. **Select** the SmartArt chart, **point** to the frame, and **move** the chart so it is centered under the National Sector graphic.

14. Feel free to insert a different SmartArt diagram in a blank area of the worksheet. Explore options to add shapes, change colors, and change styles on the Design ribbon.
*Depending on the chart type, some options will be dimmed (unavailable) on the Ribbon.*

15. **Save** 🖫 the changes and **close** the workbook.

# Apply Your Skills

## Use Shapes Tools

*In this exercise, you will create a worksheet that includes a chart. You will use an arrow and a text box to emphasize the chart.*

1. Choose **File→New** to start a new workbook, if necessary.

2. **Maximize** ▣ the window.

3. **Enter** and **format** the worksheet data as shown at the end of this exercise.

4. **Create** the chart as shown. Include the **legend** above the chart.

5. Create the **text box** and apply a **shape style**.

6. Draw the **arrow** as a perfect horizontal line and apply a **shape style**.

7. **Print** the worksheet, chart, and shapes on a single page.

8. **Save** 🖫 with the name **as-Q1 Sales** in the Lesson 10 folder and **close** the workbook. *Your worksheet should look similar to the following illustration.*

|  | A | B | C | D | E | F | G | H |
|---|---|---|---|---|---|---|---|---|
| 1 | **Lee's Deli** | | | | | | | |
| 2 | **1st Quarter Profit (three stores)** | | | | | | | |
| 3 | | | | | | | | |
| 4 | **Location** | **January** | **February** | **March** | | | | |
| 5 | Graham | $  11,278 | $  11,615 | $  11,795 | | | | |
| 6 | Hillsborough | 12,003 | 12,780 | 14,014 | | | | |
| 7 | Mebane | 7,898 | 5,750 | 7,956 | | | | |
| 8 | Total | $  31,179 | $  30,145 | $  33,765 | | | | |
| 9 | | | | | | | | |

Chart: ■ January  ■ February  ■ March

$16,000
$14,000
$12,000
$10,000
$8,000
$6,000
$4,000
$2,000
$-

Graham    Hillsborough    Mebane

Why are the Mebane profits lower?

# Format Clip Art and a Shape

*In this exercise, you will insert a clip art image and draw a star shape that contains text. You will crop, resize, and move objects. You also will a apply shape style.*

1. **Open** the as-Revenue Star workbook from the Lesson 10 folder.

2. **Maximize** 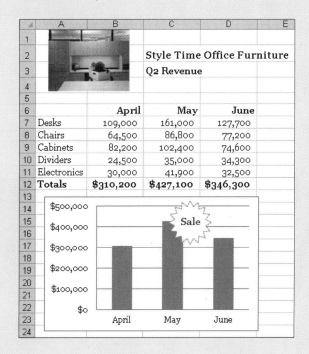 the window.

3. **Insert** two blank rows above **row 1**.

4. Move the titles in the **range A3:A4** to the **range C2:C3**.

5. Search for a **clip art photograph** (not an illustration) of office furniture. Choose an appropriate image from the results, and **insert** it on the worksheet.

6. **Crop** away some of the edges around the photograph image.

7. **Scale** the image smaller and move it into **position** in the **range A1:B4**.

8. If necessary, use the **Corrections** options on the Ribbon to adjust the sharpness, brightness, or contrast of the image.

9. Choose the **16-point star shape tool**, hold down [Shift] to draw a perfect circle about one inch wide, and type **Sale** in the shape.

10. Apply a **shape style** that complements the chart colors.

11. **Move** the star shape onto the chart as shown in the illustration at the end of this exercise.

12. If necessary, **resize** the star to display its text completely. Use the size options on the Ribbon to ensure that the shape's width and height are equal to maintain a perfect circle.

13. **Save** the changes and **close** the workbook.
    *The worksheet should look similar to the following illustration. Your photo and shape style may be different.*

| | A | B | C | D | E |
|---|---|---|---|---|---|
| 1 | | | | | |
| 2 | | | Style Time Office Furniture | | |
| 3 | | | Q2 Revenue | | |
| 4 | | | | | |
| 5 | | | | | |
| 6 | | April | May | June | |
| 7 | Desks | 109,000 | 161,000 | 127,700 | |
| 8 | Chairs | 64,500 | 86,800 | 77,200 | |
| 9 | Cabinets | 82,200 | 102,400 | 74,600 | |
| 10 | Dividers | 24,500 | 35,000 | 34,300 | |
| 11 | Electronics | 30,000 | 41,900 | 32,500 | |
| 12 | Totals | $310,200 | $427,100 | $346,300 | |

# Create SmartArt

*In this exercise, you will insert and customize a SmartArt graphic.*

1. **Open** as-Accounting from the Lesson 10 folder.

2. **Maximize** ▣ the window.

3. In **cell B6**, create a formula that calculates the **profit** (not shown in the illustration below).

4. Copy the formula in **cell B6** to **cell C6**.

5. Add a **SmartArt graphic** to the worksheet, using the **Equation** chart type as shown from the Relationship category.

6. **Type** the text **Revenue, Expenses,** and **Profit (Loss)** into the graphics as shown.

7. **Right-click** the Plus (+) shape in the SmartArt chart, and choose **Change Shape→Equation Shapes→Minus** from the context menu.

8. **Select** the entire chart and apply a **bevel effect**. (Your bevel effect may be different from that shown.)

9. **Resize** and **move** the chart under the worksheet data.

10. **Save** 🖫 the changes and **close** the workbook.
    *The worksheet should look similar to the following illustration. The bevel effect you applied to the SmartArt graphic may be different.*

|   | A | B | C | D |
|---|---|---|---|---|
| 1 | **Income Projection** | | | |
| 2 | in Millions | | | |
| 3 | | Current Year | Next Year | |
| 4 | Revenue | 87.3 | 95.1 | |
| 5 | Expenses | 80.8 | 81.2 | |
| 6 | Profit (Loss) | 6.5 | 13.9 | |
| 7 | | | | |
| 8 | | | | |
| 9 | Revenue ▬ Expenses ═ Profit (Loss) | | | |
| 10 | | | | |

# Critical Thinking & Work-Readiness Skills

*In the course of working through the following Microsoft Office-based Critical Thinking exercises, you will also be utilizing various work-readiness skills, some of which are listed next to each exercise. Go to* labyrinthelab.com/ workreadiness *to learn more about the work-readiness skills.*

## 10.1 Insert a Picture

Kevin Hottel, business analyst, wants to create a total sales worksheet for the CEO. He wants to use a picture file to make the report more professional and interesting. Open **ct-Sales** (Lesson 10 folder). Sort the data by Customer and subtotal by Sales. In cell A1, insert the MyVirtualCampus logo (Lesson 10 folder). Design your list appropriately. Save your work as **ct-Sales [Your Last Name]**. Keep the file open. How does the logo enhance the business use of the report? Type your answer in a Word document named **ct-Questions** saved to your Lesson 10 folder.

## 10.2 Insert a Shape

Kevin wants to emphasize the highest sales amount by adding a shape so the CEO can see at a glance the school with the greatest sales. Open ct-Sales [Your Last Name] (Lesson 10 folder), if necessary. Insert a blue star by Draper University's total sales. Resize and position the shape to fit within the top and bottom borders of a cell. Then, format the shape with a glow effect. Save your work and keep the file open for the next exercise.

## 10.3 Use SmartArt

Kevin wants to organize the colleges by their areas using SmartArt. Open ct-Sales [Your Last Name] (Lesson 10 folder), if necessary. Insert a SmartArt graphic with the Vertical Box List design. Enter one area number per shape, and use the Tab key to enter the appropriate college names under each area. Position the box list to the right of the worksheet list. Save your work and close the file.

# Using Templates and Protecting Workbooks

## LEARNING OBJECTIVES

After studying this lesson, you will be able to:

- Use existing workbooks and Office templates as the basis for new workbooks
- Create and modify custom templates
- Protect workbooks and worksheet contents
- Set a password to limit workbook access
- Add a digital signature to a workbook

As Excel becomes an integral part of your business toolkit, you may find a need to use certain workbooks repeatedly. For example, many salespeople need to fill out monthly expense reports, sales forecasts, and call reports. In this lesson, you will use predesigned Office templates and create custom templates as the basis for these and other frequently used workbook designs. Some projects require several people to work together on a workbook. To prevent others from changing important information such as formulas, you will learn how to lock and unlock certain cells, turn on worksheet protection, and set a password. You will also attach a digital signature to certify that your file has not been altered since you last saved it.

# Fundraising Event Template

My Virtual Campus Corporation markets a social networking intranet to colleges and universities. Like many other businesses, the company supports community and charitable organizations with cash donations and encourages its employees to

volunteer their time. Brett Martin is the public relations representative. She helps organize team running events to raise funds for a national cancer research organization. Because the race result reports usually look the same, Brett needs to create a template workbook as the basis for future event workbooks. The template will contain the text labels and formulas common to all events. Brett will turn on protection for specific cells, which prevents inadvertent modification by others who use the workbook. She will set a password for worksheet access and create a digital signature to assure event participants that the file is authentic. With these features in every workbook, Brett will "race" through her reporting tasks.

| 8 | | | Race Results | | |
|---|---|---|---|---|---|
| 9 | | | [Type event name here] | | |
| 10 | | | [Enter month and day here] | | |
| 11 | | | | | |
| 12 | Place | Team | Team Captain | Points | |
| 13 | 1 | | | | |
| 14 | 2 | | | | |
| 15 | 3 | | | | |
| 16 | 4 | | | | |
| 17 | 5 | | | | |
| 18 | | Average | | #DIV/0! | |

[Type a message or select the graphic and press Delete.]

Brett's template contains all the basic headings and formulas used for a typical race results report. Each template gives a fresh start with the same design.

| | A | B | C | D | E | |
|---|---|---|---|---|---|---|
| 8 | | | Race Results | | | |
| 9 | | | Coastal Classic | | | |
| 10 | | | | | | |
| 11 | Place | Team | Team Captain | Points | | |
| 12 | 1 | Herrera Insurance | Eric Tsang | 403.61 | | |
| 13 | 2 | Jordan Brands | Jenny Ralberg | 400.32 | | |
| 14 | 3 | Phi Delta | Marcus Daly | 391.45 | | |
| 15 | 4 | KMI | Sarah Kaluza | 382.90 | | |
| 16 | 5 | Ridgeline Dental | Anthony Neu | 376.44 | | |
| 17 | | Average | | 390.94 | | |
| 18 | | | | | | |
| 19 | | | | | | |
| 20 | | | | X | Brett Martin | |
| 21 | | | | | | |
| 22 | | | | Brett Martin | | |
| 23 | | | | Public Relations Representative | | |

A seven-point improvement over last year!

After the event directors use the template to fill in the data for a specific race, Brett includes a digital signature to authenticate the file.

# 11.1 Using Templates

**Video Lesson**    labyrinthelab.com/videos

You may use Excel's predesigned templates or create your own templates as the basis for new workbooks.

## Template Features

Any Excel workbook may be saved as a template. Templates, therefore, may include any type of cell entries, formatting, pictures, shapes, charts, and formatting available in Excel that you wish to reuse for a new workbook. A workbook filename includes the extension .xlsx, as in Richmond Race Results.xlsx, although the operating system may be set to hide extensions from view. When you save a workbook as a template, the filename contains the extension .xltx. That extension tells Excel to open a *copy of the template so that the original remains unchanged and available for reuse as many times as you like. The t*emplate file does not change when you edit workbooks based on that template. You may, however, open the template to make revisions. Those revisions will appear only in new workbooks based on the revised template.

## Creating a New Workbook from a Template

The New tab of Backstage view displays the options for creating a new workbook. You may create a new, blank workbook; create a new workbook based on an existing workbook; or create a new workbook based on a template.

You may use the New from Existing command to create a new workbook based on an existing workbook that was not saved as a template.

### Choosing a Template

You may choose from among three types of templates: installed sample templates, custom templates in the default templates folder or another location, and Office.com Templates. They are shown in the following illustration.

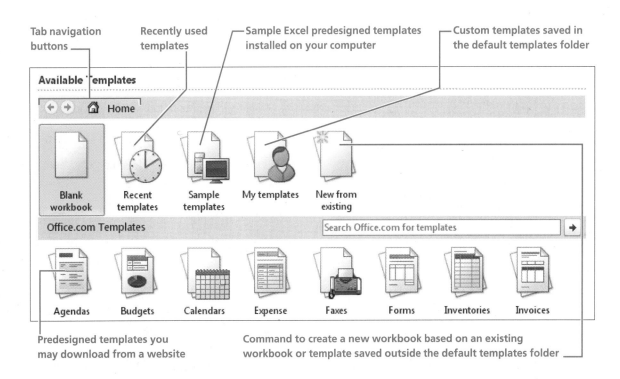

Tab navigation buttons

Recently used templates

Sample Excel predesigned templates installed on your computer

Custom templates saved in the default templates folder

Predesigned templates you may download from a website

Command to create a new workbook based on an existing workbook or template saved outside the default templates folder

## Office.com Templates

If connected to the Internet, you may choose from a variety of templates located on the Microsoft website, including calendars, budgets, calculators, and accounting worksheets. Selecting one of these displays a preview of the template worksheet on the right in the New tab of Backstage view. The Download command transfers the template from the website to your computer.

# Template Storage Locations

Excel's installed templates reside on the computer's hard drive or on a network drive, depending on the Office installation. Office.com templates are placed in your computer's Templates folder after downloading, and you may edit them to meet your specific needs.

Custom templates that you create are saved by default to the Templates folder on your computer. To avoid hunting for your custom templates, save them in this folder. You may not have user privileges to save on some computers or networks. In that case, save to another file storage location. To use the template, you must navigate to that location.

Want to know where that Templates folder is on your computer? Check the last Quick Reference task in the following table.

| Task | Procedure |
|------|-----------|
| Create a workbook based on an existing workbook | ▪ Choose File→New.<br>▪ Choose New from Existing, navigate to the workbook's location, select the workbook, and click Create New. |
| Create a workbook based on an Excel installed template | ▪ Choose File→New.<br>▪ Choose Sample Templates, select a template, and click Create. |
| Create a workbook based on an Office.com template | ▪ Choose File→New.<br>▪ Choose a category under Office.com Templates, select a template, and click Download. |
| Reuse a recently used template | ▪ Choose File→New.<br>▪ Choose Recent Templates and select a template. |
| View the path to the Templates folder | ▪ Choose File→Save as 🗎.<br>▪ Change the Save as Type option to Excel Template.<br>▪ Follow the step for your version of Windows:<br>  ◆ Win 7/Vista: Click the folder button at the left of the address bar in the Save As dialog box or drop down the Look In list. This displays the path to the Templates folder.<br>  ◆ Win XP: Drop down the Look In list. This displays the path to the Templates folder.<br>▪ Cancel the Save As command. |

## DEVELOP YOUR SKILLS 11.1.1

# Create a New Workbook from an Excel Template

*In this exercise, you will use an installed template to create a new workbook.*

### Open a New Workbook Based on a Template

1. Choose **File→New** to display the New tab of Backstage view.

2. **Double-click** Sample Templates.

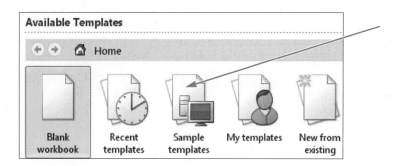

3. Follow these steps to select the installed template named Expense Report:
*If Expense Report is not available, choose another template.*

Ⓐ Select **Expense Report**.　　　　　Ⓑ Notice the displayed preview and then click the **Create** button.

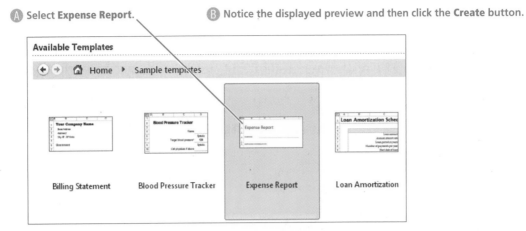

*Excel opens a new workbook containing an expense report form. Notice that the Excel title bar displays ExpenseReport1, indicating that you are working in a copy of the template rather than the original file. (ExpenseReport1 is a temporary document name for display only.)*

4. **Scroll** through the worksheet and **click** cells containing a dollar sign ($) to view their formulas in the Formula Bar. The orange-filled cells are formatted as a table.

## Revise and Save the Workbook

5. Fill in part of the form by **typing** text and numbers into some of the cells.

6. **Save** 🖫 the workbook as **Expense Report** in the Lesson 11 folder in your file storage location.
*Notice that the Save As dialog box opens so that you may type a filename and that the Save as Type shows Excel Workbook, the normal workbook file format.*

7. **Close** ☒ the workbook.

# 11.2 Customizing Templates

**Video Lesson**   labyrinthelab.com/videos

If a predesigned template does not suit your needs, you may create a workbook and save it as a template. You may revise your custom template, but workbooks based on the previous template version do not update.

## Creating Your Own Templates

To create a template, first create a workbook as usual with the cell entries, formatting, graphics, and other settings that you want to reuse. You then choose the Save As command to change the file format to a template.

| | A | B | C |
|---|---|---|---|
| | | Forecast | Forecast |
| 3 | Product | Units | Dollars |
| 4 | **Billing** | | |
| 5 | **MyCareer** | | |
| 6 | **MyResume** | | |
| 7 | **Upgrade Protection** | | |
| 8 | | - $ | - |

The formulas in this routine report are ready to calculate data entered.

| QUICK REFERENCE | USING CUSTOM TEMPLATES |
|---|---|
| **Task** | **Procedure** |
| Create a custom template | ▪ Create the workbook as usual. <br> ▪ Choose File→Save or Save As to display the Save As dialog box. <br> ▪ Type the filename, choose Excel Template in the Save as Type list, and click Save to store the template in the Templates folder. If you do not have user privileges to save in that folder, use a file storage location of your choice. |
| Create a new workbook based on a custom template saved in the Templates folder | ▪ Choose File→New. <br> ▪ In the New tab of Backstage view, choose My Templates and select a template. |
| Create a new workbook based on a custom template saved outside the Templates folder | ▪ Choose File→New. <br> ▪ In the New tab of Backstage view, select New from Existing, navigate to the template's location, select the template, and click Create New. |
| Modify a custom template stored in the default Templates folder | ▪ Choose File→New. <br> ▪ In the New tab of Backstage view, choose My Templates and select a template. <br> ▪ Make the desired changes in the template. <br> ▪ Choose File→Save or Save As. <br> ▪ Choose Excel Template in the Save as Type list, select the original filename, click Save, and click Yes to confirm. |

## Create a New Template

*In this exercise, you will save your workbook as a template in your file storage location. You will not save templates to the hard drive or network drive because many computer classrooms prevent students from accessing those drives. See the preceding Quick Reference table for procedures to save and reuse templates from the Templates folder of a computer's hard drive.*

1. **Open** the Richmond Race Results workbook from the Lesson 11 folder.

2. **Maximize** 🔲 the window.

### Make the Worksheet Generic

*First you will make the workbook generic by removing data specific to the Richmond race. Then you will save the workbook as a template so that it may be used by the race directors.*

3. Select **cell B9** and replace *Richmond 5K Run* with the generic heading **[Type event name here]**.

4. **Select** the text in the callout graphic and **replace** with the generic text **[Type a message or select the graphic and press Delete.]**.

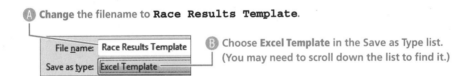

5. **Delete** the race results from the **range B12:D16**.
   *The race directors will fill in the names and scores for a particular race each time they use the template as the basis for a new workbook. Notice that the D17 formula cell displays an error message because you deleted the data. Do not worry. When the directors enter their race results, the formula will calculate correctly.*

### Save the Workbook as a Template

6. Select **cell B9**.
   *It is a good practice to leave a specific cell selected before saving. When you start a new workbook, the pointer will be in that cell ready for typing the event name.*

7. Choose **File→Save As** 🖫 and follow these steps to save the workbook as a template:

Ⓐ **Change** the filename to **Race Results Template**.

| File name: | Race Results Template |
|---|---|
| Save as type: | Excel Template |

Ⓑ Choose **Excel Template** in the Save as Type list. (You may need to scroll down the list to find it.)

8. Navigate to the Lesson 11 folder in your file storage location, and click **Save**. (Do **not** save in the default Templates folder.)
   *The Excel title bar now displays Race Results Template as the filename. The original Richmond Race Results file remains unchanged.*

9. **Close** ☒ the template workbook.

## Base a New Workbook on the Template

*Use the following steps to access templates stored in locations such as a USB drive that prevent them from appearing in My Templates. Do not use the Open command to use such templates because you would be editing the template file rather than creating a new workbook based on the template.*

10. Choose **File→New**.

11. In the New tab of Backstage view, select **New from Existing** and navigate to the Lesson 11 folder, if necessary.

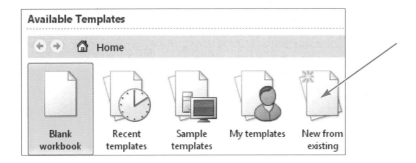

12. Select **Race Results Template**, and click **Create New**.
    *A new generic workbook based on the template appears, and the temporary document name Race Results Template1 appears in the title bar.*

## Customize and Save the New Workbook

13. Follow these steps to enter the data for the Coastal Classic race:

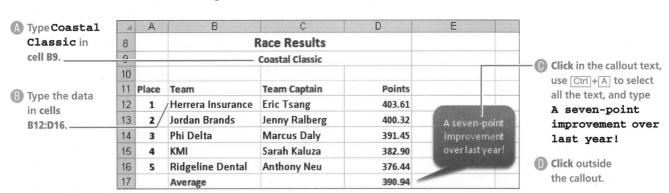

Ⓐ Type **Coastal Classic** in cell B9.

Ⓑ Type the data in cells B12:D16.

Ⓒ **Click** in the callout text, use ⎡Ctrl⎤+⎡A⎤ to select all the text, and type **A seven-point improvement over last year!**

Ⓓ **Click** outside the callout.

14. Click the **Save** 💾 button on the Quick Access toolbar to display the Save As dialog box.
    *Notice that the Save as Type setting is set to Excel Workbook. You are working with a new workbook based on the Race Results template. Your changes will be saved in the new workbook, leaving the underlying template unchanged.*

15. Type **Coastal Classic Race Results** as the filename, verify that the Lesson 11 folder is selected in your file storage location, and click **Save**.

16. **Close** ☒ the workbook.

# Modifying Custom Templates

Video Lesson    labyrinthelab.com/videos

You may modify a custom template after it has been created.

To modify a template, you must open it from within Excel. If you open the template from a folder window, you will simply create a new workbook.

## Browsing for a Template

You can use the My Templates command to base a new workbook on a template in the default Templates folder and the New from Existing command for a template outside that folder. As an alternative, you may use a computer or folder window to navigate to a custom template and issue the Open command. Note that double-clicking a template file does not open the original template for editing but rather creates a new workbook based on the template.

### DEVELOP YOUR SKILLS 11.2.2
## Modify the Template

*In this exercise, you will open the custom template, make a change, and resave.*

### Open the Template

1. Choose **File→Open** 📂.

2. **Navigate** to the Lesson 11 folder.

3. Choose **Race Results Template** and click **Open**.
   *Look at the Excel title bar and notice the name Race Results Template. You are now working with the original template—not a workbook based on the template.*

### Modify the Template and Save the Changes

*Next you will add a row and format a cell for the date.*

4. Insert a **blank row** at **row 10**.

5. Select **cells B10:D10** and choose **Home→Alignment→Merge & Center** 🔳 from the Ribbon.

6. Select **cell B10** and choose **Home→Cells→Format** 🔲 **→Format Cells** 🔲 from the Ribbon.

7. Follow these steps in the Format Cells dialog box to set a date format that displays the month and day in figures:

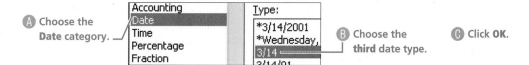

8. In **cell B10**, type **[Enter month and day here]**.

9. Select **cell B9** to position the pointer for data entry when a new workbook is created.

| Race Results |
|---|
| [Type event name here] |
| [Enter month and day here] |

10. **Save** 🖫 the changes and **close** ⊠ the template.

**Test the Modified Template**

11. Choose **File→New**.

12. In the New tab of Backstage view, select **New from Existing** and navigate to your file storage location containing the template, if necessary.

13. Select the **Race Results Template**, and click **Create New**.
    *A new workbook based on the modified template appears.*

14. Select **cell B10** and enter **October 28**.
    *The date formatted as 10/28 replaces the generic instruction.*

15. **Close** ⊠ the new workbook without saving it.

# 11.3 Protecting Workbooks and Worksheets

**Video Lesson** labyrinthelab.com/videos

The protection options prevent your workbooks and worksheets from being accidentally or intentionally modified. Use protection to prevent inexperienced users from damaging workbooks. Excel offers three levels of protection:

■ **Workbook Level Protection**—Protects the structure of the entire workbook, preventing changes to the way worksheets are displayed

■ **Worksheet Level Protection**—Restricts changes to certain objects on worksheets

■ **Cell Level Protection**—Limits access to certain cells on worksheets

## Protecting the Workbook Structure

Protecting a workbook prevents structural changes from being made to the workbook. For example, you cannot delete, rename, copy, or move worksheets while the structure is protected. You may also protect a workbook window to prevent users from changing the window size and position. With Windows protection on, worksheets display consistently every time the workbook is opened. You may turn off workbook protection to make changes and then turn it on again.

### Structure Protection Settings

The Protect Workbook  command displays the dialog box shown in the following illustration. There are two types of protection you can choose. You may use both types simultaneously if desired. Using an optional password allows you to control who can switch this protection on and off.

- **Structure**—Protects worksheets from being reordered, copied, or deleted within the workbook
- **Windows**—Prevents users from changing the workbook window size and position

The Protect Workbook command allows you to create a password so no one else can delete worksheets or alter their order.

### DEVELOP YOUR SKILLS 11.3.1
## Protect a Workbook

*In this exercise, you will protect a workbook template. Assume that you added a worksheet to the Race Results template and deleted the callout on the Results worksheet. You will open the template and protect the workbook structure and window.*

### Open a Template

1. Choose **File→Open** 📂.

2. **Navigate** to the Lesson 11 folder.

3. Choose the **Protected Template** file and click **Open**.
   *Look at the Excel title bar and notice the name Protected Template. You are now working with the original template—not a workbook based on the template.*

### Protect the Entire Workbook

*You wish to standardize the look of the worksheet window each time the workbook is opened and prevent inexperienced users from deleting the worksheet.*

*Notice the two sets of quick-sizing buttons at the top-right corner of the Excel window. The top buttons size the program window and the bottom three buttons size the worksheet within the program window. The bottom sizing buttons will disappear once you protect the windows on the worksheet.*

4. Choose **Review→Changes→Protect Workbook**  from the Ribbon.

5. Place a checkmark in both the **Structure** and **Windows** boxes and click **OK**.
   *Notice that the bottom set of quick-sizing buttons has been removed from the window. The Windows protection option prevents you from sizing and moving the worksheet windows within the program window. If desired, you can still size and move the program window.*

6. Try **dragging** the Results worksheet tab to another location in the workbook order.
   *An icon indicates the action cannot be performed because the workbook is protected.*

7. **Double-click** the Results worksheet tab to try changing its name.
   *A message indicates that the workbook is protected.*

8. Click **OK** to close the message box.
   *At this point you are prevented from modifying the workbook structure. You still may work normally within the worksheet, however.*

## Unprotect and Protect the Workbook

*Notice that the Protect Workbook command is highlighted when toggled on. The highlight disappears when you click the command again to turn off protection.*

9. Choose **Review→Changes→Protect Workbook**  from the Ribbon.

10. **Double-click** the Results worksheet tab and notice that now you could change the name if desired.

11. **Click** anywhere in the worksheet to cancel the renaming action.

12. Choose the **Protect Workbook** command, place a checkmark in both the **Structure** and **Windows** boxes, and click **OK**.

13. **Save**  the template workbook and leave it **open**.

# Protecting Worksheet Elements

Video Lesson    labyrinthelab.com/videos

You may turn on protection for individual worksheets within a workbook. The Protect Sheet command even allows you to restrict activity on the worksheet to specific actions, such as selecting cells, formatting rows and columns, and inserting or deleting rows and columns. Choosing the Protect Sheet command from the Review ribbon is faster, but you also may access the command from a menu on the Home ribbon or on the Info tab in Backstage view.

The Protect Sheet dialog box allows you to restrict specific activities when protection is switched on.

## Turning Protection On and Off

Although it might appear that you would turn worksheet protection on and off by using the Protect Worksheet and Contents of Locked Cells option, that is not the case. That option always should have a checkmark. Clicking OK actually turns on worksheet protection.

## Allowing User Changes

By default only two user options are selected in the Protect Sheet dialog box, giving users permission only to click on cells. If you remove those checkmarks, users may scroll through the worksheet but may not select any cell. You may specify certain items that users still are allowed to change in a protected worksheet, such as editing graphics, deleting rows, and formatting columns.

# Password Protection

For the highest level of protection, type a password in the Protect Sheet dialog box. Users must enter the password to unprotect the worksheet and make further changes. The Protect Structure and Windows dialog box also contains a password option.

**If you forget your workbook protection password, you must re-create the workbook, as you cannot get into the file. You will not assign workbook protection passwords in this lesson.**

| Task | Procedure |
|------|-----------|
| Set workbook level protection | ▪ Choose Review→Changes→Protect Workbook 🔒 from the Ribbon. |
| | ▪ In the Protect Structure and Windows dialog box, place a checkmark in the Structure box and/or Windows box. |
| | ▪ (Optional) Enter a password if you wish to password-protect the protection settings. Retype the password when prompted. |
| Unprotect a workbook | ▪ Choose Review→Changes→Protect Workbook 🔒 from the Ribbon. (The button is shaded when protection is on and unshaded when protection is off.) |
| | ▪ Enter the workbook protection password if prompted. |
| Protect a worksheet | ▪ Choose Review→Changes→Protect Sheet 🔒 from the Ribbon. |
| | ▪ Place a checkmark by any items that users should have permission to change. |
| | ▪ (Optional) Enter a password if you wish to password-protect the protection settings. Retype the password when prompted. |
| Unprotect a worksheet | ▪ Choose Review→Changes→Unprotect Sheet 🔒 from the Ribbon. |
| | ▪ Enter the worksheet protection password if prompted. |
| Unlock ranges of cells in a worksheet and protect all other cells | ▪ Select the desired cell range(s) in the worksheet to be unprotected/unlocked. |
| | ▪ Choose Home→Cells→Format→Lock Cell 🔒 from the Ribbon to toggle the lock setting to off. |
| | ▪ Choose Home→Cells→Format 🔒→Protect Sheet from the Ribbon. |
| Unlock one or more graphics in a worksheet and protect all other graphics | ▪ Select the graphic(s) in the worksheet to be unlocked. |
| | ▪ Choose Format→Size dialog box launcher from the Ribbon. |
| | ▪ Choose the Properties category. |
| | ▪ Remove the checkmark from the Locked box. Also remove the checkmark from the Lock Text box, if you wish a shape's text to be editable. |
| | ▪ Choose Home→Cells→Format 🔒→Protect Sheet from the Ribbon. |

## DEVELOP YOUR SKILLS 11.3.2

# Protect a Worksheet

*In this exercise, you will explore worksheet protection with and without a password.*

### Protect a Worksheet

*A Scoring worksheet in the workbook has been added to explain how race participants are rated. You prefer that other users not be able to change any information in this worksheet.*

1. Display the **Scoring** worksheet in the Protected Template.

2. Choose **Review→Changes→Protect Sheet** 🔒 from the Ribbon.

3. Take a moment to browse the protection options and then click **OK**.

4. **Click** any cell in the worksheet and try entering new text or numbers.
   *Excel displays a message box indicating that the cell cannot be changed.*

5. Click **OK** to close the message box.

## Unprotect the Sheet

*The Scoring worksheet still should be active. Assume that you need to edit the worksheet.*

6. Choose **Review→Changes→Unprotect Sheet** ⊞ from the Ribbon.
   *The command toggles between Protect Sheet and Unprotect Sheet. The Protect Sheet and Unprotect Sheet commands also are available in the Format menu of the Home ribbon.*

7. **Click** any empty cell in the worksheet and enter any number or text.
   *With worksheet protection off, you may make any changes.*

8. **Undo** ⤺ the change.

## Set a Worksheet Password

*The Scoring worksheet still should be active. You wish to set a password for this worksheet because without that higher level of protection, users could unprotect the sheet and inadvertently make changes.*

9. Choose the **Protect Sheet** command from the Ribbon.

10. In the Protect Sheet dialog box, type **abc123** in the Password to Unprotect Sheet box and click **OK**.

11. In the confirm dialog box, retype the **password** and click **OK**.
    *You turned on worksheet protection and set a password to prevent users from unprotecting the sheet without authorization.*

12. **Click** any cell in the worksheet and try entering new text or numbers.
    *Excel displays a message box indicating that the cell cannot be changed because worksheet protection is turned on.*

13. Click **OK** to close the message box.

## Type the Password

*You will use the password to unprotect the worksheet.*

14. Choose the **Unprotect Sheet** command from the Ribbon.

15. Type **abc123** in the Password box and click **OK**.
    *The password is no longer in effect. If you want to password-protect the worksheet again, you must repeat the steps.*

## Protect the Worksheet Without a Password

16. Choose the **Protect Sheet** command from the Ribbon and click **OK** without setting a password.
    *At this point only the Scoring worksheet is protected.*

17. **Save** 🖫 the template workbook and leave it **open**.

# Protecting Cells

Video Lesson    labyrinthelab.com/videos

You may protect the contents and formatting of certain cells from being changed. You also may hide formulas so that they do not display in the Formula Bar or when you use Ctrl+` to display formulas. All cells in a worksheet are locked by default until you unlock them. Why, then, have you been able to edit all locked cells in the lesson up to this point? The cells' locked or unlocked condition has no effect until *worksheet protection* is turned on. *With protection on, you cannot change locked cells.*

## The Protection Tab

You use the Protection tab of the Format Cells dialog box to change options for selected cells. There are two cell protection options you may set:

- **Locked**—Check or uncheck this option to lock/unlock currently selected cells on the worksheet.
- **Hidden**—This option affects only the display of formulas and does not hide labels, values, or formula results.

The Locked option causes the selected cells to be protected.

The Hidden option affects only the display of formulas within the selected cells.

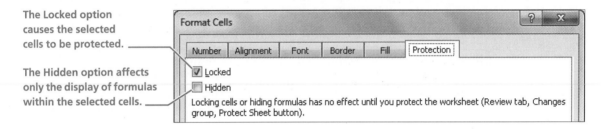

## Unlocking Cells in a Protected Worksheet

When the Locked option is unchecked, selected cells are unlocked. Unlocked cells may be edited even though the overall worksheet is protected. This way, you can protect formulas and labels while allowing data entry in specific parts of the worksheet. You must unlock the cells before protecting the worksheet.

## The Changes Area

For rapid data entry into unlocked cells, you may tap Tab after entering data in each cell. When you reach the end of a row within the changes area and tap Tab, the pointer wraps to the next row.

## To Lock or Not to Lock

Because cells may be locked or unlocked, you may be wondering which option to use. If your worksheet contains only a few cell ranges that users are allowed to change, unlock those cells. The rest of the worksheet remains locked when you turn on worksheet protection. If most of the worksheet needs to be accessible for updating, you may want to choose Select All, select Unlock, and then lock just the cells that you want to protect.

Use the Ctrl key to select multiple cell ranges and then select Unlock, Lock, or Hidden to apply the option to multiple ranges at once.

# Unlock Cells in a Worksheet

*In this exercise, you will unlock a range of cells in the Results worksheet of the Protected Template. You will then turn on protection to prevent labels and the formula from being changed.*

*Before You Begin: The Protected Template workbook should be open in Excel. If it is not, repeat steps 1–3 of Develop Your Skills 11.3.1. Worksheet protection should be off in the Results worksheet.*

## Unlock Cells in the Results Worksheet

*You will set a changes area for data entry in the Results worksheet.*

1. In the Results worksheet of the Protected Template workbook, select the **range B13:D17**. *This range includes all cells that will change for each racing event.*

2. Choose **Home→Cells→Format** from the Ribbon and notice the **Lock Cell** button on the menu.
   *The shaded button indicates that the selected cells are currently locked.*

3. Complete the command by choosing **Lock Cell** 🔒 to toggle the lock setting to off.

4. With the range still selected, choose **Home→Cells→Format** and notice the Lock Cell button. (Do **not** click the Lock Cell command.)
   *The button is not shaded, indicating that the selected cells are unlocked.*

5. **Click** on a worksheet cell to exit the Format menu without choosing a command.

6. Issue the command to unlock **cells B9:B10**.
   *Remember that these actions have no effect on unlocked and locked cells until you protect the worksheet in the next step.*

## Protect the Sheet and Test Cell Attributes

7. Choose **Home→Cells→Format→Protect Sheet** 🔲 from the Ribbon and click **OK**.

8. Select **cell A13** and try entering data in the cell.
   *A message box appears to indicate that the cell is protected.*

9. Click **OK** to close the message box.

10. Select **cell B13**, type **800**, and **press** ⎘Tab⎚.
    *Excel lets you enter the number because you unlocked the cell prior to protecting the sheet. Using Tab speeds cell data entry in the changes area.*

11. **Undo** the cell entry.

12. Select **cell B9** to position the pointer for data entry when a new workbook is created.

13. **Save** 💾 the changes.

14. Choose **File→Close** 🗂 to close the workbook without exiting Excel.
    *Because the workbook window is protected, the window's Close button is unavailable.*

## Create a New Workbook

*After designing a template, you will find it a good practice to test its use.*

15. Choose **File→New**.

16. In the New tab of Backstage view, select **New from Existing** and navigate to the Lesson 11 folder, if necessary.

17. **Choose Protected Template**, and click **Create New**.
    *A new generic workbook based on the template appears.*

## Enter Sample Data

*The pointer is in cell B9 ready for data entry.*

18. Type **Deer Creek Run** in **cell B9**.

19. Type **April 17** in **cell B10**.
    *The date formatted as 4/17 displays.*

20. Enter the following data:

| Place | Team | Team Captain | Points |
|---|---|---|---|
| 1 | Sole Survivors | Diana Luna | 392.41 |
| 2 | Canton Medical | John Gordon | 388.16 |
| 3 | Road Warriors | Aaron Brooks | 384.50 |
| 4 | Duarte Supply | Gloria Ochoa | 325.84 |
| 5 | Chau Family | Min Chau | 317.55 |

21. **Verify** that other cells are locked by trying to enter data in a few cells.

22. **Save** 🖫 the workbook as **Deer Creek Race Results** in the Lesson 11 folder.

23. Choose **File→Close** to close the workbook.

# 11.4 Creating Digital Signatures

**Video Lesson**   labyrinthelab.com/videos

A digital signature authenticates that your workbook originated from you, came from a reliable source, and was not altered—possibly by a virus—after the digital signature was applied. Digital signatures are sometimes called digital IDs.

If anyone (or a computer virus) modifies the worksheet in any way, the digital signature is removed when the changes are saved. The absence of the digital signature may indicate a security problem. You must remove a digital signature to change your workbook, and then you may reapply the digital signature.

## When to Use a Digital Signature

You may use a digital signature when giving workbooks or templates to others as email attachments, as a downloadable file on your organization's intranet, from a website, or on a disk. In addition, you may send a document to someone for an electronic signature as you would a paper document.

## Creating a Digital Certificate

You add a digital signature to a file by attaching a digital certificate. If no certificate is installed when you use the Add a Digital Signature command, a dialog box appears to allow you to get a certificate. You may obtain a digital certificate using one of the following methods:

■ **Via Self Signature**—You may create your own digital certificate, although its use is limited. The authenticity of the digital signature can be verified only on your own computer.

■ **Via Digital Certificate**—Digital certificates may be obtained from third-party vendors, which check identification before issuing a certificate. If you post workbooks on an intranet or the Internet, your network administrator usually will provide you with an authentic digital certificate.

This dialog box displays if a digital certificate (digital ID) is not installed.

 Your network security administrator may provide the digital certificates for your organization, so check with that person before creating your own. You will not obtain or install a third-party digital certificate in this lesson. You may not have user permission to create a digital certificate on your classroom computer.

# Create a Digital Certificate

*In this exercise, you will create a temporary digital certificate on your local computer.*

*Although you will not install a digital certificate from a third party in this lesson, you would use most of the following steps in doing so.*

1. **Open** the Coastal Classic Race Results workbook from the Lesson 11 folder.
   *You created this workbook in Develop Your Skills 11.2.1.*

2. Choose **File→Info**. Click the **Protect Workbook** button in Backstage view and choose **Add a Digital Signature** from the menu.
   *If a digital signature already exists on your computer, the dialog boxes may differ from those described in the next steps.*

3. In the Microsoft Excel dialog box, click **OK**.
   *If a digital ID is already installed on the computer, the Sign dialog box appears. Otherwise, the Get a Digital ID dialog box appears.*

4. If the **Sign** dialog box is visible, skip to **step 8**; otherwise continue with **step 5**.

5. **Read** the descriptions for the two options in the Get a Digital ID dialog box.
   *It's not necessary to purchase a digital ID in order to sign a document. In this case, you will simply create your own self-signature.*

6. Choose **Create Your Own Digital ID** and click **OK**.
   *The Create a Digital ID dialog box appears. Here you can add descriptive information for your self-signature.*

7. Follow these steps to fill in the digital ID information for Brett Martin:

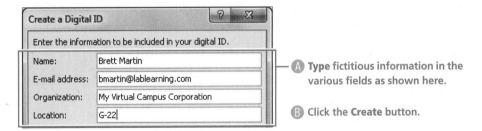

Excel creates the digital ID, which is stored in your computer. The Sign dialog box displays.

8. Leave the Sign dialog box **open** for the next exercise.

# Creating a Digital Signature

**Video Lesson**   labyrinthelab.com/videos

Your digital signature may be embedded in the workbook with or without a signature line visible on a worksheet.

## Electronic vs. Written Signature Lines

Paper forms and other documents often contain signature lines. You may add similar signature lines electronically to Excel workbooks and templates by using the Signature Line menu on the Insert Ribbon. The recipient adds an electronic signature next to the X by typing the name or adding a picture of a handwritten signature. A digital signature is added automatically to the file to authenticate the recipient's identity.

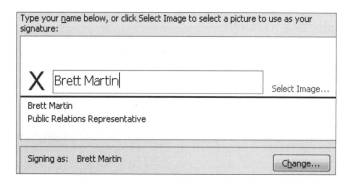

Entering an electronic signature that will be visible in the worksheet

## Invisible Signatures

If a signature line is not necessary, you may add just the digital signature, which does not display on any worksheet. However, the signature is visible in the Signatures task pane (see the next topic). So this signature is not literally invisible, it's just not openly displayed like the formal signature line described in the previous topic.

## Checking Signature Details

The Status Bar displays the Signatures 👤 button whenever you open a digitally signed workbook. Clicking this button displays the Signatures task pane, where you may view the signature details to verify that there is no problem with the signature. When a signed document is attached to email, the recipient should look in the email message for the Signatures button and a Signed By line.

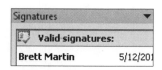

The Signatures task pane displays the digital signature name and certificate expiration date. View other details from the name's drop-down menu.

| Task | Procedure |
|------|-----------|
| Create a self-signature certificate on the local computer and create an invisible digital signature | ■ Choose File→Info→Protect Workbook menu ▼→Add a Digital Signature.<br>■ If the Microsoft Excel dialog box displays, click OK.<br>■ If the Get a Digital ID dialog box displays, choose Create Your Own Digital ID and click OK.<br>■ Type your information in the Create a Digital ID dialog box and click OK.<br>■ Fill in the Purpose for Signing This Document box, if desired, and click Sign. |
| Remove a digital certificate | ■ Launch Internet Explorer. (Depending on your browser version, you may need to modify the next steps.)<br>■ Choose Tools→Internet Options, and display the Content tab.<br>■ Under Certificates, click the Certificates button.<br>■ Display the Personal tab, choose the certificate, click Remove, click Yes, and then click Close. |
| Apply an invisible digital signature (digital certificate installed) | ■ Choose File→Info→Protect Workbook menu ▼→Add a Digital Signature.<br>■ Fill in the Purpose for Signing This Document box, if desired, and click Sign. |
| Remove a digital signature | ■ Choose File→Info→View Signatures if the Signatures pane is not already displayed.<br>■ Drop down the menu on the signature name and choose Remove Signature. |
| Add a visible signature line to a worksheet | ■ Choose Insert→Text→Signature Line menu ▼→Microsoft Office Signature Line from the Ribbon.<br>■ In the Signature Setup dialog box, type the text to appear under the signature line, and select any desired options. |
| Sign a signature line | ■ Double-click the signature line in the worksheet.<br>■ In the Sign dialog box, do one of the following:<br>  ◆ Type your name next to the X.<br>  ◆ Click Select Image, navigate to the folder containing the image file, select the file, and click Select.<br>  ◆ Write a handwritten signature next to the X using a tablet PC. |

## DEVELOP YOUR SKILLS 11.4.2

# Apply a Digital Signature

*In this exercise, you will add a digital signature to the a workbook and view details about the digital signature.*

*Before You Begin: You must have completed Develop Your Skills 11.4.1, and the Coastal Classic Race Results workbook should be open.*

*Now that you have created a digital certificate, you may add a digital signature to the workbook.*

1. If the Sign dialog box is not open from the last exercise, choose **File→Info→Protect Workbook menu ▼→Add a Digital Signature** from the Ribbon and click **OK**.

2. Read the information in the Sign dialog box, type **Race results certification** in the Purpose for Signing This Document box, and click **Sign**.

*Typing the purpose is optional for a digital signature.*

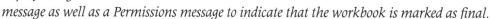

3. Click **OK** to confirm.

*The Info tab of Backstage view displays a Signed Workbook message as well as a Permissions message to indicate that the workbook is marked as final.*

4. Choose **View Signatures** next to the Signed Workbook message; **read** the message above the worksheet.

*The user may choose to edit the workbook, which removes the digital signature.*

*The Signatures task pane displays with Brett's name as a valid signature and the digital certificate's date.*

5. Follow these steps to display signature details:

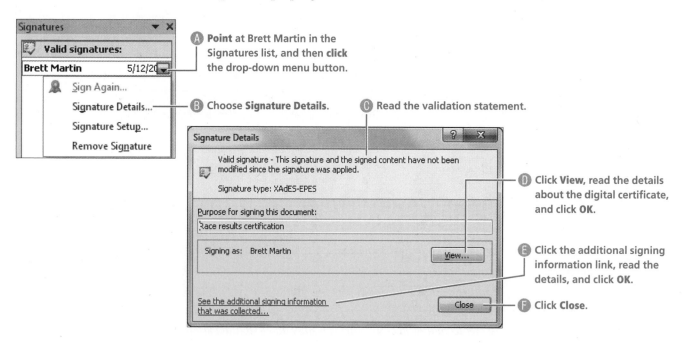

(A) **Point** at Brett Martin in the Signatures list, and then **click** the drop-down menu button.

(B) Choose **Signature Details**.

(C) Read the validation statement.

(D) Click **View**, read the details about the digital certificate, and click **OK**.

(E) Click the additional signing information link, read the details, and click **OK**.

(F) Click **Close**.

*Notice that the Excel title bar displays [Read-Only]. Also notice that the Save button is dimmed in the Quick Access toolbar.*

# Removing Digital Signatures

**Video Lesson** labyrinthelab.com/videos

You display the Signatures task pane to view signatures that have been created. A digital signature may be removed at any time by using the drop-down menu on each signature name or by choosing Edit Anyway in the message bar above the worksheet window. Note, however, that you would remove a digital *certificate* in Internet Explorer, not in Excel.

## DEVELOP YOUR SKILLS 11.4.3
## Remove a Digital Signature

*In this exercise, you will remove the digital signature from the Excel workbook file, reapply it, and then remove the digital certificate from the computer.*

### Remove the Digital Signature

*Because a digital signature verifies that a document has not changed since the digital signature was applied, Excel does not allow any changes to this document. Assume that you want to change the document, so you need to remove the digital signature.*

1. Point to **Brett Martin** in the signatures list, click the **drop-down menu button**, and choose **Remove Signature**.
   *Excel prompts you to confirm that the signature should be permanently removed from the document. However, you can reapply the signature and shortly will do so.*

2. Choose **Yes** to confirm the removal, and then click **OK**.
   *The document is now available for changes.*

### Reapply the Digital Signature

*Assume that you changed some data. You will reapply the digital signature.*

3. Choose **File→Info→Protect Workbook menu ▾**→Add a Digital Signature from the Ribbon, click **OK**, click **Sign,** and click **OK**.
   *Adding a digital signature was quicker this time because the digital certificate already exists.*

4. **Close** Backstage view, and **close** the Signatures task pane.

5. **Close** ⊠ the workbook.
   *You are not prompted to save.*

### Remove the Digital Certificate from the Local Computer

*You will remove the digital certificate to restore the local computer to its original condition.*

6. Launch **Internet Explorer.**
   *Depending on your browser version, you may need to modify the next steps.*

7. Choose **Tools→Internet Options**, and display the **Content** tab.

8. In the Certificates section, click the **Certificates** button.

9. In the Certificates dialog box, display the **Personal** tab, if necessary.

10. Select the Brett Martin certificate, and then click the **Remove** button.
    *Internet Explorer displays a prompt that you cannot decrypt data that was encrypted with the certificate and asks you to confirm the removal.*

11. Choose **Yes** to confirm removal of the certificate.

12. Click the **Close** button to close the Certificates dialog box.

13. Click **OK** to close the Internet Options dialog box.
    *You have removed the digital certificate to restore the setup for other users.*

14. **Exit** Internet Explorer.

## 11.5 Concepts Review

| Concepts Review | labyrinthelab.com/excel10 |

*To check your knowledge of the key concepts introduced in this lesson, complete the Concepts Review quiz by going to the URL listed above. If your classroom is using Labyrinth eLab, you may complete the Concepts Review quiz from within your eLab course.*

# Reinforce Your Skills

## Use a Workbook as a Template

*In this exercise, you will use the Fall Gold Results workbook as the basis for a new workbook. To accomplish this, you will use the New from Existing option in the New Workbook dialog box.*

### Create the New Workbook

1. Choose **File→New** to display the New tab of Backstage view.

2. Click **New from Existing**.
   *The New from Existing Workbook dialog box appears. This box lets you locate an existing workbook to be used as the basis of a new workbook.*

3. **Navigate** to the Lesson 11 folder in your file storage location.

4. Choose the **rs-Fall Gold Results** workbook and click the **Create New** button.
   *A new workbook identical to the Fall Gold Results workbook appears. Notice that the Excel title bar displays the temporary display name Fall Gold Results1, indicating that this is a copy of the original file.*

5. **Maximize** 🔲 the window.

### Modify the Workbook

6. Click in **cell B9** and change the word *Gold* to **Bronze**.

7. Change the scores in **column D** as follows: **38, 41, 45, 50, 53**
   *The Average function in cell D17 will recalculate the average based on the new numbers.*

8. **Click** in the callout and edit the phrase to **two-point**.

9. Apply a different **shape style** to the callout.
   *Choose a style with a color that blends with other colors in the worksheet.*

### Save the Workbook

10. Click **Save** 💾 in the Quick Access toolbar.
    *The Save As dialog box appears, allowing you to save the workbook with a new name. The New from Existing command in the New tab of Backstage view allows you to use an existing workbook just like you would use a template.*

11. **Save** the workbook as **rs-Fall Bronze Results** in the Lesson 11 folder.
    *Make certain to delete the number 1 from the filename before completing the save.*

12. **Close** ☒ the workbook.

# Unlock a Graphic in a Template

*You have learned how to unlock certain cells to allow changes when worksheet protection is turned on. In this exercise, you will unlock a graphic so that it may be changed.*

1. Use the **Open** 📂 command to open rs-Sailing Event Template in the Lesson 11 folder. Verify that the Excel title bar displays the template filename and does not include a number.
   *You are working in the original template file rather than a workbook copy.*

2. **Maximize** ▣ the window.

3. Display the **Results** worksheet, if necessary.

4. Choose **Review→Change→Unprotect Sheet** 🔓 from the Ribbon.
   *You must unprotect the sheet to unlock a graphic.*

5. Select the **callout**.

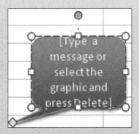

6. With the callout selected, choose the Drawing Tools Format ribbon and click the dialog box launcher button in the Size group on the Ribbon.
   *The Format Shape dialog box displays with the Size options in view. You will unlock this graphic so that users may change its text or delete the graphic when it is not needed.*

7. Select the **Properties** category at the lower-left of the dialog box, make certain that **Locked** and **Lock Text** are unchecked, and click **Close**.

8. Choose **Review→Change→Protect Sheet** 🔒 from the Ribbon and click **OK** in the Protect Sheet dialog box.
   *New workbooks based on this template will allow users to edit the callout, but the other worksheet graphics are still locked.*

9. Select **cell B9** to position the pointer for data entry when a new workbook is created.

10. **Save** 💾 and **close** the template.

# Create a Template

*In this exercise, you will create a template that will be used for quarterly forecasts at Zephron Industries. All Zephron sales reps will use the template as a basis for quarterly sales forecasts. The template includes three worksheets: a data sheet, a column chart sheet, and a pie chart sheet. You will format the data worksheet, remove the sample data, and save the workbook as a template. This way, the sales reps need only enter their data, and the charts already are created for them.*

## Set Up the Worksheet Using Sample Data

*You will set up the worksheet in the next few steps. You will include sample data to test the template. The data will be deleted prior to saving the template.*

1. **Open** 📂 the **rs-Sales Forecast** workbook from the Lesson 11 folder and **maximize** the window.

2. Display the **Revenue Forecast** worksheet to view the bar chart and then display the **Revenue Breakdown** worksheet to view the pie chart.

3. In the Data Sheet worksheet, click the **Select All** ◢ button.

4. Choose **Home→Cells→Format** ▦ **→Column Width** and set the column widths to **13**.

## Design the Worksheet

5. Use the **Merge & Center** �centericon button on the Ribbon to center the title and subtitle in **rows 1** and **3** across **columns A–C**.

6. In **cell C10**, create a formula to sum the **Forecast Dollars** values.

7. Apply a fill color and font color to the cells containing data in **rows 1–3**, **5**, and **10**. The example uses a **dark fill color** and a **white font color**.

8. Format the **range B6:C9** in **Comma Style** with **no decimal places**, as shown. Format the total forecast dollars in **Accounting style** with **no decimals**.

| ◢ | A | B | C |
|---|---|---|---|
| 1 | Zephron Quarterly Sales Forecast | | |
| 2 | | | |
| 3 | Sales Rep - Donna Wilson | | |
| 4 | | | |
| 5 | Product | Forecast Units | Forecast Dollars |
| 6 | GPS Systems | 230 | 21,900 |
| 7 | Cell Phones | 560 | 24,000 |
| 8 | Netbooks | 725 | 165,000 |
| 9 | PCs | 120 | 92,400 |
| 10 | Total | | $  303,300 |

## Delete the Sample Data and Save the Workbook as a Template

9.  Select the numbers in the **range B6:C9** in the **Data Sheet** worksheet.

10. **Tap** Delete to delete the data.
    *The total in cell C10 displays as a dash (zero). The formula is still intact, however, so the total will recalculate when new data are entered in the cells. The charts will be meaningless until data are entered into the Data Sheet.*

11. Select **cell B6** to set the pointer in the data entry area when a workbook is opened.

12. Choose **File→Save As** and set the Save as Type to **Excel Template**.

13. Change the filename to `rs-Sales Forecast Template` and save it to the Lesson 11 folder (not the Templates folder).

14. Leave the template **open** for the next exercise.
    *You will set protection options in the next exercise.*

---

### REINFORCE YOUR SKILLS 11.4

# Use and Modify a Template

*The Sales Forecast Template that you created in Reinforce Your Skills 11.3 contains text, formatting, formulas, and charts. Creating a template with such items is especially useful for inexperienced users who may have learned only how to enter data. In this exercise, you will protect chart sheets and worksheet cells to prevent users from inadvertently altering the design.*

*Before You Begin: You must have completed Reinforce Your Skills 11.3, and the rs-Sales Forecast Template workbook should be open.*

## Protect a Template

1.  If necessary, **open** rs-Sales Forecast Template from the Lesson 11 folder.

2.  Verify that the Excel title bar displays the template filename and does not include a number.
    *You are working in the original template file rather than a workbook copy.*

3.  **Maximize** 🔲 the window, if necessary.

4.  Display the **Revenue Forecast** worksheet.
    *No values display in the chart because you deleted them in the previous exercise.*

5.  Choose **Review→Change→Protect Sheet** 🔒 from the Ribbon and click **OK** in the Protect Sheet dialog box.

6.  Choose the command to **protect** the Revenue Breakdown worksheet also.
    *This chart also contains no values, and the labels overlap. Next you will set a changes area by unlocking cells and turning on worksheet protection.*

7.  Display the **Data Sheet** worksheet.

8.  Select the **range B6:C9**.

9.  Choose **Home→Cells→Format→ Lock Cell** 🔒 from the Ribbon to unlock the selected cells.

10. Choose the command to **protect** the Data Sheet worksheet.

11. Select **cell B6** to position the pointer for data entry when a new workbook is created.

12. **Save** 🖫 and **close** the template.
*You will use the template to create a new workbook in the next exercise.*

---

**REINFORCE YOUR SKILLS 11.5**

# Use a Template

*In this exercise, you will create a new workbook based on the rs-Sales Forecast Template, and then enter data.*

*Before You Begin: You must have completed Reinforce Your Skills 11.3 and Reinforce Your Skills 11.4.*

## Create a New Workbook Based on the Template

1. Choose **File→New→New from Existing**.

2. Navigate to the Lesson 11 folder, **select** rs-Sales Forecast Template, and click **Create New**.
*A new workbook based on the Sales Forecast Template file appears. Notice that no data currently exists in cells B6:C9.*

3. **Maximize** 🗖 the window, if necessary.

4. Display the **Revenue Forecast** worksheet to view the bar chart and then display the **Revenue Breakdown** worksheet to view the pie chart.
*Notice that these chart sheets currently do not display charts because the Data Sheet cells are empty. The charts will be generated as you enter data in the next step.*

5. **Enter** the numbers shown to the right into **columns B and C** of the Data Sheet. After typing each number, **tap** Tab.
*The pointer will wrap to the next row of the changes area for rapid data entry.*

| | A | B | C |
|---|---|---|---|
| | | Forecast | Forecast |
| 5 | Product | Units | Dollars |
| 6 | GPS Systems | 200 | 20,500 |
| 7 | Cell Phones | 590 | 25,000 |
| 8 | Netbooks | 750 | 167,000 |
| 9 | PCs | 120 | 90,300 |

*The Total for Forecast Dollars should equal $302,800. The data are formatted with the Comma Style and Accounting number format that you already set in the template.*

6. Display the **Revenue Forecast** worksheet and then display the **Revenue Breakdown** worksheet.
*Notice that the charts have been generated.*

7. Click **Save** 🖫 in the Quick Access toolbar to display the Save As dialog box.

8. Change the filename to **rs-Wilson Forecast** and **save** to the Lesson 11 folder.
*The workbook has been saved and the template is ready to be used for future forecasts.*

9. **Close** ⊠ the workbook.

## Create a Digital Signature

*In this exercise, you will create a digital certificate and apply a digital signature to a workbook.*

### Create a Digital Certificate on the Local Computer

*You will create a temporary digital certificate rather than install a digital certificate from a third party.*

1. **Open** 📂 the rs-Sales workbook from the Lesson 11 folder.

2. Choose **File→Info→Protect Workbook menu ▾→Add a Digital Signature**.
   *If a digital signature already exists on your computer, the dialog boxes may differ from those described in the next steps.*

3. In the Microsoft Excel dialog box, click **OK**.

4. Choose **Create Your Own Digital ID** and click **OK**.
   *You are creating a self-signature digital certificate on your local computer.*

5. In the Create a Digital ID dialog box, **type** your information (make up details as necessary) and click **Create**.
   *The Sign dialog box displays.*

### Add a Digital Signature to a Workbook

6. Now that you have created a digital certificate, you may use the Sign dialog box to add a digital signature to the workbook.

7. Type **Sales** in the Purpose for Signing This Document box, and click **Sign**.

8. Click **OK** to confirm.
   *The Info tab indicates the file is a Signed Workbook and has been marked as final.*

9. Click the **View Signatures** button in the Info tab of Backstage view.
   *The Signatures task pane displays as shown with your name as a valid signature and the digital certificate's date.*

   *Notice that the Excel title bar displays [Read-Only]. Also notice that the Save button is dimmed in the Quick Access toolbar. The digital signature ensures recipients that the file was not altered, possibly by a computer virus. The Marked as Final message bar above the worksheet allows you to remove the digital signature and edit the file, if necessary.*

10. **Close** ☒ the task pane.

11. Choose **File→Exit**.
    *You are not prompted to save. (Excel saved the workbook when you added the digital signature.)*

## Remove the Digital Certificate from the Local Computer

*You will remove the digital certificate to restore the local computer to its original condition.*

12. **Launch** Internet Explorer.

    *Depending on your browser version, you may need to modify the next steps.*

13. Choose **Tools→Internet Options**, and display the **Content** tab.

14. Under Certificates, click the **Certificates** button.

15. In the Certificates dialog box, display the **Personal** tab, if necessary.

16. Select your certificate, click **Remove**, click **Yes**, click **Close**, and then click **OK**.

    *You have removed the digital certificate to restore the setup for other users.*

# Apply Your Skills

## Create and Use a Template

*In this exercise, you will create a template for the Redmont School District. Each school within the district will use the template to create a budget workbook and an accompanying chart. They will use the New from Existing command in the New Workbook dialog box to base their new workbooks on the template you create.*

### Create the Template

1. Start **Excel** and **open** the as-Budget Allocation workbook from the Lesson 11 folder.

2. **Maximize** the window.
   *The worksheet contains sample data and an embedded pie chart.*

3. **Delete** the sample data in the **range B4:B8**, and then **deselect** the range.

4. Select an appropriate cell to be ready for data entry in new workbooks based on this template.

5. Display a **print preview** to verify that the workbook and chart will print on **one page**.
   *Notice that a footer displays the filename in the center section.*

6. **Close** the print preview without printing.

7. **Save** as a template named **as-Budget Allocation Template**. Make certain to save your template in the Lesson 11 folder, **not** the Templates folder.

8. **Close** the template.

### Create a New Workbook Based on the Template

9. Use the **New from Existing** command in Backstage view to create a new workbook based on the as-Budget Allocation Template file.

10. **Rename** the Sheet1 tab to **Barrett**.

11. Type **Barrett School** in **cell C1**.

12. **Enter** the data shown into the **range B4:B8**. The chart in your new workbook should display the new percentages. You may adjust the position of any chart data labels, if necessary.

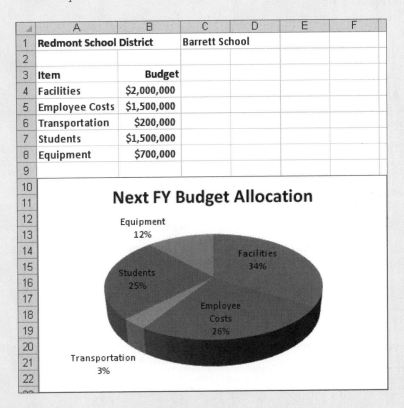

13. **Save** 💾 with the name **as-Barrett Budget** in the Lesson 11 folder and **close** the workbook.

## Protect a Template

*In this exercise, you will protect specific cells in a worksheet and protect a workbook template.*

1. **Open** the as-Budget Template file from the Lesson 11 folder.
   *You should be working in the original template file rather than a workbook copy.*

2. **Maximize** 🔲 the window.

### Protect the Template

3. Unlock the **range B4:B8** and **cell C1** so that the user may enter data only in those cells. The user should not be allowed to change any other cells.

4. **Protect** the Budget worksheet.

5. **Protect** the template so that users may not delete or insert any sheet tabs.

6. **Save** 💾 the template.

7. Have your instructor or a teaching assistant initial that you successfully applied cell protection, worksheet protection, and workbook protection to the template. _____

8. Leave the template **open**.
*You will apply a digital signature to the template in the next exercise.*

## Apply a Digital Signature

*In this exercise, you will create a digital ID and use it to apply a digital signature to a workbook.*

1. **Open** the as-Budget Template from the Lesson 11 folder if it is not already open.
*You should be working in the original template file rather than a workbook copy.*

2. **Maximize** ☐ the window.

### Create a Digital ID

3. Create a **digital ID** on your computer with your name, a made-up email address, and the name of your class.

### Apply a Digital Signature

4. **Apply** a digital signature to the template.

5. Have your instructor or a teaching assistant initial that you successfully applied a digital signature to the document. _____

6. **Close** ☒ the template.

# Remove a Digital Signature

*In this exercise, you will remove a digital signature from a workbook and remove the digital ID from the computer.*

*Before You Begin:* You must have completed Apply Your Skills 11.3 .

### Remove the Digital Signature

1. **Open** as-Budget Template from the Lesson 11 folder.
*The Marked as Final message should display above the worksheet because you applied a digital signature in the previous exercise.*

2. **Remove** the digital signature from the template.

3. Have your instructor or a teaching assistant initial that you successfully removed the digital signature. _____

4. **Close** ☒ the template and **exit** Excel.

### Remove the Digital ID

5. **Remove** the digital ID from the computer.

6. Have your instructor or a teaching assistant initial that you successfully removed the digital ID. _____

# Critical Thinking & Work-Readiness Skills

*In the course of working through the following Microsoft Office-based Critical Thinking exercises, you will also be utilizing various work-readiness skills, some of which are listed next to each exercise. Go to labyrinthelab.com/ workreadiness to learn more about the work-readiness skills.*

## 11.1 Create a New Workbook from an Excel Template

Elizabeth Zain is the western regional sales account manager for My Virtual Campus. She wants each office to use the same template when submitting purchase orders. Verify that your Internet connection is active. Open a new Excel file. Locate the Office.com templates, search for purchase order templates, and open the Purchase Order (Simple Blue Design) template. Customize the template by inserting the company logo into cell A1 using the MyVirtualCampus file (Lesson 11 folder). Revise the template to reflect the western region using cell A3. Save your work as **ct-Purchase Order Form [Your Last Name]**. Close the file when you are finished.

**WORK-READINESS SKILLS APPLIED**

- Exercising leadership
- Improving or designing systems
- Selecting technology

## 11.2 Create Your Own Template

Ms. Green is a tennis instructor at Western State College who uses web applications through My Virtual Campus. She teaches five classes each semester and wants to convert an existing class to a template for consistent use with each class. She will emphasize the class meeting time using a colored shape. Open ct-Green (Lesson 11 folder). Use the Count function to calculate the number of students absent on any given day. Protect these formula cells. Locate and insert the horizontal scroll shape from the Stars and Banners category, and enter generic text in the shape to indicate the class meeting time. Delete all data for specific students. Save your work as a template with the name **ct-Green [Your Last Name]** in the Lesson 11 folder. Close the file when you are finished.

**WORK-READINESS SKILLS APPLIED**

- Managing the self
- Organizing and maintaining information
- Improving or designing systems

## 11.3 Protect a Worksheet

Elizabeth Zain wants to create a worksheet projecting next year's profit based on the past two years of revenue and expenses. She also wants to protect the formula she creates from any changes. Open ct-My Virtual Campus Profit. Create a formula to subtract the expenses from the revenue given for each year. Lock the formula cells. Test the cell integrity. Password-protect your worksheet, and then remove password protection. Save your work as **ct-My Virtual Campus Profit [Your Last Name]**. Close the file when you are finished.

**WORK-READINESS SKILLS APPLIED**

- Selecting technology
- Using arithmetic/ mathematics
- Managing the self

# Creating PivotTables and Macros

## LEARNING OBJECTIVES

After studying this lesson, you will be able to:

- Create PivotTables and change their fields
- Create PivotCharts from PivotTable or worksheet data
- Set macro security to protect workbook data
- Record and run macros to automate tasks
- Add custom task buttons to worksheets

Excel has many features to help you perform sophisticated data analyses, including the PivotTable and the PivotChart. PivotTables let you summarize worksheet data dynamically to view them in various ways. In this lesson, you will arrange your data with simple drag-and-drop commands and have Excel automatically create summary formulas in the rows and columns. You also will create PivotCharts to achieve the same power and flexibility for charting data. Many Excel workbooks are used on a recurring basis. Examples include monthly expense accounts, sales forecasts, and lists of various types. Often, the same tasks are performed in these workbooks over and over. Excel allows you to create macros to automate repetitive tasks. In addition, Excel lets you assign macros to shortcut keys, buttons on the Quick Access toolbar, and custom buttons or other graphics in a worksheet. In this lesson, you will create macros and custom buttons in an Excel workbook.

# Simplifying Repetitive Tasks

Raritan
Clinic
East

Pediatric Diagnostic Specialists

Raritan Clinic East, an incorporated medical practice that serves a patient community ranging in ages from newborn to 18 years, is planning to construct a pediatric oncology facility. In addition, a companion facility will provide temporary housing to physicians specializing in ground-breaking cancer treatments and long-term housing for family members of the children who are receiving treatments. Sandra Chavez-Hall is the chief development officer for the clinic's foundation. She coordinates a fundraising campaign to solicit contributions from private donors, charitable organizations, industry sources, and government grants to build the two facilities. Sandra will use PivotTables and PivotCharts to analyze the contributions by various criteria.

| 3 | Row Labels | Sum of Year 1 | Sum of Year 2 |
|---|---|---|---|
| 4 | ⊟Level 1 | 117,267,482 | 118,272,625 |
| 5 | Corporate Sponsorship | 17,460,000 | 20,300,000 |
| 6 | Federal Government Grant | 49,899,591 | 47,894,948 |
| 7 | Individual Sponsorship | 12,500,000 | 15,000,000 |
| 8 | State Government Grant | 37,407,891 | 35,077,677 |
| 9 | ⊟Level 2 | 6,254,063 | 7,511,682 |
| 10 | Corporate Grant | 1,250,000 | 1,425,000 |
| 11 | Corporate Sponsorship | 250,000 | 200,000 |
| 12 | Individual Sponsorship | 2,500,000 | 2,500,000 |
| 13 | Medical Center/Large Facility | 100,000 | 90,250 |
| 14 | Medical Ctr Contribution | 654,063 | 596,432 |
| 15 | Organized Labor/Union Contribution | 750,000 | 700,000 |
| 16 | Private Grant | 750,000 | 2,000,000 |
| 17 | ⊞Level 3 | 1,317,583 | 1,204,419 |
| 18 | ⊞Level 4 | 202,100 | 85,500 |
| 19 | ⊞Level 5 | 58,287 | 109,509 |
| 20 | ⊞Level 6 | 15,186 | 6,827 |
| 21 | Grand Total | 125,114,701 | 127,190,562 |

Levels 3–6 are collapsed to display only the subtotals.

The PivotTable shows the contributions organized by sponsor categories within each pledge level. You can easily rearrange the design to view the data in other ways.

Sandra also maintains a contributions-to-date summary report. She uses macros to record the steps used in sorting the data. By attaching each macro to a button on a worksheet, she can sort the report with one click.

| | A | B | C | D | E | F | G |
|---|---|---|---|---|---|---|---|
| 1 | | Raritan Clinic East  Pediatric Diagnostic Specialists | Capital Campaign | Insert Sponsor | Sort by Leader | | |
| 2 | | | | | | | |
| 3 | Pledge | Team Leader | Sponsor Category | Sponsor Name | Year 1 | Year 2 | To Date |
| 4 | Level 3 | Abbott | Organization Contribution | Child Advocate Society | 50,000 | 50,000 | 100,000 |
| 5 | Level 3 | Abbott | Organization Contribution | Kelsey Foundation | 0 | 50,000 | 50,000 |
| 6 | Level 4 | Abbott | Organization Contribution | Hands Across Foundation | 20,000 | 15,500 | 35,500 |
| 7 | Level 4 | Abbott | Organization Contribution | Chamber of Commerce | 10,000 | 12,500 | 22,500 |
| 8 | Level 5 | Abbott | Organization Contribution | Accountancy Association | 0 | 15,000 | 15,000 |
| 9 | Level 5 | Abbott | Organization Contribution | Business Roundtable | 0 | 15,000 | 15,000 |

Macros were created to perform repetitive tasks; then they were assigned to buttons in row 1.

# 12.1 Creating PivotTables

Video Lesson     labyrinthelab.com/videos

PivotTables are powerful data analysis tools. They let you summarize data in various ways and instantly change the view you use. You can create normal Excel lists and tables to sort and filter data and produce subtotals. A PivotTable not only subtotals groups of related data, but also goes a step further and compares one group to another. Compared with performing similar data analyses on a standard worksheet, PivotTables offer tremendous speed and flexibility.

## Arranging the Source Data

You create PivotTables from columns or from a table in an Excel worksheet. The data should contain no blank rows or columns. Converting a list to a table is recommended when records will be added after the PivotTable is created. The additional table data are included automatically when the PivotTable is refreshed or updated. Data in a list are not included automatically. The following examples explain two PivotTables based on the same worksheet list.

| | A | B | C | D | E | F |
|---|---|---|---|---|---|---|
| 3 | Pledge Level | Team Leader | Sponsor Category | Sponsor Name | Year 1 | Year 2 |
| 4 | Level 5 | Abbott | Organization Contribution | Accountancy Association | 0 | 15,000 |
| 5 | Level 4 | Faber | Corporate Sponsorship | Accurate Biomedical | 10,000 | 10,000 |
| 6 | Level 1 | Lemus | Federal Government Grant | Admin for Children & Fam | 5,129,874 | 8,075,333 |
| 7 | Level 3 | Faber | Corporate Sponsorship | Alpha Supplies Corp. | 125,000 | 50,000 |
| 8 | Level 6 | Nguyen | Individual Contribution | Andres Padilla | 0 | 500 |

The worksheet data on which the sample PivotTables are based

## PivotTable Example 1

You could sort the preceding table by pledge level or sponsor category; however, you could not easily compare totals for the various pledge levels in each sponsor category. This is where the PivotTable comes into use. A PivotTable can summarize some or all of the data in any number of ways, and it creates grand totals for you. Each column in a PivotTable is a *field*. Examine the PivotTable and notice that the Sponsor Category field from the table is used for the row labels, the Pledge Level field for the column labels, and the Year 2 field for the data area and grand totals. Each row displays the amount given by each sponsor group in the various pledge levels.

This PivotTable summarizes contributions from all sponsor groups.

| Sum of Year 2 Row Labels | Column Labels Level 1 | Level 2 | Level 3 | Level 4 | Level 5 | Level 6 | Grand Total |
|---|---|---|---|---|---|---|---|
| Corporate Grant | | 1,425,000.00 | | 0.00 | | | 1,425,000.00 |
| Corporate Sponsorship | 20,300,000.00 | 250,000.00 | 350,000.00 | 22,500.00 | 28,750.00 | | 20,951,250.00 |
| Federal Government Grant | 47,894,948.00 | | | | | | 47,894,948.00 |
| Individual Contribution | | | | | 4,100.00 | 2,080.00 | 6,180.00 |
| Individual Sponsorship | 15,000,000.00 | 2,500,000.00 | 413,579.00 | 15,000.00 | 4,475.00 | 595.00 | 17,933,649.00 |
| Local Business Contribution | | | | | 2,634.00 | 992.00 | 3,626.00 |
| Local Government Grant | | | 243,500.00 | | | | 243,500.00 |
| Medical Center/Large Facility | | 90,250.00 | | | | | 90,250.00 |
| Medical Ctr Contribution | | 596,432.00 | 122,340.00 | | | | 718,772.00 |
| Organization Contribution | | | 50,000.00 | 28,000.00 | 39,050.00 | 3,160.00 | 120,210.00 |
| Organized Labor/Union Contribution | | 700,000.00 | | | | | 700,000.00 |
| Physician Office Contribution | | | 25,000.00 | 20,000.00 | 30,500.00 | | 75,500.00 |
| Private Grant | | 2,000,000.00 | 0.00 | | | | 2,000,000.00 |
| State Government Grant | 35,077,677.00 | | | | | | 35,077,677.00 |
| Grand Total | 118,272,625.00 | 7,561,682.00 | 1,204,419.00 | 85,500.00 | 109,509.00 | 6,827.00 | 127,240,562.00 |

The amount given by each sponsor group is displayed by pledge level.

Filter buttons allow you to sort and filter the sponsor groups and pledge levels.

PivotTables automatically total the rows and columns and calculate a grand total.

# PivotTable Example 2

Using the same table data, you may view the data differently—in this case, summarized first by pledge level and then by sponsor category. To create this type of view, the PivotTable layout shown in the following illustration contains the Pledge Level and then Sponsor Category fields for row labels, no column labels, and the Year 2 field for the data area and totals.

This PivotTable layout summarizes contributions first by pledge level and then by sponsor category.

Buttons allow you to collapse and expand the level of detail.

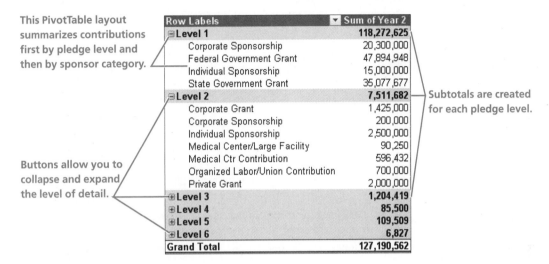

Subtotals are created for each pledge level.

In this lesson, you will learn how to lay out both of these types of PivotTables and much more.

# How PivotTables Work

Each area of the PivotTable plays a role in data organization. The PivotTable Field List task pane displays after you define the worksheet range to be used. The areas of the task pane are explained in the following illustration showing the settings for the preceding PivotTable Example 1.

You may choose some or all columns from the worksheet data to appear in the PivotTable.

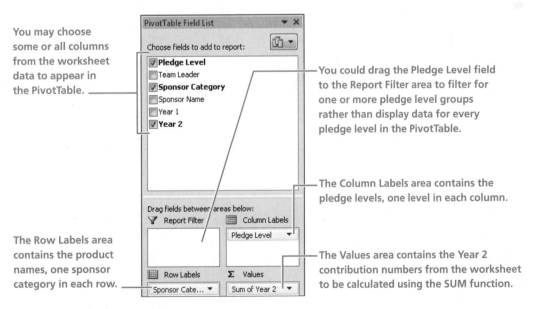

You could drag the Pledge Level field to the Report Filter area to filter for one or more pledge level groups rather than display data for every pledge level in the PivotTable.

The Column Labels area contains the pledge levels, one level in each column.

The Row Labels area contains the product names, one sponsor category in each row.

The Values area contains the Year 2 contribution numbers from the worksheet to be calculated using the SUM function.

You must select a cell in the PivotTable to display the PivotTable Field List task pane.

You design a PivotTable by choosing the columns (fields) to be included from the worksheet. Excel initially places all text columns that you choose into the Row Labels area and all selected number columns into the Values area for summing. If this is not your desired layout, you can drag and drop various fields into the correct areas of the task pane. Where you place fields determines how the PivotTable summarizes the data. By choosing different fields or dragging and dropping a field, you may quickly compare data in various ways. You may choose from several functions—such as SUM, COUNT, and AVERAGE—to calculate fields containing values.

| QUICK REFERENCE | CREATING A PIVOTTABLE |
|---|---|
| **Task** | **Procedure** |
| Create a PivotTable from a worksheet range or table | ▪ Select a cell in the worksheet range or table. |
| | ▪ Choose Insert→Tables→PivotTable [icon] from the Ribbon. |
| | ▪ Verify the worksheet range or table name in the Create PivotTable dialog box and click OK to place the PivotTable on a new worksheet. |
| | ▪ In the PivotTable Field List task pane, place a checkmark by each worksheet field to be included in the design, selecting the fields in the order they should appear as row labels and values columns. |
| | ▪ If necessary, drag and drop a field name to the correct area: Report Filter, Row Labels, Column Labels, or Values. |
| Name a PivotTable | ▪ Choose Options→PivotTable, type the name in the PivotTable name text box (spaces are allowed), and tap [Enter]. |
| Display the PivotTable Field List task pane | ▪ Select any cell within the PivotTable. |
| | ▪ If the task pane is turned off, choose Options→Show→Field List from the Ribbon. |

## DEVELOP YOUR SKILLS 12.1.1
# Create PivotTables

*The best way to understand the dynamic capabilities of a PivotTable is to create one. In this exercise, you will create PivotTables from a worksheet range and a table.*

**Review the Worksheet Data**

1. Start **Excel** and **open** the Sponsors workbook from the Lesson 12 folder in your file storage location.

2. **Maximize** [icon] the window.
   *The Sponsors Sheet worksheet contains the data you will use to create two PivotTables. Look at the column headings and the various records in the rows. Each record contains data for a specific donor or government grant for the building project. Notice the dollar amounts contained in the Year 1 and Year 2 columns.*

## Create a PivotTable from a Worksheet Range

*You will create a PivotTable that summarizes Year 2 by pledge level with subtotals for each sponsor category (corporation, individual, organization, state government agency, and so on).*

3. Select **cell B4**.
   *You should select a cell within the worksheet range or table before you create the PivotTable. The range should contain no blank rows or columns.*

4. Choose **Insert→Tables→PivotTable** 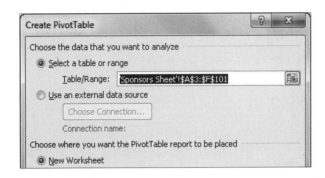 from the Ribbon.
   *The Create PivotTable dialog box appears.*

5. Verify the suggested range as shown, notice that the default is to place the PivotTable on a new worksheet, and click **OK**.
   *A new worksheet appears and contains an empty PivotTable placeholder. The PivotTable Field List task pane also displays. If the task pane is turned off, choose Options→Show→Field List from the Ribbon.*

6. **Rename** Sheet1 as **PivotTable by Sponsor Category**.

7. Select **cell A1**, which is outside the boundary of the PivotTable outline.
   *Notice that the PivotTable Field List task pane disappears. You must select a cell within the PivotTable placeholder to display the task pane.*

8. Select **cell A3** within the PivotTable placeholder to restore the task pane.
   *Notice that the PivotTable Field List task pane contains a list of all the data fields in the worksheet range. You will choose only some of them.*

9. Follow these steps to define the PivotTable in the task pane:

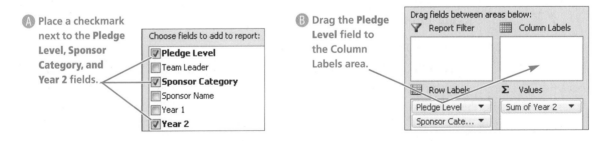

*In the resulting PivotTable, notice that the sponsor categories are displayed one per row, the six pledge levels are displayed one per column, and the Year 2 contributions data are summarized with totals for each sponsor category in column H and each pledge level in row 19. The Level 1 label is not aligned over its numbers in cell B4, and you will fix this in a later exercise.*

| | A | B | C | D | E | F | G | H |
|---|---|---|---|---|---|---|---|---|
| 3 | Sum of Year 2 | Column Labels | | | | | | |
| 4 | Row Labels | Level 1 | Level 2 | Level 3 | Level 4 | Level 5 | Level 6 | Grand Total |
| 5 | Corporate Grant | | 1425000 | | 0 | | | 1425000 |
| 6 | Corporate Sponsorship | 20300000 | 250000 | 350000 | 22500 | 28750 | | 20951250 |
| 7 | Federal Government Grant | 47894948 | | | | | | 47894948 |
| 8 | Individual Contribution | | | | | 4100 | 2080 | 6180 |
| 9 | Individual Sponsorship | 15000000 | 2500000 | 413579 | 15000 | 4475 | 595 | 17933649 |
| 10 | Local Business Contribution | | | | | 2634 | 992 | 3626 |
| 11 | Local Government Grant | | | 243500 | | | | 243500 |
| 12 | Medical Center/Large Facility | | 90250 | | | | | 90250 |
| 13 | Medical Ctr Contribution | | 596432 | 122340 | | | | 718772 |
| 14 | Organization Contribution | | | 50000 | 28000 | 39050 | 3160 | 120210 |
| 15 | Organized Labor/Union Contribution | | 700000 | | | | | 700000 |
| 16 | Physician Office Contribution | | | 25000 | 20000 | 30500 | | 75500 |
| 17 | Private Grant | | 2000000 | 0 | | | | 2000000 |
| 18 | State Government Grant | 35077677 | | | | | | 35077677 |
| 19 | Grand Total | 118272625 | 7561682 | 1204419 | 85500 | 109509 | 6827 | 127240562 |

## Name the PivotTable

10. Choose **Options→PivotTable** from the Ribbon, type **BySponsorCategory** in the Pivot-Table name text box, and **tap** Enter.

## Create a PivotTable from a Worksheet Table

*The steps for creating a PivotTable from a worksheet table are the same as for a worksheet range. This time your PivotTable will group the data by pledge level with the sponsor categories in alphabetical order within each pledge level.*

11. Display the **Sponsors Table** worksheet in the Sponsors workbook.

12. With any table cell selected, choose **Insert→Tables→PivotTable** from the Ribbon.

13. Verify that the suggested range is the **Sponsors_Table** and click **OK**.

14. **Rename** the new sheet as **PivotTable by Pledge Level**.

15. In the PivotTable Field List task pane, place a checkmark next to field names *in this order*: **Pledge Level, Sponsor Category, Year 2**.
*The task pane and the PivotTable results should display as shown. The records are grouped by pledge level with the sponsor categories in alphabetical order within each pledge level. The Year 2 subtotal displays for each pledge level, and a grand total appears at the bottom of the column. With this layout, you did not need to create any column labels.*

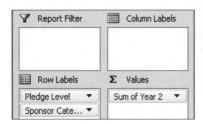

| 3 | Row Labels | Sum of Year 2 |
|---|---|---|
| 4 | ⊟Level 1 | 118,272,625 |
| 5 | Corporate Sponsorship | 20,300,000 |
| 6 | Federal Government Grant | 47,894,948 |
| 7 | Individual Sponsorship | 15,000,000 |
| 8 | State Government Grant | 35,077,677 |
| 9 | ⊟Level 2 | 7,511,682 |
| 10 | Corporate Grant | 1,425,000 |
| 11 | Corporate Sponsorship | 200,000 |

16. Choose **Options→PivotTable** from the Ribbon, type **By Pledge Level** in the Pivot-Table name text box, and **tap** Enter .
    *Notice that you can type a PivotTable name with or without spaces.*

17. **Save** 🖫 the changes to your workbook.

# Formatting a PivotTable

**Video Lesson**    labyrinthelab.com/videos

Values and subtotals in the PivotTable do not automatically display the formatting from the original worksheet cells. You may set number formatting for a value field. You also may select and format one or more specific cells in the PivotTable. For example, you may align the column labels using commands on the Home tab of the Ribbon. The PivotTable Tools Design contextual tab contains a large selection of PivotTable styles to apply color, shading, and gridlines with one mouse click. The report layout displays in Compact Form by default, or you may choose from two other layouts. The subtotals may be displayed at the top or bottom of each group or hidden.

| | A | B |
|---|---|---|
| 3 | Row Labels ▾ | Sum of Year 2 |
| 4 | ⊟Level 1 | 118,272,625 |
| 5 | Faber | 20,300,000 |
| 6 | Lemus | 82,972,625 |
| 7 | Weinstein | 15,000,000 |
| 8 | ⊟Level 2 | 7,561,682 |
| 9 | Debowski | 700,000 |

The Compact Form report layout with a PivotTable style applied

| | A | B | C |
|---|---|---|---|
| 3 | Pledge Leve ▾ | Team Leader ▾ | Sum of Year 2 |
| 4 | ⊟Level 1 | Faber | 20,300,000 |
| 5 | | Lemus | 82,972,625 |
| 6 | | Weinstein | 15,000,000 |
| 7 | **Level 1 Total** | | **118,272,625** |
| 8 | ⊟Level 2 | Debowski | 700,000 |
| 9 | | Faber | 200,000 |

The Tabular Form report layout with filter buttons for each row label field

| QUICK REFERENCE | FORMATTING A PIVOTTABLE |
|---|---|
| **Task** | **Procedure** |
| Apply number formatting to a field | Right-click a column cell in the PivotTable, choose Number Format from the pop-up (context) menu, and choose options from the Format Cells dialog box. (Do not choose the Format Cells command from the context menu, which formats the selection rather than entire columns.) |
| Change the subtotals or grand totals display | Choose Design→Layout→Subtotals 🖼 or Grand Totals 🖼 and choose an option from the Ribbon. |
| Apply a PivotTable style | Choose Design→PivotTable Styles and choose a style from the Ribbon. |
| Apply a report layout | Choose Design→Layout→Report Layout 🖼 and choose the Compact (default), Outline, or Tabular layout from the Ribbon. |

## Format a PivotTable

*In this exercise, you will format the PivotTables that you created in the previous exercise. You will format selected cells, apply number formatting to values columns, choose a PivotTable style, and explore the report layout choices.*

### Format PivotTable Data

1. Display the **PivotTable by Sponsor Category** worksheet in the Sponsors workbook. *You may need to use the navigation buttons at the left of the worksheet tabs to bring the desired tab into view.*

2. Select the **range B4:H4** and **right-align** the labels to match the number alignment in their columns.

3. Choose **Design→Layout→Grand Totals menu ▼** from the Ribbon. Experiment by choosing each option and observe its result. Choose **On for Rows and Columns** when you are finished.

4. If necessary, **select** any cell in the PivotTable to redisplay the PivotTable Field List task pane.

5. Follow these steps to format the Year 2 contribution numbers in the PivotTable:

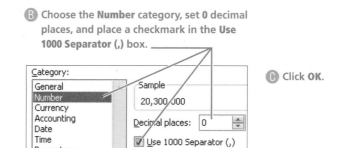

Ⓐ **Right-click** any number in the **range B5:H19**, and choose **Number Format** from the context menu.

Ⓑ Choose the **Number** category, set **0** decimal places, and place a checkmark in the **Use 1000 Separator (,)** box.

Ⓒ Click **OK**.

*All number columns are displayed with the formatting that you chose because they all are part of the Sum of Year 2 field.*

|  | A | B | C | D |
|---|---|---|---|---|
| 3 | Sum of Year 2 | Column Labels ▼ | | |
| 4 | Row Labels ▼ | Level 1 | Level 2 | Level 3 |
| 5 | Corporate Grant | | 1,425,000 | |
| 6 | Corporate Sponsorship | 20,300,000 | 250,000 | 350,000 |
| 7 | Federal Government Grant | 47,894,948 | | |

### Apply a PivotTable Style

6. Display the **PivotTable by Pledge Level** worksheet.

7. Choose the **Design→PivotTable Styles→More ▼** button, scroll through the available styles, and choose **PivotStyle Medium 9**. *This style shades the subtotal rows.*

8. Choose **Design→Layout→Report Layout→Show in Outline Form** from the Ribbon.
*This layout divides the Pledge Level and Sponsor Category fields into separate columns. Both column headings display a filter button.*

9. Choose **Design→Layout→Report Layout→Show in Tabular Form** from the Ribbon.
*This layout displays a subtotal row below its detail rows.*

10. Choose **Design→Layout→Report Layout→Show in Compact Form** to return to the original layout.

11. **Save** 💾 the changes to your workbook.

# Changing PivotTable Fields

| Video Lesson | labyrinthelab.com/videos

You may add or remove fields on a PivotTable simply by adding or removing the checkmark next to the field name in the PivotTable Field List task pane. The PivotTable will automatically reconfigure to display the new data. You also may change the order of fields within the row and column areas. One of the most powerful ways of manipulating data is to move a field from the row area to the column area or vice versa. This is called *pivoting the field* (thus the name PivotTable). The display of the data field rotates to give you an entirely different view of your data, as illustrated in the two PivotTables you created in the previous exercise. There, you positioned the Region field to display as columns in the first PivotTable and as rows in the second.

## Change PivotTable Fields

*In this exercise, you will add fields to the PivotTable and reorder the display of fields. You also will pivot the view.*

### Add a Values Field

1. Display the **PivotTable by Pledge Level** worksheet, if necessary.
*The PivotTable contains data only for Year 2. Now you will add Year 1.*

2. Place a checkmark next to **Year 1** in the task pane to add this field to the PivotTable.
*The Year 1 values are summed with subtotals and a grand total. Notice that Excel automatically added a ∑ Values entry in the task pane Column Labels area because the PivotTable now contains two Sum columns.*

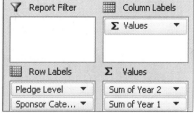

3. **Right-click** any cell in the **Sum of Year 1** column of the PivotTable, and choose **Number Format** from the context menu.

4. In the Format Cells dialog box, choose the **Number** category, set **0** decimal places, place a checkmark in the **Use 1000 Separator (,)** box, and click **OK**.

5. Repeat **steps 3 and 4** to format the **Sum of Year 2** column.

## Reorder Fields

6. **Drag** Sum of Year 2 below Sum of Year 1 in the Values area.

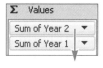

| 3 | Row Labels | ▼ | Sum of Year 1 | Sum of Year 2 |
|---|---|---|---|---|
| 4 | ⊟ Level 1 | | 117,267,482 | 118,272,625 |
| 5 | Corporate Sponsorship | | 17,460,000 | 20,300,000 |
| 6 | Federal Government Grant | | 49,899,591 | 47,894,948 |
| 7 | Individual Sponsorship | | 12,500,000 | 15,000,000 |
| 8 | State Government Grant | | 37,407,891 | 35,077,677 |
| 9 | ⊟ Level 2 | | 6,254,063 | 7,561,682 |
| 10 | Corporate Grant | | 1,250,000 | 1,425,000 |
| 11 | Corporate Sponsorship | | 250,000 | 250,000 |

*The PivotTable now displays the columns for both years in the order listed in the Values area of the task pane.*

## Add and Then Remove a Labels Field

7. Place a checkmark by the **Sponsor Name** field in the top section of the PivotTable Field List task pane.

   *Notice the order of the fields in the Row Labels area. Now the sponsors and their contribution amounts are displayed within each sponsor category. Adding or deleting row labels allows you to control the level of detail displayed in a PivotTable.*

| 4 | Row Labels | ▼ | Sum of Year 1 | Sum of Year 2 |
|---|---|---|---|---|
| 5 | ⊟ Level 1 | | 117,267,482 | 118,272,625 |
| 6 | ⊟ Corporate Sponsorship | | 17,460,000 | 20,300,000 |
| 7 | Jensen Pharmaceutical | | 7,500,000 | 10,000,000 |
| 8 | Medical Solutions Corp. | | 5,460,000 | 4,300,000 |
| 9 | Open Systems | | 4,500,000 | 6,000,000 |
| 10 | ⊟ Federal Government Grant | | 49,899,591 | 47,894,948 |
| 11 | Admin for Children & Fam | | 5,129,874 | 8,075,333 |

8. Remove the checkmark by the **Sponsor Category** field and **Sponsor Name** field in the PivotTable Field List task pane.

9. Add a checkmark by the **Team Leader** field.

   *The team leader totals appear within each pledge level. Notice that some team leaders appear in multiple pledge levels. This view makes it easy to compare Year 1 and Year 2 data.*

## Pivot the View

10. Drag the **Team Leader** field from the Row Labels area to the Column Labels area below the Σ Values field.

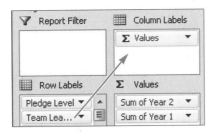

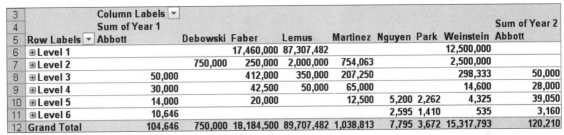

| 3 | Column Labels ▼ | | | | | | | | Sum of Year 2 |
|---|---|---|---|---|---|---|---|---|---|
| 4 | Sum of Year 1 | | | | | | | | |
| 5 Row Labels ▼ | Abbott | Debowski | Faber | Lemus | Martinez | Nguyen Park | Weinstein | Abbott |
| 6 ⊞ Level 1 | | | 17,460,000 | 87,307,482 | | | 12,500,000 | |
| 7 ⊞ Level 2 | | 750,000 | 250,000 | 2,000,000 | 754,063 | | 2,500,000 | |
| 8 ⊞ Level 3 | 50,000 | | 412,000 | 350,000 | 207,250 | | 298,333 | 50,000 |
| 9 ⊞ Level 4 | 30,000 | | 42,500 | 50,000 | 65,000 | | 14,600 | 28,000 |
| 10 ⊞ Level 5 | 14,000 | | 20,000 | | 12,500 | 5,200 2,262 | 4,325 | 39,050 |
| 11 ⊞ Level 6 | 10,646 | | | | | 2,595 1,410 | 535 | 3,160 |
| 12 Grand Total | 104,646 | 750,000 | 18,184,500 | 89,707,482 | 1,038,813 | 7,795 3,672 | 15,317,793 | 120,210 |

*You just pivoted the team leader field to be displayed in columns rather than rows. This view allows you to compare each team leader's overall performance among the various pledge levels, but comparing Year 1 to Year 2 is more difficult than in the previous view.*

11. **Undo** 🔄 the pivot you performed in the previous step.

12. **Save** 💾 the changes to your workbook.

# Filtering a PivotTable with AutoFilter

**Video Lesson** labyrinthelab.com/videos

You may set the PivotTable to filter, or include, specific items in the data summaries. The totals and subtotals are recalculated for the selected items. The Row Labels and Column Labels headings have an AutoFilter button that displays the same sorting and filtering options that are available on the columns of worksheet lists and tables.

This is the field to be filtered is selected in the list.

The heading contains an AutoFilter button.

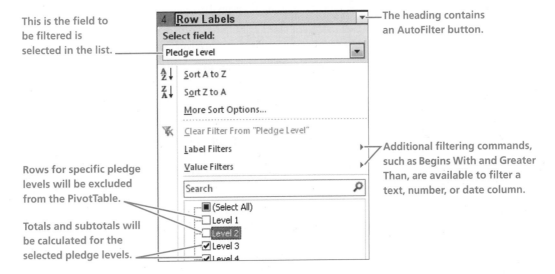

Additional filtering commands, such as Begins With and Greater Than, are available to filter a text, number, or date column.

Rows for specific pledge levels will be excluded from the PivotTable.

Totals and subtotals will be calculated for the selected pledge levels.

# Filtering PivotTables with Slicers

New to Excel 2010, slicers are menu frames displayed on the worksheet that contain all filtering choices in one field. You can choose items or clear a filter without having to drop down a list. Selected items are highlighted in slicers, making it easy to see which criteria have been applied to the PivotTable filter. Slicer frames may be resized, moved, and formatted with styles for a consistent appearance. Slicers also may be shared in other worksheets of the same workbook for use with multiple PivotTables based on the same data set. Changing the filtering selections in a shared slicer causes all connected PivotTables to update automatically.

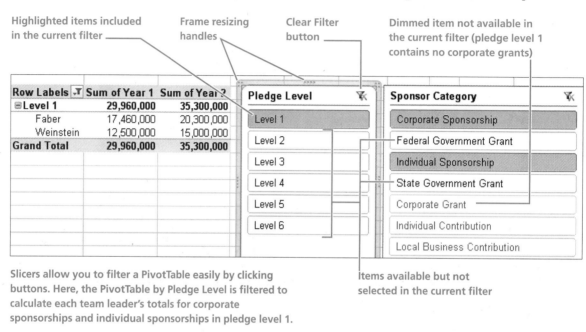

Highlighted items included in the current filter —

Frame resizing handles

Clear Filter button —

Dimmed item not available in the current filter (pledge level 1 contains no corporate grants)

Items available but not selected in the current filter

Slicers allow you to filter a PivotTable easily by clicking buttons. Here, the PivotTable by Pledge Level is filtered to calculate each team leader's totals for corporate sponsorships and individual sponsorships in pledge level 1.

| QUICK REFERENCE | CHANGING PIVOTTABLE FIELD ORDER AND FILTERING A PIVOTTABLE USING AUTOFILTER AND SLICERS |
|---|---|
| **Task** | **Procedure** |
| Change the field order in rows or columns | ▪ Drag a field name above or below another field in an area list at the bottom of the PivotTable Field List task pane. |
| Remove a field | ▪ Uncheck the field name from the PivotTable Field List task pane. |
| Filter for specific items using AutoFilter | ▪ Click the AutoFilter ▼ button next to Row Labels, Column Labels, or a specific column label, if available, in the PivotTable.<br>▪ Choose a field from the fields available in the filtering list.<br>▪ Remove the checkmark form the desired item(s), or choose Label Filters, Value Filters, or Date Filters, depending on the type of data in the column. |
| Filter for specific items using slicers | ▪ Select any cell in the PivotTable.<br>▪ Choose Options→Sort & Filter→Insert Slicer ▤ from the Ribbon. (Or, choose Design→Filter→Slicer.)<br>▪ Place a checkmark next to the desired fields in the Insert Slicers dialog box, and click OK.<br>▪ Choose one or more items in slicers, as desired. To select additional items in a slicer, hold down Ctrl while clicking each item. To remove items from a multiple selection, hold down Ctrl while clicking each item. |

| Task | Procedure |
|------|-----------|
| Clear a filter from a slicer | ■ Choose the Clear Filter button in the upper-right corner of the desired slicer. |
| Move and resize a slicer | ■ Point to a slicer's frame or title bar and drag to the desired location on the worksheet. <br> ■ Drag a corner or side handle on the slicer frame to resize the slicer. |
| Display slicer buttons in multiple columns | ■ Select the slicer. <br> ■ Choose Options→Buttons→Columns , and choose the number of columns from the Ribbon. |
| Apply a style to a slicer | ■ Select the slicer. <br> ■ Choose Options→Slicer Styles, and choose a style from the Ribbon. |
| Connect a slicer to additional PivotTables based on the same data set in the workbook | ■ Select the slicer. <br> ■ Choose Options→Slicer→PivotTable Connections from the Ribbon. <br> ■ Place a checkmark by the PivotTable name(s) to which you wish to connect the slicer. |

## DEVELOP YOUR SKILLS 12.1.4

# Filter a PivotTable with Slicers

*In this exercise, you will display slicers on a PivotTable worksheet. You will move, resize, and format the slicers to fit around the PivotTable. Then, you will select items from the slicers to filter the PivotTable to look at the data in various ways.*

### Insert Slicers

1. Display the **PivotTable with Slicers** worksheet in the Sponsors workbook. (**Scroll** to the right in the worksheet tabs to locate the tab, if necessary.)
   *The PivotTable displays the Sponsor Categories field as rows and the Sum of Year 1 and Sum of Year 2 fields as columns.*

2. **Select** any cell in the PivotTable to display the PivotTable Tools in the Ribbon, if necessary.

3. Choose **Options→Sort & Filter→Insert Slicer** from the Ribbon.

4. Place a checkmark next to the **Pledge Level, Team Leader,** and **Sponsor Category** fields in the Insert Slicers dialog box; click **OK**.

5. Select **cell A1** to hide the PivotTable Field List task pane, if still displayed.

## Move and Resize Slicers

6. Follow these steps to move and resize the Sponsor Category slicer:

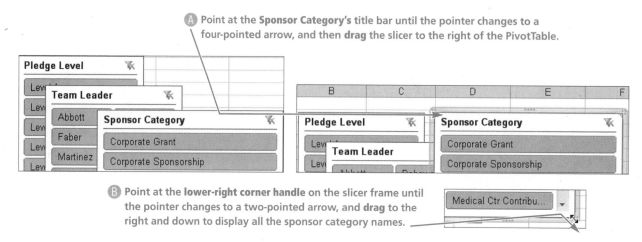

Ⓐ Point at the **Sponsor Category's** title bar until the pointer changes to a four-pointed arrow, and then **drag** the slicer to the right of the PivotTable.

Ⓑ Point at the **lower-right corner handle** on the slicer frame until the pointer changes to a two-pointed arrow, and **drag** to the right and down to display all the sponsor category names.

7. Drag the **Pledge Level** slicer and **Team Leader** slicer to **row 20** as shown.

8. Click the **Pledge Level** title to display the slicer's frame, and then **hold down** ⎡Shift⎤ and click on the **Team Leader** title.

*Frames appear around the two slicers to indicate both are selected. If you click a slicer button by mistake, click the Clear Filter button in the upper-right corner of the slicer and repeat step 8.*

9. Choose **Options→Buttons→Columns** ⊞ from the Ribbon, and change the number of columns from 1 to **2**.

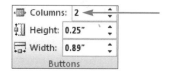

## Apply Slicer Styles

10. Click the **Sponsor Category** title in the slicer at the right of the PivotTable, choose **Options→Slicer Styles**, and choose any style from the Ribbon.

11. Repeat **step 10** to apply styles of your choice to the **Pledge Level** slicer and **Team Leader** slicer.

## Filter the PivotTable

12. Choose **Level 1** in the Pledge Level slicer.

| Pledge Level | |
|---|---|
| Level 1 | Level 2 |
| Level 3 | Level 4 |
| Level 5 | Level 6 |

| Team Leader | |
|---|---|
| Faber | Lemus |
| Weinstein | Abbott |
| Debowski | Martinez |
| Nguyen | Park |

The Team Leader slicer shows that Faber, Lemus, and Weinstein are included in the PivotTable totals. The buttons are dimmed for the other team leaders because they did not solicit any contributions at pledge level 1.

| Row Labels | Sum of Year 1 | Sum of Year 2 |
|---|---|---|
| Corporate Sponsorship | 17,460,000 | 20,300,000 |
| Federal Government Grant | 49,899,591 | 47,894,948 |
| Individual Sponsorship | 12,500,000 | 15,000,000 |
| State Government Grant | 37,407,891 | 35,077,677 |
| **Grand Total** | **117,267,482** | **118,272,625** |

| Sponsor Category |
|---|
| Corporate Sponsorship |
| Federal Government Grant |
| Individual Sponsorship |
| State Government Grant |
| Corporate Grant |

*Four sponsor categories are displayed in the PivotTable, matching the four highlighted buttons in the Sponsor Category slicer. These are the only types of sponsors to contribute at level 1, the highest dollar level.*

13. Click the **Clear Filter** button on the Pledge level slicer to restore all data in the Pivot-Table.

14. Select **Corporate Sponsorship** in the Sponsor Category slicer.
    *The Sum of Year 2 total in the PivotTable is 20,951,250. The slicers show that Pledge Levels 1–5 and team leader Faber are included.*

15. **Hold down** Ctrl and select **Individual Sponsorship**.
    *The PivotTable and slicers reflect the additional category. You can use* Ctrl *+click to select additional items or deselect them in a slicer.*

16. Experiment by **selecting** and **deselecting** various criteria in the slicers; **clear filters** from all slicers when you are finished.

17. **Save** the changes to the workbook.

# Editing PivotTable Calculations

Video Lesson    labyrinthelab.com/videos

You are not limited to summing values in a PivotTable, and you may create additional formulas.

## Changing the Function for a Values Area Item

By default, the subtotals and grand totals in a PivotTable sum the values in a field. You may use the Summarize Values By command to change the SUM function to a different function, such as AVERAGE, MAX, or COUNT. Not all Excel functions are available by using this command.

If the Values area of the PivotTable Field List task pane contains only one entry, all Sum columns will change to the function you selected. If multiple entries exist in the Values area, you may change the function for one entry at a time.

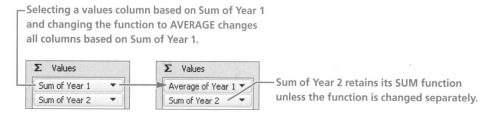

Selecting a values column based on Sum of Year 1 and changing the function to AVERAGE changes all columns based on Sum of Year 1.

Sum of Year 2 retains its SUM function unless the function is changed separately.

## Creating a Calculated Field

Some functions not available with the Summarize Values By command described previously may be typed in the Insert Calculated Field dialog box. A calculated field is a column that you create manually in the PivotTable. This field contains a formula using values from one or more existing fields. For example, the formula could subtract the value in one field from another to find the difference, as shown in the following illustration. You enter the formula once, and Excel displays the formula result in every record of the PivotTable. For accuracy, you should select field names from the list rather than type their names in creating the formula for a calculated field.

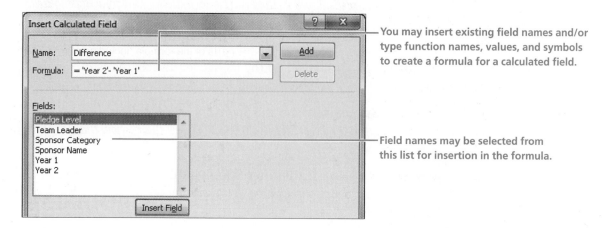

You may insert existing field names and/or type function names, values, and symbols to create a formula for a calculated field.

Field names may be selected from this list for insertion in the formula.

## Converting Column Data to a Calculation

The Show Values As command creates formulas using preset options. For example, you can calculate percentages of a total, the difference between values in two columns, a running total, or a ranked order. If you want to display the original column data along with the converted data, simply drag and drop the field name from the field list to the Values area to create a duplicate field.

# Refreshing PivotTable Data

PivotTables do not automatically update after the source data is changed.

PivotTables often are created with data from sources external to the Excel workbook containing the PivotTables. For example, the source data may be in another Excel workbook or an Access database. After you change the source data—even if in a worksheet range or table within the same workbook—you must refresh the PivotTables manually. Using the Ribbon, you may refresh just the active PivotTable or all PivotTables in the workbook. You also may set a PivotTable option to refresh data from external sources when the workbook is opened.

**FROM THE KEYBOARD**
Ctrl + Alt + F5 to refresh all data sources

| QUICK REFERENCE | EDITING PIVOTTABLE CALCULATIONS AND REFRESHING DATA |
|---|---|
| **Task** | **Procedure** |
| Change the function used to calculate subtotals and grand total(s) | ■ Select a number cell in any column of the PivotTable that contains the existing calculation.<br>■ Choose Options→Calculations-→Summarize Values By menu ▼, and choose a different function from the Ribbon.<br>■ If desired, repeat for any other calculation listed separately in the Values area of the PivotTable Field List task pane. |
| Create a calculated field to the right of existing PivotTable columns | ■ Select any cell within the PivotTable.<br>■ Choose Options→Calculations→Fields, Items, & Sets menu ▼→Calculated Field from the Ribbon.<br>■ Type a name in the Name box of the Insert Calculated Field dialog box.<br>■ Edit the formula =0 to the desired formula by double-clicking field names and typing other parts of the formula, including math symbols (such as + or *). |
| Modify a formula in a calculated field | ■ Choose Options→Calculations→Fields, Items, & Sets menu ▼→Calculated Field from the Ribbon.<br>■ Choose the calculated field name in the Name drop-down list (not the Field list) of the Insert Calculated Field dialog box.<br>■ Edit the formula and click Modify. |

| Task | Procedure |
|---|---|
| Delete a calculated field | ▪ Choose Options→Calculations→Fields, Items, & Sets menu ▼→Calculated Field from the Ribbon. |
| | ▪ Choose the calculated field name in the Name drop-down list (not the Field list) of the Insert Calculated Field dialog box. |
| | ▪ Click Delete. |
| Convert all data in a field to percentages of a total or calculate a difference, running total, or ranked order | ▪ If a duplicate field is desired to retain the original column data, drag and drop the field name from the upper part of the PivotTable Field List into the Values area. |
| | ▪ Choose a number cell in the desired column of the PivotTable where you want to convert data. |
| | ▪ Choose Options→Calculations→Show Values As menu ▼, and choose the desired preset option from the Ribbon to convert all data in the field. |
| Refresh PivotTables after changing source data | ▪ Choose Options→Data→Refresh menu ▼ from the Ribbon and choose one of the following: |
| | ♦ Refresh to update the active PivotTable. |
| | ♦ Refresh All (or use Ctrl + Alt + F5 ) to update all PivotTables in the workbook. |

# Change PivotTable Calculations

*In this exercise, you will change the default SUM to a different function. You will create a calculated field to set a 110 percent contributions goal for each team leader. You also will change a value in the original source table and observe the effect upon PivotTables.*

1. Display the **PivotTable by Pledge Level** worksheet.

## Change a Function

2. Select a number cell in **column B** of the PivotTable. Then, choose **Options→Calculations→Summarize Values By menu ▼→Average** from the Ribbon.
   *The column heading changes to Average of Year 1 in the PivotTable and the Values area of the task pane. The subtotals and grand total now calculate averages. Notice that the Sum of Year 2 column did not change. You must edit the function separately for each calculation listed in the Values area of the task pane. You will leave Sum of Year 2 as is.*

## Create a Calculated Field

*Assume that you set a goal for all team leaders to increase contributions by 110 percent in Year 3.*

3. Choose **Options→Calculations→Fields, Items, & Sets menu ▼→Calculated Field** from the Ribbon.

4. Follow these steps to create a calculated field in the Insert Calculated Field dialog box:

Ⓐ Type **Goal 110% Year 2** in the **Name** box.

Ⓑ Tap [Tab] to highlight =0 in the Formula box. Type an **equals (=)** sign to begin the formula.

Ⓒ **Double-click** Year 2 and type **\*110%** (make certain to type the asterisk) to finish the formula.

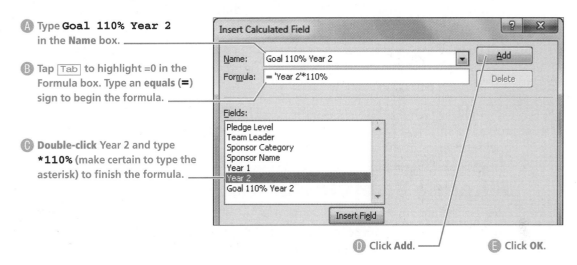

Ⓓ Click **Add.**          Ⓔ Click **OK.**

*The calculated field displays as the last column of the PivotTable.*

| 3 | Row Labels ▼ | Average of Year 1 | Sum of Year 2 | Sum of Goal 110% Year 2 |
|---|---|---|---|---|
| 4 | ⊟**Level 1** | **13,029,720** | **118,272,625** | **130,099,888** |
| 5 | Faber | 5,820,000 | 20,300,000 | 22,330,000 |
| 6 | Lemus | 17,461,496 | 82,972,625 | 91,269,888 |
| 7 | Weinstein | 12,500,000 | 15,000,000 | 16,500,000 |

## Change Worksheet Data

*Cell C10 of the PivotTable shows that team leader Faber is responsible for $250,000 of Level 2 contributions in Year 2. Next, you will change a value in the table upon which the PivotTable is based.*

5. Display the **Sponsors Table** worksheet. (Do not select the Sponsors Sheet tab.)

6. In **cell F98** for Year 2, change 250,000 to **200000**.

7. Display the **PivotTable by Pledge Level** worksheet.
   *Notice that Faber's level 2 amount in Year 2 still appears as 250,000 in cell C10. Changes to the source data do* not *automatically update in the PivotTables.*

## Refresh PivotTables

8. Choose **Options→Data→Refresh menu ▼→Refresh All** from the Ribbon.
   *Faber's amount now appears as 200,000, and the goal was recalculated in cell D10. Any other PivotTables or PivotCharts based on the same source data would also be updated.*

9. **Save** 💾 the changes to your workbook.

## 12.2 Creating PivotCharts

**Video Lesson**   labyrinthelab.com/videos

A PivotChart presents data from a PivotTable. There are two ways to create a PivotChart.

1. You may chart an existing PivotTable by choosing a chart type from the Insert ribbon as for a normal Excel chart.

2. You may use the PivotChart command to create a PivotTable and PivotChart from the source data at the same time. The chart builds as you choose fields in the PivotTable Field List task pane.

The field(s) in the values area of the PivotTable are displayed as data series in the chart. The row labels in the PivotTable are used as the axis labels in the chart, and the column labels are the data series in the chart legend.

### Filtering PivotCharts

The PivotChart may be filtered using the AutoFilter buttons on the chart, AutoFilter buttons on the PivotTable, or slicers added to the worksheet. (See the previous filtering topics in this lesson.) The filtering is applied to the related PivotTable as well.

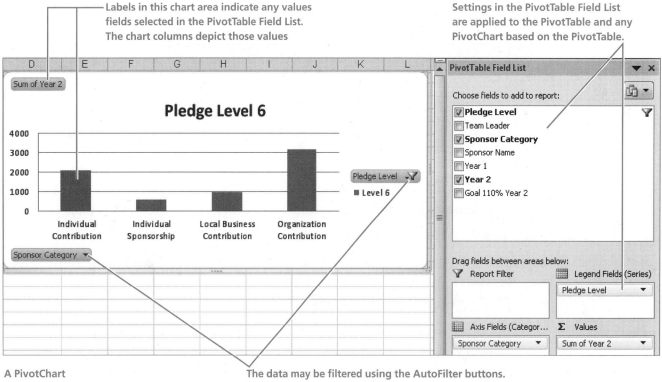

Labels in this chart area indicate any values fields selected in the PivotTable Field List. The chart columns depict those values

Settings in the PivotTable Field List are applied to the PivotTable and any PivotChart based on the PivotTable.

A PivotChart

The data may be filtered using the AutoFilter buttons. This chart is filtered to display only pledge level 6.

Copy a PivotTable before creating a PivotChart. Any changes to the chart update in the PivotTable copy. The design in the original PivotTable will be preserved for further analysis.

# Formatting and Printing PivotCharts

You format PivotCharts using the same Ribbon commands as for normal Excel charts. You choose from the same variety of chart styles, including column, line, and pie. You format chart objects just as you would on a normal Excel chart. Some chart formatting, such as data labels, is not preserved after a PivotChart is refreshed. When a PivotChart is selected, the Print command will print only the chart. By first selecting a worksheet cell, you can print both the PivotTable and PivotChart as displayed on the worksheet.

| QUICK REFERENCE | WORKING WITH PIVOTCHARTS |
|---|---|
| **Task** | **Procedure** |
| Create a PivotChart from an existing PivotTable | ■ Select any cell within the PivotTable. <br> ■ Choose Insert→Charts, and choose a chart type from the Ribbon. The chart is created next to the PivotTable. |
| Create a PivotTable and PivotChart concurrently from a worksheet range or table | ■ Select any cell in the worksheet range or table. <br> ■ Choose Insert→Tables→PivotTable menu ▼→PivotChart from the Ribbon. <br> ■ Verify the worksheet range or table name in the Create PivotTable with PivotChart dialog box and click OK to place the PivotTable and PivotChart placeholders on a new worksheet. <br> ■ Choose options for the PivotTable in the PivotTable Field List task pane. These options also create a column PivotChart automatically. |
| Modify PivotChart format | ■ Select the chart and choose from the Design, Layout, and Format Ribbons as for a normal Excel chart. |
| Filter data in a PivotChart | ■ Choose the AutoFilter button on the PivotChart for the desired field, and choose filtering options from the drop-down list. <br> *or* <br> ■ Choose Analyze→Data→Insert Slicer, choose the desired slicer(s), and click OK. <br> ■ Choose the desired filtering criteria from the slicer(s). |

## Create a PivotChart

*In this exercise, you will create a PivotChart from an existing PivotTable.*

1. Display the **PivotChart** worksheet of the Sponsors workbook. (**Scroll** to the **right** in the worksheet tabs to locate the tab, if necessary.)

### Create a PivotChart

2. **Select** any cell within the PivotTable and choose **Insert→Charts→Column**. Below 2-D Column in the chart types menu, choose **Clustered Column**. <br> *A new column chart is created immediately from the settings in the PivotTable Field List.*

*Notice that while the PivotChart is selected, the Column Labels area of the PivotTable Field list task pane is labeled Legend Fields (Series). The Row Labels area is labeled Axis Fields (Categories).*

3. **Point** at the chart frame and **drag** the chart just below the PivotTable.

4. Place a checkmark next to **Year 2** in the PivotTable Field List.
*The Sum of Year 2 column displays in the PivotTable, and the PivotChart displays an additional column for the Sum of Year 2 series.*

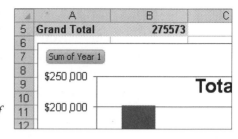

## Filter the PivotTable and PivotChart

*Notice that the PivotTable has been filtered to display pledge Levels 4–6. The PivotChart matches this filtering. You will use the AutoFilter button on the chart to remove pledge level 4. You could also use the Row Labels AutoFilter button on the PivotTable.*

5. Follow these steps to filter the PivotChart:

Ⓐ Choose the **Pledge Level AutoFilter** button at the lower-left corner of the PivotChart.

Ⓑ **Scroll** down the list.

Ⓒ Remove the checkmark next to **Level 4.**

☐ Level 3
☐ Level 4
☑ Level 5
☑ Level 6

Ⓓ Click **OK.**

## Format the PivotChart

6. **Select** the chart, if necessary.

7. Choose **Design→Type→Change Chart Type→Column→Clustered Cylinder** from the Ribbon and click **OK.**
*The chart is reconfigured to the new chart type. You may use chart formatting commands on any PivotChart.*

8. Choose **Layout→Labels→Chart Title→Centered Overlay Title** from the Ribbon, type **Levels 5 and 6** (your text appears in the Formula Bar), and **tap** Enter.

9. Feel free to add other formatting to the chart. For example, the values labels on the vertical axis could be formatted as Currency with no decimals, as shown here.

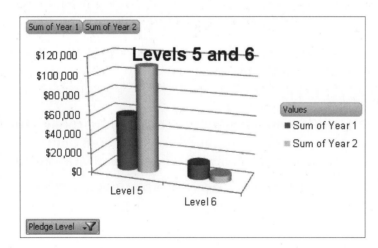

10. **Save**  the changes.

11. Use `Ctrl`+`W` or the **Close** button shown to close the workbook but leave Excel **open**.

# 12.3 Changing Macro Security

**Video Lesson**   labyrinthelab.com/videos

A macro is a recorded set of mouse and keyboard actions that can be played back at any time. Macros are useful for automating routine tasks, especially if those tasks are lengthy. Though macros are a huge timesaver for your frequently used procedures, they also are a prime way to pass viruses to computers. Therefore, be cautious about opening workbooks containing macros that you receive from others.

## Security Levels

You change macro security in the Trust Center section within Excel Options. Your setting there is in effect for all Excel workbooks that you open on your computer. The setting is not embedded in any workbooks that you save and share with others. You may choose among four different levels of security in Excel that control whether macros in an opened workbook are available or disabled:

- **Enable all macros**—You are not protected from potentially unsafe macros. This option is not recommended for general use.

- **Disable all macros except digitally signed macros**—This option automatically disables unsigned macros and enables macros from publishers you previously added to the trusted publishers list in the Trust Center. An invisible digital signature or visible signature line may be added to an Excel workbook.

- **Disable all macros with notification**—This is the default option, and it displays a message allowing you to enable macros in the specified workbook if you wish or use the workbook without enabling the macros.

- **Disable all macros without notification**—Only macros in workbooks that you placed in a trusted location of the Trust Center are allowed to run. All other digitally signed and unsigned macros are disabled.

If you have antivirus software installed, the file will be scanned for viruses before it is opened regardless of the security level you set.

Your network system administrator may set macro security and prevent users from changing it.

| QUICK REFERENCE | CHANGING MACRO SECURITY |
|---|---|
| **Task** | **Procedure** |
| Change macro security | Choose File→Options 📄→Trust Center→Trust Center Settings button→ Macro Settings, and choose a macro security option. |

# Verify Macro Security

*In this exercise, you will verify the macro security setting on your computer. Then you will open a workbook and enable its macros.*

1. Choose **File→Options** 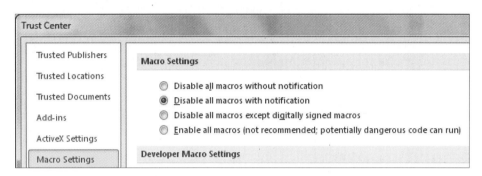→**Trust Center**. Click the **Trust Center Settings** button and choose the **Macro Settings** category from the left side of the window. Choose **Disable All Macros with Notification** if not already selected.

2. Choose the **Message Bar** category from the left side of the window. Verify that the following option is selected: **Show the Message Bar in All Applications When Content, Such As ActiveX and Macros, Has Been Blocked**.

3. Click **OK** twice to exit the Excel Options window.

4. **Open** the Macro Test workbook from the Lesson 12 folder in your file storage location. *A Security Warning message displays below the Ribbon to alert you that macros are disabled. If you do not respond, the message will disappear after you begin working in the workbook.*

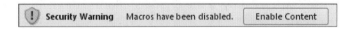

5. Click the **Enable Content** button next to the Security Warning. *The macros are enabled.*

6. Click the **Sort by Leader** button. *The worksheet list should sort in order by team leader, indicating that the macro worked successfully.*

7. **Close** the workbook without saving changes.

# 12.4 Recording Macros

**Video Lesson** labyrinthelab.com/videos

Excel's macro recording feature saves your keystrokes and the commands you issue for a task. For example, you may record steps to choose page layout options and print a document by clicking the appropriate commands in the Ribbon. You then may play back a recorded macro at a later time. This is similar to using a video camera. You turn it on, press the record button, and stop recording when finished. You may replay the recording as many times as you want. Similarly, macros play back recorded keystrokes and mouse actions.

 After the Record Macro button is clicked in the Status Bar, the Stop Recording button appears.

## Naming a Macro

You should name your macros. If you do not, Excel names them Macro1, Macro2, and so on. Name your macros following the same rules that are used for defined names for ranges. Macro names may not contain spaces but may include capital letters or underscores to separate words. For example, you may name a macro FormatTitle or Format_Title.

## Recording Macro Steps

Most actions you perform are recorded in the macro. These include mouse actions, choosing Ribbon commands, selecting options in dialog boxes, using cursor keys to navigate the worksheet, and typing text. Any mistakes and corrections you make during recording also are saved in the macro. You may decide not to rerecord the macro, however, if the final result is correct.

 You should practice the procedure you wish to automate before you actually record the macro. This will help you avoid mistakes during the recording process.

## Storing Macros

Macros are available only in the workbook in which you create them unless you assign them to the Personal Macro Workbook.

### Current Workbook

Some macros are useful only in a particular workbook. For example, you may develop a macro to sort worksheet rows in a specific manner. The macro is useful only in the workbook in which it is created, so you would choose the storage option This Workbook.

### Personal Macro Workbook

The Personal.xlsb file is a hidden file that makes its macros available in all open workbooks on your computer system. For example, you may create a macro to format headings with a consistent style to be used in various workbooks. You will assign a macro to the Personal Macro Workbook and delete macros from it in a Skill Builder exercise of this lesson.

# Saving a Workbook Containing Macros

If you attempt to save a workbook containing macros using the normal Excel Workbook file format, Excel displays the message "The following features cannot be saved in macro-free workbooks: VB Project." Clicking No in the message box displays the Save As dialog box, where you should choose the Excel Macro-Enabled Workbook file format. The file is saved with the extension .xlsm in the file name to indicate that it contains a macro.

| File name: | Contributions with Macros |
|---|---|
| Save as type: | Excel Macro-Enabled Workbook |

| QUICK REFERENCE | RECORDING A MACRO |
|---|---|
| **Task** | **Procedure** |
| Record a macro | ■ Create the worksheet and prepare to record the macro. |
| | ■ Click the Record Macro 🔲 button on the Status Bar in the lower-left corner of the window. |
| | ■ Right-click the Status Bar and choose Macro Recording in the context menu if the button does not display. Tap Esc to hide the context menu.) |
| | ■ Type a descriptive name in the Macro Name box (spaces are not allowed) and fill in other options as desired. |
| | ■ Click OK to begin recording. |
| | ■ Execute the commands and actions you want the macro to record. |
| | ■ Click the Stop Recording 🔲 button on the Status Bar when you have finished recording. |
| Delete a macro | ■ Choose View→Macros→View Macros 🔲 (the top part of the button) from the Ribbon or use Alt + F8. |
| | ■ Choose the desired macro name and click Delete. |
| Save a workbook containing macros | ■ Choose Save 🔲 and click No in the message box or choose Save As. |
| | ■ Choose Excel Macro-Enabled Workbook from the Save as Type list in the Save As dialog box. |

## DEVELOP YOUR SKILLS 12.4.1

# Record a Macro

*In this exercise, you will record a macro to sort a table first by team leader and then by the contributions to date. You will save the workbook in the macro-enabled file format.*

*Before You Begin: Macro security should be set to Disable All Macros with Notification from Develop Your Skills 12.3.1.*

## Open the Workbook

1. **Open** the Contributions workbook.

   *Take a moment to review the worksheet. Notice that it contains a table of sponsors and that each sponsor has been assigned to a team leader. Also notice that the list is sorted in order by sponsor name, and the table's AutoFilter column heading buttons are turned off. The goal of the next few exercises is to sort the table and add new sponsors to the table. You will record macros to automate the sorting process.*

## Record the Sort_by_Leader Macro

2. Click the **Record Macro** 🖳 button on the Status Bar at the bottom-left corner of the window. (**Right-click** the Status Bar and choose **Macro Recording** in the context menu if the button does not display. **Tap** Esc to hide the context menu.)
*The Record Macro dialog box appears.*

3. Follow these steps to name the macro and begin the recording process:

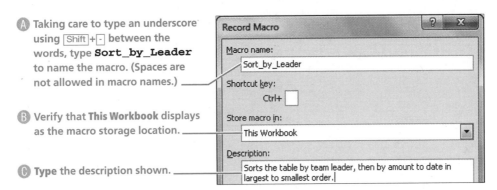

Ⓐ Taking care to type an underscore using Shift+- between the words, type **Sort_by_Leader** to name the macro. (Spaces are not allowed in macro names.)

Ⓑ Verify that **This Workbook** displays as the macro storage location.

Ⓒ **Type** the description shown.

4. Click **OK**, and the macro will begin recording your actions.
*If you make any mistakes, just correct the errors as you would normally. Major errors may be fixed either by stopping the recording and starting over or by editing the macro in the Visual Basic Editor (not covered in this lesson).*

5. Select **cell B4** in the table.
*This step ensures that the proper data is selected prior to sorting whenever the macro is run.*

6. Choose **Data→Sort & Filter→Sort** from the Ribbon.

7. Follow these steps to set the Sort parameters and initiate the Sort:

Ⓐ Click the drop-down button on the Sort By list and choose **Team Leader**.

Ⓑ Click the **Add Level** button.

Ⓒ Choose **To Date** from the list.

Ⓓ Choose **Largest to Smallest** from the list.

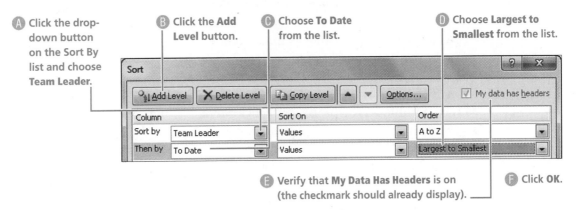

Ⓔ Verify that **My Data Has Headers** is on (the checkmark should already display).

Ⓕ Click **OK**.

8. Click the **Stop Recording** ▪ button on the Status Bar at the bottom-left corner of the window.

*Your actions have been saved in the macro. The list is sorted as shown in the following illustration. Keep in mind that the macro recorded this sort sequence.*

| | A | B | C | D | E | F | G |
|---|---|---|---|---|---|---|---|
| 3 | Pledge | Team Leader | Sponsor Category | Sponsor Name | Year 1 | Year 2 | To Date |
| 4 | Level 5 | Abbott | Organization Contribution | Accountancy Association | 0 | 15,000 | 15,000 |
| 5 | Level 4 | Faber | Corporate Sponsorship | Accurate Biomedical | 10,000 | 10,000 | 20,000 |
| 6 | Level 1 | Lemus | Federal Government Grant | Admin for Children & Fam | 5,129,874 | 8,075,333 | 13,205,207 |
| 7 | Level 3 | Faber | Corporate Sponsorship | Alpha Supplies Corp. | 125,000 | 50,000 | 175,000 |
| 8 | Level 6 | Nguyen | Individual Contribution | Andres Padilla | 0 | 500 | 500 |
| 9 | Level 5 | Weinstein | Individual Sponsorship | Anonymous | 500 | 500 | 1,000 |
| 10 | Level 6 | Weinstein | Individual Sponsorship | Anonymous | 300 | 200 | 500 |
| 11 | Level 6 | Weinstein | Individual Sponsorship | Anonymous | 235 | 145 | 380 |
| 12 | Level 6 | Weinstein | Individual Sponsorship | Anonymous | 0 | 250 | 250 |
| 13 | Level 4 | Faber | Corporate Sponsorship | Aspen Medical Services | 20,000 | 0 | 20,000 |
| 14 | Level 6 | Park | Local Business Contribution | Breeze Auto Sales | 560 | 622 | 1,182 |
| 15 | Level 2 | Lemus | Private Grant | BTP Foundation | 50,000 | 950,000 | 1,000,000 |
| 16 | Level 5 | Abbott | Organization Contribution | Business Roundtable | 0 | 15,000 | 15,000 |

## Save the Workbook as Macro-Enabled

9. Click **Save** 💾.
   *A message displays as shown. The VB Project indicated is a Visual Basic Project module containing your macro.*

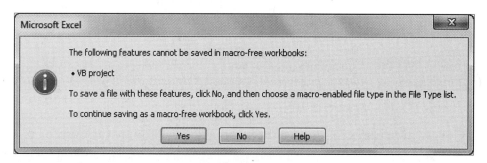

10. Click **No** to display the Save As dialog box.

11. Edit the **File Name** to `Contributions with Macros`.

12. Drop down the Save As type list, choose **Excel Macro-Enabled Workbook**, and click **Save**.
    *The macro is saved as part of the workbook named Contributions with Macros.xlsm. If you were to close the workbook, the macro would be available the next time you opened the workbook. The Disable All Macros with Notification security setting is in effect, so you still can control whether macros actually are enabled in an opened workbook.*

## 12.5 Running Macros

labyrinthelab.com/videos

You may run macros in a variety of ways. The method you use depends on how the macro was assigned. You may create a macro and assign it to a shortcut key, graphic, or Quick Access toolbar button. An unassigned macro must be run by using the Macros command on the Ribbon and selecting a macro. This procedure may be used to run any macro recorded in the current workbook, even if the macro was assigned. The keyboard shortcut Alt + F8 may be used to display the Macro dialog box.

**FROM THE KEYBOARD**
Alt + F8 to view macros

| **QUICK REFERENCE** | **RUNNING A MACRO** |
|---|---|
| **Task** | **Procedure** |
| Run an unassigned or assigned macro from the Ribbon | ▪ Choose View→Macros→View Macros 🗔 from the Ribbon or use Alt + F8. ▪ Choose the desired macro name and click Run. |
| Run an assigned macro | ▪ Use the shortcut key or click the assigned graphic, worksheet button, or Quick Access toolbar button. |

### DEVELOP YOUR SKILLS 12.5.1
### Run an Unassigned Macro

*In this exercise, you will sort the contributions table manually in a different order and then run the Sort_by_Leader macro.*

*Before You Begin: You must have completed Develop Your Skills 12.4.1, and the Contributions with Macros workbook should be open. Macro security should be set to Disable All Macros with Notification from Develop Your Skills 12.3.1. If you reopened the Contributions with Macros workbook and the Security Warning message appears under the Ribbon, choose Enable Macros.*

1. Select **cell D4** and choose **Data→Sort & Filter→Sort A to Z** ↕ from the Ribbon.
   *The contributions table is sorted alphabetically by sponsor name. Now you will run the macro you created in the previous exercise.*

2. Choose **View→Macros→View Macros** 🗔 from the Ribbon.

3. Choose the **Sort_by_Leader** macro and click **Run** in the Macro dialog box.
   *The list is sorted by team leader, then by the To Date amount in highest to lowest order within each team leader's rows. The macro saves you time because you did not need to choose the Sort command and set options manually.*

4. **Save** 🖫 the changes to the workbook.

# 12.6 Assigning Macros

**Video Lesson**   labyrinthelab.com/videos

You may run a macro from within the Macro dialog box. However, macros are more accessible if you assign them to shortcut keys, custom buttons or graphics on a worksheet, or buttons on the Quick Access toolbar. You then run the macro by issuing the shortcut key or clicking the object to which the macro is assigned.

## Assigning Macros to Shortcut Keys

Excel lets you assign a macro to a shortcut key as you name the macro. You may run the macro simply by using the shortcut key combination. You must use Ctrl or Ctrl+Shift as part of the shortcut key combination. Any shortcut you assign will override an existing Excel command shortcut. For example, you may assign Ctrl+B to a macro, but that combination would no longer choose Bold from the Ribbon.

If you are in the habit of using Microsoft's command shortcuts, use Ctrl+Shift for your macro shortcuts.

### DEVELOP YOUR SKILLS 12.6.1
## Assign a Macro to a Shortcut Key

*In this exercise, you will create a macro to add a new sponsor to the table and assign the macro to a shortcut key. You will run the macro to add a sponsor. Then you will assign a shortcut key to the macro you created in the previous exercise and use its shortcut key to sort the list.*

*Before You Begin: You must have completed Develop Your Skills 12.4.1 and 12.5.1, and the Contributions with Macros workbook should be open. Macro security should be set to Disable All Macros with Notification from Develop Your Skills 12.3.1. If you reopened the Contributions with Macros workbook and the Security Warning message now appears under the Ribbon, choose Enable Macros.*

### Assign a Shortcut Key and Record the Insert_Student Macro

*You will record a new macro that automates the process of inserting a new sponsor record just below the table header row.*

1. Click the **Record Macro** 📇 button on the Status Bar.
   *The Record Macro dialog box appears.*

2. Follow these steps to name a new macro:

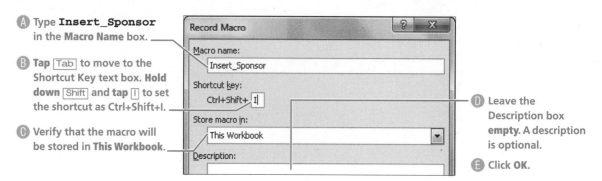

Ⓐ Type **Insert_Sponsor** in the **Macro Name** box.

Ⓑ **Tap** Tab **to move to the Shortcut Key text box. Hold down** Shift **and tap** I **to set the shortcut as Ctrl+Shift+I.**

Ⓒ Verify that the macro will be stored in **This Workbook**.

Ⓓ Leave the Description box **empty.** A description is optional.

Ⓔ Click **OK.**

*In the next few steps, you will perform the actions to be recorded in the macro. You will insert a blank table row below the column headings and copy cell formatting to the blank cells.*

3. Select **cell A4**.

4. Taking care not to select the menu ▼ button, choose **Home→Insert** from the Ribbon.
   *A blank row is inserted at row 4, and its cells are formatted like the column headings.*

5. Select the **range A5:G5**, and choose **Home→Clipboard→Format Painter** 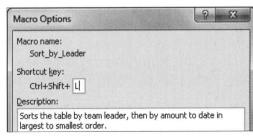 from the Ribbon.

6. Select **cell A4** to apply the cell formatting from row 5 to the blank row 4.

7. Select **cell A4** again to position the pointer for data entry.

8. Click the **Stop Recording** ⬛ button on the status bar.

## Run the Macro to Add New Students

9. Delete the blank **row 4** that you inserted while creating the macro.

10. Use Ctrl + Shift + I to run the Insert_Sponsor macro. (Hold down Ctrl, then also hold down Shift, and then tap I. Release Ctrl and Shift.)
    *The pointer moves to cell A4 and blank cells are inserted. New sponsors always will be added to a new row below the header row.*

    *If your macro did not work correctly, choose View→Macros→Macros→Insert_Sponsor, and then click Delete. Then repeat steps 1–10, choosing Yes when asked if you wish to replace the macro.*

11. **Add** the following sponsor to the table. **Tap** Tab after entering the Year 2 value, and the To Date total will be calculated automatically.

| 4 | Level 6 | Weinstein | Individual Contribution | Raul T. Garcia | 0 | 500 | 500 |
|---|---------|-----------|-------------------------|----------------|---|-----|-----|

12. **Run** the Insert_Sponsor macro again and add this sponsor to the table:

| 4 | Level 6 | Weinstein | Individual Contribution | Wayne Zobe | 0 | 300 | 300 |
|---|---------|-----------|-------------------------|------------|---|-----|-----|

## Assign a Shortcut Key to the Sort_by_Instructor Macro

13. Choose **View→Macros→View Macros** 🔳 from the Ribbon.

14. Choose the **Sort_by_Leader** macro and click **Options** in the Macro dialog box.

15. In the Shortcut Key text box, **press** Shift, and **tap** L to set the shortcut key to Ctrl+Shift+L. Click **OK**.

16. Click **Cancel** to exit the Macro dialog box.

17. Use Ctrl + Shift + L to run the macro.
    *The table is sorted by team leader and then by To Date amount in highest to lowest order within each team leader group. The Raul T. Garcia record moves to row 98 in the Weinstein team leader group. The Wayne Zobe record moves to row 101.*

18. **Save** 💾 the changes to the workbook.

# Assigning Macros to Custom Buttons

**Video Lesson** labyrinthelab.com/videos

A macro assigned to a custom button is run whenever the button is clicked. The easiest way to create a custom button is to add a shape, such as a rectangle, to the worksheet. You then assign a macro to the button. You may position custom buttons anywhere in a worksheet. To avoid deleting buttons in error, do not place them in rows or columns that could be deleted in the future. A custom button may also contain a descriptive label to help identify its function or the macro that is assigned to it.

You may create custom buttons using the Button (Form Control) tool on the Developer tab. To display this tab, choose File→Options from the Ribbon, select Customize Ribbon at the left of the Excel Options dialog box, and place a checkmark next to Developer in the Main Tabs list at the right. The Developer tab contains commands for working with macros.

| QUICK REFERENCE | ASSIGNING A MACRO |
|---|---|
| **Task** | **Procedure** |
| Assign a macro to a shortcut key as the macro is created | ▪ Click the Record Macro [icon] button on the Status Bar.<br>▪ While filling in options in the Macro dialog box, click in the Shortcut Key text box and key a single letter, or hold [Shift] and key the letter. |
| Assign a macro to a shortcut key after the macro is created | ▪ Choose View→Macros→View Macros [icon] from the Ribbon.<br>▪ Choose the macro name and click Options in the Macro dialog box.<br>▪ In the Macro Options dialog box, click in the Shortcut Key text box and key a single letter, or hold [Shift] and key the letter. |
| Assign a macro to a custom button or graphic on the worksheet | ▪ Record the macro.<br>▪ Insert a shape, picture, or clip art image on the worksheet. Right-click the object and choose Assign Macro from the context menu. Choose the desired macro from the Assign Macro dialog box.<br>▪ To display a text label in a shape used as a custom button, select the button in the worksheet and type the desired text in the button.<br>▪ If necessary, resize the button or graphic, drag it to the desired worksheet location, and align multiple buttons. |

## DEVELOP YOUR SKILLS 12.6.2

## Assign Macros to Custom Buttons

*In this exercise, you will create buttons and assign the Insert_Sponsor and Sort_by_Leader macros to them.*

*Before You Begin: Macro security should be set to Disable All Macros with Notification from Develop Your Skills 12.3.1. If you reopened the Contributions with Macros workbook and the Security Warning message appears under the Ribbon, choose Enable Macros.*

### Create Buttons

1. Choose **Insert→Illustrations→Shapes→Rectangles→Rectangle** [icon] shape tool from the Ribbon.

2. Drag the mouse to draw a button on **cell D1**.

3. Copy and paste the button to cell **E1**.

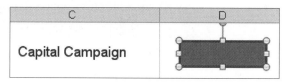

### Name Buttons

4. Select the **first button** and type `Insert Sponsor`; do *not* tap Enter.

5. Select the **second button** and type `Sort by Leader`.
   *Button text may contain spaces because it is only a label.*

6. **Click** outside the button to deselect it.

7. If necessary, **align** the buttons: Select the first button, use Shift +click to select the second button, and choose **Format→Arrange→Align→ Align Top** from the Ribbon.
   *Formatting the buttons is easier if completed before you assign macros to the buttons. If you wish, you may change the colors and outline in custom buttons.*

### Assign Macros to Buttons

8. **Deselect** the two buttons.

9. **Right-click** the Insert Sponsor button and choose **Assign Macro** from the context menu.

10. In the Assign Macro dialog box, choose **Insert_Sponsor** from the list and click **OK**.

11. Use the preceding steps to assign the **Sort_by_Leader** macro to its button.

### Run Macros Using the Buttons

12. **Deselect** the button.

13. Click the **Insert Sponsor** button to run the Insert_Sponsor macro. (Deselect the button and select again if the pointer does not display as a hand as you select the button.)
    *A new row appears just below the header row.*

14. Add this sponsor to the new row:

| 4 | Level 3 | Abbott | Organization Contribution | Kelsey Foundation | 0 | 50,000 | 50,000 |
|---|---------|--------|---------------------------|-------------------|---|--------|--------|

15. Click the **Sort by Leader** button to run the Sort_by_Leader macro.
    *The new row is sorted into the worksheet as row 5.*

16. **Save** 💾 the changes and **close** the workbook.
    *Now you have learned to create simple macros to automate routine tasks. You ran macros using the Ribbon, shortcut keys, and custom buttons on the worksheet.*

## 12.7 Concepts Review

**Concepts Review**   labyrinthelab.com/excel10

*To check your knowledge of the key concepts introduced in this lesson, complete the Concepts Review quiz by going to the URL listed above. If your classroom is using Labyrinth eLab, you may complete the Concepts Review quiz from within your eLab course.*

# Reinforce Your Skills

## Create a PivotTable and a PivotChart

*In this exercise, you will create a PivotTable and PivotChart simultaneously from a worksheet table. You will practice placing and pivoting fields to change your view of the data.*

1. **Start** Excel and **open** the rs-Jan Sales PivotTable workbook from the Lesson 12 folder.
   *The January Sales worksheet displays one month's activity at Avery Internet Auto Sales. Before you create a PivotTable, take a moment to look over the layout of the data fields and records. For example, notice that there is just one field for numeric data in this table.*

### Create the PivotTable and PivotChart

2. Select **cell A4**.
   *This tells Excel to use the table data when you create the PivotTable.*

3. Choose **Insert→Tables→PivotTable** ⊞ **menu ▼→PivotChart** from the Ribbon, verify **JanSales** as the table data to be used, and click **OK** to create a PivotTable and PivotChart in a new worksheet.

4. **Rename** the Sheet1 sheet tab to **PivotTable**.
   *The PivotTable Field List task pane is displayed. If it does not and you made certain the chart is selected, choose Analyze→Show/Hide→Field List. You may turn on/off the pane as needed.*

5. In the PivotTable Field List task pane, place a checkmark in the **Sold By** and **Price** checkboxes.
   *The PivotTable displays the total sales for each salesperson using the Sum of Price field in the values area of the PivotTable Field List task pane. The chart is selected, so the task pane displays Axis Fields (Categories) and Legend Field areas.*

6. **Select** a cell in the PivotTable, and the same areas now are titled Row Labels and Column Labels to reflect those items in the PivotTable.

## Add a Field

*Since you may need to know which types of cars each salesperson sold during January, you will place a new field in the row field's area.*

7. Place a checkmark in the **Type** box on the task pane to add the field to the Row Labels area.

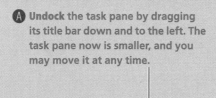

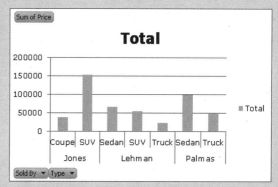

*The PivotTable and PivotChart expand to display the sales of the various types of vehicles sold by each salesperson. It might also be interesting to summarize how the revenue at the dealership breaks down by vehicle type, so in the next step you will pivot the Type field from the row area to the column area.*

## Arrange Items in the Window

*You may not see the entire PivotTable and PivotChart as items change in the window.*

8. Follow these steps to maximize space:

**Ⓐ Undock** the task pane by dragging its title bar down and to the left. The task pane now is smaller, and you may move it at any time.

**Ⓑ Resize** the PivotTable Field List by dragging its bottom border up or down to keep desired options visible.

**Ⓒ** To prevent the PivotChart from covering the PivotTable in the next step, **move** the PivotChart to the right by dragging the chart frame. until the left edge of the chart is in column G.

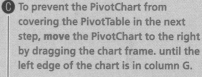

## Pivot the View

9. Drag the **Type** field to the Column Labels area.

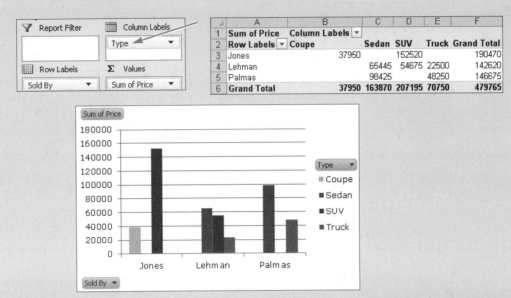

| | A | B | C | D | E | F |
|---|---|---|---|---|---|---|
| 1 | Sum of Price | Column Labels | | | | |
| 2 | Row Labels | Coupe | Sedan | SUV | Truck | Grand Total |
| 3 | Jones | 37950 | | 152520 | | 190470 |
| 4 | Lehman | | 65445 | 54675 | 22500 | 142620 |
| 5 | Palmas | | 98425 | | 48250 | 146675 |
| 6 | Grand Total | 37950 | 163870 | 207195 | 70750 | 479765 |

*The Grand Total line at the bottom of the PivotTable displays the revenue for each type of car. The chart displays columns for each car type.*

## Add a Field and Pivot the View

10. Place a checkmark in the **New/Preowned** box on the task pane to add the field to the Row Labels area and observe the effect in the PivotTable and the PivotChart.

11. Drag the **New/Preowned** field above Sold By in the Row Labels area of the task pane as shown.

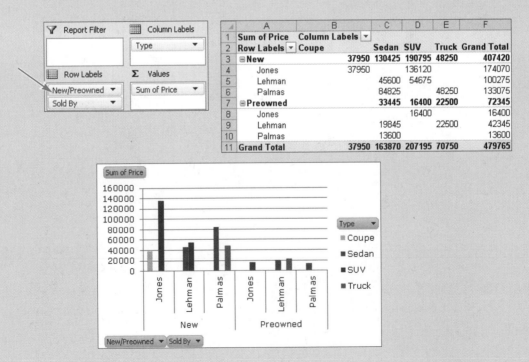

| | A | B | C | D | E | F |
|---|---|---|---|---|---|---|
| 1 | Sum of Price | Column Labels | | | | |
| 2 | Row Labels | Coupe | Sedan | SUV | Truck | Grand Total |
| 3 | ⊟New | | 37950 | 130425 | 190795 | 48250 | 407420 |
| 4 | Jones | 37950 | | 136120 | | 174070 |
| 5 | Lehman | | 45600 | 54675 | | 100275 |
| 6 | Palmas | | 84825 | | 48250 | 133075 |
| 7 | ⊟Preowned | | 33445 | 16400 | 22500 | 72345 |
| 8 | Jones | | | 16400 | | 16400 |
| 9 | Lehman | | 19845 | | 22500 | 42345 |
| 10 | Palmas | | 13600 | | | 13600 |
| 11 | Grand Total | 37950 | 163870 | 207195 | 70750 | 479765 |

*This view clearly shows that revenue is much greater for new cars than preowned, as might be expected.*

12. Move the PivotChart to below the PivotTable so both fit on **one printed page**.

13. **Drag** the PivotTable Field List task pane to the right edge of the screen, until the task pane is docked.

14. **Select** a cell in the PivotTable to deselect the PivotChart.
*Only the chart would print when the chart is selected.*

15. **Save** 🖫 the changes and **close** the workbook.
*As you have seen, PivotTables and PivotCharts help you display and analyze data in various ways with a minimum of setup steps.*

<br>

### REINFORCE YOUR SKILLS 12.2
# Filter a PivotTable

*In this exercise, you will filter to exclude data items from a PivotTable. You also will use a slicer to filter by a field not displayed in the PivotTable.*

1. **Open** the rs-Feb Sales PivotTable workbook.
*Look at the table data in the February Sales worksheet. A PivotTable and a PivotChart were created using this data.*

2. Display the **PivotTable** worksheet.
*You will not use the field buttons in the PivotChart, so they were turned off in the Analyze ribbon.*

3. **Select** a cell within the PivotTable to display the PivotTable Field List task pane, if necessary.

### Use AutoFilter

4. Follow these steps in the PivotTable to suppress the display of data for Walk-In sales:

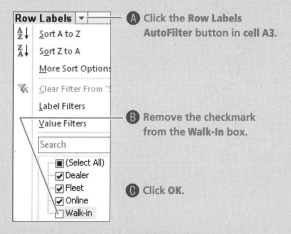

Ⓐ Click the **Row Labels** AutoFilter button in **cell A3**.

Ⓑ Remove the checkmark from the **Walk-In** box.

Ⓒ Click **OK**.

*Notice that no data is displayed for Walk-In sales, and the Row Headers filter button displays a filter icon. You may use this method to switch the display of individual data items on and off for any field in the Row Labels or Column Labels.*

5. Display the **Row Labels** filter list again and choose **Clear Filter from "Source."**

## Delete and Add Fields in the PivotTable

6. In the PivotTable Field List task pane, remove the checkmark from the **Source** box.

7. Place a checkmark in the **Financing** box to add the field to the PivotTable.
   *The pie chart displays bank/credit union financing as 46 percent, dealer financing as 42 percent, and cash as 12 percent for all vehicles sold.*

## Filter with a Slicer

*Notice that the New/Preowned field does not have a checkmark in the PivotTable Field List, so the field does not appear in the PivotTable. At times, you may wish to maintain a simplified PivotTable and PivotChart design. You can use slicers to filter for fields that are not displayed. Next, you will filter for new and preowned vehicles.*

8. Choose **Insert→Filter→Slicer** ▦ from the Ribbon.

9. In the Insert Slicers dialog box, place a checkmark next to **New/Preowned**, and click **OK**.
   *The New/Preowned slicer displays on the worksheet window, and the PivotTable Filter List task pane is hidden.*

10. Point to the **New/Preowned** title in the slicer, and **drag** the slicer frame so it is not covering the PivotTable or PivotChart.

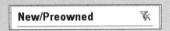

11. Choose **New** in the slicer.
    *The Sum of Price column in the PivotTable and the PivotChart percentages have changed to include only new vehicles. The pie chart displays Dealer financing as 46 percent but Cash financing as only 6 percent of new vehicles sold.*

12. Choose **Preowned** in the slicer.
    *The values and percentages update to include only preowned vehicles. Now you can see that dealer financing is only 21 percent and the majority of preowned vehicle purchases were paid in cash.*

13. **Select** the PivotChart, choose **Design→Chart Styles→More** ▾, and choose a **chart style** that displays good contrast between the colors of the text and pie slices.

14. Change the **page orientation** or **resize** the chart, if necessary, to fit the PivotTable and PivotChart on one printed page.

15. **Save** ▦ the changes and **close** the workbook.

# Create a Macro for the Personal Macro Workbook

*In this exercise, you will create a macro that selects an entire worksheet, formats all cells with bold, and widens the columns. You will assign the macro to the personal macro workbook to make it available for use in other workbooks you may open.*

## Begin Recording the Macro

1. **Start** a new workbook.

2. Click the **Record Macro button**  on the Status Bar.

3. **Type** the macro name **FormatSheet** in the Record Macro dialog box.

4. Set the Store Macro In option to **Personal Macro Workbook**.

> **NOTE** Choose This Workbook instead if you cannot save a macro to the Personal Macro Workbook on your computer system.

5. Click **OK** (and replace the macro if it already exists) to begin the recording process.

## Set Worksheet Formats

6. Use Ctrl + A to select the entire worksheet.

7. Use Ctrl + B to bold all cells.

8. Choose **Home→Cells→Format** ▦ **→Column Width** to display the Column Width dialog box, type **12**, and **tap** Enter to choose **OK**.

9. Select **cell A1** to deselect the highlighted cells.

10. Click the **Stop Recording** ■ button on the Run the Macro status bar.

11. Choose **File→Close** 🗀 and choose **not** to save when Excel asks if you want to save the workbook.

## Run the Macro

12. Start a new workbook and choose **View→Macros→View Macros** 🖹 (the top part of the button) to display the Macro dialog box.
    *Any macro with PERSONAL.XLSB! in its name has been saved to the Personal Macro Workbook and is available to all open workbooks.*

13. Choose the **PERSONAL.XLSB!FormatSheet** macro and click the **Run** button. (Choose FormatSheet rather than PERSONAL.XLSB!FormatSheet if you saved the macro to This Worksheet.)
    *The column and text formats are set. Keep in mind that you may apply virtually any formatting to cells, columns, rows, text, or numbers with a macro.*

## Delete the Macro from the Personal Macro Workbook

*Macros stored in the Personal Macro Workbook cannot be removed with the Delete button in the Macro dialog box. Just read the next steps and complete step 20 if you saved the macro to This Workbook rather than Personal Macro Workbook.*

14. Choose **View→Macros→View Macros** 📄 from the Ribbon.

15. Follow these steps to delete the FormatSheet macro from the Personal Macro Workbook:

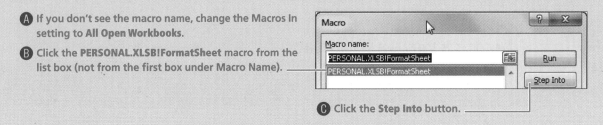

Ⓐ If you don't see the macro name, change the Macros In setting to **All Open Workbooks**.

Ⓑ Click the **PERSONAL.XLSB!FormatSheet** macro from the list box (not from the first box under Macro Name).

Ⓒ Click the **Step Into** button.

*The macro code displays in the Microsoft Visual Basic for Applications window.*

16. In the Microsoft Visual Basic for Applications window, choose **Tools→Macros**.

17. In the Macros dialog box, set the Macros In option to **VBA Project (PERSONAL.XLSB)**.

18. Choose the **FormatSheet** macro, click **Delete**, and click **OK** to confirm.

19. **Close** ⬛ the Microsoft Visual Basic for Applications window to reveal the Excel workbook window.
    *In this exercise, you deleted the macro to keep the computer system "clean." Normally, you would leave macros stored in the personal macro workbook so they could be used in all workbooks.*

20. **Close** the empty workbook without saving it.

# Apply Your Skills

## Create a PivotTable

*In this exercise, you will create a PivotTable to calculate the cost of care and shelter for healthy and sick animals at Capital City Animal Shelter.*

1. **Open** the as-April Expenses workbook from the Lesson 12 folder.

2. Examine the April Expense Report worksheet. Identify the fields you will use in the PivotTable.

### Create the PivotTable

3. Create a **PivotTable** on a new worksheet.

4. **Rename** the new sheet with a descriptive name of your choice.

5. **Rename** the PivotTable as **April Expenses**.

6. Set up fields for the PivotTable so that the rows summarize the data by **cats/dogs** and then by **age**.

7. Set up fields so that the columns compare the cost of caring for **healthy** and **sick** animals.

8. Set up fields to total the cost of **care** and **shelter**.

### Format the PivotTable

9. **Apply** a PivotTable style.

10. Format all numbers with **Comma Style and two decimal places**.
    *When you finish, your PivotTable should match the following figure, except for field labels.*

Your PivotTable displays some additional labels. They were removed from this figure because they would display a significant part of the exercise solution.

|  | A | B | C | D |
|---|---|---|---|---|
| 3 | **Sum of Total Costs** | **Column Labels** ▾ |  |  |
| 4 | **Row Labels** ▾ | **Healthy** | **Sick** | **Grand Total** |
| 5 | ⊟ **Cat** | **349.75** | **292.25** | **642.00** |
| 6 | Adult | 349.75 | 182.50 | 532.25 |
| 7 | Kitten |  | 109.75 | 109.75 |
| 8 | ⊟ **Dog** | **919.50** | **448.00** | **1,367.50** |
| 9 | Adult | 564.00 | 67.00 | 631.00 |
| 10 | Pup | 355.50 | 381.00 | 736.50 |
| 11 | **Grand Total** | **1,269.25** | **740.25** | **2,009.50** |

### Change Worksheet Data and Update the PivotTable

11. In the April Expenses worksheet, change the cost per day in **cell F1** to **$5.25**.

12. Do whatever is necessary to **update** the PivotTable to reflect the change you just made.

13. **Save** 💾 the changes and **close** the workbook.

# Create a PivotTable and PivotChart

*In this exercise, you will create a PivotTable and PivotChart that display the cost of care and shelter for sick and healthy animals summarized by animal type and health. The chart will be a stacked column chart.*

1. **Open** the as-May Expenses workbook.

2. Examine the May Expense Report worksheet. Identify the fields you will use to create the PivotTable and its accompanying PivotChart.

## Create the PivotTable and PivotChart

3. Create a **PivotTable** and **PivotChart** together on a new worksheet.

4. **Rename** the new sheet with a descriptive name of your choice.

5. **Rename** the PivotTable as `May Expenses`.

6. Set up fields for the PivotTable and PivotChart so that the table and chart summarize the data by **cats/dogs** and then by **health**.

7. Set up fields so that the **shelter cost** and **veterinary cost** are calculated separately.

8. Format all numbers in the PivotTable with **Comma Style and no decimal places**.

## Format the PivotChart

9. Change the chart type to **Stacked Column**.

10. Apply a PivotChart **style** and a **chart layout** of your choice.
*When you finish, your PivotTable and PivotChart should match the following figure, except for field labels.*

Your PivotTable displays one additional label. It was removed from this figure because it would display a significant part of the exercise solution.

Your PivotChart style and layout may differ from that shown.

| ⊿ | A | B | C |
|---|---|---|---|
| 1 | | Sum of Shelter Cost | Sum of Veterinary Cost |
| 2 | ⊟ Cat | 594 | 75 |
| 3 | Healthy | 325 | 40 |
| 4 | Sick | 270 | 35 |
| 5 | ⊟ Dog | 1,155 | 265 |
| 6 | Healthy | 869 | 90 |
| 7 | Sick | 286 | 175 |
| 8 | Grand Total | 1,749 | 340 |

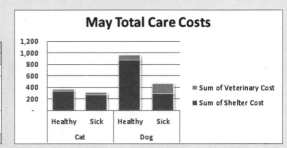

11. Change the **page orientation** and make any other adjustments necessary to fit the Pivot-Table and PivotChart on **one printed page**.

12. **Save** 🖫 the changes and **close** the workbook.

# Create a Macro that Inserts the Date

*In this exercise, you will create a macro that inserts the phrase **Today's Date** in cell A1 and the TODAY() function in cell A2. The macro also will format the two cells. You will assign the macro to the current workbook only.*

1. Start a **new workbook** containing three blank worksheets.

2. Select **cell A10**.

## Record the Macro

3. Begin **recording** a new macro.

4. **Name** the macro **TodaysDate**, assign the shortcut keystroke **Ctrl+Shift+D** to the macro, and store it in **This Workbook**. Your macro should record all of the actions in **steps 5–11**.

5. Select **cell A1**.

6. Type **Today's Date** into **cell A1**.

7. Enter the formula **=TODAY()** in **cell B1**.
   *This function displays the current date in the cell.*

8. Left-align the date in **cell B1**.

9. Format **cells A1:B1** with size 12, bold, and a blue color for text.

10. Set the width of **column A** to **20**.

11. Select **cell B1**.

12. **Stop** the macro recording.

13. **Save** 🖫 as a Macro-Enabled Workbook with the name **as-Today's Date** in the Lesson 12 folder in your file storage location.

## Test the Macro Using the Ribbon Command

14. Display the **Sheet2** worksheet.

15. Run the macro using the **Run** command in the Macro dialog box.
    *If your macro does not insert text, format the text, and widen column A as specified in steps 5–11, then delete the macro and rerecord it.*

## Test the Macro Shortcut Key

16. Display the **Sheet3** worksheet.

17. **Test** the macro using the ⌈Ctrl⌉+⌈Shift⌉+⌈D⌉ keystroke combination.

18. Have your instructor or a teaching assistant initial that you have successfully run the macro. _____

19. **Save** as **as-Today's Date** again and **close** the workbook.

# Create Macros and Assign Buttons

*In this exercise, you will create a defined name for a list, create two macros, assign buttons to them, and finally run the macros using the buttons.*

1. **Open** the as-Holiday Donations workbook.

2. Display the **November Donations** worksheet, if not already displayed.

3. **Create** two macros for use in this workbook only and **assign** them to buttons as shown in the following table. The table describes the button text, macro names, and macro functions for each button. Position the buttons above the list in rows 3:4.

| Button Text | Macro Name | Macro Function |
|---|---|---|
| Sort by Patron | Sort_by_Patron | Sort the patron list in rows 6–16 in A to Z order based on the patron last names and first names in columns A:B. |
| Sort by Details | Sort_by_Details | Sort the the patron list in rows 6–16 from largest to smallest based on the donation details in column D. |

4. **Save** 💾 as a Macro-Enabled Workbook in the Lesson 12 folder in your file storage location.

## Test the Macros

5. Manually **sort** the list in A to Z order by the type of donation in **column C**.

6. **Test** the Sort_by_Patron macro.

7. **Test** the Sort_by_Details macro.

8. Have your instructor or a teaching assistant initial that you have successfully run the macros. _____

9. **Save** 💾 again and **close** the workbook.

# Critical Thinking & Work-Readiness Skills

*In the course of working through the following Microsoft Office-based Critical Thinking exercises, you will also be utilizing various work-readiness skills, some of which are listed next to each exercise. Go to* labyrinthelab.com/workreadiness *to learn more about the work-readiness skills.*

## 12.1 Create a PivotTable and PivotChart

Dr. Edward Jackson, chief operating officer of Raritan Clinic East, would like a PivotTable and a PivotChart created from data to show a summary of patients' daily drug charges in each hospital station by doctor name. Open ct-Raritan Clinic East Patients (Lesson 12 folder). Look at the Patients worksheet. Title the list appropriately and descriptively. You will adjust column widths in a later exercise. Perform a two-column sort by Station then by Doctor. Insert both a Pivot-Table and PivotChart into a new worksheet and rename the worksheet **PivotChart**. Set up the PivotTable to display daily cost totals by station and then by doctor name. Format the chart for appropriate size and appearance. Save your work as **ct-Raritan Clinic East Patients [Your Last Name]**. Keep the file open.

**WORK-READINESS SKILLS APPLIED**

- Organizing and maintaining information
- Using computers to process information
- Seeing things in the mind's eye

## 12.2 View Details using the PivotChart

Dr. Edward Jackson would now like to see a summary of patients. Open ct-Raritan Clinic East Patients [Your Last Name], if necessary. Using options on the PivotTable Field List and the PivotChart, display the doctor specialty and doctor names, and then graph only Dr. Lawrence's patients. Resize and move the chart, if necessary. Format the PivotChart worksheet to print on one page. Save your work, and keep the file open.

**WORK-READINESS SKILLS APPLIED**

- Seeing things in the mind's eye
- Organizing and maintaining information
- Using computers to process information

## 12.3 Create Macros

You have decided to help Dr. Edward Jackson be more productive by adding macros the Patients worksheet. If necessary, open ct-Raritan Clinic East Patients [Your Last Name]. On the Patients worksheet, create a macro to automatically insert today's date in cell H1 and right align it. Create another macro to autofit the column widths. Test the macros by running them. Then, save as a macro-enabled workbook. Close your file when you are finished.

**WORK-READINESS SKILLS APPLIED**

- Showing responsibility
- Making decisions
- Selecting technology

# Using Financial Functions and Data Analysis

## LESSON OUTLINE

## LEARNING OBJECTIVES

After studying this lesson, you will be able to:

- Use the PMT and FV functions to analyze loans and investments
- Adjust one or more variables using the Goal Seek and Solver tools
- Create what-if models in the Scenario Manager

Several Excel tools allow you to perform a *what-if analysis* on worksheet data. For example, you might ask, "What if our company obtained a loan for 9 percent rather than 8 percent?" By changing the interest rate used in a formula to various rates, you could see the effect on the monthly loan payment. Excel's built-in financial functions may be used for various types of calculations. In this lesson, you will use the PMT (Payment) function to determine the monthly payment for a business loan. You also will use the FV (Future Value) function to determine the future value of investments. Excel provides other tools to help you find solutions to what-if questions. In this lesson, you will use Goal Seek and Solver to answer a variety of questions. Excel also provides the Scenario Manager to view alternative scenarios with up to 32 input variables for advanced data analysis.

# Analyzing a Fundraising Campaign

**Raritan Clinic East**

Pediatric Diagnostic Specialists

Sandra Chavez-Hall coordinates a fundraising campaign to build two new facilities at Raritan Clinic East. The clinic will borrow an initial amount to begin the planning process, until Raritan's foundation raises enough contributions to start building. Sandra will set up an Excel worksheet that calculates the loan repayment schedule using the PMT (Payment) function and a variety of input variables. Major funding for the building projects will be provided by various grants and sponsors. One contribution plan allows corporate and individual sponsors to make monthly payments toward their pledge amounts. These payments will be invested, and Sandra will use the FV (Future Value) function to forecast the total earned. Then she will use Excel's Goal Seek and Solver tools to explore various financing scenarios. She will use the Scenario Manager to view various models comparing fundraising goals and expenses.

|   | A | B |
|---|---|---|
| 1 | Loan Analysis | |
| 2 | | |
| 3 | Phase 1 Site Plan Cost | $580,473.95 |
| 4 | | |
| 5 | Loan | |
| 6 | Loan Amount | $480,473.95 |
| 7 | Interest Rate | 5.45% |
| 8 | Number of Months | 60 |
| 9 | Monthly Payment | $ 9,166.67 |
| 10 | Total Interest | $ 69,525.96 |
| 11 | | |
| 12 | Total Cost | |
| 13 | Down Payment | $100,000.00 |
| 14 | Total Loan Payments | $549,999.92 |
| 15 | Total  Financed Cost | $649,999.92 |

The Goal Seek and Solver tools help determine the maximum Phase 1 site plan cost and loan interest rate that will keep the total financed cost within budget.

| Scenario Summary | | | | | |
|---|---|---|---|---|---|
| | Current Values: | Scenario 1 | Scenario 2 | Scenario 3 | Scenario 4 |
| **Changing Cells:** | | | | | |
| Cash_Contributions | 2,000,000 | 1,000,000 | 1,500,000 | 2,000,000 | 3,250,000 |
| In_Kind_Contributions | 25,000 | 50,000 | 50,000 | 25,000 | 53,000 |
| Grants | 25,000 | 30,000 | 50,000 | 25,000 | 200,000 |
| Interest_Income | 25,000 | 20,000 | 20,000 | 25,000 | 80,000 |
| **Result Cells:** | | | | | |
| Projected_Net_Income | $ 1,965,000 | $ 990,000 | $ 1,510,000 | $ 1,965,000 | $ 3,473,000 |
| Targeted_Expenses_vs._Income | 5.30% | 10.00% | 6.79% | 5.30% | 3.07% |
| Total_Income | $ 2,075,000 | $ 1,100,000 | $ 1,620,000 | $ 2,075,000 | $ 3,583,000 |

Scenario Manager compiles a report to compare the results of several scenarios.

# 13.1 Creating Financial Functions

**Video Lesson** labyrinthelab.com/videos

Excel provides more than 50 financial functions that calculate important financial numbers. For example, Excel has basic financial functions for determining monthly payments on loans, the total interest paid on loans, the future value of investments, and other such questions. Excel also has advanced financial functions for calculating depreciation of assets, internal rates of return, and other more advanced business topics.

## PMT and FV Functions

The PMT (Payment) and FV (Future Value) functions are the most useful financial functions for the average Excel user. The PMT function calculates the required payment for a loan when you specify the loan amount, interest rate, and number of payments you will make. The FV function calculates the total amount you will have in an investment when you specify the deposit amount, interest rate, and number of deposits.

## Financial Function Syntax

You may enter financial functions using the Insert Function dialog box or by typing them. You may use the actual values or cell references in the formulas. Keep in mind that using the cell reference offers more flexibility. For example, you may easily change the number of deposits in an FV function without having to edit the formula. Like all other functions, financial functions have a specific syntax you must follow. The generic format of the PMT and FV functions are shown in the following table.

| Function | Syntax |
|---|---|
| PMT (Payment) | PMT (rate, periods, loan amount) |
| FV (Future Value) | FV (rate, periods, payment) |

Most car loans and fixed-rate mortgages have payment amounts that remain constant throughout the term of the loan. The PMT and FV functions can be used when the payment amount remains constant. The various arguments in the PMT and FV functions are outlined in the following table.

| Argument | Description |
|---|---|
| Periods | This is the number of payments made for a loan or deposits for an investment. Most loans have a monthly payment period, so you should specify the number of months instead of the number of years. For example, use 60 as the number of periods for a five-year auto loan (5 years*12 months per year). |
| Rate | This is the interest rate for each period of the loan or investment. Although loans are quoted as annual rates, payments usually are made monthly. Therefore, you will need to divide the interest rate by 12 in the formula. For example, a 7 percent annual rate would be expressed as 7%/12. |
| Payment | This is the amount invested in each period. The payment must be the same for each period. |
| Loan amount | This is the amount borrowed. |

| Argument | Description |
|---|---|
| Present value (optional) | This is the starting balance of an investment, such as the current amount in a savings account. You are not required to enter the argument if the starting balance is 0 (zero). |
| Future value (optional) | This is the balance you wish to have at the end of an investment. You are not required to enter the argument if the balance will be 0 (zero). |
| Type (optional) | This indicates when the payments are due. You are not required to enter the default argument 0 (zero) if payments are made at the end of the period, such as the last day of each month. Enter 1 if payments are due at the beginning of the period. |

### Converting Negative Numbers to Positive

Excel treats payments as debits (money you owe), so the PMT and FV functions display the result as a negative number. This is a convention that bankers and other financial professionals use. Placing a minus (−) sign before the cell reference for the loan amount or payment in the formula changes the result to a positive number, which may be more easily understood.

A minus (−) sign may be entered before the loan amount or payment in a PMT or FV formula. As an alternative, the minus sign may be entered just before the function name, as in =−PMT or =−FV. Placing the minus sign in either location converts the result to a positive number.

### DEVELOP YOUR SKILLS 13.1.1

## Use the PMT and FV Functions

*In this exercise, you will set up a loan worksheet that will calculate the monthly payment on a construction loan using the PMT function. You also will use the FV function to calculate the monthly deposit required to save the $10,000 down payment.*

### Create a PMT Function

1. **Start** Excel and **open** the Fundraising workbook from the Lesson 13 folder in your file storage location.

2. **Maximize** 🔲 the window, if necessary.
   *The $700,000 site plan cost and $100,000 down payment are already entered in the Loan worksheet.*

3. In the Loan worksheet, select **cell B6** and enter the formula **=B3−B13**.
   *The result is $600,000. The loan amount is the site plan cost minus the down payment. The PMT function will use the loan amount as one of its arguments.*

4. Select **cell B7** and enter **6%** as the interest rate.

5. Select **cell B8** and enter **60** as the number of months.

6. Select **cell B9** and enter the formula **=PMT(B7,B8,B6)**.
   *The result equals ($37,125.43). Remember that the generic PMT function syntax is =PMT(rate, periods, loan amount). Notice that the B7, B8, and B6 references in the function refer to the interest rate, number of months, and loan amount in the worksheet.*

   *Excel formats the payment in Currency Style, red, and in parentheses. The red color and parentheses indicate a negative number. You will convert this number to a positive number in the following steps.*

   *Finally, notice that $37,125.43 seems a very large payment because the interest rate in cell B7 is an annual rate of 6 percent. The borrower would not pay 6 percent interest per month. The interest rate must be divided by 12 (the number of months in a year) to calculate a monthly interest rate in the function. You will do this in the following steps.*

7. Select **cell B9**.

8. Click in the **Formula Bar**, position the insertion point after the equals (=) sign in the formula, and **type** a minus (–) sign.

9. Position the insertion point after **cell B7** in the formula and type **/12** to divide the **cell B7** rate by 12, and **complete** the entry.
   *The completed formula is =–PMT(B7/12,B8,-B6). The new payment equals $11,599.68. This payment certainly will be more affordable. The minus sign converts the number to a positive, and the B7/12 argument establishes a 0.5 percent per month rate.*

10. Format **cell B9** in Accounting format with two decimal places.

11. Select **cell B14** and enter the formula **=B9*B8**.
    *Total loan payments equal $695,980.86.*

12. Select **cell B10** and enter the formula **=B14-B6**.
    *Total loan interest equals $95,980.86. The loan amount in cell B6 is subtracted from the total payments to determine the total interest.*

13. Select **cell B15** and enter the formula **=B13+B14**.
    *The total cost equals $795,980.86 to finance the phase 1 site plan. Your worksheet should match the following illustration.*

|   | A | B |
|---|---|---|
| 1 | Loan Analysis | |
| 2 | | |
| 3 | Phase 1 Site Plan Cost | $700,000.00 |
| 4 | | |
| 5 | Loan | |
| 6 | Loan Amount | $600,000.00 |
| 7 | Interest Rate | 6.00% |
| 8 | Number of Months | 60 |
| 9 | Monthly Payment | $ 11,599.68 |
| 10 | Total Interest | $ 95,980.86 |
| 11 | | |
| 12 | Total Cost | |
| 13 | Down Payment | $100,000.00 |
| 14 | Total Loan Payments | $695,980.86 |
| 15 | Total Financed Cost | $795,980.86 |

14. **Save** 🖫 the changes to the workbook.

## Create the FV Function

*Corporate and individual sponsors may make monthly payments to the capital campaign. These contributions will be invested to earn interest.*

15. Display the **Investment** worksheet of the Fundraising workbook.

16. Select **cell B5**, and type **0** to indicate that the sponsor will make no initial contribution.
    *The cell displays a hyphen (–) to indicate zero.*

17. Select **cell B7**, and enter **2.5%** for the annual interest rate.

18. Select **cell B8**, and enter **36** for the number of monthly payments.

19. Select **cell B6**, and enter the formula **=B3/B8**. *The formula divides the $300,000 pledge amount by 36 months. The monthly contribution is $8,333.*

20. Select **cell B9**.

21. Follow these steps to choose the FV (Future Value) function:

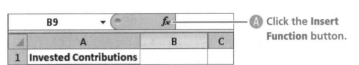

|   | A | B |
|---|---|---|
| 1 | Invested Contributions | |
| 2 | | No initial contribution |
| 3 | Pledge Amount | $300,000.00 |
| 4 | | |
| 5 | Starting Balance | $        - |
| 6 | Monthly Contribution | $     8,333 |
| 7 | Interest Rate | 2.5% |
| 8 | Number of Months | 36 |
| 9 | Total Investment | |

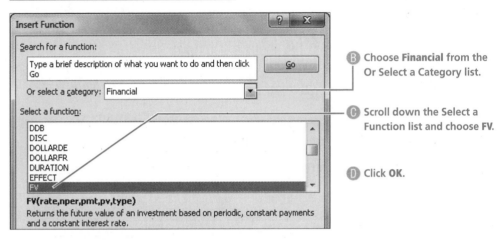

Ⓐ Click the **Insert Function** button.

Ⓑ Choose **Financial** from the Or Select a Category list.

Ⓒ Scroll down the Select a Function list and choose **FV**.

Ⓓ Click **OK**.

22. Follow these steps to specify the function arguments:

Ⓐ If necessary, drag the **Function Arguments** dialog box aside so that the range **A1:B9** is visible.

Ⓑ Click in the **Rate** box, select **cell B7** in the worksheet, and type **/12**. This divides the annual interest rate by 12 months.

Ⓒ Click in the **Nper** box and select **cell B8** in the worksheet to set the number of payment periods.

Ⓓ Click in the **Pmt** box. Type a minus (−) sign and click **cell B6** to set the payment amount to a negative value.

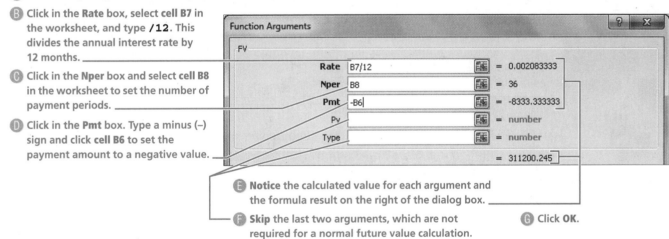

Ⓔ **Notice** the calculated value for each argument and the formula result on the right of the dialog box.

Ⓕ **Skip** the last two arguments, which are not required for a normal future value calculation.

Ⓖ Click **OK**.

*The completed formula is =FV(B7/12,B8,-B6), and the result $311,200.24 appears in cell B9. With deposits of $8,333 per month in an investment fund earning 2.5 percent, the contributions would total this amount in three years.*

## Include Optional Arguments

*What if sponsors were required to contribute an initial payment of 25 percent of the total pledge amount and make payments on the first of each month? In the next steps, you will modify the FV formula.*

23. Select **cell E5**, and enter the formula **=E3*25%** for the initial contribution.
    *The result is $75,000.*

24. Copy the **range B6:B9** to the **range E6:E9**.

25. Select **cell E6**, and click in the **Formula Bar**.

26. Making certain to type the **parentheses**, edit the formula to **=(E3-E5)/E8**.
    *The monthly contribution now is $6,250. It is based on $225,000, the remainder of the pledge amount after the sponsor makes the initial contribution.*

27. Select **cell E9**, and click the **Insert Function** $f_x$ button at the left of the Formula Bar to display the Insert Function dialog box.

28. Follow these steps to enter optional arguments:

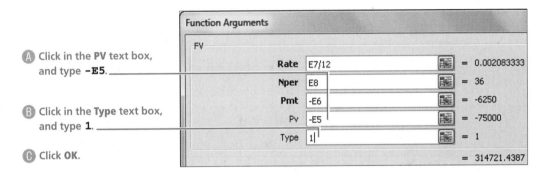

Ⓐ Click in the **PV** text box, and type **-E5**.

Ⓑ Click in the **Type** text box, and type **1**.

Ⓒ Click **OK**.

*The revised formula is =FV(E7/12,E8,-E6,-E5,1). The new total investment is $314,721.44. The -E5 argument is entered as a negative number. It indicates the starting balance, or the present value of the investment before the monthly payments begin. The Type argument of 1 indicates that payments will be made at the beginning of each month. The total future value of the investment in cell E9 is larger with these two payment options as compared to cell B9.*

29. Change the number of months to 24 in **cells B8** and **E8**.
    *By experimenting with the values for rate, number of periods, and payment used in the FV function, you may create various plans for saving the desired amount or meeting the sponsor's budget for the monthly payment. In the next exercises, you will use Excel's tools to automate this analysis.*

30. **Save** 🖫 the changes, and leave the workbook **open**.

# 13.2 Using Data Analysis Tools

**Video Lesson**  labyrinthelab.com/videos

Excel provides several tools to perform advanced what-if analyses. Goal Seek is best used when you know the formula answer you want but not the specific value in one cell that would achieve the answer. The Solver sets the values of multiple cells to produce the desired result that you specify for a target cell. You also may set minimum and maximum values for Solver to use in calculations. Scenario Manager saves a model worksheet with various changes to values so that you may compare the scenarios side by side.

## Using Goal Seek

With Goal Seek you set a goal for a specific formula result. For example, you will set a monthly payment goal of $10,000 in the Loan worksheet. The goal cell must contain a formula, which is a PMT function in this example. You will instruct Goal Seek to adjust the down payment to achieve the desired monthly payment.

| QUICK REFERENCE | USING GOAL SEEK |
| --- | --- |
| **Task** | **Procedure** |
| Set up a Goal Seek solution | ▪ Test the worksheet with sample data to make certain that formulas are functioning properly. |
| | ▪ Select the cell for which you want to set a goal. The cell must contain a formula. |
| | ▪ Choose Data→Data Tools→What-If Analysis 📖→Goal Seek from the Ribbon. |
| | ▪ Type the desired goal value in the To Value box. |
| | ▪ Click in the By Changing Cell box and choose the worksheet cell for which Goal Seek will adjust the value. |

### DEVELOP YOUR SKILLS 13.2.1
## Use Goal Seek

*In this exercise, you will use Goal Seek to adjust the down payment based on a specific monthly payment that you enter. Then you will adjust the interest rate.*

### Use Goal Seek to Adjust the Down Payment

*Assume that you wish to see the effect on the down payment that Raritan Clinic would be required to pay if the monthly payment were $10,000 rather than $11,599.68 as previously calculated.*

1. Display the **Loan** worksheet of the Fundraising workbook.

2. Select **cell B9**.
   *Choosing the cell for which you wish to set a goal prior to starting Goal Seek will ensure that you set the goal for the correct cell. The currently selected cell reference displays in the Set Cell box when you open Goal Seek.*

3. Choose **Data→Data Tools→What-If Analysis** 📖→**Goal Seek** from the Ribbon.

4. Follow these steps to set the Goal Seek parameters:
*You may either type cell references or use point mode in the Goal Seek dialog box.*

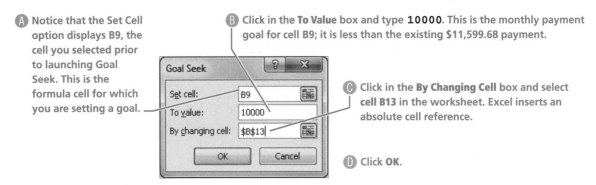

Ⓐ Notice that the Set Cell option displays B9, the cell you selected prior to launching Goal Seek. This is the formula cell for which you are setting a goal.

Ⓑ Click in the **To Value** box and type **10000**. This is the monthly payment goal for cell B9; it is less than the existing $11,599.68 payment.

Ⓒ Click in the **By Changing Cell** box and select **cell B13** in the worksheet. Excel inserts an absolute cell reference.

Ⓓ Click **OK**.

*The Goal Seek Status dialog box indicates that Goal Seek found a solution for the goal. The down payment in the worksheet has been adjusted to $182,744.39. As you can see, a higher down payment is required with a $10,000 monthly payment.*

5. Click **Cancel** in the Goal Seek Status dialog box to undo the change to the down payment.

## Use Goal Seek to Adjust the Interest Rate

*You wish to know what the loan interest rate would have to be if the monthly payment were $12,000.*

6. Make certain **cell B9** is still selected and choose **Data→Data Tools→What-If Analysis→Goal Seek** from the Ribbon.

7. Type **12000** in the **To Value** box to set the monthly payment goal.

8. Click in the **By Changing Cell** box, and then select **cell B7** (the interest rate cell) in the worksheet.

9. Click **OK**, and the interest rate is changed to 7.42 percent.

10. Move the **Goal Seek Status** dialog box, if necessary, to see **cell B7**.

11. Click **OK** again to confirm the change to the interest rate.

12. **Save** 💾 the changes.

## Change Values in a What-If Analysis

*After seeking a goal, you also may experiment with the what-if analysis by changing the site plan cost or other values directly in the worksheet. The cells you change should contain values and not formulas.*

13. Select **cell B3** and change the **site plan cost** to **$500,000**.
*What impact does this change have on the other amounts?*

14. Feel free to experiment with Goal Seek. When you are finished, **close** ⊠ the workbook **without** saving the changes.

# Using Solver

Video Lesson    labyrinthelab.com/videos

 Goal Seek is easy to use but is somewhat limited. Goal Seek adjusts only one variable at a time. Excel's Solver tool can solve problems when more than one variable requires adjustment. In fact, you may specify up to two hundred variables, but all variables must appear in a formula related to the objective cell. You may specify a precise objective cell value, as with Goal Seek, or you may specify that Solver determine the Max (maximum) or Min (minimum) value. For example, you may specify a monthly payment of $300 for an auto loan. In addition, Solver lets you specify one or more constraints. Constraints give you extra control by limiting a cell's possible range of values in the suggested solution. You may not set a constraint for any cell that is used in the objective cell's formula. Instead, you must enter the desired value in the appropriate worksheet cell. The new Solver version in Excel 2010 includes a choice of three solving methods. The default GRG Nonlinear method is appropriate for many typical business problems that have a smooth nonlinear solution.

See the Excel Help for more information about the Solver's three solving methods: GRG Nonlinear, Simplex LP for linear problems, and Evolutionary for other problems.

Solver changes the values in these two worksheet cells to meet the specified objective and restraint. In this example, the solution will display an optimum car purchase price and loan interest rate.

A specific value is set for the objective cell, a $300 monthly car payment in this example.

Constraint rules limit how the solution is calculated. As shown here, the total vehicle cost cannot be greater than $28,000.

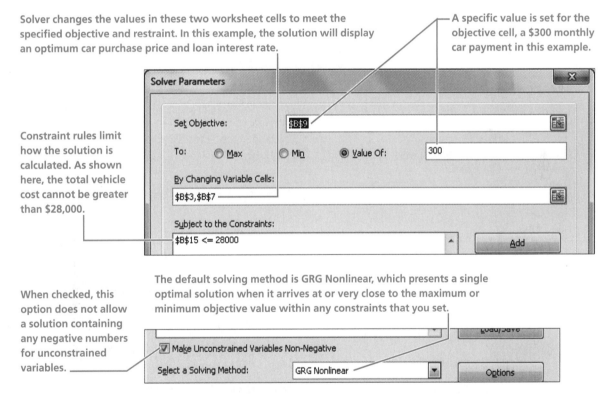

When checked, this option does not allow a solution containing any negative numbers for unconstrained variables.

The default solving method is GRG Nonlinear, which presents a single optimal solution when it arrives at or very close to the maximum or minimum objective value within any constraints that you set.

Solving for optimum values in two cells based on an objective cell value and a constraint rule

## *Installing Solver*

Solver is not part of the typical Office 2010 installation but is an add-in program. The Solver command displays in an Analysis group on the Data ribbon after installation.

 Your network administrator may not grant permission to install add-in programs.

| Task | Procedure |
|------|-----------|
| Install or remove an add-in tool | ■ Choose File→Options ▣ →Add-Ins. |
| | ■ Choose Excel Add-Ins to the right of Manage at the bottom of the window, and click Go. |
| | ■ In the Add-Ins dialog box, place a checkmark in the box for each desired add-in. Removing checkmarks uninstalls add-ins that are currently installed. |
| Set up a Solver solution | ■ Test the worksheet with sample data to make certain that formulas are functioning properly. |
| | ■ Choose Data→Analysis→Solver ▣ from the Ribbon. |
| | ■ If desired, click the Reset All button to clear previously set options in the Solver Parameters dialog box. |
| | ■ Click in the Set Objective box and choose the worksheet cell for which you want to set a goal. |
| | ■ Choose Max or Min; or, choose Value Of and type a desired goal value for the objective cell in the text box. |
| | ■ Click in the By Changing Variable Cells box and choose one or more worksheet cells whose values you want Solver to adjust. Type a comma between cell references. |
| | ■ If desired, click the Add button and set one or more constraint rules in the Add Constraint dialog box. |
| | ■ Place a checkmark next to Make Unconstrained Variables Non-Negative if only positive numbers are acceptable in the solution for these variables. |
| | ■ Click Solve in the Solver Parameters dialog box. |
| | ■ Read the message in the Solver Results dialog box, choosing Keep Solver Solution or Restore Original Values. |
| Save Solver results as a scenario to view again later | ■ Click Save Scenario in the Solver Results dialog box. |
| | ■ Type a scenario name. |

## DEVELOP YOUR SKILLS 13.2.2

# Use Solver

*In this exercise, you will use Solver to determine the site plan cost and interest rate required to achieve the total financed cost that you specify.*

*Before You Begin: Solver must be installed using the procedure given in the preceding Quick Reference table.*

## Reset to Original Values

1. **Open** the Fundraising workbook from the Lesson 13 folder.

2. In the **Loan** worksheet, **reenter** the original value of **6%** in cell B7. Make certain that **cell B3** contains $700,000.00, **cell B8** contains 60, and **cell B13** contains $100,000.00. *All worksheet cells should contain the values or formulas you created in Develop Your Skills 13.1.1.*

## Use Solver to Adjust the Cost and Interest Rate

3. Choose **Data→Analysis→Solver** ?→ from the Ribbon.

4. Follow these steps to set the objective cell value and specify the variable cells:

(A) Click the **Reset All** button and click **OK** to confirm the reset if any previous entries display in the dialog box.

(B) **Click** in the Set Objective box (if not already selected), and select **cell B15** in the worksheet.

(C) Choose **Value Of** and enter **650000** in the text box to set a specific total financed cost.

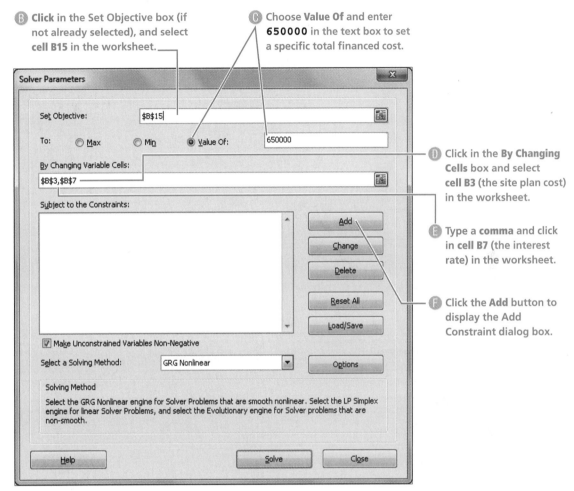

(D) Click in the **By Changing Cells** box and select **cell B3** (the site plan cost) in the worksheet.

(E) Type a **comma** and click in **cell B7** (the interest rate) in the worksheet.

(F) Click the **Add** button to display the Add Constraint dialog box.

*Excel converts the objective cell and variable cells to absolute cell references as you entered them in the Solver Parameters dialog box.*

5. Follow these steps to specify a constraint:

(A) Select **cell B10** (total interest) in the worksheet to enter an absolute cell reference in this box.

(B) Make certain the operator is set to <= (less than or equal to).

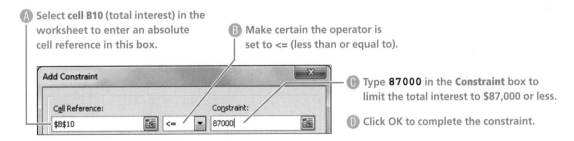

(C) Type **87000** in the **Constraint** box to limit the total interest to $87,000 or less.

(D) Click OK to complete the constraint.

*The constraint rule appears in the Subject to the Constraints list of the Solver Parameters dialog box.*

6. Take a moment to review the options you have set in the Solver Parameters dialog box.

7. Click the **Solve** button, and the Solver will go to work.

*When the Solver has completed its calculations, the Solver Results dialog box should report that a solution has been found that meets all conditions.*

8. Follow these steps to accept the proposed solution:

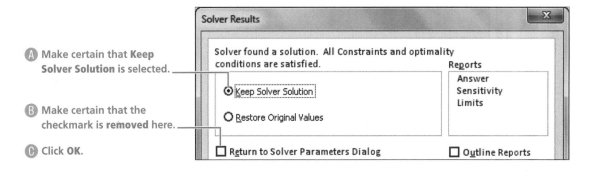

Ⓐ Make certain that **Keep Solver Solution** is selected.

Ⓑ Make certain that the checkmark is **removed** here.

Ⓒ Click **OK**.

*The completed solution should match the following example.*

|   | A | B |
|---|---|---|
| 1 | Loan Analysis | |
| 2 | | |
| 3 | Phase 1 Site Plan Cost | $580,473.95 |
| 4 | | |
| 5 | Loan | |
| 6 | Loan Amount | $480,473.95 |
| 7 | Interest Rate | 5.45% |
| 8 | Number of Months | 60 |
| 9 | Monthly Payment | $ 9,166.67 |
| 10 | Total Interest | $ 69,525.96 |
| 11 | | |
| 12 | Total Cost | |
| 13 | Down Payment | $100,000.00 |
| 14 | Total Loan Payments | $549,999.92 |
| 15 | Total Financed Cost | $649,999.92 |

Solver suggested a $580,473.95 site plan cost and 5.45 percent interest rate for the two variables you specified.

The monthly payment recalculates as $9,166.67. No constraint was placed on this formula.

The total financed cost is just below $650,000, and total interest is below $87,000, the limits you set.

## Use Solver to Adjust the Cost

*You determine that a maximum $11,000 monthly payment is acceptable, and a local bank offers a 6 percent business loan. You wish to know the maximum site plan cost you can negotiate, but your research shows that $650,000 is the lowest bid you are likely to receive.*

9. Choose **Data→Analysis→Solver** 📊 from the Ribbon.

10. Click **Reset All** to clear the previous options, and click **OK** to confirm.

11. Follow these guidelines to set options in the Solver Parameters dialog box:

Ⓐ Set the **monthly payment goal** to $11000.

Ⓑ Set the **site plan cost** to adjust.

Ⓒ Click **Add** to display the Add Constraint dialog box.

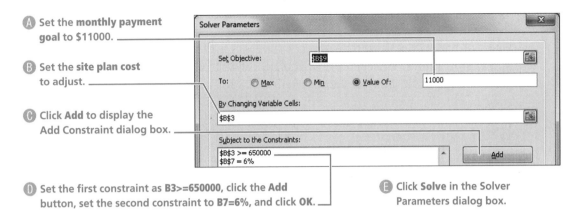

Ⓓ Set the first constraint as **B3>=650000**, click the **Add** button, set the second constraint to **B7=6%**, and click **OK**.

Ⓔ Click **Solve** in the Solver Parameters dialog box.

*Solver reports it could not find a solution. The interest rate still is 5.45% in cell B7 because the constraint for interest rate was ignored. You may not set a constraint for any cell used in the objective cell's formula, =−PMT(B7/12,B8,B6). You must enter the desired interest rate in the worksheet.*

12. Choose **Restore Original Values** make certain that the checkmark is removed next to Return to Solver Parameters Dialog, and click **OK**.

13. In **cell B7**, change the interest rate to **6%**.

14. Choose **Data→Analysis→Solver** 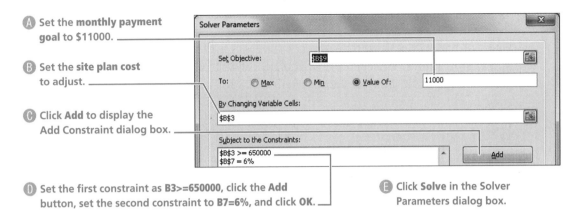.

15. Select the constraint rule **$B$7=6%**, and click the **Delete** button.

16. Click **Solve** to use the other options that you previously set.
    *This time a solution was found. The site plan cost equals $668,981.85. This is the maximum price that you may negotiate on to meet the $11,000 monthly payment goal. Notice that the monthly payment in cell B9 is rounded up to $11,000.01, which Solver found to be the optimum solution.*

17. Click **OK** to accept the proposed solution.

18. **Save** the changes to the workbook.

**Experiment with Solver**

19. Take a few minutes to experiment with Solver.
    *Depending on the variables and constraints you create, Solver may report that no solution was found or suggest a 0 (zero) or negative amount in one or more cells. If this occurs, choose Restore Original Values and solve again after editing the options.*

20. When you have finished, **close** the workbook **without** saving changes.

# Scenario Manager

Video Lesson    labyrinthelab.com/videos

Excel provides the Scenario Manager to create and save what-if models with up to 32 variables. This allows you to model virtually any what-if scenario. Scenario Manager does not solve for a specific variable value to achieve a formula result as Goal Seek and Solver do. You may, however, save a Solver solution as a scenario.

## What Is a Scenario?

A scenario is a group of values assigned to cells in a what-if model. The model calculates formula results based on the values you enter in the scenario. Scenarios are given names to identify them, and they are saved and organized using the Scenario Manager.

## Managing Scenarios

You may create and manage a large number of scenarios in the Scenario Manager. This way, you may compare various scenarios and the results they achieve. The Scenario Manager also lets you display and print a summary of all scenarios. The scenario summary does not automatically update when you change any scenario values. You must create a new summary.

## Adding Scenarios

Selecting the variable cells in the worksheet before issuing the Scenario Manager command is recommended. The Ctrl key is used to select noncontiguous cell ranges. The Scenario Manager has an Add button that allows you to create new scenarios. Each scenario may contain different values. The following illustration shows the Scenario Values dialog box with values entered for the variable cells. If you enter a formula for a variable, Excel will convert the result to a value.

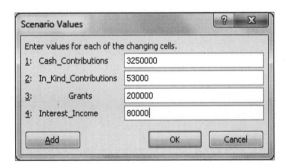

The entered values are applied to cells in the worksheet, thus forming a scenario.

| Task | Procedure |
|------|-----------|
| Create a scenario | ■ Create defined names for all worksheet cells containing variables or result formulas affected by the variables. |
| | ■ Select the worksheet cells containing the desired variables but do not select any cells containing result formulas. |
| | ■ Choose Data→Data Tools→What-If Analysis→Scenario Manager from the Ribbon. |
| | ■ Click the Add button in the Scenario Manager dialog box. |
| | ■ In the Add Scenario dialog box, type a scenario name. |
| | ■ In the Scenario Values dialog box, edit values as desired. |
| Display a scenario in a worksheet | ■ Choose the desired scenario name in the Scenario Manager dialog box. |
| | ■ Click the Show button. |
| Edit a scenario | ■ Choose the desired scenario name in the Scenario Manager dialog box. |
| | ■ Click the Edit button. |
| | ■ In the Scenario Values dialog box, edit values as desired. |
| Display and print a summary of all scenarios | ■ Click the Summary button in the Scenario Manager dialog box. |
| | ■ Choose Scenario Summary or Scenario PivotTable Report. |
| | ■ Click in the Result Cells box and choose one or more worksheet cells containing result formulas based on the scenario values. Type a comma between cell references. Excel places the report on a new worksheet. |
| | ■ Print the scenario report worksheet, if desired. |
| Remove a scenario summary worksheet | ■ Right-click the Scenario Summary worksheet tab at the lower-left corner of the workbook window, and choose Delete from the context menu. |
| | ■ Click Delete to confirm deletion of the worksheet. |

## DEVELOP YOUR SKILLS 13.2.3
# Use the Scenario Manager

*In this exercise, you will use a model to analyze fundraising goals with certain budgeted expenses that are necessary to raise the funds. You understand that a lower expense-to-income percentage indicates that resources are being used more effectively. Therefore, you will take a closer look at each component of the projected income to set achievable goals. You will create a model and use Scenario Manager to set up and manage multiple scenarios.*

### Set Up the Model

1. **Open** the Campaign Scenarios workbook from the Lesson 13 folder.

2. In the **Campaign Analysis** worksheet, enter the model values in the **range B4:B7** as shown.
   *Notice that the formula to sum the total income already has been entered in cell B8. The expenses and their sum formula have been entered in the range B11:B15.*

| | A | B |
|---|---|---|
| 1 | Capital Campaign Net Income Model | |
| 2 | | |
| 3 | *Income Goals* | |
| 4 | Cash Contributions | 1,000,000 |
| 5 | In-Kind Contributions | 50,000 |
| 6 | Grants | 30,000 |
| 7 | Interest Income | 20,000 |
| 8 | Total Income | $ 1,100,000 |

3. Select **cell B17**, and review the formula =B8-B15 in the Formula Bar.
*The generic formula is Projected Net Income = Total Income – Total Expenses.*

4. In **cell B18**, enter the formula **=B15/B8**.
*The result equals 0.1. Notice that this formula divides the total expenses by the total income to compare the two amounts.*

5. Format **cell B18** as **bold** and **Percent Style** with **two decimal places**.
*Expenses are 10.00 percent of net income. This model is the starting point from which you will create scenarios to see the effect on the Targeted Expenses vs. Income percentage.*

## Name the Variable Cells and Results Cells

*In the next few steps, you will name the variable cells in the model using the Create from Selection command in the Formulas ribbon. Naming the variable cells is beneficial because the names, rather than cell references, will appear in the Scenario Manager dialog box. You also will name some results cells containing formulas because they will appear in a summary report.*

6. Select the **range A4:B8**, which includes the income labels and the cell values to which they refer.

7. With the **range A4:B8** still selected, **hold down** ⌈Ctrl⌉ and select the **range A17:B18**, which includes labels and formula cells.
*Both ranges should appear selected.*

| ◢ | A | B |
|---|---|---|
| 1 | Capital Campaign Net Income Model | |
| 2 | | |
| 3 | *Income Goals* | |
| 4 | Cash Contributions | 1,000,000 |
| 5 | In-Kind Contributions | 50,000 |
| 6 | Grants | 30,000 |
| 7 | Interest Income | 20,000 |
| 8 | Total Income | $ 1,100,000 |
| 9 | | |
| 10 | *Targeted Expenses* | |
| 11 | Web/Social Media Development | 25,000 |
| 12 | Print Materials | 10,000 |
| 13 | Events | 50,000 |
| 14 | Salaries - Grant Proposals | 25,000 |
| 15 | Total Expenses | $ 110,000 |
| 16 | | |
| 17 | Projected Net Income | $ 990,000 |
| 18 | Targeted Expenses vs. Income | 10.00% |

8. Choose **Formulas→Defined Names→Create From Selection** 🖼 from the Ribbon.

9. Place a checkmark in the **Left Column box** (if not already checked) and click **OK**.

10. Choose **Formulas→Defined Names→Name Manager** 🖨 to view all defined names and their Refers To entries.

11. Widen the **Name** column and **Refers To** column, if necessary, to view entire entries in the Name Manager dialog box.

12. Close the **Name Manager** dialog box.

## Create the First Scenario

13. Taking care not to select cell B8, select the **range B4:B7** as shown to the right.
    *Only the income variables will be adjusted in the Scenario Manager. Usually it is best to preselect the cells as you did here, though you may always select the cells once the Add Scenario dialog box is displayed.*

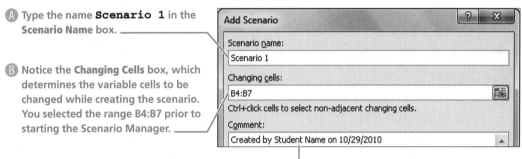

| ▲ | A | B |
|---|---|---|
| 3 | *Income Goals* | |
| 4 | **Cash Contributions** | 1,000,000 |
| 5 | **In-Kind Contributions** | 50,000 |
| 6 | **Grants** | 30,000 |
| 7 | **Interest Income** | 20,000 |
| 8 | Total Income | $ 1,100,000 |

14. Choose **Data→Data Tools→What-If Analysis** 📊**→Scenario Manager** from the Ribbon.
    *The dialog box should indicate that no scenarios are currently defined.*

15. Click the **Add** button to add a new scenario.

16. Follow these steps to set scenario options in the Add Scenario dialog box:

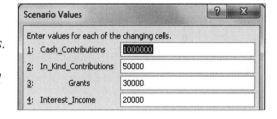

Ⓐ Type the name **Scenario 1** in the **Scenario Name** box.

Ⓑ Notice the **Changing Cells** box, which determines the variable cells to be changed while creating the scenario. You selected the range B4:B7 prior to starting the Scenario Manager.

Ⓒ Edit the username in the **Comment** box to your name.    Ⓓ Click **OK**.

*The Scenario Values dialog box appears as shown; do not make any changes in the dialog box. Review the defined names displayed to the left of the variable boxes. Notice that Excel filled in the variable boxes with the current values from the range B4:B7 that you selected in the worksheet.*

17. Click **OK** to complete the scenario.
    *The Scenario Manager dialog box displays the scenario name you just created. This scenario will serve as a starting point and a comparison for other scenarios.*

## Add Another Scenario

18. Click the **Add** button in the Scenario Manager dialog box.

19. Enter the name **Scenario 2** in the **Add Scenario** dialog box, make certain the Changing Cells are **B4:B7**, edit the Comment to include your name, and click **OK**.

20. Change the variables for **Cash_Contributions** and **Grants**, as shown to the right.

21. Click **OK** in the Scenario Values box.
    *Scenario 1 and Scenario 2 now appear in the Scenario Manager dialog box.*

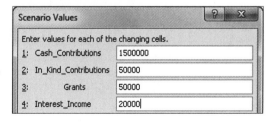

### Show the Results

22. Make certain **Scenario 2** is chosen, and click the **Show** button in the Scenario Manager dialog box. (Move the dialog box to view the worksheet values, if necessary.)
*Excel substitutes the scenario values into the model. The formula in cell B18 calculates the Targeted Expenses vs. Income result, which equals 6.79 percent.*

23. Choose **Scenario 1** and click the **Show** button.
*As you can see, the Scenario Manager rapidly lets you see the results of various scenarios.*

24. Now add **two new scenarios** using the data in the following table:

| Variable | Scenario 3 Scenario Value | Scenario 4 Scenario Value |
|---|---|---|
| Cash Contributions | 500,000 | 3,250,000 |
| In-Kind Contributions | 25,000 | 53,000 |
| Grants | 25,000 | 200,000 |
| Interest Income | 25,000 | 80,000 |

25. Use the **Show** button to display the results of each scenario.

### Edit a Scenario

26. Choose **Scenario 3** in the Scenario Manager dialog box and click the **Show** button.
*The Expenses vs. Net Sales equals 19.13 percent. This percentage is much too high. Fortunately, the Scenario Manager lets you adjust scenario values until a desired result is achieved.*

27. With **Scenario 3** still chosen, click the **Edit** button.

28. Click **OK** in the Edit Scenario box.

29. Change the **Cash Contributions** value to **2000000** in the Scenario Values dialog box and click **OK**.

30. Click the **Show** button again, and the result equals 5.30 percent.
*You can use these scenarios to determine which income items need to be adjusted to achieve an acceptable percentage.*

### Display a Summary of All Scenarios

31. Click the **Summary** button in the Scenario Manager dialog box.
    *Notice that you may display a scenario summary or a scenario PivotTable report.*

32. Follow these steps to select Scenario Summary report options:

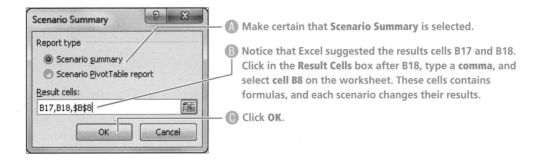

*Excel inserts the summary on a new worksheet named Scenario Summary. Review the summary, which displays the results data in the order you chose in the previous step. You may print a summary as you would print any other worksheet. You also may remove a summary by deleting its worksheet.*

33. **Save** 💾 and **close** the workbook.

# 13.3 Concepts Review

| Concepts Review | labyrinthelab.com/excel10 |
|---|---|

*To check your knowledge of the key concepts introduced in this lesson, complete the Concepts Review quiz by going to the URL listed above. If your classroom is using Labyrinth eLab, you may complete the Concepts Review quiz from within your eLab course.*

# Reinforce Your Skills

## Use the PMT Function and Solver

*In this exercise, you will use the PMT function to calculate mortgage payments for a 30-year fixed mortgage. The generic syntax of the PMT function is repeated below for your convenience. You also will use Solver to determine the purchase price and interest rate required for a specified total cost.*

*Payment Function Syntax =PMT(rate, periods, loan amount)*

*Before You Begin: The Solver add-in must be installed on your computer system to complete the last steps of this exercise.*

### Create a PMT Function

1. **Start** a new workbook and set up the worksheet shown to the right using a formula in **cell B5** to calculate the loan amount as **Purchase Price – Down Payment**.

|  | A | B |
|---|---|---|
| 1 | **30-Year Mortgage Analysis** |  |
| 2 |  |  |
| 3 | Purchase Price | 260,000.00 |
| 4 | Down Payment | 25,000.00 |
| 5 | Loan Amount | 235,000.00 |
| 6 | Interest Rate | 9.00% |
| 7 | Number of Years | 30 |
| 8 | Monthly Payment |  |
| 9 | Total Interest |  |
| 10 | Total Cost of Home |  |

2. Select **cell B8** and enter the formula **=-PMT(B6/ 12,B7*12,B5)**.
   *The result equals $1,890.86. Notice that the formula has a minus (–) sign after the equals (=) sign. Also, the first argument divides the interest rate in cell B6 by 12 because payments will be made monthly. Likewise, the second argument multiplies the number of years in cell B7 by 12 months in a year. Excel formats the result with the Currency Style because you used the PMT function.*

3. Select **cell B9** and enter **=B8*B7*12-B5** to calculate the total interest.
   *The result equals $445,710.73. Take a few moments to study the formula and notice that it calculates the total payments over the term of the loan and subtracts the loan amount. Also notice that the number of months is determined by multiplying the number of years in cell B7 by 12.*

4. Select **cell B10** and enter **=B9+B3** to calculate the total cost of the home.

5. **Format** all dollar amounts in **Comma Style with two decimal places**. Format the percentage with **two decimal places**.

### Create a Pie Chart

*You will create a pie chart that compares the two costs—purchase price and total interest.*

6. Select the noncontiguous **ranges A3:B3** and **A9:B9**, as shown.
   *This selection allows the pie chart to compare the Purchase Price to the Total Interest.*

|  | A | B |
|---|---|---|
| 1 | **30-Year Mortgage Analysis** |  |
| 2 |  |  |
| 3 | Purchase Price | 260,000.00 |
| 4 | Down Payment | 25,000.00 |
| 5 | Loan Amount | 235,000.00 |
| 6 | Interest Rate | 9.00% |
| 7 | Number of Years | 30 |
| 8 | Monthly Payment | $1,890.86 |
| 9 | Total Interest | 445,710.73 |
| 10 | Total Cost of Home | 705,710.73 |

7. Choose **Insert→Charts→Pie** 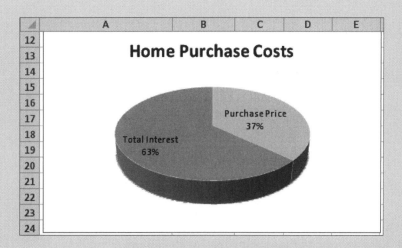 **→Pie in 3D** and create the following embedded pie chart.

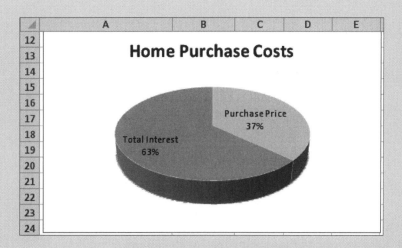

8. Use **Layout 1** and resize the chart smaller if needed. Position the pie chart in **row 12** below the data.

## Use a What-If Analysis

*Notice that the monthly payment in cell B8 is approximately $1,891.*

9. Select **cell B6**.

10. Change the **Interest Rate** to **6%** and notice the impact on the monthly payment and the chart slices.

11. Experiment with various interest rates. Also, try changing the down payment and note the impact on the monthly payment.

12. When you are finished, make certain that the **purchase price** is **260,000** and change the **down payment** back to **25000** and the **interest rate** to **6%**.

## Use Solver

*What interest rate and purchase price are needed to achieve a monthly payment of $1,500, an interest rate not to exceed 7 percent, and total interest not to exceed $300,000? You will use Solver to find these values.*

13. Select **cell B8** and choose **Data→Analysis→Solver** from the Ribbon.
*The Solver Parameters dialog box displays.*

14. Verify that the **Set Objective**: box displays cell $B$8.

15. Choose the **Value Of** option and type **1500** for the monthly payment.

16. Click in the **By Changing Variable Cells** text box, select **cell B3** in the worksheet for the purchase price, type a **comma**, and select **cell B6** for the interest rate.

17. Click the **Add** button and create a constraint for the interest rate not to exceed **7%**.

**18.** Add a constraint for the **total interest** not to exceed **300000**.

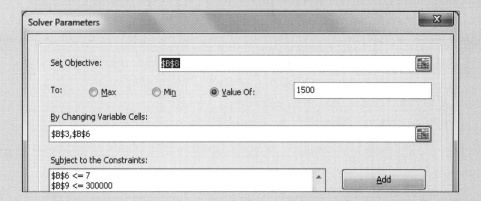

**19.** Click **Solve** and **OK** to accept Solver's suggested solution.

*The new purchase price should be $271,203.84 with an interest rate of 6.15 percent. Solver may suggest a different solution, but the variables should meet all the requirements that you set in the dialog box.*

**20. Save** 💾 as **rs-Home Mortgage** in the Lesson 13 folder, and then **close** the workbook.

|   | A | B |
|---|---|---|
| 1 | **30-Year Mortgage Analysis** | |
| 2 | | |
| 3 | Purchase Price | 271,203.84 |
| 4 | Down Payment | 25,000.00 |
| 5 | Loan Amount | 246,203.84 |
| 6 | Interest Rate | 6.15% |
| 7 | Number of Years | 30 |
| 8 | Monthly Payment | $1,500.00 |
| 9 | Total Interest | 293,796.12 |
| 10 | Total Cost of Home | 564,999.95 |

## REINFORCE YOUR SKILLS 13.2

# Use the FV Function

*In this exercise, you will use the Future Value (FV) function to determine the future value of a college fund. This is important if you are saving for a college education, but the worksheet also may be used to determine the future value of nearly any investment that has consistent contributions. The generic syntax of the FV function is repeated below for your convenience.*

*Future Value Function Syntax =FV(rate, periods, payment)*

**1. Start** a new workbook.

**2.** Use the **Column Width** command to set the width of **column A** to 19 and **column B** to 14.

**3. Enter** the data shown to the right.

**4.** Format the interest rate in **cell B3** as a **percentage** with **two decimal places**.

|   | A | B |
|---|---|---|
| 1 | **College Fund** | |
| 2 | | |
| 3 | Interest Rate | 8.00% |
| 4 | Number of Years | 18 |
| 5 | Monthly Contribution | 200 |
| 6 | Future Value | |

**5.** Select **cell B6** and enter the function **=FV(B3/12,B4*12,-B5)**.

*The result equals $96,017.23. Notice that the formula has a minus (–) sign between the comma and B5. Otherwise, the FV function would return a negative number. Also, notice that the interest rate in cell B3 is divided by 12 to produce a monthly rate. The number of years in cell B4 is multiplied by 12 to produce the total number of monthly payments.*

**6. Save** 💾 as **rs-Original College Fund** in the Lesson 13 folder.
*You will continue to use this workbook in the next exercise.*

# Use Goal Seek

*In this exercise, you will use Goal Seek to determine the interest rate required to save $200,000 by contributing $300 monthly for 18 years.*

*Before You Begin: You must have completed Reinforce Your Skills 13.2, and the rs-Original College Fund workbook should be open.*

## Use Goal Seek

1. Choose **File→Save As** 🖼, name the new workbook **rs-College Fund Goal**, and **save** it in the Lesson 13 folder.

2. Select **cell B5** and change the **monthly contribution** to **300**.
   *Notice that this increases the future value of the investment to approximately $144,000. In the next few steps, you will use Goal Seek to determine the interest rate necessary to achieve a future value of $200,000 with a monthly contribution of $300 for 18 years.*

3. Select **cell B6** and choose **Data→Data Tools→What-If Analysis** 🗒 **→Goal Seek** from the Ribbon.

4. Set the **To Value** option to **200000**.

5. Set the **By Changing Cell** option to **B3** (the interest rate cell).

6. Click **OK** and notice that a 10.91 percent interest rate is required.

7. Click **OK** in the Goal Seek Status dialog box to accept the change to the interest rate.

8. Use **Goal Seek** to determine the interest rate required to achieve a $275,000 future value with a $325 monthly contribution.

| | A | B |
|---|---|---|
| 1 | **College Fund** | |
| 2 | | |
| 3 | Interest Rate | 12.92% |
| 4 | Number of Years | 18 |
| 5 | Monthly Contribution | 325 |
| 6 | Future Value | $275,000.00 |

9. **Save** 💾 and **close** the workbook.

# Use the Scenario Manager

*In this exercise, you will use the Scenario Manager to project the profit for a new toy manufacturer named KidCraft. Donna Williams, the founder of KidCraft, needs to set up the model as part of her business plan. She is trying to raise funds, and a business plan and financial model are a crucial part of this process.*

## Create the Worksheet

1. **Start** a new workbook.
   *In the next steps, you will create the worksheet shown to the right.*

2. **Enter** the labels in **column A** and the values in the **range B3:B8**.

3. Use the **SUM** function in **cell B9** to calculate the expenses in the range B5:B8.

4. Calculate the **Gross Profit** in **cell B11** as the Forecasted Revenue – Total Costs.

5. Calculate the **Net Profit** in **cell B12** as the Gross Profit*70%.

|  | A | B |
|---|---|---|
| 1 | KidCraft FY5 Projected Income | |
| 2 | | |
| 3 | Forecasted Revenue | $ 345,000 |
| 4 | | |
| 5 | Employee Costs | 62,000 |
| 6 | Capital Expenditures | 75,900 |
| 7 | Manufacturing | 58,650 |
| 8 | Marketing and Sales | 55,200 |
| 9 | Total Costs | $ 251,750 |
| 10 | | |
| 11 | Gross Profit | $ 93,250 |
| 12 | Net Profit | $ 65,275 |

6. **Format** the values with the **Comma Style** and **Accounting** formats shown.

7. **Rename** the worksheet tab as **Projected Income**.

## Name the Cells

8. Select the **range A3:B12**.

9. Choose **Formulas→Defined Names→Create from Selection** 📖 from the Ribbon.

10. Make certain that the **Left Column box** is checked, and click **OK**.
    *The names are defined for the cells in column B. This will be helpful when you use the Scenario Manager.*

## Create the First Scenario

*The first scenario will be based on existing values in the worksheet.*

11. Select **cell B3**, and then **press and hold** Ctrl while you drag to select the **range B5:B8**.
    *The blank cell B4 and the total cost in cell B9 should not be included in the selection. You will create scenarios by changing the selected cells.*

12. Choose **Data→Data Tools→What-If Analysis** 🔢 **→Scenario Manager** from the Ribbon.
    *The dialog box should indicate that no scenarios are currently defined.*

13. Click the **Add** button to add a new scenario.

14. Type the name **Scenario 1**, edit the **Comment** box to include your name, and click **OK**.
*The Scenario Values dialog box displays.*

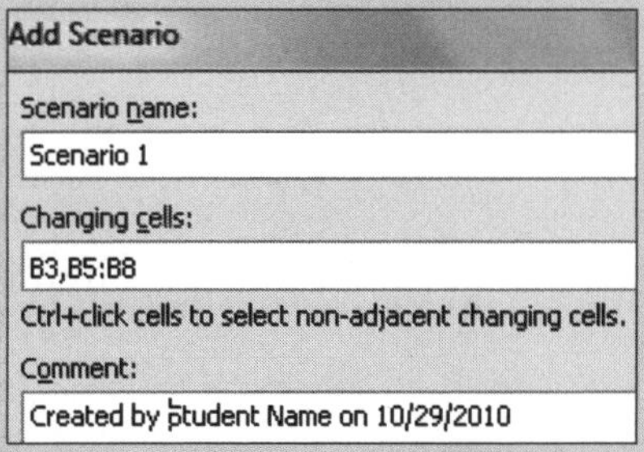

15. Click the **Add** button to complete Scenario 1 and display the Add Scenario dialog box.
*You may create additional scenarios without returning to the initial Scenario Manager dialog box.*

**Add Scenario**

Scenario name:

Scenario 1

Changing cells:

B3,B5:B8

Ctrl+click cells to select non-adjacent changing cells.

Comment:

Created by Student Name on 10/29/2010

## Add Other Scenarios

16. Type the name **Scenario 2** and click **OK**.

17. Change only the Forecasted Revenue number to **500000** and click **Add**.

18. Now add **two new scenarios** using the data in the following table, making certain that you click **OK** after entering values for Scenario 4 rather than using Add as you will do for Scenario 3.

| Variable | Scenario 3 Scenario Value | Scenario 4 Scenario Value |
|---|---|---|
| Forecasted Revenue | 700,000 | 700,000 |
| Employee Costs | 80,000 | 80,000 |
| Capital Expenditures | 35,000 | 42,000 |
| Manufacturing | 98,000 | 85,000 |
| Marketing and Sales | 85,000 | 70,000 |

19. Use the **Show** button in the Scenario Manager dialog box to show the results of each scenario.

## Display a Summary of All Scenarios

20. Click the **Summary** button in the Scenario Manager dialog box.

21. Choose the **Scenario Summary** option; set results cells for the Total Costs, Gross Profit, and Net Profit; and click **OK**. *Excel inserts the summary on a new worksheet, shown here.*

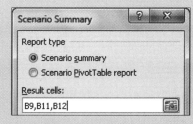

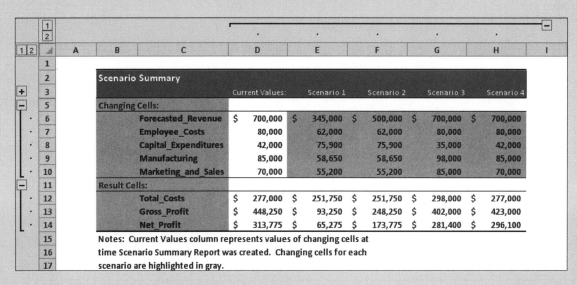

22. **Save** 💾 as **rs-Financial Scenarios** in the Lesson 13 folder and **close** the workbook.

# Apply Your Skills

## APPLY YOUR SKILLS 13.1
## Use the FV Function and Solver

*In this exercise, you will calculate the future value of a mutual fund investment. Then you will use Solver to determine the rate of return needed to achieve a specific future value.*

*Before You Begin: The Solver add-in must be installed on your computer system to complete this exercise.*

1. **Create** the worksheet shown at right.

2. Taking care to display the answer as a **positive** number, use the **FV** function to calculate the future value in **cell B6**.

3. **Format** all cells as shown and adjust the column widths.

| | A | B |
|---|---|---|
| 1 | Investment Projections | |
| 2 | | Utilities Mutual Fund |
| 3 | Projected Annual Rate of Return | 11.00% |
| 4 | Number of Years | 20 |
| 5 | Monthly Contribution | $             300 |
| 6 | Future Value | $ |

4. Use **Solver** to determine the annual rate of return needed to achieve a future value of $300,000 with a monthly contribution of $400 or less. Accept Solver's suggested answer.

5. **Save** 🖫 with the name **as-Mutual Fund** in the Lesson 13 folder of your storage location and **close** the workbook.

## APPLY YOUR SKILLS 13.2
## Use the PMT Function and Goal Seek

*In this exercise, you will calculate the monthly payment for a home equity loan. Then you will use Goal Seek to determine the amount you could borrow with a monthly payment of $200.*

1. **Create** the worksheet shown at right.

2. Taking care to display the answer as a **positive** number, use the **PMT** function to calculate the monthly payment in **cell B7**.

3. **Format** all cells as shown and adjust the column widths.

| | A | B |
|---|---|---|
| 1 | Home Equity Loan Analysis | |
| 2 | | Credit Union |
| 3 | Interest Rate | 6.00% |
| 4 | Number of Years | 10 |
| 5 | Loan Amount | $15,000.00 |
| 6 | Monthly Payment | |

4. Use **Goal Seek** to determine what the loan amount could be if the monthly payment were $200, and accept Goal Seek's suggested answer.

5. **Save** 🖫 with the name **as-Home Equity Loan** in the Lesson 13 folder and **close** the workbook.

# Use Scenario Manager

*In this exercise, you will use Scenario Manager to project salaries and expenses by creating three scenarios for a budget worksheet.*

1. **Open** the as-Budget Scenarios workbook from the Lesson 13 folder of your storage location.

2. Create **Scenario 1** using the existing model data in the Budget worksheet. Use only the **Sales** and **Customer Support** costs as variables.

3. Create **Scenarios 2 and 3** using the data in the following table:

| Variable | Scenario 2 | Scenario 3 |
|---|---|---|
| Sales | 2,500,000 | 2,000,000 |
| Customer Support | 100,000 | 85,000 |

4. Show **Scenario 3** in the worksheet.

5. **Display** a scenario summary report to include the following results: Salaries and Wages Total, Staffing Expenses Total, Sales Staffing Ratio, and Customer Support Staffing Ratio.

6. **Save** 🖫 and **close** the workbook.

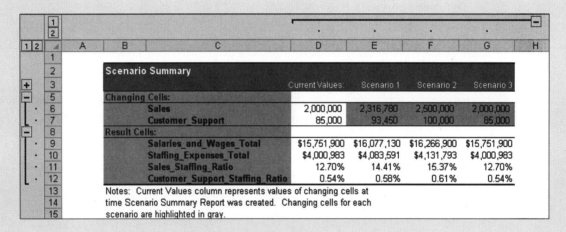

# Critical Thinking & Work-Readiness Skills

*In the course of working through the following Microsoft Office-based Critical Thinking exercises, you will also be utilizing various work-readiness skills, some of which are listed next to each exercise. Go to* labyrinthelab.com/ workreadiness *to learn more about the work-readiness skills.*

## 13.1 Use the PMT Function

Sandra Chavez-Hall is ready to start planning the fundraising for building Phase 2 at Raritan Clinic East. Raritan will get a business loan to help pay the startup costs. Set up a new worksheet for Sandra. Use the PMT formula to determine the monthly payment needed if the loan amount is $1,500,000, the annual interest rate is 7%, and number of years is 5. Then, create a formula to calculate the total cost of the loan. The generic formula is Total Loan Cost = Monthly Payment * Number of Payments. Save your work as **ct-Raritan Clinic Phase 2 [Your Last Name]** in the Lesson 13 folder. Keep the file open.

## 13.2 Use the FV Function and Goal Seek

Raritan Clinic East will solicit contributions for the total loan cost. The contributions will be invested in a fund that pays interest. Sandra wants to calculate the total investment after three years. Open ct-Raritan Clinic Phase 2 [Your Last Name], if necessary. Create an appropriate formula for Sandra. Use the FV function to show the total investment if monthly contributions are $50,000, the annual interest rate is 4%, and the number of years is 3. Then, use Goal Seek to determine the monthly contributions needed to achieve a future value equal to the total loan cost. You calculated the loan cost in the previous exercise. Save your work and keep the file open.

## 13.3 Use Scenario Manager

Before publicizing the fundraising goals, Sandra wants to understand the economics behind the interest rate and watch the interest as it accrues. Sandra is aware that the investment interest may vary, but she is not certain how much it affects her goals. Use the Scenario Manager to help her understand how the fluctuation of just one percentage point can influence the total investment. If necessary, open ct-Raritan Clinic Phase 2 [Your Last Name]. Use Scenario 1 to retain the present future value information. Create Scenario 2 to show what will happen if the interest rate drops to 3%. Prepare a scenario summary sheet that displays both scenarios. Save and close the file when you are finished.

# Applying Advanced Functions and Auditing

## LEARNING OBJECTIVES

After studying this lesson, you will be able to:

- Use 3-D cell references in formulas to summarize workbook data
- Create a lookup formula to locate a value or text in a list
- Use subtotal formulas to calculate data in filtered lists
- Build formulas with criteria IF functions and logical functions to perform actions based on criteria
- Use text functions to reformat data
- Correct formula errors using the auditing tools

Complex worksheets for decision making often require advanced functions based on the values in other cells. You may set up detailed worksheets with an identical design for various categories or time periods of a project and summarize the data on a separate worksheet. In this lesson, you will use 3-D cell references in formulas to create the summary calculations. The HLOOKUP and VLOOKUP functions help to use one piece of information to find another in a list. You will use the VLOOKUP function to locate the fundraising award for each team member. With the criteria IF and SUBTOTAL functions, you may sum, average, or count values when specific criteria are satisfied. You also may use logical functions, such as AND or NOT, to specify various criteria in formulas. Excel's text functions help you to reformat data imported into an Excel workbook from another program. For example, you will use the SUBSTITUTE function to replace a misspelled job title with the correct title. In addition, you will learn how to work with formula auditing tools, which are particularly useful in locating errors in complex formulas that are dependent on other formulas.

# Summarizing Fundraising Performance

**Pediatric Diagnostic Specialists**

Sandra Chavez-Hall coordinates a fundraising campaign to build two new facilities at Raritan Clinic East. To track the performance of her team members, Sandra uses an Excel workbook with a worksheet for each month. To combine the data from the monthly worksheets into a quarterly summary worksheet, Sandra uses 3-D cell references in SUM formulas.

| B5 | | | $fx$ | =SUM(October:December!B5) |
|---|---|---|---|---|

| | A | B | C |
|---|---|---|---|
| 1 | Raritan Clinic East *Pediatric Diagnostic Specialists* | **Capital Campaign** | |
| 2 | | **October-December** | |
| 3 | | | |
| 4 | | **Contributions** | |
| 5 | Cash Contributions | $ 207,895 | |
| 6 | In-Kind Contributions | $ 25,382 | |
| 7 | Grants | $ 1,612,200 | |
| 8 | **Total Contributions** | **$ 1,845,477** | |
| 9 | | | |
| 10 | **Total Direct Expenses** | **$ 43,583** | |
| 11 | | | |

**Summary** / October / November / December

A worksheet formula containing a 3-D cell reference to cell B5 on three worksheets

Sandra also needs to calculate monthly contributions raised by the Raritan Clinic Foundation team members. Sandra uses the VLOOKUP function and a lookup table to determine whether team members receive an award. She also uses the lookup table to display a message that indicates each team member's goal achievement status.

| | A | B | C | D | E | F | G |
|---|---|---|---|---|---|---|---|
| 4 | **Team Leader** | **Goal** | **Amount Raised** | **Over (Under) Goal** | **Award Rate** | **Award Points** | **Achieved Goal?** |
| 5 | Abbott | $25,000 | $31,810 | $6,810 | 5% | 1,591 | Above Goal |
| 6 | Debowski | $100,000 | $95,350 | ($4,650) | 1% | 954 | Below Goal |
| 7 | Faber | $60,000 | $52,500 | ($7,500) | 0% | - | Under Achiever |
| 8 | Lemus | $100,000 | $110,350 | $10,350 | 7% | 7,725 | Over Achiever |

| Over (Under) Goal | Award Rate | Message |
|---|---|---|
| ($100,000) | 0% | Under Achiever |
| ($5,000) | 1% | Below Goal |
| $0 | 3% | At Goal |
| $5,000 | 5% | Above Goal |
| $10,000 | 7% | Over Achiever |

A worksheet using VLOOKUP and a lookup table to find the award percentage and the goal achievement status

# 14.1 Using 3-D Cell References in Formulas

**Video Lesson**   labyrinthelab.com/videos

You can create a workbook containing detail worksheets and a summary worksheet. You may use a linking formula in the summary worksheet to refer to the contents of a cell in a single detail worksheet. Excel also allows you to perform calculations using the contents of the same cell address in multiple worksheets, which is called a 3-D cell reference. Contrast the following linking formula and normal summing formula with a formula containing a 3-D cell reference.

| Type of Formula | Example | What It Does |
|---|---|---|
| Linking | =Supplies!C6 | Gets the contents from cell C6 in the Supplies worksheet |
| Normal | =Supplies!C6 + Utilities!C6 | Sums cell C6 from the Supplies and Utilities worksheets only |
| 3-D | =SUM(Supplies:Equipment!C6) | Sums cell C6 in all worksheets from Supplies through Equipment in the workbook |

## Why Use a 3-D Reference?

Using a 3-D reference provides two advantages over normal cell references in a multisheet formula. First, you do not have to click the cell in each worksheet to build the formula. Also, the formula automatically includes the specified cell from additional worksheets that you insert within the worksheet range.

 Deleting a worksheet or moving a worksheet tab to outside the range in the 3-D reference removes that worksheet's values from the formula result.

## Creating a 3-D Reference

Functions that you may use to create 3-D references include SUM, AVERAGE, COUNT, MAX, MIN, and some statistical functions. A formula may contain a single cell or a cell range as a 3-D reference. Remember that the cells being referenced must be the identical cell addresses in all detail worksheets. You cannot, for example, use cell B2 from one worksheet and cell C3 from another. But, you may, for example, use the range B2:E2 from all the worksheets. The cell or range must also contain the same type of data, such as values.

| Task | Procedure |
|------|-----------|
| Create a 3-D reference | ■ Design all worksheets so that the cell contents to be calculated are in the identical cell addresses.<br>■ Select the cell to contain the formula in the summary worksheet.<br>■ Type the function beginning, such as =SUM(.<br>■ Click the first sheet tab and hold down [Shift] while clicking the last sheet tab to be referenced.<br>■ In the sheet currently displayed, select the cell or range to be referenced, and complete the formula. |

### DEVELOP YOUR SKILLS 14.1.1

# Create 3-D Cell References

*In this exercise, you will create 3-D cell references to one cell in several worksheets. You will also create a 3-D reference to a cell range.*

1. **Start** Excel and **open** the Campaign Summary workbook from the Lesson 14 folder in your file storage location.

2. **Maximize** ▣ the window.
   *You will create 3-D references on the Summary worksheet to sum values from the other three worksheets.*

3. Display the **October** worksheet to see that the worksheet design for **rows 1–8** is identical to that of the Summary worksheet. Display the **November** worksheet, and then display **December** to see that they contain an identical structure.

4. Display the **Summary** worksheet.

## Create a 3-D Cell Reference Formula for Contributions

5. Follow these steps to create a formula that adds the values in cell B5 from each of the monthly contributions worksheets:

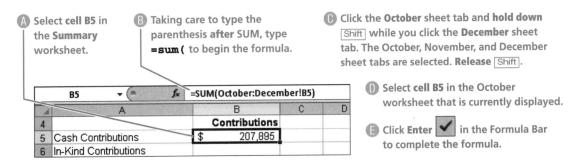

Ⓐ Select **cell B5** in the **Summary** worksheet.

Ⓑ Taking care to type the parenthesis **after** SUM, type **=sum (** to begin the formula.

Ⓒ Click the **October** sheet tab and **hold down** [Shift] while you click the **December** sheet tab. The October, November, and December sheet tabs are selected. **Release** [Shift].

Ⓓ Select **cell B5** in the October worksheet that is currently displayed.

Ⓔ Click **Enter** ✓ in the Formula Bar to complete the formula.

*The Formula Bar displays =SUM(October:December!B5). Notice that an exclamation (!) point separates the worksheet names from the cell address. The formula result is $207,895, which is the total cash contributions from cell B5 in the October, November, and December worksheets.*

6. Use **Autofill** to copy the formula in **cell B5** to the range **B6:B7**.

7. **Deselect** the highlighted range.

8. Select **cell B7** and look in the Formula Bar to see that the 3-D reference is included in the formula that you copied.

## Create a 3-D Cell Range Formula for Total Direct Expenses

*Now you will calculate the total direct expenses to generate the contributions and grants. You will use the SUM function for the same cell range across the three monthly worksheets.*

9. Display the **October** worksheet.
   *Review the expense data in rows 11–14. The other monthly worksheets are designed identically with values in the range B11:B14.*

10. Display the **Summary** worksheet.

11. Select **cell B10**.

12. Choose **Home→Editing→AutoSum** $\Sigma$ from the Ribbon.

13. Click the **October** sheet tab.

14. **Hold down** [Shift] while you click the **December** sheet tab to select all monthly sales worksheets, and then **release** the [Shift] key.

15. Drag to select **cells B11:B14** in the October worksheet.
    *Although the October worksheet is displayed, you are specifying the cells to be summed in all the detail sheets that you selected.*

16. Click **Enter** ✔ in the Formula Bar to complete the formula.
    *The Formula Bar displays =SUM(October:December!B11:B14). The formula result is $43,563.*

| | A | B | C |
|---|---|---|---|
| 1 | Raritan Clinic East | **Capital Campaign** | |
| 2 | Pediatric Diagnostic Specialists | **October-December** | |
| 3 | | | |
| 4 | | **Contributions** | |
| 5 | Cash Contributions | $ 207,895 | |
| 6 | In-Kind Contributions | $ 25,382 | |
| 7 | Grants | $ 1,612,200 | |
| 8 | **Total Contributions** | $ **1,845,477** | |
| 9 | | | |
| 10 | **Total Direct Expenses** | $ 43,563 | |

17. **Save** 💾 the changes, **close** the workbook, and leave Excel **open**.

# 14.2 Introducing Lookup Functions

Video Lesson    labyrinthelab.com/videos

The VLOOKUP (Vertical Lookup) and HLOOKUP (Horizontal Lookup) functions are used to retrieve a piece of data from a lookup table located somewhere in the same worksheet, a separate worksheet, or a different workbook. In this lesson, you will look up the award percentage rate, which depends on the the team leader's fundraising over or under the goal. The dollar increment values display down the first column of a vertical lookup table or across the first row of a horizontal lookup table. You may use either format and its matching function.

Take care to place a lookup table outside rows or columns that might be deleted in the future.

|  | E | F |
|---|---|---|
|  | **Over (Under) Goal** | **Award Rate** |
| 15 | | |
| 16 | ($100,000) | 0% |
| 17 | ($5,000) | 1% |
| 18 | $0 | 3% |
| 19 | $5,000 | 5% |
| 20 | $10,000 | 7% |

A vertical lookup table containing dollar amounts under or over the fundraising goal amounts and their corresponding award rates

The same data arranged in a horizontal lookup table

|  | A | B | C | D | E | F |
|---|---|---|---|---|---|---|
| 15 | **Over (Under) Goal** | ($100,000) | ($5,000) | $0 | $5,000 | $10,000 |
| 16 | **Award Rate** | 0% | 1% | 3% | 5% | 7% |

## Lookup Function Syntax

The generic parts of the HLOOKUP and VLOOKUP functions are identical, as shown in the following table.

| Function | Syntax |
|---|---|
| HLOOKUP (Horizontal Lookup) | HLOOKUP(lookup value, table array, column index number, range lookup) |
| VLOOKUP (Vertical Lookup) | VLOOKUP(lookup value, table array, column index number, range lookup) |

The following table outlines the arguments of the VLOOKUP function.

| Argument | Description |
|---|---|
| Lookup value | The value in the worksheet to be looked up in the first column of the table array |
| Table array | The cell range containing the lookup table, which may be expressed as absolute cell references or a defined name |
| Column index number | The column number in the table array that contains the corresponding data to be retrieved |
| Range lookup (optional; the default is TRUE) | A logical value that specifies a search for an exact or approximate value in the table array (TRUE) or an exact match only (FALSE) |

# How the VLOOKUP Function Works

The formula =VLOOKUP(D5,Award_Table,2) is used as an example to explain how the search takes place in the lookup table. Cell D5 contains the lookup value $6,810. The defined name Award_Table indicates that the search takes place in the table array located in the range $E$16:$G$20. The search is conducted down the first column of the table array until the highest value not greater than the lookup value is located. The number 2, the column index number in the formula, indicates that the corresponding award rate will be retrieved from the second column of the lookup table.

Cell E5 contains the VLOOKUP formula to find Abbott's award rate based on $6,810 in funds raised over the goal.

Excel searches for the lookup value $6,810 down the first column of the lookup table. The search stops at $5,000 on row 19 because the lookup value is at least $5,000 but not $10,000.

| | A | B | C | D | E |
|---|---|---|---|---|---|
| 4 | Team Leader | Goal | Amount Raised | Over (Under) Goal | Award Rate |
| 5 | Abbott | $25,000 | $31,810 | $6,810 | 5% |
| 6 | Debowski | $100,000 | $95,350 | ($4,650) | 1% |
| 7 | Faber | $60,000 | $52,500 | ($7,500) | 0% |

| | E | F |
|---|---|---|
| 15 | Over (Under) Goal | Award Rate |
| 16 | ($100,000) | 0% |
| 17 | ($5,000) | 1% |
| 18 | $0 | 3% |
| 19 | $5,000 | 5% |
| 20 | $10,000 | 7% |

Traveling along row 19, the search moves to column 2 of the lookup table, as specified by the column index number in the function.

The award rate 5 percent is returned to cell E5.

When a lookup formula will be copied to other cells, the cell range of the table array should be expressed in the formula as a defined name or absolute cell references, such as $E$16:$F$20.

## Specifying the Range Lookup Argument

Excel uses the default range lookup argument TRUE so the search is conducted in the first column of the table array for either an exact match of $6,810 or the closest value that is not greater than $6,810. At times, you may want to search only for an exact match of the lookup value. The formula =VLOOKUP(A5,Employee_Records,2,FALSE) includes the FALSE range lookup argument, which restricts the search to an exact match. Assume that cell A5 contains the last name Abbott. A search for an exact match is conducted in the first column of the Employee_Records table array. If Abbott is not found, Excel displays #N/A in the formula cell to indicate a Value Not Available error.

# Sorting a Table Array

The rows in the table array must be sorted in lowest to highest (A to Z) order in the first column when the TRUE range lookup argument is used. This way, you can be assured that VLOOKUP will stop at the proper row and return the correct value. Sorting the table array is not required when the FALSE range lookup argument is used.

# Use VLOOKUP

*In this exercise, you will set up a three-column table array and then use the VLOOKUP function to calculate award points and display messages.*

## Create a Table Array

1. **Open** the Awards workbook from the Lesson 14 folder, and display the **December** worksheet.

   *You will create the table array in the range E16:G20 and assign a defined name to that range. The labels in row 15 are optional and not part of the table array.*

2. Complete the **table array** by entering the numbers and text shown in the following illustration. Use a **minus sign** (–) to enter the negative numbers in cells E16 and E17. *The number formatting is already applied to the blank cells.*

   |    | E | F | G |
   |----|---------------------|----------------|----------------|
   |    | Over<br>(Under)<br>Goal | Award<br>Rate | Message |
   | 15 |  |  |  |
   | 16 | ($100,000) | 0% | Under Achiever |
   | 17 | ($5,000) | 1% | Below Goal |
   | 18 | $0 | 3% | At Goal |
   | 19 | $5,000 | 5% | Above Goal |
   | 20 | $10,000 | 7% | Over Achiever |

## Assign a Range Name to the Table Array

*In the next few steps, you will assign a defined name to the table array. Naming a range for a table array is optional. You would use absolute cell references in the lookup formula if you did not use a defined name.*

3. Follow these steps to create the range name:

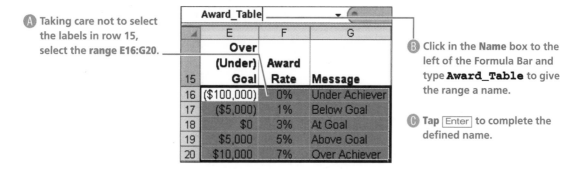

A Taking care not to select the labels in row 15, select the range **E16:G20.**

B Click in the **Name** box to the left of the Formula Bar and type **Award_Table** to give the range a name.

C Tap ⏎Enter to complete the defined name.

4. **Deselect** the table array.

## Create a VLOOKUP Formula for the Award Rate

*You will use the VLOOKUP function to calculate the award rate for each team leader in column E.*

5. **Enter** the formula **=VLOOKUP(D5,Award_Table,2)** in **cell E5**.
   *The 5 percent award rate is returned from the lookup table to cell E5.*

6. Take a few moments to study the three arguments in the function you just entered and understand how the lookup works.

7. Use **Autofill** to copy the formula from **cell E5** down to the **range E6:E12**.

8. Select **cell E7** and review the formula in the Formula Bar.
   *The award rate returned from the lookup table is 0 percent. Notice that all arguments are the same for this function, except that the relative cell reference tells VLOOKUP to look up the value from cell D7.*

## Calculate the Award Points

*The formula Over (Under) Goal * Award Rate calculates the team member's award points.*

9. **Enter** the formula **=C5*E5** in cell F5.
   *The result equals 1,591.*

10. Use **AutoFill** to copy the commission formula in **cell F5** down for the other team members.

| | A | B | C | D | E | F | G |
|---|---|---|---|---|---|---|---|
| 4 | **Team Leader** | **Goal** | **Amount Raised** | **Over (Under) Goal** | **Award Rate** | **Award Points** | **Achieved Goal?** |
| 5 | Abbott | $25,000 | $31,810 | $6,810 | 5% | 1,591 | |
| 6 | Debowski | $100,000 | $95,350 | ($4,650) | 1% | 954 | |
| 7 | Faber | $60,000 | $52,500 | ($7,500) | 0% | - | |
| 8 | Lemus | $100,000 | $110,350 | $10,350 | 7% | 7,725 | |
| 9 | Martinez | $70,000 | $66,000 | ($4,000) | 1% | 660 | |
| 10 | Nguyen | $45,000 | $48,000 | $3,000 | 3% | 1,440 | |
| 11 | Park | $30,000 | $31,680 | $1,680 | 3% | 950 | |
| 12 | Weinstein | $70,000 | $67,000 | ($3,000) | 1% | 670 | |

## Create a VLOOKUP Formula for the Goal Achievement Messages

11. Select **cell G5** and enter the function **=VLOOKUP(D5,Award_Table,3)**.

    *The message Above Goal is returned. Notice that you used the same arguments for this function that you did in cell E5 except that the last argument is 3 instead of 2. This instructs VLOOKUP to return the message text from column 3 of the table array.*

12. Use **AutoFill** to copy the quota message formula in **cell G5** down for the other team members.

    *Rows 5–20 should match the following illustration.*

| ▲ | A | B | C | D | E | F | G |
|---|---|---|---|---|---|---|---|
| 4 | **Team Leader** | **Goal** | **Amount Raised** | **Over (Under) Goal** | **Award Rate** | **Award Points** | **Achieved Goal?** |
| 5 | Abbott | $25,000 | $31,810 | $6,810 | 5% | 1,591 | Above Goal |
| 6 | Debowski | $100,000 | $95,350 | ($4,650) | 1% | 954 | Below Goal |
| 7 | Faber | $60,000 | $52,500 | ($7,500) | 0% | - | Under Achiever |
| 8 | Lemus | $100,000 | $110,350 | $10,350 | 7% | 7,725 | Over Achiever |
| 9 | Martinez | $70,000 | $66,000 | ($4,000) | 1% | 660 | Below Goal |
| 10 | Nguyen | $45,000 | $48,000 | $3,000 | 3% | 1,440 | At Goal |
| 11 | Park | $30,000 | $31,680 | $1,680 | 3% | 950 | At Goal |
| 12 | Weinstein | $70,000 | $67,000 | ($3,000) | 1% | 670 | Below Goal |
| 13 | | | | | | | |
| 14 | | | | | | | |
| 15 | | | | | **Over (Under) Goal** | **Award Rate** | **Message** |
| 16 | | | | | ($100,000) | 0% | Under Achiever |
| 17 | | | | | ($5,000) | 1% | Below Goal |
| 18 | | | | | $0 | 3% | At Goal |
| 19 | | | | | $5,000 | 5% | Above Goal |
| 20 | | | | | $10,000 | 7% | Over Achiever |

13. Select **cell F16** and change the rate to **1%**.

    *The rate in cell E7 changed from 0 percent to 1 percent, and the corresponding award points in cell F7 now is 525.*

14. Click **Undo** 🔄 to change the entry back to 0% in cell F16.

15. Select **cell G16** and change the message to **Counsel**.

    *Notice that the result in cell G7 changed to Counsel because you changed the message in the lookup table.*

16. Click **Undo** 🔄 to change the entry back to *Under Achiever*.

17. **Save** 💾 the changes, and leave the workbook **open**.

# 14.3 Using the SUBTOTAL Function to Calculate Filtered Lists

Video Lesson    labyrinthelab.com/videos

You can filter a worksheet list to display only the records that meet certain criteria. For example, you can filter to display records that did not meet the monthly fundraising goal. If the records are in an Excel table, formulas in the total row use the SUBTOTAL function and automatically recalculate for the filtered records. When the records have not been converted to a table, you may use the SUBTOTAL function to calculate values in the filtered list.

## SUBTOTAL Function Syntax

The generic parts of the SUBTOTAL function are shown in the following table.

| Function | Syntax |
| --- | --- |
| SUBTOTAL | SUBTOTAL(function number, range1, [range2],…) |

The following table outlines the arguments of this function.

| Argument | Description |
| --- | --- |
| Function number | The arithmetic operation that will be performed |
| Range1 | The range containing the values to be calculated |
| Range2, range3, and so on | (Optional) Additional ranges, cell references, or specific values to be included in the calculation |

The following table describes the basic functions you may use. See Excel Help for additional statistical functions to calculate standard deviation and variance.

| Function Number | Function | Operation Performed |
| --- | --- | --- |
| 1 | AVERAGE | Averages the range |
| 2 | COUNT | Counts cells containing numbers in the range |
| 3 | COUNTA | Counts nonblank cells in the range |
| 4 | MAX | Returns the largest number in the range |
| 5 | MIN | Returns the smallest number in the range |
| 6 | PRODUCT | Multiples all values contained in the formula arguments |
| 9 | SUM | Adds the range |

## How the SUBTOTAL Function Works

The formula =SUBTOTAL(9,C5:C20) is used as an example to explain the function result. The range to be calculated is C5:C20. SUBTOTAL differs from a normal SUM or AVERAGE formula because SUBTOTAL ignores any rows that are not displayed in the filter result. In this example, the argument 9 indicates that the SUM function will calculate the values in the filtered range.

A function formula may be created using the Insert Function button on the Formula Bar, Formula AutoComplete, or the Function Library on the Formulas ribbon, or by typing the formula directly in the cell or Formula Bar.

# Use the SUBTOTAL Function

*In this exercise, you will filter a list to display team leaders who achieved at least $50,000 in fundraising. Then you will use the SUBTOTAL function to sum and average the filtered values.*

## Sum the Entire List

1. **Open** the Awards workbook from the Lesson 14 folder, if necessary, and display the **December** worksheet.

2. Select **cell C13**, choose **Home→Editing→AutoSum** $\boxed{\Sigma}$ from the Ribbon, and click **Enter** in the Formula Bar.
   *The result should be $502,690, which is the total raised in December. Notice that the Formula Bar displays =SUM(C5:C12).*

## Filter the List

3. Select **cell A4**, and choose **Data→Sort & Filter→Filter** $\boxed{\text{Y}}$ from the Ribbon.
   *Each column heading in row 4 displays an AutoFilter button.*

4. In **cell C4**, choose the Amount Raised column heading **AutoFilter** $\boxed{\blacktriangledown}$ button.

5. Point to **Number Filters** in the context (or pop-up) menu, and choose **Greater Than**.

6. In the **Custom AutoFilter** dialog box, enter **50000** in the text box as shown, and **tap** $\boxed{\text{Enter}}$ to choose **OK**.

*The list displays five records for team members who achieved $50,000 or more. Notice that the SUM result in cell C13 still displays $502,690 rather than the total for just the filtered records. The sum is not recalculated automatically.*

## Sum the Filtered List

7. Select **cell C13**, and choose **Home→Editing→AutoSum** $\Sigma$ from the Ribbon.

| ▲ | C | D | E |
|---|---|---|---|
| 4 | **Amount Rais** ▼ | **Over (Under) G** ▼ | **Award Rate** ▼ |
| 6 | $95,350 | ($4,650) | 1% |
| 7 | $52,500 | ($7,500) | 0% |
| 8 | $110,350 | $10,350 | 7% |
| 9 | $66,000 | ($4,000) | 1% |
| 12 | $67,000 | ($3,000) | 1% |
| 13 | =SUBTOTAL(9,C5:C12) | | |
| 14 | SUBTOTAL(function_num, ref1, [ref2], ...) | | |

*Now Excel recognizes that the list has been filtered. The formula =SUBTOTAL(9,C5:C12) appears in the Formula Bar. The argument 9 indicates that the filtered range will be summed.*

8. Click the **AutoSum** $\Sigma$ button again to complete the formula.
*The result should be $391,200, which is the subtotal for the five filtered records.*

## Average the Filtered List

9. Follow these steps to create a subtotal formula that averages the Over (Under) Goal amount for the filtered records:

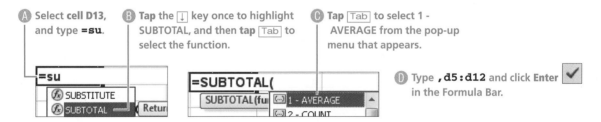

Ⓐ Select **cell D13**, and type **=su**.

Ⓑ **Tap** the ↓ key once to highlight SUBTOTAL, and then **tap** Tab to select the function.

Ⓒ **Tap** Tab to select 1 - AVERAGE from the pop-up menu that appears.

Ⓓ Type **,d5:d12** and click **Enter** ✓ in the Formula Bar.

*The formula =SUBTOTAL(1,D5:D12) appears in the Formula Bar. Notice that you included the entire list range D5:D12 even though the filter does not display cell D5. The result should be −1,760. Although the five team leaders raised the highest amounts, their average is below the goal.*

10. Use **Format Painter** 🖌 to apply the formatting from **cell D12** to **cell D13**.
*The result should appear as ($1,760).*

11. Apply additional formatting of your choice to the **range C13:D13** so that the subtotals are noticeable.

12. **Save** 💾 the changes, and leave the workbook **open**.

# 14.4 Creating Formulas Using Criteria IF Functions

**Video Lesson**    labyrinthelab.com/videos

Excel also provides functions that average, count, or sum cells that meet one or more criteria. The AVERAGEIF, COUNTIF, and SUMIF functions calculate using one criterion. The AVER-AGEIFS, COUNTIFS, and SUMIFS functions calculate using multiple criteria that you specify. Only cells meeting all the criteria are averaged, counted, or summed.

## Function Syntax

The generic parts of the two types of functions are shown in the following table.

| Function | Syntax |
|----------|--------|
| AVERAGEIF | AVERAGEIF(range, criteria) |
| COUNTIF | COUNTIF(range, criteria) |
| SUMIF | SUMIF(range, criteria, sum range) |
| AVERAGEIFS | AVERAGEIFS(range1, criteria1, range2, criteria2) |
| COUNTIFS | COUNTIFS(range1, criteria1, range2, criteria2) |
| SUMIFS | SUMIFS(sum range, range1, criteria1, range2, criteria2) |

The AVERAGEIFS, COUNTIFS, and SUMIFS functions may include up to 127 ranges and corresponding criteria.

The following table outlines the arguments of these functions.

| Argument | Description |
|----------|-------------|
| Range | The cells to be compared with the criteria |
| Criteria | Enclosed in quotation (") marks, the comparison value, text, or expression using a comparison operator, such as =, >, <, >=, <=, or <> (not equal to) |
| Sum range | The potential cells to be summed |

## How the SUMIF Function Works

The formula =SUMIF(C5:C12,">=30000",C5:C12) is used as an example to explain the function result. The range to be evaluated is C5:C12. Enclosed in quotation marks ("), the criterion is greater than or equal to 30,000. The sum range C5:C12 contains the potential cells to be summed. Excel performs the logical test C5:C12>=30000. Only the values of cells containing at least 30,000 in the range C5:C12 are summed. The formula also could be entered as =SUMIF(C5:C12,">=30000") without the last argument because the range and sum range are the same.

The range will be used both to evaluate for criteria and to calculate the result if the sum range is not specified in a SUMIF formula.

# How the COUNTIFS Function Works

The formula =COUNTIFS(F5:F12,"Yes",G5:G12,"Yes") is used as an example to explain the function result. The range F5:F12 is evaluated for cells containing the text *Yes*. *Also, the range* G5:G12 is evaluated for *Yes*. Only records meeting both criteria are counted.

| | A | B | C | D | E | F | G | |
|---|---|---|---|---|---|---|---|---|
| 4 | Team Leader | Nov. Goal | Nov. Raised | Dec. Goal | Dec. Raised | Achieved Nov. Goal? | Achieved Dec. Goal? | |
| 5 | Abbott | $25,000 | $24,500 | $25,000 | $31,810 | | Yes | |
| 6 | Debowski | $90,000 | $92,200 | $100,000 | $95,350 | Yes | | |
| 7 | Faber | $40,000 | $44,475 | $60,000 | $52,500 | Yes | | |
| 8 | Lemus | $80,000 | $79,620 | $100,000 | $110,350 | | Yes | |
| 9 | Martinez | $70,000 | $52,170 | $70,000 | $66,000 | | | |
| 10 | Nguyen | $25,000 | $25,250 | $45,000 | $48,000 | Yes | Yes | — The COUNTIFS function |
| 11 | Park | $25,000 | $27,570 | $30,000 | $31,680 | Yes | Yes | finds two team leaders |
| 12 | Weinstein | $50,000 | $45,650 | $70,000 | $67,000 | | | who meet both criteria of |
| 13 | | | | | | *Count:* | *2* | *Yes in columns F and G.* |

## Create a SUMIF Function

*In this exercise, you will use the SUMIF function to add cells containing $30,000 or greater in monthly fundraising.*

1. Display the **November** worksheet of the Awards workbook.

2. Enter **Raised at Least $30,000** in **cell A13**.

3. Widen **column A** to fit the text in **cell A13**.

4. Use **Format Painter** to copy the number format from **cell C12 to C13**.

5. Format the **range A13:C13** as bold.
   *Next you will create a formula that adds the values in cells where the amount raised is at least $30,000.*

6. Select **cell C13** and click the **Insert Function** $f_x$ button in the Formula Bar.

7. Follow these steps to find the SUMIF function:

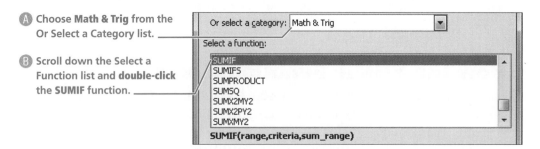

Ⓐ Choose **Math & Trig** from the Or Select a Category list.

Ⓑ Scroll down the Select a Function list and **double-click** the **SUMIF** function.

*The Function Arguments dialog box appears for the SUMIF function.*

8. If necessary, move the **Function Arguments** dialog box out of the way of **column C** by dragging its title bar.

9. Follow these steps to specify the SUMIF function arguments:

Ⓐ Select the **range C5:C12** in the worksheet as the range to be evaluated.

Ⓑ Click in the **Criteria** box and type **>=30000**. Excel will add quotation marks to the argument.

Ⓒ Leave the Sum_Range box **empty** because the cells are the same as for the range.

Ⓓ Click **OK**.

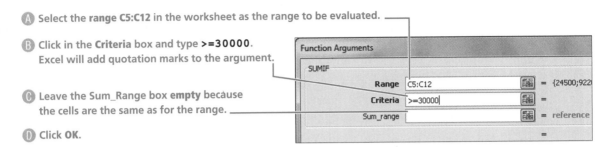

10. Review the completed formula in the Formula Bar.
*The formula is =SUMIF(C5:C12, ">=30000").*
*The result is $314,115.*

| | A | B | C | D |
|---|---|---|---|---|
| 12 | Weinstein | $50,000 | $45,650 | ($4,350) |
| 13 | **Raised at Least $30,000** | | **$314,115** | |

C13   *fx* =SUMIF(C5:C12,">=30000")

11. **Save** 💾 the changes, and leave the workbook **open**.

# 14.5 Using Logical Functions in Formulas

**Video Lesson**   labyrinthelab.com/videos

In the preceding topic, you used the SUMIF function to sum values that met certain criteria. Excel provides several logical functions that allow you to customize your criteria when comparing data. The IF function is the basis of many formulas used for decision making. The IF function performs a logical test that you design. You can use the AND, OR, and NOT functions in IF formulas to specify one or more criteria to be checked. AND requires that all conditions be met, but OR is satisfied with any one of the conditions. Excel displays *TRUE* or performs the specified action when the criteria are met. Excel displays *FALSE* or performs a different action when the criteria are not met.

## IF, AND, OR, and NOT Function Syntax

The following table describes the generic parts of the logical functions IF, AND, OR, and NOT.

| Function | Syntax |
|---|---|
| IF | IF(logical test, value if true, value if false) |
| AND | AND(condition1, condition2,...) |
| OR | OR(condition1, condition2,...) |
| NOT | NOT(condition) |

The following table outlines the arguments of these logical functions.

| Argument | Description |
|---|---|
| Logical test | The condition being checked using a comparison operator, such as =, >, <, >=, <=, or <> (not equal to) |
| Value if true | The value, text in quotation (") marks, or calculation returned if the logical test result is found to be true |
| Value if false | The value, text in quotation (") marks, or calculation returned if the logical test result is found to be false |
| Condition | A logical expression to be evaluated as true or false; one of multiple expressions evaluated by an AND function or an OR function |

## How Logical Functions Work Together

The formula =IF(AND(B5>=25000,B5<=50000),D5,"") is used as an example to explain the function results shown in the following illustration.

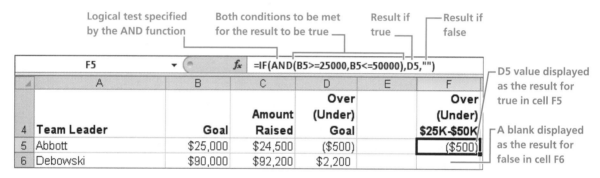

An IF function containing an AND function for the logical test

Excel performs the logical test AND(B5>=25000, B5<=50000). Parentheses surround the AND function's multiple arguments. The first argument seeks a monthly fundraising goal equal to or greater than $25,000. The second argument limits the goal to $50,000 or less. The logical test, therefore, searches for goals between $25,000 and $50,000. The AND function requires that all specified conditions be met for the result to be true. If a value is not between $25,000 and $50,000, the result of the logical test is false. D5 is the value-if-true argument in the IF function, and the contents of cell D5 will be displayed in the formula cell when true. The value-if-false argument "" (quotation marks without any text between them) indicates that the formula cell will be blank when false.

The logical test NOT(L5=M5) could be used in an IF formula to ensure that two values are not identical. If the value in L5 is not equal to the value in M5, the value-if-true action is performed. If the values are equal, the value-if-false action is performed.

## IFERROR Function Syntax

The IFERROR function checks a formula for an error. The generic parts of the IFERROR logical function are shown in the following table.

| Function | Syntax |
|---|---|
| IFERROR | IFERROR(value, value if error) |

The following table outlines the arguments of the IFERROR function.

| Argument | Description |
|---|---|
| Value | The formula being checked for an error |
| Value if error | The value, text in quotation (") marks, or calculation returned if the formula result is found to be an error |

Excel checks formulas and returns the following error types described in the following table.

| Error Type | Description | Common Cause |
|---|---|---|
| #DIV/0! | Value is divided by 0 | Divisor cell referenced in the formula contains 0 or is empty |
| #N/A | Value not available | Cell referenced in the formula is empty |
| #NAME? | Text in a formula is not recognized | Misspelled or nonexistent range name in formula |
| #NULL! | Nonadjacent areas referenced in a formula | The existence of a space character instead of punctuation, such as a comma (,) |
| #NUM! | Invalid numeric value in a formula or function | Nonnumeric text in a function that requires a numeric argument |
| #REF! | Invalid cell reference | The editing or deletion of cell(s) referenced in the formula |
| #VALUE! | Incorrect data type used in a formula | Cell referenced in the formula contains text rather than a value |

## How the IFERROR Function Works

Inexperienced Excel users may not recognize Excel's error types, such as #N/A, displayed in formula result cells. Adding the IFERROR function to a formula allows you to display a descriptive message rather than the error type, as shown in the following illustration on the right. You also may define messages, such as "NA" (Not Applicable) or "0," to display when error results are acceptable.

Cell C5 contains text rather than a value, triggering an error message.

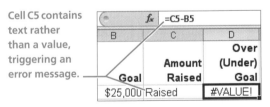

The defined error message is enclosed within quotation marks (").

The formula result displays the normal #VALUE! error message when an error is found.

The IFERROR function displays a "CHECK DATA" message when an error is found.

The IFERROR function should not be confused with the ISERROR function. First available in Excel 2007, IFERROR requires only a value-if-error action to be specified. Earlier Excel versions require a lengthier IF(ISERROR(logical test),value-if-true, value if false) formula structure.

# Use Logical Functions

*In this exercise, you will use the IF and AND functions to create a formula. The formula result displays the difference between the goal and the amount raised for team leaders whose fundraising goals were between $25,000 and $50,000.*

## Use the IF Function

1. Display the **November** worksheet in the Awards workbook, if necessary.

2. Select **cell F5**, and choose **Formulas→Function Library→Logical** 🐾 **→IF** from the Ribbon.
   *You may use the Function Library as an alternative to the Insert Function button on the Formula Bar.*

3. If necessary, move the **Function Arguments** dialog box out of the way by dragging its title bar until you can see **columns B–D**.

## Specify an Argument Using the AND Function

4. Follow these steps to enter the IF function arguments:

Ⓐ Taking care to type the punctuation as shown, enter
**and(B5>=25000,B5<=50000)** in the **Logical_Test** box.

| | | |
|---|---|---|
| Function Arguments | | |
| IF | | |
| Logical_test | AND(B5>=25000,B5<=50000) 🔢 | = TRUE |
| Value_if_true | D5 🔢 | = -500 |
| Value_if_false | "" 🔢 | = "" |
| | | = -500 |

Ⓑ Tap ⎘Tab to select the Value_If_True box, and select **cell D5** in the worksheet.

Ⓒ Tap ⎘Tab to select the Value_If_False box, and type **""** (use ⇧Shift+' twice to type the quotation marks).

*In the Function Arguments dialog box, notice that the logical test evaluates as TRUE at the right of its text box. Both arguments that you specified with the AND function are true. The Value_If_True result is –500.*

5. Click **OK**.

6. Use **Format Painter** 🖌 to apply the formatting from **cell D5** to **cell F5**.
   *The result in cell F5 should appear as ($500).*

## Copy the IF Formula

7. Use **AutoFill** to copy the formula in **cell F5** to the **range F6:F12**.

| | A | B | C | D | E | F |
|---|---|---|---|---|---|---|
| 4 | **Team Leader** | **Goal** | **Amount Raised** | **Over (Under) Goal** | | **Over (Under) $25K-$50K** |
| 5 | Abbott | $25,000 | $24,500 | ($500) | | ($500) |
| 6 | Debowski | $90,000 | $92,200 | $2,200 | | |
| 7 | Faber | $40,000 | $44,475 | $4,475 | | $4,475 |
| 8 | Lemus | $80,000 | $79,620 | ($380) | | |
| 9 | Martinez | $70,000 | $52,170 | ($17,830) | | |
| 10 | Nguyen | $25,000 | $25,250 | $250 | | $250 |
| 11 | Park | $25,000 | $27,570 | $2,570 | | $2,570 |
| 12 | Weinstein | $50,000 | $45,650 | ($4,350) | | ($4,350) |
| 13 | **Raised at Least $30,000** | | **$314,115** | | | |

*Values appear in column F for five records that meet both conditions you specified with the AND function. The other formula cells in column F appear blank, which you specified as the Value_If_False argument.*

8. **Save** 💾 the changes, **close** the workbook, and leave Excel **open**.

# 14.6 Using Functions to Format Text

**Video Lesson** labyrinthelab.com/videos

Workbook data may be imported from sources other than Excel. These data may not be formatted as you wish. For example, employee names may be contained in one column. Sorting and filtering the names would be much easier if the names were separated into three columns for last name, first name, and middle name. Some names may not begin with a capital letter. Excel's text functions can help you clean up the data.

## Creating Formulas with Text Functions

You create the formulas in a blank area of a worksheet to duplicate the data using the formats that you specify. You may use the Paste Values command to convert the formulas into values. Then you may delete the original unformatted data, if you wish. You may specify the text argument in a formula as a cell reference, another formula that results in text, or specific text surrounded by quotation marks.

 If you are familiar with Excel macros and VBA (Visual Basic for Applications), you may program a macro that converts text in a range of cells or an entire worksheet rather than use functions.

# Changing the Case of Text with PROPER, LOWER, and UPPER

The PROPER function changes the first letter of each word in the text to uppercase and the other letters of the word to lowercase. The LOWER function changes all text to lowercase, and UPPER converts all text to uppercase. You should check the converted text for unintended results. For example, the PROPER function converts "JAMES DENTON II" to "James Denton Ii." You may edit such cells manually. The syntax of these functions is shown in the following table.

| Function | Syntax |
|---|---|
| PROPER | PROPER(text) |
| LOWER | LOWER(text) |
| UPPER | UPPER(text) |

In the illustration of the three function formulas below, the original text is in column A. The PROPER, LOWER, and UPPER formulas and their results are in column B.

Cell B10 contains the formula =PROPER(A10). Excel formats each word to begin with a capital letter and display lowercase for the other letters.

Cell B11 contains the formula =LOWER("AND"). In this case, text is not retrieved from cell A11. Enclosed in quotation marks in the formula, the text argument AND is formatted in lowercase in the formula result cell.

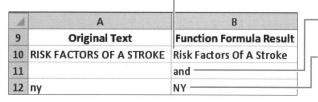

Cell B12 contains the formula =UPPER(A12). The contents of cell A12 are formatted in uppercase.

The results of the PROPER, LOWER, and UPPER functions

# Using SUBSTITUTE to Replace Text

The SUBSTITUTE function changes the specified text characters to a different set of characters. The function, which is case sensitive, looks for an exact match. If an exact match is not found, the original text is displayed in the formula result cell.

The generic parts of the function are shown in the following table.

| Function | Syntax |
|---|---|
| SUBSTITUTE | SUBSTITUTE(text, old text, new text, [instance number]) |

The following table outlines the arguments of the SUBSTITUTE function.

| Argument | Description |
|---|---|
| Text | The text to be searched |
| Old text | The text to be replaced, which may be in a cell, returned by a formula result, or enclosed in quotation (") marks as the function argument |
| New text | The text to be substituted for the old text |
| Instance number | (Optional) The occurrence of old text to be replaced within the full text, as in 2 to substitute only the second instance of "e" in "Indexed." All instances, if the instance number is omitted |

The formula =SUBSTITUTE(I5,"Nurse Aid,""Nurse Aide") is used as an example to illustrate the function arguments and results shown below. The formula was entered in cell B5 and copied down column B. In this example, the optional instance number argument is not included because the text appears only once in the cell contents.

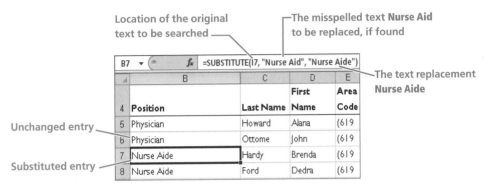

The SUBSTITUTE function only replaces text for which it finds an exact match.

## Calculating the Text Length with LEN

The LEN function counts the characters, including spaces, in the specified text string, which may be in a cell, returned by a formula result, or enclosed in quotation (") marks as the function argument. The LEN function often is used with other functions to obtain a desired result. The syntax of the function is shown in the following table.

| Function | Syntax |
| --- | --- |
| LEN | LEN(text) |

You can use the LEN function to locate some input errors in cells. In the following example, the formula =LEN(F5) counts the characters in a phone number. The formula was copied down column G. Cell F8 contains the number 555-00027. The formula result is 9. Any result other than 8 indicates an input error.

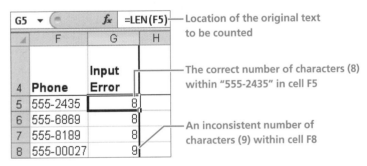

The LEN function counts the total characters in the specified text.

The Conditional Formatting command in the Home ribbon may be used to highlight cells containing abnormal results.

# Using FIND to Locate Text

The FIND function locates a specific text string within text. The result returns the starting character position of the found text. You may specify an optional character number at which Excel is to start the search. Excel counts characters from the left of the text to arrive at this character. The FIND function may be used with other functions to obtain a desired result. The syntax of the FIND function is shown in the following table.

| Function | Syntax |
|----------|--------|
| FIND | FIND(find text,within text,[character start number)] |

The following table describes the arguments of the FIND function.

| Argument | Description |
|----------|-------------|
| Find text | The text to be found |
| Within text | The text in which the search will take place, which may be in a cell, returned by a formula result, or enclosed in quotation (") marks as the function argument |
| Character start number | (Optional) The starting character for the search, counted from the left in the searched text; the first character, if the start number is omitted |

The function =FIND (" ",K5) is used to explain the function arguments in the following illustration. The search is performed in the contents of cell K5. A space is found at the sixth character of the text, and the function result is 6.

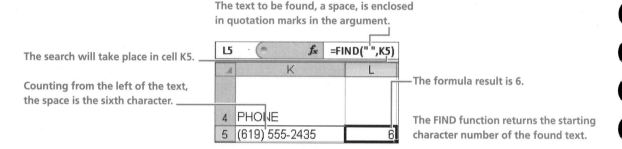

The text to be found, a space, is enclosed in quotation marks in the argument.

The search will take place in cell K5.

Counting from the left of the text, the space is the sixth character.

The formula result is 6.

The FIND function returns the starting character number of the found text.

# Using LEFT, MID, and RIGHT to Extract Text

Data copied into an Excel worksheet may contain extra characters that you do not want. You can use the LEFT, MID, and RIGHT functions to extract a certain number of characters, depending on their location in the text string. For example, you can use the RIGHT function to extract the last four digits of a social security number. The MID function counts the characters from the left until it arrives at the starting character number you specified. The extracted characters display in the formula result cell, and the original text is not affected. The syntax of these functions is shown in the following table.

| Function | Syntax |
|----------|--------|
| LEFT | LEFT(text,[number of characters]) |
| MID | MID(text,character start number, number of characters) |
| RIGHT | RIGHT(text,number of characters) |

The arguments in the LEFT, MID, and RIGHT functions are described in the following table.

| Argument | Description |
|---|---|
| Text | The text characters to be counted or extracted |
| Number of characters | (Optional for the LEFT and RIGHT functions) The total characters to be extracted; the first character, if this argument is omitted |
| Character start number | (Optional for the LEFT and RIGHT functions) The starting character to be extracted, counted from the left in the text; the first character, if the start number is omitted |

The following illustration of the formula =LEFT(M5,3) explains the basic use of the LEFT function to extract text. Notice that the original text in cell M5 remains unchanged, and the result displays in the N5 formula cell.

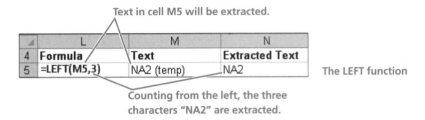

The LEFT function

The formula =RIGHT(M6,4) in cell N6 is used below to explain the basic use of the MID function to extract text.

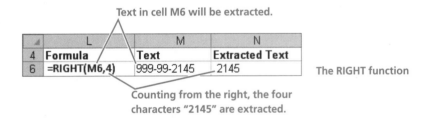

The RIGHT function

The formula =MID(M7,4,3) in cell N7 explains the basic use of the MID function to extract text. Remember that the start number and number-of-characters arguments are required for this function.

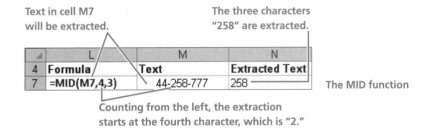

The MID function

### Splitting Names

The formulas in the following table use multiple functions to extract a last name, first name, and middle name into separate columns. Function formulas work well to perform this task when the names do not have the same number of units. For example, a middle name may be included for some names, but not for others. In the following formulas, the FIND function looks for a space in the name, expressed by the argument " " as a space surrounded by quotation marks. To locate the middle name, the argument LEN(C7&D7) sums the character length of the first name and last name. Do not be concerned if you do not understand the complexity of the formulas, but you may challenge yourself to think about how they work. These formulas may be used when no spaces exist within a name unit. For example, the first name must be "LaRonda" or "Laronda" rather than "La Ronda." Any names with spaces, titles, or suffixes, such as "Dr." or "Jr.," would need to be cleaned up manually.

| Formula | Text Extracted | Original Text | Result |
|---|---|---|---|
| =RIGHT(J5,LEN(J5)-FIND(" ",J5,1)) | Last name | Jose Edgar Garcia | Garcia |
| =LEFT(J5,FIND(" ",J5)) | First name | Jose Edgar Garcia | Jose |
| =IF(LEN(C7&D7)+2>=LEN(J7),"",  MID(J7,LEN(D7)+2,LEN(J7)-LEN(C7&D7)-2)) | Middle name | Jose Edgar Garcia | Edgar |

The Text to Columns command in the Data ribbon can split names into separate columns. The names, however, must all contain the same number of name units. If some names contain a middle name, then all other names must contain a blank field for the middle name unit.

### DEVELOP YOUR SKILLS 14.6.1
## Use Functions to Format Text

*In this exercise, you will use various text functions to clean up data. You will substitute text to correct a misspelling. You will split the area codes and phone numbers into two columns. You also will check the length of the phone numbers to identify any input errors. Finally, you will examine formulas that split employee names into columns for last name and first name, as well as format the names with the proper case.*

### Use the SUBSTITUTE Function

1. **Open** the Data Clean Up workbook from the Lesson 14 folder.
   *Take a few moments to review the data in columns H–K. "Nurse Aid" is misspelled in column I, and some names in column J do not display the correct case. You wish to split the phone numbers into two columns. You will create text formulas in columns B and E–G to reformat some of the data.*

2. Select **cell B7**, and choose **Formulas→Function Library→Text** 🄰→**SUBSTITUTE** from the Ribbon.

3. If necessary, move the **Function Arguments** dialog box out of the way by dragging its title bar until you can see **row 7**.

4. Follow these steps to complete the Function Argument dialog box:

Ⓐ Select **cell I7** in the worksheet as the text to use.

Ⓑ Type **Nurse Aid** in the **Old_Text** box. Excel will add the quotation marks.

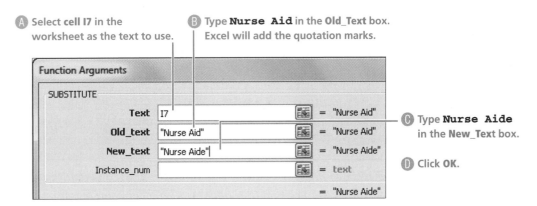

Ⓒ Type **Nurse Aide** in the **New_Text** box.

Ⓓ Click **OK**.

*Cell B7 displays* Nurse Aide. *The Formula Bar displays =SUBSTITUTE(I7,"Nurse Aid","Nurse Aide"). The SUBSTITUTE function replaced the original text. If this did not happen, make certain that you typed the text entries exactly as instructed, including the capital letter at the beginning of each word.*

5. Copy **cell B7** and paste in the **range B5:B8**.
   *The original text* Physician *from cells I5 and I6 displays in cells B5 and B6. The original cells did not contain* Nurse Aid, *and no replacement was necessary.*

## Split the Phone Numbers

*In the next steps, you will split the phone numbers so that the area code appears in column E and the remainder in column F.*

6. Select **cell E5**, and choose **Formulas→Function Library→Text Ⓐ→LEFT** from the Ribbon.

7. Follow these steps to complete the Function Arguments dialog box:

Ⓐ Select **cell K5** in the worksheet as the text to use.

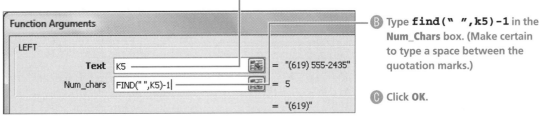

Ⓑ Type **find(" ",k5)-1** in the **Num_Chars** box. (Make certain to type a space between the quotation marks.)

Ⓒ Click **OK**.

*The Formula Bar displays =LEFT(K5,FIND(" ",K5)-1). Cell K5 contains the text (619) 555-2435. The FIND function locates the space after the area code in cell K5. Including the space, the number of characters in (619) is six. You entered −1 to subtract the space character. The Num_Chars argument then evaluates as 5. The result in cell E5 is (619).*

8. Use the **AutoFill** handle to copy **cell E5** down to the **range E6:E8**.

9. Select **cell F5**, and choose **Formulas→Function Library→Text Ⓐ→RIGHT** from the Ribbon.

10. Follow these steps to complete the Function Arguments dialog box:

Ⓐ Select **cell K5** in the worksheet as the text to use.

Ⓑ Type `len(k5)-find(" ",k5)` in the **Num_Chars** box. (Make certain to type a space between the quotation marks.)

Ⓒ Click **OK**.

*The Formula Bar displays =RIGHT(K5,LEN(K5)-FIND(" ",K5)). The result in cell F5 is 555-2438. The formula extracted eight characters of the phone number from the right of the entry.*

*This Num_Chars argument is more complex in this formula. The LEN function calculates 14 characters as the text length in cell K5. Again, the FIND function locates the space after the area code. The six characters up through the space are subtracted from fourteen. The Num_Char argument evaluates as eight characters counted from the right.*

11. Use the **AutoFill** handle to copy **cell F5** down to the **range F6:F8**.
    *Notice that the phone number in cell F8 contains one extra digit.*

## Use the LEN Function

12. Select **cell G5**, and enter the formula `=len(f5)`.

13. Use the **AutoFill** handle to copy **cell G5** down to the **range G6:G8**.
    *Cell G8 displays 9 as the character length, indicating an input error. You can use the LEN function to locate some input errors based on the character length in cells.*

## Examine Function Formulas That Split the Names

14. Select **cell C5**, and review the formula in the Formula Bar.
    *The formula is =PROPER(RIGHT(J5,LEN(J5)-FIND(" ",J5))). This formula extracts the last name from the text ALANA HOWARD in cell J5. The RIGHT, LEN, and FIND functions are similar to those you used to extract the phone numbers in column F. The PROPER function capitalizes the first letter of the result and changes the other letters to lowercase. The result in cell C5 is Howard.*

15. Select **cell D5**, and review the formula in the Formula Bar.
    *The formula is =PROPER(LEFT(J5,FIND(" ",J5)-1)). This formula extracts the first name from the text ALANA HOWARD in cell J5. The LEFT and FIND functions are similar to those you used to extract the five-character area codes in column E. The PROPER function adjusts the case of the text. The result in cell D5 is Alana.*

16. **Save** 💾 the changes, **close** the workbook, and leave Excel **open**.

# 14.7 Tracing Formulas

**Video Lesson**    labyrinthelab.com/videos

Excel's auditing tools are useful for analyzing complex formulas that are dependent on other formulas. The auditing tools are also quite helpful for locating errors in formulas.

## The Formula Auditing Tools

The Formula Auditing tools are used primarily for displaying and hiding cell tracers. Cell tracers are arrows that identify precedent and dependent cells of formulas. The Formula Auditing group of the Formulas ribbon is shown at right.

The Formula Auditing tools on the Formulas Ribbon

## Tracing Precedents

The Trace Precedents ⊡ command displays arrows that point from the cells referenced by a formula to the cell containing the formula. A formula may reference cells containing values and/or cells that contain other formulas. Thus, a formula may have several levels of precedents. Repeating the Trace Precedents command adds the next level to the display. The following illustrations show the Awards workbook with the precedent cell tracers (arrows) displayed for the award points formula in cell F6. The first level includes cells C6 and E6, referenced in the formula. Cell E6 contains its own formula for the award rate. The second level displays the precedent for that formula, which depends on a lookup table.

| F6 | ▼ | fx | =C6*E6 | | |
|---|---|---|---|---|---|

| | A | B | C | D | E | F |
|---|---|---|---|---|---|---|
| 4 | Team Leader ▼ | Go ▼ | Amount Rais ▼ | Over (Under) Go ▼ | Award Rate ▼ | Award Poin ▼ |
| 6 | Debowski | $100,000 | $95,350 | ($4,650) | 1% | 954 |

*The filled dots indicate that cells C6 and E6 are precedents.*

*The arrow points from the precedent cells to the formula cell that references them.*

The first level of precedents for the formula C6*E6

| | A | B | C | D | E | F | G |
|---|---|---|---|---|---|---|---|
| 4 | Team Leader ▼ | Go ▼ | Amount Rais ▼ | Over (Under) Go ▼ | Award Rate ▼ | Award Poin ▼ | Achieved Goal? ▼ |
| 6 | Debowski | $100,000 | $95,350 | ($4,650) | 1% | 954 | Below Goal |
| 7 | Faber | $60,000 | $52,500 | ($7,500) | 0% | - | Under Achiever |
| 8 | Lemus | $100,000 | $110,350 | $10,350 | 7% | 7,725 | Over Achiever |
| 9 | Martinez | $70,000 | $66,000 | ($4,000) | 1% | 660 | Below Goal |
| 12 | Weinstein | $70,000 | $67,000 | ($3,000) | 1% | 670 | Below Goal |
| 13 | | | $391,200 | ($1,760) | | | |
| 14 | | | | | | | |
| 15 | | | | | Over (Under) Goal | Award Rate | Message |
| 16 | | | | | ($100,000) | 0% | Under Achiever |
| 17 | | | | | ($5,000) | 1% | Below Goal |
| 18 | | | | | $0 | 3% | At Goal |
| 19 | | | | | $5,000 | 5% | Above Goal |
| 20 | | | | | $10,000 | 7% | Over Achiever |

*The second level showing the lookup table as a precedent for the VLOOKUP formula in cell E6*

## Trace and Clear Precedent Arrows

*In this exercise, you will trace to cells that make up the formula in cell F6 and then trace precedents for cell G6.*

1. Select **cell F6** in the **December** worksheet of the Awards workbook.

2. Choose **Formulas→Formula Auditing→Trace Precedents** 📄 from the Ribbon.
   *Tracer arrows appear, indicating that the formula in cell F6 is dependent on cells C6 and E6. Next you will look for any precedents to those two cells.*

3. Choose **Formulas→Formula Auditing→Trace Precedents** 📄 again in the Ribbon.
   *A tracer arrow from the table array in rows 16–20 to cell E6 appears. This shows that the formula in cell E6 depends on the table array. Cell C6 has no precedents because it does not contain a formula.*

4. Choose **Formulas→Formula Auditing→Remove Arrows** 📄 **menu ▼→Remove Precedent Arrows** from the Ribbon to hide the second level of tracer arrows.
   *Now only the first precedent level displays.*

5. Choose **Formulas→Formula Auditing→Remove Arrows** 📄 to hide all tracer arrows.
   *This command removes all levels at one time.*

6. Select **cell G6** and choose **Formulas→Formula Auditing→Trace Precedents** 📄 from the Ribbon.
   *The formula in cell G6 clearly is dependent on cell D6 and cell E16 in the table array.*

7. Choose **Formulas→Formula Auditing→Remove Arrows** 📄 to hide all tracer arrows.

8. You made no changes, so just leave the workbook **open**.

## Tracing Dependents

| Video Lesson | labyrinthelab.com/videos |

The Trace Dependents 📄 command shows you the dependents for a selected cell. Dependents are formula cells that reference the selected cell. Repeating the Trace Dependents command displays an additional set of arrows that trace the next level of dependents until all dependent cells are identified.

# Trace Dependents

*In this exercise, you will trace to cells that are dependent on the value in cell C6.*

*Before You Begin: You must have completed Develop Your Skills 14.4.1, 14.5.1, 14.6.1, and 14.7.1.*

1. **Open** the Awards workbook, display the **December** worksheet, and select **cell C6**.

2. Choose **Formulas→Formula Auditing→Trace Dependents** ⬚ from the Ribbon.
   *As indicated by the three arrow heads shown here, cells C13, D6, and F6 include a reference to cell C6 in their formulas. You will trace the dependents for those three cells in the next step.*

| | C | D | E | F | G |
|---|---|---|---|---|---|
| 4 | Amount Rais⯆ | Over (Under) G⯆ | Award Rate ⯆ | Award Poin⯆ | Achieved Goal? ⯆ |
| 6 | $95,350 | ($4,650) | 1% | 954 | Below Goal |
| 7 | $52,500 | ($7,500) | 0% | - | Under Achiever |
| 8 | $110,350 | $10,350 | 7% | 7,725 | Over Achiever |
| 9 | $66,000 | ($4,000) | 1% | 660 | Below Goal |
| 12 | $67,000 | ($3,000) | 1% | 670 | Below Goal |
| 13 | $391,200 | ($1,760) | | | |

3. Repeat the **Trace Dependents** ⬚ command.
   *Additional tracer arrows point from cell D6 to cells E6 and G6. The filled dot in cell D6 indicates that the cell is a precedent for cell E6, which has a formula dependent on cell D6. Another tracer arrow points from cell D6 to the subtotal formula in cell D13.*

| | C | D | E | F | Ach |
|---|---|---|---|---|---|
| 4 | Amount Rais⯆ | Over (Under) G⯆ | Award Rate ⯆ | Award Poin⯆ | G |
| 6 | $95,350 | ($4,650) | 1% | 954 | Below |
| 7 | $52,500 | ($7,500) | 0% | - | Under |
| 8 | $110,350 | $10,350 | 7% | 7,725 | Over A |
| 9 | $66,000 | ($4,000) | 1% | 660 | Below |
| 12 | $67,000 | ($3,000) | 1% | 670 | Below |
| 13 | $391,200 | ($1,760) | | | |

4. Choose **Formulas→Formula Auditing→Remove Arrows** ⬚ to remove the tracer arrows.

5. Select **cell G16** in the table array and choose the **Trace Dependents** ⬚ command.
   *A number of tracer arrows are drawn from cell G16 to cells with formulas dependent on the data in that cell.*

6. Repeat the **Trace Dependents** ⬚ command until all dependent cells are revealed.

7. Use the **Remove Arrows** ⬚ command to remove the tracer arrows.

8. **Close** the workbook and leave Excel **open**.

# 14.8 Auditing Formula Errors

**Video Lesson**   labyrinthelab.com/videos

Cells with formulas sometimes display error messages such as #VALUE!, #NAME!, or #DIV/0!. A formula may display an incorrect result rather than a message. Errors may be caused by incorrect cell entries in precedent cells, empty cells, incorrect or missing defined names, or incorrect formulas. Excel can help you identify cells that contain errors that prevent the display of correct formula results.

If error checking does not appear to be working, ensure that Enable Background Error Checking and the desired Error Checking Rules have a checkmark in the Formulas category of the Excel Options dialog box.

## Auditing Single Cells

Excel continuously checks for common errors as you work, depending on the error checking options selected in the Excel Options dialog box. Excel alerts you to inconsistent formulas and other potential errors by displaying a small triangle icon in the upper left of a cell. You may handle marked cells one cell at a time. An error checking menu is available while the cell is selected to get help, show calculation steps, edit the formula, or ignore the error. The menu commands vary depending on the error type. Excel marks a SUM formula when it determines that adjacent cells are not included in the sum range. If the range is correct, you would choose the Ignore Error command from the menu.

Error checking menu containing commands to get help, solve, or ignore the error ⎯

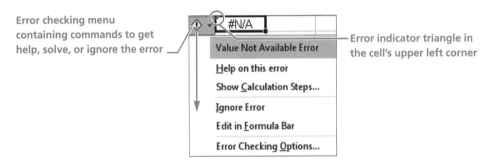

Error indicator triangle in the cell's upper left corner

## Error Checking in Multiple Cells

The Error Checking ⬦ command on the Formulas ribbon allows you to navigate and respond to error messages throughout the work-sheet, similar to the spell checker. The Error Checking dialog box summarizes each error and provides the same commands as the error checking menu available on a single cell.

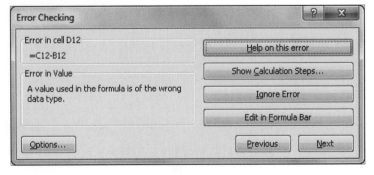

# Tracing Errors

The Trace Error command on the Formulas ribbon draws arrows that point from any precedent cells to the selected cell containing the error message.

| QUICK REFERENCE | AUDITING FORMULAS |
|---|---|
| **Task** | **Procedure** |
| Audit a single cell marked as containing an error | ▪ Select the cell containing a triangle icon in its upper-left corner.<br>▪ Click the error checking button to the left of the cell and choose a command from the menu. |
| Audit all cells marked as containing an error | ▪ Choose Formulas→Formula Auditing→Error Checking 🗸 from the Ribbon.<br>▪ Choose a command in the Error Checking dialog box.<br>▪ Click Resume after editing a formula to view the next error. |
| Trace precedents for a cell displaying an error message | ▪ Select the cell displaying the error message.<br>▪ Choose Formulas→Formula Auditing→Error Checking→Trace Error from the Ribbon to display tracer arrows. |
| Restore triangle icons for ignored errors | ▪ Choose File→Options 🔳→Formulas category.<br>▪ Under Error Checking, click Reset Ignored Errors. |
| Show calculation steps in any formula | ▪ Select a cell containing a formula.<br>▪ Choose Formulas→Formula Auditing→Evaluate Formula 🔍 from the Ribbon.<br>▪ In the Evaluate Formula dialog box, click Step In to view more information about an underlined expression, if desired, and then click Step Out to display the result.<br>▪ Click Evaluate to display the result of the next underlined expression.<br>▪ Continue clicking Evaluate until all expressions are evaluated and the formula result displays. |

## DEVELOP YOUR SKILLS 14.8.1
## Check Errors in Formulas

*In this exercise, you will respond to formula error messages using Excel's error checking commands.*

### Enable Error Checking

1. **Open** the Error Check workbook from the Lesson 14 folder.
2. Choose **File→Options** 🔳 **→Formulas** category.

3. Follow these steps to review the error checking options, but do not make any changes unless your instructor directs:

(A) Make certain that the **Enable Background Error Checking** box has a checkmark.

**Error Checking**

☑ Enable background error checking

Indicate errors using this color: [color] ▾    [Reset Ignored Errors]

(B) Review the items in the **Error Checking Rules** area of the Excel Options dialog box.

**Error checking rules**

☑ Cells containing formulas that result in an error ⓘ
☑ Inconsistent calculated column formula in tables ⓘ
☑ Cells containing years represented as 2 digits ⓘ
☑ Numbers formatted as text or preceded by an apostrophe ⓘ
☑ Formulas inconsistent with other formulas in the region ⓘ

☑ Formulas which omit cells in a region ⓘ
☑ Unlocked cells containing formulas ⓘ
☐ Formulas referring to empty cells ⓘ
☑ Data entered in a table is invalid ⓘ

(C) Hover the mouse over any information icon to display a **ScreenTip** that explains the option.

4. Click **Cancel** (or **OK** if your instructor directs you to change any options).

## Edit a Formula to Correct an Error

5. Notice that a #REF! error message displays in **cell G9**.

6. Select **cell G9**.
   *The Formula Bar displays =VLOOKUP(D9,Award_Table,4). The formula in cell G9 is dependent on the value in cell D9 and the table array in rows 16–20.*

7. Point to the **error checking menu button** to the left of the selected cell.

| 7,725 | Over Achiever |
| ⬦ 0 | #REF! |
| 1,440 | Below Goal |

   *A ScreenTip displays possible causes of the error, including a reference error in the function. Cell D9 and the defined name Award_Table appear to be correct in the formula. The column index number, however, refers to a nonexisting column 4 in the table array. The column index number should refer to column 3.*

8. Click the **error checking menu button** to the left of **cell G9** and choose **Edit in Formula Bar** from the menu.

9. Replace **4** with **3** in the formula and **tap** [Enter] to complete the entry.
   *Cell G9 now correctly displays Below Goal.*

## Check for Errors

*The Error Checking command is useful for responding to multiple error messages in a worksheet.*

10. Choose **Formulas→Formula Auditing→Error Checking** [icon] from the Ribbon.
    *The Error Checking dialog box displays, and cell D12 is selected in the worksheet.*

11. Move the dialog box, if necessary, to view **row 12** in the worksheet.

12. Click the **Help on This Error** button in the Error Checking dialog box.

13. Take a few moments to explore the help suggestions, and then **close** the Excel Help window.

14. Read the left side of the **Error Checking** dialog box.
    *The dialog box displays the cell D12 formula and analyzes the problem as to an Error in Value. Notice that the a67000 entry in cell C12 is not a value.*

15. Select **cell C12** in the worksheet, **delete** the letter "a" in the Formula Bar, and **complete** the entry.

16. Click **Resume in the Error Checking** dialog box.
    *Correcting the error in cell C12 allowed the other formulas in row 12 to display correct results. No error messages now exist in any cells.*

17. Click **OK** to respond to the message that error checking is complete.

18. **Save** 💾 the changes, **close** the workbook, and leave Excel **open**.

## Evaluating Formulas

**Video Lesson**   labyrinthelab.com/videos

The Evaluate Formula 🔍 command allows you to see what each part of a formula includes. You may evaluate any formula, but this tool is particularly helpful with multiple-operator formulas. For example, in the formula =B13*(1-$F$18), the Evaluate Formula dialog box would show you the actual value of B13. The formula is easier to analyze than just looking at the cell reference. As you step through the evaluation process, you will see the actual values and calculations that make up the complete formula.

### DEVELOP YOUR SKILLS 14.8.2
### Evaluate a Formula

*In this exercise, you will evaluate the projected contributions formula in the Calculations worksheet of a financial report.*

1. **Open** the Financial Report workbook from the Lesson 14 folder.
   *This workbook contains two worksheets. The Factors worksheet contains values that are used in formulas on the Calculations worksheet.*

2. Select **cell B6** in the **Calculations** worksheet.
   *This cell contains the projected contributions formula =Factors!B2*Factors!B3*B5. Notice that the cell references include the Factors worksheet name because they are on a different worksheet.*

3. Choose **Formulas→Formula Auditing→Evaluate Formula** 🔍 from the Ribbon.
   *The Evaluate Formula dialog box displays the formula with the first expression underlined to indicate cell B2 in the Factors worksheet.*

4. Click the **Evaluate** button in the Evaluate Formula dialog box.
   *The first part of the formula, Factors!B2, is evaluated, and the cell's actual value of 1.05 is displayed in the dialog box.*

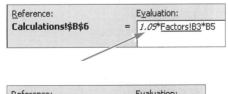

5. Click the **Evaluate** button to evaluate the next part of the formula.
   *The second expression of the formula evaluates as 10000, the actual value of cell B3 in the Factors worksheet.*

6. Click **Evaluate**.

   *The italicized result shows that the prior calculation 1.05%\*10000 equals 10500. This product will be multipled by cell B5 in the Calculations worksheet.*

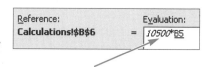

| Reference: | | Evaluation: |
|---|---|---|
| **Calculations!$B$6** | = | *10500*\*B5 |

7. Continue to click the **Evaluate** button until the final answer of 2,100,000 is displayed in the Evaluate Formula dialog box.

   *With every click of the Evaluate button, each part of the formula is displayed, showing you step by step how the final result of $2,100,000 is calculated.*

8. Click **Restart** in the Evaluate Formula dialog box to repeat the evaluation process.

9. This time click **Step In** to preview the upcoming evaluation, and then click **Step Out** to complete the evaluation.

10. Continue using **Step In** and **Step Out** when the expression includes a cell reference, and then use **Evaluate** for the final steps of the formula evaluation.

11. When finished, close the **Evaluate Formula** dialog box.

12. **Close** the workbook **without** saving; you made no changes.

## 14.9 Concepts Review

**Concepts Review**  labyrinthelab.com/excel10

*To check your knowledge of the key concepts introduced in this lesson, complete the Concepts Review quiz by going to the URL listed above. If your classroom is using Labyrinth eLab, you may complete the Concepts Review quiz from within your eLab course.*

# Reinforce Your Skills

## Create 3-D Cell References

*In this exercise, you will add a new worksheet to the workbook and use a 3-D cell reference to add values from several worksheets.*

### Copy a Worksheet

1. **Open** the rs-Project Budget workbook from the Lesson 14 folder.

2. Display each worksheet in the workbook to see that they have an identical design.
   *Cell B9 of each worksheet contains the total number of days to complete a task.*

3. **Right-click** on the worksheet tab to copy the **Site Design Team** worksheet, then position the copy first in the worksheet order.

4. **Rename** the new worksheet as **Budget**.

5. Change the label in **cell A1** to **Website Development Budget**.

6. Change **cell A3** to **Estimated Cost Per Day** and center the label.

7. Delete the labels and values in the **range A4:B9**.

8. Type and align the entries in **cells A4 and A6** as shown in the following illustration.

| | A | B |
|---|---|---|
| 1 | Website Development Budget | |
| 2 | | |
| 3 | Estimated Cost Per Day | Days to Complete |
| 4 | $700 | 65 |
| 5 | | |
| 6 | Budget | |

### Enter a 3-D Cell Reference

*You will use a 3-D cell reference to cell B9 in the four task worksheets to calculate the total number of worker-days for the entire project.*

9. Select **cell B4**.

10. Tap ⌸.

11. Type **s** to display functions beginning with the letter *s* in the **Formula AutoComplete** function list. (Choose **File→Options→Formulas→Working with Formulas→ Formula AutoComplete** to turn the option on if the function list does not appear.)

12. Type **u** to display the SUM function in the **AutoComplete** list.

13. **Tap** ⬇ twice to highlight SUM, and then **tap** ⌷Tab⌷ to select SUM.
    *The function =SUM( displays in the cell and the Formula Bar.*

14. Click the **Site Design Team** sheet tab.

15. **Hold down** ⌷Shift⌷ while you click the **Shopping Cart** sheet tab.

16. Select **cell B9** in the currently displayed worksheet.

17. Click **Enter** ☑ in the Formula Bar to complete the formula.
    *The result equals 63 total days. The formula totaled cell B9 from all four worksheets.*

18. Examine the 3-D cell reference in the Formula Bar.
    *The formula displays as =SUM('Site Design Team:Shopping Cart Team'!B9). A colon (:) indicates the range of worksheet names, and an exclamation (!) point separates the worksheet reference from the cell reference. Single quotation marks (') surround the sheet name because they contain spaces.*

    *The 3-D reference must refer to the same cell in each of the detail worksheets, but you may create the formula in any cell.*

### Create the Cost Formula

19. In **cell B6** of the **Budget** worksheet, enter the formula **=A4*B4** to calculate the budget needed to complete the website development project.

20. Format the budget amount as **Currency format with no decimal places**, if not already formatted so.

### Test the 3-D Cell Reference

21. Display the **Site Design Team** worksheet and change the value in **cell B8** to **4**.
    *Take note of the new sum in cell B9.*

22. Display the **Budget** worksheet, and verify that the total number of days increased to 65 in **cell B4** and the budget increased to $45,500 in **cell B6**.
    *3-D cell references allow you to calculate the values in several worksheets on a single summary worksheet.*

23. **Save** 💾 the changes and **close** the workbook.

---

### REINFORCE YOUR SKILLS 14.2
# Create a Table Array and HLOOKUP Function

*In this exercise, you will use a table array and the VLOOKUP function to assign the letter grades A–F to students based on their test scores. Then you will learn to use the Transpose command to convert the table array for use with the HLOOKUP function. You also will review how to edit properties for a defined name.*

### Create a Table Array

1. **Open** the rs-Test 1 Grades workbook from the Lesson 14 folder.

2. Enter the table array data in the **range F5:G9** as shown to the right.
    *Notice that you listed the test score values in ascending (lowest to highest) order so that the VLOOKUP function will assign the proper grade. In a moment, you will create a formula to determine the letter grades in column D.*

| | F | G |
|---|---|---|
| 3 | **Grade Table** | |
| 4 | **Test Scores** | **Letter Grade** |
| 5 | 0 | F |
| 6 | 60 | D |
| 7 | 70 | C |
| 8 | 80 | B |
| 9 | 90 | A |

3. Taking care not to select the labels in rows 3 and 4, select the **range F5:G9**.

4. Click in the **Name** box on the left of the Formula Bar, and type `Grade_Table`.

5. Tap [Enter] to assign Grade_Table as the defined name for the table array.
   *You may always use the absolute cell range for a table array and reference that range in the lookup formula. A defined name, however, usually is clearer.*

## Use the VLOOKUP Function

6. Select **cell D4** and click the **Insert Function**  button in the Formula Bar.

7. Choose **All** from the Select a Category list in the Insert Function dialog box.

8. Tap [V] to jump to the functions beginning with the letter *V* in the Select a Function list.

9. Continue **tapping** [V] until VLOOKUP is highlighted, and then **tap** [Enter] to choose VLOOKUP.

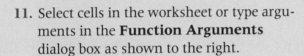

10. Move the **Function Arguments** dialog box aside until you can see **columns D–G**.

11. Select cells in the worksheet or type arguments in the **Function Arguments** dialog box as shown to the right.

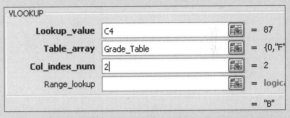

12. Click **OK**.
    *The grade result should be B. Take a few moments to understand how this formula works. VLOOKUP searched down the left column of the table array for the lookup value 87 (the value in cell C4). It stopped at 80 because the lookup value is at least 80 but not 90. Traveling along row 8, the lookup proceeded to the second column in the table array and returned the letter grade B from cell G8.*

13. Use **AutoFill** to copy the formula down the column for the other students.
    *The worksheet should match the following illustration.*

|  | A | B | C | D | E | F | G |
|---|---|---|---|---|---|---|---|
| 3 | Last | First | Test Scores | Letter Grade |  | Grade Table | |
| 4 | Espinoza | Marlo | 87 | B |  | Test Scores | Letter Grade |
| 5 | Kim | Alicia | 95 | A |  | 0 | F |
| 6 | Savant | Susan | 34 | F |  | 60 | D |
| 7 | Warren | Reed | 67 | D |  | 70 | C |
| 8 | Lee | Jimmy | 82 | B |  | 80 | B |
| 9 | Soth | Ashley | 91 | A |  | 90 | A |
| 10 | Sulai | Raj | 94 | A |  |  |  |
| 11 | Brown | Bernice | 78 | C |  |  |  |

14. **Save**  the changes.

## Sort the List and Delete a Record

*Notice that the lookup table is located in the same rows as the student data. In the next steps, you will see how this may cause a problem.*

15. Select **cell A4** and choose **Data→Sort & Filter→Sort A to Z** ![Sort A to Z icon] from the Ribbon.
    *The student records are sorted in alphabetical order by last name, and Excel protected the table array from being included in the sort. Notice that two students have a B grade.*

16. **Right-click** row 8 and choose **Delete** from the context menu to remove Susan Savant's record.

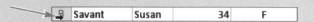

| 8 | Savant | Susan | 34 | F |

*As you can see, row 8 included the table array data for the B grade. The formula now returns a C grade instead of B for two students.*

17. Click **Undo** ![Undo icon] to restore row 8.

## Convert the Table Array from Vertical to Horizontal

*Rows 1 and 2 would not likely be deleted, so they are a safer location for the lookup table. You will convert the vertical array to horizontal to fit in these two rows.*

18. Select the **range F4:G9** (including the labels) and use ⌐Ctrl⌐+⌐C⌐ to copy.

19. Select **cell E1** and choose **Home→Paste menu ▼→Transpose** ![Transpose icon] from the Ribbon.
    *The copied cells are pasted in a horizontal orientation rather than vertical. Transpose means "to switch or reverse." The command is available if you copy cells but not if you cut them.*

20. Center the test scores in the **range F1:J1** so that they align with their matching grades.

21. Widen **column E** so that the labels display completely.

22. Select the **range F4:G9** and **tap** ⌐Delete⌐.
    *The grade formulas in column D display the #N/A error message because cells F5:G9 now are empty. You will rebuild the formula using the HLOOKUP function.*

## Edit the Defined Name

*Next you will display the Name Manager dialog box and update the Refers To range for one of the defined names.*

23. Choose **Formulas→Defined Names→Name Manager** ![Name Manager icon] from the Ribbon.

24. Select **Grade_Table**.

25. Click the **Collapse** ![Collapse icon] button next to Refers To in the bottom right of the dialog box.

26. Taking care not to select the labels in column E, select the **range F1:J2**.

27. Click the **Expand** ![Expand icon] button to display Name Manager.

28. Click **Close**, and then click **Yes** to confirm.
    *The grade formulas currently return the value 60.*

## Use the HLOOKUP Function

29. Select **cell D4**, edit the first letter to **H** so the function name reads *HLOOKUP*, and **complete** the formula.

    *The formula now is =HLOOKUP(C4,Grade_Table,2). The only difference between VLOOKUP and HLOOKUP is the orientation of the table array. Occasionally you may decide to use a horizontal table array for a better worksheet design.*

30. Use **AutoFill** to copy the **D4** formula down for the other students.

| | A | B | C | D | E | F | G | H | I | J |
|---|---|---|---|---|---|---|---|---|---|---|
| 1 | Test 1 Grade Calculations | | | | Test Scores | 0 | 60 | 70 | 80 | 90 |
| 2 | | | | | Letter Grade | F | D | C | B | A |
| 3 | Last | First | Test Scores | Letter Grade | | | Grade Table | | | |
| 4 | Brown | Bernice | 78 | C | | | | | | |
| 5 | Espinoza | Marlo | 87 | B | | | | | | |
| 6 | Kim | Alicia | 95 | A | | | | | | |
| 7 | Lee | Jimmy | 82 | B | | | | | | |
| 8 | Savant | Susan | 34 | F | | | | | | |
| 9 | Soth | Ashley | 91 | A | | | | | | |
| 10 | Sulai | Raj | 94 | A | | | | | | |
| 11 | Warren | Reed | 67 | D | | | | | | |

31. **Save** 🖫 the changes and **close** the workbook.

## REINFORCE YOUR SKILLS 14.3

# Use the VLOOKUP Function and Error Checking

*In this exercise, you will create a simple financial worksheet that uses tax rates from a table array to calculate the Net Profit. The tax rate calculations have been simplified to make the data easy to understand. You will use Error Checking to locate the source of a formula error.*

## Calculate the Five-Year Growth Using Percentages

1. **Open** the rs-Financial Projections workbook from the Lesson 14 folder.

   *The owner of King's Bakery is projecting sales growth of 27 percent for each of the next five years. These calculations appear in rows 4–9.*

## Use Error Checking and Create a Formula

*The gross profit is equal to the projected sales in row 4 minus the expenses in rows 5–9. You will calculate the gross profit with a formula that uses the SUM function to sum the expenses and then subtracts the result from the projected sales.*

2. In **cell B10**, enter **=B4-(B5:B9)**.

   *Cell B10 should display an error.*

3. Choose **Formulas→Formula Auditing→Error Checking** 🔷 from the Ribbon.

   *Take a moment to read the information on the left side of the Error Checking dialog box, which cannot pinpoint the exact location of the error.*

4. Click the **Show Calculation Steps** button in the dialog box.

   *Cell B4 is evaluated as 400000, which is correct.*

5. Click the **Evaluate** button in the Evaluate Formula dialog box.
*The next formula expression –(B5:B9) evaluates as a #VALUE! error. Evaluating the formula helped to locate the problem area in the formula. The function SUM is missing.*

6. Click **Close** in the Evaluate Formula dialog box.

7. Click the **Edit in Formula Bar** button in the Error Checking dialog box.

8. Click in the **Formula Bar** between the minus (–) sign and the parenthesis, type **SUM,** and tap Enter.
*The result equals $15,000. You may nest functions like SUM inside a formula.*

## Calculate the Total Taxes Using the VLOOKUP Function

9. Drop down the **Name** list to the left of the Formula Bar and choose **Tax_Table**.
*The tax table at the bottom of the worksheet is selected. This table array was assigned the defined name Tax_Table when the worksheet was first created.*

10. In **cell B11**, enter `=B10*VLOOKUP(B10,Tax_Table,2)`.
*The result equals $1,500. In this example, the total taxes are calculated as the gross profit in cell B10 multiplied by the tax rate returned by the VLOOKUP function.*

## Calculate the Net Profit and Format All Cells

11. In **cell B12**, enter a formula to calculate the net profit as Gross Profit–Total Taxes.
*The result equals $13,500.*

12. Use **AutoFill** to copy the formulas in the **range B10:B12** across the rows.
*Rows 10–12 should match the following illustration.*

| 10 | Gross Profit | $ 15,000 | $ 61,850 | $ 127,530 | $ 218,041 | $ 341,148 |
|----|--------------|----------|----------|-----------|-----------|-----------|
| 11 | Total Taxes | $ 1,500 | $ 15,463 | $ 47,186 | $ 85,036 | $ 133,048 |
| 12 | Net Profit | $ 13,500 | $ 46,388 | $ 80,344 | $ 133,005 | $ 208,100 |

13. **Save** the changes and **close** the workbook.

### REINFORCE YOUR SKILLS 14.4

# Use the COUNTIF and COUNTIFS Functions

*In this exercise, you will use the COUNTIF function to count students who achieved a minimum test score on one test and COUNTIFS for multiple tests.*

## Create a COUNTIF Formula

1. **Open** the rs-Test 3 Grades workbook from the Lesson 14 folder.
*In the next steps, you will create a formula to count students who earned at least 70 points on Test 1.*

2. Select **cell C13** and click the **Insert Function** button in the Formula Bar.

3. Choose the **Statistical** category and **double-click** the COUNTIF function in the list.
*The Function Arguments dialog box displays.*

4. Select **cells C4:C11** in the worksheet for Range.

5. Type **>=70** in the Criteria box and click **OK**.

   *The result is 6. Excel added quotation (")
   marks around the criteria in the formula
   =COUNTIF(C4:C11,">=70").*

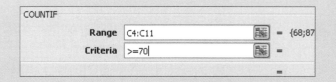

6. Copy the formula in **cell C13** to the **range D13:E13**.

## Create a COUNTIFS Formula

*In the next steps, you will create a formula to count students who earned at least 70 points on every test.
Only records meeting all the criteria in the COUNTIFS formula are counted.*

7. Select **cell E14** and click the **Insert Function** $f_x$ button in the Formula Bar.

8. Choose the **Statistical** category and **double-click** the COUNTIFS (not COUNTIF) function in the list.

   *The Function Arguments dialog box displays.*

9. Select the **range C4:C11** in the worksheet for Criteria Range1.

10. Type **>=70** in the **Criteria1** box.

    *Excel will add quotation (") marks around the criteria when you click the next text box.*

11. Click in the **Criteria Range2** box and select the **range D4:D11** in the worksheet.

12. Copy ">=70" from the **Criteria1** box and paste it in the **Criteria2** box.

13. Click in the **Criteria Range3** box and select the **range E4:E11** in the worksheet.

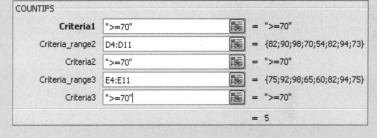

14. Tap [Tab] to display the **Criteria3** box.

    *Only five text boxes display in the dialog box at one time.*

15. Paste ">=70" in the **Criteria3** box.

16. Click **OK**.

    *The result is 5, indicating that five students
    earned a minimum score of 70 on each of the
    three tests. The COUNTIFS function may have
    up to 127 sets of criteria ranges and criteria.*

    *Your worksheet should look like the illustration
    to the right.*

17. **Save** 🖫 the changes and **close** the workbook.

| | A | B | C | D | E |
|---|---|---|---|---|---|
| 1 | **Test 3 Grade Calculations** | | | | |
| 2 | | | | | |
| 3 | **Last** | **First** | **Test 1** | **Test 2** | **Test 3** |
| 4 | Brown | Bernice | 68 | 82 | 75 |
| 5 | Espinoza | Marlo | 87 | 90 | 92 |
| 6 | Kim | Alicia | 95 | 98 | 98 |
| 7 | Lee | Jimmy | 82 | 70 | 65 |
| 8 | Savant | Susan | 34 | 54 | 60 |
| 9 | Soth | Ashley | 91 | 82 | 82 |
| 10 | Sulai | Raj | 94 | 94 | 94 |
| 11 | Warren | Reed | 75 | 73 | 75 |
| 12 | | | | | |
| 13 | **Count >= 70** | | 6 | 7 | 6 |
| 14 | **All tests** | | | | 5 |

# Use the Subtotal Function

*In this exercise, you will filter a list to display students who have taken Level 1 Excel training tests. Then you will use the SUBTOTAL function to count just the filtered records. You also will create a SUBTOTAL formula to find the maximum value among the filtered test values.*

## Name and Filter the List

1. **Open** rs-Training Roster from the Lesson 14 folder.

2. Select **cell C3**, and choose **Data→Sort & Filter→Filter** ▽ from the Ribbon.
   *Each column heading in row 3 displays an AutoFilter button.*

3. In **cell C3**, choose the Level column heading **AutoFilter** ▾ button.

4. Point to **Number Filters** in the context menu, and choose **Equals**.

5. In the **Custom AutoFilter** dialog box, enter **1** and **tap** [Enter] to choose **OK**.
   *There should be eight records showing.*

## Count Filtered Items

6. Select **cell C22**.

7. **Type** the formula **=subtotal(2,c4:c21)** and **tap** [Enter].
   *The result should be 8. The argument 2 performs a count of only the displayed values in the filtered range C4:C21.*

## Find the Maximum Value

8. Copy the formula in **cell C22** to **cell D22**.

9. Edit the formula to change the argument from **2** to **4**.
   *The result should be 100. In the formula =SUBTOTAL(4,D4:D21), the argument 4 performs a MAX function on only the displayed values in the filtered range D4:D21.*

10. Use the **Format Painter** to copy the number formatting from **cell D19** to **cell D22**.

11. Choose **Data→Sort & Filter→Clear** ▨ from the Ribbon to remove the filter.
    *The SUBTOTAL formulas in row 22 recalculate for all 18 records.*

12. **Save** ▨ the changes, and leave the workbook **open**.
    *You will continue to use this workbook in the next exercise.*

# Use the AND and OR Functions

*In this exercise, you will use the AND function to list students who completed Level 1 and earned a score of 100 on the test. You will use the OR function to list students who earned either a score of 100 on the test or a letter grade of A for the class.*

*Before You Begin: You must have completed Reinforce Your Skills 14.5, and the rs-Training Roster workbook should be open.*

## Use the AND Function

1. Type **100 and A** in **cell F3**, and type **100 or A** in **cell G3**.

2. Select **cell F4**, and choose **Formulas→Function Library→Logical** 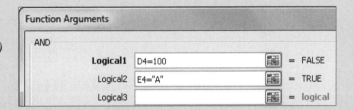 **→AND** from the Ribbon.
   *The Function Arguments dialog box opens. You may use the Function Library as an alternative to using the Insert Function button on the Formula Bar.*

3. Type **D4=100** in the **Logical1** box.

4. Type **E4="A"** in the **Logical2** box, and click **OK**.
   *The formula =AND(D4=100,E4="A") displays in the Formula Bar. The result appears as FALSE because the Logical2 condition was not met.*

5. Use **AutoFill** to copy the formula in **cell F4** to the **range F5:F21**.
   *The result is TRUE in cells F9 and F20. Two students met both conditions.*

## Use the OR Function

6. Select **cell G4**, and choose **Formulas→Function Library→Logical** 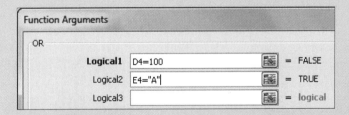 **→OR** from the Ribbon.
   *The Function Arguments dialog box opens.*

7. If necessary, move the **Function Arguments** dialog box out of the way by dragging its title bar until you can see **columns D–G**.

8. For the **Logical1** entry, select **cell D4** in the worksheet and type **=100**.

9. For the **Logical2** entry, select **cell E4** in the worksheet and type **="A"** and then click OK.

*The formula =OR(D4=100,E4="A") displays in the Formula Bar. The result appears as TRUE because either the Logical1 or Logical2 condition was met.*

10. Use **AutoFill** to copy the formula in **cell G4** to the **range G5:G21**.

## Add the IF Function

*Now you will modify the formula by using the IF function to display* Yes *if true or a blank if false.*

11. Select **cell G4**.

12. In the **Formula Bar**, click between the equals (=) sign and O.

13. Taking care to include the parenthesis, type **IF(** and then **tap** the ⌐End⌐ key on the keyboard to position the **insertion point** at the end of the formula.

14. Type **,"Yes","")** and click the **Enter** ☑ button on the Formula Bar to complete the formula.
    *The formula is =IF(OR(D4=100,E4="A","Yes","")). The OR function serves as the argument to be evaluated as true or false by the IF function.*

15. Use **AutoFill** to copy the formula in **cell G4** to the **range G5:G21**; center-align the range.
    *Displaying* Yes *or a blank makes it easier to read the results.*

16. **Save** 🖫 the changes and **close** the workbook.

# Apply Your Skills

## Use Auditing Tools

*In this exercise, you will respond to messages about possible formula errors.*

1. **Open** the as-Vehicle Sales workbook in the Lesson 14 folder.

2. Display the **Robert Sales** worksheet.
   *Cell E15 displays a triangle icon in the upper-left corner of the cell.*

3. Trace precedents for the formula in **cell E15** and determine whether the formula includes the appropriate cell range. Leave the tracer arrow displayed.

4. Use the error checking menu on **cell E15** to review possible causes for the triangle icon alert. Determine whether the formula for new vehicle sales is correct or needs to be changed. Choose an appropriate command in the menu to remove the triangle icon from the cell.

5. Display the **Sales Summary** worksheet.

6. Use the **Error Checking** dialog box to find and repair formulas containing errors. Each linking formula should point to the grand total sales in a salesperson's worksheet.
   *The formula results are shown in the following illustration.*

| | A | B | C |
|---|---|---|---|
| 1 | Ritzer's Auto Sales | | |
| 2 | Sales for January | | |
| 3 | | | |
| 4 | Sales | | |
| 5 | New | | |
| 6 | Used | | |
| 7 | Grand Total | | |
| 8 | | | |
| 9 | | | |
| 10 | | | |
| 11 | | | |
| 12 | Salesperson | | Total Sales |
| 13 | Robert | Bendel | $251,190 |
| 14 | David | Johnson | $122,620 |
| 15 | Gwen | Wenski | $193,160 |

7. **Save** 💾 the changes.
   *You will continue to use this workbook in the next exercise.*

# Create 3-D Cell References

*In this exercise, you will use 3-D cell references in formulas.*

*Before You Begin: You must have completed Apply Your Skills 14.1, and the as-Vehicle Sales workbook should be open.*

1. Display the **Sales Summary** worksheet in the as-Vehicle Sales workbook.

2. In the appropriate cell, create a formula with a **3-D cell reference** that sums new vehicle sales for the three sales-people.

3. Create similar **formulas** for sales of used vehicles and the grand totals.
   *The formula results are shown in the illustration to the right.*

4. **Save** 🖫 the changes and **close** the workbook.

| | A | B |
|---|---|---|
| 1 | Ritzer's Auto Sales | |
| 2 | **Sales for January** | |
| 3 | | |
| 4 | **Sales** | |
| 5 | New | $ 452,780 |
| 6 | Used | $ 114,190 |
| 7 | **Grand Total** | $ 566,970 |

# Create a Table Array and VLOOKUP Function

*In this exercise, you will use the VLOOKUP function to determine how many free rentals the customer receives.*

1. **Open** the as-Frequent Renters workbook from the Lesson 14 folder.

2. Set up the **table array** under the worksheet data as shown here:

| | A | B | C | D | E |
|---|---|---|---|---|---|
| 1 | **Jenco Equipment Rentals - Frequent Renter Awards** | | | | |
| 2 | | | | | |
| 3 | | **Customer** | | **Frequent Renter Points Earned** | **Number of Free Rentals** |
| 4 | Hansen | Leslie | A | 6 | 1 |
| 5 | Liu | Shen | | 17 | 3 |
| 6 | Ortiz | Maria | D | 3 | 0 |
| 7 | Park | Young | Min | 22 | 4 |
| 8 | Randall | Lynn | G | 11 | 2 |
| 9 | Salcedo | Nicolas | | 4 | 0 |
| 10 | Tate | Deborah | M | 14 | 2 |
| 11 | | | | | |
| 12 | | | | **Free Rentals Table** | |
| 13 | | | | **Frequent Renter Points** | **Free Rentals** |
| 14 | | | | 0 | 0 |
| 15 | | | | 5 | 1 |
| 16 | | | | 10 | 2 |
| 17 | | | | 15 | 3 |
| 18 | | | | 20 | 4 |
| 19 | | | | 25 | 5 |

3. Assign the defined name **Free_Rentals_Table** to the table array.

4. Use the VLOOKUP function in **column E** to determine the number of free rentals each customer should receive. The function should use the frequent renter points earned in column D as the lookup value and search the Free_Rentals_Table for the correct number of free rentals.

5. **Save** 🔲 the changes and **close** the workbook.

## Use the NOT Function

*In this exercise, you will create a NOT function to indicate whether a person has or has not worked exactly 40 hours per week.*

1. **Open** the as-Weekly Payroll workbook from the Lesson 14 folder.

2. In **cell I4**, create a NOT function that indicates whether Millie Aberdeen has worked 40 hours this week. The result TRUE or FALSE should display in the cell.

| Reg Hours Worked | Overtime Hourly Rate | Overtime Hours Worked | Gross Pay | Did Not Work 40 hours |
|---|---|---|---|---|
| 40 | $18.00 | 4 | $552.00 | FALSE |

3. Copy the formula in **cell I4** down **column I** for the other employees.
   *A TRUE result indicates the employee did not work exactly 40 hours.*

4. Apply conditional formatting to the **column I** formula cells to draw attention to the TRUE results.

5. **Save** 🔲 the changes and **close** the workbook.

# Critical Thinking & Work-Readiness Skills

*In the course of working through the following Microsoft Office-based Critical Thinking exercises, you will also be utilizing various work-readiness skills, some of which are listed next to each exercise. Go to* labyrinthelab.com/workreadiness *to learn more about the work-readiness skills.*

## 14.1 Use the Error Checking Feature

**WORK-READINESS SKILLS APPLIED**

- Serving customers/clients
- Showing responsibility
- Using computers to process information

Sandra Chavez-Hall, chief development officer for Raritan Clinic East Foundation, requests a daily operating report from her administrative assistant. The report is almost ready to give to Sandra. Your job is to finish it. Open ct-Raritan Clinic East Patient Roster (Lesson 14 folder). Run the error-checking function and fix the two formulas with errors. Make certain the formulas work correctly and that the worksheet contains no errors. Save your work as **ct-Raritan Clinic East Patient Roster [Your Last Name]**. Keep the file open.

## 14.2 Use the COUNTIF Function

**WORK-READINESS SKILLS APPLIED**

- Solving problems
- Using computers to process information
- Organizing and maintaining information

In order to cover appointments for two doctors attending a conference, the operations director needs to check on the number of patients scheduled for doctor appointments today. Open ct-Raritan Clinic East Patient Roster [Your Last Name], if necessary. Create a COUNTIF formula in cell F2 to show how many patients Dr. R. Lawrence has today. In cell F3, show how many patients Dr. J. Ottome has scheduled. Save your work and keep the file open.

## 14.3 Define a Table Array and Use the VLOOKUP Function

**WORK-READINESS SKILLS APPLIED**

- Serving customers/clients
- Using computers to process information
- Reasoning

The operations director is researching drug trials to help patients pay for their medications. In this case, she is examining the Pickard Trial to see how it may help with the specific patients' drug costs. If necessary, open ct-Raritan Clinic East Patient Roster [Your Last Name]. Define data provided in columns L and M as a table array for drug costs that this particular grant will reimburse. Name the table array **Trial_Reimbursement**. Use the VLOOKUP function to create formulas in the range H7:H16. The formulas should look up the drug cost in the table array and return the reimbursement percentage. Conditional formatting has been applied to the formula range. Save and close the file when you are finished.

# Using Advanced Formatting and Analysis Tools

## LESSON OUTLINE

## LEARNING OBJECTIVES

After studying this lesson, you will be able to:

- Group worksheets for efficient data entry
- Consolidate data from multiple worksheets by position and category
- Set data validation rules to restrict data entry
- Remove duplicate records from data
- Create data tables to perform what-if analyses
- Develop trendlines and sparklines to analyze chart data

You can summarize data using such features as linking formulas and 3-D cell references in formulas. In this lesson, you will consolidate data from detail worksheets by position and category. Occasionally, you may need to set up multiple worksheets before data common to all of them are available. You will group worksheets to enter the data into multiple worksheets simultaneously. Many Excel workbooks are designed by experienced users but used by individuals with little Excel experience. Excel's Data Validation tool can assist users of all levels with data entry by forcing values to fall within a specified range. When data are combined or imported from different sources, duplicate records may exist. Excel's Remove Duplicates tool may be used to delete them. Data tables assist with what-if analyses by adjusting variables in a formula. Trendlines are another aid to analysis, helping you perceive and forecast trends in chart data. You also will create sparklines, or mini charts, to present changing data patterns in cells right next to the worksheet data.

# Consolidating and Validating Data

**Raritan Clinic East**

Pediatric Diagnostic Specialists

Sandra Chavez-Hall is the chief development officer at Raritan Clinic East. She will present quarterly fundraising results to the clinic's foundation board using charts and tables, but first she must gather the numbers for the contributions achieved. Sandra needs a workbook to store detailed information in separate sheets. She will use Excel's consolidation feature to summarize the data into a summary sheet without manually creating formulas. In addition, she will use data validation and other tools to format the workbook and create sparklines to show trends in data. Sandra will use a data table to forecast net income for an upcoming fundraising event.

|  | A | B | C | D | E | F |
|---|---|---|---|---|---|---|
| 1 | Raritan Clinic East Pediatric Diagnostic Specialists | **Capital Campaign** | | | | |
| 2 | | **All Sources** | | | | |
| 3 | | | | | | |
| 4 | **Pledge Level** | **Q1** | **Q2** | **Q3** | **Q4** | **By Quarter** |
| 5 | Level 1 | 16,541,676 | 30,201,177 | 32,114,970 | 38,409,659 | |
| 6 | Level 2 | - | 2,000,000 | 2,253,988 | 2,000,075 | |
| 7 | Level 3 | 202,373 | 222,645 | 479,673 | 412,892 | |
| 8 | Level 4 | 100,891 | 50,000 | 51,209 | - | |
| 9 | Level 5 | 8,647 | 13,043 | 17,921 | 18,676 | |
| 10 | Level 6 | 1,262 | 2,889 | 4,600 | 6,435 | |
| 11 | **Total Contributions** | **16,854,849** | **32,489,754** | **34,922,361** | **40,847,737** | **125,114,701** |

A consolidated worksheet summarizing quarterly totals from multiple source sheets

— Sparkline

Variables for tickets sold

|  | A | B | C | D | E | F | G |
|---|---|---|---|---|---|---|---|
| 1 | **Net Income $ Goal** | **Net Income % Goal** | | | | | |
| 2 | $ 75,000 | 70% | | | | | |
| 3 | | | | **Ticket Sales Above (Below) Goal** | | | |
| 4 | | | **Tickets Sold** | | | | |
| 5 | | | 600 | 650 | 700 | 750 | 800 |
| 6 | **Ticket Price** | $ 100 | (33,000) | (29,500) | (26,000) | (22,500) | (19,000) |
| 7 | | $ 150 | (12,000) | (6,750) | (1,500) | 3,750 | 9,000 |
| 8 | | $ 200 | 9,000 | 16,000 | 23,000 | 30,000 | 37,000 |
| 9 | | $ 250 | 30,000 | 38,750 | 47,500 | 56,250 | 65,000 |
| 10 | | $ 300 | 51,000 | 61,500 | 72,000 | 82,500 | 93,000 |

Variables for ticket price

A data table showing the various results when two variables are adjusted in a formula; the data table formula is hidden in cell B5

# 15.1 Working with Grouped Worksheets

**Video Lesson**    labyrinthelab.com/videos

You may temporarily group two or more worksheets to save time when entering data, creating formulas, and formatting worksheets. When worksheets are grouped, whatever you type is entered on all sheets simultaneously. The same is true of formatting. For example, changing the column width on one worksheet also affects the same column on the other grouped worksheets. You may copy data from an ungrouped worksheet and paste to all worksheets in a group.

## Grouping Worksheets

By grouping worksheets, you work with them as a set. For example, imagine that you used a budget template to create a workbook with 12 monthly worksheets. Rather than typing or pasting the same row labels multiple times, you may group the sheets and type the labels just once. You may group contiguous or noncontiguous worksheets using the Shift and Ctrl keys, just as you do when selecting multiple cells. In this lesson, you will work with contiguous worksheets. When worksheets are grouped, their sheet tabs change color, and *[Group]* displays in the window's title bar.

| Quarterly Summary [Group] | | | |
|---|---|---|---|
| A | B | C | D |
| 4 **Pledge Level** | **Q1** | **Q2** | |
| 5 Level 1 | 5,176,926 | 5,026,177 | 9,93 |
| 6 Level 2 | - | - | 1,00 |
| 7 Level 3 | 100,000 | 100,000 | 2 |

Summary    **Cash**    In-Kind    Grants    Ticket Sales

The title bar indicates that worksheets are grouped.

The sheet tabs turn white when worksheets are grouped.

## Ungrouping Worksheets

Grouping and ungrouping actually are selecting and deselecting procedures. The Ungroup Sheets command in the sheet tab pop-up, or context, menu removes the grouping so that you may work in one worksheet at a time.

If all sheets in a workbook are grouped, you may simply click on any sheet tab, other than the first one, to ungroup them.

## DEVELOP YOUR SKILLS 15.1.1

# Group Worksheets

*In this exercise, you will explore the structure of summary and detail worksheets. You will group four worksheets, enter new data, copy existing data, and apply formatting to all sheets simultaneously.*

### Explore the Workbook

1. **Start** Excel and **open** the Quarterly Summary workbook from the Lesson 15 folder in your file storage location.

2. Take a few moments to study the **Summary** and **three source** worksheets.
*The number cells are empty in the Summary sheet. Later in this lesson, these cells will receive data from the Cash, In-Kind, and Grants sheets through the Consolidation command. Some row and column headings are missing from the four worksheets. You will group the worksheets and type the labels once.*

### Group Worksheets

3. Follow these steps to group the four worksheets:

Ⓐ Click the **Summary** sheet tab.

Ⓑ **Hold down** Shift and **click** the Grants sheet tab. **Release** Shift.

*The four sheets are now grouped. Notice [Group] in the title bar and that the grouped sheet tabs are white.*

### Enter Data in Grouped Worksheets

*The ranges A14:A17 and B4:E4 are empty in all four worksheets. You will enter data once into these cells for all grouped worksheets.*

4. In **cell A14**, type **Web/Social Media Development** and **tap** Enter.

5. Continue entering the following labels in **cells A15:A17: Print Materials, Events**, and **Salaries - Grant Proposals**.

6. In **cell B4**, type **Q1** and **right-align** the label. Apply **bold**.

7. Use **AutoFill** to extend the series through **cell E4**.
   *The range B4:E4 should display Q1, Q2, Q3, and Q4.*

8. **Deselect** the highlighted cells.

### Ungroup the Worksheets

9. **Right-click** the Summary sheet tab and choose **Ungroup Sheets** from the context menu.

10. Display each of the **source** worksheets.
    *Notice that the labels you entered in the ranges A14:A17 and B4:E4 are now on all of the worksheets.*

### Copy and Paste Cells to Grouped Worksheets

*Some row headings on the Summary worksheet should be included on the source worksheets.*

11. Display the **Summary** worksheet.

12. Select the **range A5:A10**, and use Ctrl+C to copy.

13. Display the **Cash** worksheet and select **cell A5**, the destination cell.

14. **Hold down** Shift and click the **Grants** sheet tab to select all source sheets.

15. Use Ctrl+V to paste.
    *The labels were pasted to cells A5:A10 in the three source worksheets.*

16. Deselect the cells.

### Format Grouped Worksheets

*Now you will apply formatting to cells in a worksheet group.*

17. Display the **Summary** worksheet.

18. **Tap** Esc to clear the marquee surrounding the **range A5:A10**.

19. **Group** the four worksheets again.

20. Follow these steps to select the desired cells to format:

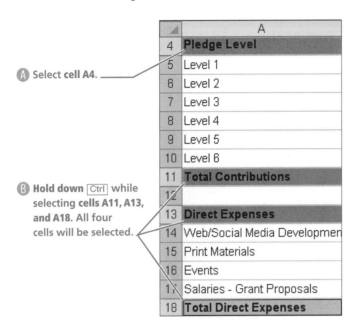

A Select **cell A4**.

B Hold down Ctrl while selecting **cells A11, A13, and A18**. All four cells will be selected.

21. Choose **Home→Styles→Cell Styles→Themed Cell Styles→20% - Accent6**, and then apply **Bold** from the Ribbon.
    *The selected cells display a light purple fill.*

22. **Deselect** the cells.

23. Take a few moments to view the changes that were made to each worksheet.
    *All the worksheets should have the same formatting as the Summary sheet.*

24. Experiment with **grouping** and **ungrouping** contiguous and noncontiguous sheets.
    *Remember, use the Shift key to group contiguous sheets and the Ctrl key to group noncontiguous sheets.*

25. When finished, make certain to **ungroup** the worksheets.

26. **Save** the changes, and leave the workbook **open**.

# 15.2 Consolidating Worksheet Data

Video Lesson    labyrinthelab.com/videos

Excel's Consolidate  command combines values from source worksheets into a destination worksheet. You select an entire range, and all its value and formula cells (but not text cells) are consolidated simultaneously to the destination worksheet. Only one range may be consolidated from each source worksheet. The calculation results are values rather than formulas unless you select the Create Links to Source Data option. When the results are values, you must repeat the Consolidate command if values change later in the source worksheets. You may redisplay the Consolidate dialog box to add a reference range for any worksheet added to the workbook, and you may delete any reference range.

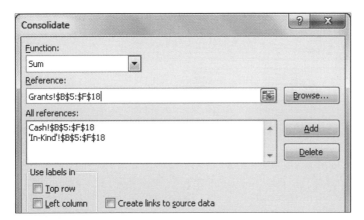

A consolidation reference being created to the Grants worksheet in the Consolidate dialog box

The Browse button in the Consolidate dialog box allows you to navigate to other workbooks and consolidate data from them.

## Consolidation Functions

The SUM function is the most commonly used consolidation function. You also may use AVERAGE, MIN, MAX, and some other statistical functions when consolidating. You choose the desired function in the Consolidate dialog box when you set up the consolidation.

## Types of Consolidation

You may consolidate data using either of the following methods:

- **By Position**—This method is useful when all worksheets have the same layout. To consolidate by position, specify the same range in all worksheets. Excel uses the function you choose to consolidate values in the same cell of each of the specified worksheets.

- **By Category**—This method is used when the supporting worksheets have different layouts but identical row or column labels that refer to the common data. A worksheet may contain labels for categories that other worksheets do not include. Excel uses the row and column headings to determine which rows or columns to consolidate with the other consolidation ranges you specify. The consolidation produces one row or column in the summary sheet for each unique row or column encountered in the supporting sheets. The consolidated data contains no blank rows or text formatting from the source worksheets, but you can format the summary sheet results after the consolidation.

# Creating Links to Source Data

By default, consolidated data is not linked to the source cells. The Create Links to Source Data option does create linking formulas on the summary worksheet. For example, cell C5 contains the linking formula =Cash!$B$5 as shown in the following illustration. The consolidated data are formatted as an outline that may be expanded to view the source data or collapsed to view the totals. Any changes to source data on the original worksheets will update in the summary sheet.

Level 1 is expanded to display the data from three source worksheets, one sheet per row. The source workbook name for each sheet displays in column B. All three sheets are in the same Quarterly Summary workbook in this example.

Cell C5 in the Summary sheet contains a linking formula to refer to the cell B5 value in the Cash worksheet.

The Level 1 total for Q1 is the sum of the three linked cells in the range C5:C7.

| C5 | | fx =Cash!$B$5 | | |
|---|---|---|---|---|
| | A | B | C | D | E |
| 4 | Pledge Level | | Q1 | Q2 | |
| 5 | | Quarterly Summary | 5,176,926 | 5,026,177 | 9,9 |
| 6 | | Quarterly Summary | 11,364,750 | 21,175,000 | 22,1 |
| 7 | | Quarterly Summary | - | - | |
| 8 | Level 1 | | 16,541,676 | 30,201,177 | 32,1 |
| 12 | Level 2 | | - | 2,000,000 | 2,2 |
| 16 | Level 3 | | 202,373 | 222,645 | 4 |

The labels for each quarter were entered manually after the consolidation. Only values are transferred from the source sheets.

Data consolidated by category and linked in an outline format to the source data

The column A text labels are included in the summary because the Left Column option was selected in the Consolidate dialog box to create a consolidation by category.

| QUICK REFERENCE | CONSOLIDATING DATA |
|---|---|
| **Task** | **Procedure** |
| Consolidate by position or category | ■ Select a cell in the destination worksheet to be used as the starting point for the consolidation. *By category:* This range should include column and/or row labels. |
| | ■ Choose Data→Data Tools→Consolidate from the Ribbon. |
| | ■ Choose a consolidation function (usually SUM) in the Consolidate dialog box. |
| | ■ Click in the Reference box. |
| | ■ Click the sheet tab of the first source worksheet and select the data range. *By category:* The range must include either row or column labels. |
| | ■ Click the Add button to add the range to the All References list. |
| | ■ Click the next source sheet tab, and click Add to add the same range to the All References list. *By category:* Select a different range, if desired. |
| | ■ Continue adding the remaining source sheet ranges. *By category:* Place a checkmark in the Top Row box in the Use Labels In area if you included column labels or in the Left Column box if you included row labels. |
| | ■ Place a checkmark in the Create Links to Source Data box, if desired, and click OK. Using this option avoids having to update the consolidation manually after changes are made to the source data. |
| | ■ Format the consolidated data in the summary sheet as necessary. |
| Update the consolidation manually after changing values in source worksheets | ■ Choose Data→Data Tools→Consolidate from the Ribbon and click OK. |

# Consolidate Data

*In this exercise, you will use the Consolidate command to consolidate the pledge level contributions and expenses related to fund raising. You will consolidate from the Cash, In-Kind, and Grants worksheets by position. This is possible because all worksheets have the same layout.*

## Consolidate by Position

1. Display the **Summary** worksheet in the Quarterly Summary workbook.

2. Select **cell B5** as the starting point for the consolidated data.

3. Choose **Data→Data Tools→Consolidate** from the Ribbon.

4. If necessary, move the **Consolidate** dialog box until **cell B5** in the Summary sheet and the sheet tabs at the bottom of the Excel window are visible.

5. Follow these steps to set consolidation options in the Consolidate dialog box:

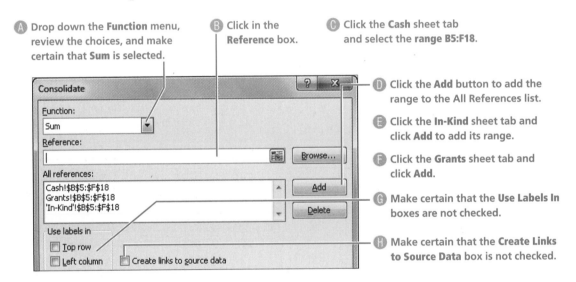

Ⓐ Drop down the **Function** menu, review the choices, and make certain that **Sum** is selected.

Ⓑ Click in the **Reference** box.

Ⓒ Click the **Cash** sheet tab and select the **range B5:F18**.

Ⓓ Click the **Add** button to add the range to the All References list.

Ⓔ Click the **In-Kind** sheet tab and click **Add** to add its range.

Ⓕ Click the **Grants** sheet tab and click **Add**.

Ⓖ Make certain that the **Use Labels In** boxes are not checked.

Ⓗ Make certain that the **Create Links to Source Data** box is not checked.

*Review the references in the All References list. You build a consolidation range by adding references to this list.*

6. Click **OK**.

*Excel consolidates the data into the Summary sheet. The Summary worksheet should display the consolidated numbers shown in the following illustration.*

| 4 | Pledge Level | Q1 | Q2 | Q3 | Q4 | |
|---|---|---|---|---|---|---|
| 5 | Level 1 | 16,541,676 | 30,201,177 | 32,114,970 | 38,409,659 | |
| 6 | Level 2 | - | 2,000,000 | 2,253,988 | 2,000,075 | |
| 7 | Level 3 | 202,373 | 222,645 | 479,673 | 412,892 | |
| 8 | Level 4 | 100,891 | 50,000 | 51,209 | - | |
| 9 | Level 5 | 8,647 | 13,043 | 17,921 | 18,676 | |
| 10 | Level 6 | 1,262 | 2,889 | 4,600 | 6,435 | |
| 11 | Total Contributions | 16,854,849 | 32,489,754 | 34,922,361 | 40,847,737 | 125,114,701 |
| 12 | | | | | | |
| 13 | Direct Expenses | | | | | |
| 14 | Web/Social Media Developmen | 3,500 | 3,500 | 3,500 | 37,000 | |
| 15 | Print Materials | 947 | 977 | 1,699 | 864 | |
| 16 | Events | 12,589 | 22,753 | 10,465 | 45,872 | |
| 17 | Salaries - Grant Proposals | 6,000 | 6,000 | 6,000 | 6,000 | |
| 18 | Total Direct Expenses | 23,036 | 33,230 | 21,664 | 89,736 | 167,666 |

## Examine the Results

*Notice that the number format in the range B5:F18 was transferred from the source worksheets sheets to the summary sheet. The bold text formatting, however, was not transferred.*

7. Select any cell in the **range B5:F18** in the Summary worksheet.

*The Formula Bar displays a value rather than a formula. The Consolidate command sums the values in the specified ranges and enters the results as values in the Summary sheet. You would need to give the Consolidate command again if the numbers in the detail worksheets were updated. Assume that you did not switch on Create Links to Source Data in the Consolidate dialog box because you will not update the data.*

8. **Save** 🖫 the changes, and leave the workbook **open**.

# 15.3 Working with Data Validation

Video Lesson | labyrinthelab.com/videos

Excel's data validation tool lets you restrict data entry in cells. The default validation setting for a cell is Any Value, meaning that until you specify a validation setting and criteria, any value may be entered in the cell.

## Restricting Data Entry Using Criteria

You may restrict both the type and range of acceptable values. For example, you may want to restrict data entry to whole numbers between 0 and 100,000. You may also create an input message and error alert message to guide the user in entering acceptable data. An input message appears whenever the restricted cell is selected. An error message appears whenever data entry is attempted and the data is not of the correct type or within the accepted range.

Data validation operates only when the user attempts to type directly in a cell. No alert occurs when cell contents result from using the fill handle, Paste command, or an incorrect cell reference in a formula.

The following table describes the available validation criteria.

| Type | Entries Must Be |
| --- | --- |
| Any Value | No restrictions; may display an input message without checking for valid entries |
| Custom | A formula, expression, or reference to a calculation in another cell |
| Dates | Dates |
| Decimal | Numbers or fractions |
| List | Only those in a specified list |
| Text Length | A specific number of characters |
| Time | Times |
| Whole Number | Integers without decimal places |

If the values in the worksheet are formatted with decimal places, use Decimal rather than Whole Number.

## Copying a Data Validation Rule

A data validation rule must be created while a single worksheet is selected and cannot be set up while worksheets are grouped. You may, however, copy a cell containing a validation rule. Then, you may use the Validation option of the Paste Special command on the Ribbon to apply a data validation rule from that cell to other cells on the same worksheet, another sheet, or grouped sheets. You may edit a validation rule. The Apply These Changes to All Other Cells with the Same Settings option in the Data Validation dialog box updates cells only in the active worksheet. You must use the Validation option of the Paste Special command to apply the revised rule to cells on other sheets.

# Set Up Data Validation

*In this exercise, you will set up data validation in a specified cell range and create an error alert message for incorrect entry attempts. You will use the Text Length option to restrict the Level 1–6 label entries. You also will create a data validation rule using a drop-down list to indicate that each fundraising goal was met or not met.*

## Set Data Validation for Numeric Entries

*First, you will set up a data validation rule for the direct expense values. You usually would set up the rule before entering the data, but you will reenter some values to test the rule.*

1. Display the **Cash** worksheet of the Quarterly Summary workbook.

2. Select the values in the **range B14:E17** as shown in the following illustration. (Make certain that the expense labels in column A and the total cells in row 18 are **not** selected.)

| | A | B | C | D | E |
|---|---|---|---|---|---|
| 14 | Web/Social Media Development | 1,500 | 1,500 | 1,500 | 35,000 |
| 15 | Print Materials | 500 | 500 | 500 | 563 |
| 16 | Events | 12,321 | 22,753 | 10,465 | 45,657 |
| 17 | Salaries - Grant Proposals | - | - | - | - |
| 18 | **Total Direct Expenses** | **14,321** | **24,753** | **12,465** | **81,220** |

3. Choose **Data→Data Tools→Data Validation** 🔲 from the Ribbon.

4. Follow these steps to set the data entry restrictions:

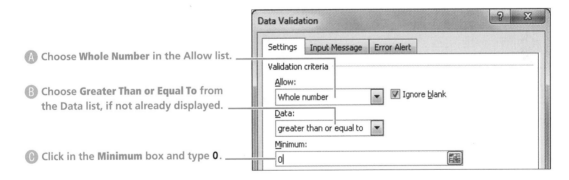

Ⓐ Choose **Whole Number** in the Allow list.

Ⓑ Choose **Greater Than or Equal To** from the Data list, if not already displayed.

Ⓒ Click in the **Minimum** box and type **0**.

5. Display the **Input Message** tab in the dialog box.
   *Notice that you may create an input message that appears whenever a restricted cell is selected. You will not use this option in this exercise. You will use an error alert message instead.*

6. Display the **Error Alert** tab.

7. Follow these steps to set an error alert message:

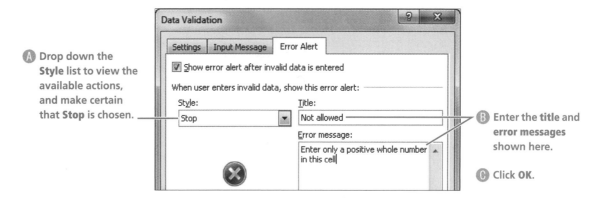

**A** Drop down the **Style** list to view the available actions, and make certain that **Stop** is chosen.

**B** Enter the **title** and **error messages** shown here.

**C** Click **OK**.

## Test the Data Validation

8. Select **cell B14** in the **Cash** sheet.

9. **Type** the negative number **–1000** and **tap** Enter.
   *The error alert message appears. The data validation restriction allows you to enter only a positive whole number in this cell.*

10. Click the **Retry** button in the message box.
    *Retry lets you edit an incorrect entry, while Cancel deletes the entry.*

11. Type **1000.50** and **tap** Enter.
    *Once again, the entry is not accepted because it is not a whole number.*

12. Click the **Retry** button and **enter** the original number **1500**.

## Validate Label Entries Using Text Length

13. Select the **range A5:A10**.
    *Notice that all text entries are seven characters in length in the selected range. You will create a data validation rule based on the text length.*

14. Choose **Data→Data Tools→Data Validation** 📋 from the Ribbon.

15. Follow these steps to set up the data entry restriction:

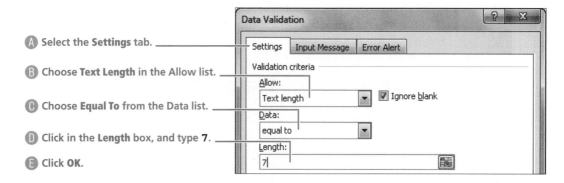

**A** Select the **Settings** tab.

**B** Choose **Text Length** in the Allow list.

**C** Choose **Equal To** from the Data list.

**D** Click in the **Length** box, and type **7**.

**E** Click **OK**.

*You did not set an input message, and the default error alert message will apply for this rule.*

16. Select **cell A5**.

17. Type **Level 22** and **tap** Enter.
    *The default error message displays.*

18. Click the **Cancel** button in the error message
    dialog box to leave the original entry
    unchanged.

## Copy and Paste a Data Validation Rule

*You cannot set up a data validation rule while sheets are grouped, but you may paste a validation format to a range in a group.*

19. **Right-click** cell B14, and choose **Copy** from the context menu.
    *This cell is formatted with the data validation rule for direct expense values you set up. In the next few steps, you will apply only the validation formatting to the direct expenses range of the In-Kind and Grants worksheets.*

20. Select the **In-Kind** sheet tab, **hold down** Shift, and
    select the **Grants** sheet tab.
    *The two grouped sheet tabs have a white background.*

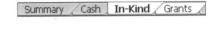

21. Select the **range B14:E17**.

22. Choose **Home→Clipboard→Paste menu ▼→Paste Special** from the Ribbon.
    *If an error message appears because you chose the Paste command rather than the Paste menu, click Cancel and repeat this step.*

23. Choose **Validation** in the Paste
    Special dialog box, and click **OK**.

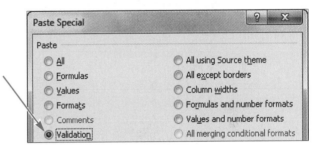

24. Select **cell B14** to deselect the range in
    both grouped sheets.

25. **Right-click** the Grants sheet tab, and
    choose **Ungroup Sheets** from the
    context menu.
    *Now only the Grants worksheet is active.*

26. Type **web** in cell B14 of the **Grants** worksheet, and **tap** Enter.
    *The Not Allowed error message displays because you applied the data validation rule.*

27. Click **Cancel** in the error message dialog box to restore the original value.

28. **Save** 💾 the changes, and leave the workbook **open**.

# Creating Drop-Down Lists for Data Entry

Video Lesson    labyrinthelab.com/videos

The data validation List option allows you to restrict data entry for a cell to a choice contained in a drop-down list. For example, the acceptable entries for a product's status could be *In Stock* and *Reorder*. An error message displays if the user attempts to type an entry.

## *Specifying List Items*

You may type the list items separated by commas (,) in the Data Validation dialog box. As a recommended alternative, you may enter the list choices in cells down a column of a worksheet and give the range where the entries are stored. Revising the list choices often is easier with the in-worksheet method. Including a blank cell at the end of the list range allows the user to reset the cell contents to a blank when appropriate. You may wish to lock the cell range containing the list entries and turn on worksheet protection (see the Excel Help topic about locking cells and protecting a worksheet, if necessary).

## *Specifying Other Options*

The In-Cell Dropdown option must be checked for the drop-down list to be displayed in the specified cells. The Ignore Blanks option must be unchecked if you wish to prevent users from typing entries in cells formatted with a list.

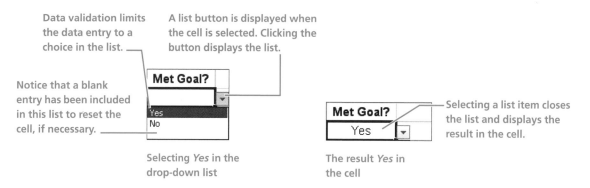

Data validation limits the data entry to a choice in the list.

A list button is displayed when the cell is selected. Clicking the button displays the list.

Notice that a blank entry has been included in this list to reset the cell, if necessary.

Selecting *Yes* in the drop-down list

Selecting a list item closes the list and displays the result in the cell.

The result *Yes* in the cell

| QUICK REFERENCE | VALIDATING DATA ENTRIES |
|---|---|
| **Task** | **Procedure** |
| Set validation criteria and messages except for a list | ■ Select the cells to be validated. |
| | ■ Choose Data→Data Tools→Data Validation ▦ from the Ribbon. |
| | ■ Choose the desired category from the Allow list. (Choose Custom if you wish to enter a formula.) |
| | ■ Choose the criteria for data to be entered in the cells. |
| | ■ If desired, set an input message and/or error alert message using the tabs in the Data Validation dialog box. |

| Task | Procedure |
|---|---|
| Set validation criteria and messages for a list | ■ Type the list items in a named worksheet range. The range may include a blank entry, if desired.<br><br>■ Select the cells to be validated.<br><br>■ Choose Data→Data Tools→Data Validation ▦ from the Ribbon.<br><br>■ Choose List from the Allow list.<br><br>■ Remove the checkmark next to Ignore Blank, and place a checkmark next to In-Cell Dropdown.<br><br>■ Click in the Source box, and select the named range containing the list items in the worksheet.<br><br>■ If desired, set an input message and/or error alert message using the tabs in the Data Validation dialog box. |
| Copy a validation rule to other cells | ■ Right-click the cell containing the validation rule, and choose Copy from the context menu.<br><br>■ Select the cell range that will receive the validation formatting.<br><br>■ Choose Home→Clipboard→Paste menu ▼→Paste Special from the Ribbon.<br><br>■ Choose the Validation option in the Paste Special dialog box. |
| Locate cells formatted with data validation rules in the active worksheet | ■ Choose Home→Editing→Find & Select ▦→Validation from the Ribbon. The data validation cells will be selected. |

# Use a Drop-Down List

*In this exercise, you will set data validation to restrict data entry to items in a drop-down list.*

### Create and Name the List

1. Display the **Summary** worksheet of the Quarterly Summary workbook.

2. Type **Yes** in **cell G1**.

3. Type **No** in **cell G2**.

4. Select the **range G1:G3**.
   *This range will contain the entries in the drop-down list. Notice that you included a blank cell so users may reset a cell to a blank when necessary.*

5. Click in the **Name** box to the left of the Formula Bar.

6. Type **List** and **tap** ⏎ Enter to assign the name to the range.

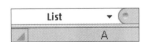

### Set Data Validation

7. In **cell G4**, type **Met Goal?** Center align the entry, and choose **bold**, if necessary.

8. Select the **range G5:G10**; **center-align** the cells.
   *The range should still be selected.*

9. Choose **Data→Data Tools→Data Validation** ▦ from the Ribbon.

10. Follow these steps to set up the data entry restriction:

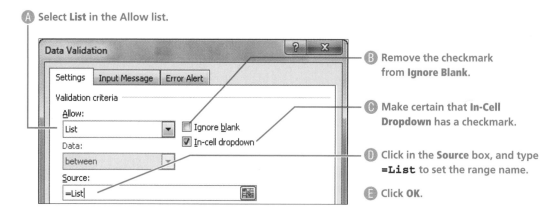

Ⓐ Select **List** in the Allow list.

Ⓑ Remove the checkmark from **Ignore Blank**.

Ⓒ Make certain that **In-Cell Dropdown** has a checkmark.

Ⓓ Click in the **Source** box, and type **=List** to set the range name.

Ⓔ Click **OK**.

*You did not enter an input message, and the default error alert message will be used.*

## Use the List to Enter Data

11. Select **cell G5**.

12. Follow these steps to enter data from the drop-down list:

Ⓐ Click the **drop-down list button**.

Ⓑ Choose **Yes** from the list.

Ⓒ Verify that **Yes** displays in the cell.

13. Select **cell G6**, and choose **No** from the in-cell drop-down list.

14. Select **cell G7**, and choose **No**.
*Assume that now you wish to reset this entry to a blank until you obtain more information.*

15. Click the **drop-down list button** on **cell G7**, and choose the **blank item** below No.
*Cell G7 is now blank. Providing a blank choice in the list allows the user to reset the cell entry.*

16. Select **cell G8**, type **Maybe**, and **tap** ⌑Enter⌑.
*An error message appears because you unchecked the Ignore Blanks option in the Data Validation dialog box. With the option off, the user is not allowed to type an entry into the cell.*

17. Read the error message, and click **Cancel**.

18. **Save** 🖫 the changes, and leave the workbook **open**.

# 15.4 Circling Invalid Data

**Video Lesson**   labyrinthelab.com/videos

At times, data may already be entered in worksheet cells before data validation rules are created. Some cells then may contain invalid data, so you should use the Circle Invalid Data command to find them. The command does just what the name implies: it places circles around any data that does not conform to the validation rules set for the cells. Once the data is circled, you may ignore or correct an entry. The red circles are easy to spot and do not print.

Circles around invalid data are temporary. Even if you don't clear the circles before you close the file, they will be gone when you reopen the file. You may, however, choose the Circle Invalid Data command again.

| QUICK REFERENCE | CIRCLING INVALID DATA |
| --- | --- |
| **Task** | **Procedure** |
| Circle invalid data entered prior to creation of validation rules | ■ Choose Data→Data Tools→Data Validation menu ▼→ Circle Invalid Data from the Ribbon.   ■ Edit or ignore circled cells, as desired. |
| Remove validation circles | ■ Perform any one of the following:   ◆ Enter valid data in the cells.   ◆ Choose Data→Data Tools→Data Validation menu ▼→ Clear Validation Circles from the Ribbon.   ◆ Close the workbook. |

## DEVELOP YOUR SKILLS 15.4.1
## Circle Invalid Data

*In this exercise, you will reset data validation for a range of cells and then circle invalid data. You will edit values flagged as invalid. Finally, you will consolidate data again to update the totals on the Summary sheet.*

### Change Data Validation for a Range

*In the first steps, you will revise a data validation rule only for the expense values in the Cash worksheet.*

1. Display the **Cash** worksheet of the Quarterly Summary workbook.

2. Taking care not to select the totals in row 18, select the expense values in the **range B14:E17**.

3. Choose **Data→Data Tools→Data Validation** from the Ribbon.

4. Display the **Settings** tab in the Data Validation dialog box, if necessary.
   *Recall that you set validation options to a whole positive number earlier in this lesson.*

5. Follow these steps to restrict expense values to a maximum of $32,000:

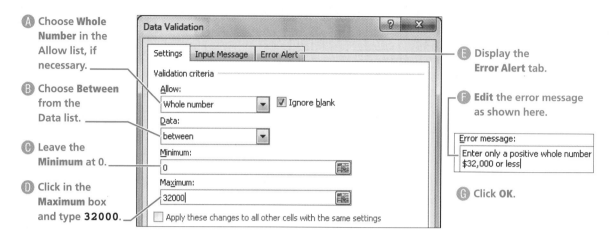

Ⓐ Choose **Whole Number** in the Allow list, if necessary.

Ⓑ Choose **Between** from the Data list.

Ⓒ Leave the **Minimum** at 0.

Ⓓ Click in the **Maximum** box and type **32000**.

Ⓔ Display the **Error Alert** tab.

Ⓕ **Edit** the error message as shown here.

Ⓖ Click **OK**.

## Test Data Validation

6. Enter **41500** in **cell B15**.

7. Read the error message, click **Retry,** and enter **1200**.

## Circle Invalid Data

8. Choose **Data→Data Tools→Data Validation menu ▼→Circle Invalid Data** 📇 from the Ribbon.
   *Red circles appear around the cells that do not meet the validation set for those cells.*

| 13 | Direct Expenses | | | | |
|----|-----------------|-------|--------|--------|--------|
| 14 | Web/Social Media Development | 1,500 | 1,500 | 1,500 | 35,000 |
| 15 | Print Materials | 1,200 | 500 | 500 | 563 |
| 16 | Events | 12,321 | 22,753 | 10,465 | 45,657 |
| 17 | Salaries - Grant Proposals | - | - | - | - |

9. Select **cell E14** and enter **1500**.
   *Notice that the red circle disappeared after you completed a valid entry.*

## Clear Validation Circles

10. Leave the value in **cell E16** as is.
    *At times you may want to keep previous values in the worksheet even if they do not meet the validation rules.*

11. Choose **Data→Data Tools→Data Validation menu ▼→Clear Validation Circles**  from the Ribbon.
    *The remaining validation circle disappears.*

### Consolidate Data

*You edited some values on the Cash worksheet in this exercise. Recall that a consolidated worksheet is not updated automatically unless the links option is switched on. In the next few steps, you will consolidate data again manually on the Summary worksheet.*

12. Display the **Summary** worksheet.
    *Notice that the direct expense total in cell F18 is 167,666 from the previous consolidation.*

13. Select **cell B5**.
    *Cell B5 is the starting cell in the consolidation cell range B5:F18.*

14. Choose **Data→Data Tools→Consolidate**  from the Ribbon.
    *The Consolidate dialog box appears with the ranges still set for the Cash, Grants, and In-Kind worksheets.*

15. Click **OK**.
    *The sums are recalculated, and cell F18 should display 134,866.*

16. **Save** 💾 the changes, and **close** the workbook.

## 15.5 Removing Duplicate Records

**Video Lesson**   labyrinthelab.com/videos

When you combine or import records into a worksheet, duplicate records may then exist in multiple rows of the worksheet. Excel provides several methods to identify and remove duplicates that contain the same cell entries as those in another row. The records are not considered duplicates if the data are formatted differently.

> **NOTE**
> Filtering for unique records does not delete any duplicate records, but the Remove Duplicates command does delete them.

### Filtering for Unique Records

You may perform an advanced filter to temporarily hide duplicate records. You may filter a list or table in place, as shown in the following illustration. You also may choose to copy unique records to another area of the same worksheet or a different worksheet.

Duplicate records in rows 5 and 7 are hidden temporarily.

|   | A | B | C |
|---|---|---|---|
| 3 | **Pledge Level** | **Team Leader** | **Sponsor Category** |
| 4 | Level 5 | Abbott | Organization Contrib |
| 6 | Level 4 | Faber | Corporate Sponsors |
| 8 | Level 1 | Lemus | Federal Government |
| 9 | Level 3 | Faber | Corporate Sponsors |
| 10 | Level 6 | Nguyen | Individual Contributio |

The result of an advanced filter for unique records

# Removing Duplicates

The Remove Duplicates ▦ command on the Ribbon deletes duplicate records from a list. You specify the columns in which Excel is to look for an exact match. Choosing all columns will ensure that only the records that match in every cell will be deleted. You may undo the action if the result is not what you expect.

| QUICK REFERENCE | FILTERING AND REMOVING DUPLICATE RECORDS |
|---|---|
| **Task** | **Procedure** |
| Filter to hide duplicate records in a list or table | ■ Select any cell in the list or table. <br> ■ Choose Data→Sort & Filter→Advanced ▦ from the Ribbon. <br> ■ Verify that the default list range is correct in the Advanced Filter dialog box. <br> ■ Choose to filter the list in place or copy to another location. <br> ■ Place a checkmark next to Unique Records Only. |
| Remove duplicate records from a list or table | ■ Select any cell in the list or table. <br> ■ Choose Data→Data Tools→Remove Duplicates ▦ from the Ribbon. <br> ■ Verify that a checkmark is next to My Data Has Headers if column headings are included as the first row of data. <br> ■ Select the desired columns that contain duplicate data. (Select all columns to require an exact match of all data in rows.) |

DEVELOP YOUR SKILLS 15.5.1

# Filter Unique Records and Remove Duplicates

*In this exercise, you will perform an advanced filter to hide duplicate records. You also will remove duplicates permanently.*

## Perform an Advanced Filter

1. **Open** the Combined Contributions workbook from the Lesson 15 folder.
   *Duplicate records exist in rows 4–5 and 6–7.*

2. Select **cell D4**.

3. Choose **Data→Sort & Filter→Advanced** ▦ from the Ribbon.

4. Follow these steps to filter the list for unique records:

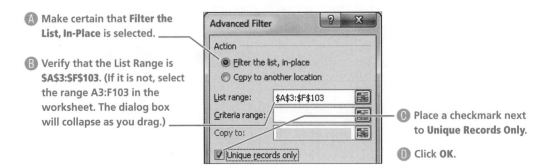

Ⓐ Make certain that **Filter the List, In-Place** is selected.

Ⓑ Verify that the List Range is **$A$3:$F$103**. (If it is not, select the range A3:F103 in the worksheet. The dialog box will collapse as you drag.)

Ⓒ Place a checkmark next to **Unique Records Only.**

Ⓓ Click **OK.**

*The duplicate rows 5 and 7 are hidden, and the Status Bar at the lower-left corner of the window indicates that 98 unique records were found.*

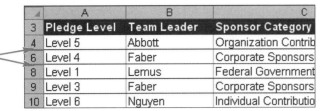

5. Choose **Data→Sort & Filter→Clear** from the Ribbon.
   *The duplicate records reappear in the list. Filtering did not delete the records.*

## Remove Duplicates

6. Make certain that **cell D4** or another cell in the list is selected.

7. Choose **Data→Data Tools→Remove Duplicates** from the Ribbon.

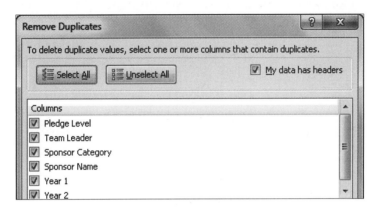

*Notice that all columns are selected with a checkmark in the Remove Duplicates dialog box.*

8. Make certain **My Data Has Headers** has a checkmark in the upper-right corner of the dialog box, and click **OK**.
   *Excel looks for an exact match in all columns of records to find duplicate rows.*

9. Read the message indicating that two records were removed, and click **OK**.
   *The Remove Duplicates command deleted the records without asking for confirmation. You could undo the command if the results were incorrect.*

10. **Save** and **close** the workbook.

# 15.6 Using Data Tables

**Video Lesson**   labyrinthelab.com/videos

Data tables are different from the tables that allow you to sort, filter, and create totals for data. Data tables preview the effect that changing some values would have on a formula's result. A data table is structured around a specific formula to perform a what-if analysis. Various values from a list are substituted for either one or two cell references in the formula. The Data Table command calculates the formula result for each value listed.

## One-Variable Data Tables

One-variable data tables compute results for various values substituted for a cell reference in a formula. For example, the data table may display the result for a FV (Future Value) formula with the monthly payment as a variable in increments of $20. This example is shown in the following illustration, where the empty Payment cell (B5) is known as the input cell. Each value from Payment column C of the data table is substituted in the input cell, and its corresponding Future Value result displays in column D.

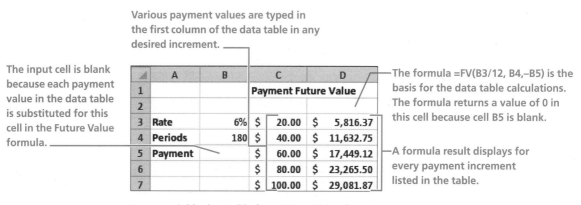

Various payment values are typed in the first column of the data table in any desired increment.

The input cell is blank because each payment value in the data table is substituted for this cell in the Future Value formula.

The formula =FV(B3/12, B4,–B5) is the basis for the data table calculations. The formula returns a value of 0 in this cell because cell B5 is blank.

A formula result displays for every payment increment listed in the table.

A one-variable data table for a Future Value formula

## Two-Variable Data Tables

You will work with two-variable data tables in this lesson. While a one-variable data table has one input cell, this type has two input cells. Values are substituted for two cell references in the formula. The following illustration shows the layout of a two-variable data table using the same Future Value formula as in the previous example. Take a few moments to review this illustration carefully.

The formula =FV(B3/12, B4,–B5) is the basis for the data table calculations. The formula returns a value of 0 in this cell because cells B3 and B5 are blank.

Various payment values are typed into the first column of the data table, and rates are entered into the first row.

The input cells are blank because each rate and payment value in the data table are substituted for these cells in the Future Value formula.

| ▲ | A | B | C | D | E | F | G |
|---|---|---|---|---|---|---|---|
| 1 | | | Payment | Future Value | | | |
| 2 | | | $ - | 4% | 5% | 6% | 7% |
| 3 | Rate | | $ 20.00 | $ 4,921.81 | $ 5,345.78 | $ 5,816.37 | $ 6,339.25 |
| 4 | Periods | 180 | $ 40.00 | $ 9,843.62 | $ 10,691.56 | $ 11,632.75 | $ 12,678.49 |
| 5 | Payment | | $ 60.00 | $ 14,765.43 | $ 16,037.34 | $ 17,449.12 | $ 19,017.74 |
| 6 | | | $ 80.00 | $ 19,687.24 | $ 21,383.12 | $ 23,265.50 | $ 25,356.98 |
| 7 | | | $ 100.00 | $ 24,609.05 | $ 26,728.89 | $ 29,081.87 | $ 31,696.23 |

A two-variable data table for a Future Value formula

A formula result displays for every combination of rate and payment listed in the table.

## QUICK REFERENCE — CREATING DATA TABLES

| Task | Procedure |
|---|---|
| Create a one-variable data table | ▪ Enter a formula in the worksheet. The formula must include a reference to one input cell outside the data table. |
| | ▪ Enter input variable values down the column (under the formula cell) to substitute for one cell address in the formula. |
| | ▪ Select the data table, including the formula cell, all input variable values, and the cells that will hold the calculated results. |
| | ▪ Choose Data→Data Tools→What-If Analysis 📊→Data Table from the Ribbon. |
| | ▪ In the Data Table dialog box, specify the column input cell that is outside the data table and used in the formula. |
| Create a two-variable data table | ▪ Enter a formula as the upper-left cell in the data table. The formula must include references to two input cells outside the data table. |
| | ▪ Enter input variable values across the first row (to the right of the formula cell) to substitute for one cell address in the formula. |
| | ▪ Enter input variable values down the first column (under the formula cell) to substitute for one cell address in the formula. |
| | ▪ Select the data table, including the formula cell, all input variable values, and the cells that will hold the calculated results. |
| | ▪ Choose Data→Data Tools→What-If Analysis 📊→Data Table from the Ribbon. In the Data Table dialog box, specify the row input cell and column input cell that are outside the data table and used in the formula. |

## Create a Two-Variable Data Table

*In this exercise, you will create a data table with two variables. The data table formula will calculate the amount above or below the net income goal for a fundraising event for each combination of ticket price and tickets sold.*

### Set Up the Data Table

1. **Open** a new, blank workbook.

2. Enter the following data into **Sheet1**, formatting the numbers and text as shown.

| | A | B | C | D | E | F | G |
|---|---|---|---|---|---|---|---|
| 1 | Net Income $ Goal | Net Income % Goal | | | | | |
| 2 | $ 75,000 | 70% | | | | | |
| 3 | | | | Ticket Sales Above (Below) Goal | | | |
| 4 | | | Tickets Sold | | | | |
| 5 | | | 600 | 650 | 700 | 750 | 800 |
| 6 | Ticket Price | $ 100 | | | | | |
| 7 | | $ 150 | | | | | |
| 8 | | $ 200 | | | | | |
| 9 | | $ 250 | | | | | |
| 10 | | $ 300 | | | | | |

*A two-variable data table is always set up this way. One set of variables is placed immediately to the right of the formula (the tickets sold from 600 to 800 in this exercise). The other set of variables is placed immediately below the formula (the dollar amounts). The Tickets Sold and Ticket Price labels may be placed anywhere as long as they do not interfere with the table.*

3. Select **cell B5**.
   *You will create a formula with references to two input cells. Any two blank cells may be used as the input cells as long as they are outside the data table range. You will use cell B3 as the tickets sold (row) variable and cell B4 as the ticket price (column) variable.*

4. **Enter** the formula **=(B2\*B3\*B4)–A2** in **cell B5**.
   *The result equals –75000, the entire net income goal, because cells B3 and B4 used in the formula are blank. This formula first calculates the net income as 70 percent of tickets sold at the specified price. From the result, the $75,000 net income goal is subtracted to calculate the dollar amount of ticket sales that is above or below the goal. A positive number is acceptable.*

5. Select **cell B5**, and change the text color to **white** to **hide** the formula result.
   *The result of the formula cell is not a relevant value for your ticket sales analysis.*

## Complete the Data Table

*The final steps in creating the data table are selecting the table range and issuing the Data Table command.*

6. Select the **range B5:G10** as shown.

| | A | B | C | D | E | F | G |
|---|---|---|---|---|---|---|---|
| 4 | | | Tickets Sold | | | | |
| 5 | | | 600 | 650 | 700 | 750 | 800 |
| 6 | Ticket Price | $ 100 | | | | | |
| 7 | | $ 150 | | | | | |
| 8 | | $ 200 | | | | | |
| 9 | | $ 250 | | | | | |
| 10 | | $ 300 | | | | | |

*When selecting the range for a data table, you must include the formula, variables, and cells that will hold the calculated results in the selection. Notice that the text labels and input cells are not included.*

7. Choose **Data→Data Tools→What-If Analysis** →**Data Table** from the Ribbon.

8. Follow these steps to choose the input cells:

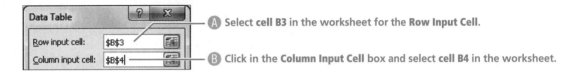

Ⓐ Select **cell B3** in the worksheet for the **Row Input Cell**.

Ⓑ Click in the **Column Input Cell** box and select **cell B4** in the worksheet.

*The Row Input Cell is the cell in which you want the row variables (tickets sold) to be substituted. Likewise, the Column Input Cell substitutes the column variables (ticket prices). If you look at the formula in cell B5, you will see that these substitutions make sense.*

9. Click **OK** in the Data Table dialog box.
   *The data table is completed as shown in the following illustration.*

| | A | B | C | D | E | F | G |
|---|---|---|---|---|---|---|---|
| 3 | | | Ticket Sales Above (Below) Goal | | | | |
| 4 | | | Tickets Sold | | | | |
| 5 | | | 600 | 650 | 700 | 750 | 800 |
| 6 | Ticket Price | $ 100 | (33,000) | (29,500) | (26,000) | (22,500) | (19,000) |
| 7 | | $ 150 | (12,000) | (6,750) | (1,500) | 3,750 | 9,000 |
| 8 | | $ 200 | 9,000 | 16,000 | 23,000 | 30,000 | 37,000 |
| 9 | | $ 250 | 30,000 | 38,750 | 47,500 | 56,250 | 65,000 |
| 10 | | $ 300 | 51,000 | 61,500 | 72,000 | 82,500 | 93,000 |

10. Select the **range C6:G10**, and choose **Comma Style with no decimals** from the Ribbon.
    *Notice the positive numbers in the data table. Any positive number indicates that net income would be above the goal. At a ticket price of $150, more than 700 tickets must be sold to achieve the desired net income amount. Any ticket price of $200 or more would achieve the goal, but a higher price might result in fewer tickets sold.*

11. **Save** the changes as **Tickets Data Table** in the Lesson 15 folder in your file storage location.

12. Feel free to experiment with your data table. For example, try changing the ticket prices in **column B** to increments of $25 rather than $50. How would the results change if the net income percentage in cell B2 were 65%?

*The data table will be recalculated each time you change a variable.*

13. When you are finished, **close** the workbook **without** saving again.

## 15.7 Creating Trendlines

**Video Lesson**    labyrinthelab.com/videos

Trendlines are used on charts for data analysis and prediction. A trendline visually displays the trend (increasing or decreasing) of one data series in a chart. There are several types of trendlines available, each suited to the display of particular types of data. For example, a linear trendline works well with data that follow a fairly straight path. A moving average trendline smoothes out fluctuations in data by averaging two or more adjacent data points for each trendline data point.

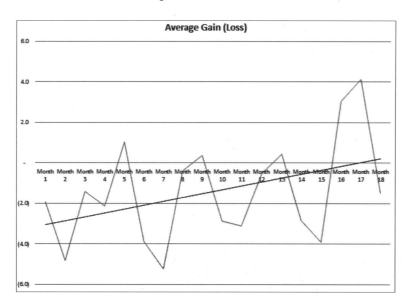

This linear trendline depicts the upward trend for average weight of patients enrolled in a clinical study over 18 months.

 You cannot add a trendline to certain types of charts, such as 3-D, pie, and area charts.

## Add a Trendline

*In this exercise, you will add a trendline to an existing chart. You will format the trendline to show trends based on various time periods.*

### Insert a Trendline

1. **Open** the Contributions Trend workbook from the Lesson 15 folder.
   *The Summary worksheet and trend chart summarize net sales for four quarters of a year.*

2. Display the **Trend Chart** worksheet.

3. **Select** the chart.

4. Choose **Chart Tools Layout→Analysis→Trendline** 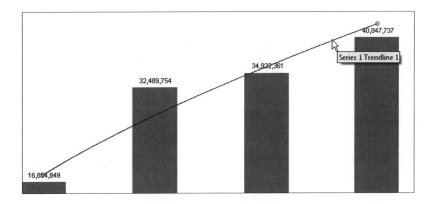→**Linear Trendline** from the Ribbon.
   *The new trendline appears. This best-fit line indicates that net sales are increasing at an excellent rate.*

### Edit the Trendline

5. Taking care to position the tip of the pointer arrow against the trendline as shown, select the **trendline**. (If the trendline does not display handles at its endpoints, reposition the tip of the mouse pointer at the trendline and select again.)

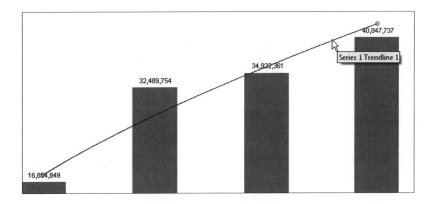

6. Choose **Layout→Analysis→Trendline→Linear Forecast Trendline**.
   *The trendline lengthens to forecast net sales in the next two quarters.*

7. Select the trendline, and choose **Layout→Analysis→Trendline** 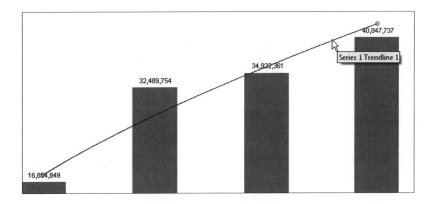→**More Trendline Options** from the Ribbon.

8. In the **Forecast** area in the lower part of the Format Trendline dialog box, change **Forward** from 2.0 periods to **1**.

9. Take a few moments to view the other options in the dialog box.

10. Click **Close**.
    *The trendline now forecasts only one quarter in the future, a more conservative analysis.*

11. With the trendline still selected, choose **Layout→Analysis→Trendline→Two Period Moving Average** from the Ribbon.

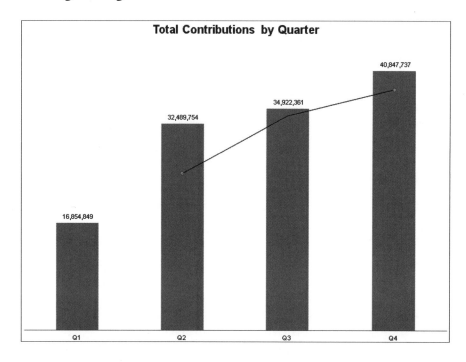

*The trendline shortens to begin at the second quarter and displays an angle to reflect the fewer number of data points being averaged for each point on the trendline. This type of trendline follows data fluctuations. To use trendline options effectively, an understanding of statistics in math is helpful.*

12. **Save** 🖫 the changes, and leave the workbook **open**.

# 15.8 Creating Sparklines in Cells

**Video Lesson** labyrinthelab.com/videos

Sparklines appear as miniature charts in worksheet cells. New in Excel 2010, sparklines allow you to show the data graphically without all the steps required in creating a normal chart. You also may select a cell range and create sparklines for every row or column at once. Changes to data are reflected immediately in sparklines right next to the data. Each sparkline charts the data in one row or column.

| | A | B | C | D | E | F |
|---|---|---|---|---|---|---|
| 4 | **Pledge Level** | **Q1** | **Q2** | **Q3** | **Q4** | **By Quarter** |
| 5 | Level 1 | 16,541,676 | 30,201,177 | 32,114,970 | 38,409,659 | |
| 6 | Level 2 | - | 2,000,000 | 2,253,988 | 2,000,075 | |
| 7 | Level 3 | 202,373 | 222,645 | 479,673 | 412,892 | |
| 8 | Level 4 | 100,891 | 50,000 | 51,209 | - | |
| 9 | Level 5 | 8,647 | 13,043 | 17,921 | 18,676 | |
| 10 | Level 6 | 1,262 | 2,889 | 4,600 | 6,435 | |
| 11 | **Total Contributions** | **16,854,849** | **32,489,754** | **34,922,361** | **40,847,737** | **125,114,701** |

Sparklines in column F with dot markers to show upward and downward trends for each pledge level of contributions during the year

## Formatting Sparklines

You may format sparklines as lines, columns, or win-loss columns. The win-loss format shows the increase or decrease as compared to a previous period. You may format sparklines with styles and choose to display data points in various ways. For example, the Markers option displays a dot for each value along a sparkline formatted as a line. The same formatting must be applied to sparklines created all at once, while unique formatting may be applied to each sparkline created one at a time.

| QUICK REFERENCE | CREATING TRENDLINES AND SPARKLINES |
|---|---|
| **Task** | **Procedure** |
| Add a trendline to a chart | ■ Display the chart to which you wish to add a trendline.<br>■ Choose Chart Tools Layout→Analysis→Trendline from the Ribbon.<br>■ Choose a trendline type.<br>■ Select a data series in the Add a Trendline Based on Series dialog box, if more than one exists in the chart. |
| Change the trendline type | ■ Select the trendline.<br>■ Choose Chart Tools Layout→Analysis→Trendline from the Ribbon.<br>■ Choose a trendline type. |
| Format the trendline | ■ Select the trendline.<br>■ Choose the desired options on the Format ribbon. |
| Add objects specific to the chart type and trendline type | ■ Select the trendline.<br>■ Display the Chart Tools Layout ribbon and choose options from those displayed in the Analysis group. |
| Create a sparkline | ■ Select the cell to contain the sparkline, or select a cell range to place a sparkline in each row or column.<br>■ Choose the Insert ribbon, and choose the desired sparkline type from the Sparklines group on the Ribbon.<br>■ In the Create Sparklines dialog box, select the data range containing the source values.<br>■ Verify the location range of cells to contain the sparkline(s), and click OK. |
| Format a sparkline | ■ Select the desired cell(s) containing a sparkline.<br>■ Choose the desired options on the Sparkline Tools Design ribbon. |

## Create Sparklines

*In this exercise, you will create sparklines in a fundraising summary worksheet to show upward and downward trends in the contributions raised each quarter.*

### Create Sparklines as Line Charts

1. Display the **Summary** sheet in the Contributions Trend workbook.

2. Select the **range F5:F10**.
   *These cells will contain the sparklines for each contribution level.*

3. Choose **Insert→Sparklines→Line** 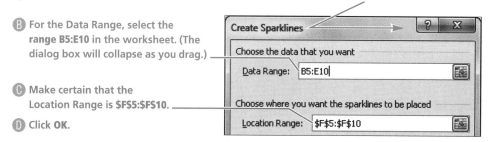 from the Ribbon.

4. Follow these steps to complete the Create Sparklines dialog box:

Ⓐ Move the dialog box, if necessary, to view **column B** in the worksheet.

Ⓑ For the Data Range, select the **range B5:E10** in the worksheet. (The dialog box will collapse as you drag.)

Ⓒ Make certain that the Location Range is **$F$5:$F$10**.

Ⓓ Click **OK**.

*A sparkline appears in each cell of the range.*

5. Choose **Sparkline Tools Design→Show→Markers** from the Ribbon to place a checkmark next to Markers.

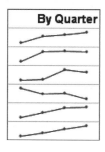

*The sparklines display a dot marker for each quarter, thus making the upward and downward trends easier to understand.*

6. Read the other options in the Design ribbon, and then **deselect** the range.

7. **Save** the changes.

### Create Sparklines as Column Charts

8. Select **cell F14**, and choose **Insert→Sparklines→Column** from the Ribbon.

9. In the **Create Sparklines** dialog box, set the Data Range to **B14:E14**, verify that the Location Range is **$F$14**, and click **OK**.
   *This time you created a single sparkline.*

10. Repeat **steps 8–9** to create a column sparkline in **cell F15**. Then, repeat twice more for **cells F16 and F17**.

| | B | C | D | E | F |
|---|---|---|---|---|---|
| 13 | **Q1** | **Q2** | **Q3** | **Q4** | **By Quarter** |
| 14 | 3,500 | 3,500 | 3,500 | 37,000 | |
| 15 | 947 | 977 | 1,699 | 864 | |
| 16 | 12,589 | 22,753 | 10,465 | 45,872 | |
| 17 | 6,000 | 6,000 | 6,000 | 6,000 | |

*Notice the values in the range B14:E14. The sparkline chart in cell F14 represents these values in relation to each other. The fourth column in the sparkline is larger to represent the value 37,000 as compared to the value 3,500 in the other three cells. The columns in cell F17 are an equal size because the values in the range B17:E17 are equal. The sparklines do not compare values from one row to values in another row.*

## Format Sparklines

11. Select **cell F15**, and follow these steps to change the sparkline style:

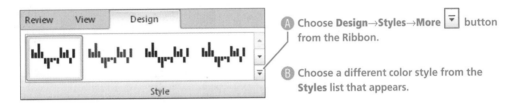

Ⓐ Choose **Design→Styles→More** ⬛ button from the Ribbon.

Ⓑ Choose a different color style from the **Styles** list that appears.

*Notice that you could format a single sparkline because you created each sparkline separately in the range F14:F17.*

12. Repeat the above step **twice** to apply different sparkline styles to **cells F16 and F17**.

13. Select **cell F5**.
   *The range F5:F10 is surrounded by an outline to indicate that the six sparklines are selected. You previously created these sparklines all at once.*

14. Choose **Design→Style→More** ⬛ button, and choose a different style from the Ribbon.

15. Feel free to experiment with any other options in the Show group of the Design ribbon to format the sparklines.

16. **Save** 💾 the changes, and **close** the workbook.

# 15.9 Concepts Review

**Concepts Review**   labyrinthelab.com/excel10

*To check your knowledge of the key concepts introduced in this lesson, complete the Concepts Review quiz by going to the URL listed above. If your classroom is using Labyrinth eLab, you may complete the Concepts Review quiz from within your eLab course.*

# Reinforce Your Skills

## Group Worksheets and Consolidate Data by Category

*In this exercise, you will complete a workbook that tracks compensation paid to independent contractors. The employer issues 1099 statements (similar to W-2 forms) to independent contractors at the end of the year for their income tax returns. The workbook contains a Year-to-Date worksheet as well as worksheets for each month. You will group the worksheets and enter the headings for all the sheets. In addition, you will use the Consolidate by Category option to consolidate the monthly data in the Year-to-Date worksheet.*

### Browse the Workbook

1. **Open** the rs-Consolidated Compensation workbook from the Lesson 15 folder.
   *Notice that the Year-to-Date worksheet has column headings in row 3 but no data. The Consolidation command will insert the data.*

2. Display the **January** worksheet.
   *Six 1099 recipients are listed with their respective number of hours and compensation. This recipient list is different for each month because these temporary contractors come and go on a regular basis.*

3. Select **cell C4**.
   *Notice that the compensation is calculated as the hours multiplied by $21.35. The Consolidate command will combine the hours and compensation from the monthly worksheets. You can consolidate cells with both values and formulas, as in this exercise.*

4. Display the **February** worksheet.
   *Seven recipients are listed for February. Several of these recipients differ from those in the January worksheet.*

5. Display the **March** worksheet and notice that, again, the recipient list has changed.
   *In a later step, you will use the Consolidate command for the Year-to-Date worksheet. You cannot consolidate by position, as you did in the Quarterly Summary workbook previously in this lesson, because the monthly sheets have different layouts. The list of independent contractors varies.*

### Group Multiple Worksheets

*Next you will group the worksheets to prepare for data entry and formatting.*

6. Display the **Year-to-Date** worksheet.

7. **Hold down** ⟨Shift⟩ and click the **March** sheet tab.
   *Notice that the sheets are now grouped so that whatever you do on one worksheet occurs simultaneously on all worksheets in the group.*

### Enter and Format Labels Across Worksheets

8. Select **cell A1** in the Year-to-Date worksheet and enter **Compensation**.

9. Merge and center the label in **cell A1** across **cells A1:C1**.

10. With cells A1:C1 still selected, choose **Home→Styles→Cell Styles→Themed Cell Styles→Accent1** (white text with dark blue fill) from the Ribbon.

11. Select **cells A3:C3** and choose **Home→Styles→Cell Styles→Themed Cell Styles→ 20% - Accent1** (black text with light blue fill) from the Ribbon.

12. **Deselect** the highlighted cells.

13. **Right-click** the Year-to-Date sheet tab and choose **Ungroup Sheets** from the context menu.

14. Edit **cell A1** in the Year-to-Date worksheet to `1099 Recipient Compensation`.

15. Display each of the **monthly** worksheets.
    *Notice that the formatting you applied while the worksheets were grouped appears on every worksheet. You edited the title in cell A1 while the worksheets were ungrouped, so only the Year-to-Date worksheet reflects that change.*

## Select Data to Consolidate

16. Display the **Year-to-Date** worksheet and select **cell A4** as the starting point for the consolidated data.

17. Choose **Data→Data Tools→Consolidate** from the Ribbon.
    *In the next few steps, you will specify the range references you wish to consolidate. You will do this by selecting the ranges in the various sheets and adding them to the All References list.*

18. Follow these steps to set consolidation options in the Consolidate dialog box:

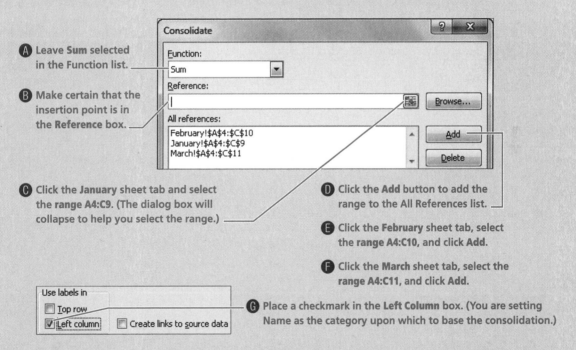

A Leave **Sum** selected in the Function list.

B Make certain that the insertion point is in the **Reference** box.

C Click the **January** sheet tab and select the **range A4:C9**. (The dialog box will collapse to help you select the range.)

D Click the **Add** button to add the range to the All References list.

E Click the **February** sheet tab, select the **range A4:C10**, and click **Add**.

F Click the **March** sheet tab, select the **range A4:C11**, and click **Add**.

G Place a checkmark in the **Left Column** box. (You are setting Name as the category upon which to base the consolidation.)

*Review the references in the All References list. You build a consolidation by adding references to this list. Notice that the row labels in column A are included in the references. The Consolidate command will use the labels in the left column (column A) to determine which rows to consolidate from the monthly sheets. Excel will create one consolidated row in the Year-to-Date worksheet for each name. For example, the name Dennis Johnson appears in two worksheets. Excel will create one Dennis Johnson row in the Year-to-Date sheet summing his numbers.*

19. Click **OK** in the Consolidate dialog box.
*The Year-to-Date worksheet displays the consolidated numbers shown in the following illustration.*

| | A | B | C |
|---|---|---|---|
| 1 | 1099 Recepient Compensation | | |
| 2 | | | |
| 3 | Name | Hours | Compensation |
| 4 | Johnson, Dennis E. | 27 | 576.45 |
| 5 | Lake, Cheryl Y. | 77 | 1,643.95 |
| 6 | Parson, Robin J. | 67 | 1,430.45 |
| 7 | Williams, Scott G. | 35 | 747.25 |
| 8 | Richardson, Eddie | 46 | 982.10 |
| 9 | Jones, William T. | 51 | 1,088.85 |
| 10 | Thomas, Wanda M. | 65 | 1,387.75 |
| 11 | Wilson, Leslie A. Jr. | 38 | 811.30 |
| 12 | Simpson, Lakisha D. | 12 | 256.20 |
| 13 | Ellis, Ellen E. | 10 | 213.50 |
| 14 | Williams, Stewart M. | 8 | 170.80 |

*Notice that each name appears just once in the consolidated list. Feel free to browse through the monthly sheets. You will notice that the consolidated numbers are sums of the numbers for the individual months.*

20. **Deselect** the highlighted range.

## Add Another Worksheet

*You can easily consolidate the data again by adding a consolidation range for any monthly worksheet added later. In the next few steps, you will add an April worksheet and reconsolidate the data.*

21. Copy the **March** worksheet and name the new sheet **April**.

22. In the **April** worksheet, select **rows 6 and 7** and use the **Delete** command to remove them.
*Scott Williams and Eddie Richardson did not receive compensation in April.*

23. Add the recipients and hours shown to **rows 10 and 11**.
*Excel will automatically calculate the compensation in cells C10 and C11 when you* [Tab] *through the cells during data entry.*

| 10 | Sanchez, Pedro | 23 | 491.05 |
|---|---|---|---|
| 11 | Yee, Doness U. | 21 | 448.35 |

## Consolidate Again

24. Display the **Year-to-Date** worksheet.

25. Select all consolidated data in the **range A4:C14** and **tap** the [Delete] key.
*It is best to delete the existing data before reconsolidating because the new consolidation will overwrite the existing data. If the new consolidation has fewer rows than the original consolidation, there will be leftover (and incorrect) rows at the bottom of the consolidated data.*

26. Select **cell A4** and choose **Data→Data Tools→Consolidate** ⊞ from the Ribbon.
*Notice that the consolidation ranges you chose are still in the All References list. Now you need only add the April range.*

27. Make certain that the insertion point is in the **Reference** box.

28. Click the **April** sheet tab and select the **range A4:C11** in the worksheet.

29. Click the **Add** button in the dialog box.

30. Click **OK** to complete the consolidation.
    *The updated consolidation includes 13 unique names in rows 4–16.*

31. **Deselect** the highlighted range.

32. **Save** 🖫 the changes, and **close** the workbook.

REINFORCE YOUR SKILLS 15.2
## Construct a Loan Payment Data Table

*In this exercise, you will create a two-variable data table. The data table will calculate monthly payments on a car loan using various interest rates and payment periods.*

### Set Up the Data Table

1. **Start** a new workbook and **enter** the data shown. Make certain that the numbers in **column B** are formatted with percent symbols.

| ⊿ | A | B | C | D | E | F | G |
|---|---|---|---|---|---|---|---|
| 1 | Car Loan Analysis | | | | | | |
| 2 | | | | | | | |
| 3 | Opening Balance | | $   22,000 | | | | |
| 4 | | | | | | | |
| 5 | | | Months | | | | |
| 6 | | | 36 | 42 | 48 | 54 | 60 |
| 7 | Rate | 2% | | | | | |
| 8 | | 3% | | | | | |
| 9 | | 4% | | | | | |
| 10 | | 5% | | | | | |
| 11 | | 6% | | | | | |
| 12 | | 7% | | | | | |
| 13 | | 8% | | | | | |
| 14 | | 9% | | | | | |

2. Select **cell B6**, the upper-left corner cell of the data table.
   *In the next step, you will enter a formula that uses the PMT function. The PMT function calculates payments using a monthly interest rate, number of payments, and opening balance as arguments.*

3. **Enter** the formula = **–PMT(B5/12,A6,C3)** and **complete** the entry.
   *The result displays as #NUM! because cells B5 and A6 (the input cells for the data table) are empty. You will respond to this message later. The formula is interpreted as follows.*

   *The B5/12 reference is the interest rate argument. The B5 reference is divided by 12 because the payments will be made monthly, and the rates in column B are annual rates. The interest rates in column B will be substituted into input cell B5 when the Data Table command is issued.*

   *The A6 reference is the second input cell. The months in row 6 will be substituted into this cell when the Data Table command is issued.*

   *Cell C3 contains the loan amount. The PMT function always returns a negative number, so you added a minus (–) sign to reverse the formula result to a positive number.*

## Complete the Data Table

4. Select the **range B6:G14** and choose **Data→Data Tools→What-If Analysis** 📊 **→Data Table** from the Ribbon.

5. Enter **A6** as the **row input** cell and **B5** as the **column input** cell.

6. Click **OK** and the table is calculated.

7. Taking care not to select the months in row 6 or rates in column B, select the **range C7:G14**.

8. Format the selected cells as **Comma Style with two decimal places**.

## Adjust the Loan Amount

*Now imagine that you want to see the same analysis for a different loan amount. This is easily accomplished by changing the loan amount in cell C3.*

9. Select **cell C3** and change 22000 to **25000**.

10. **Complete** the entry, and the data table will recalculate.
    *Assume that your budget allows a maximum payment of $550. Read across each row of the data table to determine the loan length. For example, at the 2 percent rate, the loan term must be 48 months.*

| ◢ | A | B | C | D | E | F | G |
|---|---|---|---|---|---|---|---|
| 3 | Opening Balance | | $ 25,000 | | | | |
| 4 | | | | | | | |
| 5 | | | Months | | | | |
| 6 | | #NUM! | 36 | 42 | 48 | 54 | 60 |
| 7 | Rate | 2% | 716.06 | 616.81 | 542.38 | 484.49 | 438.19 |
| 8 | | 3% | 727.03 | 627.78 | 553.36 | 495.49 | 449.22 |
| 9 | | 4% | 738.10 | 638.87 | 564.48 | 506.65 | 460.41 |
| 10 | | 5% | 749.27 | 650.08 | 575.73 | 517.96 | 471.78 |
| 11 | | 6% | 760.55 | 661.41 | 587.13 | 529.42 | 483.32 |
| 12 | | 7% | 771.93 | 672.86 | 598.66 | 541.04 | 495.03 |
| 13 | | 8% | 783.41 | 684.42 | 610.32 | 552.81 | 506.91 |
| 14 | | 9% | 794.99 | 696.11 | 622.13 | 564.73 | 518.96 |

## Respond to an Alert

*If the Enable Background Error Checking option is switched on in Excel Options, the PMT formula cell displays a small triangle icon in the upper left of the cell to alert you to the #NUM! error. For the purpose of the data table, this is not actually an error.*

11. Select **cell B6**, click the **alert** button displayed to the left of the cell, and choose **Ignore Error** from the context menu.
    *If you determine that #NUM! would confuse other workbook users, you may format the cell with a white font to "hide" the message, or you could hide the cell and turn on worksheet protection.*

12. **Save** as **rs-Loan Data Table** in the Lesson 15 folder; then **close** the workbook.

# Work with Trendlines and Sparklines

*In this exercise, you will add a trendline to the data on an existing chart. You will create sparklines to chart the net sales performance for each quarter during a four-year period.*

## Create and Format a Trendline

1. **Open** the rs-Trendline workbook from the Lesson 15 folder and take a moment to review the data.
   *The Net Sales worksheet depicts the quarterly net sales over the course of four years.*

2. Display the **Trend Chart** worksheet.
   *This chart displays the four years of data. Notice that the data pattern fluctuates up and down. A linear trendline would not provide much help in analyzing the trends.*

3. Select the chart and choose **Chart Tools Layout→Analysis→Trendline→More Trendline Options** from the Ribbon.

4. Move the **Format Trendline** dialog box to one side of the workbook window as you work so that you can view the trendline.

5. Under **Trend/Regression Type** in the Format Trendline dialog box, choose **Polynomial**.
   *This trendline type is useful for tracking fluctuations in data. Inspecting the columns in the chart indicates several significant changes over the four-year period.*

6. Use the spinner button to set the **Order** option to **4** as shown.
   *Each click displays an additional rise or dip in the trendline.*

*One way to compare the accuracy of a trendline is to display its R-squared value. The closer a trendline's R-squared value is to 1, the better it fits the data.*

7. Place a checkmark in the **Display R-squared Value on Chart** option near the bottom of the dialog box.
   *The R-squared value displays near the end of the trendline as $R^2 = 0.5312$.*

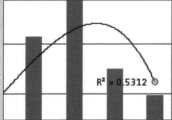

8. Change the **Order** option to **6** next to Polynomial and click **Close**.
   *The trendline displays $R^2 = 0.6286$. Since its value is closer to 1, this trendline represents a more accurate forecast. An ideal trendline would have an $R^2$ value very close to 1.*

9. **Save** the changes.

## Create Sparklines

10. Display the **Sales Change** worksheet.
    *On this sheet, the data are rearranged by each quarter of the fiscal year. You will create sparklines to quickly chart the changes from year to year and identify the lowest year in each row.*

11. Select the **range F5:F8**.

12. Choose **Insert→Sparklines→Line** from the Ribbon.

13. On the Sparkline Tools Design ribbon, navigate to the **Show** group and place a checkmark next to both **Markers** and **Low Point**.
    *The markers indicate each fiscal year on a sparkline. Notice that the low point has a slightly different color than the other markers. Next, you will choose a color with more contrast so the low point stands out.*

14. Choose **Design→Style→Marker Color→Low Point**, and choose a contrasting theme color.
    *Now the sparklines present the lower sales performance in fiscal years 1 and 3 more clearly.*

| ◢ | A | B | C | D | E | F |
|---|---|---|---|---|---|---|
| 1 | **Net Sales** | | | | | |
| 2 | Fiscal Years 1–4 | | | | | |
| 3 | | | | | | |
| 4 | **Quarter** | **FY 1** | **FY 2** | **FY 3** | **FY 4** | **Change** |
| 5 | Q1 | $1,375,950 | $3,072,567 | $ 1,376,950 | $3,072,567 | ⟋⟍⟋ |
| 6 | Q2 | $2,975,324 | $3,254,087 | $ 1,484,565 | $4,235,210 | ⟋⟍⟋ |
| 7 | Q3 | $4,195,000 | $2,752,200 | $ 1,257,535 | $2,752,200 | ⟍⟍⟋ |
| 8 | Q4 | $2,000,058 | $2,484,384 | $ 2,005,486 | $2,484,384 | ⟋⟍⟋ |

15. **Save** the changes, and **close** the workbook.

# Apply Your Skills

## Consolidate Data by Category

*In this exercise, you will consolidate the shares bought and sold each month into a summary investment portfolio worksheet.*

1. **Open** as-Consolidated Portfolio from the Lesson 15 folder in your file storage location.
   *The workbook contains a Beginning Balance worksheet showing the number of shares owned at the beginning of the year. The January and February worksheets include the shares purchased, reinvested, and sold.*

2. Copy a worksheet to create the **March** worksheet and **Portfolio Activity** worksheet shown in the illustrations below. (Copying will ensure that the column widths and cell formats are the same as in the other worksheets.) Make certain to enter the data in the correct cells as shown because you will consolidate the data by position later in this exercise.

| | A | B | C | D | E |
|---|---|---|---|---|---|
| 1 | **March** | | | | |
| 2 | | | | | |
| 3 | **Investment Name** | **Shares Purchased** | **Shares Reinvested** | **Shares Sold** | **Net Shares** |
| 4 | Prigem | | | 12.39 | (12.39) |
| 5 | American Fund | 40.52 | 1.23 | | 41.75 |
| 6 | Guardian Balanced Fund | 12.31 | 4.70 | | 17.01 |

| | A | B | C | D | E |
|---|---|---|---|---|---|
| 1 | **Portfolio Activity** | | | | |
| 2 | | | | | |
| 3 | **Investment Name** | **Shares Purchased** | **Shares Reinvested** | **Shares Sold** | **Net Shares** |

3. **Rename** the sheet tabs using the entries from **cell A1**.

4. Use the **Consolidate** command to combine the Beginning Balance and three monthly worksheets into the **Portfolio Activity** worksheet.
   *The names of eight investments and their consolidated numbers should result.*

5. **Sort** the investments into alphabetical order on the **Portfolio Activity** worksheet.

6. **Save** 🖫 the changes, and **close** the workbook.

# Construct a Mortgage Payment Data Table

*In this exercise, you will create a data table to calculate monthly payments for a home mortgage using various interest rates and periods.*

1. **Start** a new workbook.

2. Begin creating the **data table** by typing labels in cells as needed.

3. **Enter** the loan amount **$200,000** in **cell C3**.

4. **Enter** interest rates from **6%, 6.5%**, and up through **8.5%** in **column B**.

5. **Enter** the number of *months* for loan periods of 15, 20, 25, and 30 years in **row 6**.

6. Use the **PMT** function to create a formula in the appropriate cell. You used the PMT function in Reinforce Your Skills 15.2.

7. Issue the **Data Table** command.

8. **Format** the values in the data table as **Comma Style with two decimal places**.

9. Optional: Apply a **conditional format** that changes the font and fill color when a data table value is less than 1,550.01.

10. Clear any **alert** or **error message** that appears in a cell.

11. **Save** 🖫 with the name **as-Mortgage Data Table** in the Lesson 15 folder; then **close** the workbook.

# Present Data with Sparklines

*In this exercise, you will add a trendline to a column chart.*

1. **Open** the as-Projected Revenue workbook.

2. Create sparklines in **column G** to present the projected yearly changes in revenue, gross profit, and net profit.

3. **Format** the sparklines appropriately.

4. **Save** 🖫 the changes, and **close** the workbook.

# Critical Thinking & Work-Readiness Skills

*In the course of working through the following Microsoft Office-based Critical Thinking exercises, you will also be utilizing various work-readiness skills, some of which are listed next to each exercise. Go to* labyrinthelab.com/ workreadiness *to learn more about the work-readiness skills.*

## 15.1 Group Sheets and Summarize Data

Sandra Chavez-Hall, chief development officer for Raritan Clinic East Foundation, has asked you to summarize direct expenses for Quarter 1. Open ct-Expense Summary (Lesson 15 folder). Group the January, February, and March sheets, and apply Comma Style to the numbers in column B. Then, copy cell B4 from the January worksheet to the Summary, February, and March worksheets by grouping sheets as necessary. Consolidate the January, February, and March expenses into column B of the Summary sheet. Save as **ct-Expense Summary [Your Last Name]**, and then close the file.

**WORK-READINESS SKILLS APPLIED**

- Solving problems
- Thinking creatively
- Arithmetic/ mathematics

## 15.2 Create a Two-Variable Data Table

Sandra is ready to study the mortgage payments for Phase 2. She requests a two-variable data table. Your job is to set it up for her. Open a new workbook. Create a two-variable data table for a mortgage of $1,500,000. Enter a set of variables to the right of the data table formula as the months for 10, 15, 20, and 25 years. Create the set of variables below the formula as interest rates of 7.5%, 7.75%, 8%, 8.25%, 8.5%, 8.75%, and 9%. Save your work as **ct-Phase 2 [Your Last Name]** in your Lesson 15 folder, and then close the file.

**WORK-READINESS SKILLS APPLIED**

- Solving problems
- Using computers to process information
- Arithmetic/ mathematics

## 15.3 Display Trends in Cells

The operations director at Raritan Clinic East needs to evaluate the cost of three drugs used at the clinic. She has data showing the cost of each drug over a period of five years. Open ct-Drug Cost (Lesson 15 folder). Use sparklines to show the cost trend for each of the three drugs. Apply appropriate formatting to the sparklines. Then, type a brief label in one cell to describe the purpose of the sparklines. Save and close the file when you are finished.

**WORK-READINESS SKILLS APPLIED**

- Seeing things in the mind's eye
- Interpreting and communicating information
- Using computers to process information

# Collaborating in Excel

## LESSON OUTLINE

## LEARNING OBJECTIVES

After studying this lesson, you will be able to:

- Create folders to organize project documents
- Manage and print comments in workbooks
- Track and consolidate changes made by multiple authors to a single workbook copy
- Prepare and share workbooks for collaboration
- Merge multiple versions of a shared workbook

Collaborating on projects is a typical business activity. The Internet simplifies exchanging documents and other types of information to coordinate geographically diverse activities. However, the lack of face-to-face contact also places a premium on sharing information efficiently. In this lesson, you will learn how to participate in workbook collaboration. You will set up folders for project files, place comments into an Excel workbook, and prepare the workbook to be distributed to other people. The ability to create shared workbooks is one of Excel's most powerful collaboration features. You can set up a workbook that several other users can access simultaneously on a network server, or intranet. Excel's change history tracking feature can help you avoid and resolve potential conflicts when data is edited by multiple users. You will learn how to merge all of the users' changes automatically into one workbook.

# Collaborating on Grant Reports

**Raritan Clinic East**

Pediatric Diagnostic Specialists

Grace Vargas is the grant and contract coordinator for Raritan Clinic East. She administers grant funds awarded to the medical center to support various research studies and uses Excel for several of the project activities. Grace administers a Connections medical research grant project that involves Raritan's cardiology and orthopedics departments. She must assemble financial data from both departments each quarter and submit it to the granting agency to show how the funds were spent. Grace and her colleagues use email and an intranet to transmit information back and forth in the form of messages and Excel workbooks.

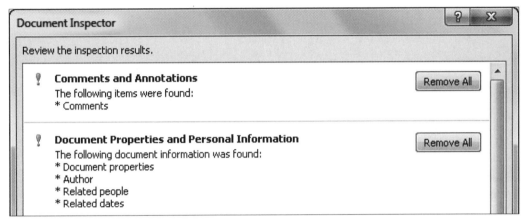

Grace uses the Document Inspector tool to remove items containing personal information prior to sharing the workbook with coworkers.

Grace and her colleagues use comments to ask questions and make suggestions. Comments can also help everyone involved in the project understand special formulas and values contained in worksheet cells.

When Grace points at the cell containing the comment marker, the comment pops up with Terry's question about a formula in the draft budget report.

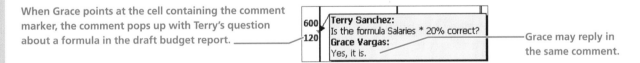

Grace may reply in the same comment.

Grace may also share a workbook with others working on the project. As they return revisions to the workbook, Grace uses Excel's Compare and Merge Workbooks command. Excel automatically enters all revisions from the other workbooks and marks them to be accepted or rejected. This allows Grace to review everyone's revisions in a single workbook.

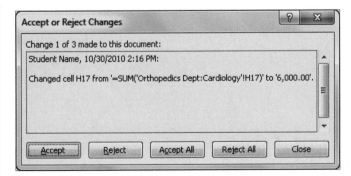

Grace may accept or reject each change that other collaborators made to the workbook.

# 16.1 Creating Folders in Excel

**Video Lesson**   labyrinthelab.com/videos

When you work on a project, you usually will create one or more folders on your computer to store the documents and other types of files with which you will work. This topic will give you practice in creating folders and teach you techniques to access the new folders quickly.

## Working with Project Folders

Depending on the size of the project and the number of files you must organize, you may need to create more than one folder. You may create a main folder for the project as well as subfolders inside of it for major types of documents or major sections of the project. The following diagram displays an example of project folders.

The Grant Project main folder for the project is selected in the address bar of the window. The folder contents appear below.

Subfolders hold documents for each quarterly report.

Various files that apply to the entire grant project are kept in the main folder

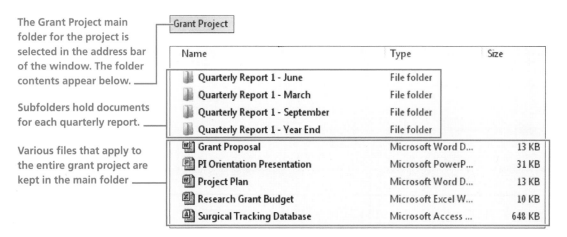

## Creating Folders

You don't need to leave Excel to create a new folder. Simply choose the Open or Save As command, and then click the New Folder button (or Create New Folder button, depending on your Windows version) on the dialog box toolbar. You may create a single folder or several. If desired, you may also create folders inside other folders.

   A new folder ready for typing the folder name

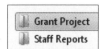   The newly named folder

## Renaming Folders

You may rename folders from within Excel by right-clicking the folder and choosing Rename from the context menu. Or you may click once on the folder, pause one second, and click again to select the folder name for renaming.

   A folder name ready for renaming

## Create and Rename a Project Folder

*In this exercise, you will create a folder from within the Excel program.*

1. Start **Excel** and choose **File→Open** 📂.

2. Follow these steps to begin creating the new folder:

**NOTE** The dialog box may appear slightly different depending on your Windows version.

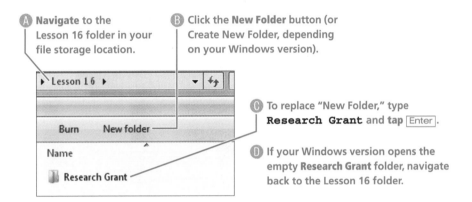

Ⓐ **Navigate** to the Lesson 16 folder in your file storage location.

Ⓑ Click the **New Folder** button (or Create New Folder, depending on your Windows version).

Ⓒ To replace "New Folder," type **Research Grant** and tap Enter.

Ⓓ If your Windows version opens the empty **Research Grant** folder, navigate back to the Lesson 16 folder.

*The new folder appears at the top of the file list. It is now ready to store files.*

3. **Right-click** the Research Grant folder and choose **Rename** from the bottom of the context menu.
   *The folder name is selected for renaming.*

4. Type **Grant Project** and tap Enter.

5. Click the **Cancel** button in the Open dialog box.
   *This cancels the Open command, not the creation of the new folder.*

6. Leave the Excel window **open**.

## Organizing Workbooks in Folders

**Video Lesson** labyrinthelab.com/videos

Many computer users store their files in the Documents or My Documents folder found on most Windows systems. Sometimes you will store files in a separate folder such as the one you just created. This allows you to place your project on a portable drive to use at another computer. Excel's Open and Save As dialog boxes allow you to move or copy files to different folders and to delete files from within Excel.

| Task | Procedure |
| --- | --- |
| Create a new folder | ■ Choose File→Open . <br> ■ Navigate to the folder that will contain the new folder. <br> ■ Click the New Folder button in the dialog box toolbar. <br> ■ Type the folder name and tap Enter. |
| Rename a folder | ■ Choose File→Open . <br> ■ Navigate to the folder containing the folder to be renamed. <br> ■ Right-click the desired folder, type the new name, and tap Enter. |
| Copy or move files | ■ Choose File→Open . <br> ■ Navigate to the folder containing the files to be copied or moved. <br> ■ Select the desired file. Use Ctrl or Shift to select multiple files. <br> ■ Use Ctrl+C to copy or Ctrl+X to cut the files. <br> ■ Navigate to the destination folder. <br> ■ Use Ctrl+V to paste the files. |

## DEVELOP YOUR SKILLS 16.1.2

# Move and Copy Files to a Folder

*In this exercise, you will move and copy some files into the folder you created in the previous exercise and then open a workbook from that folder.*

### Move a File to a Folder

1. Choose **File→Open** , and navigate to the Lesson 16 folder in your file storage location.

2. **Single-click** the Shared Budget file to select it.

3. Use Ctrl+X from the keyboard to cut the file.
   *The file's icon is dimmed to indicate the cut.*

4. **Double-click** the Grant Project folder to open it.

5. Use Ctrl+V from the keyboard to paste the file.

The file display may appear slightly different depending on your Windows version and the type of view selected.

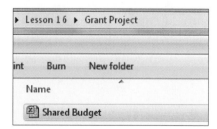

*The Shared Budget file appears in the Grant Project folder.*

6. Navigate back to the Lesson 16 folder in the **Open** dialog box.
   *The Shared Budget file is no longer in the Lesson 16 folder because you moved the file rather than copying it.*

## Copy Three Files to a Folder

*In the next few steps, you will place a copy of three files in the Grant Project folder. The original files will remain in the Lesson 16 folder.*

7. Follow these steps to copy the files:

(A) Scroll down the list, if necessary, until the **budget** files are visible.

(B) Select the **Connections Grant Cardiology Budget** file.

| Lesson 16 |
| as-Animal Shelter Expenses |
| as-Crisis Intervention Budget |
| Connections Grant Cardiology Budget |
| ct-Bed Count |
| ct-Shared Bed Count Cardiology |
| ct-Shared Bed Count Surgery |
| ct-Shared Bed Count |
| Distributed Budget |
| Merged Budget 1 |
| rs-Corey's Grant Budget |

(C) **Hold down** Ctrl and click both the Distributed Budget file and the Merged Budget 1 file; then **release** Ctrl.

*The* Ctrl *key allows you to select multiple adjacent or nonadjacent files.*

8. Use Ctrl+C from the keyboard to **copy** the files to the Clipboard.
   *The files' appearance does not change, but the files have been copied.*

9. **Scroll up**, if necessary, until the Grant Project folder is visible at the top of the file list, and then **double-click** the folder to open it.

10. Use Ctrl+V from the keyboard to **paste** the files.
    *The files are copied into the Grant Project folder.*

11. Navigate back to the Lesson 16 folder.

12. **Select** the original three files you selected in **step 7, tap** Delete, and choose **Yes** to confirm the deletion.
    *You will use the file copies in the Grant Project folder during this lesson.*

## Open a File in the Folder

13. Open the **Grant Project** folder.
    *Navigating to a folder and opening files from it is easy as long as you keep track of the locations of your folders.*

14. Open the **Connections Grant Cardiology Budget** workbook file, and leave the file **open** for the next exercise.

# 16.2 Inserting and Viewing Comments

**Video Lesson**   labyrinthelab.com/videos

Excel's Comment feature is a great tool for online collaboration. A comment is a text note that you can embed inside a workbook cell without cluttering the normal view of the workbook. You may display all comments on a worksheet and even print them.

## When to Use a Comment

Comments are an excellent way to handle many situations. You may want to insert a comment:

- To document the formula or value in a cell.
- To record a question about the worksheet data to be followed up later.
- To ask a question of an online collaborator without placing it into the normally printed page of the workbook.

## Viewing Comments

When someone inserts a comment, Excel places a small red triangle at the top-right corner of the cell. When you point at the cell containing the red triangle, Excel displays the name of the author and the text of the comment. You also may display or hide one or all comments using commands in the Comments group on the Review Ribbon. The following illustration shows a cell and its associated comment.

Pointing at the cell containing the red triangle will pop up the comment.

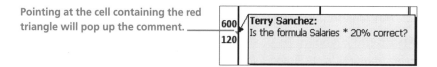

## Navigating Through Comments

You may jump from one comment to the next with the Next and Previous commands in the Ribbon. Using these commands is especially useful in large worksheets. When you reach the last comment in the workbook, the Next command starts over with the first comment in the workbook. The following figure displays the Comments group commands on the Ribbon.

These buttons navigate backward and forward through the comments.

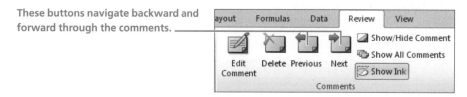

# Review Comments

*In this exercise, you will review comments inserted into the workbook by Terry Sanchez.*

1. Follow these steps to display some comments on the Cardiology worksheet of the Connection Grant Cardiology Budget workbook:

Ⓐ Point at this cell containing a **comment triangle** and read Terry Sanchez's comment.

| | A | B | C | D | E | F | G | H |
|---|---|---|---|---|---|---|---|---|
| 9 | EXPENSES | | | | | | | |
| 10 | PROJECT STAFF | | | | | | | |
| 11 | Salaries | | 1,462 | 600 | 1,224 | 600 | 1,224 | 600 |
| 12 | Benefits | | 284 | 120 | 194 | 120 | 194 | 120 |
| 13 | | | | | | | | |
| 14 | OPERATING COSTS | | | | | | | |
| 15 | Curriculum development | | 1,010 | | 1,010 | | 1,010 | |
| 16 | Staff development | | | | | | 216 | |
| 17 | Supplies | | | | 400 | | | 8,000 |

Ⓑ Point at each of these cells and read the comments.

2. Choose **Review→Comments→Show All Comments** 🗐 from the Ribbon.
*All comments on the worksheet are displayed when you choose this command.*

3. Choose **Review→Comments→Show All Comments** 🗐 from the Ribbon again to toggle off the display of the comments.

4. Choose **Review→Comments→Next** 🗐 from the Ribbon

5. Repeat the **Next** command to view the second comment.

6. Choose **Review→Comments→Previous** 🗐 from the Ribbon.
*The Next and Previous commands are useful for navigating through comments one by one.*

7. Issue the **Next** command three times until prompted that you are at the end of the workbook.

8. Click **OK** in the Microsoft Excel dialog box to start over at the first comment.

9. Select any cell to hide the comment, and leave the workbook **open**.

## Setting the Username

**Video Lesson**    labyrinthelab.com/videos

Before you insert comments, you should set the username to identify that the comment came from you. You make this setting in the Excel Options window in the General category. Once you set the username, Excel will keep this setting until the username is changed to something else.

You may not have permission rights to change the username on a classroom computer. The computer number may display as the username on a network of computers, or all computers may have the same username.

## Inserting and Deleting Comments

**FROM THE KEYBOARD**

Shift + F2 to insert comment

You may insert a comment into any cell with the New Comment  command on the Ribbon or by right-clicking a cell and choosing Insert Comment from the context menu. A comment is specific to a cell; you cannot assign a comment to a range of cells. You cannot insert more than one comment box in a cell, but you may add to an existing comment. After you give the command, a comment box appears in which you may type the text of the comment. Clicking outside the comment box hides it when Show All Comments is turned off. The Delete command on the Review ribbon will remove the selected comment from its cell.

## Adding to Comments

You may add to comments made by other authors by clicking in the comment box and typing. If the comment is not displayed, you may select the cell and choose Edit Comment from the Ribbon or context menu. Typing your name in bold is recommended to identify your portion of the comment.

The New Comment command on the Ribbon changes to Edit Comment when a comment box is selected.

### *Example of an Edited Comment*

As you read comments inserted by your co-worker in another department, you notice one that asks a question. Rather than insert a new comment, you decide to add your answer by editing the existing comment. You also may apply

a different text color to this edit so that the other readers can readily distinguish your addition from the original comment.

## Formatting Comment Text

You may change most text attributes for your comment using commands on the Home Ribbon, but the Font Color command is not available on the Ribbon. Instead, you should use the Format Comment command in the context menu to display a dialog box, where you may change the font color.

## Positioning and Sizing a Comment

A comment box may be moved by dragging its border or using the cursor keys to nudge the box. You may resize a comment box by dragging any of the eight resizing handles that appear around its edge. A comment box does not expand automatically to display all the text of a lengthy comment. You may use cursor keys to scroll through text in a comment, but resizing the comment box will ensure that everyone can read the entire comment.

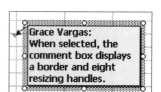

| Task | Procedure |
|---|---|
| Associate your name with new comments | ▪ Choose File→Options ⊞→General category.<br>▪ Under Personalize Your Copy of Microsoft Office, enter your name in the User Name box. |
| Insert a comment in a worksheet cell | ▪ Select the desired cell.<br>▪ Choose Review→Comments→New Comment ⊞ from the Ribbon (or right-click on the desired cell and choose Insert Comment from the context menu).<br>▪ Type the desired text in the comment box.<br>▪ Click outside the comment box to complete the comment. |
| Make a comment pop up and then hide it | ▪ Point at the cell containing the comment triangle for about one second to make the comment box pop up.<br>▪ Point at any other cell to hide the comment. |
| Show or hide a comment | ▪ Select the cell containing the comment triangle.<br>▪ Choose Review→Comments→Show/Hide Comment ⊞ from the Ribbon (or right-click the cell and choose Show/Hide Comments from the context menu). |
| Show or hide all comments in a workbook | ▪ Choose Review→Comments→Show All Comments ⊞ from the Ribbon. |
| Navigate through comments | ▪ Choose Review→Comments→Next ⊞ from the Ribbon to find the next comment.<br>▪ Choose Review→Comments→Previous ⊞ from the Ribbon to go back one comment. |
| Add to a comment | ▪ Select the cell containing the comment.<br>▪ Choose Review→Comments→Edit Comment ⊞ from the Ribbon (or right-click on the cell with the comment and choose Edit Comment from the context menu) if the comment box is not visible.<br>▪ Edit the comment text normally. You may change the text color of your addition if you like.<br>▪ Click outside the comment box to complete the comment. |
| Format comment text | ▪ Select the desired comment cell.<br>▪ Choose Review→Comments→Edit Comment ⊞ or Edit Comment from the Ribbon, as needed (or right-click the cell and choose the command from the context menu).<br>▪ Select existing text or position the insertion point for new next.<br>▪ Choose Home→Cells→Format ⊞→Format Comment from the Ribbon (or right-click inside the comment box and choose Format Comment from the context menu).<br>▪ Change the font, size, and color, as desired. |
| Move and resize a comment | ▪ Display the comment.<br>▪ Drag its border to move the comment box.<br>▪ Drag one of the eight resizing handles to resize. |
| Delete a comment | ▪ Select the desired comment cell.<br>▪ Choose Review→Comments→Delete Comment ⊞ from the Ribbon (or right-click on the cell and choose Delete Comment from the context menu). |

# Insert and Add to Comments

*In this exercise, you will insert a new comment into a cell and edit an existing comment with an answer to a question. Then you will move comments so that the underlying cells are visible.*

*Before You Begin: Verify with your instructor, staff, or class notes whether you have permission to change the username on your computer. Verify the procedure for restoring the original username if you do have permission.*

## Set the Username

1. Choose **File→Options** . Display the **General** category, if not already displayed.

2. Under Personalize Your Copy of Microsoft Office, notice the current **User Name**.

Click Cancel and skip to step 5 if you do not have permission to change the username on your computer.

3. As directed by your instructor, write the current username *exactly as shown* so that you may restore that name at the end of this exercise, or write the restoration procedure in the space provided:

_____

4. Change the existing username in the User Name box to **your first name and last name**, and click **OK** to save the change.

## Insert a Comment

5. Verify that the Connections Grant Cardiology Budget workbook in the Grants Project folder is **open**.

6. **Right-click** cell G20 and choose **Insert Comment** from the context menu.
*A comment box appears. Notice that the username is exactly as entered in the User Name box.*

7. Type the following comment in the comment box:

   **Participation in the League for Innovation conference**.

8. **Tap** Enter, and then select **cell G20** to close the Edit Comment box and hide your comment.

9. Point at **cell G20** to pop up your comment.

## Add to a Comment

10. **Right-click** cell D12 and choose **Edit Comment** from the context menu.
*The comment box appears and displays Terry Sanchez's question followed by the insertion point (text cursor).*

11. Use Ctrl+B to turn on bold, **type** your name followed by a colon (:), **tap** Enter, and use Ctrl+B to turn off bold.

12. **Drag down** the center-bottom handle of the comment box to enlarge the box, if necessary.

13. **Right-click** anywhere in the comment text and choose **Format Comment** from the context menu.

14. In the Format Comment dialog box, drop down the **Color** list, choose a new text color, such as Blue, and then click **OK**.

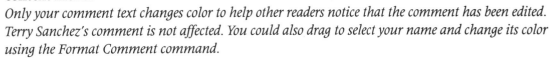

15. **Type** the following: **Yes, it is**.

16. Select **cell D12** to close the comment box.

17. **Right-click** cell D12 and choose **Show/Hide Comments** from the context menu.

    *Only your comment text changes color to help other readers notice that the comment has been edited. Terry Sanchez's comment is not affected. You could also drag to select your name and change its color using the Format Comment command.*

## Move a Comment

18. Choose **Review→Comments→Show All Comments** 🗗 from the Ribbon to display all comments.

    *Notice that some comments cover worksheet data or overlap another comment. You will move a comment off the data portion of the workbook.*

19. Click in the **cell D12** comment box to select it.

20. Follow these steps to change the location of a comment on the worksheet:

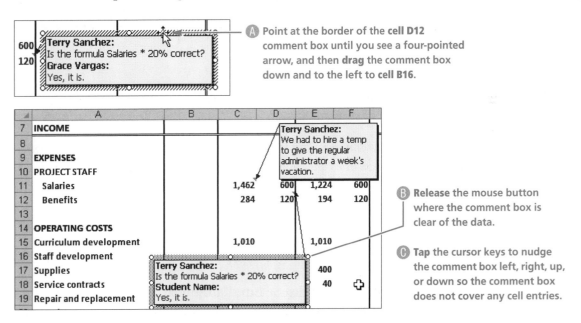

*A line still connects the comment to its cell. You may move a comment box to any location on the worksheet so it is out of the way of important data. This may be necessary before you print the comments on the worksheet, as you will learn to do in the next topic.*

## Delete a Comment and Save the Workbook

21. **Right-click** cell H17 and choose **Delete Comment** from the context menu.
    *The triangle icon disappears from the cell to indicate that it no longer contains a comment.*

22. **Save** 🖫 the changes, and leave the workbook **open** for the next exercise.

# Printing Comments

**Video Lesson**    labyrinthelab.com/videos

Excel's default setting is to suppress the printing of comments. To print the comments in a workbook, you choose a comments printing mode in the Page Setup dialog box. You may print each currently displayed comment where it appears on the worksheet or print all comments (whether displayed or not) on a separate sheet.

| QUICK REFERENCE | PRINTING COMMENTS |
|---|---|
| **Task** | **Procedure** |
| Print the comments in a workbook | ■ If you are going to print comments as they appear on the worksheets, display all comments that you want printed.<br>■ Choose Page Layout→Page Setup dialog box launcher from the Ribbon.<br>    [ Page Setup    ⬚ ] ◄———<br>■ Display the Sheet tab in the Page Setup dialog box.<br>■ Under Print, choose a print mode from the Comments list. |
| Switch off printing comments | ■ Choose Page Layout→Page Setup dialog box launcher from the Ribbon.<br>■ Under Print, choose (None) from the Comments list. |

## DEVELOP YOUR SKILLS 16.2.3
# Print Comments

*In this exercise, you will make settings to control the printing of comments. Then you will print the worksheet with comments printed on a separate sheet. Finally, you will switch off the printing of comments and restore the original username if you changed it to your name.*

1. Choose **Review→Comments→Show All Comments** 🗐 from the Ribbon to display all comments, if not already displayed.
   *Notice that all of the comments on the worksheet are displayed. One of the page setup options prints comments as they are currently displayed on the worksheet.*

2. Choose **Page Layout→Page Setup dialog box launcher** 🔲 from the Ribbon.

3. Display the **Sheet** tab in the Page Setup dialog box.

4. Under Print, drop down the Comments list and choose **As Displayed on Sheet**.

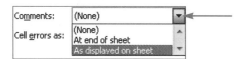

5. Click the **Print Preview** button near the bottom of the Sheet tab in the dialog box.
   *Excel displays the Print tab of Backstage view. The comments will print exactly as shown. You moved a comment in Develop Your Skills 16.2.2 to avoid covering important worksheet data.*

6. Click the **Page Setup** link at the bottom-left corner of Backstage view.

7. Display the **Sheet** tab in the Page Setup dialog box.

8. Choose **At End of Sheet** from the Comments list, and click **OK**.
   *The Print tab of Backstage view displays the worksheet in the preview.*

9. Click the **Next Page** button at the bottom of Backstage view to display page 2.
   *A second sheet has been added to the printout. This prints the comments along with their cell references. Since the comments print on a separate sheet, they will not cover any of the data as they could with the As Displayed on Sheet option.*

10. Click the **Print** 🖨 button at the upper-left corner of Backstage view to print the worksheet with a separate comments page.

11. Retrieve the printout from the printer.

## Switch Off Printing Comments

12. Choose **Page Layout→Page Setup dialog box launcher** ⌁ from the Ribbon.

13. Display the **Sheet** tab in the Page Setup dialog box.

14. Choose **(None)** from the Comments list and click **OK**.
    *Now the printing of comments is suppressed until you switch on this option again.*

15. **Save** 💾 the changes, and **close** the workbook. Leave Excel **open**.

 Skip steps 16–17 if you did not change the username in Develop Your Skills 16.2.2. If you did change the username, refer to the procedure that you wrote in step 3 of that exercise to restore the original username, which may vary from the following steps.

## Restore the Username

16. Choose **File→Options** 🔳. Display the **General** category, if not already displayed.

17. Under **Personalize Your Copy of Microsoft Office**, carefully **type** the original username that you wrote down during Develop Your Skills 16.2.2 in the User Name box and click **OK**.

# 16.3 Preparing Workbooks for Distribution

Video Lesson   labyrinthelab.com/videos

Assume that you created a workbook and checked its contents for accuracy. You wouldn't want your colleagues or clients to make changes or view confidential information unless authorized. You can perform a few more steps to enhance data security before sharing the workbook with other people.

## Inspecting Workbooks for Personal Information and Hidden Data

The Document Inspector tool can search for certain items in a workbook that you may not wish other people to see. The following table gives examples of data that you may include in a search and items that will *not* be found.

| Examples of items that may be included in a search | Examples of items NOT included in a search |
| --- | --- |
| ■ Hidden worksheets, rows, and columns | ■ Hidden cells |
| ■ Comments in cells | ■ Comments resulting from edits by multiple authors |
| ■ Document properties, such as the author's name | ■ Data entered in out-of-the-way areas of a worksheet |
| ■ Headers and footers | ■ White text on a white background |
| ■ Comments next to named ranges in the Name Manager | ■ A shape covering worksheet data |
| ■ Objects formatted as hidden or invisible | ■ Invisible objects pasted from Web pages |
| | ■ Hyperlinks and other workbook metadata that give the path to the source data's storage location |

When the Document Inspector displays the search result, you may choose to remove items from the workbook from within the search result. The removal may be permanent, and you cannot choose specific instances within a category. For example, you may choose to remove all document property types listed in the search result but not just some of them. You may, however, choose not to remove all in Document Inspector and instead delete any single item manually in the workbook as you would normally.

The workbook contains comments and document properties that could contain personal information.

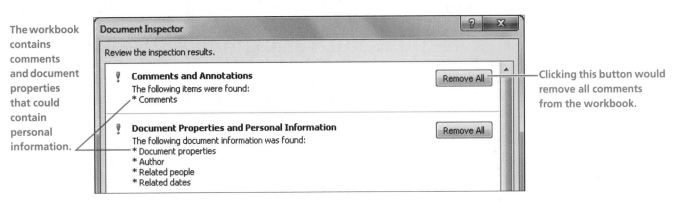

Clicking this button would remove all comments from the workbook.

The Document Inspector report

Some removed content cannot be restored. If you are uncertain, close Document Inspector, locate and remove items manually, and inspect again.

# Marking a Workbook as Final

The Mark as Final command in the Info tab of Backstage view saves the workbook and sets the file as read-only. A co-worker can view the workbook but cannot enter, change, or format data. This feature is not foolproof, though. Anyone who opens the workbook can turn off the "final" status.

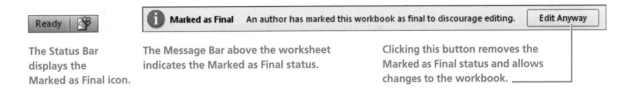

| The Status Bar displays the Marked as Final icon. | The Message Bar above the worksheet indicates the Marked as Final status. | Clicking this button removes the Marked as Final status and allows changes to the workbook. |
|---|---|---|

# Granting a User Permission to View or Edit a Workbook

In addition to locking cells on a worksheet and protecting the workbook, you may control who may open a workbook and whether they may edit, print, or copy data from it. You also may set a permission expiration date. Your network administrator may set up rights management on your intranet server. As an alternative, you may sign up for a Windows Live account and use the free Windows Rights Management Services Client software to embed your chosen permissions and restrictions in the workbook file. When users try to open the file, they receive a message to connect to the licensing server. If the user's credentials are verified as valid, the server downloads a license to use the file and the workbook opens. Otherwise, a message indicates that the user does not have permission rights for the file.

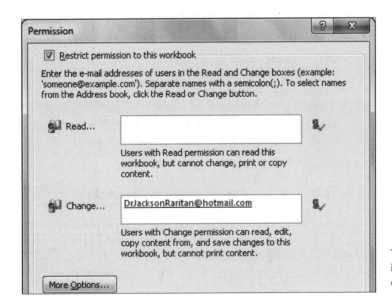

This Permission dialog box indicates that one user may open and change the workbook.

The Status Bar displays an icon to indicate that a permission policy is applied to the workbook.

| QUICK REFERENCE | INSPECTING, MARKING AS FINAL, AND RESTRICTING ACCESS TO WORKBOOKS |
|---|---|
| **Task** | **Procedure** |
| Inspect a workbook for hidden data and personal information | ▪ Save a copy of the original workbook in case you need to recover hidden data or document attributes. |
| | ▪ Choose File→Info, and choose Check for Issues menu ▼→Inspect Document in the Info tab of Backstage view. |
| | ▪ Check or uncheck the desired options for inspection. |
| | ▪ Click Inspect. |
| | ▪ In the Document Inspector dialog box, click Remove All next to any item to remove all instances of that item, or click Close and remove items manually from the workbook. |
| Mark a workbook as final | ▪ Choose File→Info, and choose Protect Workbook menu ▼→Mark as Final in the Info tab of Backstage view. |
| | ▪ Click OK to confirm, and click OK in the message box. The Permissions indicator will be highlighted in Backstage view. |
| Remove final status from a workbook | ▪ Follow one of these steps: |
| | ◆ Click the Edit Anyway button in the Message Bar above the worksheet. |
| | *or* |
| | ◆ Choose File→Info, and choose Protect Workbook menu ▼→Mark as Final in the Info tab of Backstage view to toggle off the option. |
| Allow access to a workbook only to certain people | ▪ Save the workbook. |
| | ▪ Choose File→Info, and choose Protect Workbook menu ▼→Restrict Permission by People→Restricted Access in the Info tab of Backstage view. |
| | ▪ Follow the prompts to sign up for the Information Rights Management Services, if necessary. |
| | ▪ Follow the prompts to use an existing Windows Live ID or create an account ID, and then log in with your email address and password. |
| | ▪ In the Select User dialog box, choose the desired user account for granting permission, and click OK. |
| | ▪ In the Permissions dialog box, place a checkmark next to Restrict Permission to This Workbook, and enter the users' email addresses in the Read box and Change box, as desired. |
| | ▪ To set an expiration date, click the More Options button, and enter an expiration date. |
| Remove restrictions for accessing a workbook | ▪ Choose File→Info, and choose Protect Workbook menu ▼→Restrict Permission by People→Unrestricted Access in the Info tab of Backstage view. |
| | ▪ Click Yes to confirm that anyone can open and edit the workbook. |
| Access a restricted workbook after permission is granted | ▪ Make certain your Internet or network connection is active. |
| | ▪ Choose File→Open, navigate to the storage location containing the desired file, and double-click the file. A blank workbook appears. |
| | ▪ Click OK when prompted to connect to the licensing server. After your credentials are verified, the workbook appears. |

## Inspect and Mark a Workbook as Final

*In this exercise, you will use Document Inspector to search for data items you may not wish other people to see when you share the workbook. You also will mark the workbook as final to help prevent unintended changes.*

### Use Document Inspector

1. **Open** the Distributed Budget workbook from the Grant Project folder in the Lesson 16 folder.

2. Choose **File→Save As** , change the filename to **Distributed Budget Final**, make certain that the **Grant Projects** folder is active, and click **Save**.
   *The file copy is saved in the Grant Project folder within the Lesson 16 folder. Inspecting a copy of the original workbook is recommended to preserve original data that may be lost during inspection.*

3. Choose **File→Info,** and choose **Check for Issues menu ▾→Inspect Document** in the Info tab of Backstage view.

*The Document Inspector dialog box displays seven selected categories. You could deselect any categories, if desired.*

4. Read the inspection categories, and then click **Inspect** at the bottom of the dialog box.
   *The inspection report appears.*

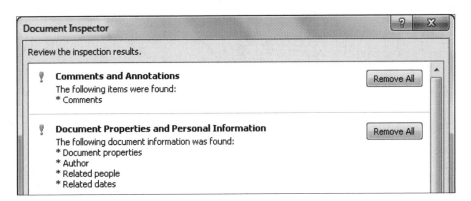

*Two categories of data that may contain personal information were found in the workbook. Each category is indicated by a red exclamation (!) mark. Under the Comments and Annotations category, notice that Comments were found. Also, several types of document properties were found.*

5. Click **Remove All** at the right of Comments and Annotations.

*The Comments and Annotations category now indicates that all comment items were successfully removed.*

6. Click **Remove All** at the right of Document Properties and Personal Information.

*All seven categories now display a blue checkmark.*

7. Close the **Document Inspector** dialog box.

*Notice that only the size, last modified date, and created date properties remain at the right of the Info tab in Backstage view. The author name was removed.*

8. **Tap** Esc to exit Backstage view, and notice that all comments were removed.

*You cannot undo to restore the comments. The Remove All button should be used with care.*

| Properties ▼ | |
| --- | --- |
| Size | 20.0KB |
| Title | Add a title |
| Tags | Add a tag |
| Categories | Add a category |
| **Related Dates** | |
| Last Modified | Today, 7:19 PM |
| Created | 2/18/1998 4:29 PM |
| Last Printed | 6/26/2010 4:52 PM |
| **Related People** | |
| Author | Add an author |
| Last Modified By | Student Name |

## Mark the Workbook as Final

9. Choose **File→Info**, and choose **Protect Workbook menu ▼→Mark as Final** in the Info tab of Backstage view.

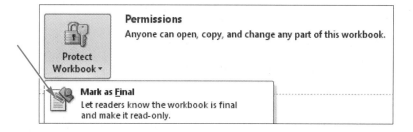

10. Read the Microsoft Excel message, and click **OK**.

11. Read another message, if one appears, and click **OK**.

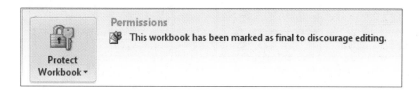

*The Permissions heading changes color and indicates the workbook status.*

12. **Tap** Esc to exit Backstage view, and read the Message Bar about the workbook.

13. Select any cell in the worksheet, and attempt to enter data.

*You cannot type into a cell. Notice that formatting comments on the Ribbon are dimmed.*

14. Click the **Edit Anyway** button in the Message Bar.

*The Marked as Final status is removed, and the document may be edited and formatted as usual.*

15. **Save** 💾 the changes, and **close** the workbook.

# 16.4 Sharing Workbooks Without a Network

In a workgroup environment, several team members may need to access the same workbook simultaneously. For example, they may be independently checking data, entering data into areas of a project workbook assigned to them, or updating rapidly changing data. You may set up a shared workbook for other users to edit. If your organization does not have a computer network available, you may distribute the shared workbook using either of the following methods:

1. Sending one copy to the first team member to make changes and then routing the same file to the next user

2. Giving each user his/her own copy in which to make changes

You will set the workbook as shared, track changes made by the various users, and review the changes. The Excel commands that you use will vary depending on the method.

# 16.5 Tracking Changes to Workbooks

**Video Lesson**  labyrinthelab.com/videos

When several people make changes to the same workbook, one person usually is assigned to review and approve each change. Excel can maintain a change history that tracks each change to the workbook. The change history displays the username of the person who made each change along with the original and new contents of each cell. The change history lets you review each change and accept or reject it. A changed cell may be identified by its border and a triangle in the upper-left corner. Each user's changes are marked in a different color.

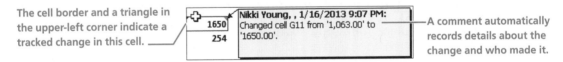

The cell border and a triangle in the upper-left corner indicate a tracked change in this cell.

Nikki Young, , 1/16/2013 9:07 PM:
Changed cell G11 from '1,063.00' to '1650.00'.

A comment automatically records details about the change and who made it.

## Example of Tracked Changes at Work

You turn on the Track Changes feature and then give the workbook file to your assistant. You ask him to contact two grant and contract specialists and then input any expenditures not yet included in the workbook. You turn on the Track Changes feature so you can quickly see and review all changes your assistant makes. You may also turn on the Track Changes feature for one workbook copy before passing it from one person to another for changes and then back to the project manager to approve the changes. Switching on Track Changes also sets that workbook to be shared. In this case, you need not also use the Share Workbook command described later in this lesson.

| Task | Procedure |
|------|-----------|
| Switch on tracking changes for a workbook | ■ Choose Review→Changes→Track Changes ▦→Highlight Changes from the Ribbon. |
| | ■ Make certain that the box next to Track Changes While Editing has a checkmark. This option also sets the workbook to be shared. |
| | ■ Under When, Who, and Where in the Highlight Changes dialog box, choose the options for the changes that should be highlighted. |
| | ■ Set whether you wish the changed cells to be highlighted on the screen and click OK. |
| | ■ Choose Yes when prompted to save the workbook. You must save the workbook to activate tracking changes. |
| Switch off tracking changes | ■ Choose Review→Changes→Track Changes ▦→Highlight Changes from the Ribbon. |
| | ■ Remove the checkmark from the box next to Track Changes While Editing. Note that the change history will be erased. |

# Track Changes to a Workbook

*In this exercise, you will switch on the Track Changes feature and then edit several workbook cells. As you work, your edits will be recorded for later review.*

1. **Open** the Shared Budget workbook from the Grant Project folder, which is within the Lesson 16 folder in your file storage location.

## Check the Username

*Because Track Changes records the name of each user who edits the workbook, you will check the username and change it to your own name, if necessary.*

2. Choose **File→Options** ▦. Display the **General** category, if not already displayed.

3. Under Personalize Your Copy of Microsoft Office, notice the name in the **User Name** box.

 Click Cancel and skip to step 5 if you do not have permission rights to change the username on your computer.

4. Change the existing name in the **User Name** box to your first name and last name, and click **OK**.

## Switch On Track Changes

5. Choose **Review→Changes→Track Changes** 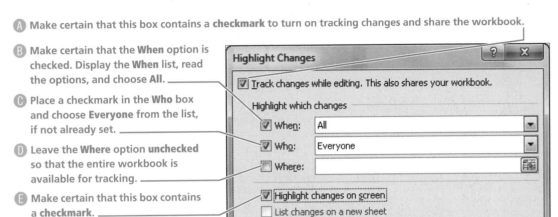 →**Highlight Changes** from the Ribbon.

6. Follow these steps to set up tracking changes:

(A) Make certain that this box contains a **checkmark** to turn on tracking changes and share the workbook.

(B) Make certain that the **When** option is checked. Display the **When** list, read the options, and choose **All**. ⎯⎯⎯

(C) Place a checkmark in the **Who** box and choose **Everyone** from the list, if not already set. ⎯⎯⎯

(D) Leave the **Where** option **unchecked** so that the entire workbook is available for tracking. ⎯⎯⎯

(E) Make certain that this box contains a **checkmark**. ⎯⎯⎯

7. Click **OK** to close the dialog box, and then click **OK** when prompted to save the workbook. *You must save the file to activate the tracking changes feature. Now Excel is set up to record every change made to the workbook. Notice that [Shared] appears after the filename in the title bar at the top of the window, as shown in the following illustration. You will learn more about sharing workbooks later in this lesson.*

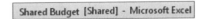

## Edit the Workbook

8. Display the **Orthopedics Dept** worksheet.

9. Select **cell E21**, which currently has a value of 2,308, and enter **1725**.
*Notice the border around the cell and the small triangle in the upper-left corner. This mark tells you that the cell has been edited since Track Changes was activated.*

10. **Right-click** cell E21 and choose **Insert Comment** from the context menu. Type the comment **Network server was repaired.**

11. Click **outside** the comment box.

12. Point at **cell E21** but do not click. In the pop-up box that appears, read the change history and your comment for cell E21.

13. If the comment box remains visible when you point to a different cell, choose **Review→Comments→Show All Comments** from the Ribbon to turn off the display of comments.

14. Select **cell G16** and **enter** a value of **725**.

15. Select **cell G11** and change the value to **5844**.

16. **Save** 🖫 the changes.
*You are finished editing the workbook. Now read on to see how the workbook author reviews the edits.*

# Reviewing Tracked Changes

**Video Lesson**  labyrinthelab.com/videos

You may review changes to a workbook that has the Track Changes feature switched on. When you review changes, Excel can jump from one change to the next, giving you the opportunity to accept or reject each change. After you have reviewed a change, Excel keeps a record of the change until you deactivate the Track Changes feature. The following list describes your review options.

- **Accept**—An accepted change is kept in the cell. The change history records the old value that was replaced.
- **Reject**—A rejected change restores the old value in the cell. The change history records the new value that was rejected.
- **Accept All or Reject All**—All changes that have not yet been reviewed may be rejected or accepted with a single command.

## The Change History

After you have reviewed changes to a worksheet, the change history retains a copy of the reviewed cells, including their old and new values and any rejected values. Thus, even after you accept a change, you may refer to the change history and manually reinstate an old or rejected value. You may view the change history by displaying a separate History worksheet. This worksheet is deleted automatically when you save the workbook, but you may give the command again.

When you switch off track changes, the change history is erased.

| QUICK REFERENCE | REVIEWING TRACKED CHANGES |
|---|---|
| **Task** | **Procedure** |
| Review and approve changes to a workbook | ■ Choose Review→Changes→Track Changes →Accept/Reject Changes from the Ribbon.<br>■ Choose OK when prompted to save the workbook.<br>■ Choose the categories of changes you wish to review in the Select Changes to Accept or Reject dialog box and click OK.<br>■ Use the buttons in the Accept or Reject Changes dialog box to navigate through the changes and accept or reject them as desired. |
| View the change history for a workbook | ■ Choose Review→Changes→Track Changes →Accept/Reject Changes from the Ribbon.<br>■ Place a checkmark in the box next to List Changes on a New Sheet and click OK. The new History worksheet will remain visible until you give the Save command. |

# Review the Changes

*In this exercise, you will take on the role of Grace Vargas reviewing the changes.*

*Before You Begin: You may not have permission rights to change the username on your computer. If directed by your instructor, close the Shared Budget workbook and open it on a different computer. That way, you may still use a different username while reviewing the changes.*

## Set the Username

1. Choose **File→Options** . Display the **General** category, if not already displayed.

2. Under Personalize Your Copy of Microsoft Office, notice the current **User Name**.

Click Cancel and skip to step 4 if you do not have permission rights to change the username on your computer.

3. Enter **Grace Vargas** in the User Name box, and click **OK** to save the change.
*Notice that the borders around the changed cells have changed color. This alerts you that the cells were changed by someone other than Grace Vargas, the current user.*

## Accept or Reject Changes

4. Choose **Review→Changes→Track Changes** **→Accept/Reject Changes** from the Ribbon.
*A dialog box appears in which you can select the changes to accept or reject.*

5. Follow these steps to examine your choices:

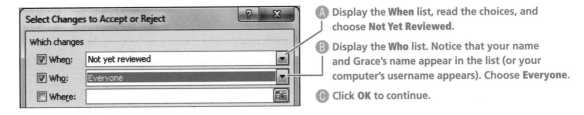

Ⓐ Display the **When** list, read the choices, and choose **Not Yet Reviewed**.

Ⓑ Display the **Who** list. Notice that your name and Grace's name appear in the list (or your computer's username appears). Choose **Everyone**.

Ⓒ Click **OK** to continue.

*The Accept or Reject Changes dialog box appears so that you may navigate from one changed cell to the next, as shown in the following illustration.*

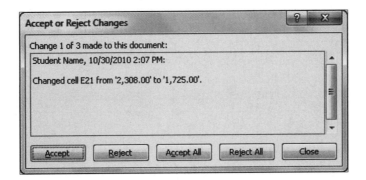

6. If necessary, drag the title bar to move the **Accept or Reject Changes** dialog box so that **cell E21** is visible.
*Notice that the first cell that you changed already has a marquee around it.*

7. Point at **cell E21**, but do not click.
*Notice that you cannot view the comment. Before reviewing a changed worksheet, you may want to display or review any comments first.*

8. Click the **Accept** button to accept this change to the workbook.
*Notice that cell E21 no longer has a change box around it. The change has been reviewed. The marquee moves on to the next changed cell, G16. You recognize this figure as advance payment for travel by a medical staff member to a training seminar. You decide to reject this change because you know that this expense should not be recorded until next quarter, when the training actually takes place.*

9. Click the **Reject** button.
*Cell G16 reverts to its old value, which is blank.*

10. Click the **Accept** button for **cell G11**.
*Notice that the change boxes have returned to cells E21 and G11, where you accepted the change. These cells will remain marked until you switch off Track Changes.*

11. Scroll down so that **row 16** is at the top of the window.
*This allows enough space to view the comment in cell E21, which you will do next.*

12. Point at **cell E21**.
*Notice that the entry from the change history appears for this cell as in the previous exercise. It tells you the name of the person who changed the cell, the old and new values, and the name of the person who entered the comment.*

13. Scroll up until **row 1** is visible.

14. **Save** 💾 the workbook.
*The change history is not complete unless you save the workbook. Next you will create a change history worksheet.*

### View the Change History

15. Choose **Review→Changes→Track Changes 📝→Highlight Changes** from the Ribbon.

16. Place a checkmark in the box next to **List Changes on a New Sheet** near the bottom of the dialog box and click **OK**.

| | A | B | C | D | E | F | G | H | I | J | K |
|---|---|---|---|---|---|---|---|---|---|---|---|
| 1 | Action Number | Date | Time | Who | Change | Sheet | Range | New Value | Old Value | Action Type | Losing Action |
| 2 | 1 | 5/21/2010 | 10:22 PM | Student Name | Cell Change | Orthopedics Dept | E21 | 1725 | 2308 | | |
| 3 | 2 | 5/21/2010 | 10:22 PM | Student Name | Cell Change | Orthopedics Dept | G16 | 725 | <blank> | | |
| 4 | 3 | 5/21/2010 | 10:22 PM | Student Name | Cell Change | Orthopedics Dept | G11 | 5844 | 1063 | | |
| 5 | 4 | 5/21/2010 | 10:35 PM | Grace Vargas | Cell Change | Orthopedics Dept | G16 | <blank> | | Result of rejected action | 2 |
| 6 | | | | | | | | | | | |
| 7 | The history ends with the changes saved on 5/21/2010 at 10:35 PM. | | | | | | | | | | |

*The History worksheet appears. (Your Date, Time, and Who entries will vary from the illustration.) The change history maintains a complete record of every change to the workbook. Notice that the last action line even describes how cell G16 reverted to blank as a result of a rejected change.*

17. **Save**  the workbook.
   *The temporary History worksheet disappears after you save the workbook, and the first worksheet in the workbook is displayed.*

## Switch Off Track Changes

*Now that you have reviewed the changes, you no longer need to track them.*

18. Choose **Review→Changes→Track Changes** **→Highlight Changes** from the Ribbon.

19. Remove the checkmark from the **Track Changes While Editing** box and click **OK**.

20. Click **Yes** when asked to confirm removal of the change history and workbook sharing.
   *Wait briefly as Excel deletes the hidden change history data from the workbook.*

21. Display the **Orthopedics Dept** worksheet.
   *Notice that the changed cells contain the accepted values but no longer display borders.*

22. **Close** the workbook, and leave Excel **open**.

## Restore the Username

 Skip steps 23 and 24 if you did not change the username. If you did change the username, refer to the procedure you wrote in step 3 in Develop Your Skills 16.2.2 to restore the original username, which may vary from the following steps.

23. Choose **File→Options**. Display the **General** category, if not already displayed.

24. Under **Personalize our Copy of Microsoft Office**, carefully **type** the original username you wrote down during Develop Your Skills 16.2.2 in the User Name box and click **OK**.

# 16.6 Merging Multiple Workbooks

**Video Lesson** labyrinthelab.com/videos

 You may choose to share a workbook by distributing a copy to each user rather than placing it on a network server. The Compare and Merge Workbooks command gives you the capability to merge the multiple copies of the workbook containing all user changes into a single workbook. This saves you the tedium of opening each workbook individually and then selecting, copying, and pasting the necessary cells into the primary workbook. The files to be merged must all be copies of the *original* workbook, and the copies must have unique filenames. For example, users may add their initials to the filename, such as mw-Budget and tg-Budget.

 You may only merge the edited copies of the workbook when it has been set up as a shared workbook with Track Changes. The Compare and Merge Workbooks command is dimmed for normal (unshared) Excel workbooks.

## Example of a Merge

You create a shared workbook. You send the workbook to several people by email as an attachment and request that the recipients fill in data on specific sections. After the workbook copies are returned, you use the Compare and Merge Workbooks command to merge them into your original shared workbook. You will not have to look for, copy, and paste the data. Then, you use the Accept/Reject Changes command to resolve any changes that multiple users made to the same cell.

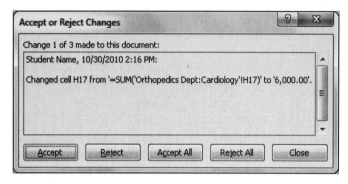

The Compare and Merge Workbooks command displays all changes made to a cell.

The Compare and Merge Workbooks command does not appear on the Ribbon. You must add it to the Quick Access toolbar or a main tab on the Ribbon.

## What Happens When Workbooks Are Merged

Excel performs several operations when you merge workbooks. The details are described in the following table.

| Change | Description |
|--------|-------------|
| Data is merged into the currently active workbook | Whichever copy of the shared workbook you have open when you give the Compare and Merge Workbooks command is the one that receives the merged data. The copies of the workbook you are merging from do not receive merged data. |
| Merged data replaces original data | Data merged from other workbook(s) will replace any data already existing in the same cells of the workbook into which you are merging. |
| A change history is recorded | Excel records all changes that occur during the merge, including where the data came from and who made the change. You may review the changes and accept any one change to a cell. |

## Merged Cells Compared to Merged Workbooks

Do not confuse the Compare and Merge Workbooks command with merged cells. Merged cells allow you to combine a range of cells and center a label across the cells. You cannot merge cells in a shared workbook. You must either merge cells before sharing the workbook or turn off sharing.

| Task | Procedure |
|------|-----------|
| Add the Compare and Merge Workbooks command to the Quick Access toolbar | ■ Choose File→Options→ , and choose the Quick Access Toolbar category in the Excel Options dialog box.<br>■ Choose Commands Not in the Ribbon from the Choose Commands From list.<br>■ Scroll down the list, select Compare and Merge Workbooks, and click the Add button. |
| Merge multiple copies of a shared workbook | ■ Set up the workbook to be shared. Distribute copies of the original shared workbook to others who will contribute data. The files must have unique filenames.<br>■ After the workbook copies are edited and returned, open the one file into which all others will be merged.<br>■ Make certain that all other workbooks to be merged are closed.<br>■ Choose Compare and Merge Workbooks ⬤ from the Quick Access toolbar.<br>■ In the dialog box, select the workbook to be merged or use Ctrl or Shift to select multiple files. |
| Review merged changes to a workbook | ■ Choose Review→Changes→Track Changes ▣→Accept/Reject Changes from the Ribbon.<br>■ Choose the types of changes you wish to review and click OK.<br>■ Use the buttons in the dialog box to navigate through the changes and accept or reject changes as desired. |

## Protecting Elements in a Shared Workbook

You may protect worksheet elements before setting the workbook to be shared. For example, you may lock or unlock cells and then turn on worksheet protection. The Protect and Share Workbook command sets the workbook to be shared and provides two additional protection levels. The share and track changes features are dimmed in dialog boxes to prevent users from switching them off in an individual copy of a shared workbook. You may also set a password to ensure that only designated users may alter this protection. This password is distinct from any passwords set to protect cells or worksheets.

When you use the Protect and Share Workbook command, the shared workbook is automatically created and the Track Changes feature is activated. Thus, you do not have to execute the Share Workbook command separately.

| Task | Procedure |
|------|-----------|
| Share a workbook and protect the change history from being disabled | ■ Choose Review→Changes→Protect and Share Workbook from the Ribbon.<br><br>■ In the Protect Shared Workbook dialog box, place a checkmark in the box next to Sharing with Track Changes.<br><br>■ Enter a password, if desired, and reenter the password when prompted to confirm. Users must enter the password to alter protection.<br><br>■ If desired, choose Review→Changes→Share Workbook from the Ribbon and set options in the Advanced tab of the Share Workbook dialog box. |
| Switch off workbook sharing and password protection for the change history | ■ Choose Review→Changes→Unprotect Shared Workbook from the Ribbon.<br><br>■ Enter the password.<br><br>■ Click Yes to confirm removing the workbook from shared use. |

## DEVELOP YOUR SKILLS 16.6.1

# Merge Two Workbooks

*In this exercise, you will merge changes from a copy of a shared workbook into the original shared workbook.*

*Before You Begin: The Compare and Merge Workbooks command should be available on the Quick Access toolbar, or you must have permission rights to add the command.*

### Set the Username

Skip to step 3 if you do not have permission rights to change the username on your computer.

1. Choose **File→Options**. Display the **General** category, if not already displayed.

2. Under **Personalize Your Copy of Microsoft Office**, enter your **first and last name** in the User Name box and click **OK**.

### Create a Shared Workbook with Track Changes Protection

*In this section of the exercise, you will create a protected shared workbook. You will then create a second copy of the workbook with a different name.*

3. **Open** the Merged Budget 1 workbook.

4. Choose **Review→Changes→Protect and Share Workbook** from the Ribbon.

5. Place a checkmark in the box next to **Sharing with Track Changes** and click **OK**.
   *You just turned on workbook sharing and track changes, and you protected both features. Excel warns you that the workbook will now be saved.*

6. Click **OK** to confirm saving the shared workbook.

7. Choose **Review→Changes→Share Workbook** ⊞ from the Ribbon.
*Notice that the Allow Changes by More than One User option is dimmed. Users cannot switch off workbook sharing, nor can they switch off change tracking in the Highlight Changes dialog box.*

8. Click **Cancel** to exit the dialog box without making any changes.

## Copy the Shared Workbook

*You will save a second copy with a different name. You can do this to create as many copies of the shared workbook as you need. Excel will still recognize these variously named workbooks as being shared with the original workbook.*

9. Choose **File→Save As** 🖫. Change the number from 1 to **2** in the filename and click **Save**.
*The new filename is Merged Budget 2. Notice that the title bar displays [Shared] after the filename.*

## Enter Data in the Workbook Copy

10. Display the **Cardiology** worksheet.
*When you merge data into a workbook, the new data in a cell being merged always replaces any data already in the cell. You will place a new value in one of the cells and see how Excel helps you catch any potential problems during the merge.*

11. Select **cell H17** and enter **6000** as the new value.

12. Enter **600** in **cell H11**.

13. Enter **120** in **cell H12**.

14. **Close** the workbook and choose to **save** when you are asked to save the changes.
*You cannot merge from an open workbook.*

## Merge the Workbooks

*Now that the Cardiology worksheet is edited, you will merge the changes into the original workbook.*

15. Verify that the **Compare and Merge Workbooks** ⬤ command is installed on the Quick Access toolbar. If it is not, follow these steps to install the command:

Ⓐ Choose **File→Options** 🖹 →Quick Access Toolbar category.

Ⓑ Choose **Commands Not in the Ribbon** from the **Choose Commands From** list.

Ⓒ Scroll down the command list and select **Compare and Merge Workbooks**.

| Choose commands from: ⓘ |
| --- |
| Commands Not in the Ribbon ▾ |
| Compare and Merge Workbooks... |
| 🖉 Constrain Numeric |

Ⓓ Click the **Add** button in the center of the dialog box.

Ⓔ Click **OK**.

16. **Open** the Merged Budget 1 workbook.

17. Display the **Cardiology** worksheet.
*Notice that no data values are entered into cells H11 and H12 of this worksheet.*

18. Choose **Compare and Merge Workbooks** ⊙ from the Quick Access toolbar.
    *A dialog box opens from which you can select one or more files to merge. To select more than one file from the list, you would hold down the [Ctrl] key as you make your selections. In this exercise, you will merge just one file.*

19. **Double-click** the Merged Budget 2 workbook to merge it into your open workbook.
    *Excel saves the workbook as it processes the merge. All data for the Cardiology worksheet have been merged into place. Notice that the newly merged number 6000 in cell H17 that you entered into the Merged Budget 2 workbook has replaced the old figure of 8000. However, you still have the opportunity to review the changes and reject incorrect merge results.*

## Visually Review the Changes

*You will use two methods to survey the results. First, you will perform a visual review of highlighted changes. Then you will use the Accept/Reject Changes command to review them.*

20. Choose **Review→Changes→Track Changes** 📝 **→Highlight Changes** from the Ribbon.

21. Follow these steps to display the change history worksheet:

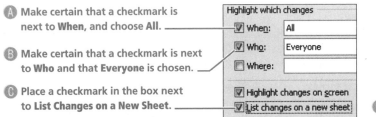

Ⓐ Make certain that a checkmark is next to **When**, and choose **All**.

Ⓑ Make certain that a checkmark is next to **Who** and that **Everyone** is chosen.

Ⓒ Place a checkmark in the box next to **List Changes on a New Sheet**.

Ⓓ Click **OK**.

22. Examine **columns H and I** of the History worksheet. These columns display a new and an old value for **cell H17**.

23. Display the **Cardiology** worksheet.
    *Notice the change box around the changed cell, another visual indication that a change you might not want has taken place. You could manually change this cell if necessary. However, you will use the Accept/Reject Changes command instead.*

## Accept and Reject Changes

24. Choose **Review→Changes→Track Changes** 📝 **→Accept/Reject Changes** from the Ribbon.

25. Make certain that the dialog box is set as shown at right, and click **OK**.
    *The first change is displayed. In fact, it's the only one we need to worry about.*

26. Click **Reject** to replace 6000 with the old value.
    *Now you see the next change on the Cardiology worksheet. You know that this and the next change values are good. Rather than click Accept for changes one by one, you can simply accept them all.*

27. Click **Accept All** to accept all remaining changes.
    *That saved some time! Now you will turn off sharing on this workbook.*

### Disable Sharing for the Workbook

28. Choose **Review→Changes→Unprotect Shared Workbook**  from the Ribbon.
    *Although protection has been removed, the workbook is still shared. You must use the Share Workbook command to switch off sharing.*

29. Choose **Review→Changes→Share Workbook** from the Ribbon.

30. On the **Editing** tab, uncheck the box next to **Allow Changes by More than One User at the Same Time**, and click **OK**.

31. Click **Yes** to confirm removing the workbook from shared use.
    *Now that the workbook is no longer shared, you cannot perform any additional merge commands. You would need to share the workbook again and then create additional copies to merge with this workbook. Notice that the change boxes are no longer visible because the change history has also been deactivated.*

32. **Save** the changes, and **close** the workbook.

### Restore the Username

Skip steps 33 and 34 if you did not change the username. If you did change the username, refer to the procedure that you wrote in step 3 in Develop Your Skills 16.2.2 to restore the original username, which may vary from the following steps.

33. Choose **File→Options** and display the **General** category, if not already displayed.

34. Under **Personalize Your Copy of Microsoft Office**, carefully **type** the original username that you wrote down during Develop Your Skills 16.2.2 in the User Name box and click **OK**.

### Remove a Button from the Quick Access Toolbar

*Your instructor may request that you skip the next step.*

35. **Right-click** the Compare and Merge Workbooks button on the Quick Access toolbar, and choose **Remove from Quick Access Toolbar** in the context menu.

## 16.7 Concepts Review

Concepts Review    labyrinthelab.com/excel10

*To check your knowledge of the key concepts introduced in this lesson, complete the Concepts Review quiz by going to the URL listed above. If your classroom is using Labyrinth eLab, you may complete the Concepts Review quiz from within your eLab course.*

# Reinforce Your Skills

## Create a New Folder

*In this exercise, you will create a new folder for a project from within Excel's Save As dialog box.*

1. **Open** the rs-Expense Report workbook from the Lesson 16 folder in your file storage location.

2. Choose **File→Save As** 🗎 from the Ribbon.

3. Follow these steps to create a new folder:
   *Your dialog box may appear slightly different from what is shown here, depending on your version of Windows.*

Ⓐ Navigate to the Lesson 16 folder in your storage location, if not already displayed.

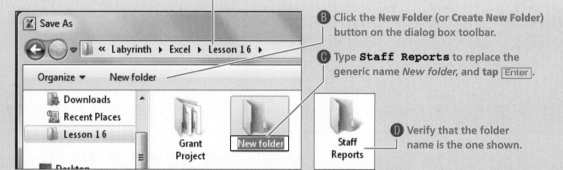

Ⓑ Click the **New Folder** (or **Create New Folder**) button on the dialog box toolbar.

Ⓒ Type **Staff Reports** to replace the generic name *New folder*, and tap ⌨Enter.

Ⓓ Verify that the folder name is the one shown.

Skip to **step 5** if your Windows version opened the empty Staff Reports folder.

4. **Double-click** the Staff Reports folder in the Save As dialog box to open the folder.
   *Notice the new folder name in the Save In box. Excel immediately opened the new folder after you named it.*

5. **Save** the workbook in the folder you just created, and leave the workbook **open**.
   *Now you have two copies of this workbook file in your file storage location: one where you opened the file originally and one in the new folder. You will use the copy in the Staff Reports folder in the next exercise.*

# Work with Comments

*In this exercise, you will add comments to a workbook. You will also edit, move, delete, and print comments.*

*Before You Begin: You must have completed Reinforce Your Skills 16.1, and the rs-Expense Report workbook should be open. The Microsoft Office username should be set to your name if you have permission to do so (see steps 1–4 in Develop Your Skills 16.2.2).*

## Insert Comments

1. Select **cell B11** and then choose **Review→Comments→New Comment** 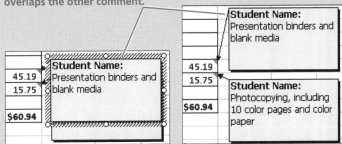 from the Ribbon. **Enter** the following comment: **Presentation binders and blank media**

2. **Right-click** cell B12 and choose **Insert Comment** from the context menu. Enter the following comment: **Photocopying, including 10 color pages**

3. **Enter** the following comment in **cell I19**: **Travel to/from airport at 50 cents per mile**

4. **Enter** the following comment in **cell E22**: **Find receipt**

5. **Save** the changes.

## Display and Hide the Comments

6. Choose **Review→Comments→Show All Comments** from the Ribbon.
   *Notice that the comments for cells B11 and B12 overlap. You need to move them to new positions.*

7. Follow these steps to move a comment:

   **A** Click in the comment box for **cell B11**.

   **B** Point at the **comment box border** until the pointer displays four arrows, and then **drag** the comment up so that it no longer overlaps the other comment.

8. Move the comment for **cell B12** down.

9. Move the comment for **cell I19** up so it is above row 18 and no longer overlaps the data in **cells J19 and K19**.

## Delete and Edit Comments

10. **Right-click** cell E22 and choose **Delete Comment** from the context menu.

11. Click in the comment box for **cell B12**, type **and color paper** at the end of the comment, and click **outside** the comment box.

## Print the Comments

12. Choose **Page Layout→Page Setup dialog box launcher** from the Ribbon.

| Page Setup | ☐ |
| --- | --- |

13. Display the **Sheet** tab in the Page Setup dialog box.

14. Under Print, drop down the **Comments** list and choose **As Displayed on Sheet**. Click **OK**.

15. Click **Print Preview** to make certain that the worksheet and comments will print on one page.

16. **Print** 🖨 the workbook and retrieve your printout from the printer.

17. **Save** 💾 the changes and **close** the workbook.

---

### REINFORCE YOUR SKILLS 16.3

# Share a Workbook and Review Changes

*In this exercise, you will set up a workbook to be routed to Corey Owens, a co-worker. First, you will inspect the document for potential security issues; then you will protect and share the workbook. Next, you will review the changes in a workbook that Corey returns to you. Finally, you will create the History worksheet to display the change history.*

*Before you Begin: The Microsoft Office username should be set to your name if you have permission to do so (see steps 1–4 in Develop Your Skills 16.2.2).*

## Use Document Inspector

1. **Open** the rs-Workforce Grant Budget workbook from the Lesson 16 folder.

2. Choose **File→Info**, and choose **Check for Issues menu ▾→Inspect Document** in the Info tab of Backstage view.

3. Choose to **save** the workbook if asked to save.
   *The Document Inspector dialog box displays. A workbook must retain certain document properties to be shared, so you will not inspect for properties and personal information.*

4. Remove the checkmark from **Document Properties and Personal Information**, and then click **Inspect**.
   *After a few moments, the Document Inspector report displays. The report should not indicate any potential problems.*

5. **Close** the Document Inspector and **exit** Backstage view.

## Turn On Workbook Sharing and Track Changes

6. Choose **Review→Changes→Protect and Share Workbook** 🗔 from the Ribbon.

7. Switch on **Sharing with Track Changes** but do **not** set a password.

8. Click **OK**, and then click **OK** again to confirm saving the workbook.
*The word* [Shared] *appears after the filename in the title bar. Any changes that users make will be highlighted in the workbook.*

9. **Close** the workbook.
*Now the workbook is ready to distribute so that coworkers can input their data.*

## Review Changes in a Workbook

*Assume that your coworker Corey Owens edited and returned the shared workbook to you.*

10. **Open** the rs-Corey's Grant Budget workbook from the Lesson 16 folder.

11. Choose **Review→Changes→Track Changes→Highlight Changes** from the Ribbon.
*Notice that the Track Changes While Editing option is checked. Track Changes was switched on automatically when the command was given to share the workbook.*

12. In the **Highlight Changes** dialog box, choose options to highlight all changes from everyone and click **OK**.

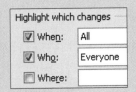

13. Choose **Review→Changes→Track Changes** 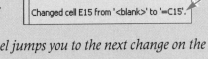 **→Accept/Reject Changes** from the Ribbon.

14. Set options as shown in the following illustration.

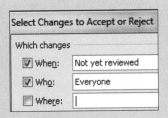

15. Click **OK** in the Select Changes to Accept or Reject dialog box.

16. Click **Accept** to accept the first edit in **cell C15**.

17. Read the details of the next change and notice that Corey entered a formula.
*Users may enter values, text, or formulas in cells.*

18. Accept this edit in **cell E15** and the next change for **cell G15**.
*Notice that now the Q2 Budget worksheet is displayed. Excel jumps you to the next change on the second worksheet in the workbook.*

19. Click **Reject** to restore **cell E21** in the Q2 Budget worksheet to blank.
*After you have reviewed all of the changes, the dialog box disappears. Notice that the change boxes are still displayed, however. They remain until you switch off Track Changes.*

20. **Save** the workbook.

## Display and Print the Change History

*Excel can display the change history of the workbook. This can be useful for reviewing edits.*

21. Choose **Review→Changes→Track Changes** 📝→**Highlight Changes** from the Ribbon.

22. Place a **checkmark** in the box next to **List Changes on a New Sheet** and click **OK**.
*A History worksheet appears, listing all Corey's changes to the workbook that you accepted. Notice that the change to cell E21 of the Q2 Budget worksheet does not appear because you rejected it. Therefore, the original value was restored. Your Who, Date, and Time entries will vary from the following illustration.*

| | A | B | C | D | E | F | G | H | I | J | K |
|---|---|---|---|---|---|---|---|---|---|---|---|
| 1 | Action Number | Date | Time | Who | Change | Sheet | Range | New Value | Old Value | Action Type | Losing Action |
| 2 | 1 | 6/26/2010 | 11:22 PM | Corey Owens | Cell Change | Q1 Budget | C15 | 2,000.00 | <blank> | | |
| 3 | 2 | 6/26/2010 | 11:22 PM | Corey Owens | Cell Change | Q1 Budget | E15 | "=C15 | <blank> | | |
| 4 | 3 | 6/26/2010 | 11:22 PM | Corey Owens | | Q1 Budget | G15 | "=C16 | <blank> | | |
| 5 | 4 | 6/26/2010 | 11:22 PM | Corey Owens | Cell Change | Q2 Budget | E21 | 500 | <blank> | | |
| 6 | 5 | 6/26/2010 | 11:23 PM | Student Name | Cell Change | Q2 Budget | E21 | <blank> | | Result of rejected action | 4 |
| 7 | | | | | | | | | | | |
| 8 | The history ends with the changes saved on 6/26/2010 at 11:23 PM. | | | | | | | | | | |

23. **Print** 🖨 the History worksheet and retrieve your printout from the printer.

24. **Close** the workbook.

REINFORCE YOUR SKILLS 16.4

# Merge Workbooks

*In this exercise, you will merge data from three copies of a shared workbook. Each copy was created from the original shared workbook and then changed by various coworkers.*

*Before You Begin: The Compare and Merge Workbooks* ⊙ *command should be available on the Quick Access toolbar, or you must have permission rights to add the command. The Microsoft Office username should be set to your name if you have permission to do so (see steps 1–4 in Develop Your Skills 16.2.2).*

## Merge Data into the Shared Workbook

1. Verify that the **Compare and Merge Workbooks** ⊙ command is installed on the Quick Access toolbar. If it is not, follow these steps to install the command:

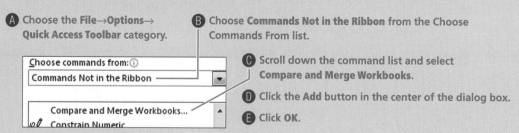

Ⓐ Choose the **File→Options→ Quick Access Toolbar** category.

Ⓑ Choose **Commands Not in the Ribbon** from the Choose Commands From list.

Ⓒ Scroll down the command list and select **Compare and Merge Workbooks**.

Ⓓ Click the **Add** button in the center of the dialog box.

Ⓔ Click **OK**.

2. **Open** the rs-Merged Budget 1 workbook from the Lesson 16 folder.
*Look at the title bar at the top of the Excel window. Notice that this is a shared workbook.*

3. Choose **Compare and Merge Workbooks**  from the Quick Access toolbar, and click **OK** if a message appears that the workbook needs to be saved before continuing.
*The Select Files to Merge into Current Workbook dialog box appears. Remember that you may merge only copies of workbooks made from the original shared workbook. The files on your file storage location have already been created and edited from the rs-Merged Budget 1 file you are sharing.*

*Next you will choose the three edited copies of the workbook that were returned by your coworkers.*

4. Navigate to the Lesson 16 folder and **click** rs-Merged Budget 2.

5. **Hold down** Shift and select rs-Merged Budget 4.

rs-Expense Report
rs-Merged Budget 1
rs-Merged Budget 2
rs-Merged Budget 3
rs-Merged Budget 4
rs-Workforce Grant Budget

*Three files should appear selected for merging, including rs-Merged Budget 3. Using Shift includes all files between the first and last in the selection. During the next step, watch the Status Bar at the bottom of the Excel window to monitor the progress of the command. You also will see the values update in the Curriculum Development and Faculty/Staff Professional Development rows.*

6. Click **OK** to start the merge.
*After a few moments, all data is merged into the Q1 Budget worksheet and Q2 Budget worksheet. Excel automatically saved the rs-Merged Budget 1 file after the merge.*

## Accept and Reject Changes

7. Choose **Review→Changes→Track Changes** [icon]→**Accept/Reject Changes** from the Ribbon.

8. Make certain that the **Accept or Reject Changes** dialog box is set as shown at right, and click **OK**.
*The dialog box displays a conflict for cell C15.*

| Select Changes to Accept or Reject |
| --- |
| Which changes |
| ☑ When: Not yet reviewed |
| ☑ Who: Everyone |
| ☐ Where: |

9. **Resolve** the conflict by choosing Oscar Valencia's change of 1,000 and then click **Accept**.
*Another conflict for cell E21 of the Q2 Budget worksheet is displayed. Lawrence Harris changed your original value of 1,000 to 5,000. You know that is not correct.*

10. Click **Reject** to restore the **cell E21** value to 1,000. (Do not click Accept.)

11. Click **Accept All** to accept the remaining changes.

12. **Save** [icon] the workbook.

## Display the Change History

13. Choose **Review→Changes→Track Changes** 📝**→Highlight Changes** from the Ribbon.

14. Choose **All** from the **When** list. Make certain that **Who** has a **checkmark** and **Everyone** is chosen.

15. Place a **checkmark** in the box next to **List Changes on a New Sheet**, and click **OK**.
    *A History worksheet appears, listing all changes to the workbook that you accepted. Compare Action Numbers 2 and 10. You rejected Lawrence Harris's change to cell E21 of the Q2 Budget worksheet. Both changes to cell C15 are listed; the second change "won" because you accepted Oscar Valencia's number. The last change listed for a cell is the one that appears in the merged worksheet. Your Who, Date, and Time entries will vary from the illustration below.*

| | A | B | C | D | E | F | G | H | I | J | K |
|---|---|---|---|---|---|---|---|---|---|---|---|
| 1 | Action Number | Date | Time | Who | Change | Sheet | Range | New Value | Old Value | Action Type | Losing Action |
| 2 | 1 | 6/27/2010 | 5:39 PM | Lawrence Harri | Cell Change | Q1 Budget | C15 | 4,500 | <blank> | | |
| 3 | 2 | 6/27/2010 | 5:39 PM | Lawrence Harri | Cell Change | Q2 Budget | E21 | 5,000.00 | 1,000.00 | | |
| 4 | 3 | 6/27/2010 | 5:41 PM | Iridza Paloma | Cell Change | Q1 Budget | C16 | 500 | <blank> | | |
| 5 | 4 | 6/27/2010 | 5:41 PM | Iridza Paloma | Cell Change | Q1 Budget | E16 | =C16 | <blank> | | |
| 6 | 5 | 6/27/2010 | 5:41 PM | Iridza Paloma | Cell Change | Q1 Budget | G16 | =C16 | <blank> | | |
| 7 | 6 | 6/27/2010 | 5:41 PM | Iridza Paloma | Cell Change | Q2 Budget | G20 | 500 | <blank> | | |
| 8 | 7 | 6/27/2010 | 5:43 PM | Oscar Valencia | Cell Change | Q1 Budget | C15 | 1,000.00 | <blank> | | |
| 9 | 8 | 6/27/2010 | 5:43 PM | Oscar Valencia | Cell Change | Q1 Budget | E15 | 1,500.00 | <blank> | | |
| 10 | 9 | 6/27/2010 | 5:43 PM | Oscar Valencia | Cell Change | Q1 Budget | G15 | 2,000.00 | <blank> | | |
| 11 | 10 | 6/27/2010 | 5:43 PM | Student Name | Cell Change | Q2 Budget | E21 | 1000 | | Result of rejected action | 2 |
| 12 | | | | | | | | | | | |
| 13 | The history ends with the changes saved on 6/27/2010 at 5:56 PM. | | | | | | | | | | |

16. **Print** 🖨 the History worksheet and retrieve your printout from the printer.
    *Normally you would remove workbook sharing after approving changes. In this exercise, however, you will leave the change history available to re-create the History worksheet, if necessary.*

17. **Save** 💾 and **close** the workbook.

# Apply Your Skills

APPLY YOUR SKILLS 16.1

## Add Comments to a Workbook

*In this exercise, you will insert a new comment and edit an existing comment on a worksheet.*

*Before You Begin: The Microsoft Office username should be set to your name if you have permission to do so (see steps 1–4 in Develop Your Skills 16.2.2).*

1. **Open** the as-Crisis Intervention Budget workbook from the Lesson 16 folder in your file storage location.

2. **Add** the following comment in **cell C6**: `Added an evening volunteer coordinator to the hotline staff.`

3. Edit the comment in **cell D7** by adding the following text below the existing comment text: `Repairs were completed by November 18 within the originally estimated cost.`

4. **Display** all comments.

5. **Move** comments below the data area so that all data is visible while the comments are displayed.

6. **Resize** comments as necessary to display all text in a comment.

7. Make certain that the worksheet and comments fit on **one page**.

8. **Print** 🖨 the workbook with comments on the same sheet (not on a separate sheet).

9. **Save** 💾 and **close** the workbook.

APPLY YOUR SKILLS 16.2

## Track Changes to a Workbook

*In this exercise, you will set the workbook to track changes and make several edits in a worksheet. You will then review the edits and turn off the Track Changes feature.*

1. **Open** the as-Animal Shelter Expenses workbook from the Lesson 16 folder.
   *This workbook does not have data in it yet. You will enter data during the various Assessment exercises.*

2. Set the workbook to **highlight and track changes** and use the appropriate options.

3. In **cell B5** of the Expense Report worksheet, create a linking formula to **cell E9** on the Cats worksheet.

4. In **cell B6**, create a linking formula to **cell E9** on the Dogs worksheet.

5. Create a formula in **cell B7** that sums the **range B5:B6**.

6. **Save** 💾 the workbook.

7. **Display** and **print** the change history for the workbook.

| | A | B |
|---|---|---|
| 4 | Animal | Total Costs |
| 5 | Cats | $ - |
| 6 | Dogs | $ - |
| 7 | Total Costs | $ - |

8. Give the command to **accept or reject changes** and **approve all** changes you made to the workbook.

9. **Turn off** Track Changes and click **Yes** when alerted that the change history and workbook sharing will be removed.

10. **Save** 🖫 the workbook and leave it **open** for the next exercise.

### APPLY YOUR SKILLS 16.3
# Share a Workbook

*In this exercise, you will share a workbook file and then create two copies of it to merge in the next exercise.*

*Before You Begin: You must have completed Apply Your Skills 16.2, and the as-Animal Shelter Expenses workbook should be open.*

1. **Share** the workbook.

2. Create **two copies** of the shared workbook, one named **as-Animal Shelter Cats** and the other named **as-Animal Shelter Dogs**.
   *Remember that each must be a copy of the original workbook. You cannot copy the Cats workbook to create the Dogs workbook.*

3. **Close** any workbook still open.

### APPLY YOUR SKILLS 16.4
# Merge Workbooks

*In this exercise, you will edit the two copies of the shared workbook you created in Apply Your Skills 16.3. Then you will merge the contents of the edited workbooks into the as-Animal Shelter Expenses workbook.*

*Before You Begin: You must have completed Apply Your Skills 16.2 and Apply Your Skills 16.3, and the as-Animal Shelter Expenses workbook should be open. The Compare and Merge Workbooks command should be available on the Quick Access toolbar.*

## Edit and Merge Workbook Copies

1. **Open** the as-Animal Shelter Cats workbook from the Lesson 16 folder.

2. **Type** new data into the Cats worksheet to match the data items shaded in gray in the following illustration.

| Animal | Age | Health | Date Arrived | Shelter Cost |
|--------|--------|---------|-------------|-------------|
| Cat | Adult | Healthy | 1-May | $ 82.50 |
| Cat | Adult | Healthy | 9-May | $ 60.50 |
| Cat | Kitten | Healthy | 10-May | $ 57.75 |
| Cat | Adult | Healthy | 30-May | $ 2.75 |

3. **Save** 🖫 and **close** the as-Animal Shelter Cats workbook.

4. **Open** the as-Animal Shelter Dogs workbook.

5. **Type** new data into the Dogs worksheet to match the data items shaded in gray in the following illustration.

| Animal | Age | Health | Date Arrived | Shelter Cost |
|--------|-------|---------|-------------:|-------------:|
| Dog | Adult | Healthy | 2-May | $ 79.75 |
| Dog | Adult | Healthy | 8-May | $ 63.25 |
| Dog | Pup | Sick | 15-May | $ 44.00 |
| Dog | Adult | Healthy | 20-May | $ 30.25 |

6. **Save** 🖫 and **close** the as-Animal Shelter Dogs workbook.

7. **Open** the as-Animal Shelter Expenses workbook.

8. **Merge** the contents of the as-Animal Shelter Cats and as-Animal Shelter Dogs workbooks into the as-Animal Shelter Expenses workbook.
   *Your data should appear in the Cats and Dogs worksheets. The Expense Report worksheet should display totals as shown on the right.*

|  | A | B |
|---|-----------|-------------:|
| 4 | Animal | Total Costs |
| 5 | Cats | $ 203.50 |
| 6 | Dogs | $ 217.25 |
| 7 | Total Costs | $ 420.75 |

## Mark the Document as Final

9. Remove **workbook sharing** and mark the document as **final**.

10. **Close** the as-Animal Shelter Expenses workbook.

## Restore the Username

Skip steps 11–12 if you did not change the username. If you did change the username, refer to the procedure that you wrote in step 3 in Develop Your Skills 16.2.2 to restore the original username, which may vary from the following steps.

11. Choose **File→Options** 🖹 and display the **General** category, if not already displayed.

12. Under **Personalize Your Copy of Microsoft Office**, carefully type the original username that you wrote down during Develop Your Skills 16.2.2 in the User Name box and click **OK**.

# Critical Thinking & Work-Readiness Skills

*In the course of working through the following Microsoft Office-based Critical Thinking exercises, you will also be utilizing various work-readiness skills, some of which are listed next to each exercise. Go to labyrinthelab.com/ workreadiness to learn more about the work-readiness skills.*

## 16.1 Share a Workbook

**WORK-READINESS SKILLS APPLIED**

- Serving clients/ customers
- Organizing and maintaining information
- Selecting technology

Dr. Edward Jackson, chief operating officer for Raritan Clinic East, is studying the efficiency of patient bed availability. Your job is to set up a shared workbook for him. Open ct-Bed Count (Lesson 16 folder). Protect the workbook for sharing with track changes, and save with the name **ct-Bed Count [Your Last Name]** in the Lesson 16 folder. Create a file copy for both Cardiology and Surgery. Close the files when you are finished.

## 16.2 Merge Edited Copies of a Shared Workbook

**WORK-READINESS SKILLS APPLIED**

- Serving clients/ customers
- Organizing and maintaining information
- Selecting technology

Dr. Jackson wants to look at the bed space occupied on May 18 and has asked for your help. Open ct-Shared Bed Count(Lesson 16 folder), and merge it with the data from ct-Shared Bed Count Cardiology and ct-Shared Bed Count Surgery (also in the Lesson 16 folder). Highlight all changes, and accept the changes to cells C6 and C7 on the Surgery sheet. Save your work and keep the file open.

## 16.3 Work with Comments

**WORK-READINESS SKILLS APPLIED**

- Serving clients/ customers
- Acquiring and evaluating information
- Reading

Deion Jennett is Dr. Jackson's administrative assistant. He wants to do a final review of the comments before turning the report over to Dr. Jackson to make sure they are all appropriate to room/bed space, and asks for your help. Open ct-Shared Bed Count, if necessary. Delete any comments that are not related to the room space, and adjust comments so that they do not overlap worksheet data. Create and print the change history. Then, save the workbook. Close the file when you are finished.

# Sharing Workbooks on Networks and the Internet

## LESSON OUTLINE

## LEARNING OBJECTIVES

After studying this lesson, you will be able to:

- Share workbooks for simultaneous collaboration on an intranet
- Share workbooks via the web in Windows Live SkyDrive
- Edit workbooks online using Excel Web App 2010

An organization's employees and clients may work from different locations and in different time zones. They often need the capability to access documents 24/7 from a central storage location. Desktop and mobile devices allow people to view and collaborate on documents from almost anywhere. In this lesson, you will learn how to set up a workbook that several other users can access simultaneously on a network server, or intranet. Cloud computing is a technology that allows users to share and edit files using software stored centrally on the Internet. You will learn how to store workbooks online in Windows Live SkyDrive and edit a workbook with the Excel 2010 Web App from any computer with Internet access.

# Sharing Workbooks in a Central Storage Location

**Raritan Clinic East**

**Pediatric Diagnostic Specialists**

Grace Vargas is the grant and contract coordinator for Raritan Clinic East. She needs to upload various documents on her medical center's network server so other employees can view them. In addition, she will ask employees in various departments to update the expense numbers in a budget workbook stored on the server. First, Grace will set up the workbook in Excel for sharing on the intranet. Then, Raritan's network administrator will create a network folder where Grace will upload her workbook file. Grace realizes that some employees who are traveling will need to access documents from a wireless device, such as a mobile phone, that may not have Excel installed or the capability to connect to Raritan's intranet. She decides to store certain documents on Windows Live SkyDrive. Other collaborators only need a web browser on their devices to access the documents. Or, they can download a workbook to a computer that has Excel installed, edit, and then upload the file back to SkyDrive.

| | Action Number | Date | Time | Who | Change | Sheet | Range | New Value | Old Value | Action Type | Losing Action |
|---|---|---|---|---|---|---|---|---|---|---|---|
| 2 | 1 | 5/21/2010 | 11:16 PM | Student Name | Cell Change | Orthopedics Dept | C15 | 3,250.00 | 1,134.00 | | |
| 3 | 2 | 5/21/2010 | 11:16 PM | Student Name | Cell Change | Orthopedics Dept | G16 | 350 | <blank> | | |
| 4 | 3 | 5/21/2010 | 11:38 PM | Grace Vargas | Cell Change | Orthopedics Dept | H18 | 700 | <blank> | | |
| 5 | 4 | 5/21/2010 | 11:38 PM | Grace Vargas | Cell Change | Orthopedics Dept | G15 | 1,450.00 | <blank> | | |
| 6 | | | | | | | | | | | |
| 7 | The history ends with the changes saved on 5/21/2010 at 11:38 PM. | | | | | | | | | | |

Grace uses the workbook's change history to track all updates that users make to the shared workbook stored on the network server.

Shared folder created on Windows Live SkyDrive

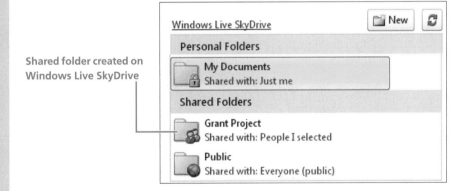

Grace may use Excel to upload a workbook to a shared folder on Windows Live SkyDrive and give permission to other people to edit the workbook or only to view it.

# 17.1 Sharing Workbooks on a Network

**Video Lesson** labyrinthelab.com/videos

Excel's Share Workbook 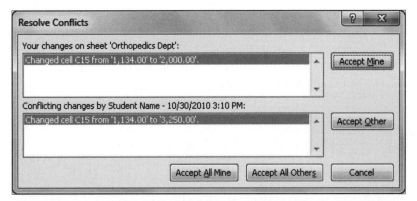 command lets you set up a workbook for sharing and choose options for recording a history of changes to the workbook. Then you can review the change history for any conflicts between entries to the same cells and see how they were resolved. When the shared workbook is stored on a network drive on your organization's intranet and you have the file open, you may have Excel give you automatic updates of all user changes. When sharing files, you should give users clear instructions about the data that they should and should not change.

## Characteristics of Shared Workbooks

When you set up a workbook for sharing on a network, several features work together to coordinate the use of the workbook.

- **Shared Access**—Multiple users can access the same file at once and see which other users currently have the file open.

- **User Settings**—Users may save their own printing and filtering settings as a custom view with the file.

- **Change History**—The change history is activated automatically whenever you create a shared workbook. This feature must be active as long as the workbook is shared.

- **Resolving Conflicts**—When changes are saved to a shared workbook, Excel displays a dialog box to help you review and resolve any conflicts between what you and another user have entered.

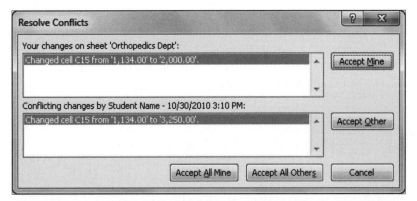

The Resolve Conflicts dialog box appears after two users change the same cell and save a shared workbook.

## Simultaneous Access to Shared Workbooks

When you share a workbook on a network drive, several users can open and change the workbook simultaneously. Changes saved by multiple users are recorded in the change history for later review. When two users change the same cell and the second user gives the Save command, Excel analyzes the change history and alerts the second user to review both changes and choose one. Excel cannot keep both changes in one cell.

If more than one person tries to open a standard (unshared) Excel workbook, the second person to open the workbook will receive a warning message and must open a read-only copy in order to view the file.

## Disabled Features in Shared Workbooks

Several Excel features are disabled when a workbook is shared, whether on a network drive or distributed to individual users. For example, you cannot delete a worksheet or add tables and charts in a shared workbook. Nor can you change passwords to protect worksheets—although password protection applied before the workbook is shared remains in effect. For a complete list of disabled features, see the Use a Shared Workbook to Collaborate topic in Excel Help.

| QUICK REFERENCE | SHARING A WORKBOOK |
| --- | --- |
| **Task** | **Procedure** |
| Set up a workbook to be shared | ■ Choose Review→Changes→Share Workbook ▦ from the Ribbon. |
| | ■ In the Editing tab of the Share Workbook dialog box, place a checkmark in the box next to Allow Changes by More Than One User at the Same Time. |
| | ■ Display the Advanced tab in the dialog box, choose any desired options, and click OK. |
| | ■ Click OK to confirm saving the workbook. |
| | ■ Copy the workbook to a network drive or other location where the entire workgroup has access to it, or make multiple copies of the original file and distribute a copy to each user. |

### DEVELOP YOUR SKILLS 17.1.1
## Set Up and Edit a Shared Workbook

*In this exercise, you will set up the Shared Budget workbook to be shared. Then you will open the workbook in two different Excel windows simultaneously to simulate multiple users working in a shared workbook on a network drive.*

*Before You Begin: Verify with your instructor, staff, or class notes whether you have permission to change the username on your computer. Verify the procedure for restoring the original username if you do have permission.*

### Set the Username

1. Choose **File→Options**. Display the **General** category, if not already displayed.

2. Under Personalize Your Copy of Microsoft Office, notice the current **User Name.**

Click Cancel and skip to step 5 if you do not have permission to change the username on your computer.

3. As directed by your instructor, write the current username *exactly as shown* so you may restore that name at the end of this exercise. Or, write the restoration procedure in the space provided:

_____

4. Change the existing username in the User Name box to **Grace Vargas**, and click **OK** to save the change.

## Set Up the Shared Workbook

5. **Open** the Shared Budget workbook from the Lesson 17 folder in your file storage location.

6. Choose **Review→Changes→Share Workbook** 📊 from the Ribbon.

7. On the **Editing** tab, place a checkmark in the box next to **Allow Changes by More than One User at the Same Time**.

8. Display the **Advanced** tab and read the various options.

9. Make certain that the **Ask Me Which Changes Win** option is chosen near the bottom of the dialog box, as shown at right. *This option ensures that you can review and accept or reject any conflicting changes to cells whenever you save the workbook.*

> Conflicting changes between users
> ⦿ A̲sk me which changes win
> ⦾ T̲he changes being saved win

10. Click **OK**, and then click **OK** again to confirm saving the workbook. *Notice that* [Shared] *appears on the title bar next to the filename. This tells you that sharing has been enabled for this workbook.*

> Shared Budget [Shared] - Microsoft Excel

11. Choose **Review→Changes→Track Changes** 📝**→Highlight Changes** from the Ribbon. *Notice that the Track Changes While Editing option is checked. Track Changes was switched on automatically when you gave the command to share the workbook.*

12. Make certain that **When** is set to **Since I Last Saved**.

13. Place a checkmark in the box next to **Who** and make certain that **Everyone** is chosen in the Who list. *This sets the change history to display change boxes around the changes that everyone makes in the workbook. Remember that Grace Vargas (or your computer's username) is the username set in the Excel Options dialog box, so Excel considers her to have created this shared workbook.*

14. Click **OK** in the dialog box. Click **OK** again in the dialog box with the message No Changes Were Found with the Specified Properties. *Initially, Excel finds that no changes have yet been made after the workbook was saved.*

## Edit the Shared Workbook

*Now you will play the role of Grace editing some data in the workbook.*

15. Display the **Orthopedics Dept** worksheet.

16. Select **cell C15** and enter **2000** as the new value for the cell.

17. Select **cell H18**, a blank cell, and enter **700**.

18. Select **cell G15**, a blank cell, and enter **1450**.

19. Do **not** save yet. *You set the When option to track changes from the last save. Saving now would not track the changes you just made.*

### Start a Second Copy of Excel

*Now you will work as if you are accessing the workbook simultaneously with Grace.*

This new window will be referred to as the second Excel window for the remainder of this exercise and the following exercise.

20. Display the **Start** menu in Windows and navigate to Excel to open a **second** Excel program window.

### Change the Username

Skip to step 23 if you do not have permission rights to change the username on your computer.

21. Choose **File→Options** . Display the **General** category, if not already displayed.

22. Under **Personalize Your Copy of Microsoft Office**, enter your first name and last name in the User Name box and click **OK** to save the change.
*Now when you open the workbook, Excel will recognize you as a different user making changes to the workbook.*

### Open a Second Copy of the Workbook

23. **Open** the Shared Budget workbook from the Lesson 17 folder in your file storage location.
*Notice that* [Shared] *appears just to the right of the filename on the title bar. You now have this file open in two Excel program windows at once. This is possible only with a shared workbook, not a standard Excel workbook.*

24. Choose **Review→Changes→Share Workbook** from the Ribbon, and notice that two users are listed under Who Has This Workbook Open Now (if you were allowed to change the username).

25. Click **Cancel** to exit the dialog box without making any changes.

26. Display the **Orthopedics Dept** worksheet, select **cell C15**, and enter **3250** as the new value for the cell.
*This new value will conflict with the 2000 entry Grace made in step 16. However, as you will see later, Excel will help you catch conflicts like this. Notice also that, unlike the first copy, this second copy of the shared workbook does not display change boxes. The changes are being saved to the change history, though, and will be displayed later in the exercise when you review the changes.*

27. Select **cell G16** and enter **350**.
*This value does not conflict with any value entered by Grace.*

28. **Save** the changes and leave the **second** Excel window open.
*Excel saves the changes to this second copy of the shared workbook in the change history. Later, Excel will use the change history to enter the data into Grace's copy of the workbook in the first Excel window and to resolve the conflict in cell C15.*

## Switch to the First Workbook and Resolve Conflicts

29. Follow these steps to switch to Grace Vargas' copy of the workbook:
*Your buttons may look different. If they appear side by side, click the Microsoft Excel button to the left.*

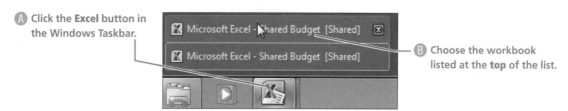

Ⓐ Click the **Excel** button in the Windows Taskbar.

Ⓑ Choose the workbook listed at the **top** of the list.

*The first Excel window becomes the active window, and you are back to viewing Grace's work in this copy of the shared workbook. Notice that the changes you made in the second Excel window are not yet visible. They are in the change history. The changes won't be visible until Grace gives the Save command on her copy of the shared workbook.*

30. **Save** 🖫 the workbook in the first Excel window.

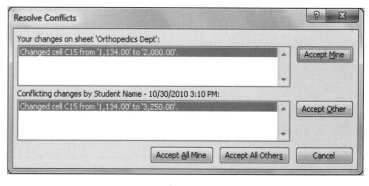

*A Resolve Conflicts dialog box appears. This alerts Grace that her change conflicts with a change you made and saved in the second Excel window a few moments ago. Notice that Excel displays the name, time, and other details of the conflicting change. Based on her knowledge of the project, Grace recognizes that the higher figure is correct.*

31. Click the **Accept Other** button on the right side of the dialog box.

32. Click **OK** to acknowledge the message that the workbook has been updated with the various changes.
*Notice that the 350 in cell G16 of the second Excel window was entered automatically because it did not conflict with any other edits to the workbook.*

## Review Changes to the Shared Workbook

*Now you will look over the change boxes on the worksheet and review the change history worksheet.*

33. Choose **Review→Changes→Track Changes** 📝 **→Highlight Changes** from the Ribbon.

34. Follow these steps to review the change history:

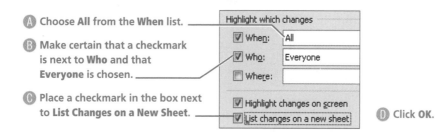

Ⓐ Choose **All** from the **When** list.

Ⓑ Make certain that a checkmark is next to **Who** and that **Everyone** is chosen.

Ⓒ Place a checkmark in the box next to **List Changes on a New Sheet.**

Ⓓ Click **OK.**

*The History worksheet appears. Your Date, Time, and Who columns will differ from the illustration.*

| | A | B | C | D | E | F | G | H | I | J | K |
|---|---|---|---|---|---|---|---|---|---|---|---|
| 1 | Action Number ▼ | Date ▼ | Time ▼ | Who ▼ | Change ▼ | Sheet ▼ | Range ▼ | New Value ▼ | Old Value ▼ | Action Type ▼ | Losing Action ▼ |
| 2 | 1 | 5/21/2010 | 11:16 PM | Student Name | Cell Change | Orthopedics Dept | C15 | 3,250.00 | 1,134.00 | | |
| 3 | 2 | 5/21/2010 | 11:16 PM | Student Name | Cell Change | Orthopedics Dept | G16 | 350 | <blank> | | |
| 4 | 3 | 5/21/2010 | 11:38 PM | Grace Vargas | Cell Change | Orthopedics Dept | H18 | 700 | <blank> | | |
| 5 | 4 | 5/21/2010 | 11:38 PM | Grace Vargas | Cell Change | Orthopedics Dept | G15 | 1,450.00 | <blank> | | |
| 6 | | | | | | | | | | | |
| 7 | The history ends with the changes saved on 5/21/2010 at 11:38 PM. | | | | | | | | | | |

*As you may expect, all changes are recorded here. Notice, however, that the 2000 entry made in cell C15 of the first Excel window is not recorded. That was the cell with the conflicting changes. Since you dismissed the 2000 value and kept the 3250 value, the change history does not record the conflict, just the resolution.*

35. Display the **Orthopedics Dept** worksheet.
    *Notice that change boxes have appeared around all four of the cells that were changed earlier in this exercise.*

36. **Save** 💾 the workbook in the **first** Excel window.
    *Notice that the History worksheet disappears after the save. However, you may still see the change boxes.*

37. Leave both Excel windows **open** for the next exercise.

## Switching Off Sharing

| Video Lesson | labyrinthelab.com/videos |
|---|---|

You may want to switch off sharing only temporarily or after a project is completed. When you switch off sharing, the change history is erased and any unsaved changes by other users are lost. You should not turn off sharing to a workbook unless you are satisfied that everyone's data have been saved and that any conflicts have been resolved satisfactorily. Once you disable the sharing feature for a workbook, there is no turning back.

Before you turn off sharing, make certain that all other network users have saved their changes and closed the workbook. Otherwise, their changes will be lost.

| QUICK REFERENCE | DISABLING WORKBOOK SHARING |
|---|---|
| **Task** | **Procedure** |
| Disable workbook sharing | ▪ Print or copy the History worksheet to another workbook, if desired. |
| | ▪ Make certain that all other users have saved their work. Otherwise, any unsaved changes are lost. |
| | ▪ Choose Review→Changes→Share Workbook ⊞ from the Ribbon. |
| | ▪ In the Editing tab of the Share Workbook dialog box, remove the checkmark in the box next to Allow Changes by More than One User at the Same Time. |
| | ▪ Click Yes when you are warned that the change history will be erased and that other users will not be able to save their work. |

## Stop Sharing the Workbook

*In this exercise, you will disable sharing for the workbook. This command will also erase the change history and deactivate the Track Changes feature.*

1. Verify that the active window is the **first** Excel window with Grace's work and the change boxes displayed. (If the change boxes do not display, choose **Review→Changes→Track Changes**, and click **OK**.)

2. Choose **Review→Changes→Share Workbook**  from the Ribbon, and select the **Editing** tab in the Share Workbook dialog box, if necessary.
   *Notice that the Who Has This Workbook Open Now list on the dialog box displays both Excel users. You should see your own name (or computer username) on the second line along with the time you opened the workbook in the second window. Although you could use the Remove User button near the bottom of the dialog box to close the other window, it is much more polite to contact the user and provide an opportunity to save the workbook. Otherwise, the unsaved changes will be lost.*

3. Click **Cancel** to close the dialog box.

### Turn Off Workbook Sharing

4. Make the **second** Excel window active by clicking the Excel button on the Windows Taskbar and selecting the bottom file in the list (or clicking the button to the right if the buttons are side by side on the Taskbar). Then **close** that Excel window without saving any changes.

5. Choose **Review→Changes→Share Workbook**  from the Ribbon.
   *The Who Has This Workbook Open Now list now shows just one open copy of the shared workbook. Now it is safe for Grace to turn off sharing for this workbook.*

6. Uncheck the **Allow Changes by More than One User at the Same Time** option and click **OK**.

7. Click **Yes** to confirm removing the workbook from shared use.
   *Now this workbook may be opened by only one user at a time.*

8. **Close** the workbook and click **Yes** if prompted to save the changes.

### Restore the Username

Skip steps 9 and 10 if you did not change the username. If you did change the username, refer to the procedure you wrote in step 3 in Develop Your Skills 17.1.1 to restore the original username, which may vary from the following steps.

9. Choose **File→Options.** Display the **General** category, if not already displayed.

10. Under **Personalize Your Copy of Microsoft Office,** carefully **type** the original username you wrote down during Develop Your Skills 17.1.1 in the User Name box and click **OK**.

11. **Exit** Excel.

| Video Lesson | labyrinthelab.com/videos |
|---|---|

You may not always be at your computer or have access to your hard drive when you need to edit a file. For example, you may need to edit an important work document from home, but have no access to your work computer. With Windows Live™ SkyDrive, you can store your files online so they are available from any computer with an Internet connection. With Office Web Apps 2010, you or your colleagues can edit those files residing on SkyDrive even if the actual Microsoft Office programs are not installed on the computer being used.

## Creating a Windows Live ID Account

SkyDrive and Office Web Apps 2010 require you to have a Windows Live ID to sign in before the service can be used. A Windows Live ID is simply a free account with a Microsoft service such as Hotmail (email), Messenger (instant messaging), or Xbox LIVE (online gaming).

Adjust the steps in the following Quick Reference table if the Windows Live website has been updated.

| QUICK REFERENCE | CREATING AND USING A WINDOWS LIVE ID |
|---|---|
| **Task** | **Procedure** |
| Create a free Windows Live ID | ■ Verify that your Internet connection is active.<br>From Excel:<br>■ Choose File→Save & Send→Save to Web.<br>■ In the Save to Windows Live area of Backstage view, click Sign Up for Windows Live.<br>■ Fill in the form to create your Windows Live ID.<br>From a web browser:<br>■ Start Internet Explorer or another web browser, type **www.live.com** in the Address box at the top of the window, and tap Enter.<br>■ Click the Sign Up button on the Windows Live web page.<br>■ Fill in the form to create your Windows Live ID. |
| Sign in to Windows Live with an existing ID | From Excel:<br>■ Choose File→Save & Send→Save to Web.<br>■ In the Save to Windows Live area of Backstage view, click Sign In.<br>■ Enter your Windows Live ID email address and password, if not already displayed, and click OK.<br>From a web browser:<br>■ Start Internet Explorer or another web browser, type **www.live.com** in the Address box at the top of the window, and tap Enter.<br>■ Click the Sign In button on the Windows Live web page.<br>■ Enter your Windows Live ID email address and password, if not already displayed, and click Sign In. |

## Create a Windows Live ID Account

| WebSim | labyrinthelab.com/excel10 |
| --- | --- |

*In this exercise, you will sign up for a Windows Live ID by creating a new Hotmail email address. Then you will log off Windows Live.*

1. **Type** the URL for the student web page (listed above) in the address bar of your web browser and **tap** Enter.

2. From the left navigation bar, click **Lessons 12–18** and then **Lesson 17**; then click the **Develop Your Skills 17.2.1: Create a Windows Live ID Account** link.
   *The WebSim loads. The browser is open to the Windows Live homepage. Websites are updated frequently, and the actual web pages may vary from those shown in the WebSim.*

3. Work your way through the **on-screen exercise instructions**.

4. Click the **Back to Course** link at the top-right corner of your screen.

## Storing Files on SkyDrive

| Video Lesson | labyrinthelab.com/videos |
| --- | --- |

SkyDrive is a free service provided by Microsoft that allows you to store your files online. This online storage provides several benefits.

- You can access your files from any computer with an Internet connection.
- You don't need to worry about losing the files from your hard drive crashing or USB drive breaking because your files are stored on the SkyDrive servers. You should, however, make backup copies of important files.

Adjust the steps in the following Quick Reference table if the Windows Live website has been updated.

| QUICK REFERENCE | SAVING AND ACCESSING FILES ON SKYDRIVE |
| --- | --- |
| **Task** | **Procedure** |
| Navigate to SkyDrive in Windows Live | ■ Choose Windows Live→SkyDrive from the menu bar at the top of the Windows Live web page. |
| Navigate to SkyDrive in Excel | ■ Choose File→Save & Send→Save to Web. |
|  | ■ Click Windows Live SkyDrive in the Save to Windows Live SkyDrive area of Backstage view, if necessary. |
|  | ■ Log into Windows Live, if necessary. |

| Task | Procedure |
|------|-----------|
| Upload a workbook in SkyDrive | ▪ Start your web browser, log into Windows Live, and navigate to SkyDrive. |
|  | ▪ Open the folder into which you wish to add the file. |
|  | ▪ Click the Add Files link. |
|  | ▪ Click a Browse button or choose Select Documents from Your Computer, depending on the command available. Navigate to the folder containing the desired file, and double-click the filename. |
| Save a workbook in Excel to a SkyDrive folder | ▪ Open the workbook that you wish to save to SkyDrive. |
|  | ▪ Choose File→Save & Send→Save to Web. |
|  | ▪ In the Save to Windows Live SkyDrive area of Backstage view, select the SkyDrive folder into which you wish to save the file. |
|  | ▪ Click Save As 🖾 under the folders list. |
|  | ▪ In the Save As dialog box, verify the folder name, name the file, and click Save. |
| Access a file stored on SkyDrive | ▪ Start your web browser and navigate to www.live.com. |
|  | ▪ Sign in with your Windows Live ID and choose SkyDrive. |
|  | ▪ Select the folder containing the file that you wish to access. |
|  | ▪ Select the desired file to view it. Alternatively, point to the file you want to access and click an action, such as Edit in Browser, Share, or More. |

## DEVELOP YOUR SKILLS 17.2.2
# Add a File on Windows Live SkyDrive

**WebSim**   labyrinthelab.com/excel10

*In this exercise, you will sign into Windows Live SkyDrive and upload a workbook file to an existing shared folder.*

1. If necessary, **type** the URL listed above into the address bar of your web browser and **tap** ⏎ Enter .

2. From the left navigation bar, click **Lessons 12–18** and then **Lesson 17**; then click the **Develop Your Skills 17.2.2: Add a File on Windows Live SkyDrive** link.
   *The WebSim loads. The browser is open to the Windows Live homepage. Websites are updated frequently, and the actual web pages may vary from those shown in the WebSim.*

3. Work your way through the **on-screen exercise instructions**.

4. Click the **Back to Course** link at the top-right corner of your screen.

## Saving a File to SkyDrive in Excel

**Video Lesson**   labyrinthelab.com/videos

As you learned in the previous exercise, you may upload Excel workbooks after logging in to Windows Live in your web browser. As an alternative, you may log in to Windows Live and save a workbook to SkyDrive from within Excel.

## Save a File in Excel to Windows Live SkyDrive

| WebSim | labyrinthelab.com/excel10 |
|---|---|

*In this exercise, you will save a file to Windows Live SkyDrive from within Excel. You will save the workbook file using Backstage view.*

1. If necessary, **type** the URL listed above into the address bar of your web browser and **tap** Enter.

2. From the left navigation bar, click **Lessons 12–18** and then **Lesson 17**; then click the **Develop Your Skills 17.2.3: Save a File in Excel to Windows Live SkyDrive** link. *The WebSim loads. The Shared Budget workbook is open in Excel.*

3. Work your way through the **on-screen exercise instructions**.

4. Click the **Back to Course** link at the top-right corner of your screen.

# Editing Files with Office Web Apps 2010

| Video Lesson | labyrinthelab.com/videos |
|---|---|

Files that have been saved to SkyDrive can be edited online using Office Web Apps 2010. These applications can be considered as free online versions of Microsoft Office programs, but with limited functionality. Initially, Microsoft planned to support editing only in Word, Excel, PowerPoint, and OneNote documents with Office Web Apps 2010. The apps may feature different capabilities at a later time. The benefits and limitations of Office Web Apps 2010 are summarized in the following table.

| Benefits of Office Web Apps 2010 | Limitations of Office Web Apps 2010 |
|---|---|
| ▪ Files can be edited from any computer with an Internet connection | ▪ Requires a Windows Live ID |
| ▪ No need for Microsoft Office to be installed | ▪ Fewer features and capabilities than the full Microsoft Office applications |
| ▪ Document content and formatting are maintained between the Web App and the full Office application | |

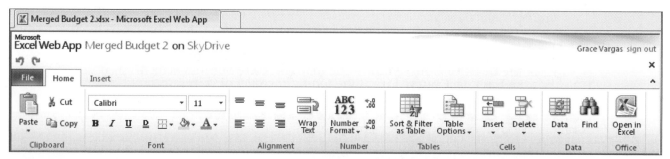

The Excel Web App features a similar Ribbon as in the full version of Excel, but lacks much of the functionality.

Adjust the steps in the following Quick Reference table if the Office Web Apps have been updated.

| Task | Procedure |
|------|-----------|
| Edit a workbook on SkyDrive using the Excel Web App | ▪ In SkyDrive, open the folder containing the file to be edited.<br>▪ Click the desired file to view the workbook.<br>▪ Choose Edit in Browser from the menu bar above the worksheet to open the workbook in the Excel Web App.<br>▪ Respond to accept the service agreement if a message appears.<br>▪ Edit the workbook. The Ribbon does not contain all of the commands that are in the full Excel version.<br>▪ When you are finished editing, click either Close ☒ or Sign Out at the upper-right above the Ribbon. The file is saved automatically. |
| Edit a workbook on SkyDrive using the full Excel version | ▪ In SkyDrive, open the folder containing the file to be edited.<br>▪ Click the desired file to view the workbook.<br>▪ Choose Open in Excel from the menu bar above the worksheet to open the workbook in Excel on your computer.<br>▪ Click OK to respond to the message about opening web files.<br>▪ Edit the workbook, click Save, and close Excel.<br>▪ In the SkyDrive window, your changes may not appear automatically. Close and reopen the workbook on SkyDrive to verify that the changes were saved. |

### DEVELOP YOUR SKILLS 17.2.4

## Edit a Workbook Using the Excel Web App

**WebSim**    labyrinthelab.com/excel10

*In this exercise, you will access a workbook on Windows Live SkyDrive. Assume that you are using a computer with Internet access but without Excel installed. You will edit the workbook using the Excel Web App.*

1. If necessary, **type** the URL listed above into the address bar of your web browser and **tap** Enter.

2. From the left navigation bar, click **Lessons 12–18** and then **Lesson 17**; then click the **Develop Your Skills 17.2.4: Edit a Workbook Using the Excel Web App** link.
   *The WebSim loads. Assume that you have signed in to Windows Live SkyDrive. Internet Explorer displays the Grant Project folder in your SkyDrive storage location.*

3. Work your way through the **on-screen exercise instructions**.

4. Click the **Back to Course** link at the top-right corner of your screen.

## Sharing Files with SkyDrive

**Video Lesson**    labyrinthelab.com/videos

In addition to editing files stored on SkyDrive with Office Web Apps 2010, you can share files and allow others to edit or comment on them. Alternatively, you can share files and allow others to only view or comment on them.

## Creating and Sharing SkyDrive Folders

When you share a file on SkyDrive, you actually share the SkyDrive folder containing the file. Therefore, all files stored in the SkyDrive folder are shared. You can easily create additional SkyDrive folders to more easily manage permissions. For example, you can create one folder that stores files you allow others to edit and create another folder that stores files you allow the same people to only view. Files you store in the Public folder are available to anyone with a Windows Live ID who knows their location.

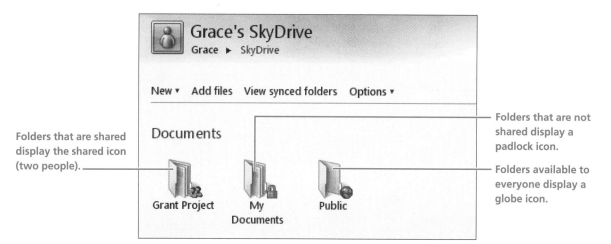

Folders that are shared display the shared icon (two people).

Folders that are not shared display a padlock icon.

Folders available to everyone display a globe icon.

| QUICK REFERENCE | WORKING WITH SKYDRIVE FOLDERS |
|---|---|
| **Task** | **Procedure** |
| Create a folder in SkyDrive | ■ Navigate to SkyDrive. |
| | ■ Choose New ▼ menu→Folder from the web page menu bar above the SkyDrive folder icons. |
| | ■ Type a folder name in the Name box. |
| | ■ Leave the Share With setting as Just Me, or click Change to set up sharing with other people. |
| | ■ Click Next to begin adding files to the folder. (Click Cancel if you do not wish to add files at this time.) |
| Share a SkyDrive folder | ■ In SkyDrive, select the folder to open it. |
| | ■ Choose Share ▼ menu→Edit Permissions from the web page menu bar. |
| | ■ Enter the email address of the person with whom you would like to share the folder and tap Enter. Repeat this step to add additional people, if desired. |
| | ■ Choose the desired permission level from the list next to each person's email address. |
| | ■ Click Save. |
| | ■ Type a message to include in the invitation email, and click Send. (Click Skip This if you do not wish to send an invitation.) |
| Access a shared folder | ■ Click the link to the shared folder in the invitation email you received from the file's owner. |
| | ■ Click the View Folder button in the email. |
| | ■ Point to the file you wish to view or edit and choose an action. |

## Create a SkyDrive Folder

| WebSim | labyrinthelab.com/excel10 |
| --- | --- |

*In this exercise, you will create a SkyDrive folder to store shared documents.*

1. If necessary, **type** the URL listed above into the address bar of your web browser and **tap** Enter.

2. From the left navigation bar, click **Lessons 12–18** and then **Lesson 17**; then click the **Develop Your Skills 17.2.5: Create a SkyDrive Folder** link.
   *The WebSim loads and the SkyDrive start page appears. You are already logged in as GraceVargasRaritan@hotmail.com.*

3. Work your way through the **on-screen exercise instructions**.

4. Click the **Back to Course** link at the top-right corner of your screen.

## Moving Files

| Video Lesson | labyrinthelab.com/videos |
| --- | --- |

Because permissions are set on folders and not individual files, you may find it necessary to move files from one SkyDrive folder to another.

## Move Files

| WebSim | labyrinthelab.com/excel10 |
| --- | --- |

*In this exercise, you will move a file from one SkyDrive folder to another.*

1. If necessary, **type** the URL listed above into the address bar of your web browser and **tap** Enter.

2. From the left navigation bar, click **Lessons 12–18** and then **Lesson 17**; then click the **Develop Your Skills 17.2.6: Move Files** link.
   *The WebSim loads and the SkyDrive start page appears. You are already logged in as GraceVargasRaritan@hotmail.com.*

3. Work your way through the **on-screen exercise instructions**.

4. Click the **Back to Course** link at the top-right corner of your screen.

## Setting the Folder Permission Level

| Video Lesson | labyrinthelab.com/videos |
| --- | --- |

Once a folder is created, you can set its permission level, allowing others to view or edit the files inside. SkyDrive lets you set global permissions and share a folder with the general public, or you can specify individuals by their email addresses. Any files stored in the folder will inherit the folder's permissions. While granting permission, you may send an email to invite the specified people to access the shared folder.

## Share a Folder Using Permissions

| WebSim | labyrinthelab.com/excel10 |
| --- | --- |

*In this exercise, you will share a SkyDrive folder and all the files within.*

1. If necessary, **type** the URL listed above into the address bar of your web browser and **tap** Enter.

2. From the left navigation bar, click **Lessons 12–18** and then **Lesson 17**; then click the **Develop Your Skills 17.2.7: Share a Folder Using Permissions** link.
   *The WebSim loads and the SkyDrive page appears. The contents of the For Revision folder are displayed. You are already logged in as GraceVargasRaritan@hotmail.com.*

3. Work your way through the **on-screen exercise instructions**.

4. Click the **Back to Course** link at the top-right corner of your screen.

## Accessing Shared Files

| Video Lesson | labyrinthelab.com/videos |
| --- | --- |

Once a file has been shared with you, accessing it is simple. You click the View Folder button in the invitation email, log in with your Windows Live ID if prompted, and edit the file just as if it were one of your own files on SkyDrive. Make certain you keep the invitation email because using the View Folder button is the easiest way to access the files.

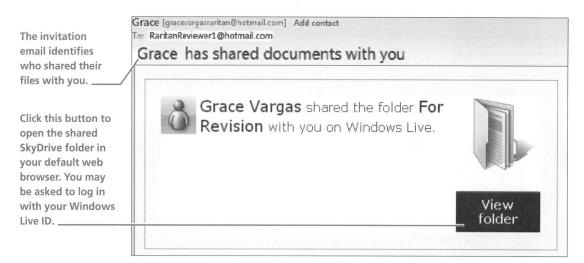

The invitation email identifies who shared their files with you.

Click this button to open the shared SkyDrive folder in your default web browser. You may be asked to log in with your Windows Live ID.

Grace [gracevargasraritan@hotmail.com]  Add contact
To:  RaritanReviewer1@hotmail.com
**Grace  has shared documents with you**

**Grace Vargas** shared the folder **For Revision** with you on Windows Live.

View folder

# 17.3 Concepts Review

| Concepts Review | labyrinthelab.com/excel10 |
| --- | --- |

*To check your knowledge of the key concepts introduced in this lesson, complete the Concepts Review quiz by going to the URL listed above. If your classroom is using Labyrinth eLab, you may complete the Concepts Review quiz from within your eLab course.*

# Reinforce Your Skills

## Set Up a Workbook for a Network Share

*In this exercise, you will create a shared workbook for access by other users on a network.*

1. **Open** the rs-Network Share Budget workbook from the Lesson 17 folder.

2. Choose **Review→Changes→Share Workbook** ⊞ from the Ribbon.

3. Place a **checkmark** in the box next to **Allow Changes by More than One User at the Same Time**.

4. Display the **Advanced** tab and follow these steps to set options in the dialog box.

| | |
|---|---|
| **Track changes**<br>◉ Keep change history for: [7] ⬍ days<br>◯ Don't keep change history | Ⓐ **Set 7 days in the Keep Change History For box.** |
| **Update changes**<br>◉ When file is saved<br>◯ Automatically every: [15] ⬍ minutes<br>    ◉ Save my changes and see others' changes<br>    ◯ Just see other users' changes | Ⓑ **Make certain that the other settings match the illustration.** |
| **Conflicting changes between users**<br>◉ Ask me which changes win<br>◯ The changes being saved win | |

*Saving the change history for seven days rather than 30 days reduces the potential size of the file. The longer changes are kept and the more changes that are tracked, the larger the workbook file will become.*

5. Click **OK**, and then click **OK** again to approve saving the workbook.
*Notice the word* [Shared] *to the right of the filename in the title bar.*

6. Choose **Review→Changes→Track Changes** 📝**→Highlight Changes** from the Ribbon.
*Notice that the Track Changes feature has been switched on. This was done automatically when you set the workbook for sharing. Notice also that the When setting is Since I Last Saved. This causes the highlight around changes to disappear each time you save the workbook. However, all changes will still be listed in the Change History.*

7. Click **Cancel** in the dialog box.

8. Have your instructor or a teaching assistant initial that you have successfully shared the workbook. _____

9. **Close** the workbook.
*The workbook is now ready to be placed on a network drive for multiple users to open and work on the file simultaneously.*

# Create a Windows Live ID

*In this exercise, you will create a Windows Live ID to use in later exercises as you work in Windows Live SkyDrive.*

*Before You Begin: It is recommended that you use the Internet Explorer browser for the textbook exercises. You may use the Firefox or Safari browsers if Internet Explorer is not available.*

 Websites are updated frequently, and the actual web pages may vary from those shown in the exercises of this book. Adjust the step instructions if the Windows Live website has been updated.

## Create a Windows Live ID Account

1. **Start** your web browser.

2. Type **www.live.com** in the address bar of the web browser, and **tap** Enter.
   *The Windows Live homepage includes a link to sign up for a Hotmail email account and a link to sign into Windows Live.*

3. Click the **Sign Up** button at the bottom-left of the web page.

4. Complete the form to create your Windows Live ID. Do **not** click the I Accept button at the bottom of the page yet.

5. Write down your Windows Live ID and password for future reference:
   - Windows Live ID:_____@hotmail.com
   - Password:_____

   *It is recommended that you use this account only for the exercises in this book. Your account information is not secure, as anyone can look over your shoulder and learn your account password.*

6. Click **I Accept** at the bottom of the page to complete the registration.
   *Your Windows Live account is created, and your Hotmail page appears. You could access Windows Live SkyDrive from this window. However, you will sign out now.*

## Sign Out from Windows Live

7. Click Sign Out at the upper-right corner of the browser window.
   *You are signed out of Hotmail and redirected to another Microsoft web page.*

8. Leave your web browser **open** and continue with the next exercise.

# Create a Folder and Share a Workbook in Windows Live SkyDrive

*In this exercise, you will sign in to Windows Live. You will access SkyDrive, create a new shared folder, and upload an Excel workbook to the folder. Then you will sign out of Windows Live.*

*Before You Begin: You must have completed Reinforce Your Skills 17.2, and your web browser should be open.*

## Sign In to Windows Live

1. Type **www.live.com** in the address bar of the web browser, and **tap** Enter.
   *The Windows Live sign-in page displays.*

2. Type the **Windows Live ID** (such as yourname22@hotmail.com) that you created in step 5 of Reinforce Your Skills 17.2, and **tap** Tab.

3. Type your **password**, and **tap** Enter to sign in.
   *Your Windows Live homepage displays.*

## Navigate to SkyDrive

4. Point at **Windows Live** in the upper-left corner of your homepage window and choose **SkyDrive** from the menu.
   *Your SkyDrive web page displays. You can choose SkyDrive on the navigation menu as shown below to move back to this view whenever you wish to view your folder list, create a folder, or open a different folder.*

## Create a Folder in SkyDrive

5. Notice that the My Documents folder was created automatically. Its icon has a padlock to indicate that the folder is not shared with anyone but you.

6. Choose **New ▾ menu→Folder** from the menu bar above the My Documents folder.
   *The Create a Folder page displays.*

7. Type **Budget Drafts** as the folder name.

## Share the Folder

*In the next few steps, you will change the folder permissions to share the folder with another co-worker.*

8. Click **Change** to the right of Share With: Just Me. (If you accidentally continued to the next screen, click Just Me instead. Then, click Edit Permissions in the Permissions for Budget Drafts screen.)

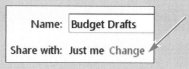

9. Under Add Specific People, type **nikkiyoung@raritan.com** in the Enter a Name or an E-Mail Address box, and **tap** Enter.
   *The email address displays with a checkmark and Nikki Young's current permission rights near the bottom of the window. Nikki's email account does not actually exist, so you will not use it to access any files.*

10. Click the permission rights menu ▼ arrow, and choose **Can Add, Edit Details, and Delete Files**, if not already selected.

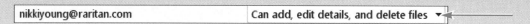

11. Click **Next** to display the Budget Drafts folder page.

## Add a Workbook File to the Folder

*Some of the next steps contain an alternate instruction for you to follow if the Silverlight add-in program is installed on your computer.*

12. Choose **Add Files** from the Budget Drafts folder menu bar.

13. Click the **Browse** button for the first Add Document text box. (If the Add Document text boxes do not display, choose **Select Documents from Your Computer** instead.)

14. Navigate to the Lesson 17 folder in your file storage location and **double-click** the rs-Orthopedics Dept Budget workbook.

15. Click the **Upload** button. (If the file uploaded automatically, click the **Continue** button at the bottom of the window instead.)
    *The file uploads, and the icon for the rs-Orthopedics Dept Budget file displays in the folder.*

16. Click **Sign Out** in the upper-right corner of the window to exit Windows Live.

17. **Close** your web browser window.

# Edit a Workbook with Excel Web App

*In this exercise, you will save a workbook from within Excel to a folder in your Windows Live SkyDrive storage location. Then, you will edit the workbook in Excel Web App as if you are working from a computer that does not have Excel installed.*

*Before You Begin: You must have completed Reinforce Your Skills 17.2.*

## Create a New Workbook in Excel

1. **Start** a new, blank workbook in Excel.

2. **Enter** data of your choice in a few cells.

3. **Format** the data appropriately, such as applying colors, changing alignment, or adjusting column widths.

## Save the Workbook to Windows Live SkyDrive

4. Choose **File→Save & Send→Save to Web**.
   *The Save to Windows Live SkyDrive pane displays in Backstage view.*

5. Click the **Sign In** button in the Windows Live SkyDrive pane.

6. In the dialog box that appears, enter the **email address** and **password** you created in Reinforce Your Skills 17.2, and **tap** Enter.
   *You are now logged in to Windows Live, and your folder list appears as shown. The Budget Drafts folder displays only if you completed Reinforce Your Skills 17.3.*

7. Choose the **My Documents** folder under Personal Folders, if not already selected.
   *The folder name is highlighted. Under My Documents, notice that Shared With: Just Me indicates you have not shared the folder. Other people cannot access documents you place in this folder. You could change the folder permission properties, if you wished.*

8. Click the **Save As** button.
   *After a few moments, the Save As dialog box appears. The address bar displays an alphanumeric entry for your SkyDrive main folder and ^.Documents (or a similar name) to indicate that My Documents is the currently active folder.*

9. Enter the filename **rs-SkyDrive Workbook** and click **Save**.
*Your workbook has been saved to SkyDrive, and the workbook redisplays in Excel. You could continue editing and then save again to SkyDrive, if you wished.*

10. **Exit** Excel.

## Edit the Workbook in Excel Web App

*Now assume that you are using a computer in an Internet café. You wish to edit your workbook, but this computer does not have Excel installed.*

11. **Start** your web browser and navigate to **www.live.com**.

12. **Sign in** with your Windows Live ID and password. (See step 5 of Reinforce Your Skills 17.2, if necessary.)

13. Choose the **My Documents** folder, if it is not open already.
*The My Documents folder page appears and contains the rs-SkyDrive Workbook folder you just saved.*

14. **Click** the rs-SkyDrive Workbook file.
*The workbook displays below a menu of available actions.*

15. Try to change the contents of any cell.
*The cell contents are not changed. Currently, you only may view the workbook. To edit the workbook, you must choose either the Open in Excel or Edit in Browser command.*

16. Click **Edit in Browser** in the menu.

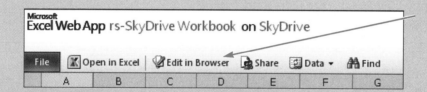

*You are now viewing your workbook in Excel Web App. Notice that fewer tabs and commands are available on the Ribbon than in the full version of Excel. The Web App, however, allows you to edit the workbook when Excel isn't installed on the computer you are using.*

17. Take a moment to browse through the **File**, **Home**, and **Insert** tabs of the Ribbon to become familiar with the commands available, and then return to the Home tab.

18. Experiment by editing a cell's entry, applying various formatting to cells, and cutting and pasting data to a different row or column.
*Notice that the context, or popup, menu is not available when you right-click a cell or cell range.*

## Sign Out from Windows Live

19. Click **Sign Out** at the upper-right corner when you finish editing the workbook.
*Signing out or clicking the Back button in the browser window automatically saves your changes and closes the workbook.*

20. **Close** your web browser.

# Apply Your Skills

## Create and Share a Folder on SkyDrive

*In this exercise, you will sign in to your Windows Live account. Then you will navigate to SkyDrive and create a new folder.*

1. **Start** your web browser and navigate to **www.live.com**.

2. **Sign in** using the Windows Live ID and password you created in step 5 of Reinforce Your Skills 17.2. (Follow steps 3–6 of that exercise if you did not create a Windows Live account.)

3. Navigate to your **SkyDrive** storage location in Windows Live.

4. Create a new folder named **Raritan Shared Documents** in SkyDrive. Choose options to **share** the folder with nikkiyoung@raritan.com. Allow Nikki to **view** documents in the folder but not to edit or delete them. If you are asked to send a notification to Nikki, click **Skip This**. Do not send a notification to her fictitious email address.

5. Leave your browser window **open** and continue with the next exercise.

## Add a File to the SkyDrive Folder

*In this exercise, you will upload a workbook to your Raritan Shared Documents folder on Windows Live SkyDrive.*

*Before You Begin: You must have completed Apply Your Skills 17.1. Your web browser should be open, and you should be signed in to your Windows Live account.*

1. Navigate to the **Raritan Shared Documents** folder in Windows Live SkyDrive, if necessary. You created this folder in Apply Your Skills 17.1.

2. Add the as-Cardiology Dept Budget workbook from the Lesson 17 folder in your file storage location to the **Raritan Shared Documents** folder in SkyDrive.

3. Click **Sign Out** in the top-right area of the web page.

4. Leave your browser window **open** and continue with the next exercise.

# Edit a Workbook Using Excel Web App

*In this exercise, you will upload a workbook to your Raritan Shared Documents folder on Windows Live SkyDrive.*

*Before You Begin: You must have completed Apply Your Skills 17.1 and 17.2. Your web browser should be open, and you should be signed in to your Windows Live account.*

1. Navigate to the **Raritan Shared Documents** folder in Windows Live SkyDrive, if necessary. You created this folder in Apply Your Skills 17.1.

2. Choose the as-Cardiology Dept Budget workbook. You added this file in Apply Your Skills 17.2.

3. Choose to edit the workbook using **Excel Web App**.

4. Select **cell E11,** and change the May grant salaries to **1597**.
   *The total grant amount in cell I11 should be 4,283.*

5. Click the **Back** button in your web browser.

6. **Open** the as-Cardiology Dept Budget workbook, and verify that the change was saved.

7. Have your instructor or a teaching assistant initial that you successfully saved the revised as-Cardiology Dept Budget workbook in the Raritan Shared Documents folder on SkyDrive: _____

8. **Sign out** from Windows Live, and **close** your browser window.

# Critical Thinking & Work-Readiness Skills

*In the course of working through the following Microsoft Office-based Critical Thinking exercises, you will also be utilizing various work-readiness skills, some of which are listed next to each exercise. Go to labyrinthelab.com/ workreadiness to learn more about the work-readiness skills.*

## 17.1 Set Up a Workbook for a Network Share

Elias Carpenter is a nurse supervisor at Raritan Clinic East. He coordinates a free testing program to screen patients for diabetes. He uses Excel to keep a record of the screening costs. These costs include medical and office supplies as well as physician, medical professional, and administrative time. Your job is to set up his workbook to be shared on Raritan Clinic's intranet, or network. Open ct-Diabetes Screening Clinic (Lesson 17 folder). Save with the name **ct-Diabetes Screening Clinic [Your Last Name]** in the Lesson 17 folder. Take a few moments to review the worksheets. Two sheets contain PivotTables that organize the personnel costs by patient age group and test result. Then, set up the workbook to be shared on the network so that multiple users can enter data simultaneously. Display each tab in the Ribbon and determine which commands are unavailable until sharing is switched off. Close the workbook when finished.

**WORK-READINESS SKILLS APPLIED**
- Understanding systems
- Participating as a member of a team
- Reasoning

## 17.2 Create a SkyDrive Folder and Add a File

Elias will be away from Raritan Clinic while attending a conference and cannot access the Raritan Clinic intranet then. In this scenario, he wishes to use Windows Live SkyDrive to continue working on his unshared workbook. Log in to Windows Live using the ID and password you created in Reinforce Your Skills 17.1. Navigate to SkyDrive and create a folder named **Diabetes Screening**. Upload the *original* ct-Diabetes Screening Clinic workbook (Lesson 17 folder) to the newly created folder. Leave SkyDrive open for the next exercise.

**WORK-READINESS SKILLS APPLIED**
- Selecting technology
- Applying technology to a task
- Organizing and Maintaining information

## 17.3 Edit a Workbook Stored on SkyDrive

Elias is attending the conference and needs to change some personnel costs in his workbook. He is using a computer that has the full version of Excel 2010 installed. Log in to Windows Live, if necessary. Open the ct-Diabetes Screening Clinic workbook from the Diabetes Screening folder on SkyDrive. You may choose to edit the workbook either in Excel or Excel Web App. In the Costs worksheet, sort the records by screening result. Change the personnel cost to $30 for all patients whose test result indicated Type 1 or Type 2 diabetes. Do *not* change the cost for patients whose test result was normal or borderline. Use the Data tab of the Ribbon (Excel) or the HomeData menu ▼ (Excel Web App) to refresh all connections so that the costs update in the PivotTable worksheets. Save the workbook, and close it in SkyDrive. Reopen the workbook in SkyDrive to verify the changes were saved. Sign out from Windows Live when you are finished.

**WORK-READINESS SKILLS APPLIED**
- Applying technology to a task
- Organizing and Maintaining information
- Making decisions

# Integrating Excel with Other Programs

## LEARNING OBJECTIVES

After studying this lesson, you will be able to:

- Save workbooks for use with prior Excel versions
- Convert workbooks to text, PDF, and XPS file formats
- Share Excel data with Word, PowerPoint, and Access
- Import text and data from external sources into Excel workbooks
- Save workbook elements as a web page

Information is shared electronically in many ways. In this lesson, you will learn how to make Excel 2010 workbooks compatible with prior Excel versions so that all project collaborators may share data. You will learn how to convert workbooks to other file formats, including PDF and XPS for document sharing. A program other than Excel may be the basis for a project. For example, you often will create reports using Word and make presentations using PowerPoint. Through the power of application integration, you may link or embed Excel data, tables, and charts in those documents. You also will bring data into Excel from external sources such as a plain-text file or Word document. Documents often are shared electronically as web pages. You will learn how to save an entire workbook as a web page, as well as save a single worksheet and selected elements from a sheet.

# Producing an Annual Report

**Raritan Clinic East**

Pediatric Diagnostic Specialists

Deion Jenett is administrative assistant to Dr. Edward Jackson, the chief operating officer at Raritan Clinic East. Deion is halfway through a project to produce Raritan's annual report. He coordinates the efforts of the production team to get various parts of the publication ready for printing and publishing to the clinic's website. Deion assembles information about the production tasks and the schedule into an Excel workbook and then publishes the workbook in a universal file format so everyone can review it. As part of his normal job duties, Deion also merges Excel workbook data into forms or letters addressed to multiple recipients.

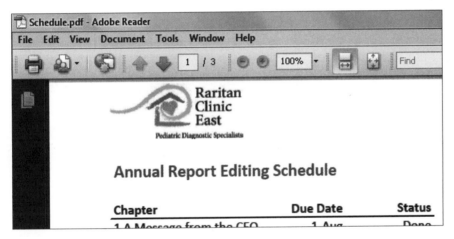

Deion saves an Excel workbook as a PDF file, a universal file format that may be viewed by anyone in a PDF reader.

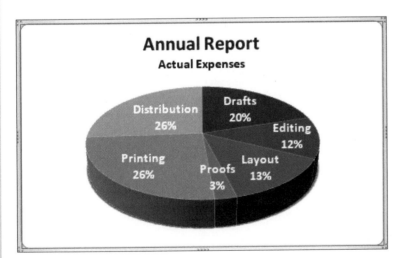

The Copy and Paste commands are used to import a linked Excel chart into a PowerPoint slide.

| Employee Name: | «First» «Last» |
| Employee ID: | «Exployee ID» |
| Job Title: | «Position» |

| Employee Name: | Nadia Andrews |
| Employee ID: | NA34 |
| Job Title: | Nurse Aide |

Data from an Excel workbook is inserted into merge fields, and then Word's Mail Merge feature is used to assemble personalized forms.

# 18.1 Maintaining Compatibility with Previous Versions of Excel

**Video Lesson** labyrinthelab.com/videos

You can open and work with Excel workbooks saved in Excel 2010 or earlier versions such as Excel 97, 2000, 2003, and 2007. At times, you will need to share your workbooks and templates with others who have one of the earlier Excel versions or may not have Excel installed. You must ensure that files are saved in a format that those users can open.

## About File Formats

A file format is a structure for storing data in a computer file. An application program uses specific file formats to save anything that you create in that program. The format that an application program normally uses to save files is called its *native* file format. For example, Word saves files using the format Word Document (.docx), and a web page editor may use the HTML file format.

### Identifying a File's Format

When you give Excel's Save As  command, you may choose from a number of file formats in the Save As Type list in the Save As dialog box. The default is Excel Workbook. While browsing filenames in Excel or Windows Explorer, you may identify files that are compatible with Excel by viewing the icons next to the filenames. You may also read the extension at the end of the filename, if extensions are displayed. For example, the extension .xls indicates a spreadsheet workbook saved for use with a previous Excel version.

> Can't view any filename extensions? See the Working with File Formats Quick Reference table on page 700 for the procedure to switch on their display.

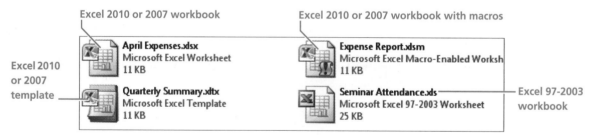

The file's icon and extension in the filename identify the file type

The following table shows the file formats that you may use to save workbooks for various Excel versions along with their file extensions.

> All Excel filename extensions begin with the letters *xl* and contain additional letters that have special meanings. In Excel 2010, the third letter is *s* for spreadsheet (workbook), *t* for template, or *a for add-in. The fourth letter x indicates that the file is* without macros, and *m* indicates that it does have macros.

| File Type | Excel Version | Description | File Extension |
|-----------|---------------|-------------|----------------|
| Excel Workbook | 2010 or 2007 | Workbooks without macros | .xlsx |
| Excel Macro-Enabled Workbook | 2010 or 2007 | Workbooks with macros | .xlsm |
| Excel Template | 2010 or 2007 | Template workbooks without macros | .xltx |
| Excel Macro-Enabled Template | 2010 or 2007 | Template workbooks with macros | .xltm |
| Excel 97-2003 Workbook | 97–2003 | Workbooks with or without macros | .xls |
| Excel 97-2003 Template | 97–2003 | Template workbooks with or without macros | .xlt |
| Excel Binary Workbook | 97–2007 | Non-XML workbooks | .xlsb |
| Microsoft Excel 5.0/95 Workbook | 95 | Early-version workbooks | .xls |

## Excel 2010 Open XML File Formats

As you can see from the preceding table, Excel 2010 has more file formats than most previous versions to help identify files containing macros and reduce the file size, which is beneficial when you share files. The file structure, called Open XML, is based on the Extensible Markup Language (XML) used by software developers. XML is is one standard for the exchange of structured data on the Internet.

## Earlier Excel File Formats

Versions prior to Excel 2010 and 2007 use different file formats than XML. For this reason, some Excel 2010 and 2007 features are not viewable in the earlier versions. Files saved in these formats display the words *[Compatibility Mode]* in the Excel title bar as shown in the following illustration.

Schedule [Compatibility Mode] - Microsoft Excel

You have the following two options to enable users of earlier versions to open and work with your Excel 2010 file.

- **Save in a Non-XML File Format**—You may save your workbook in a file format that removes the incompatible features.
- **Use the Compatibility Pack**—Users may download and install a file converter that hides the incompatible features.

| Task | Procedure |
|------|-----------|
| Save a workbook in an Excel 97-2003 file format | ■ Choose File→Save As ⬛→Excel 97-2003 Workbook. (Two files will now exist if you previously saved the file in Excel Workbook format.)<br>■ Correct any issues reported by the Compatibility Checker. |
| Display filename extensions | ■ Open Windows Explorer.<br>■ Choose (Win 7/Vista) Organize→Folder and Search Options or (Win XP) Tools→Folder Options.<br>■ Display the View tab, and under Advanced Settings remove the checkmark next to Hide Extensions for Known File Types. |
| Identify the format of files | ■ Choose File→Open 📂 or open Windows Explorer.<br>■ Navigate to the folder containing the file(s) in your file storage location.<br>■ Display the Files of Type list and choose All Files if working in Excel's Open dialog box.<br>■ Click the Views ▤ ▼ menu button on the dialog box or Explorer toolbar and choose Details.<br>■ Look at the icon next to the filename, read the filename extension (if displayed), and read the file type. |

## DEVELOP YOUR SKILLS 18.1.1
# Save a Workbook for an Earlier Excel Version

*In this exercise, you will save an Excel 2010 workbook in a file format compatible with an earlier version of Excel. You will view file details to identify file formats.*

## Save the Workbook

1. **Start** Excel and **open** the Schedule workbook from the Lesson 18 folder in your file storage location.

2. **Maximize** ▣ the window.
   *This workbook contains three worksheets. Notice that the words [Compatibility Mode] do not appear after the filename in the title bar. This workbook was saved in Excel 2010, and all its features are visible.*

3. Choose **File→Save As** ⬛.
   *The Save As dialog box opens.*

4. Follow these steps to save the workbook in Excel 97–2003 file format:
   *Filenames in your dialog box will display extensions if the Windows Explorer option is set to do so. Filename extensions are not displayed in the illustrations of this exercise except those Excel displays. No other filenames now appear in the dialog box because you are currently filtering for only this Excel 97–2003 type. Other files do exist in the folder, but they are not in this file format.*

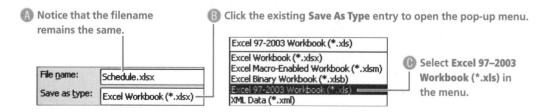

Ⓐ Notice that the filename remains the same.

Ⓑ Click the existing **Save As Type** entry to open the pop-up menu.

| File name: | Schedule.xlsx |
| Save as type: | Excel Workbook (*.xlsx) |

Excel 97-2003 Workbook (*.xls)
Excel Workbook (*.xlsx)
Excel Macro-Enabled Workbook (*.xlsm)
Excel Binary Workbook (*.xlsb)
Excel 97-2003 Workbook (*.xls)
XML Data (*.xml)

Ⓒ Select **Excel 97–2003 Workbook (*.xls)** in the menu.

5. Click **Save**.

*No alerts appeared because Excel found no compatibility issues in this workbook. This file could be opened and edited in Excel versions 97 through 2003.*

## Identify the Format of Files

*Next you will display the filenames in the Lesson 18 folder and review their file formats.*

6. Choose **File→Open** 📂, and navigate to the Lesson 18 folder, if not already displayed.

7. Follow these steps to display details about the files in the folder:
*Your dialog box displays more files than shown here. The dialog box may vary slightly from the illustration depending on your Windows version.*

Ⓐ Click the **Views menu ▼** button on the dialog box Menu Bar, and choose **Details** from the menu.

Ⓑ Point at the border at the right of the **Type** column heading until the pointer resembles a double-pointed arrow. **Double-click** the border to widen the Type column. (Drag the border to the right if you have trouble double-clicking.)

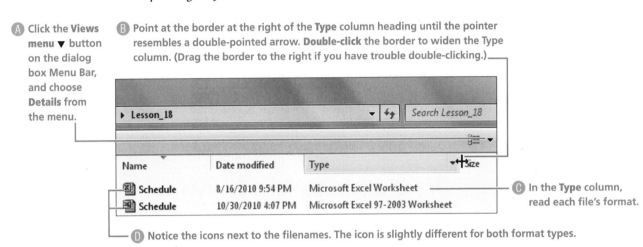

| Name | Date modified | Type | Size |
|---|---|---|---|
| Schedule | 8/16/2010 9:54 PM | Microsoft Excel Worksheet | |
| Schedule | 10/30/2010 4:07 PM | Microsoft Excel 97-2003 Worksheet | |

Ⓒ In the **Type** column, read each file's format.

Ⓓ Notice the icons next to the filenames. The icon is slightly different for both format types.

*Also, each filename displays a filename extension, such as .xlsx, if the display option is switched on in Windows.*

8. Click **Cancel** to exit the Open dialog box.

9. **Close** the workbook, and leave Excel **open**.

# Checking for Excel Version Compatibility

**Video Lesson**   labyrinthelab.com/videos

The Compatibility Checker scans your workbook and identifies any features that would not be included if you were to save the workbook in a non-XML (nonnative) file format. The report summarizes various incompatibilities as significant or minor, and it provides a Find button to help you locate each occurrence in the workbook. You may decide to proceed if the compatibility check reports only a minor loss of fidelity, such as table formatting. Significant issues usually must be resolved. The dialog box contains an option that, when switched on, will check for compatibility every time the workbook is saved.

The Compatibility Checker automatically scans any file that you save in a non-XML format even if you did not run the Checker before giving the Save As command.

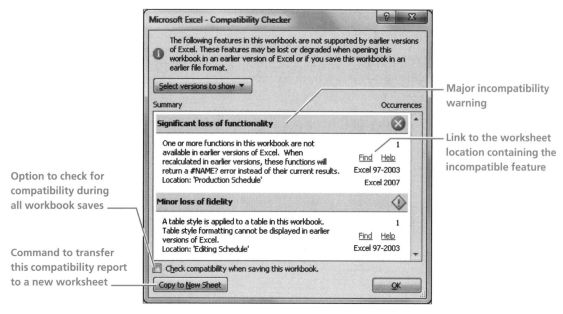

**Option to check for compatibility during all workbook saves**

**Command to transfer this compatibility report to a new worksheet**

**Major incompatibility warning**

**Link to the worksheet location containing the incompatible feature**

A report displayed by the Compatibility Checker before or while a file is saved

# Check Excel Version Compatibility

*In this exercise, you will run the Compatibility Checker to check for compatibility issues before attempting to save a file in the Excel 97-2003 file format.*

1. **Open** the Compatibility Check workbook from the Lesson 18 folder.
   *Notice that the Editing Schedule worksheet contains a table style, which is not supported in older Excel versions.*

## Run the Compatibility Checker

*If you accidentally close the Compatibility Checker window in the following steps, just give the command again.*

2. Choose **File→Info**. In the Info tab of Backstage view, choose **Check for Issues menu ▾**, and choose **Check Compatibility**.
   *After a few moments, the Microsoft Excel – Compatibility Checker window appears with its report of two issues found in the workbook.*

3. **Scroll** through the window and read both messages.

4. Click the **Help** link under Minor Loss of Fidelity.
   *The Excel Help window appears so you may search for information to help resolve table compatibility issues.*

5. **Close** the Help window.

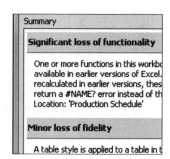

6. In the Compatibility Checker window, **scroll up** and click the **Find** link under Significant Loss of Functionality.
*The pointer jumps to cell D13 on the Production Schedule worksheet. This cell contains a formula using the WORKDAY.INTL function. This function is new in Excel 2010 and is not backward compatible. You would edit the workbook to correct this significant compatibility issue before saving. However, you are not required to make any corrections in this exercise.*

7. Notice that the Compatibility Checker window is closed because you used the Find link.
*You may run the Compatibility Checker again as needed, and any resolved issues will no longer display.*

**Use Save As**

*Next, you will give the Save As command with the intent to save the file for an earlier Excel version. Remember that two compatibility issues still exist in the workbook.*

8. Choose **File→Save As** 📇.

9. In the Save As dialog box, drop down the **Save As Type** list, and choose **Excel 97-2003 Workbook**.

| File name: | Compatibility Check.xls |
|---|---|
| Save as type: | Excel 97-2003 Workbook (*.xls) |

10. Click **Save**.
*The Compatibility Checker window appears. Excel automatically runs the checker whenever you attempt to save a workbook in a non-XML file format. Notice the buttons at the bottom of the dialog box. The Continue button would save the file with the issues unresolved. That might be appropriate for minor compatibility issues but is not the action that you want to take now.*

11. Click **Copy to New Sheet**.
*The compatibility issues report, including cell locations, is transferred to a separate worksheet for documentation and printing. You could use this information to continue resolving any compatibility issues until the workbook would be ready for saving.*

12. **Close** the workbook without saving again.

## Using the Compatibility Pack

Video Lesson    labyrinthelab.com/videos

A free compatibility download from Microsoft allows users of previous Excel 2000, XP (2002), and 2003 versions to open and work with Excel 2010 files. Users are prompted to download and install the Microsoft Office Compatibility Pack the first time they attempt to open an Excel 2010 file. Thereafter, any opened Excel 2010 files will be converted automatically. Any formatting or other features specific to Excel 2010 do not display when the file is opened in the previous version but are preserved when the file is reopened in Excel 2010. Having that capability may be worth asking other users to take the time to install the Compatibility Pack.

If asking others to install the Compatibility Pack could cause a problem—perhaps inconveniencing your best customers—you may opt to save files in the Excel 97-2003 file format as previously described in this lesson. Just remember that some Excel 2010 features may be removed permanently from those files.

# Converters

A converter is a small program that allows an application program such as Excel to open files that are not in the program's native file format. For example, you may need to import data from a Word document into a worksheet. Excel features a variety of converters that are installed automatically. You also may download and install additional converters that may become available as new file formats are introduced. For example, when a new version of an application program is released, it often introduces a new native file format.

## *Example of Using a Converter*

You send a workbook saved in an Excel 2010 file format to another user who uses Excel 2003. The other user installs the Compatibility Pack, which includes converter programs. When she opens your Excel 2010 file, it is converted to a format that is compatible with her Excel version. Any incompatible features will be hidden.

| QUICK REFERENCE | CHECKING WORKBOOK COMPATIBILITY WITH EARLIER EXCEL VERSIONS |
|---|---|
| **Task** | **Procedure** |
| Check a workbook for features incompatible with earlier Excel versions | ■ With the workbook open, choose File→Info. In the Info tab of Backstage view, choose Check for Issues menu ▼, and choose Check Compatibility. |
|  | ■ Click the Find link in the Compatibility Checker dialog box to locate the first incompatible cell, if any issues are reported. |
|  | ■ Edit the worksheet to correct a major incompatibility. |
|  | ■ Run Compatibility Checker again to verify that the previous issue is no longer reported. Find and, if necessary, correct any additional major issues. Correct minor issues as necessary. |
| Install the Microsoft Office Compatibility Pack | ■ Start Internet Explorer, navigate to the Microsoft Office 2010 Downloads web page, enter *Compatibility Pack* in the Search box, and initiate the search. |
|  | ■ Follow instructions to download and install the Microsoft Office Compatibility Pack for Word, Excel, and PowerPoint 2007 file formats. This Compatibility Pack also is used for Excel 2010. |

# 18.2 Converting Workbooks to Other File Formats

Video Lesson    labyrinthelab.com/videos

At times, you may need to save worksheet data to use in a program other than Excel or upload a worksheet onto a web page. You may choose from several file formats in the Save As dialog box, such as XML Data or Web Page. This topic explains two common methods of sharing data between incompatible programs or with users who do not have the original program.

## Text File Formats

Text file formats are commonly used to export data to or from another program that is incompatible with Excel. All worksheet formatting, such as fonts, colors, and graphics, is removed. Two types of text files are used most often in conjunction with Excel: comma delimited and tab delimited.

### Comma Delimited

A comma delimited text file uses a comma to separate two columns of data. The following illustration shows an example of Excel data converted in a comma delimited file. When saving a workbook in this file format, you would choose CSV (Comma Delimited) from the Save As Type list. The filename extension .csv is added to the filename.

```
First,Last,Phone,City
Deion,Jenett,619-555-7823,San Diego
Jacqueline,Chan,303-555-8989,Denver
Jason,Stevens,540-555-2220,Bristol
```
Excel column data converted to the comma delimited format

### Tab Delimited

A tab delimited file uses a tab character to separate two columns of data. In the following example of a tab delimited file, each small arrow represents a non-printing tab code. When saving a workbook in this file format, you would choose Text (Tab Delimited) from the Save As Type list. The filename extension .txt is added to the filename.

| First → | Last → | Phone → | City |
|---------|--------|---------|------|
| Deion → | Jenett → | 619-555-7823 | → San Diego |
| Jacqueline → | Chan → | 303-555-8989 | → Denver |
| Jason → | Stevens → | 540-555-2220 | → Bristol |

Excel column data converted to the tab delimited format

## Limitations of File Formats

Some file formats will not save all information in the workbook file. For example, a tab delimited file won't save data on multiple worksheets or any cell formatting. Excel will warn you about features, formatting, or data you might lose in the new file format. When you save a workbook to a non-Excel file format, a second file is created. The original workbook file is not changed.

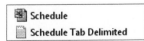

Icons and filenames for an original Excel workbook and a version saved in tab delimited format

### *Example of a File Format Limitation*

You decide to convert a workbook to tab delimited format. Excel warns you that only the currently selected worksheet can be saved to the new file. So, you perform a save command for each worksheet in the workbook. Now each worksheet is contained in a separate file. You also notice that comments on the worksheets are not saved in the tab delimited format.

| QUICK REFERENCE | CONVERTING WORKSHEET DATA TO A TEXT FORMAT |
|---|---|
| **Task** | **Procedure** |
| Save workbook data in comma delimited or tab delimited format | ■ Choose File→Save As . <br> ■ In the Save As dialog box, choose CSV (Comma Delimited) or Text (Tab Delimited) from the Save As Type list. <br> ■ Enter the name in the File Name box and click Save. |

## DEVELOP YOUR SKILLS 18.2.1
# Convert Excel Data to Text

*In this exercise, you will use the Save As command to save a copy of a worksheet in a different file format. You will then use the Notepad application to view the workbook in its new file format.*

### Convert a Worksheet to Text

1. **Open** the original Schedule workbook that is in the Excel Workbook file format. Its icon is shown to the right. Display the **Details** view to determine the correct file in the Save As dialog box, if necessary.

   > **Schedule**
   > Microsoft Excel Worksheet
   > 11 KB

2. Display the **Editing Schedule** worksheet, if not already displayed.

3. Choose **File→Save As** [icon].

4. Follow these steps to save the workbook in the tab delimited file format:

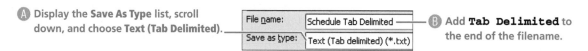

Ⓐ Display the **Save As Type** list, scroll down, and choose **Text (Tab Delimited)**.

File name: Schedule Tab Delimited

Save as type: Text (Tab delimited) (*.txt)

Ⓑ Add **Tab Delimited** to the end of the filename.

5. Click the **Save** button and read the warning box.
   *Excel warns you that the selected file type cannot save a file containing multiple worksheets. It will save only the active worksheet.*

6. Click **OK** to acknowledge the warning, and then review the next warning box that appears.
   *Excel now warns you that the tab delimited file format may not be compatible with features in your workbook file. Features other than the text in cells, such as cell formatting, will be removed in the resulting file.*

7. Choose **Yes** to continue the conversion to the tab delimited format.
   *Excel completes the conversion. Notice that the worksheet tab has been renamed to the new filename. Although the name of the new file appears in the Excel title bar, you are not really viewing the converted file. You must open the newly converted file to see the changes.*

8. Use ⌈Ctrl⌉+⌈W⌉ to close the workbook. Choose **not** to save when you are asked if you wish to save the workbook.

## View the Converted Data

9. Choose **File→Open**  and navigate to the Lesson 18 folder, if necessary.
   *Notice that the newly converted file is not listed. That's because Excel is displaying only workbook files. A tab delimited file is saved in text format. In the next step, you will tell Excel to display all text format files.*

10. Choose **Text Files** from the Files of Type list, as shown below. Your dialog box may differ depending on your Windows version.

| File name: | ▼ | Text Files | ▼ |
| --- | --- | --- | --- |

*Three files with this file format display. You used the Open dialog box only to navigate to and view file-names. In the next step, you will open the file using a different program. The Notepad applet is a simple text editor that comes with Windows. It allows you to view exactly what the data in your converted file looks like.*

11. Follow these steps to open the text file in Notepad:

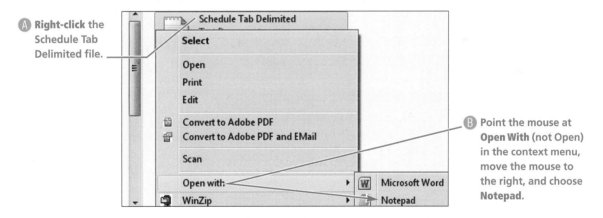

Ⓐ **Right-click** the Schedule Tab Delimited file.

Ⓑ Point the mouse at **Open With** (not Open) in the context menu, move the mouse to the right, and choose **Notepad**.

*The file opens in Notepad, the Windows text editor program. Notice that the file contains only plain text separated by tabs. The original worksheet's cell formatting and the logo graphic were removed. This file format, however, may be the only means of bringing the data into certain programs that are not compatible with Excel.*

12. **Close** the Notepad window. Choose **not** to save if you are asked to save changes to the file.

13. **Cancel** Excel's Open dialog box.

# PDF and XPS File Formats

**Video Lesson** labyrinthelab.com/videos

The PDF (Portable Document Format) and XPS (XML Paper Specification) file formats may be applied to Excel workbooks and many other types of documents. These file formats allow colleagues to view and print a workbook with all formatting intact even if they don't have any Excel version, and it also prevents them from making any changes or accessing any hidden information. For example, a user who installs the free Adobe Acrobat Reader may view a PDF document. You may use either the Save As command in the File tab or the Create PDF/XPS command in the Save & Send tab of Backstage view to publish the document. You may publish a selected range, a worksheet, or the entire workbook.

Personal information from the document's properties, such as your Microsoft Office user name, are saved with the PDF or XPS document unless you choose Options and uncheck Document Properties.

| QUICK REFERENCE | PUBLISHING A WORKBOOK IN PDF OR XPS FORMAT |
|---|---|
| **Task** | **Procedure** |
| Publish a PDF or XPS document | ■ To save part of a workbook, display the desired worksheet. Select a range, if desired. |
| | ■ Choose File→Save As, or choose File→Save & Send→Create PDF/XPS Document→Create PDF/XPS from Backstage view. |
| | ■ Enter the workbook name in the File Name box. |
| | ■ Choose PDF (or choose XPS Document) from the Save As Type list. |
| | ■ Choose an Optimize For option, and then choose other options as desired. |
| | ■ Click Save (or click Publish if you chose the Create PDF/XPS command in Backstage view). |

## DEVELOP YOUR SKILLS 18.2.2
# Publish Excel Data as a PDF Document

*In this exercise, you will convert a workbook to the PDF file format, and then you will view the file in a PDF reader program.*

*Before You Begin: Your computer must have a PDF reader such as Adobe Acrobat Reader installed.*

1. **Open** the original Schedule workbook. Its icon is shown to the right. If necessary, change Files of Type to Excel Files to see the filename.

2. Choose **File→Save As** 🔖, and choose **PDF** in the Save As Type list.
*The PDF publishing options appear along the bottom of the Save As dialog box. The filename Schedule should already be entered, and the file type is PDF. Notice that the Open File After Publishing option is switched on if your computer has a PDF reader installed.*

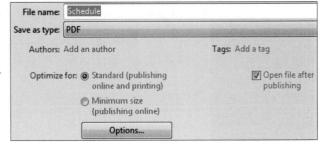

3. Click the **Options** button near the lower-left corner of the dialog box.

4. Under **Publish What** in the Options dialog box, choose **Entire Workbook**.
*Notice that you may publish a selected range, the active worksheet, the entire workbook, or a table (available when a table range is selected). The Ignore Print Areas option is used to disregard any print area set in Excel.*

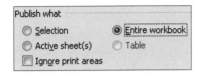

5. Click **OK**.

6. Click the **Save** button in the Save As dialog box.
*After a few moments, the published workbook displays in an Adobe Acrobat (or other PDF reader) window. This occurs because the Open File After Publishing option was switched on. Depending on the PDF reader you use, the filename Schedule.pdf usually appears in the window's title bar.*

7. **Maximize** the PDF reader window.

8. Use the following tools to browse through the document (your reader window may differ from the one shown):

Ⓐ If the worksheet is not readable, click the **decrease magnification** button or **increase magnification** button multiple times until it is readable.

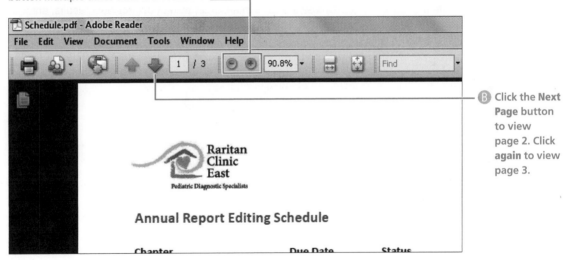

Ⓑ Click the **Next Page** button to view page 2. Click **again** to view page 3.

*The toolbar buttons allow you to print or select and copy text and objects, but you cannot alter anything in this document.*

9. **Close** the reader window.

10. **Close** the Schedule workbook, and leave Excel **open**. Choose **not** to save if you are asked to save.

# 18.3 Using Excel Tables with Word Mail Merge

**Video Lesson**    labyrinthelab.com/videos

You may wish to send multiple customers a letter or an envelope containing marketing materials. Word's mail merge feature helps you prepare a standard message (called the main document) and personalize each copy with the customer's name, address, most recent order date, and other data unique to that customer. You may use a list or table from an Excel worksheet as a data source for these and other documents in Word. In this lesson, you will work with tables. A table should be set up with each field (column) containing one type of data, such as the order date. You insert various field names in the main document to personalize the message. When the mail merge is completed, data from each record (row) of the data source replace the field names, and you have a personalized document copy for each record.

For a successful mail merge, break up data into its smallest segments. For example, each of the following segments in an address list should be in a separate column: title, first name, middle initial, last name, street, city, state, and ZIP code.

| QUICK REFERENCE | USING EXCEL TABLES WITH WORD MAIL MERGE |
|---|---|
| **Task** | **Procedure** |
| Create the table and name the worksheet in Excel | ▪ Create the table in an Excel workbook. For best results, enter the table column headings in row 1 of the worksheet.<br>▪ Double-click the sheet tab, type the sheet name, and tap Enter.<br>▪ Save the workbook. |
| Start the mail merge in Word | Do one of the following:<br>▪ Open the desired main document.<br>▪ Start a new, blank document in Word.<br>▪ Choose Mailings→Start Mail Merge→Start Mail Merge and choose the document type from the Ribbon. |
| Choose an Excel worksheet as the data source | ▪ Choose Mailings→Start Mail Merge→Select Recipients →Use an Existing List from the Ribbon.<br>▪ In the Select Data Source dialog box, select the Excel file containing the table and click Open.<br>▪ In the Select Table dialog box, choose the desired worksheet, place a checkmark in the box next to First Row of Data Contains Column Headers, and click OK. |
| Select records | ▪ Choose Mailings→Start Mail Merge→Edit Recipient List from the Ribbon.<br>▪ Use options to sort, filter, find, and deselect records, as desired. |

| Task | Procedure |
|------|-----------|
| Complete the main document | ■ Type text and use Mailings→Write & Insert Fields→Insert Merge Field  from the Ribbon. |
| Preview the merged copies | ■ Choose Mailings→Preview Results→Preview Results from the Ribbon.<br>■ Use navigation buttons in the Preview Results group on the Ribbon to view the document for any one record. |
| Print or email the completed document copies | ■ Choose Mailings→Finish→Finish & Merge →Print Documents (or Send E-mail Messages) from the Ribbon. |

After starting the mail merge, you use commands in sequence on the Mailings Ribbon from left to right. The next command usually is dimmed until you complete the preceding step.

## DEVELOP YOUR SKILLS 18.3.1
# Mail Merge Excel Table Data in Word

*In this exercise, you will merge a form document with employee data from an Excel table to fill in the form with each employee's name, identification number, and so on.*

### View the Table Data

1. **Open** the Employee List workbook from the Lesson 18 folder in your file storage location. If necessary, change Files of Type to **All Excel Files** to see the filename in the Open dialog box.

2. Display the **Orthopedics** worksheet.
   *Notice that the table's column headings are in row 1 of the worksheet. This helps you work with the data more easily during the merge. Each column (field) contains a specific category of data, such as last name. Each row (record) contains the data for one employee.*

3. **Close** the workbook.

### Start the Merge

4. Start **Word** and **open** Seminar Form from the Lesson 18 folder.
   *This is the main document that you will merge with employee data from the Excel table. You may also start with a new, blank document and enter the necessary information for the main document.*

   *Next you will use commands on the Mailings Ribbon. After using a Ribbon command, you will use the command to its right until you complete the merge.*

5. Choose **Mailings→Start Mail Merge→Start Mail Merge** from the Ribbon.
   *Notice that the formatting choices on the menu include letters, envelopes, labels, an address directory, and a normal document. You would select one of these to start the main document if one were not already created.*

6. **Press** Esc to cancel the menu.

## Connect to the Data Source

7. Choose **Mailings→Start Mail Merge→Select Recipients** 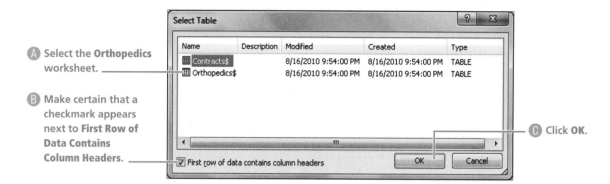**→Use Existing List** from the Ribbon.

8. In the **Select Data Source** dialog box, navigate to the Lesson 18 folder in your file storage location, choose the Employee List workbook, and click **Open**.

9. Follow these steps to select the Orthopedics worksheet:

Ⓐ Select the **Orthopedics** worksheet.

Ⓑ Make certain that a checkmark appears next to **First Row of Data Contains Column Headers.**

Ⓒ Click **OK**.

10. Choose **Mailings→Start Mail Merge→Edit Recipient List** from the Ribbon.

11. In the **Mail Merge Recipients** dialog box, click in the checkbox next to employees Gonzalez, Howard, and Lawrence to deselect the department's physicians and department chief.

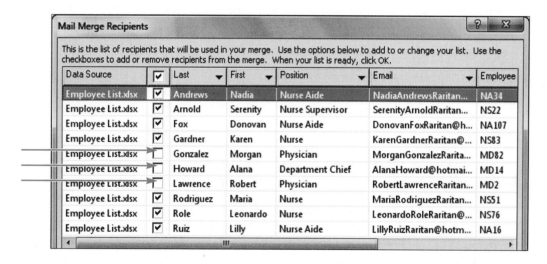

*Notice the commands to sort, filter, and find records in the lower half of the dialog box. You may also perform these tasks by clicking the triangle next to a column heading, which displays a menu. You may edit the worksheet and refresh the list from within this dialog box.*

12. Click **OK** in the Mail Merge Recipients dialog box.

## Insert Merge Fields

*You will insert field names in the form. Word will substitute one employee's data in those locations on each copy of the form.*

13. **Click** in the blank to the right of Employee Name in the form.

14. Choose **Mailings→Write & Insert Fields→Insert Merge Field** ▤ menu ▾→**First** from the Ribbon, and then **tap** $\boxed{\text{Spacebar}}$.

15. Choose **Mailings→Write & Insert Fields→Insert Merge Field** ▤ menu ▾→**Last** from the Ribbon.

16. Use the preceding step to add the **Employee ID** and **Position** fields as shown in the following illustration.

| Employee Name: | «First» «Last» |
|---|---|
| Employee ID: | «Employee_ID» |
| Job Title: | «Position» |

*You may insert field names within a paragraph or in a mailing address to create a business letter, envelope, or labels. You type punctuation and spaces between words as necessary.*

17. **Click** in the blank to the right of Dept. Head and type **Alana Howard, MD**.

| Dept. Head: | Alana Howard, MD |
|---|---|

*You typed directly in the form because all employees have the same department head. All text typed in the main document appears in every individualized copy.*

18. **Click** in the blank to the right of Department and type **Orthopedics**.

19. Choose **Mailings→Write & Insert Fields→Highlight Merge Fields** 📄 from the Ribbon.
*The field names are identified with a gray background to show you the location of inserted fields in the entire document.*

20. Choose **Mailings→Write & Insert Fields→Highlight Merge Fields** 📄 from the Ribbon again to toggle off the highlighting.
*If displayed, the highlighting would appear in printed copies, which is not desirable.*

## Preview the Form Copies

21. Choose **Mailings→Preview Results→Preview Results** 🔍 from the Ribbon.
*The view switches to the form for the first employee in the table. (If the tenth record displays, click the First Record button in the Preview Results group on the Ribbon.)*

22. Choose **Mailings→Preview Results→Next Record** in the Ribbon. Click the button again to view the next few records.
*Records 5–7 for Gonzalez, Howard, and Lawrence do not display because you unchecked them in step 11 of this exercise.*

## Print a Copy

23. Choose **Mailings→Finish→Finish and Merge** 📄→**Print Documents** from the Ribbon.

24. In the Merge to Printer dialog box, choose **Current Record** and click **OK**.

25. Click **OK** in the Print dialog box to print one copy of the form.

26. Retrieve the printout from the printer.

27. **Save** 💾 the changes, and exit **Word**.

# 18.4 Sharing Excel Data with Access

**Video Lesson**    labyrinthelab.com/videos

Access, a software application in Microsoft Office, stores data in tables that look similar to Excel worksheets. While you usually may format data and create calculations more easily in Excel, the database capabilities of Access allow you to filter large amounts of data using queries and to combine data from multiple sources to create various reports. When you import an Excel worksheet into a new Access table, you have the option to link the data. Then, any updates made to the original worksheet data in Excel are shown when you reopen the database and the related Access table. Without linking, the data is not updated in Access. Linked data cannot be edited in Access.

 If the original linked Excel workbook is moved or deleted, its link is broken and the data is not available in Access. The Linked Table Manager command in Access allows you to give the new location if the file was moved. Make frequent backups of linked workbooks in case a file is deleted inadvertently.

| QUICK REFERENCE | IMPORTING EXCEL DATA INTO ACCESS |
|---|---|
| **Task** | **Procedure** |
| Import worksheet data as a new Access table or into an existing table | ■ Open the Access database.<br>■ Choose External Data→Import→Excel from the Ribbon.<br>■ In the Get External Data – Excel Spreadsheet dialog box, click Browse and choose the desired workbook.<br>■ Choose an import option and click OK.<br>■ In the Import Spreadsheet Wizard dialog box, place a checkmark in the box next to First Row Contains Column Headings.<br>■ Continue choosing options and clicking Next in the wizard.<br>■ Enter the name for the new or existing Access table and click Finish.<br>■ Respond to any message box that appears.<br>■ Display All Tables in the Navigation Pane, and double-click the table to open it. |

## DEVELOP YOUR SKILLS 18.4.1
## Import Worksheet Data into Access

*In this exercise, you will import employee data from an Excel worksheet as a new table in the database. Then you will import the same worksheet but set a link to observe the difference.*

1. Start **Access**.
   *The New tab of Backstage view, where you may start a new database, appears. You wish to open an existing database.*

2. Click **Open** 📂 on the File tab, navigate to the Lesson 18 folder, and **open** the Raritan Employees database.

3. If a security warning appears above the database, click **Enable Content**.
   *The title bar displays the name of the database and (Access 2007) to indicate the version in which it originally was created. The design of this database is not yet complete. The Navigation Pane on the left contains the names of various tables, queries, forms, and reports that make up the database.*

## Import a Worksheet as a New Table

4. Choose **External Data→Import & Link→Excel** [icon] from the Ribbon.

5. In the Get External Data – Excel Spreadsheet dialog box, click **Browse** and choose the **Nurse Aides** workbook from the Lesson 18 folder.
*Read the three options for importing worksheet data in the dialog box.*

6. Make certain that the **Import the Source Data into a New Table in the Current Database** option is selected, and then click **OK**.
*The Import Spreadsheet Wizard dialog box appears and displays a preview of the Nurse Aides worksheet. (If the workbook contained multiple worksheets, you would be prompted to select one.) Notice that the column headings display as the first data row as shown to the right. They should be above row 1, and you will correct this in the next step.*

| 1 | Nurse Aide ID | Last Name | First Name |
|---|---|---|---|
| 2 | NA1 | Hardy | Brenda B. |

7. Place a checkmark in the box next to **First Row Contains Column Headings**.
*The column headings display above the first row of data. Remember to choose this option, or the worksheet data will not import correctly.*

8. Click **Next** and review the options.
*The wizard displays options to format the worksheet columns as fields in the database. You will not change any options.*

9. Click **Next**, review the options, and click **Next** again.

10. In the **Import to Table** box, change the existing name to **Employees**.
*You are naming the new Access table. You need not use the worksheet name.*

11. Click **Finish**, and click **Close** in the next window. (Do not select the Save Import Steps option.)
*The new Employees table name displays under the Tables group in the Navigation Pane on the left.*

| Tables |
|---|
| Employees |
| General Employees |

12. **Double-click** Employees to open the table.
*Notice that Access added* ID *as the first field in the table and automatically numbered the records. Depending on the database design, you may want to delete this field in the Import Spreadsheet Wizard dialog box while importing the data.*

## Import as a Linked Worksheet

*Now you will import the same data by linking to the original worksheet to observe the difference.*

13. Choose **External Data→Import→Excel** [icon] from the Ribbon.

14. In the Get External Data – Excel Spreadsheet dialog box, click **Browse** and choose the **Nurse Aides** workbook.

15. Choose **Link to the Data Source by Creating a Linked Table** and click **OK**.

16. Place a checkmark in the box next to **First Row Contains Column Headings**.

17. Click **Next**.
*This time no field options appear because you are linking to the worksheet.*

18. Leave the Linked Table Name as **Nurse Aides**, and then click **Finish**. Click **OK** when alerted that the link has been completed.

*Notice that the icon next to All Staff in the Navigation Pane indicates a linked Excel worksheet.*

> Conflicting changes between users
> ● A_sk me which changes win
> ○ _The changes being saved win

19. **Double-click** Nurse Aides in the Navigation Pane to open the table.

20. **Click** in any cell and try to type a different entry.
    *You cannot edit the data from within Access. You may only edit the original worksheet in Excel.*

21. **Exit** ⊠ Access. Click **Yes** if prompted to save the table design.

## 18.5  Inserting Excel Charts in PowerPoint

**Video Lesson**   labyrinthelab.com/videos

Using the Paste command is usually the best method for inserting an existing Excel chart in PowerPoint. If no chart yet exists, you may create one entirely in PowerPoint using the same commands and options as in Excel, as long as Excel is installed on the same computer.

PivotCharts are converted to normal charts when pasted in a presentation. You may adjust formatting but cannot adjust fields and calculations.

### Linking Compared to Embedding

You may choose to paste a chart by converting the chart to a picture, embedding, or linking. The embedding and linking options are more useful because you can edit the chart data. Embedding places a standalone copy of the chart in the destination document. Sharing the PowerPoint presentation is simplified because the original workbook need not be distributed with the presentation. Any changes to the workbook, however, are not updated in the document holding the embedded copy. Linking a chart means that if the worksheet data is updated and saved, the chart automatically updates in the PowerPoint presentation. When you choose to paste, the embedding and linking options also allow you convert the chart to the theme of the destination document or retain the original colors and fonts.

Embedding a chart in another document gives users access to the entire workbook upon which the chart is based. If that is not desirable, you should copy a worksheet and its chart to a separate workbook.

The Paste menu with options to embed, link, or convert the chart to a picture

Take care not to delete the original linked worksheet data or the workbook file because the link would be broken. Distributing the presentation via email would also break the link to the original workbook storage location.

| Task | Procedure |
|------|-----------|
| Link or embed an Excel chart on a slide | ■ Create and save the worksheet and chart in Excel. |
| | ■ Right-click in a blank area of the chart and choose Copy from the context menu. |
| | ■ Close the workbook. |
| | ■ Open the desired presentation in PowerPoint and create a slide using a layout containing a content placeholder. |
| | ■ Right-click the content placeholder and choose the desired option under Paste from the context menu. |
| Update a linked chart in PowerPoint | ■ Right-click on the chart and choose Edit Data from the context menu. |
| | ■ Edit the worksheet upon which the chart is based. |
| | ■ Close the workbook and choose to save when asked if you want to save. |
| Edit an embedded chart on a slide | ■ Right-click on the chart and choose Edit Data from the context menu. |
| | ■ In the displayed Excel worksheet, edit the desired data. |
| | ■ Close the workbook; you are not asked to save it. |

## DEVELOP YOUR SKILLS 18.5.1
# Link a Chart in PowerPoint

*In this exercise, you will copy a chart from an Excel workbook and paste the chart onto a PowerPoint slide. Then you will change a value on the linked worksheet from within PowerPoint to update the chart.*

1. **Open** the AR Project Expenses workbook.

2. **Right-click** in a blank area of the chart and choose **Copy** from the context menu.

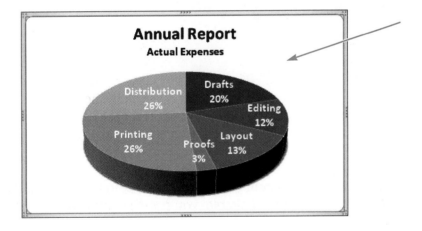

3. Leave the workbook **open**.
   *The chart is copied to the Clipboard.*

4. Start **PowerPoint** and open the Project Budget presentation from the Lesson 18 folder.

5. Select **slide 2 in** the Slides tab at the left of the window.
   *This slide has the Title and Content layout.*

6. Follow these steps to paste the chart on slide 2:

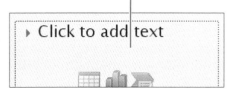

Ⓐ In the Slide Pane, **right-click** in a blank area within the content placeholder to display the context menu.

Ⓑ In the context menu, point to each button under Paste Options to read its ScreenTip. Choose **Use Destination Theme & Link Data**.

*Because you selected the placeholder prior to pasting, the chart fills the placeholder and you need not resize or center the chart on the slide. The chart's colors change to match the theme of the presentation.*

7. **Close** ⊠ Excel and leave PowerPoint **open**.

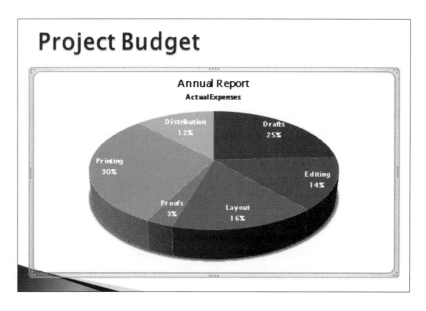

## Update the Linked Chart

*Next you will change a worksheet value and the chart from within PowerPoint.*

8. **Right-click** anywhere on the chart and choose **Edit Data** from the context menu.
   *Excel opens and displays the original worksheet.*

9. In **cell D14**, notice that Distribution is 12 percent of the total expenses. Scroll to the **right**, if necessary, to see that 12 percent is also shown in the Distribution pie slice.

10. Change **cell C14** to **1000**.
   *The percentage changes to 26 percent.*

11. **Close** the workbook and choose to **save** when asked if you want to save.
   *Saving the changes will update the linked chart in PowerPoint. Notice that Distribution is now 26 percent in the PowerPoint chart.*

12. **Close** PowerPoint and choose to **save** when asked if you want to save.

# 18.6 Importing External Data

**Video Lesson** labyrinthelab.com/videos

You can bring data from other application programs into Excel. This is called *importing*. For example, if a coworker types some information in Word, you may import this data directly into an Excel worksheet. Excel can import a variety of data into your workbooks. You may import data from as many sources as needed to complete a document. Converters are installed in Excel to import data from many popular applications.

 If Excel can't import a specific type of data, check in the source application to see if you can save the data in another file format that is compatible with Excel. Some loss of formatting may occur.

The three methods that you may use to import data into an Excel worksheet are the following:

- **Copy and Paste**—You may use standard copy and paste commands to bring text, images, and charts into a worksheet.
- **Drag and Drop**—You may select data in another application program, use the mouse to drag the selection into an Excel worksheet, and release the mouse button.
- **Import a File**—The Get External Data command on the Data ribbon is used to import an entire text file, Access table, web page table, or data from other sources such as a network server.

## Using Copy and Paste

You may copy and paste data between another application and an Excel workbook. For example, you may copy and paste a table or text from a Word document into an Excel worksheet. You simply select the data in the other document window, cut or copy the selection, and paste it into the desired cell in the Excel window. You may also use the Paste Special command to paste data, such as images, into Excel in a specific format.

## Importing Data with Drag and Drop

You may drag and drop data between another application window and an Excel workbook. For example, you may drag and drop a table or text from a Word document into an Excel worksheet. You select the data to be imported and then drag and drop it onto the desired worksheet. When you use this technique, the data is cut from the source file. However, if you then close the source file without saving, the original data will be retained.

| Task | Procedure |
|------|-----------|
| Import text data with Copy and Paste | ■ Open the application window. <br> ■ Select the text in the source document and choose Home→Clipboard→Copy (or use Ctrl + C). <br> ■ Select the desired cell of the worksheet and choose Home→Clipboard→Paste (or use Ctrl + V). <br> ■ Format the pasted text as desired. |
| Import text data with Drag and Drop | ■ Display the Excel worksheet window and an application window containing the text data side by side. <br> ■ Drag to select the text data in the other program. Point to the selection, drag toward the Excel window, point to a cell in the worksheet, and release the mouse button. |

## DEVELOP YOUR SKILLS 18.6.1

# Import Data between Documents

*In this exercise, you will insert a logo at the top of a worksheet and then use the Copy and Paste commands to add the logo to other worksheets. You will drag and drop text from a Word document into the workbook. Finally, you will copy a table and text from Word and paste it in the workbook.*

### Insert and Duplicate the Logo

1. **Open** the AR Production Schedule workbook and **maximize** the window.

2. Select **cell A1** on the Editing Schedule worksheet, if not already selected, and then choose **Insert→Illustrations→Picture** from the Ribbon.

3. Navigate to the Lesson 18 folder in your file storage location, if not already displayed. *Excel displays only one picture file in the Insert Picture dialog box. Notice that Files of Type near the bottom of the dialog box is set to All Pictures.*

4. **Double-click** Raritan Clinic Logo to insert the image in **cell A1**.

5. With the image still selected, choose **Format→Size→Shape Height**, type **.64**, and **tap** Enter.

6. **Right-click** the image and choose **Copy** from the context menu.

7. Display the **Layout Schedule** worksheet.

8. **Right-click** cell A1 and choose **Paste** from the context menu. *The Clipboard retains the most recently copied or cut items. Thus, you can paste the logo multiple times after you give the Copy command.*

9. Display the **Production Schedule** worksheet and paste the logo into **cell A1**.

## Drag and Drop Text

*Another staff member used Word to compose her status list. You will use drag and drop to copy a heading from her Word document into Excel.*

10. Display the **Layout Schedule** worksheet.

11. Start **Word** and **open** the AR Layout Schedule document.

12. **Right-click** in a blank area of the Windows taskbar at the bottom of the screen and choose **Show Windows Side by Side** (or **Tile Windows Vertically,** depending on your Windows version) from the context menu.
*The Excel and Word windows display side by side. This will make it easy for you to drag and drop from one window to the other. If any other window also displays, minimize it and repeat the Show Windows Side by Side (or Tile Windows Vertically) command.*

13. Click the **AR Layout Schedule** button in the Windows taskbar to activate the Word document.

14. Follow these steps to drag and drop text into the worksheet:

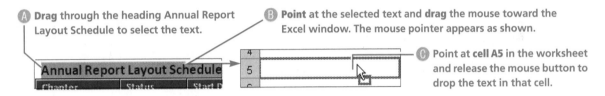

(A) **Drag** through the heading Annual Report Layout Schedule to select the text.

(B) **Point** at the selected text and **drag** the mouse toward the Excel window. The mouse pointer appears as shown.

(C) **Point** at **cell A5** in the worksheet and release the mouse button to drop the text in that cell.

*Notice that the heading text disappeared from the Word document. A drag and drop cuts the selection from the source document. Leave the Word document open.*

15. In the Excel window, **click** the first navigation button on the workbook tabs toolbar at the lower left of the window to display and select the Editing Schedule tab, as shown to the right.

16. Use the **Format Painter** on the Ribbon to copy the formatting from **cell A5** in the Editing Schedule worksheet to **cell A5** that you just added in the Layout Schedule worksheet.

## Copy and Paste a Word Table and Text

*Now you will transfer the remainder of the Word document. You could use drag and drop, but you may find copying and pasting to be easier for a longer selection.*

17. **Maximize** the Word window.

18. Follow these steps to copy the Word table and legend text:

Ⓐ **Point** to the left of the word *Chapter* outside the table and **drag** straight down to select the table and the Key legend text.

Ⓑ Use Ctrl + C to copy the selection.

| Chapter | Status | Start Date | Due Date |
|---|---|---|---|
| 1—A Message from the CEO | þ | Aug 2 | Aug 3 |
| 2—Our Stories | þ | Aug 3 | Aug 6 |
| 3—New Advances | x | Aug 6 | Aug 7 |
| 4—Program Activities | x | Aug 8 | Aug 13 |
| 5—Raritan Clinic Foundation | x | Aug 13 | Aug 16 |
| 6—Financials | o | Aug 18 | Aug 20 |
| 7—Board of Directions | o | Aug 21 | Aug 24 |

Key      þ Done
     x In Progress
     o Awaiting Manuscript

19. Switch to the **Excel** window in the Windows taskbar.

20. **Maximize** the Excel window.

21. Select **cell A7** in the Layout Schedule worksheet, and then use Ctrl + V to paste.
    *Thanks to Excel's Word converter, the formatting carried over into the Excel worksheet. The table cells from Word display in separate cells of the worksheet. The tab codes in the Key legend text caused that text to be placed into two columns. Notice that Excel reformatted the dates in Custom format, such as 2-Aug.*

22. Format the **range A7 through D18** in Calibri font and a font size of 11.
    *You may format imported text just like any other text in the worksheet.*

23. **Deselect** the range.

24. Widen **column A** to display all the text in the **range A8:A14**, if necessary.

25. **Right-align** the Start Date and Due Date labels over their numbers.
    *Your worksheet should look similar to the illustration at right.*

26. **Close** Word and choose **not** to save when asked if you want to save.
    *This prevents the loss of the text that you dragged and dropped. If you were to reopen this document, all of the content would reappear.*

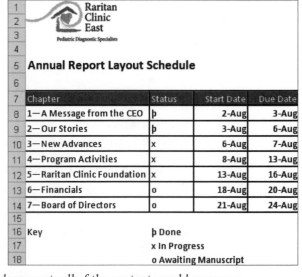

27. **Save** 💾 the changes in Excel, and leave the workbook **open**.

# Importing a Text File

Video Lesson    labyrinthelab.com/videos

The From Text 📄 command imports an entire text file into an Excel worksheet as data. The source file format may be either tab delimited (.txt) or comma delimited (.csv). When another program is not compatible with Excel, you may need to save its data as text in one of those two formats. When you import a text file, Excel examines the file to determine whether the formatting in the file will help lay out the data neatly into rows and columns. For example, if the text file is comma delimited, Excel will place each data item following a comma in a separate column. The From Text command can also help you deal with certain formatting problems that you may encounter with tab delimited or comma delimited text files.

| QUICK REFERENCE | IMPORTING A TEXT FILE INTO EXCEL |
|---|---|
| **Task** | **Procedure** |
| Import a tab delimited or comma delimited text file into an Excel worksheet | ▪ Display the worksheet in which you wish to import the text file data. <br> ▪ Choose Data→Get External Data→From Text 📄 from the Ribbon. <br> ▪ Navigate to the folder containing the text data file, select the file, and click Import. <br> ▪ Follow the instructions in the Text Import Wizard, and then click Finish. <br> ▪ In the Import Data dialog box, choose the cell where you wish to begin the data import (or choose New Worksheet). <br> ▪ Click Properties and change any desired options to refresh or format data. |

## DEVELOP YOUR SKILLS 18.6.2
# Import Data from a Text File

*In this exercise, you will import a tab-delimited text file into a worksheet.*

*Before You Begin: You must have completed Develop Your Skills 18.2.1 to create the Schedule Tab Delimited file, and the AR Production Schedule workbook should be open. If you reopened the file and a Data Connections Have Been Disabled warning appears, click the Enable Content button.*

### Import a Text File

1. Display the **Editing Schedule** worksheet of the AR Production Schedule workbook.

2. If a warning appears above the worksheet (or in a dialog box), read the warning and click **Enable Content** (or **OK**) to confirm that you trust the website source.

3. Choose **Data→Get External Data→From Text** 📄 from the Ribbon.

4. Navigate to the Lesson 18 folder, if necessary.
   *Notice that Files of Type is set to Text Files near the bottom of the dialog box. The Schedule Tab Delimited filename is displayed, but not the Word file that you used previously because its file format is Word Document (.docx).*

5. Select the Schedule Tab Delimited text file and click **Import**.
   *The Text Import Wizard dialog box appears. This wizard will guide you through the steps of importing the text file data. In the upper half of the dialog box, notice that Delimited is selected. The wizard always analyzes text files to determine whether they are a specific type of file that can aid the import process.*

6. In the preview of the text file in the lower portion of the dialog box, scroll until **row 7** is visible.

   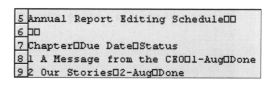

   *You want to leave out the blank rows and headings in rows 1 through 6, so you will start the import process with row 7.*

7. In the **Start Import at Row** box, enter **7** as shown to the right.

8. Click the **Next** button.

   *Step 2 of the wizard displays the next set of options. Since the file to be imported is recognized as tab delimited, Tab has already been chosen for you under Delimiters.*

9. Scroll in the **Data Preview** section to see that text displays correctly in columns.

   *The text converter places the text following a tab code into the next column.*

10. Click **Next** to continue with step 3 of the wizard.

    *This step lets you select one or more columns and change their format to text or adjust the date format. You may even exclude selected columns from being imported.*

11. Read the description of **General** format in the upper-right area of the dialog box.

    *The three columns are formatted in General format. You need not make any changes to the options.*

12. Click **Finish** to display the Import Data dialog box.

    *The wizard asks you where you want to put the data. You can specify the top-left cell of the range to receive the data.*

## Specify the Location for the Imported Text

13. Select **cell A7** in the Editing Schedule worksheet, and click **OK**.

    *The text data appear on the worksheet. Notice that the dates are converted to day/month format.*

    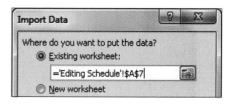

## Format the Text

14. Select the **range A7:C7** and add bold and a bottom border.

    *Your worksheet should look similar to the following illustration.*

    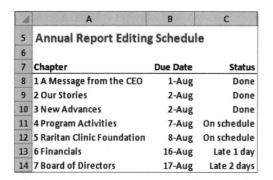

15. Add any other formatting that you think will make the text easier to read.

16. **Save** the changes, and leave the workbook **open**.

# Converting Text to Columns

Video Lesson    labyrinthelab.com/videos

The Text to Columns ⬚ command allows you to split cell entries on a worksheet into multiple columns. For example, cells containing a full employee name may be split into two columns for first name and last name. Cells containing the city and state may be split into two columns. The Convert Text to Columns wizard operates in a similar way to the Text Import Wizard you use to import a text file. You may split text by specifying a delimiter, such as a comma (,) or a space. You also may specify a column width. In the following illustration to the left, column A contains the chapter number and chapter name separated by a space. In the illustration below and to the right, the text has been split into columns A and B.

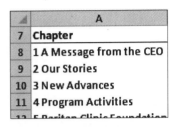

Text in a single column...

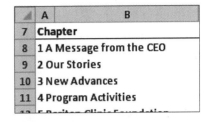

...may be split into multiple columns.

| QUICK REFERENCE | CONVERTING TEXT TO COLUMNS |
|---|---|
| **Task** | **Procedure** |
| Split text in a single column to multiple columns | ▪ Select the text in one column to be converted.<br>▪ Choose Data→Data Tools→Text to Columns ⬚ from the Ribbon.<br>▪ Follow the instructions in the Convert Text to Columns Wizard, and click Finish. |

## DEVELOP YOUR SKILLS 18.6.3
## Convert Text to Columns

*In this exercise, you will split the chapter data in column A to two columns. Currently, the chapter number and chapter name are in a single cell.*

*Before You Begin: You must have completed Develop Your Skills 18.6.2, and the AR Production Schedule workbook should be open. If you reopened the file and a Data Connections Have Been Disabled warning appears, click the Enable Content button.*

### Add a Delimiter Character to Text

1. Insert a blank column at **column B**.
   *The blank column will receive the chapter names from the split text.*

2. Select **cell A7** in the Editing Schedule worksheet.

3. Follow these steps to add a space before the word *Chapter*:

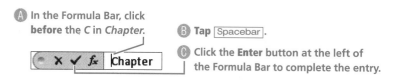

Ⓐ In the Formula Bar, click **before** the *C* in *Chapter*.

Ⓑ Tap `Spacebar`.

Ⓒ Click the **Enter** button at the left of the Formula Bar to complete the entry.

*The space you just added will become a delimiter for that cell as you split text in the next few steps.*

## Split Text into Two Columns

4. Select the **range A7:A14**.

5. Choose **Data→Data Tools→Text to Columns** ▦ from the Ribbon.
   *The Convert Text to Columns Wizard – Step 1 of 3 dialog box opens. In the upper half of the dialog box, notice that Fixed Width is selected because the data contains a space between the chapter number and chapter name.*

6. Click **Next**.
   *Step 2 of the wizard contains instructions to break the text at the desired location.*

7. **Scroll down** in the Data Preview section until **row 5** is visible.
   *Notice that the chapter numbers are in one column and the chapter titles are in a second column. Some text extends to the right of the column break line and would be placed in a third column. You will adjust the text to be placed in the second column in the next step.*

8. **Drag** the column break line from 20 to the right until it displays just to the right of *Foundation*.

9. Click **Next** to continue with step 3 of the wizard.

10. Leave the column data format set to General, and notice that the destination cell is **A7** in the dialog box.

```
            10        20        30
|   |    |    |    |    |    |    |
1 A Message from the CEO         ↑
2 Our Stories
3 New Advances
4 Program Activities
5 Raritan Clinic Foundation
```

11. Click **Finish**; click **OK** when asked if you wish to replace the contents of the destination cell.
    *Notice that the text originally after the space in each cell of column A has been moved to the new column B.*

## Adjust Column Widths

12. Point at the border between the column headings for **columns A and B**, and drag to the left to decrease the **column A** width.

| ◢ | A | B | C | D |
|---|---|---|---|---|
| 7 | | Chapter | Due Date | Status |
| 8 | 1 | A Message from the CEO | 1-Aug | Done |
| 9 | 2 | Our Stories | 2-Aug | Done |
| 10 | 3 | New Advances | 2-Aug | Done |
| 11 | 4 | Program Activities | 7-Aug | On schedule |
| 12 | 5 | Raritan Clinic Foundation | 8-Aug | On schedule |
| 13 | 6 | Financials | 16-Aug | Late 1 day |
| 14 | 7 | Board of Directors | 17-Aug | Late 2 days |

13. **Double-click** the border between the column headings for **columns B and C** to autofit the column B width.

*Rows 7–14 should look similar to the illustration.*

| | A | B | C | D |
|---|---|---|---|---|
| 7 | | Chapter | Due Date | Status |
| 8 | | 1 A Message from the CEO | 1-Aug | Done |
| 9 | | 2 Our Stories | 2-Aug | Done |
| 10 | | 3 New Advances | 2-Aug | Done |
| 11 | | 4 Program Activities | 7-Aug | On schedule |
| 12 | | 5 Raritan Clinic Foundation | 8-Aug | On schedule |
| 13 | | 6 Financials | 16-Aug | Late 1 day |
| 14 | | 7 Board of Directors | 17-Aug | Late 2 days |

14. **Save** 💾 the changes, and **close** the workbook.

# 18.7 Saving Workbook Elements as a Web Page

**Video Lesson**    labyrinthelab.com/videos

You may save a worksheet range, an entire worksheet, or a workbook with multiple sheets as a page that users may view on the web or your organization's intranet. They cannot edit the Excel data or view formulas, and some formatting may be lost when you save as a web page. You may save as either a web page with components stored in separate files or as a single web page.

For best results, the workbook upon which the web page is based should have no spaces in the filename. You may use the underscore (_) character to connect words, if desired.

## Saving as a Web Page

The Web Page option in the Save As Type list creates a main document with the filename extension .htm in the HTML (Hypertext Markup Language) format. Excel also creates a destination folder and saves workbook elements as files in that folder. You then can access individual items. For example, you may wish to replace one picture file in the folder rather than revise and republish the entire web page. You must copy both the main document and the folder to your web server.

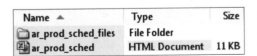

| Name ▲ | Type | Size |
|---|---|---|
| 📁 ar_prod_sched_files | File Folder | |
| 📄 ar_prod_sched | HTML Document | 11 KB |

Saving an Excel workbook as a web page results in one main document and a folder containing files necessary to display the web page.

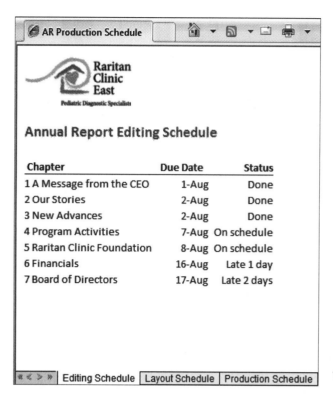

The web page as viewed in a browser

## Saving as a Single File Web Page

The Single File Web Page option in the Save As Type list is used to save all the web page elements in one file. The file is created with the filename extension .mht using the Web Archive file format. This method is useful for sending a web page as an email attachment for collaboration with others. The Web Archive file format has several limitations. A significantly larger file size results because all elements are embedded in a single file. Also, a web developer cannot edit the HTML code to update the page, and not all web browsers can open an MHT file.

## Publishing the Web Page

You must publish, or upload, your document to a web server. Your network administrator may set up a destination folder on the server for you. You may publish the web page as you save it, or you may upload it later. The Save As dialog box contains options to select the workbook portion to be saved and publish the web page. You may add a page title that would be displayed in the tab of the user's web browser. You may publish first to a drive on your computer and preview how the web page looks before uploading to a web server.

| Task | Procedure |
|------|-----------|
| Add the Web Page Preview button to the Quick Access toolbar | ■ Right-click the Quick Access toolbar, and choose Customize Quick Access Toolbar from the context menu.<br>■ In the Excel Options dialog box, choose Commands Not in the Ribbon from the Choose Commands From list.<br>■ Choose Web Page Preview from the commands list, and click Add. |
| Save a range, worksheet, or entire workbook as a web page | ■ Save the workbook with a filename containing no spaces.<br>■ Select the range or display the desired worksheet if the entire workbook is not to be saved.<br>■ Choose File→Save As 🖳.<br>■ In the Save As dialog box, choose one of the following from the Save As Type list:<br>  ◆ Web Page (creates a main document and a folder containing page elements)<br>  ◆ Single File Web Page (saves all page elements in a single file)<br>■ Choose an option for the workbook portion to be saved, and choose other options, as desired.<br>■ Click Save.<br>■ If a Microsoft Excel message about web page compatibility displays, read the message and choose Yes.<br>■ Open the web page file in a web browser, or click the Web Page Preview button on the Quick Access toolbar to check the page content. |

## DEVELOP YOUR SKILLS 18.7.1

# Save a Worksheet as a Single File Web Page

*In this exercise, you will save one worksheet from a workbook as a single web page. Then, you will preview the web page in your browser.*

*Before You Begin: A web browser, such as Internet Explorer, must be installed on your computer to view the saved web page.*

### Set the Single File Web Page Option

1. **Open** the ar_prod_sched workbook from the Lesson 18 folder.
   *Notice that the workbook name contains underscore ( _ ) characters between words. Filenames and folder names containing spaces often do not display well in a web browser.*

2. Display the **Production Schedule** worksheet.

3. Choose **File→Save As** 🖳.

4. In the Save As dialog box, choose **Single File Web Page** from the Save As Type list.
   *Other options now appear in the bottom section of the dialog box.*

### Set Web Page Options

5. For the **Save** option, choose **Selection: Sheet**.

6. Click the **Change Title** button in the bottom-right corner of the Save As dialog box.
   *The Enter Text dialog displays.*

7. In the Enter Text dialog box, type **AR Production Schedule** and click **OK**.

*The Save As dialog box reappears. The Title box displays the text you just typed. Your dialog box should resemble the one below except for the Authors.*

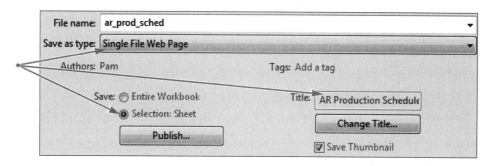

## Save and View the Web Page in a Browser

8. Click **Save**.

*The Publish as Web Page dialog box appears. Notice that the options you selected are summarized in the dialog box.*

9. Place a checkmark next to **Open Published Web Page in Browser**.

*Skip this step if your computer does not have a web browser installed.*

10. Click **Publish**.

*The web page opens in your browser. Your browser may be different than shown. The page title you specified shows in the tab and at the top of the web page.*

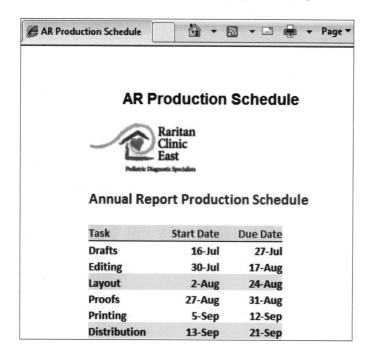

11. **Close** the browser window.

12. **Close** the workbook without saving, and **exit** Excel.

## 18.8 Concepts Review

| Concepts Review | labyrinthelab.com/excel10 |

*To check your knowledge of the key concepts introduced in this lesson, complete the Concepts Review quiz by going to the URL listed above. If your classroom is using Labyrinth eLab, you may complete the Concepts Review quiz from within your eLab course.*

# Reinforce Your Skills

## Save a Worksheet in Comma Delimited Format

*In this exercise, you will save a workbook in a nonnative file format. Then you will open the newly converted file in Excel and Notepad.*

### Save the Worksheet

1. **Open** the rs-TyncoLabs Q1 Sales workbook from the Lesson 18 workbook in your file storage location.

2. Choose **File→Save As** ![icon] from the Ribbon.

3. Display the **Save As Type** list and choose **CSV (Comma Delimited)**.

4. Change the filename to **rs-TyncoLabs Comma Delimited**.

5. Click **Save**.
   *Excel warns you that you may lose some features if you convert the data to this new file format.*

6. Choose **Yes** to continue saving in the new file format.
   *Excel saves the worksheet to the new file but continues displaying the normal Excel workbook file. To see the file in its newly converted format, you must open it.*

7. Use [Ctrl]+[W] to **close** the workbook and leave Excel **open**. Choose **not** to save when you are asked to save any changes to the file.

### Open the Converted File in Excel

8. Choose **File→Open** ![icon] from the Ribbon.
   *Notice that the newly converted file is not listed. That's because the conversion changed it from an Excel file to a text file.*

9. Display the Files of Type list and choose **Text Files**.
   *Now the converted filename should be visible.*

10. **Open** the rs-TyncoLabs Comma Delimited file.
    *Although the layout of data in specific cells is preserved, the table formatting and cell border formatting have been lost.*

11. Select **cell D5**, and then read its data in the Formula Bar.
    *Since the entire date is entered, Excel determined that this data should be displayed in Date format.*

12. Use [Ctrl]+[W] to **close** the workbook and leave Excel **open**. Choose **not** to save if you are asked to save any changes.

## Open the Converted File in Notepad

*Now you will open the converted file in a different program. The Notepad applet is a simple text editor program that comes with Windows. It will allow you to view exactly what the data in your converted file looks like.*

13. Choose **Start→All Programs→Accessories→Notepad**. (The path may be different on your computer.)

14. In the Notepad window, choose **File→Open**.
    *The Open dialog box appears. Once again, the converted file is not listed.*

15. Display the **Files of Type** list, and choose **All Files**.

16. **Open** the rs-TyncoLabs Comma Delimited file.
    *Notepad displays the data in the file. Notice the commas that separate data items. Each comma represents a column when you open the file in Excel.*

17. **Exit** Notepad. Choose **not** to save if you are asked to save any changes.

---

### REINFORCE YOUR SKILLS 18.2

# Import Data from Access

*In this exercise, you will bring data into Excel from an Access database table.*

## Import an Access Database

1. **Start** a new workbook in Excel and save it as **rs-Shelter Summary** in the Lesson 18 folder.

2. Rename the **Sheet1** tab as **Occupancy**.

3. Select **cell A1**, if not already selected.

4. Choose **Data→Get External Data→From Access**  from the Ribbon.

5. In the **Select Data Source** dialog box, navigate to the Lesson 18 folder in your file storage location.
   *Excel displays only Access files in the folder.*

6. Choose the rs-Shelter Occupancy database file and click **Open**.
   *Excel displays the three tables in the database file and asks you to select the one to be imported. In this case, you will import the Year 1 occupancy data.*

7. In the **Select Table** dialog box, choose **Shelter Occupancy – Year 1** and click **OK**.

8. In the **Import Data** dialog box, make certain that the options appear as shown in the illustration at right and click **OK**.
   *You may view data as a table, PivotTable, or PivotTable with PivotChart. You may place the imported data on the existing worksheet or a new worksheet.*

*Your imported database table should look like the following illustration. You set the data to start in cell A1 on the currently displayed worksheet.*

| | A | B | C | D | E |
|---|---|---|---|---|---|
| 1 | Week ▾ | Occupants ▾ | Male ▾ | Female ▾ | Children ▾ |
| 2 | 1 | 485 | 248 | 116 | 121 |
| 3 | 2 | 494 | 265 | 132 | 97 |

9. **Save** 💾 the changes, and leave the workbook **open** for the next exercise.

## REINFORCE YOUR SKILLS 18.3
# Import Data from Word

*In this exercise, you will bring data into Excel from a Word table.*

*Before You Begin: The rs-Shelter Summary workbook should be open from Reinforce Your Skills 18.2. If your instructor directed you to skip that exercise, start a new workbook and save as rs-Shelter Summary in the Lesson 18 folder.*

### Import from a Word Document

1. Rename the **Sheet2** tab as `Q1 Budget Summary`.

2. Start **Word** and then **open** the rs-Quarter 1 Budget document from the Lesson 18 folder. *You will use the Copy and Paste commands to import data from a Word table.*

3. If necessary, **scroll down** the document and then select the **Q1 Budget Summary** heading row and all the other rows of the budget table shown. (Do not include the title Cypress Shelter in the selection.)

| Q1 Budget Summary | | | | |
|---|---|---|---|---|
| | January | February | March | Totals |
| Mortgage & Insurance | $ 3,779 | $ 3,779 | $ 3,779 | $ 11,337 |
| Utilities | 720 | 678 | 623 | 2,021 |
| Food | 1,860 | 1,900 | 1,720 | 5,480 |
| Staff Salaries | 5,895 | 5,895 | 5,895 | 17,685 |
| Maintenance & Repairs | 325 | 370 | 1,493 | 2,188 |
| Outreach & Fundraising | 280 | 280 | 260 | 820 |
| Grand Total | $ 12,859 | $ 12,902 | $ 13,770 | $ 39,531 |

4. Choose **Home→Clipboard→Copy** 📋 from the Ribbon.

5. Close **Word**. Choose **not** to save if asked to save any changes.
*The data you copied to the Clipboard remains there even after you close the application from which you made the copy.*

6. Select **cell A1** in the Q1 Budget Summary worksheet and choose **Home→Clipboard→ Paste** from the Ribbon.
*Excel pastes the heading and table, including the text formatting that was set in the Word document.*

## Clean Up the Pasted Data

*The column widths and row heights may need to be adjusted.*

7. Adjust **column widths** as necessary.

8. Reset the **row 1** height to 18.75.

9. Select **rows 2 through 11** and reset the row height to 15.00.

10. Select the **range B4:E4**. Hold down ⌃Ctrl and select the **range B11:E11**.
    *Both ranges are highlighted.*

11. Format the selected cells as **Accounting format with no decimal places**.
    *Your worksheet should look like the following illustration.*

| ◢ | A | B | C | D | E |
|---|---|---|---|---|---|
| 1 | Q1 Budget Summary | | | | |
| 2 | | | | | |
| 3 | | January | February | March | Totals |
| 4 | **Mortgage & Insurance** | $ 3,779 | $ 3,779 | $ 3,779 | $ 11,337 |
| 5 | **Utilities** | 720 | 678 | 623 | 2,021 |
| 6 | **Food** | 1,860 | 1,900 | 1,720 | 5,480 |
| 7 | **Staff Salaries** | 5,895 | 5,895 | 5,895 | 17,685 |
| 8 | **Maintenance & Repairs** | 325 | 370 | 1,493 | 2,188 |
| 9 | **Outreach & Fundraising** | 280 | 280 | 260 | 820 |
| 10 | | | | | |
| 11 | **Grand Total** | $ 12,859 | $ 12,902 | $ 13,770 | $ 39,531 |

*As you can see, some formatting was necessary after pasting the table from Word. Also, the numbers in the Grand Total row pasted as values, not formulas.*

12. Select **cell B11** and create a formula that sums the **range B4:B9**.

13. Copy the formula in **cell B11** to the other grand total cells.

14. **Save** 🖫 the changes and leave the workbook **open** for the next exercise.

# Check Compatibility and Save a Workbook

*In this exercise, you will check a workbook's compatibility with prior Excel versions and then save for a prior version.*

*Before You Begin: You must have completed Reinforce Your Skills 18.2 and Reinforce Your Skills 18.3, and the rs-Shelter Summary workbook should be open.*

## Run the Compatibility Checker

1. Choose **File→Info→Check for Issues→Check Compatibility**.
   *After a few moments, the Microsoft Office Excel – Compatibility Checker window appears with its report of three issues causing a minor loss of fidelity.*

2. Click the **Copy to New Sheet** button in the lower-right area of the dialog box.

3. Read the report in the new worksheet that appears.
   *Two issues relate to the table in the first worksheet, and another general formatting issue is reported with three occurrences. Because these issues are reported as minor, you will not correct them.*

4. **Save** 🖫 the workbook with the Compatibility Report worksheet included.

## Use Save As

*Next you will give the Save As command to save the file for an earlier Excel version.*

5. Choose **File→Save As**, and choose **Excel 97-2003 Workbook** from the Save as Type list.

   | File name: | rs-Shelter Summary |
   |---|---|
   | Save as type: | Excel 97-2003 Workbook (*.xls) |

6. Click **Save**.
   *The Compatibility Checker window reappears to report the same issues as it did previously.*

7. Click the **Continue** button to save the file with the issues unresolved.
   *This save creates a separate workbook with the Excel 97-2003 file format. If that workbook is opened in Excel 2003, the table in the first worksheet is converted to a normal list and loses its font colors and shading, but the data is not altered.*

8. **Close** the workbook.

# Save a Workbook as a Single File Web Page

*In this exercise, you will save an Excel workbook as a single file web page.*

*Before You Begin: A web browser capable of displaying files with the .mht file extension, such as Internet Explorer, must be installed to view the published web page.*

## Save a Workbook as a Web Page

1. **Open** the rs-Budget Summary workbook from the Lesson 18 folder.

2. Choose **File→Save As** 🖫.

3. In the **Save As** dialog box, change the file name to **rs-Web Summary**.

## Set Web Page Options

4. Drop down the **Save as Type** list and choose **Single File Web Page**.

5. Click the **Change Title** button in the lower-right corner of the Save As dialog box.

6. In the **Enter Text** dialog box, type **Shelter Summary**, and click **OK**.
   *This descriptive title will display in the page tab when you open the web page in your browser.*

7. In the lower-left corner of the **Save As** dialog box, make certain the Save option is set to **Entire Workbook**.
   *Your dialog box should resemble the following illustration.*

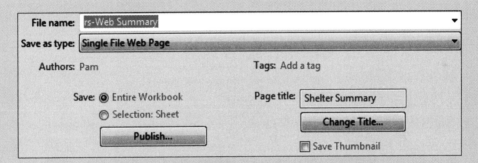

8. Click **Save**, and click **Yes** to continue saving when the Microsoft Excel compatibility message displays.
   *The workbook is saved with the filename extension .mht using the Web Archive file format. The workbook appearance does not change in Excel.*

9. **Close** the workbook file, and leave Excel **open**.

## View the Web Page

10. **Open** your web browser, such as Internet Explorer.

11. Choose **File→Open**, navigate to the Lesson 18 folder, and **open** rs-Web Summary.
    *The single file web page displays in the browser. The page title Shelter Summary displays in the page tab above the workbook data. Tabs for two worksheets display at the bottom of the browser window because you chose the Entire Workbook option while saving the web page.*

12. View the worksheets by clicking tabs at the bottom of the browser window.

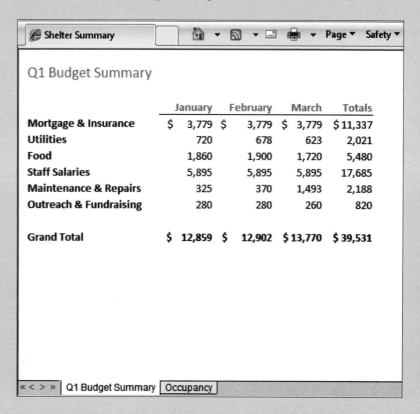

13. **Close** [X] the browser window when you are finished.

# Apply Your Skills

## Save a Worksheet in Tab Delimited File Format

*In this exercise, you will save a workbook in a different (nonnative) file format. Then you will open the converted file in Excel and print it.*

1. **Open** the as-Cypress Budget workbook from the Lesson 18 folder in your file storage location.

2. Save the Budget worksheet in the **Text (Tab Delimited)** file format with the name **as-Cypress Budget Tab Delimited**.
   *This step saves the data to a separate file, but the original workbook still appears.*

3. **Close** the workbook, and choose **not** to save when asked if you want to save changes.
   *Remember that the newly converted workbook is a text file.*

4. **Start** a new workbook.

5. **Import** the as-Cypress Budget Tab Delimited file. Start the import with **row 3** of the data (the column headings Q1, Q2 and so on). Use the General column data format for all columns. Import to **cell A1** of the worksheet.

6. After completing the import command, adjust **column widths**, if necessary, to make all text visible.

7. **Print** the worksheet.
   *Your tab delimited data should look like the following illustration.*

| | A | B | C | D | E | F |
|---|---|---|---|---|---|---|
| 1 | | Q1 | Q2 | Q3 | Q4 | Totals |
| 2 | Mortgage & Insurance | 11,337 | 11,337 | 11,337 | 11,337 | 45,348 |
| 3 | Utilities | 2,021 | 1,464 | 1,504 | 1,809 | 6,798 |
| 4 | Staff Salaries | 13,093 | 17,685 | 17,685 | 17,685 | 66,148 |
| 5 | Maintenance and Repairs | 845 | 951 | 3,113 | 724 | 5,633 |
| 6 | Outreach & Fundraising | 820 | 2,006 | 576 | 712 | 4,114 |
| 7 | Grand Totals | 28,116 | 33,443 | 34,215 | 32,267 | 128,041 |

8. **Save** 🖫 the workbook with the name **as-Delimited Import** and **close** the workbook.

# Import Data from Comma Delimited File Format

*In this exercise, you will import data into Excel from a comma delimited file and then format the data.*

1. **Start** a new workbook and save it with the name **as-Data Import** in the Lesson 18 folder.

2. Rename the **Sheet1** tab as **Imported Data**.

3. **Import** all the data (including titles) from the as-Comma Delimited Data file in the Lesson 18 folder. In the wizard, choose **Comma** as the delimiter type and make certain to preview the data. The first column will contain both animal and age data, which you will separate in a later step. Place the imported data at **cell A1** on the Imported Data worksheet.

4. After importing the data, insert a **blank column** before the **Health** column.

5. **Split** the text currently located in the **range A4:A23** into two columns for Animal and Age. Choose **Space** as the delimiter type. Preview the data to ensure that Total Costs in **cell A24** will not be split.

6. Adjust the **column widths** and add other **formatting** so that the data are easy to read.

7. Make certain that the totals in the bottom row are formulas.
   *Your formatting may vary from the following illustrations.*

| | A | B | C | D | E | F | G |
|---|---|---|---|---|---|---|---|
| 1 | Triangle Animal Shelter | | | | | | |
| 2 | March Expense Report | | | | | | |
| 3 | | | | | | | |
| 4 | Animal | Age | Health | Date Arrived | Shelter Cost | Veterinary Care | Total Costs |
| 5 | Cat | Adult | Healthy | 1-Mar | $82.50 | $10.00 | $92.50 |
| 6 | Dog | Adult | Healthy | 2-Mar | $79.75 | $10.00 | $89.75 |
| 23 | Dog | Adult | Healthy | 30-Mar | $2.75 | $10.00 | $12.75 |
| 24 | Total Costs | | | | $888.25 | $340.00 | $1,228.25 |

8. **Save** 🔲 the changes, and **close** the workbook.

# Import Data from Word

*In this exercise, you will copy and paste text and an image into Excel from a Word document and then format the data.*

1. **Start** a new workbook and save it with the name **as-EduCare Fiscal Summary** in the Lesson 18 folder.

2. Rename the **Sheet1** tab as **Year-End Report**.

3. Start **Word** and then **open** the as-EduCare Year-End Report document from the Lesson 18 folder.

4. **Drag and drop** the text Year-End Report from the Word document to **cell A1** of the Year-End Report worksheet.

5. **Copy** the Q1 through Q4 headings, data rows, and the Total row from the Word document. **Paste** them into an appropriate row of the Excel worksheet.

6. **Close** the Word document without saving.

7. **Format** the data in the worksheet, such as column widths and row heights, as necessary to make the data easy to read.

8. Do whatever is necessary to have the Total row contain **formulas**, not values. *Your worksheet may vary slightly from the following illustration.*

| | A | B | C | D | E |
|---|---|---|---|---|---|
| 1 | Year-End Report | | | | |
| 2 | | | | | |
| 3 | | Q1 | Q2 | Q3 | Q4 |
| 4 | Mortgage and Insurance | $6,779 | $6,750 | $6,750 | $6,846 |
| 5 | Utilities | 2,120 | 1,678 | 1,728 | 1,893 |
| 6 | Food | 4,860 | 4,900 | 4,720 | 5,720 |
| 7 | Staff Salaries | 8,695 | 8,695 | 8,895 | 8,895 |
| 8 | Maintenance and Repairs | 3,325 | 1,370 | 1,493 | 1,493 |
| 9 | Outreach and Fundraising | 1,280 | 1,280 | 1,260 | 1,260 |
| 10 | | | | | |
| 11 | Total | $27,059 | $24,673 | $24,846 | $26,107 |

9. **Save** 🖫 the changes, and keep the workbook **open**.

# Save a Worksheet as a Single File Web Page

*In this exercise, you will save a worksheet from an Excel workbook in the Single File Web Page file format.*

*Before You Begin: You should have completed Apply Your Skills 18.3, and the as-EduCare Fiscal Summary workbook should be open. A web browser capable of displaying files with the .mht file extension, such as Internet Explorer, must be installed to view the published web page.*

1. Check the as-EduCare Fiscal Summary workbook for **compatibility issues**. After reviewing the compatibility report, determine whether you need to take any action.

2. **Save** ⬚ the Year-End Report worksheet as a single file web page. (Do not save the entire workbook as a web page.)

3. **Open** the saved web page file in your browser, and check that it displays correctly.

4. **Close** the browser.

5. **Save** ⬚ the workbook, and then **close** it.

# Critical Thinking & Work-Readiness Skills

*In the course of working through the following Microsoft Office-based Critical Thinking exercises, you will also be utilizing various work-readiness skills, some of which are listed next to each exercise. Go to labyrinthelab.com/workreadiness to learn more about the work-readiness skills.*

## 18.1 Import Data from Access

Raritan Clinic East provides special services to families with newborn infants. You will help coordinate the data for several projects. To gather information efficiently, you have asked for the Access database source file. You have received this file and now need to import it into Microsoft Excel. Open a new Excel workbook. Import the external Access data file ct-Newborn Weights (Lesson 18 folder) as an Excel table. Delete the ID column, and sort the table by birth date in oldest to newest order. Save your workbook with the name **ct-Newborn Weights [Your Last Name]** in the Lesson 18 folder. Keep the file open.

**WORK-READINESS SKILLS APPLIED**

- Serving clients/customers
- Organizing and maintaining information
- Applying technology to a task

## 18.2 Save a Worksheet in Tab Delimited Format

Volunteers deliver congratulatory cards to each family with a newborn, and employee Jessica Allen coordinates this activity. She needs you to create a text list of patients, their newborns' birth dates, and the birth weights. The volunteers will use this information to individualize the cards. Open ct-Newborn Weights [Your Last Name], if necessary. Save the worksheet data as a text file in tab delimited format. Close the text file.

**WORK-READINESS SKILLS APPLIED**

- Serving clients/customers
- Organizing and maintaining information
- Applying technology to a task

## 18.3 Save a Worksheet as a Single File Web Page

Raritan East Clinic also supplies the local newspaper with infant birth statistics. The information is to remain static (no opportunity for anyone to change data), so you will save the data as a single file web page. You will provide this information by emailing it to the local newspaper. Open ct-Newborn Weights [Your Last Name]. Enable content if a security warning displays. Remove any personal information that could identify the patients. Then, save the worksheet as a single file web page, and enter a web page title. Open the published web page in a web browser to check the data before submitting it. Close your browser window, and close the Excel file without saving.

**WORK-READINESS SKILLS APPLIED**

- Serving clients/customers
- Organizing and maintaining information
- Applying technology to a task

# Glossary

**3-D cell reference**
Address in a formula that refers to the same single cell in adjacent worksheets of the workbook; may be used to sum or average the contents of those cells

**Adjacent**
Arrangement of cells, objects, or files that are next to each other; often may be selected as a group by using [Shift]; also known as *contiguous*

**Alignment**
Horizontal placement of text relative to the left and right margins of a cell or a page, where text is left-, right-, or center-aligned; or, vertical placement of text relative to the top and bottom margins of a cell or page, where text is top-, middle-, or bottom-aligned

**Ascending**
Sort order in which cells in a column are arranged alphabetically from A to Z, numerically from smallest to largest, or chronologically from earliest to most recent

**Auditing**
Reviewing formulas to locate errors

**AutoFill**
Feature that extends a series, copies data, or copies a formula into adjacent cells

**AutoComplete**
Feature that offers to complete a cell entry when you type the first few characters

**Backstage view**
A large window of options that displays when one of several tabs on the File tab is selected

**Calculated Field**
Column in a worksheet table or Pivot-Table containing one formula that applies to all cells in the table

**Callout**
Box or bubble containing an explanation of the item to which it points; used in charts and illustrations

**Cells**
Rectangles that make up a worksheet; the intersection of a column and row

**Change history**
Record of changes that were accepted and rejected in a workbook; the Track Changes feature must be switched on to create the change history

**Clip art**
Images, photographs, sounds, and animated GIFs that can be easily searched and inserted from the Clip Art task pane

**Color scheme**
Each document theme has 12 colors that are applied to text, backgrounds, hyperlinks, and so forth

**Comma delimited**
Text file that uses a comma to separate two columns of data; all other text formatting is removed so that data may be imported from an incompatible application

**Comments**
Notes that can be attached to cells by reviewers

**Compatibility Checker**
When an Excel 2010 workbook is saved for an earlier Excel version, the Compatibility Checker notifies the user how features specific to Excel 2010 will be handled in the earlier version

**Compatibility Pack**
Free download from Microsoft which, when installed on a system running an older version of Office, allows the user to open and edit files created in the newer Office 2010 and 2007 format

**Conditional formatting**
Formatting applied to cell contents when user-specified criteria are met

**Consolidation**
Combining values from source worksheets into a destination worksheet by position in the worksheets or by category

**Context menu**
Menu that appears when you right-click; also known as pop-up menu

**Contextual tab**
Ribbon tab that appears only when a certain object on the worksheet is selected; for example, the Table→Design contextual tab appears only when a table is selected

**Converter**
Small program that allows an application program such as Excel to open files that are not in its native file format

**Crop**
Hiding parts of a picture to make certain other elements stand out or to remove unwanted elements

**Data source**
In mail merge, the variable data that merges with the main document; controlled by merge fields

**Data table**
Analysis tool that substitutes various values from a list for either one or two cell references in a formula; the table displays results for each combination of values

**Data validation**
Procedure that checks the data being entered in a cell against a criterion; a message displays if the data is outside the criterion boundaries

**Default**
Setting that a computer program assumes you will use unless you specify a different setting

**Defined name**
Name given to a single cell or range of cells; may be used to navigate the workbook or create formulas

**Demote bullet**
Demoted bullets are indented to the right; increases the list level

**Dependents**
Cells containing formulas that refer to the selected cell; the Trace Dependents command draws an arrow from the selected cell to the dependent cells

**Descending**
Sort order in which cells in a column are arranged alphabetically from Z to A, numerically from largest to smallest, or chronologically from most recent to earliest

**Dialog box launcher**
Appears in some Ribbon groups; opens a dialog box or task pane that contains commands related to the group

**Digital certificate**
Electronic credential from a trusted source that allows the user to create a digital signature in a document

**Digital signature**
Means of authenticating the identity of a document's originator; a signed document cannot be modified

**Document Inspector**
Reviews documents for hidden data or personal information that might be stored in the document

**Document theme**
Preset design consisting of color scheme, text formatting, and placeholder positions

**Drag and drop**
Method for copying and moving text or objects; most useful when copying or moving a short distance within a worksheet or between two documents displayed side by side

**Embedded object**
Object, such as an Excel chart, inserted or pasted as embedded within a destination document; changes to an embedded object have no effect on the original object

**Field**
Column that contains a specific type of data

**File format**
Technique for storing information in a computer file; application programs normally have a special file format that they use by default

**File tab**
Expands to a menu containing commands to open, save, and print files; includes commands to prepare and distribute documents

**Filter**
Process that hides records that do not meet user-specified criteria

**Filter by Selection**
Command that displays only the records containing the same data as in the active cell

**Footer**
Text located within the bottom margin of a worksheet that repeats on all printed pages

**Format Painter**
A tool that allows you to copy formats from a cell or range and apply them to another cell or range

**Formula Bar**
Area above the worksheet in which you view, type, and edit cell entries

**Freezing**
Setting rows at the top and/or columns at the left of a worksheet to remain displayed as the worksheet is scrolled

**Function**
Predefined formula that performs calculations on table cells

**Goal Seek**
Analysis tool in Excel that calculates the value of one variable cell that is necessary to achieve a specific formula result

**Grouping**
Selecting multiple worksheets so you may enter the identical data or format cells in all grouped sheets simultaneously

**Header**
Text located within the top margin of a worksheet that repeats on all printed pages

**Header row**
First row in a table or external data source that contains text labels to describe the data in the columns below those labels

**HTML**
Hypertext Markup Language; programming language used to create web pages

**Hyperlink**
Block of text or a graphic that jumps you to another location in a workbook, to another document, or to a web page when clicked

**Import**
Retrieve data from another file saved in a file format compatible with the destination application

**Input message**
Message that instructs the user to enter data consistent with the validation rule set for a cell; also known as *validation text*

**Intranet**
Internal computer network in a company or organization in which users may access shared files and resources, such as printers

**Linked object**
Object, such as an Excel chart, created in a source file and inserted or pasted in a destination file; the object retains a link to the source file; the destination file can be updated when the source file is modified

**Linking formula**
Cell content beginning with an equals (=) sign that connects to a cell in another area of the same worksheet, a different worksheet, or a different workbook

**Live Preview**
When pointing at formatting commands on the Ribbon, Live Preview displays how the format would appear on selected text and objects without actually applying the format

**Lookup function**
Formula component that retrieves a piece of data from a lookup table located somewhere in the same worksheet, a separate worksheet, or a different workbook

**Macro**
Series of frequently used commands that can be grouped together as a single command; used to speed up repetitive tasks

**Mail Merge**
Feature in Word used to personalize standard letters, envelopes, mailing labels, and other documents by combining a main document with a data source, such as an Excel worksheet

**Main document**
In a mail merge, document that contains the content that remains constant for each recipient; controls the merge with merge fields

**Marquee**
Animated dashed line that surrounds selected cells during an operation, such as a cut or copy

**Merge fields**
Placeholders in a mail merge main document that instruct Word to insert information from a data source, such as an Excel table or list

**Merging**
Combining multiple copies of a workbook containing all user changes into a single workbook

**Mini toolbar**
Contains frequently used formatting commands; appears when you select cells, select text in a cell, or when you right-click on these

**Native file format**
Default file format used by a program

**Nonadjacent**
Arrangement of cells, objects, or files that are not next to each other; often may be selected as a group by using Ctrl; also known as *noncontiguous*

**Nonnative file format**
File format that can be used by a program, but is not the default (native) file format

**Object**
Element shared between documents, such as an Excel spreadsheet or chart

**Open XML**
File format used by Office 2010 and 2007 programs to save documents

**Orientation**
Direction in which the page is turned for viewing and printing, either portrait (short edge on top) or landscape (long edge on top)

**Outline pane**
Attached to a SmartArt frame; displays the text content of each graphic element

**PDF**
Portable Document Format; file format that allows others to view and print a document with all formatting intact even if they do not have the application that created the document

**PivotChart**
Chart view based on a PivotTable

**PivotTable**
Table view of row and column data that allows the data to be summarized and compared in multiple ways

**Precedents**
Cell addresses referenced in a formula; the Trace Precedents command draws arrows from these cells to the formula cell

**Print Preview**
Feature that allow you to see how a document will look when it is printed

**Promote bullet**
Promoted bullets are outdented to the left; decreases the list level

**Quick Access toolbar**
Graphical User Interface (GUI) that contains buttons for frequently used commands; can be customized according to your preference

**Range**
Multiple cells in adjacent rows, columns, or both rows and columns

**Record**
Collection of data in one row for one person, item, or category

**Ribbon**
Contains commands that help you perform tasks; organized in tabs that relate to a particular type of activity and groups that contain related commands

**Scaling**
Enlarging or reducing an object's overall size to a percentage of its original size

**Scenario Manager**
Analysis tool that creates and saves what-if models with up to 32 variables

**Screenshot**
A picture of a non-Excel window captured and layered on an Excel worksheet

**Select text**
Highlight text by dragging it with the mouse pointer or other techniques; used in preparation for certain tasks, such as formatting or copying text

**Shapes**
Graphic tools for drawing images in your documents

**Shared workbook**
Workbook set up to track changes that multiple users make; may be distributed to users one at a time or placed on a network server for multiple users to access simultaneously

**SkyDrive**
A web storage location provided by Microsoft Windows Live that allows you to access documents from any computer with Internet access. Also known as *Windows Live SkyDrive*.

**SmartArt**
Predesigned graphic images you can add to a document; categories include List, Hierarchy, Pyramid, and so forth

**Solver**
Analysis tool in Excel that sets the values of multiple cells used in a formula to produce the desired result that is specified for a target cell

**Sort**
To arrange data in alphabetic, numeric, or date order

**Sparkline**
Miniature chart in a worksheet cell that illustrates the direction (increasing or decreasing) of a cell range in one row or column

**Structured reference**
Method of indicating the location of a cell or other component within a table; allows formulas to adjust results automatically as rows and columns are added to the table

**Style**
Group of formats that allows you to quickly apply multiple formats at once; when a style is modified, all text with the style applied is updated with the modification; also known as *Quick Styles*

**Syntax**
The basic rules for constructing a formula, specifically one containing a function

**Tab**
Area on the Ribbon that contains groups of commands, with seven default tabs displayed on the Excel Ribbon; also, a code that sets a specific amount of space between two text items

**Tab delimited**
Text file that uses a tab code to separate two columns of data; all other text formatting is removed so that data may be imported from an incompatible application

**Table**
Grouping of worksheet cells that may be sorted, filtered, formatted with a table style, and calculated with structured references

**Table styles**
Predesigned colors and formatting that can be applied to a table

**Template**
Preformatted document that acts as a master document that can be used over and over again; can also contain text, graphics, and other objects

**Theme**
Set of formatting selections that can be applied to a document; includes colors, graphic elements, and fonts all designed to work well together

**Title Bar**
Appears across the top of the Excel window; contains the name of the application (Excel) and the name of the current document

**Toggle**
Button or setting that switches on when clicked and switches off when clicked again

**Track Changes**
Feature that, when activated, marks each change to a document; changes can then be reviewed and either accepted or rejected

**Trendline**
Line that illustrates the direction (increasing or decreasing) of one data series in a chart

**Validation rule**
Criterion used to limit the type of data or specific value entered into a cell

**Views**
Varying ways you can look at a document; optimized for specific types of work

**Web app**
A simplified version of Excel, Word, or PowerPoint used to view and edit documents on the web, especially when the full version is not installed on the computer

**What-if analysis**
Changing the value in one or more cells that are used in a formula to see the various results of the changes

**Wizard**
Sequence of steps, usually presented in a dialog box, to guide the user in completing a task

**Workbook properties**
Information about a workbook that is saved with the workbook contents

**XPS**
XML Paper Specification; file format that allows others to view and print a document with all formatting intact even if they do not have the application that created the document

**Zoom**
Command that allows you to view a document in varying levels of magnification

# Index

tracing
  dependents, 562
  errors, 565
  formulas, 561–563
  precedents, 561–562, 565
tracked changes feature, 645–651, 654, 656
transposing data, 308, 311
trendlines, 610–612, 613
two-variable data tables, 606–610

## U

Undo and Redo buttons, 44–45
ungrouping worksheets, 586, 587
UPPER function, 554
user-defined charts, 203
usernames, 59, 633, 635, 636, 646
user options for protected worksheets, 434
user permissions, 641, 642
Using, 407, 424

## V

validation of data, 594–603
value axis, charts, 204
values, field, 474, 475
versions of workbooks, managing, 698–704
vertical alignment in cells, 177, 178, 179
VLOOKUP function, 539–543

## W

watermark for printed worksheet, 276–278
web pages
  workbooks/worksheets saved as, 727–731
web pages, hyperlinking from worksheets to, 321, 323
web query, importing data, 228–230
what-if analyses, 84
Width option, Excel page layout, 267
window protection settings, 433
Word, Microsoft, and Excel data in Mail Merge, 710–713

workbooks/worksheets
  (*see also* cells)
  3-D references, 536
  change history, 648
  closing, 24
  converting files, 705–709
  copying or moving worksheets, 303–313, 317
  default number of sheets, 298, 299
  definition, 6
  deleting, 162
  digital certificates, 440–446
  disabled features, 673
  emailing, 225–228
  formatting, 114–115, 308–313
  grouping, 586–589
  hiding and unhiding, 163
  hyperlinks for, 321–325
  inserting, 162
  linking cells and formulas, 300–302
  marking as final, 641, 642, 644
  merging, 651–657, 710–713
  navigating in, 6–9
  opening, 34, 424–427
  organizing, 628–631
  outlining, 367–368
  PivotTables from, 464
  preparing for distribution, 640–644, 645
  printing, 54–57, 264–271, 326–327
  properties, 58–61
  protecting, 432–439, 653
  saving, 19–25, 484, 486, 698–704
  selecting multiple sheets, 299–300
  sharing, 645, 651–657, 672–678, 714–718
  sheet tabs, 6, 162–166
  sorting data, 248–252
  storing macros, 483, 484
  ungrouping, 586, 587
  user permissions, 641, 642
  views, 253–263
  as web pages, 727–731
wrapping text option, 119, 121
written vs. electronic signature lines, 442, 443

## X

XML file format, 699
XPS file format, 708

## Z

Zoom feature, 6, 52–53, 257

# Notes

# Notes

# Notes

# Notes

# Notes

# Notes

# Notes

# Notes

# Notes

# Notes

# Notes

# Notes

# Notes

# Notes

# Notes